The Supreme Court in the Federal Judicial System

FOURTH EDITION

The Nelson-Hall Series in Political Science
Consulting Editor: Samuel C. Patterson
The Ohio State University

Consultant in Law, Courts, and Judicial Process: Stephen L. Wasby
State University of New York at Albany

The Supreme Court in the Federal Judicial System

FOURTH EDITION

Stephen L. Wasby

STATE UNIVERSITY OF NEW YORK AT ALBANY

NELSON-HALL PUBLISHERS/CHICAGO

Library of Congress Cataloging-in-Publication Data

Wasby, Stephen L., 1937–
    The Supreme Court in the federal judicial system / Stephen L.
Wasby.—4th ed.
        p.   cm.
    Includes bibliographical references and index.
    ISBN 0-8304-13-12-X (alk. paper)
        1. United States.   Supreme Court.   2. Courts—United States.
    I. Title.
    KF8742.W38   1993
    347.73'26—dc20
    [347.30735]   92-27512
                                                                             CIP

Manufactured in the United States of America

10   9   8   7   6   5   4   3   2

The paper used in this book meets the
minimum requirements of American
National Standard for Information
Sciences—Permanence of Paper for
Printed Library Materials, ANSI
Z39.48-1984.

To the memory of my grandparents,
Frances and **Benjamin Bunshaft,**

and

Harold ("Hal") Chase
Constitutional law scholar, teacher,
Marine, and friend

The good people do is not interred with their bones,
but lives in the hearts
of those who cherish their memory.

And
for **Susan,**
my special companion

Contents

Preface

THE UNITED STATES SUPREME Court receives much attention, adulation, and criticism. Yet the American public knows far less about it than about Congress or the president. Our national legislators and particularly the president, aided by media coverage, work at making themselves highly visible. The Court, however, has no public relations apparatus and remains generally secretive about its internal processes; its rulings are supposed to speak for themselves. Moreover, there has been little public education about the Court's functioning or its place in our government, a result of the "mystery of the law," lack of attention in the educational system and in the media, and lawyers' failure to inform the lay public.

The Supreme Court's work and the justices' activities have become more visible as a result of a journalistic exposé of strategic maneuvering in the Burger Court (*The Brethren*, by Woodward and Armstrong), a study of the extrajudicial activities of Justices Brandeis and Frankfurter and of Justice Fortas, and extended interviews with several justices. Further attention was produced by Chief Justice Burger's retirement and the elevation of Justice Rehnquist to the chief justiceship, and, later, by the rejection of Judge Bork's nomination to the Court and the all-enveloping turmoil surrounding the confirmation of Justice Thomas. Although the just-noted books and interviews add a significant dimension to our knowledge of the Supreme Court's workings, none provides the general reader with adequate information about the Court. This book is written in the hope of remedying that deficiency in knowledge about the Supreme Court and of supplying a sufficient context in which to evaluate the Court's work. My intent is to provide not only understanding of what the Court has done thus far but also a basis for understanding its future actions. Justices, including chief justices, come and go, and the doctrine the Court announces may change, but the Court's basic method of deciding cases and the considerations that influence its decisions remain relatively stable.

Scholars who have devoted their attention to the Court provide much of the basis for what appears here. Their work is supplemented by data prepared specifically for this volume. I have also drawn on my own prior work while trying to avoid inflicting too much of it on the reader. Basically a synthesis of others' studies, this book reflects both emphases and gaps in the existing literature, and the reader should remember that it may take several years for detailed analyses of the Court's most recent terms to appear. In this edition, basic information is presented through the end of the Court's 1990 Term (ending in July 1991); salient information from the 1991 Term is added where appropriate.

To understand the Supreme Court, one must know about its internal procedures, including how cases are accepted for review and how those cases are decided; the Court's role at the top of our nation's judiciary—how it fits into our dual court system of separate national and state courts; and its role in the overall political system. We must therefore look not only at the Supreme Court but also at the entire national court system, the relations between federal and state courts, the Court's relations with Congress and the executive branch, and the impact of the Court's decisions. An emphasis on the federal court system as a whole is imperative if we are to provide a full understanding of the Supreme Court, but we must also keep in mind that the federal courts are not fully representative of the nation's courts. For one thing, with the exception of judges on some specialized courts, federal judges are appointed to life terms, whereas most state judges are elected. For another, the number of cases in the federal courts is small enough—despite federal judges' complaints about caseload—to allow a more deliberate pace and greater emphasis on full-dress adversary proceedings than occurs in many high-volume state courts, particularly trial courts with their frenetic pace.

The primary emphasis throughout is on the Court's *operation* rather than on the doctrines the justices announce. However, in addition to the illustrative use of cases, particular attention is given both to the Court's rulings on access to federal courts and to decisions about Congress and the presidency. The book is divided into ten chapters. Chapter 1 presents a general discussion of the Court's role in the American governmental, legal, and political system, with some attention both to history and to contemporary political controversy concerning the Court. This is followed by discussion of the structure and administration of the federal court system (Chapter 2) and the selection of federal judges (Chapter 3). Chapter 4 deals with the role of lawyers and interest groups in pursuing litigation; Chapter 5, with rules for getting into courts and the relations between federal and state courts; and Chapter 6, with the Court's exercise of choice in determining what cases to decide. Chapters 7 and 8 provide an extended consideration of the way in which the Court handles cases accepted for review, judicial interaction in deciding cases, and major considerations that enter the writing of the Court's

opinions. After an examination of the Court's review of congressional and executive branch actions in Chapter 9, the book concludes with a discussion in
Chapter 10 of public opinion about the Court and of the communication of
decisions to those affected and the impact of those rulings.

The structure I began to use with the book's second edition—based on a
restructuring of the first edition to place discussion of basic institutional matters
and judicial selection early in the volume—has been retained. The material of
the third edition has been considerably rewritten and thoroughly updated, with
newly available sources used where possible. In order to combat size creep, I
have produced a book no longer than the previous edition. No bibliography is
included, but anyone wishing to read further can easily do so by following up
items in the notes at the end of each chapter. A Table of Cases is provided where
one can find citations to cases discussed or noted in the text.

Acknowledgments are many in a work of this sort, reflecting as it does study
and exposure to others over many years. Over time, helpful and generous colleagues have provided many ideas and much information. Not all can be mentioned here, but I wish particularly to thank for their help over several editions
with particular sections David Adamany, Wayne State University; Keith O. Bo-
yum, California State University, Fullerton; George F. Cole, University of Connecticut; Jerry Goldman, Northwestern University; Joel B. Grossman, University
of Wisconsin, Madison, a sometime co-author; Arthur D. Hellman, University
of Pittsburgh Law School; Maeva Marcus, Supreme Court Documentary History
Project; Karen O'Connor, Emory University; D. Marie Provine, Syracuse University; Elliot Slotnick, The Ohio State University; and Frank Way, University of
California, Riverside. My brother, Roger Wasby, has been a helpful West Coast
clipping service. I wish especially to express my gratitude to the late Harold
Chase for his support and continuing interest in my work earlier in my career. It
is to his memory that this book is in part dedicated.

I also wish to thank the students who have raised useful and interesting
questions, prompting rethinking and rephrasing of what has been said here in the
past. In particular, I want to thank the midshipmen in my Spring 1991 Supreme
Court course at the U.S. Naval Academy, for their "barrage" of good questions;
they contributed significantly to this revision.

Thanks also go to Denise Rathbun, then of Praeger Publishers, who first
asked me to write this book, and to Steve Ferrara of Nelson-Hall, whom I consider "my publisher." Suzanne Wickham, who effectively transformed my total
lack of artistry into diagrams of the court system's structure, and Addie Napoli-
tano, who has done a superb job of manuscript preparation through more than
one edition, deserve special thanks. Mark Daly and Kenneth Slentz helped with
the proof-reading. Most important have been the helpful suggestions and moral
support of Susan Daly, who says she obstructed the project and who helped me
get away from my work when I most needed to do so.

S. L. W.

1 The Supreme Court's Roles

THE SUPREME COURT OF the United States is seen in many different ways by the American public. To some the Court is lawgiver, the nation's high tribunal and protector of the Constitution—and perhaps upholder of our liberties. Some not only see the Court as performing these functions; they *expect* it to do so and would assign it these roles, as something the Court *should* do. To others the Court is not the finder of the law but a policymaker perhaps usurping the legislative prerogative or acting as an obstacle to change—that is, as doing things it *should not* do. (See pages 353–57, 360–61.)

Whether they evaluate it positively or negatively, many people see the Supreme Court as different both from other courts in the United States and from the highest courts of other nations. After World War II, courts in an increasing number of nations were granted a power previously possessed by few courts outside the United States—the power of *judicial review,* the power to invalidate acts of other branches of the government as violating the Constitution. The U.S. Supreme Court remains unusual among highest courts of the world in not being solely a *constitutional court,* one created to hear only questions of the validity of legislative and executive actions and questions of the Constitution's meaning. Instead the Supreme Court has both the power of judicial review *and* the authority to handle all types of litigation, including cases involving interpretation of statutes and application of already-developed policy to particular fact situations. It differs from most other courts, which must accept and decide most cases brought to them, in being able to choose the cases it hears.

If this were not enough to make the Supreme Court exceptional, it is the highest court in the national judicial system. It is not only the highest of the federal courts but also the court of last resort for cases raising federal questions from the states' judicial systems. Such a position leads to the Court's performing certain functions (see pages 28–33). As the highest court, the Supreme Court thus has the final judicial word in any case involving the U.S. Constitution, and that word is binding on state courts as well as on federal judges. The Court's ability to choose its cases, coupled with its paramount position, gives its rulings the widest possible influence. Alexander Hamilton wrote in *The Federalist* that because it did not possess "either the sword or the purse" the Supreme Court would be the "least dangerous" branch, but the Court has become very important—and powerful—indeed.

The Supreme Court may have the final judicial word, but its statements are final only after Congress, the executive branch, state officials, and even the public have been able to respond. In short, the law is what the judges say it is, after everyone else has had their say. To the extent that the Court's interpretation of a statute or a constitutional provision is accepted as appropriate, it is perhaps only because the Court is the *highest* court. As Justice Jackson admonished, "We are not final because we are infallible, we are infallible only because we are final."[1] And the Court is only the final *court*—and sometimes not even that, as those who lose in the Supreme Court may be able to prevail on some other basis on remand to the lower courts, perhaps on a state law basis if the case is returned to state courts. Certainly resistance to the Supreme Court and congressional overruling of its statutory rulings (see pages 313–22) are indications of its lessened finality, and of its lesser infallibility in statutory than in constitutional matters.

People expect the Supreme Court to act like a court—or like what they think a court is. Indeed, like any other court, the Supreme Court acts within a particular legal system. In the United States, the legal system is supposedly adversary in nature, and judges are expected to rely on *precedent*, that is, decisions in past cases, just as they are also expected to decide on the basis of *principle*— some use the term *neutral principles*—rather than personal likes or whim. Both of these elements, along with the further expectation that the justices will respect the position of the states in our federal system, are part of the expectation that they will exercise *judicial restraint* rather than engage in *activism*. All these matters are elements that some feel should enter the opinions the justices write (see Chapter 8).

People react to the Court not only in terms of its procedures but also in terms of its results. They treat it not only as a legal institution deciding specific cases but also as another agency of government, making policy by its decisions just as legislators and executive agencies make policy. As it makes policy, the Court interacts with these other branches of government (see Chapter 9), and public reaction to the Court's decisions (its policy statements) forces the Court to become an actor in the political system: if the Court's actions are to have an effect and if, in the long run, the Court is to survive, the justices must take the Court's environment into account. All courts—even trial courts simply enforcing norms or sentencing defendants after accepting a guilty plea—are policymakers. However, the Supreme Court's policymaking is far more visible than the actions of most lower courts, even most state supreme courts, and, because it potentially applies to the entire nation, has far greater significance.

This chapter provides some context for our subsequent, more detailed examination of the Supreme Court in the federal judicial system. We begin with a discussion of recent controversy about the courts and the reach of their decisions. This is followed by a description of changes in the Court's importance in our political system over the course of our nation's history. Then we turn to an examination of the Supreme Court in the latter half of the twentieth century, the Warren Court (1953–69), the Burger Court (1969–86), and the Rehnquist Court (1986–). We end the chapter by returning to the theme of this introduction: the roles of the Supreme Court.

The Courts and Current Controversy

Judicial Imperialism[2]

Courts, we have been told repeatedly since the late 1970s, are "activist" rather than "self-restrained." Judges have changed "the very nature of judicial review," so that "what was once a distinctively judicial power, essentially different from legislative power, has become merely another variant of legislative power," with the judge's function no longer limited to "ascertaining and applying the will of the law." After Earl Warren became Chief Justice, the Supreme Court "assumed a role in policymaking unknown in previous American history."[3] Judges, we are told by others, are an "imperial judiciary" making decisions on "social policy" issues that judges should not decide. Moreover, we are told of "judicial incapacity"—that courts lack the skill, competence, or capacity to resolve such social policy issues.[4] Complaints of this sort have come even from within the judiciary, with Chief Justice Rehnquist commenting several years ago that it was "unhealthy" to have "so much authority" given to a small number of life-tenured justices.

In the late 1950s and early 1960s, the Court's internal security rulings produced cries of "Impeach Earl Warren!" and efforts to limit the Court's jurisdiction. Attacks on the courts, particularly the federal courts and most specifically the Supreme Court, in the 1980s were more serious and were carried out on a broader front than in 1937, when President Franklin D. Roosevelt tried to "pack" the Supreme Court. Decisions on abortion, school prayer, and school desegregation ("forced busing") provoked particularly intense reaction and efforts to remove the Court's appellate jurisdiction or the jurisdiction of all federal courts (see pages 316–18) over the subjects of those cases. Lower federal court rulings on conditions in state prisons and mental hospitals—in which some judges have specified in considerable detail how the institutions should be restructured and administered—also produced considerable hostility.[5] Judges in such cases are seen as particularly intrusive, displacing state and local officials and becoming administrators of school systems or state institutions. Appointment of federal judges for life increases critics' frustration.

In 1990, the Supreme Court decided two particularly significant cases of district judges' alleged "activism" in dealing with civil rights issues; in both the Court imposed some limits—but not major ones—on judges. One judge had found that the city of Yonkers, New York, had intentionally discriminated against racial minorities in its placement of public housing. When the city council would not pass a corrective ordinance even when given considerable time to do so, the judge held individual council members in contempt. The Supreme Court said the judge should have first held the city in contempt to try to bring about compliance. Then a district judge, attempting to implement school desegregation in Kansas City, Missouri, and, likewise finding resistance—to raising the money to fund the desegregation plan—ordered an increase in property taxes. This time the Supreme Court said the judge should have ordered the school district to have raised the taxes rather than doing so directly. In neither case did the Court touch the judges' desegregation orders, already upheld by the lower courts.[6]

Judges are seen as not only intrusive but also unaccountable. Such a view is reinforced by the Supreme Court's 1978 ruling in *Stump v. Sparkman** that judges were immune from lawsuits for damages resulting from actions they had undertaken as judges. A judge who had ordered the sterilization of a 15-year-old female at the request of the girl's mother was sued for his part in the sterilization when the daughter and her husband learned years later why she could not have children. The Supreme Court refused to say the judge's act—normally one not performed by judges—was not "judicial." However, dissenting Justice Stewart argued that "the conduct of a judge surely does not become a judicial act merely on his own say-so. A judge is not free, like a loose cannon, to inflict indiscriminate damage whenever he announces that he is acting in his judicial capacity." The Court reinforced that ruling when it refused to allow a suit against a judge who allegedly had ordered that a lawyer be brought before him with excessive force.[7] The Court did rule in *Pulliam v. Allen* (1984) that judges violating people's civil rights may be enjoined from such action and made to pay attorneys' fees to a successful plaintiff.

Criticism of the courts is deeply felt. It is intellectually appealing in a political system in which the elected branches of government are expected to be dominant; and it carries considerable political weight, particularly when the criticized rulings are seen as liberal while the nation's political tone has become more conservative. In evaluating the criticism, one must keep several matters in mind. One is that, like previous attacks on the courts, current criticism is largely prompted by critics' dislike of the courts' *results*. The attack on "government by

---

*Citations to cases mentioned in the text may be found in the Table of Cases, page 397.

judiciary" in the 1930s resulted from a preference for the program of economic regulation the Court had struck down, just as the earlier attack on "government by injunction" stemmed from a preference for laws benefiting labor unions. The liberals who criticized the Court's "activism" then did not also criticize it in the 1950s and 1960s when the Court supported civil liberties. Another point is that self-restraint would benefit the executive branch, so one needs to treat with some skepticism attacks on the Court by presidents and their attorneys general.

It is also the case that "social policy" issues, such as labor–management relations, taxation, and economic regulation of business, have long been brought to the courts for disposition. However, users of the courts have changed: those representing racial minorities, women, and the poor or disadvantaged have joined the advantaged elements of society, such as major commercial interests, in using courts to seek redress of grievances. This has led to the filing of many more civil rights cases raising current social policy questions with which the judges must deal. Here it must be kept in mind that litigation on school desegregation and institutional conditions is particularly complex and drawn out. Because considerable time is needed to prove a constitutional violation and then, once the violation is proved, to develop a remedy, a court tends to remain involved in overseeing the implementation of its decree for an extended period, perhaps many years.

The "imperial judiciary" and "judicial incapacity" arguments also tend to focus on the courts to the exclusion of other political actors. However, the *general* growth of government and additional action by legislatures and executives is a major reason for the expansion of litigation aimed at the government action. Much recent litigation concerning rights of the disadvantaged is based on congressional statutes, not on the Constitution, and such litigation results from the need to have judges interpret and enforce vague and ambiguous statutory provisions and the regulations developed to implement the statutes. (The same is true of efforts to clean up the environment.) Judges did not enact the statutes and regulations on which people base their cases, nor are they to blame for the lack of clarity. Moreover, increased judicial authority is necessary to provide continued "checks and balances" when legislative and executive authority have grown. Yet it is the courts, not Congress or executive agencies, that are blamed. Similarly, it is judges, not the officials whose actions (or inaction) have led to litigation, who are criticized. And it is federal judges who are chided for their actions, not state judges who have failed to deal effectively with governmental misconduct. As a then state chief justice observed,

> State court systems are not, or at least in the past were not, as attentive as they should have been to their responsibilities to recognize the Constitution of the United States, and the laws passed pursuant thereto as the supreme law of the land. . . . In many instances . . . state courts had not dealt in effective and aggressive ways with clear violations of federal constitutional rights occurring in the cases before them.[8]

Critics attack a judge's involvement in administering the Boston school system to produce segregation, but not the Boston School Committee's adamant refusal to obey *state* laws on school desegregation. They blame the "intrusive" action of the federal judge in the Yonkers case, not the city council's continuing refusal to locate public housing in a nondiscriminatory fashion. Long-standing prison and mental hospital conditions, often so appalling that even conservative federal judges have found the conditions in violation of the Constitution, are not given attention: judges' orders to remedy the violation are attacked. Critics of the "imperial judiciary" also seem to forget that, although judges have been willing to provide officials with considerable leeway in remedying conditions on their own, more severe remedial orders often result from officials' resistance to the initial judicial rulings.

Judges, even if not shirking their duty when cases are brought before them, may remain *reluctant* to become deeply involved in such litigation. Moreover, they cannot impose their views concerning schools or prisons until someone brings a case to court, often as a last resort after complaints to unresponsive legislators and executives. It is litigants, not judges, who initiate cases and thus establish courts' agendas, and this use of courts as a "last resort" is evidence of courts' connections to, rather than isolation from, the political process.

Critics of judges' lack of capacity claim that courts accustomed to simple bipolar complaints (A v. B) cannot handle social policy issues presented in complex polycentric (multi-actor) situations,[9] that courts carve up problems that are in reality intertwined, and that the problems with which judges deal in any one case may provide an unrepresentative slice of a larger problem that is better addressed as a whole. Preoccupied with individual cases, judges are said not to think about whether the cases represent typical situations from which precedents for later cases might be properly derived. The resultant judicial policymaking is thus piecemeal, with correction of problems only intermittent rather than continuous. Perhaps this is an accurate description of judicial policymaking, but it is an accurate description of policymaking in the other branches of government as well.[10]

Legislators, administrators, *and* judges generally begin developing policy with a problem presented by particular instances. Most legislative action, for example, occurs only after a series of complaints by constituents or interest groups, not unlike litigants' filing a case. To some degree, however, officials in all three branches contemplate other situations to which the policy they announce is intended to apply. Judges, who are expected to be subject-matter generalists, may have difficulty dealing with new areas of the law. But so do legislators, who are also generalists—not always adequately informed—who also lack an adequate basis for choosing experts to assist them. Time and preparation can, however, overcome these difficulties for both judges and legislators. Judges' supervision of institutions can also be facilitated by required periodic reports, reliance on complainants' attorneys to return to court if something is amiss, and appointment of judicial masters who can "compensate for judges' lack of familiarity with organizational routines and procedures in defendant institutions."[11]

Judicial Accountability[12]

The intensity of contemporary criticism of judges said to be insufficiently responsive to current political sentiment should not make us forget the strongly and widely held view that judges *should* be independent. Independence can result in judges' exercising discretion in ways we dislike; we do not wish judges' decisions to be purchased nor to have their decisions reflect partisan political considerations. There is also a strong argument that because of the substantial pressures against the rights of the disadvantaged, the courts, particularly the Supreme Court, need to serve as a beacon light for such rights.

The wish by many people that judges be independent does not eliminate influences that help to keep them at least somewhat accountable, if we define accountability to mean "keeping an institution's decisions in line with community political and social values and otherwise imposing constraints on the exercise of discretion."[13] Indeed, Shapiro argues that the "universal pattern" is that judging is "an integral part of the mainstream of political authority rather than . . . a separate entity."[14] This suggests clear connections with—and accountability to—the political system.

Judges are accountable *within* the legal system (legal accountability) and *to* the broader political system (political accountability). Legal accountability includes judges' socialization, their exposure to and learning of norms; legal precedents and the public nature of judicial action; reversal of judges' decisions by higher courts; and constraints imposed by courts' organizational needs. Political accountability derives from the role of public opinion—including resistance—in the judicial process, in addition to the selection and removal of judges. Within the legal system, judges are accountable primarily to lawyers or other judges, while political accountability propels judges toward the broader public or at least its more attentive members. Overlap and convergence between the types of accountability occur because lawyers participate in judicial selection and are part of the political elite.

In the United States, judges receive no formal judicial training before they become judges and only limited formal judicial training after they reach the bench. Before they become judges their most extensive relevant socialization is to their roles as lawyers. As judges, they learn most from contact with other judges, not from nonjudges and even less from nonlawyers. Legal education and training produce thorough exposure to the norm of judicial independence; to the expectation that decisions should be derived from precedent; to the idea that, when applicable precedent is lacking, they should look to "the law" as the source of decisions; and to the norm that decisions should be explained in written opinions. Precedent (see pages 270–76) affects the process by which judges arrive at the reasoned decisions expected of them; the requirement of written (or at least public) opinions, in addition to making the judicial process more open, assists in producing accountability because others can examine the justifications that judges have offered for their actions. All of these elements come together, so that instead of being "free agents" or "impersonal voices of determinate constitutional norms," "judges work within the constraints of an interpretive community and a web of institutional practices that define the limits of constitutional innovation."[15]

Cutting against accountability are unpublished opinions in the lower courts, the fact that the Supreme Court does not provide—and does not have to provide—reasons for denying review of cases, and courts' secrecy about their own internal operations. Lower courts have considerable freedom of action but the potential sanction of reversal by higher courts helps produce accountability, at least to the higher courts, in those cases litigants choose to appeal. Litigants thus become an important part of the process of producing judicial accountability. Within any court, trial or appellate, there is accountability (lateral or horizontal accountability) to other judges of the court, to other court officials, and to the lawyers who regularly practice there, as part of the dynamics that within any organization have a strong effect on everyone's everyday actions.

Political accountability may also take place through the effect of public opinion on judges. (See pages 351–62 for the Court's effects *on* public opinion.) Many judges become accustomed to responding to public opinion while holding elective public office before their judicial appointment, and the effect continues after appointment.[16] Certain aspects of public opinion are also increasingly pressed upon judges by single-issue interest groups. Even without such activity, judges are well aware of the political environment relevant to their decisions; the comment has been made that the judges "follow the election returns." And judges certainly are aware of public opinion in the form of resistance to their decisions. Because such resistance certainly lessens the effects of "judicial imperialism"—when disliked decisions are not fully implemented or when they are ignored, resisted, attacked, and overturned in other arenas (see Chapters 9 and 10)—such action may be an important way of holding courts accountable to the views held by significant segments of the public.

A key principal means by which judges might be held accountable, one directly at the intersection of legal and political accountability, is the process by which they are selected. A particular method of judicial selection can affect which political actors play a dominant role and can help to establish the values to which judges may be accountable. Partisan election is likely to magnify the importance of political party leaders, but appointive methods—such as that used in the federal judiciary (see pages 86–87) and "merit systems"—increase the relative importance played by the organized bar. At least in their first few years on the bench, appointed judges may feel more accountable to those who have appointed them than they do in the longer run when the appointing official (or even the appointing political party) may no longer be in office. (In general, time may well erode any short-term accountability.) Accountability may be built in before a judge takes the bench through the choice of appropriate nominees and through participation by lawyers' groups and other interested individuals and groups in the selection process, thus potentially reducing the need for continuing mechanisms of accountability. On the other hand, there has been increased development of means for disciplining judges and even removing them (see pages 91–96).

The Present Court and the Historical Pattern: The Court's Relative Importance

Historical perspective is important when one examines the Supreme Court's place in our political system. In order to evaluate competing claims that, from a critic's perspective, the Court is too "conservative" (or too "liberal") or too "activist" (or too "restrained"), one must first be able to penetrate rhetorical terms. These include "strict construction," "self-restraint," and "activism"—terms that refer to adherence to precedent, injection of personal values, and willingness to intervene in controversial matters (see pages 287–91). Second, one must also understand how the Court's performance at any one time compares with its performance in other periods.

Statements that the Burger Court was conservative on civil liberties issues, for example, are based on a comparison with the Warren Court, which decided a substantial majority (upward of 80 percent) of civil liberties cases in favor of the civil liberties claim. The Burger Court, by contrast, ruled against the claim over half the time. Here, however, we must be careful in our comparisons. The Burger Court had certain types of cases not before the Warren Court—women's rights and prison conditions—leaving little basis for a comparison. The Burger Court also often faced less clear-cut questions than its predecessor. If the Warren Court had answered "easy" questions—ones that now look easy, even if thought to be difficult at the time—or had established only the basic rules, later cases would pose issues of more specific application. Indeed, the cases decided by the Burger Court in its early years are said to have been "nearly 20% more difficult . . . than those decided in the early Warren Court" and then, after a decline in difficulty, increased again.[17] Thus a different picture of the Burger Court would be produced by comparing it with the Vinson Court (1946–53), generally conservative and not supportive of civil liberties claims, than with the Warren Court. In this section, based on a brief historical recapitulation of the Court's history, we focus on the variation over time in the Court's importance as a major political actor.

The Court has not always been as central or important as it now appears. It may come as somewhat of a shock, for example, to realize that when, in the Court's history, partisan conflict between Congress and the Court led to cancellation of a term of Court (something quite unlikely to happen now), the nation's business went on without interruption. The Supreme Court did not even have its own building until the 1930s: the Court met in the basement of the Capitol, and the justices did much of their work in their Washington, D.C., homes. The Supreme Court edifice across from the Capitol (brought in under cost, a miracle not likely to recur) is properly impressive, but one of the first justices to work in it said that he and his colleagues felt like "Nine Black Beetles in the Temple of Karnak."

The significance of the Supreme Court's role in the American system has varied across time and between issues. At times, the Court has seemed central to the nation's development; at other times, it has been more in the background. One of the periods of the Court's greatest centrality came in the early nineteenth century under Chief Justice John Marshall, who helped the Court achieve its earliest prominence. Through Marshall, the Court established its power to invalidate acts of Congress. The Court played a major role in establishing the national government's place in our scheme of federalism, through decisions such as *Gibbons v. Ogden*, establishing Congress's power over interstate commerce broadly defined, and *McCulloch v. Maryland*, striking down a state tax on the National Bank. Under Chief Justice Roger Taney, the Supreme Court was perhaps less obtrusive. In that period, the Court allowed the states more authority over commerce, ruling in *Cooley v. Board of Port Wardens* that where diversity was needed, states could act where the federal government had not done so. Unfortunately for Taney's reputation, the *Dred Scott* case seriously exacerbated the tensions that led to the Civil War by upsetting Congress's regulation of slavery in the territories and ruling that a slave was not a person who could sue in the courts. This case, the Court's second exercise of judicial review at the national level, was one of its "self-inflicted wounds."[18] The much closer link between the Court's rulings and party policy prior to the Civil War reduced the Court's independence and thus the centrality of its role. During and after the Civil War, the Court also played a subordinate role, its usual posture with respect to war efforts. It generally sustained Lincoln's actions and his theory of the relation between Union and Confederacy.

The Court's general prestige in the late nineteenth century was great, but the Court did not play a positive leadership role. The Court undercut post–Civil War civil rights legislation, for example, in the *Civil Rights Cases*, and then, in *Plessy v. Ferguson*, sustained state legislation requiring Negroes to ride in separate railroad cars. At the same time, the justices were saying that the Fourteenth Amendment's Due Process Clause did not include the Bill of Rights' procedural protections for criminal defendants.[19] Later the Court's conservatism led it to uphold convictions of "subversives" in cases brought in the atmosphere of World War I.[20] The Court's importance in the late nineteenth and early twentieth century also resulted from its striking down most state attempts to regulate the economy even when Congress had not acted. This was the period when "substantive due process" was at its height, with the judges reading into the Constitution their views of what was "reasonable" for the states to legislate. The Court also undid

Congress's attempts to regulate the economy, defining the commerce and taxing powers narrowly[21] and even saying that powers not expressly delegated to the federal government were reserved to the states—language like that of the Articles of Confederation.

During the New Deal period, the Court became a principal political actor by striking down much early New Deal legislation.[22] These decisions ran contrary to the political realignment reflected in President Roosevelt's election. (It was during this time that in calling a Supreme Court session to order, the court crier is alleged to have said, "May God save the United States from this Honorable Court.") Whether or not as a result of President Roosevelt's attack on the Court and his proposal to add justices (see page 326), the Court changed position, sustaining a wide variety of economic regulatory measures.[23] This change was reinforced by the departure of its four most conservative members and their replacement by justices chosen for their support of New Deal programs. After 1937, the Court regularly accepted Congress's determinations about the reach of the Commerce Clause as a vehicle for regulation of the economy—and other types of regulation, such as race relations.[24]

The Court's post-1937 restraint concerning economic regulation was not immediately accompanied by consistent judicial protection for civil liberties. In cases stemming from World War II, the Court again showed its unwillingness to protect civil liberties in war-related matters (see page 333). Most important, the Court showed its deference to the president in sustaining the relocation of Japanese-Americans in the *Korematsu* case. After World War II, blacks began to win some support for their rights in housing and graduate education,[25] but, as noted previously, the Vinson Court had an otherwise conservative record on civil liberties.[26]

The Warren Court

The Warren Court (1953–69) commands our attention because it remains the benchmark against which to measure subsequent Supreme Court action on civil liberties and civil rights. The Warren Court period was the first one in which the Court gave substantial attention to civil liberties and civil rights claims. In the long view of the Court's history, that attention, coupled with the Warren Court's *support* of civil liberties claims, made it something of an aberration. Aberration or not, its position on civil liberties and civil rights, most of it in decisions striking down state restrictions on individual rights, and the controversy surrounding its decisions, made it a central force in the American political system. Even if not as important as the president and Congress, it was highly involved in key policy issues, and the public became accustomed to the Court's being in that position.

Only with the Warren Court were minorities able to win victories they had not been able to obtain from reluctant legislatures and executives. The Court was pretty much "the only game in town" for civil liberties and civil rights policy until

Congress enacted the Civil Rights Act of 1964 and the Voting Rights Act of 1965 and the executive branch developed implementing regulations for those statutes. That led to a sharing of civil rights policymaking among the three branches but only slightly diminished the Court's centrality.

The Warren Court's first major step was the invalidation of racial segregation ("separate but equal") in education in *Brown v. Board of Education* (1954). The Court may have been leading the nation or it may have been following public opinion, at least elite public opinion, with the ruling coming only because the time was ripe[27]; the latter position does not suggest leadership. A series of decisions in 1956 and 1957 protected political dissidents caught up in government internal security investigations aimed at suspected Communists and other radicals, but the Court soon drew back from those positions. The Warren Court also required that both houses of each state legislature be apportioned on the basis of population; invalidated prayers in public schools; and expanded free speech in the areas of obscenity and libel.[28] It also regularly sustained Congress's actions to protect civil rights with respect to public accommodations, voting, and housing.[29] The justices also turned their attention to the poor, invalidating the poll tax and durational residence requirements for receiving welfare benefits.[30] The Warren Court's civil liberties record was reinforced by its easing of access to the courts for those wishing to challenge government action. This led groups to turn first to the federal courts for redress of their grievances, particularly against state and local officials, instead of using the courts as a last resort.

Producing probably the greatest controversy, the Court adopted a series of broad rules protecting criminal defendants and suspects. Of these the most notable were *Mapp v. Ohio* (improperly seized evidence inadmissible at trial—the "exclusionary rule"), *Gideon v. Wainwright* (right to counsel for indigents at trials for felonies and major misdemeanors), and *Miranda v. Arizona* (no confession admissible without suspect being warned of rights). The Court also approved "stop and frisk" practices (*Terry v. Ohio*, 1968), lifted restrictions on material that could be taken in a search, approved the use of informants, and supplied the basis for electronic surveillance with a warrant, but these rulings received far less attention. The Court also avoided some problems, such as implementation of school desegregation for over a decade after the *Brown* decision and the basic constitutional question of the right of a private proprietor to refuse service on the basis of race. Furthermore, the Court was criticized for having subordinated the interests of racial minorities to the concerns of whites and having too closely followed public opinion. The Court, it was said, had "struck down only the symbols of racism," leaving racist practices intact, and "had waltzed in time to the music of the white majority—one step forward, one step backward, and sidestep, sidestep."[31]

The Warren Court's level of support for civil liberties was not uniform but was highest at the end. Several Warren Court periods can be identified. The transition from the Vinson Court to the Warren Court was immediately visible in the 1954 *Brown v. Board of Education* school desegregation ruling, but several terms passed before the Court "succeeded impressively in freeing itself from the self-doubts that deterred constitutional development during the 1940–1953 period."[32] Chief Justice Warren himself took more than one term before joining the liberals. Not until the 1956 Term, in the Court's internal security rulings, did one see a distinctly liberal posture. This may have resulted at least as much from Justice Brennan, said to be the Warren Court's intellectual leader, as from the Chief Justice. Congressional reaction to those rulings helped lead to a decline in liberal outcomes; the Court supported civil liberties claims less than half the time in 1958–60. Only when Justice Felix Frankfurter retired in 1962 and was replaced by Justice Arthur Goldberg did the Court have a fifth reliable civil liberties vote, reinforced by Thurgood Marshall, the Court's first black member. Their presence and that of Abe Fortas, who replaced Goldberg, explains the later Warren Court's high level of support of civil liberties claims.

The Burger Court

Personnel changes are crucial for shifts in Supreme Court direction, but are only one part of it. The transition to the Roosevelt Court, which began prior to a change in personnel and was reinforced by new justices such as Hugo Black and William O. Douglas, did not take place until FDR's second term, when his first opportunities to nominate justices occurred. Considerable continuity accompanying change or transformation characterized the transition from the Warren Court to the Burger Court. All courts pass through transitional periods. As they change personnel, their policy direction changes. So does the relationship of the Court to public sentiment. At times it moves closer to public opinion, at times it appears to lead that opinion. Such changes also involve shifts in the Court's predominant role, whether as a restrained discoverer of the law or as a more active developer or maker of policy. At times the transition begins before the end of one chief justice's tenure. At other times, even with replacements of justices or a change in the person in the "center chair," there may be relatively little change. Several years may elapse before a pattern is clear. Moreover, different patterns may characterize different policy areas. The "new" Court may extend earlier rulings; maintain, consolidate, or clarify those rulings; or curtail or erode the precedents of previous years—often with substantial cumulative effect. Direct reversal of precedent may occur, but usually only after several years have elapsed.

Within three years of taking office, President Nixon was able to name not only a Chief Justice but three associate justices as well. Warren Burger became Chief Justice. He was joined first by Harry Blackmun, then by Lewis Powell and William Rehnquist. William O. Douglas, who had served on the Court longer than anyone else, departed in 1975, and President Ford named John Paul Stevens to replace him. (For a list of members of the Supreme Court from the Warren Court to the present, see Figure 1.1.) President Nixon had made the Supreme Court, and particularly its criminal procedure rulings, a subject of

Fig. 1.1   Membership of the Supreme Court (1960s to 1991)

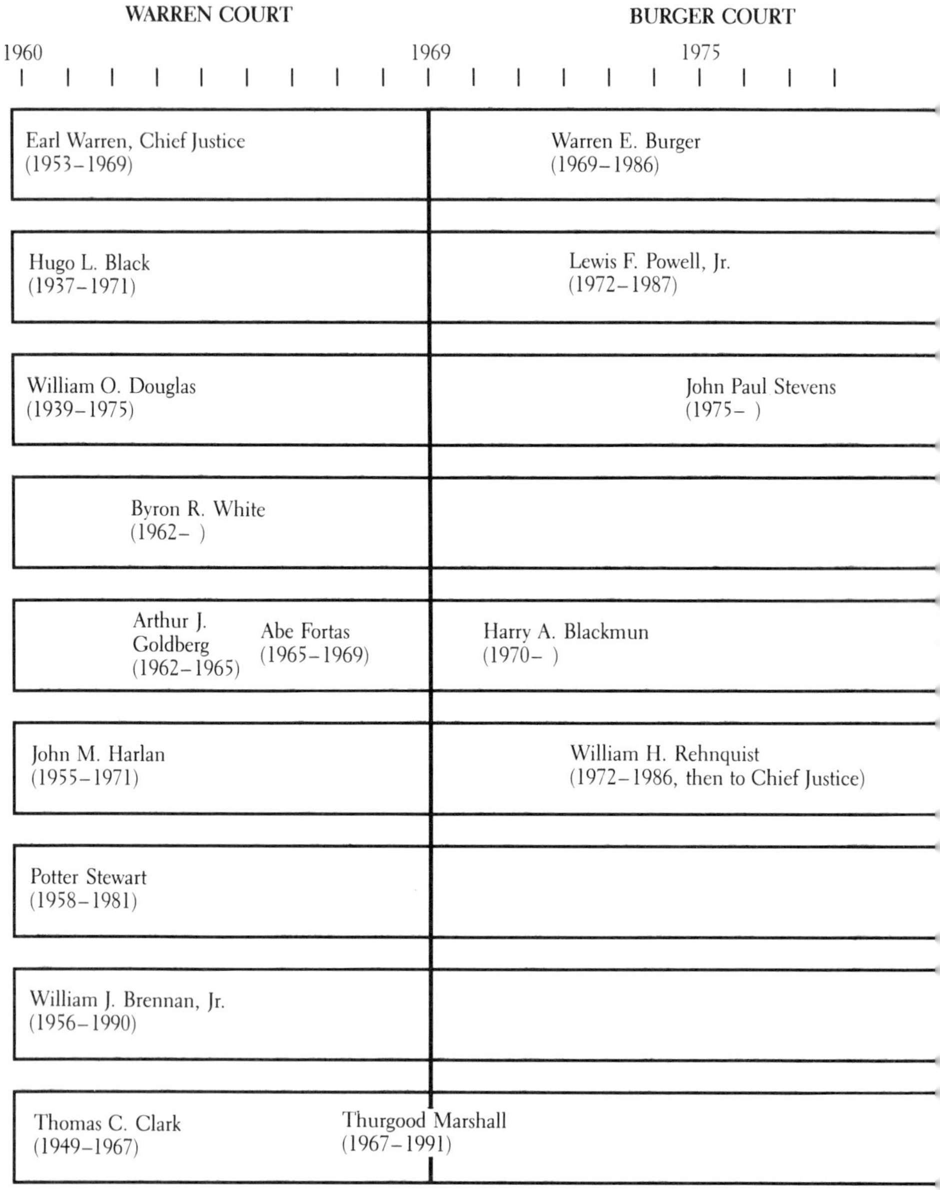

WARREN COURT	BURGER COURT
1960 · · · · · · · · · · 1969 · · · · · · · 1975 · · · · ·	

Earl Warren, Chief Justice (1953–1969)	Warren E. Burger (1969–1986)
Hugo L. Black (1937–1971)	Lewis F. Powell, Jr. (1972–1987)
William O. Douglas (1939–1975)	John Paul Stevens (1975–)
Byron R. White (1962–)	
Arthur J. Goldberg (1962–1965) Abe Fortas (1965–1969)	Harry A. Blackmun (1970–)
John M. Harlan (1955–1971)	William H. Rehnquist (1972–1986, then to Chief Justice)
Potter Stewart (1958–1981)	
William J. Brennan, Jr. (1956–1990)	
Thomas C. Clark (1949–1967) Thurgood Marshall (1967–1991)	

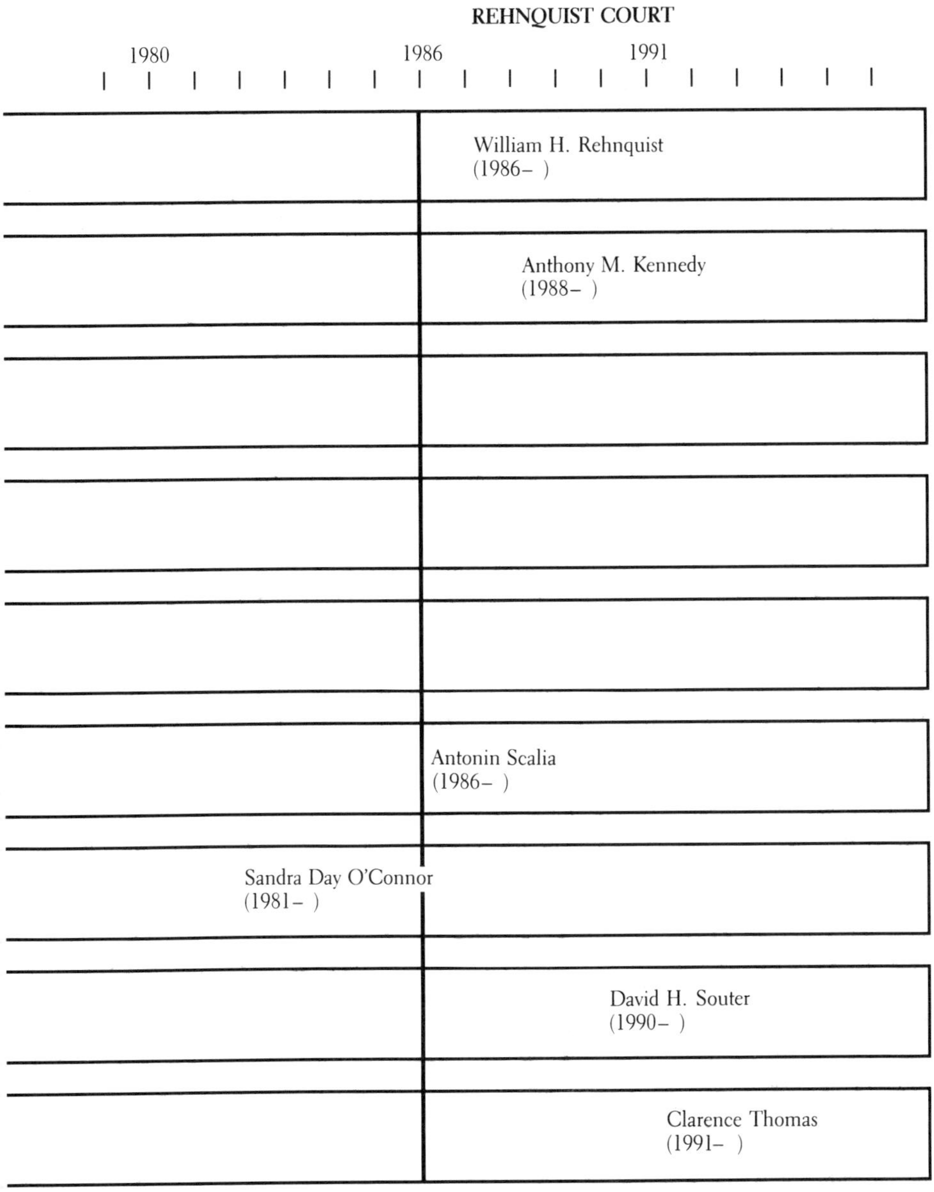

REHNQUIST COURT

1980	1986	1991

William H. Rehnquist
(1986–)

Anthony M. Kennedy
(1988–)

Antonin Scalia
(1986–)

Sandra Day O'Connor
(1981–)

David H. Souter
(1990–)

Clarence Thomas
(1991–)

campaign controversy, and he gave particular attention to the ideology of his Supreme Court nominees. The changes in personnel did bring changes in doctrine and in the Court's relationship to public opinion. However, the changes were not as great as Nixon's campaign efforts had led people to expect.

The ruling striking down the legislative veto; other important rulings on the separation of powers, the most notable of which was the crisis-resolving Watergate Tapes case (see pages 327–28); further historic decisions like those in *Roe v. Wade* (1973), providing protection for the right to an abortion, served to keep the Court almost continuously in the limelight as *a*—not *the*, but *a*—central government institution. On balance, the Burger Court was most certainly more conservative than the Warren Court. The Court was unlikely to move in any other direction. In certain areas of the law, particularly criminal procedure and most particularly search and seizure and confessions, the Court adopted a proprosecution stance. Yet the extent of change varied from area to area and the Court lacked the clear direction of the Warren Court, perhaps because it lacked firm leadership and because Justice Brennan's intellectual leadership remained although he was more frequently in the minority. Moreover, its overall record across the wide civil liberties/civil rights spectrum is also studded with liberal outcomes: support, although with unclear doctrine, for affirmative action programs; development of a woman's right to an abortion; the opening of criminal trials to the public and the press; and the development of protection for "commercial speech."

The Burger Court reinforced or even advanced some Warren Court doctrines and developed rights in some previously unexplored areas. Yet on the whole, the Court's decisions demonstrated considerable withdrawal from and undercutting of Warren Court policies affecting the entire range of civil liberties problems. Initially, Chief Justice Burger produced no great across-the-board policy change, although some areas saw more change than others. The Court limited expansion of Warren Court doctrine, but the basic picture for several years was one of marginal change and a generally unsettled pattern. The Burger Court did not at first directly overrule precedent, instead whittling away at prior rulings. Thus the 1974 Term left a picture of a "reluctant Court" that tried to make potentially important cases stand for as little as possible; a Court whose theme song was the refrain "we *only* decide"; a Court that loved to decide issues "in these particular circumstances"; and a Court that pretended not to be announcing principles even while it was announcing them.[33]

In the mid-1970s the Court consolidated its position. Even then, the Court did not become unremittingly conservative. In 1980, and even after Justice Sandra Day O'Connor replaced Justice Potter Stewart for the 1981 Term, the Court was best characterized by the headline, "Pragmatism, Compromise Mark Court: Tricky Track Record Harder to Categorize Than Pundits Predicted." Yet it did become more conservative, limiting suits for discrimination in government programs and employment, following an "accommodationist" church-state position, creating a "public safety" exception to *Miranda* and the "good faith" exception to the exclusionary rule, placing limits on prisoners' rights, and approving preventive detention for juveniles.[34] Increased tenure by the Chief Justice and the other Nixon appointees did not result in increased stability of position. This led to "drift and division" and a "lack of consistent vision" in what was called "one of the most fragmented Courts" in our history,[35] except on criminal procedure, where the justices were most (and most consistently) conservative. The Court seemed to act pragmatically rather than as the result of an agenda up to the end. In its last term it upheld antisodomy laws as applied to homosexuals while supporting affirmative action and preventing prosecutors' use of peremptory challenges to eliminate minorities from juries.[36]

Despite the rhetoric when its members were appointed, the Burger Court was not noticeably less "restrained" than its predecessor. Restraint might be inferred from increased deference to the legislative and executive branches, and from less strict tests for judging state laws and actions. This was done, however, to produce conservative rulings and was reinforced by the Court's decreased willingness to allow the federal courts to be used to resolve complaints against the government. For example, when a policeman complained that he had been improperly discharged without a hearing, the Court said, "The federal court is not the appropriate forum in which to review the multitude of personnel decisions that are made daily by public agencies. . . . The United States Constitution cannot feasibly be construed to require federal judicial review for every such error."[37]

Also evidence of activism were decisions invalidating federal and state legislative acts, which produced sharp breaks from a pattern of more than 30 years. As noted in 1979,

> In no decision did the Warren Court—nor, for that matter, did any Supreme Court since the mid-1930s—hold that an act of Congress was invalid on the ground that the lawmaking branch had exceeded its delegated powers and invaded ground reserved to the States by the Tenth Amendment. The Burger Court has done so twice. . . . In no decision did the Warren Court—nor, for that matter, did the Supreme Court for a period of over 35 years—invalidate an act of Congress or an act of the President on the ground that it usurped the other branch's constitutional powers.[38]

Yet the Burger Court had done so, and later, in its ruling invalidating the legislative veto, struck down portions of 200 federal statutes at one swell foop.

What legacy did Chief Justice Burger leave? The headline "Burger Court Leaves an Unclear Legacy" is accurate, with respect to doctrine. It may be that the Burger Court, without a strong Chief Justice, will be remembered as the period between the Warren Court and the Rehnquist Court. The Burger Court's conservatism in criminal procedure is obvious, but the picture otherwise is less clear. Thus one can agree that "the continuity and stamp of identity on the Court that Chief Justice Burger wants to personify . . . proved increasingly elusive in his Court's performance." As Justice Powell said after Burger's last term, "there has been no conservative counterrevolution by the Burger Court."[39] One reason is that Burger led neither the Court as a whole nor even his own "bloc," nor—suggesting ineffective leadership—was he able to prevent his "Minnesota Twin," Justice Blackmun, from moving far away from their early joint voting.[40]

Burger's contributions were primarily *outside* the Court rather than inside it. Taking seriously his official title of Chief Justice of *the United States*, he was the first Chief Justice since William Howard Taft (1921–29) to devote considerable effort to judicial administration, particularly but not exclusively in the federal judiciary. The range of his activities was greater than Taft's. He created institutions like the Institute for Court Management, which has provided training for court administrators, and the National Center for State Courts, which provides technical assistance to state courts and conducts research on topics of concern to them and worked for creation of the State Justice Institute, a federal agency that funds state court administration projects. He was the first Chief Justice to appoint an administrative assistant to help with his administrative tasks for both the Court and the judicial system as a whole. His efforts at legislative-executive-judicial contact led to annual meetings among leaders of the three branches to discuss administration of justice issues.[41]

Burger regularly called attention to problems like excessive litigation or inadequate training of lawyers. His comments on the latter led federal judicial districts to impose special requirements for admission to practice before the federal courts. He also called for restructuring of the circuits; elimination of three-judge district court (accomplished: see page 46) and diversity of citizenship jurisdiction (not accomplished: see page 183); and for limitations on federal judicial power over state criminal cases (accomplished by the Rehnquist Court; see pages 186–87). That position was consonant with his votes in the Court's decisions,[42] making him in this way like most other recent Chief Justices, whose "administrative and legal philosophies . . . have complemented one another."[43] He placed on the national agenda some matters that probably would not otherwise have been placed there—most specifically, the proposal for a National Court of Appeals to handle cases on national interpretation of the law (see pages 61–62).

Civil Liberties. The Burger Court's civil liberties decisions, particularly those on criminal procedure, moved the Court closer to public opinion than was the Warren Court at the height of its support for civil liberties claims. In some important civil liberties areas (for example, pregnancy-based discrimination and voting discrimination) Congress was more sympathetic to some civil rights claims.

The Court's change in position, both real and perceived, led some to turn away from the Supreme Court for resolution of their grievances. Civil liberties activity was mounted on other fronts: in Congress, in the extended if unsuccessful effort to obtain ratification of the Equal Rights Amendment (ERA), and, as suggested by liberal members of the Court such as Justice Brennan, in state courts in states where such courts were liberal. Some state high courts were willing to overturn property-tax financing of public education (when the Supreme Court was not), to invalidate zoning laws that excluded moderate- and low-income housing (after the Supreme Court refused to grant standing to those challenging such laws), and to enforce the "wall of separation" between church and state more strictly. This gave some substance to the hope that assistance in enforcing civil liberties could be found there.

These developments, coupled with the events surrounding Watergate, further deflected attention from the Court toward the president and Congress. They moved the balance of influence between the courts and the elected branches of government toward the pre–Warren Court situation in which the Court was not as predominant or central a political actor as it had been during the 1950s and 1960s. Yet the high "surprise level" in its actions and political activity to overturn its rulings (on "forced busing" and abortion) meant it remained more central than the Court of the 1940s. People continue to turn to it for whatever assistance they can obtain. "After all," said one lawyer, "it's the only Supreme Court we have."

The Burger Court's retrenchment on civil liberties and civil rights received the most attention. In Burger's first term, support for civil liberties claims fell to 55 percent. By the 1972 Term, it was down to 43.5 percent, the lowest since 1957, and decreased into the 30 percent range starting with the 1980 Term. A specific indication is the progressive decline, from the 1969 through 1979 Terms, in the rate at which interests of poor people prevailed—from 65 percent at the beginning of the period to only 30 percent in the post-1975 period.[44] Of particular importance was that state officials who challenged assertions of rights replaced civil liberties claimants as the principal victors in civil liberties cases. Closely related was the Court's willingness to upset state court decisions interpreting rights expansively. Furthermore, although during the Warren Court's heyday *no* state civil liberties ruling was overturned for exceeding the Supreme Court's civil liberties standards, the Burger Court did so both directly and, more frequently, by sending cases back to state courts for clarification of the constitutional basis of prorights rulings, although the Court in the 1969–83 Terms overturned a large proportion of cases "which the state courts decided *antithetically* to civil liberties and civil rights claimants."[45]

Despite the decrease in support for civil liberties, the Burger Court did not cut back on Warren Court rulings as much as had been expected, in part because of the strength of those rulings as precedent and the civil liberties education they had provided the public. The Burger Court actually moved forward with Warren Court doctrines in some areas and broke new ground in other areas not considered by the Warren Court. In the *Swann* case, the justices upheld lower court judges' authority to order broad remedies for school segregation, including busing. They also invalidated schemes for evading desegregation and told private schools they could not discriminate on the basis of race.[46] The Court took a strong stand against discrimination in employment. It reinforced Congress's action in passing Title VII of the 1964 Civil Rights Act, by ruling in the *Griggs* case that, even though no discrimination was intended, employment tests not related to the job could not be used if they had a discriminatory effect; the justices also supported back pay and seniority remedies for job discrimination.

However, the Court then moved in a more conservative direction by imposing tests for proving employment discrimination that were far more difficult to satisfy and by sustaining seniority provisions despite the claim that they locked in past discrimination.[47] The Court then imported the new test into cases on housing discrimination and voting rights.[48] The Court also handed down three major cases on affirmative action, the most troublesome topic in the employment discrimination area. The first and best known was the *Bakke* case (1978), where one five-justice majority narrowly invalidated a medical school's action in setting aside a specific number of seats for minorities, but another five-justice majority said that race *could* be taken into account in remedying past discrimination. In the *Weber* and *Fullilove* cases, the Court then upheld programs established by private industry and by Congress that provided positions for minorities in training programs and construction employment. And although rejecting affirmative action programs that protected minorities in the event of layoffs, the justices ended the 1986 Term with strong affirmation of affirmative action programs involving preferences in hiring.[49]

With schools, the Court's pattern was mixed. In *Milliken v. Bradley,* a 1974 ruling in a case from Detroit, the Court struck down busing across school district lines because districts outside the center city had not been shown to have discriminated. The Court also limited lower court judges' discretion to order desegregation, requiring that remedies for school segregation be tailored more narrowly than in the past. Then, showing its lack of predictability, the Court ruled that northern cities like Dayton and Columbus, Ohio, were subject to the full range of desegregation remedies for having maintained segregated school systems since before the Court's 1954 *Brown* ruling.[50]

In sex discrimination cases, women were not given as complete protection as was given racial minorities,[51] but the Court's tone was moderate-to-liberal, not conservative. Perhaps most significant as well as most controversial was the Court's invalidation, in *Roe v. Wade* and *Doe v. Bolton* (1973), of laws interfering with the right to obtain an abortion, particularly during the first trimester of pregnancy, and its striking down a variety of requirements that interfered with a woman's right to obtain an abortion. However, government restrictions on funding of abortions were upheld, federal antidiscrimination provisions that had assisted women (and minorities) were severely limited, and Congress's adoption of male-only draft registration was upheld.[52]

At first the Court advanced a strong position on separation of church and state, including outlawing many forms of aid to elementary and secondary parochial schools, and later by invalidating a statute providing for a moment of silence in the classroom.[53] Later, however, the justices handed down a number of rulings representing not a separationist but an "accommodationist" posture. Most notable was *Lynch v. Donnelly*, which upheld a city's providing a crèche at Christmastime, and a decision sustaining a state law allowing parents tax credits for tuition for parochial schools. [54]

The Court's free speech posture was mixed. In *New York Times v. United States* (1971) the justices refused to allow the government an injunction against publication of the "Pentagon Papers." They struck down "gag orders" on the press in criminal trials, and later found a First Amendment right to open trials. [55] The Court, which refused to allow radio or television coverage of its oral argument, also ruled in *Chandler v. Florida* (1982) that states could allow live electronic media coverage of trials even if defendants objected. However, grand juries were allowed to question reporters about their confidential sources. [56] The Court distinctly moved away from the Warren Court's position on obscenity in *Miller v. California* (1973), rewriting the definition of the concept to give greater scope to local community values. Its most important advance concerning free speech involved "commercial speech," to which the justices gave protection, for example, by striking down restrictions on advertising by pharmacists and lawyers. [57]

Criminal Procedure. The Burger Court's greatest retrenchment from Warren Court doctrine occurred with respect to criminal procedure, particularly searches and confessions. The majority adopted a "crime control" model rather than the Warren Court's preferred "due process" model. This was the area in which the Court most strongly supported government officials—police, prosecutors, and prison administrators. Yet, continuing to confound observers' expectations, the Court left standing both the *Miranda* requirements and the exclusionary rule, despite a campaign by Chief Justice Burger and Justice Rehnquist against the latter. However, both rules were restricted, and the "good faith" exception carved out of the latter was a major victory for law enforcement officers. The Court held the exclusionary rule inapplicable to grand jury proceedings, and made it more difficult to challenge improper searches (see page 172). The Court extended Fourth Amendment protections in the home, but searches of people (alleged drug smugglers in airports and other individuals at crime scenes) and of cars (and their contents) were generally made easier. The justices also supported law enforcement efforts by allowing searches of newspaper offices for evidence relating to a crime, installations of "bugs" and "beepers" on property and cars, aerial surveillance, and school officials' searches of students' lockers. [58]

Miranda, although never overturned, was first weakened by a ruling that confessions obtained without warnings could be used to impeach a witness's testimony at trial, [59] and later by creating a "crime scene" exception to *Miranda*—at the scene of a crime, where weapons needed to be retrieved quickly for public safety, the warnings need not be given before questions were asked (*New York v. Quarles*, 1984). The two most important Burger Court *Miranda* cases involved confessions obtained when police officers, through their statements (not explicit interrogations) played on a suspect's mental state and religious concerns to learn the whereabouts of a murder victim's body or of a murder weapon. In *Brewer v. Williams* (1977), a case which state prosecutors tried to use as a vehicle to seek to have *Miranda* overturned, the Court avoided doing so by ruling that the officers had interfered with the defendant's post-indictment right to counsel.[60] Three years later, the Court defined "interrogation" broadly, to extend beyond direct questions to statements likely to elicit an answer, but said that, on the facts of the case, the defendant had *not* been interrogated in violation of *Miranda* (*Rhode Island v. Innis*, 1980).

The Court extended the right to counsel at trial to all cases where a person was in fact to be jailed (*Argersinger v. Hamlin*, 1972), but limited the right to counsel at police lineups and on appeal. And the Court also legitimized and encouraged plea bargaining and strictly limited challenges to a conviction once a defendant, with assistance of counsel, had entered a guilty plea.[61] Nor would the justices make counsel automatically available for those whose probation or parole was being revoked or provide counsel in prison proceedings for rule violations. In all those situations, procedural protections were provided for the first time,[62] yet the Court seemed to be returning to the old "hands off" posture concerning prison matters when it turned aside attacks on conditions for pretrial detainees (those not yet convicted), deficiencies in prison conditions, and searches of prison cells.[63]

The Court's rulings on capital punishment were among its most important. The Court at first struck down the death penalty *as then applied* (*Furman v. Georgia*, 1972). Then, directly confronting the penalty's constitutionality, the Court held that the death penalty did *not* violate the Eighth Amendment's prohibition against cruel and unusual punishment, at least if the penalty were not mandatory and if aggravating *and* mitigating circumstances were considered in sentencing (*Gregg v. Georgia*, 1976). The Court went on to rule that the death penalty for rape was excessive and grossly disproportionate to the crime (*Coker v. Georgia*, 1977) and required some procedural protections for imposition of the death sentence.[64] However, the Court's majority did not hold state courts tightly to its standards and became increasingly impatient with death penalty appeals and increasingly abrupt in its treatment of them. Thus the majority complained about repeated petitions for habeas corpus, and even denied stays of execution when the issues raised by the Death Row inmate were before Court in as-yet-undecided cases.

The Rehnquist Court's First Years

The 1986 Term was Rehnquist's first as Chief Justice and the first in which Justice Scalia brought his intellectual firepower to the conservative cause on the Court. After his first term, Rehnquist was more frequently in control of the Court's majority. That occurred less through his leadership than through changing personnel on the Court. The first to retire was Justice Powell, thought by many to be a "balance" on the Court.[65] Judge Anthony Kennedy of the Ninth

Circuit replaced Powell, but only after the Senate rejected the highly controversial nomination of Judge Robert Bork and the nomination of Judge Douglas Ginsburg was withdrawn. As expected, Kennedy joined the Court's conservative side. His presence, along with the later addition of Justice David Souter to replace Justice Brennan, brought Rehnquist a solid conservative majority. Appointment of Justice Clarence Thomas to replace Justice Thurgood Marshall simply provided additional reinforcement for an already-created dominant conservative bloc. (See Figure 1.2, The Court's Membership.) Some thought that Judge Bork, although his outspoken views helped bring about his defeat, was the most highly qualified nominee to the Court in this century. Those selected after his defeat were low-key (Kennedy, Souter) or had only brief judicial experience (Souter, Thomas). In fact, their addition to the Court was said by a leading conservative to make the Court a mediocre body.[66]

Justice Marshall's departure left only Justices Blackmun and Stevens to carry the liberal banner. One could see the situation in headlines like "The Conservative Majority Solidifies" and "Conservatives Lock Up Control of High Court as Marshall Retires." That conservative dominance finally brought about the "counterrevolution" against the Warren Court that people had expected to happen soon after Warren Burger became Chief Justice. One saw it in the overturning of precedents—the Warren Court's, the Burger Court's, and even its own. As one observer noted, in the Rehnquist Court, "the spectre of politically conservative *results* and liberal judicial *methods* combined in an unusual fashion. The character of the Rehnquist Court is *not* simply that case results serve ideologically conservative ends. The methods used are frequently those of judicial liberals."[67]

As was true with the Burger Court, the Rehnquist Court's most important actions were in the area of civil liberties and civil rights. With its new Chief Justice, the Court produced expected conservatism in criminal procedure. In addition to upholding searches in a variety of situations, the Court sustained preventive detention, and upheld the death penalty against a challenge that it was applied in a racially discriminatory manner.[68] The Court supported property

Figure 1.2   The Court's Membership, 1993

	Joined Court	Appointed By
William H. Rehnquist	1972	Nixon
(became Chief Justice)	1986	Reagan
Byron R. White	1962	Kennedy
Harry A. Blackmun	1970	Nixon
John Paul Stevens	1975	Ford
Sandra Day O'Connor	1981	Reagan
Antonin Scalia	1986	Reagan
Anthony M. Kennedy	1988	Reagan
David H. Souter	1990	Bush
Clarence Thomas	1991	Bush

rights by finding land-use regulations were "takings" requiring compensation and by upholding state anti-takeover laws. At the same time, the Court was liberal on many important civil liberties and civil rights matters. Most notable were rulings upholding affirmative action programs involving hiring and promotion and allowing states to require Rotary Clubs to admit women.[69] Indeed, in the 1986 and 1987 Terms, the Court's support for civil liberties claims rose, in large measure because of the influence of Justice Brennan. The Court then settled back to a level somewhat higher than in the last Burger Court years. A look at the 1980 through 1990 Terms shows that, for all but the first and last of those years, support for civil liberties claims overall was higher than for criminal procedure civil liberties claims. The latter was an average of 12.5 percent lower, a greater gap than earlier. Except for 1986 and 1987, as just noted, overall civil liberties support was in the 30–40 percent range. It was also higher in the 1990 Term, an indication we should pay attention to *all* cases, not just the most controversial (and noteworthy) ones. Support for criminal procedure civil liberties claims was twice *below 20 percent*, was generally in the 20–30 percent range, and only once was over 40 percent. (See Figure 1.3.)

In the criminal justice area, the Court continued to expand the ability of police to search individuals and places, including cars and their contents (*Cali-*

Figure 1.3   Supreme Court Support for Civil Liberties Claims, 1980–1990 Terms

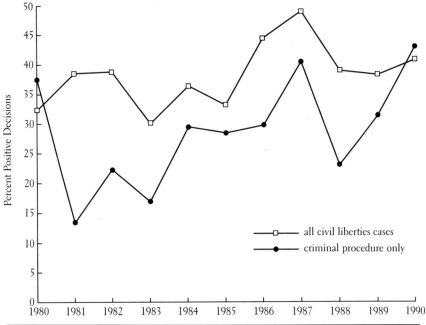

Source: Data gathered by author; graphics adapted from Thomas Church, Jr.

fornia v. Acevedo, 1991) and allowed drug testing of employees in some situations.[70] The Court further limited application of the *Miranda* rule and weakened protection against coerced confessions by ruling that their admission could be considered "harmless error."[71] Although the dissenters argued that the majority seemed impatient with death penalty cases, the majority repeatedly upheld application of the death penalty. This included allowing its use on defendants who were mentally retarded or were juveniles when they committed the crime, and reversing itself to allow the introduction of "victim impact statements" in death penalty cases.[72] In a move parallel to calls to shorten the period of review after the death penalty was imposed, the Court also severely limited the availability of federal court habeas corpus relief for convicted defendants (see pages 186–87).

The majority adopted a more "accommodationist" church-state position, especially when it upheld laws applying to all people over claims that the laws interfered with the free exercise of religion but in 1992 it strengthened the Court's position on school prayer in invalidating benedictions at public school graduations.[73] As to free speech, the most important rulings were those on flag desecration and hate speech. A closely divided Court, with conservatives Kennedy and Scalia in the majority, declared unconstitutional, as an interference with freedom of expression, those state laws that outlawed flag-burning. When Congress responded to overwhelming calls to overturn the decision by enacting a new federal law aimed at flag-burning, the same justices struck it down, too (*Texas v. Johnson,* 1989; *Eichman v. United States,* 1990). The Court also dealt a severe blow to attempts to control "hate speech" directed at racial minorities, women, or other disliked groups when it struck down a city ordinance against bias-related crime because of the crime's expressive element (*R.A.V. v. City of St. Paul,* 1992).

Abortion and affirmative action remained the two long-standing most controversial topics facing the Court. Despite calls that it do so, the Court did not overturn *Roe v. Wade.* Its 1989 5–4 ruling in *Webster v. Reproductive Health Services* demonstrated the majority's willingness to uphold limits on a woman's right to obtain an abortion and led many to think the abandonment of *Roe v. Wade* awaited only the appointment of another justice. So did rulings the following terms upholding requirements that minors notify at least one parent before obtaining an abortion and sustaining regulations that prevented family planning clinics accepting federal funds from telling their clients about the availability of abortion.[74] In 1992, in *Planned Parenthood v. Casey,* the Court firmly upheld *Roe v. Wade,* although by only a 5-4 vote, but allowed states to impose more restrictions.

The law of affirmative action remained unsettled. A 1989 ruling severely tightened the requirements for municipal governments wishing to establish "set-asides" for minority-owned businesses, but in 1990, in Justice Brennan's last decision, a majority upheld Federal Communications Commission policies assisting minorities to acquire radio and television stations.[75] The Court's withdrawal from protecting the rights of minorities and women was most visible in June 1989 rulings making plaintiffs' success in employment discrimination suits far more difficult—rulings overturned by Congress in 1991 (see page 321)—and in rulings limiting the length of time school desegregation plans had to remain in place, but the Court surprised by ruling that Mississippi's public colleges and universities remained segregated and thus must be desegregated, with no exception for "predominantly black" institutions.[76]

In general, the Supreme Court's view of civil rights has been increasingly narrow. Not only are rights defined narrowly, but the government's latitude to limit such rights is defined broadly—and the situations in which the government had the duty to protect others has also been limited, providing even less protection.[77] Over the longer run, one might expect continuing retrenchment in the protection of civil liberties and civil rights both by the Supreme Court and by the federal courts. The latter might come at least as much from President Reagan's and President Bush's appointees to those courts as from the Supreme Court's direction. This might lead to increased state court protection of liberties, begun during the Burger Court, and to an increased focus on Congress to overturn Supreme Court rulings limiting rights. The Supreme Court, while continuing to be an important actor in the American scheme, will be less central, perhaps by far, than it has been over the last three decades.

The Longer Term

Before leaving the subject of the Court's centrality in our political scheme, we should stand back from our detailed attention to look at the debate over whether the Supreme Court has interfered with the work of the other, elected branches of government, or has followed them. If the latter were the case, certainly the Court would be less central. In the 1950s, Robert Dahl, relying on the 78 cases through 1957 in which the Supreme Court had exercised judicial review to invalidate 86 provisions of federal law, asserted that the Court does not block the legislature and executive but, as a part of the dominant national alliance, actually legitimizes their work. Only half of the Court's invalidating actions came within four years of the legislation's enactment, with more than one-third of the "prompt" overrulings occurring during the Court's emasculation of the New Deal. In most instances when recent legislation was overturned, Congress reversed the Court or the Court itself did so somewhat later.

According to Dahl, seldom is the Court outside the dominant alliance for long. Moreover, the Court generally can do little without support from president and Congress. The Court might win small battles, but the justices are not likely to be successful "on matters of *major* policy, particularly if successive presidents and Congresses continue to support the policy the Court has called unconstitutional." When other political actors are unable to decide important questions, the Court can take action, but even then it does so at great risk and can succeed only if its actions are in tune with the norms of the political leadership.[78]

This position has been met directly. One argument is that Dahl over-estimated the Court's ability to legitimize; another, that Dahl *under*estimated the Supreme Court's effectiveness. David Adamany, arguing the first of these two positions, said the Court cannot legitimize unless it strikes down the acts of other branches at least occasionally. If all statutes and administrative actions were sustained, the Court's ability to legitimize would be meaningless. During constitutional crises, the Court cannot grant legitimacy because at such times justices, having been appointed earlier, are of the party opposite to that controlling the elected branches. The Court's actions invalidating legislation, more likely when one political party has dominated Congress and nominees of the other party controlled the Court, certainly do not grant legitimacy to the new coalition. Instead, conflict between the Court and the elected branches after realigning elections—those in which party control of the presidency changes and there is substantial shift in the voters' partisan identification—has "somewhat discredited and sometimes checked the lawmaking majority." In each such situation, however, the result has been "a clash that left doubtful the Court's capacity ultimately to legitimize the new regime and its policies." One hardly has legitimation when as a result of changes in personnel or its own strategic movement the Court finally adopts the dominant coalition's position. Instead there is "more the appearance of surrender to superior force."[79]

The public also does not seem to know about the Court's legitimizing role. What little the public does know is principally about cases in which majorities have been checked, not legitimized (see pages 357–58). The Court's decisions also do not eliminate substantial opposition to its policies or prevent legislative attacks on the Court and efforts to reverse its rulings. Moreover, the views of political elites, who know more than does the general public about the Court and its decisions (see page 358), are largely conditioned by the elites' political attitudes, not the Court's actions. Thus the Court does not legitimize policy for the nation through the elites; elites confer legitimacy on the courts. The Court does not itself help create respect for the political system, but commands respect because it is part of the political system. This ultimately saves the Court when a new political coalition considers limiting the justices.

Responding to Dahl differently, Jonathan Casper noted that the Court has intervened decisively in the policymaking process, holding 32 provisions of federal law unconstitutional in 28 cases from 1956 through 1974—roughly one-fourth of the instances in which national legislation had been invalidated up to that time. (Prompt overrulings of legislation—within four years of enactment—occurred in only a few of the cases. In only one, on the 18-year-old vote, and in no case involving older legislation, was the Court reversed.) Court decisions, even when ultimately overturned, delayed implementation of policies for some years after they are enacted, a further indication of the Court's effectiveness. Also important in evaluating the Court's effects are the Court's statutory interpretation rulings, which have produced important policy on a wide range of subjects.

When one assesses the Court's effectiveness, its initiatives not involving invalidation of national legislation, such as Marshall's *McCulloch v. Maryland* and *Gibbons v. Ogden* rulings, must also be taken into account, as should the Court's introduction of new issues and new participants into the political process, which may assist actors' ability "to attract adherents, mobilize resources, and build institutions."[80]

The Supreme Court's Roles

This look at the controversy in which courts are often embroiled, the Supreme Court's changing place in the American political system, and the Court's recent pattern of decisions, begins to provide some sense of the roles the Court has played, does play, and is expected to play, from its "unique position as the only institution in our society capable of an authoritative, final judicial resolution of a controversy governed by federal law." The functions the Court is supposed to perform or might perform are not important simply in the abstract but affect how the Court conducts its business.[81]

Article III of the Constitution mentions "judicial power" and indicates the reach of that power. "Judicial power" is not otherwise explained nor is the Supreme Court's work otherwise indicated. There are, however, functions, or tasks, generally associated with the highest appellate court in a nation's legal system. These functions include:

- marking boundaries between national power and state power;
- maintaining boundaries between decision-making units at any level of government;
- interpreting and clarifying statutory law and common (judge-made) law;
- delineating limits of governmental authority against claims of individual liberty;
- insuring its place as final interpreter of the Constitution and laws; and
- overseeing lower courts' interpretation and application of legal rules.[82]

> The judicial Power shall extend to all Cases, in Law and Equity, arising under this Constitution, the Laws of the United States, and Treaties made, or which shall be made, under their Authority; to all Cases affecting Ambassadors, other public Ministers and Consuls; to all Cases of admiralty and maritime Jurisdiction; to Controversies to which the United States shall be a Party; to Controversies between two or more States; between a State and Citizens of another State; between Citizens of different States; between Citizens of the same State claiming Lands under Grants of different States; and between a State, or the Citizens thereof, and foreign States, Citizens or Subjects. (Art. III, Sec. 2)

These multiple tasks do not necessarily fit together well and may in fact conflict with each other. Thus the Supreme Court, "a court of law operating within a malleable but recognizable set of rules," is both "a tribunal dispensing justice between litigants" and "a coequal branch of the federal government with a responsibility for formulating national policy while deciding specific cases."[83]

There is, however, "an unwillingness or inability to resolve conflicting visions of the Court's responsibilities."[84] And there is disagreement over particular functions. For example, in a recent case—the first flag-burning decision—the majority and minority disagreed over whether the Court should play what used to be called the role of "Republican schoolmaster," that is, moral educator: Justice Brennan, for the majority, spoke of strengthening the flag's special role through persuasion, not punishment, while Chief Justice Rehnquist, calling Brennan's words "a regrettably patronizing civics lecture," said the Court should not be speaking to the public "as if they were truant school children."[85]

The Supreme Court, when it performs the functions or tasks identified above for a highest appellate court, becomes a principal national policymaker. Some expect the Court to be such an actor; they assign it such a role. Many other actors in the American governmental system have not, however, fully or easily accepted that broad role. For many years the principal belief about the Supreme Court was that the Court did not make, but only found, the law; this is still believed by many (see page 360). The idea that there was an external, immutable truth that could be found through "right reason"—an idea that is part of the philosophical view known as *natural law,* and for which Justice Thomas had some affinity—took the form that judges found preestablished law in statutes, regulations, and particularly the Constitution, applying in specific cases the intentions of the authors of those documents. Reverence for the Supreme Court, which was thought to be "above politics," reinforced this view: the Constitution became our Bible and the Supreme Court justices our high priests, and the public transferred "our sense of the definitive and timeless character of the Constitution to the judges who expound it."[86]

The belief that courts found rather than made the law has had considerable force and has been enunciated by the justices themselves. It was stated perhaps most starkly by Justice Owen Roberts just one year before President Franklin Roosevelt attempted to "pack" the Court because of its obstruction of the New Deal:

> When an Act of Congress is appropriately challenged in the courts as not conforming to the constitutional mandate, the judicial branch of the Government has only one duty—to lay the article of the Constitution which is invoked beside the statute which is challenged and to decide whether the latter squares with the former. All the court does, or can do, is to announce its considered judgment upon the question. The only power it has, if such it may be called, is the power of judgment. This court neither approves nor condemns any legislative policy. Its delicate and difficult office is to ascertain and declare whether the legislation is in accordance with, or in contravention of, the provisions of the Constitution; and, having done that, its duty ends.[87]

This disingenuous statement—by a justice who was soon to shift his vote on the validity of economic regulation in the famous "Switch in Time That Saved

Nine" (by blunting FDR's 1937 attack on the Court)—has been called the *slot machine theory of judicial interpretation*: if you get two apples and a lemon, you lose; if three oranges appear, you win. Despite its amazingly simplistic character, this myth of what judges do has been perpetuated even by some who realize it to be a myth, because they believe that the myth makes the Court's decisions legitimate in the eyes of those affected by them. Perhaps this explains Justice Potter Stewart's remark that, "For me there is only one possible way to judge cases, and that is to judge each case on its own facts of record, under the law and the United States Constitution, conscientiously, independently, and with complete personal detachment."[88]

Myth or no myth, the Supreme Court is without doubt a policymaker, "not an impartial arbiter but a participant in social conflict [seeking] to serve twin goals of system stability and responsible government through conflict management."[89] The Court may do this in part by giving legitimacy to existing policy (but see pages 26–28). It also helps manage conflict by providing an arena in which major national issues can be debated, "by clarifying and sharpening political conflicts," by making choices in disputes "intelligible and explainable,"[90] even when the Court itself does not resolve the issues that are raised. As de-Tocqueville noted long ago, most political, economic, and social issues in the United States are transformed into legal questions that end up in court. When legislative and executive arenas are not open to debate on major issues, such as racial equality before the 1960s, those issues are particularly likely to be moved to the courts for resolution. Even when elected officials do consider important issues, they may prefer to allow ultimate resolution of those issues to be made by the justices rather than assuming responsibility themselves. However, the Court's actions may raise the level of conflict or provoke dispute rather than resolve it, as the 1973 abortion decision did. And we must remember that, for all its importance, the Supreme Court is "in vital respects a dependent body"—dependent on others for its jurisdiction, for its funding, for the nomination and confirmation of its members, and, perhaps most important, for the carrying out of its mandates.[91]

The Supreme Court's policy-making role was made clear by the Judiciary Act of 1925, called the "Judges Bill" because justices strongly urged its adoption. It gave the Court its present power to select the cases it would hear. A court required to decide all cases brought to it, like the U.S. courts of appeals, could be more easily seen as a regular "court of law," or what might be called a "court of errors and appeals," engaging primarily in "error-correction" (review of trial court decisions for error) rather than "lawmaking" or "institutional review," in which the court would "announce, clarify and harmonize" the law.[92] Yet it is hard to say that a court is not making policy when it can choose cases affecting broad classes of people and use them to announce rules intended to have general application. Indeed, although the Court does take some cases because of "human concerns," and dissenters have argued that it engages in too much "error correction" instead of attending to its "broader responsibilities," the justices themselves have made clear that the Court is expected to decide "cases of broad significance" and not "to correct every perceived error coming from the lower . . . courts."[93]

Cases of broad significance more often than not produce division in the Court. This indicates that the law can hardly be clear or obvious and makes it quite difficult to maintain the view that the justices are only finding the law. If a trial judge decides a case one way, only to be reversed by an appellate court by a vote of, say, 8–7, and the Supreme Court reverses in turn by a 5–4 vote, can one claim the law is being "found"? (One is reminded of the joke, "There stands the Supreme Court like a rock, 5–4.") The law-finding myth may not have been difficult to believe when the Court's rulings conformed closely to the nation's predominant ideology, as in the probusiness era of the late nineteenth century. However, the conflict between President Franklin Roosevelt and the Court over New Deal programs altered the view that the Court found law and produced a realization that "judicial decisions are not babies brought by judicial storks, but are born out of the travail of economic circumstances."[94] Further confirming the realization was Chief Justice Charles Evans Hughes's statement that the law is what the judges say it is, a recognition that judges exercise discretion in interpreting ambiguous language in statutes and the Constitution.

Debate continued about what the Supreme Court *should* do, but doubt about its policy-making role and the political effects of its decisions was further extinguished by resistance to and attacks on rulings of the Warren Court on such subjects as internal security, reapportionment, school prayer, and criminal procedure. The hold of the myth of the Court as lawfinder may have been further reduced by the portrayal in *The Brethren* of the very human traits of the Burger Court's justices and of their bargaining and negotiating over the Court's opinions, and from revelations about justices' continuing involvement in extrajudicial political activities (see pages 293–95).[95]

Virtually all who follow the Court's work now admit that the Court does make policy and cannot avoid doing so. Some justices have even openly acknowledged it. Justice Byron White, dissenting in *Miranda v. Arizona*, argued that the majority's ruling, while not exceeding the Court's powers, served to "underscore the obvious—that the Court has not discovered or found the law in making today's decision, nor has it derived it from irrefutable sources." Instead it had made new law "in much the same way that it has done in the course of interpreting other great clauses of the Constitution. This is what the Court historically has done. Indeed, *it is what it must do* and will continue to do until and unless there is some fundamental change in the constitutional distribution of governmental power."[96]

Although Justice Field once said, "When we become judges, we are not required to be blind to what we see as men," from time to time judges try to say that they do not engage in policy-making based on their personal values—that they act differently as judges from the way they would act in other situations. As

Justice Frankfurter put it in 1943 while dissenting when the Court invalidated the compulsory flag salute for schoolchildren:

> As judges we are neither Jew nor Gentile, neither Catholic nor agnostic. As a member of this Court I am not justified in writing my private notions of policy into the Constitution. . . . The duty of a judge who must decide which of two claims before the Court shall prevail . . . is not that of the ordinary person. [97]

Justice Blackmun, dissenting in 1972 when the majority invalidated the death penalty as then applied, said the punishment "violates childhood's training and life's experience" and that as a legislator he would sponsor legislation to repeal the penalty and as a governor he would use executive clemency to prevent people from being executed. But, he said, "There—on the Legislative Branch of the State or Federal Government, and secondarily, on the Executive Branch—is where the authority and responsibility for this kind of action lie." [98]

Such statements may continue to provide support for those who continue to believe that the Court finds the law and that it should act in special, nonpolitical ways. These beliefs are part of the context within which the Court, like any other policymaker, must act and which serve to constrain its actions. Indeed, the Supreme Court must continue to act like a court if it is to be effective. However, such statements, even if deeply felt by the person making them, may not only distract us from seeing the political values supported by the justices' votes but may well be irrelevant for those most directly affected by the Court's decisions. Whatever a judge's anguish and however moving the statement of that anguish, the ultimate consumer is interested in the judge's votes, in the specific outcome of the case, not in the judge's rhetoric, no matter how much that rhetoric interests other judges and lawyers. Thus someone on Death Row would be more interested in Justice Blackmun's vote to uphold capital punishment than in the justice's personal unhappiness about the death penalty.

Particularly if they are members of a high appellate court that decides controversial cases, judges cannot put past experience and personal values, particularly their policy views, fully to one side, although they vary in the degree to which they can do so. Some are highly predictable, for example, William O. Douglas at the liberal end of the political spectrum and William H. Rehnquist at the conservative end. Others struggle to put aside those views, although they sometimes wear them on their sleeve. For example, Justice Kennedy, joining the majority in striking down a flag-desecration statute, spoke of the "personal toll" that such a choice entailed and said the case "illustrates better than most that the judicial power is often difficult in its exercise," with judges in a situation where "sometimes we must make decisions we do not like. We make them because they are right, right in the sense that the law and the Constitution, as we see them, compel the result." [99]

If judges were readily interchangeable one for another (fungible), senators and interest groups would not display such concern about the values held by potential members of the High Court, as women's groups did about Antonin Scalia's lack of sympathy with feminist concerns; as civil rights groups did about William Rehnquist—first, at the time of his initial appointment to the Court, about opposition to a public accommodations ordinance in Phoenix, and, then at the time of his nomination to be Chief Justice, about his harassment of minority voters and the racial and religious restrictive covenants attached to deeds on property he owned; and as liberal senators did about Judge Bork's views on privacy and Judge Souter's and Judge Thomas's views on abortion.

Personal values do not, however, always dominate judges' decisions (see pages 250–61). *Judicial role conceptions*—expectations, based on others' views, of what a judge should do—can also affect judges' actions, as can other factors like the Court's internal institutional norms. Yet, because the justices' policy positions do play a major part in the Supreme Court's decisions, the Court is quite clearly a policymaker, although the political *effects* of its decisions would make it one in any event.

As a policymaker, the Supreme Court does not play a single uniform policymaking role. There are differences from one policy area to the next in the degree to which the Court makes policy. At times policymaking is evident in major single decisions; at other times policy develops cumulatively through several decisions in a policy area. In some areas, the Court may be a "policy leader"; in others, it may avoid such leadership. It may accept Congress's statement of the need for a statute or an administrative agency's rationale for a regulation, or it may make its own determination of the need and evaluation of the rationale. Such variation "might seem rather strange in an isolated and insulated court administering The Law by processes of rigorous legal logic" but is not unusual "in a political agency faced with a wide range of problems, each entailing a different constellation of political forces."[100] However, although the Court is a policymaker, it is not just any old political actor. It wears special garb, proceeds by means of special forms, and uses specialized language. It is *both* a political institution and, because of its format, procedures, and language, a legal one.

Notes

1. *Brown v. Allen*, 344 U.S. 443, at 540 (1953).

2. This section is drawn from Stephen L. Wasby, "Arrogation of Power or Accountability: 'Judicial Imperialism' Revisited," *Judicature* 65 (October 1981): 209–19.

3. Christopher Wolfe, *The Rise of Modern Judicial Review: From Constitutional Interpretation to Judge-Made Law* (New York: Basic Books, 1986), pp. ix, 3, 60, 204, 259.

4. See Donald Horowitz, *The Courts and Social Policy* (Washington, D.C.: The Brookings Institution, 1977); Nathan Glazer, "Toward an Imperial Judiciary," *The Public Interest* 40 (Fall 1975): 104–23; Raoul Berger, *Government by the Judiciary: The Transformation of the Fourteenth Amendment* (Cambridge, Mass.: Harvard University Press, 1977).

5. See the studies in Phillip J. Cooper, *Hard Judicial Choices: Federal District Court Judges and State and Local Officials* (New York: Oxford University Press, 1988).

6. *Spallone v. United States*, 110 S.Ct. 625 (1990); *Missouri v. Jenkins*, 110 S.Ct. 1650 (1990). In early 1992, the Court ruled that lower courts should use a flexible standard in determining whether to reopen consent decrees that had resulted from institutional reform litigation, although the burden

was to remain on the party wishing to reopen the decree. *Rufo v. Inmates of Suffolk County Jail*, 112 S.Ct. 748 (1992).

7. *Mireles v. Waco*, 112 S.Ct. 286 (1991).

8. Robert Sheran, interview, *The Third Branch* 13 (March 1981): 1.

9. Abram Chayes, "The Role of the Judge in Public Law Litigation," *Harvard Law Review* 89 (1976): 1281–1310.

10. For a well-developed set of criteria for examining the relative capacity of policymaking institutions, see Lief Carter, "When Courts Should Make Policy: An Institutional Approach," *Public Law and Public Policy*, ed. John Gardiner (New York: Praeger, 1977), pp 141–57.

11. Ralph Cavanagh and Austin Sarat, "Thinking About Courts: Toward and Beyond a Jurisprudence of Judicial Competence," *Law & Society Review* 14 (Winter 1980): 406.

12. For a more complete discussion, see Stephen L. Wasby, "Accountability of the Courts," *Accountability in Urban Society*, ed. Scott Greer et al. (Beverly Hills, Calif.: Sage, 1978), pp. 143–68.

13. Ibid., p. 145.

14. Martin Shapiro, *Courts: A Comparative and Political Analysis* (Chicago: University of Chicago Press, 1981), p. 20.

15. Stuart Scheingold, "Constitutional Rights and Social Change: Civil Rights in Perspective," *Judging the Constitution: Critical Essays on Judicial Lawmaking*, eds. Michael W. McCann and Gerald L. Houseman (Glenview, Ill.: Scott, Foresman, 1989), pp. 73–91.

16. For the varying effect in race relations cases, see Jack Peltason, *Fifty-Eight Lonely Men* (New York: Harcourt, Brace and World, 1961); Charles Hamilton, *The Bench and the Ballot: Southern Federal Judges and Black Voters* (New York: Oxford University Press, 1973); Micheal Giles and Thomas Walker, "Judicial Policy-Making and Southern School Segregation," *Journal of Politics* 37 (November 1975): 917–36.

17. Laurence Baum, "Measuring Policy Change in the U.S. Supreme Court," *American Political Science Review* 82 (September 1988): 909.

18. Others were said by Chief Justice Hughes to have been *Hepburn v. Griswold*, 75 U.S. 603 (1870), the first Legal Tender Case, in which the Court invalidated use of paper money to pay debts, and *Pollock v. Farmers' Loan and Trust Co.*, 157 U.S. 429 (1895), holding the income tax unconstitutional. Some have referred to more contemporary cases, like *Miranda v. Arizona*, 384 U.S. 436 (1966), or the 1973 abortion rulings (*Roe v. Wade*, 410 U.S. 113, and *Doe v. Bolton*, 410 U.S. 179), in such terms.

19. For example, *Hurtado v. California*, 110 U.S. 516 (1884) (grand jury indictment), and *Twining v. New Jersey*, 211 U.S. 78 (1908) (Fifth Amendment).

20. *Abrams v. United States*, 250 U.S. 616 (1919), and *Schenck v. United States*, 249 U.S. 47 (1919). See Richard Polenberg, *Fighting Faiths: The Abrams Case, The Supreme Court, and Free Speech* (New York: Viking Penguin, 1987). See also *Gitlow v. New York*, 268 U.S. 652 (1925).

21. On child labor legislation, see *Hammer v. Dagenhart*, 247 U.S. 251 (1918) (commerce), and *Bailey v. Drexel Furniture*, 259 U.S. 20 (1922) (taxation).

22. For example, *Schechter Poultry Corp. v. United States*, 295 U.S. 495 (1935); *United States v. Butler*, 297 U.S. 1 (1936); *Carter v. Carter Coal Co.*, 298 U.S. 238 (1936).

23. *National Labor Relations Board v. Jones & Laughlin Steel Corp.*, 301 U.S. 1 (1937); *United States v. Darby*, 312 U.S. 100 (1941).

24. There is some dispute over Congress's power to regulate state and local governments. See *National League of Cities v. Usery*, 426 U.S. 833 (1976), and *Garcia v. San Antonio Metropolitan Transit Authority*, 469 U.S. 528 (1985); see also *Gregory v. Ashcroft*, 111 S. Ct. 2395 (1991).

25. *Shelley v. Kraemer*, 334 U.S. 1 (1948) (restrictive covenants); *Sweatt v. Painter*, 339 U.S. 629 (1950); and *McLaurin v. Board of Regents*, 339 U.S. 637 (1950) (law school and graduate education). Whites-only primary elections had been invalidated during the war: *Smith v. Allwright*, 321 U.S. 649 (1944).

26. C. Herman Pritchett, *Civil Liberties and the Vinson Court* (Chicago: University of Chicago Press, 1954).

27. See Mary L. Dudziak, "Desegregation as a Cold War Imperative," *Stanford Law Review* 41 (November 1988): 61–120.

28. Reapportionment: *Reynolds v. Sims*, 377 U.S. 533 (1964); school prayer: *Engel v. Vitale*, 370 U.S. 421 (1962), and *Abington School District v. Schempp*, 374 U.S. 203 (1963); obscenity: *Roth v. United States/Alberts v. California*, 354 U.S. 476 (1957); libel: *New York Times v. Sullivan*, 376

U.S. 254 (1964). On libel, see Anthony Lewis, *Make No Law: The Sullivan Case and the First Amendment* (New York: Random House, 1991). See generally Stephen L. Wasby, *Continuity and Change: From the Warren Court to the Burger Court* (Pacific Palisades, Calif.: Goodyear, 1976), pp. 71–77.

29. Public accommodations: *Heart of Atlanta Motel v. United States*, 371 U.S. 241 (1964), and *Katzenbach v. McClung*, 379 U.S. 294 (1964); voting: *South Carolina v. Katzenbach*, 383 U.S. 301 (1966); housing: *Jones v. Mayer*, 392 U.S. 409 (1968).

30. *Harper v. Virginia Board of Elections*, 383 U.S. 663 (1963); *Shapiro v. Thompson*, 394 U.S. 618 (1960).

31. Lewis M. Steel, "Nine Men in Black Who Think White," *New York Times Magazine*, October 13, 1968, pp. 56, 117.

32. Robert G. McCloskey, "Reflections on the Warren Court," *Virginia Law Review* 51 (November 1965): 1234.

33. Paul Bender, "The Reluctant Court," *Civil Liberties Review* 2 (Fall 1975): 101.

34. *Grove City College v. Bell*, 465 U.S. 555 (1984), and *Firefighters v. Stotts*, 467 U.S. 561 (1984) (discrimination and affirmative action); *New York v. Quarles*, 467 U.S. 649 (1986) (*Miranda*); *United States v. Leon*, 468 U.S. 897 (1984), and *Massachusetts v. Sheppard*, 468 U.S. 981 (1984) ("good faith" exception); *Hudson v. Palmer*, 467 U.S. 517 (1984) (prisoners' rights); *Schall v. Martin*, 467 U.S. 253 (1984) (detention of juveniles).

35. See Benno C. Schmidt, Jr., "As Burger Continues, His Court Becomes Unstable," *New York Times*, September 30, 1984.

36. *Bowers v. Hardwick*, 478 U.S. 186 (1986) (sodomy); *Local 28 v. E.E.O.C.*, 478 U.S. 421 (1986), and *Local 39 v. City of Cleveland*, 478 U.S. 501 (1986) (affirmative action); and *Batson v. Kentucky*, 476 U.S. 79 (1986) (peremptory challenges).

37. *Bishop v. Wood*, 426 U.S. 341 at 349-50 (1976).

38. Jesse Choper, "The Burger Court: Misconceptions Regarding Judicial Restraint and Insensitivity to Individual Rights," *Syracuse Law Review* 30 (Spring 1979): 771–72. The first two cases are *Oregon v. Mitchell*, 400 U.S. 112 (1970) (18-year-olds' right to vote), and *National League of Cities v. Usery*, 426 U.S. 83 (1976) (application of the minimum wage to state and local employees); the last case is *Buckley v. Valeo*, 424 U.S. 1 (1976) (method of selecting the Federal Election Commission).

39. Schmidt, "As Burger Continues, His Court Becomes Unstable"; "Court Under Burger Foiled Conservative Hopes, Powell Says," *Los Angeles Times*, August 13, 1986, p. 20.

40. Stephen L. Wasby, "Justice Harry A. Blackmun: Transformation from 'Minnesota Twin' to Independent Voice," *The Burger Court: Political and Judicial Profiles*, eds. Charles M. Lamb and Stephen C. Halpern (Urbana, Ill.: University of Illinois Press, 1992), pp. 63–99.

41. See Edward A. Tamm and Paul C. Reardon, "Warren E. Burger and the Administration of Justice," *Brigham Young University Law Review* 1981: 447–521, particularly 452; and William F. Swindler, "The Chief Justice and Law Reform, 1921–1971," *The Supreme Court Review*, ed. Philip Kurland (Chicago: University of Chicago Press, 1971), pp. 241–64.

42. See, for example, Warren E. Burger, "Annual Report to the American Bar Association by the Chief Justice of the United States," *American Bar Association Journal* 67 (March 1981): 290–93, and "Isn't There a Better Way?" *American Bar Association Journal* 68 (March 1982): 274–77. See also Arthur B. Landever, "Chief Justice Burger and Extra-Case Activism," *Journal of Public Law* 20 (1971): 523–41.

43. Peter G. Fish, "The Office of Chief Justice of the United States: Into the Federal Judiciary's Bicentennial Decade," *The Office of Chief Justice* (Charlottesville, Va.: University of Virginia, 1984), p. 77. Indeed, he may have found it "advantageous to rephrase as a judicial administration issue a question having far-reaching substantive public policy implications." Ibid., p. 115.

44. Gayle Binion, "The Disadvantaged Before the Burger Court: The New Unequal Protection," *Law & Policy Quarterly* 4 (January 1982): 39–41.

45. Harold J. Spaeth, "Burger Court Review of State Court Civil Liberties Decisions," *Judicature* 68 (February-March 1985): 285.

46. *Runyon v. McCrary*, 427 U.S. 160 (1976) (admission to racially discriminatory private schools). See also *Bob Jones University v. United States*, 461 U.S. 574 (1983).

47. *Washington v. Davis*, 426 U.S. 229 (1976) ("intent" rather than effect required to show a constitutional violation) (employment); *Teamsters v. United States*,431 U.S. 324 (1977) and *American Tobacco Co. v. Patterson*, 456 U.S. 63 (1982) (seniority).

48. *Village of Arlington Heights v. Metropolitan Housing Development Corp.*, 429 U.S. 252 (1977) (housing); *City of Mobile v. Bolden*, 447 U.S. 55 (1980) (voting).

49. *Local 28 v. E.E.O.C.*, 478 U.S. 421 (1986); *Local 93 v. City of Cleveland*, 478 U.S. 301 (1986).

50. *Dayton Board of Education v. Brinkman*, 443 U.S. 527 (1979), and *Columbus Board of Education v. Penick*, 443 U.S. 449 (1979).

51. See *Frontiero v. Richardson*, 411 U.S. 676 (1973).

52. *Harris v. McRae*, 448 U.S. 297 (1980) (Medicaid abortion funding); *Grove City College v. Bell*, 465 U.S. 555 (1984) (sex discrimination in education aid); *Rostker v. Goldberg*, 453 U.S. 57 (1981) (draft registration).

53. *Wallace v. Jaffree*, 472 U.S. 38 (1985).

54. *Mueller v. Allen*, 463 U.S. 388 (1983).

55. *Nebraska Press Association v. Stuart*, 427 U.S. 539 (1976) (gag order); *Richmond Newspapers v. Virginia*, 448 U.S. 55 (1980).

56. *Branzburg v. Hayes*, 408 U.S. 665 (1972).

57. *Virginia State Board of Pharmacy v. Virginia Citizens Consumers Council*, 425 U.S. 748 (1976) (pharmacists); *Bates v. State Bar of Arizona*, 433 U.S. 350 (1977).

58. *Zurcher v. Stanford Daily*, 436 U.S. 547 (1978) (newspapers); *Dalia v. United States,* 441 U.S. 236 (1979); and *United States v. Knotts*, 460 U.S. 276 (1983) (beeper); *California v. Ciraolo*, 476 U.S. 207 (1986), and *Dow Chemical Co. v. United States*, 476 U.S. 227 (1986) (aerial surveillance); *New Jersey v. T.L.O.*, 469 U.S. 325 (1984) (school lockers).

59. *Harris v. New York*, 401 U.S. 222 (1971), reinforced by *Oregon v. Hass*, 420 U.S. 714 (1975).

60. After the defendant was reconvicted, the Supreme Court, ruling that the little girl's body would have been found even without defendant's statement, upheld admission of the evidence under the "inevitable discovery" rule. *Nix v. Williams*, 467 U.S. 431 (1984).

61. *North Carolina v. Alford*, 400 U.S. 25 (1970), and *Santobello v. New York*, 404 U.S. 527 (1971); *Brady v. United States*, 397 U.S. 542 (1970).

62. *Morrissey v. Brewer*, 408 U.S. 471 (1972) (parole); *Gagnon v. Scarpelli*, 411 U.S. 778 (1973) (probation); *Wolff v. McDonnell*, 418 U.S. 539 (1974) (prison discipline).

63. *Bell v. Wolfish*, 441 U.S. 520 (pretrial detainees); *Rhodes v. Chapman*, 452 U.S. 337 (1981) (double-celling); *Hudson v. Palmer*, 468 U.S. 517 (1984), and *Block v. Rutherford*, 468 U.S. 568 (1984) (searches of cells).

64. See *Gardner v. Florida*, 430 U.S. 349 (1977) (sentencing procedure); *Estelle v. Smith*, 451 U.S. 454 (1981) (limiting psychiatrist's testimony); *Bullington v. Missouri*, 451 U.S. 430 (1981) (application of double jeopardy); *Lockett v. Ohio*, 438 U.S. 586 (1978), and *Eddings v. Oklahoma*, 455 U.S. 104 (1982) (mitigating evidence).

65. Janet Blasecki, "Justice Lewis F. Powell: Swing Voter or Staunch Conservative?" *Journal of Politics* 52 (May 1990): 530–47.

66. Bruce Fein, "A Court of Mediocrity," *ABA Journal* 77 (October 1991): 74–79. For a rebuttal, see Paul R. Baier, "The Court and Its Critics," *ABA Journal* 78 (February 1992): 58–62.

67. Robert Glennon, "Will the Real Conservatives Please Stand Up?" *ABA Journal* 76 (August 1990): 50.

68. *United States v. Salerno*, 481 U.S. 739 (1987); *McCleskey v. Kemp*, 481 U.S. 279 (1987).

69. *United States v. Paradise*, 480 U.S. 149 (1987), and *Johnson v. Transportation Agency*, 480 U.S. 616 (1987); *Board of Directors of Rotary International v. Rotary Club of Duarte*, 481 U.S. 537 (1987). For updated data showing decline in the Court's support for civil liberties and its increased support for the government, see Reginald S. Sheehan, "Governmental Litigants, Underdogs, and Civil Liberties: A Reassessment of a Trend in Supreme Court Decision Making," *Western Political Quarterly* 45 (March 1992): 27–39.

70. *National Treasury Employees Union v. Von Raab*, 109 S.Ct. 1384 (1989), and *Skinner v. Railway Labor Executives Association*, 109 S.Ct. 1402 (1989).

71. *Arizona v. Fulminante*, 111 S.Ct. 1246 (1991).

72. *Penry v. Lynaugh*, 109 S.Ct. 2934 (1989); *Stanford v. Kentucky*, 109 S.Ct. 2669 (1989); *Payne v. Tennessee*, 111 S.Ct. 2547 (1991).

73. *Employment Division, Department of Human Resources of Oregon v. Smith*, 110 S.Ct. 1595 (1990); *Lee v. Weisman*, 112 S.Ct. 2649 (1992).

74. *Hodgson v. Minnesota*, 110 S.Ct. 2926 (1990), and *Ohio v. Akron Center for Reproductive Health*, 110 S.Ct. 2972 (1990); *Rust v. Sullivan*, 110 S.Ct. 1759 (1991).

75. *City of Richmond v. J. A. Croson Co.*, 109 S.Ct. 706 (1989); *Metro Broadcasting v. Federal Communication Commission*, 111 S.Ct. 2997 (1990).

76. *Board of Education of Oklahoma City v. Dowell*, 111 S.Ct. 630 (1991), and *Freeman v. Pitts*, 112 S.Ct. 1430 (1992); *United States v. Fordice*, 112 S.Ct. 2727 (1992).

77. *DeShaney v. Winnebago County Department of Social Services*, 109 S.Ct. 998 (1989).

78. Robert Dahl, *Democracy in the United States* (Chicago: Rand McNally, 1972), pp. 201–02. The original statement was Dahl, "Decision-Making in a Democracy: The Supreme Court as a National Policy-Maker," *Journal of Public Law* 7 (Fall 1957): 279–95.

79. David Adamany, "Legitimacy, Realigning Elections, and the Supreme Court," *Wisconsin Law Review* 1973: 825, 822.

80. Jonathan D. Casper, "The Supreme Court and National Policy Making," *American Political Science Review* 70 (March 1976): 3.

81. Samuel Estreicher and John E. Sexton, "A Managerial Theory of the Supreme Court's Responsibilities: An Empirical Study," *New York University Law Review* 59 (October 1984): 717.

82. Arthur D. Hellman, "The Business of the Supreme Court Under the Judiciary Act of 1925: The Plenary Docket in the 1970's," *Harvard Law Review* 91 (June 1978): 1716; D. Marie Provine, *Case Selection in the Supreme Court* (Chicago: University of Chicago Press, 1980), p. 101.

83. Walter F. Murphy, *Elements of Judicial Strategy* (Chicago: University of Chicago Press, 1964), pp. 208–09.

84. Estreicher and Sexton, "A Managerial Theory," 717.

85. *Texas v. Johnson*, 109 S.Ct. 2533, at 2547–48 (Brennan), 2555 (Rehnquist) (1989).

86. Max Lerner, "Constitution and Court as Symbols," *Yale Law Journal* 46 (1939): 1294–95.

87. *United States v. Butler*, 297 U.S. 1 at 62–63 (1936).

88. Potter Stewart, "Reflections on the Supreme Court," *Litigation* 8 (#3, Spring 1982): 8.

89. S. Sidney Ulmer, "Researching the Supreme Court in a Democratic Pluralist System: Some Thoughts on New Directions," *Law & Policy Quarterly* 1 (January 1979): 55.

90. Vincent Blasi, "The Rootless Activism of the Burger Court," *The Burger Court: The Counterrevolution That Wasn't*, ed. Blasi (New Haven, Conn: Yale University Press, 1983), p. 209.

91. Robert H. Jackson, *The Supreme Court in the American System of Government* (Cambridge, Mass.: Harvard University Press, 1955), p. 10.

92. Paul D. Carrington, Daniel J. Meador, and Maurice Rosenberg, *Justice on Appeal* (St. Paul, Minn: West Publishing Co., 1976), pp. 2–3.

93. *Boag v. MacDougall*, 454 U.S. 364 at 366 (1982) (Justice O'Connor, concurring).

94. Max Lerner, *Ideas for the Ice Age* (New York: Viking, 1941), p. 259.

95. Robert Woodward and Scott Armstrong, *The Brethren: Inside the Supreme Court* (New York: Simon and Schuster, 1979); Bruce Allen Murphy, *The Brandeis/Frankfurter Connection: The Secret Political Activities of Two Supreme Court Justices* (New York: Oxford University Press, 1982).

96. 384 U.S. 436 at 521–32 (1966); emphasis supplied.

97. *West Virginia State Board of Education v. Barnette*, 319 U.S. 624 at 647 (1943).

98. *Furman v. Georgia*, 408 U.S. 238 at 405–6, 410–11 (1972). Justice Blackmun has now said recent Court rulings raise questions about the basis of his statement. *Sawyer v. Whitley*, 112 S.Ct. 2514 at 2528-29 (1992). See also *Boyle v. United Technologies Corp.*, 487 U.S. 500 at 531 (1988).

99. *Texas v. Johnson*, 109 S.Ct., at 2548.

100. Martin Shapiro, *Law and Politics in the Supreme Court* (New York: Free Press, 1964), p. 328.

2 Elements of the Federal Judicial System

THIS CHAPTER IS INTENDED to provide a picture of the federal court system's overall structure. We look at the basic levels of the national court system and at associated specialized courts, starting with the district courts and moving to the courts of appeals, followed by a discussion of judicial administration. An examination of the Supreme Court and its position in the federal judicial system concludes the chapter.

The United States has a dual court system of separate national and state courts. It is a result of our system of federalism, although not all federal systems have two levels of courts; in some, state or provincial courts adjudicate issues of national law. We have a set of national courts including territorial courts, and each state has its own courts, giving us 52 separate court systems (the federal system, 50 states, and the District of Columbia). Each state has trial courts of general jurisdiction, that is, courts with legal authority to hear all civil and criminal cases; they are usually called district, superior, or circuit courts. All states also have specialized courts of one or more types, for example, for probate (wills and estates) or juvenile and family proceedings. Most states have an intermediate appellate court, to which all or most appeals are taken first, and a supreme court (in some states, called the court of appeals). Many states retain a fourth level of limited jurisdiction courts—the "inferior" (meaning lower) or "petty" courts—including justice-of-the-peace courts, mayors' courts, police courts, and some municipal courts established to assist with the higher volume of litigation in large urban areas. Appeals from these courts, instead of going directly to an appellate court, are often directed to the general jurisdiction trial court, sometimes for a new trial (trial *de novo*).

The Supreme Court of the United States, the only court specified in the Constitution, is our principal interest as the apex of the federal judicial system for federal questions, but we must also pay attention to the lower federal courts. The national judicial structure—the Supreme Court, courts of appeals, district courts, and magistrate judges (connected to and generally subordinate to the district courts), as well as some specialized courts such as the bankruptcy courts—is similar to most states' court systems. The Supreme Court cannot initiate cases but must rely on the lower federal courts and the state courts as the source of its business, the place where cases are initiated and where they take the shape in which they arrive at the Supreme Court and with which the justices must then work. The lower federal courts are also where most federal litigation terminates so that they make much law in areas of litigation not reviewed or seldom reviewed by the Supreme Court. The basic relations among federal courts, discussed in this chapter, are portrayed in Figure 2.1. (For relations between state courts and federal courts, see Figure 5.1 in Chapter 5.)

Development of the Federal Court System

The federal court system as we now know it assumed its present basic form only late in the nineteenth century. The system of federal courts established by Congress in the Judiciary Act of 1789 was relatively elementary. The Congress created the Supreme Court, specified by the Constitution itself (see Art. III, Sec. 1), and the district courts and circuit courts. The district courts' jurisdiction was not broad, and they dealt mainly with admiralty cases, minor federal crimes and minor cases in which the United States was plaintiff. (District judges' salaries reflected workload, something not true now.) The circuit courts were primarily trial courts for diversity of citizenship cases (suits between citizens of different states), although they tried major federal crimes and larger U.S. plaintiff cases, and they also had some appellate jurisdiction over the district courts. These courts, created under the Judiciary Act of 1789, had final authority on ı matters within their jurisdiction, with appeals limited by various technical visions. This made the Supreme Court largely a court of review for *state c* rulings.

> The judicial Power of the United States shall be vested in one supreme Court, a in such inferior Courts as the Congress may from time to time ordain and esta lish. (Art. III, Sec. 1)

In the circuit courts, which did not have their own judges, a district and two Supreme Court justices were to sit twice a year in each district ıe circuit. Almost immediately (in 1793), Congress reduced the burden o Supreme Court justices of attending court in the district so that each year on one

Figure 2.1 The Federal Court System

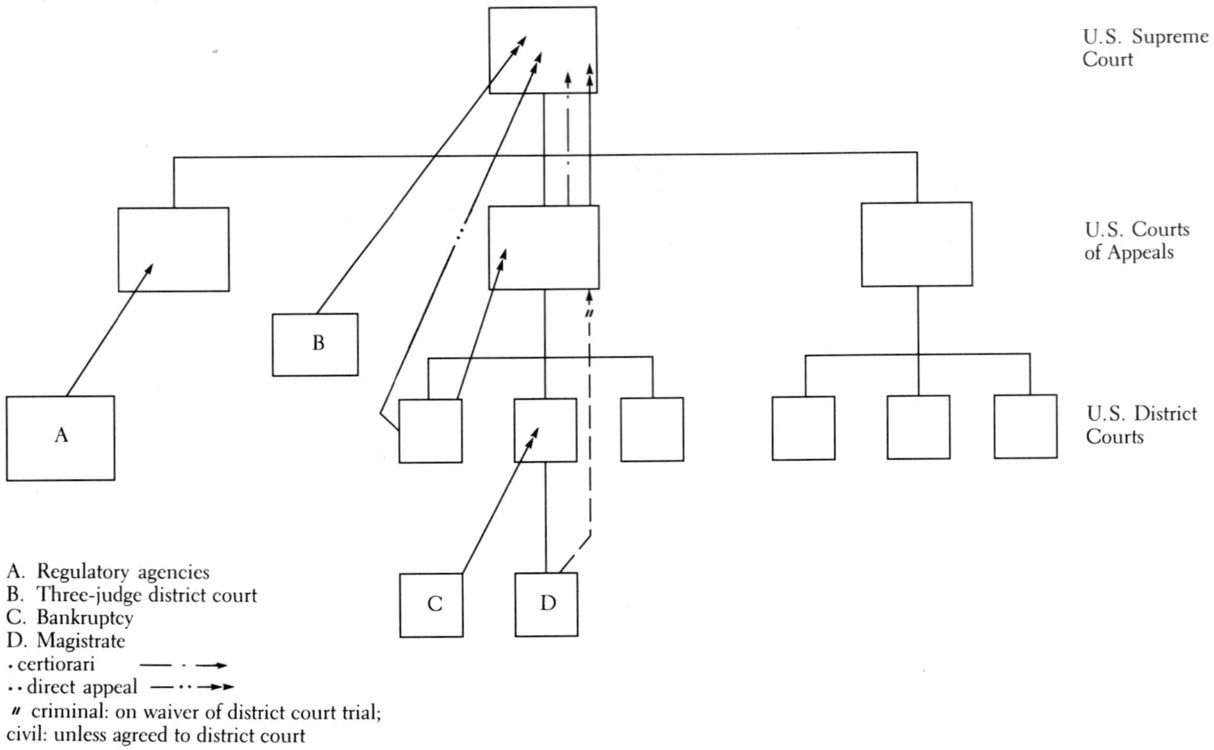

U.S. Supreme
Court

U.S. Courts
of Appeals

U.S. District
Courts

A. Regulatory agencies
B. Three-judge district court
C. Bankruptcy
D. Magistrate
· certiorari   —— · ——▸
·· direct appeal —— ·· ——▸

" criminal: on waiver of district court trial;
civil: unless agreed to district court

justice would have to sit once in each district. In 1801, the Federalists created 16 circuit court judgeships for six circuits, but in 1802 the Jeffersonian Democrats promptly repealed this action. The Act of 1801 also granted the circuit courts what we now call "federal question" jurisdiction, but the courts' opportunity to develop it was eliminated by the repealer, which the Supreme Court upheld.[1]

District judges were used increasingly in the circuit courts until after the Civil War, and the Supreme Court justice assigned to the circuit (the *circuit justice*) often did not visit certain parts of large western circuits. Because of the extreme distance from the East Coast to California, a separate circuit court—with its own circuit judges—was established for California. In 1869, nine judgeships were created specifically for the circuit courts. These circuit judges had the same authority as the Supreme Court justices assigned to the circuit, who were now required to attend only one term of circuit court in each district of the circuit every two years. A circuit justice, circuit judge, or district judge could hold circuit court, or any two could sit as a panel. Nonetheless, district judges held circuit court most of the time, creating a dual role in which they sat in review over their own district court decisions. Supreme Court justices also had this dual role when they sat on circuit and later had to review their rulings appealed to the Supreme Court, a matter that concerned them. The justices handed down some very important rulings on circuit. Included were one of the first rulings on judicial review (*Hayburn's Case*, 1792), John Marshall's ruling on executive privilege in the Aaron Burr treason trial (*United States v. Burr*, 1807), and Justice Bushrod Washington's opinion in *Corfield v. Coryell* (1823) on "privileges and immunities." Later came Chief Justice Roger Taney's ruling on military detention of civilians (*Ex parte Merryman*, 1861), which President Lincoln ignored.

Supreme Court justices are no longer subject to the rigors of riding circuit. In the early days, they had to put up with "the dangers and miseries of overturned vehicles, runaway horses, rivers in full flood, or icebound and scruffy taverns," and the early justices petitioned Congress to eliminate circuit-riding.[2] There were even more serious dangers: the life of Justice Stephen Field, on circuit in California, was threatened by a disgruntled litigant who was shot and killed by the U.S. marshal assigned to guard the justice. After the state indicted the marshal for murder, he was transferred to the federal court's jurisdiction and was exonerated, the Supreme Court ruling that his action was part of properly enforcing the nation's laws (*In Re Neagle*, 1890). Circuit duty was continued for many years because the lower courts needed help with their caseload and because the Supreme Court's caseload was not overwhelming. Congress also felt that if the justices stayed in Washington, they might be dominated by the capital's lawyers, with whom they often shared rooming houses, and not be able to keep in touch with the people. If anything, the risk now is that the justices will not have sufficient contact with the hinterlands. However, they usually attend their circuit's judicial conference and in 1984 Justice Rehnquist, who had no experience as a trial judge, "rode out to Richmond" to preside over one trial. (His ruling in that case was reversed by the court of appeals.)

In the early years of the Republic, the judges struggled to work out their jurisdiction. This was made more difficult by efforts to alter the Judiciary Act of 1789, itself a compromise, fairly soon after its adoption; some of the proposed changes would have directly affected the basic linkages between federal and state courts.[3] The judges had to decide whether there was a common law of crimes—that is, whether the judges could declare criminal improper behavior that Congress had not specified as a crime—or whether punishments not specified by Congress would be imposed. They decided against both.[4] One reason for their ruling was that Congress could have given them that jurisdiction, but did not. This illustrated the more general point that federal courts were given far less than the full jurisdiction they could have been given, and at no point has Congress bestowed on the federal courts all the jurisdiction they could have under Article III.

In the Judiciary Act of 1875, the district courts received general federal question jurisdiction. That allowed them to hear civil suits involving at least $500 if the case arose "under the Constitution, laws, or treaties of the United States." (At the same time, the jurisdictional minimum for cases coming to the Supreme Court from the circuit courts was $5,000.) Congress did not provide for review of capital (death sentence) cases until 1889 and for all cases involving "infamous crimes"—those where a sentence of imprisonment was possible—until 1891.

The failure to create any lower federal courts in the Constitution, and the limited jurisdiction given them in the early years, resulted from arguments that the state courts, bound by the Supremacy Clause (Art. VI), could be expected to enforce the Constitution. Such arguments may have had force in connection with the Constitution's ratification. We should remember that the Bill of Rights and the Judiciary Act were debated and passed at the same time, although it took a while for the former to be ratified: both were part of the anti-Federalists' concern about the role of judges and whether there should be lower federal courts, part of their concern about the size and power of the national government as a whole. Later, competing considerations came to the fore. Particularly important were the feelings of those wanting a strong national government that because state courts were not enforcing federal law adequately, an effective federal judicial mechanism was essential.

In 1891, the U.S. Courts of Appeals (as they are now called) were established, to be staffed by two circuit judges and a Supreme Court justice, for whom a district judge could substitute. The old circuit courts, which thus became courts without full-time judges, were finally abolished in 1911. This at last made district courts the dominant federal court of original jurisdiction. The presence of a regular set of intermediate appellate courts meant that the Supreme Court no longer had to accept all the cases in which its decision was sought, and the movement toward giving the Court control over what cases it would hear then began. This process of providing the Supreme Court with discretionary jurisdiction began in 1914 and continued in 1916, but received its major advance in the

Judges Bill of 1925, which provided authority to hear large categories of cases on petition for a writ of certiorari (see page 73).

The District Courts

District courts are the federal judicial system's basic trial court, hearing both a wide range of criminal offenses and diverse types of civil cases, including antitrust, commerce, patent and copyright, contract, and tort suits. Most district court civil cases involve private individuals or businesses raising federal questions or bringing suit under diversity of citizenship jurisdiction, but the United States government is a party in roughly one-fourth of the civil cases.

Each of the nation's 94 U.S. district courts is located in a single state or territory, except for the District of Wyoming, which includes the Montana and Idaho portions of Yellowstone National Park. Twenty-six states, the District of Columbia, Puerto Rico, and the nation's three territories each constitute one district; the remaining states have two to four districts each. We now give them a name like Middle, Northern, Central, or Southern, but in the mid-nineteenth century there were other names, based on geographic locations, such as the Albemarle, Pamptico, and Cape Fear Districts in North Carolina. The judges sit at locations designated by statute within these districts.

There are now 649 district court judgeships, an increase of more than 50 percent since the 1970s. Each judge is appointed by the president with the advice and consent of the Senate during "good behavior," that is, for life if the judge is not impeached (see pages 98–106). Since 1966, district judges in Puerto Rico have had lifetime appointments. The Supreme Court has treated Puerto Rico, which has commonwealth status, much like a state, for example, extending the protections of the Fourth Amendment to it and giving great weight to its courts' interpretations of Puerto Rico law.[5]

A district judge generally is appointed to a single district, but in some "floater" positions a judgeship is assigned to more than one district (for example, Eastern and Western Districts of Oklahoma) and only eventually is assigned to a single district. District courts vary considerably in the number of judgeships. There are no longer any single-judge districts. Some have as few as two judges while the largest districts—like the Southern District of New York, which includes Manhattan, and the Central District of California, including Los Angeles—have more than 25. Other large districts include the Northern District of Illinois (Chicago) and the Eastern District of Pennsylvania (Philadelphia).

District court caseloads have increased substantially throughout the century, ten times from 1904 to a peak in 1985. From 1969 to 1985, the increase was 178+ percent, greatly exceeding the increase in district judgeships (69%). (Filings may increase when judgeships are added because potential litigants believe the judges will be able to decide cases more promptly.) Early in the century, district court caseload had more criminal than civil cases; now there are far more civil cases, although the criminal ones must get first attention. Civil cases have increased not only in absolute numbers, but also in per capita terms.[6] Case filings per year—over 200,000 civil cases and over 45,000 criminal cases—have fluctuated, with civil filings down almost 25 percent since their 1985 high.

Filings have not necessarily paralleled increases in population or economic growth,[7] but can be best explained by a combination of demographic factors and governmental action.[8] They may also reflect social trends, shifts in the nation's political agenda, and Supreme Court decisions, such as those in the 1960s protecting defendants' rights and facilitating state prisoners' access to federal courts. District courts by no means have identical dockets, which vary depending on business or industry and other activities (such as major prisons) located in the district. Thus the Southern District of New York (S.D.N.Y.) has a large number of admiralty cases, as does the Eastern District of Louisiana (E.D.La.), which also has many Jones Act (personal injury to those working on the high seas) cases because of the Gulf of Mexico oil rigs.

Growth in criminal cases has resulted both from increases in crime, for example, drug offenses, and from increased public pressure to "do something" about it, and from new federal criminal statutes. The number of drug cases filed rose from 3,100 to 16,400 from 1980 to 1990, well ahead of the increase in all criminal filings. They were *more than one-fourth* of all federal criminal filings in 1991, and the backlog in drug cases increased from 1,200 to 7,400 from the end of Fiscal Year 89 to the end of FY 90 alone. The Speedy Trial Act, by imposing a strict calendar on the stages of federal criminal cases from arrest and indictment through trial and providing for dismissal of a case for failure to meet designated deadlines, means that district courts must attend to criminal cases ahead of civil cases, and the busier district courts' capacity to keep up with routine civil cases has been strained. However, the Supreme Court ruled in 1976 that district judges may *not* use workload as a reason for refusing to accept cases that are within their jurisdiction.[9]

On the civil side, where most cases involve either federal statutes or the federal government as a party, there have been increases in cases on environmental protection, job discrimination, education of the handicapped, and prison conditions. Apart from attention-getting areas like civil rights cases and prisoner petitions, we find that increases in federal civil cases have also occurred on such topics as Social Security disability benefits, contracts and torts, and "recovery cases"—mostly government cases to get overpayments of veterans' benefits and to recover defaulted student loans (watch out, reader!).

Each new federal statute tends to produce a jump in filings, but in some instances this tails off after a while as basic questions about the statute are resolved. Chief Justice Burger urged that each piece of legislation should have a *judicial impact statement*, that is, an indication of how many cases would be filed and thus the judicial resources needed to enforce the statute. The idea, the call for which has recently been renewed, was to get legislators to provide the judiciary with the resources needed to enforce the new laws—or at least to get the legislators to recognize the effects of their actions on the judiciary. Whatever the merits of such an idea, it has not served to restrain Congress, which regularly passes new statutes requiring judicial enforcement without providing additional judges and related resources. Some judges have criticized Congress for its actions in federalizing crime and for taking the position that "Whatever bothers us is a federal question" so that there appear to be no limits to federal jurisdiction.

Burger Court rulings restricting state prisoners' use of federal court coupled with use of new prison grievance mechanisms have deflected some of the grievances from the courts. The advocacy by Chief Justice Burger, some of his colleagues, and many other lawyers, of eliminating diversity of citizenship cases as one way of reducing caseload, produced only an increase in the jurisdictional dollar threshold from $10,000 to $50,000. That was followed by a 15 percent drop in diversity filings in the first year under the new rule, with the decline larger if asbestos cases are omitted. But past experience suggests that this decline will be followed by a renewed increase in filings.

Most district court decisions are final.[10] They are either not appealed, if appealed are settled prior to an appellate ruling, or, in the vast proportion of cases reviewed by the courts of appeals, are sustained—often in brief affirmances without opinion. In 1965–67, for example, roughly one-third of completed district court cases were taken to the appellate courts, but because of terminations before final submission, the proportion finally reviewed was only about one-fifth. Courts of appeals provide "sustained supervision" of district court decisions "in only a few areas of public policy."[11] They intervene, that is, alter or reverse, district court rulings in only a small portion of cases—roughly one-sixth, more for civil than for criminal.[12] Nor is appellate court review of district court output uniform across the districts within each circuit or across subject matters. When we add the fact that by no means all court of appeals rulings are carried to the Supreme Court, which grants review to only a very small percentage of those cases in which review is sought, "the great majority of district court decisions are neither reviewed nor reversed."[13] Thus district court decisions are *the* rulings in all but a very small percentage of cases decided there.

Because district court rulings on various subjects are not appealed in the same proportions, appellate review is not likely to produce uniformity in federal law nor will it necessarily protect important national interests. For example, in civil rights cases, where district judges resisted appellate rulings so that appellate supervision was most needed, appeal rates were among the lowest. The low rate of review and of appellate court reversal means that district courts follow appropriate legal doctrine less as a result of the explicit sanction of reversal by superiors than through informal controls, which include precedent, professional socialization including service with the court of appeals, anticipation of appellate judicial action, and ideological unity provided by shared regional and political backgrounds.[14]

District court cases are ordinarily heard by one judge. There are times when all the judges in a district, facing numerous cases raising a new issue of law, will sit together (*en banc*) to develop a common legal position, although application to individual cases remains with the individual judges.[15] This occurred often when judges were first considering constitutional challenges to the Sentencing Guidelines. The judges in Eastern District New York (E.D.N.Y.) also sat *en banc* to consider issues in a major racketeering trial involving organized crime.

In specified situations, three-judge district courts, composed of two district judges and a court of appeals judge, have been convened. Three-judge district courts were first established in 1903 to deal with requests for injunctions against Interstate Commerce Commission (ICC) orders. Allowing single district judges to invalidate state laws gave them too much power, so in 1910 a three-judge district court was required to enjoin enforcement of state laws; in 1913, the rule was extended to state administrative actions. In 1937 suits to invalidate federal statutes were made subject to the three-judge court requirement. Appeals from such panels go directly to the Supreme Court because of the importance of the cases and because an appeals court judge has already participated in hearing them. The Supreme Court must hear them, although it has disposed of most of them summarily.

Although they were initially created when state economic regulation was challenged, from the mid-1960s through the early 1970s, there was increased use of three-judge courts as litigants sought injunctions against state laws said to interfere with civil rights; such cases accounted for a significant portion of the Supreme Court's decisions. This increased number of mandatory appeals, which came directly to the Supreme Court without benefit of prior treatment by the courts of appeals, hindered the Court's ability to use its certiorari jurisdiction to choose the cases it would consider fully. So the justices developed doctrines to limit use of three-judge district courts and called upon Congress to eliminate them.

Congress, after earlier eliminating direct appeals of ICC orders and in government civil antitrust cases, in 1976 eliminated most three-judge district courts. Thus requests for injunctions against state laws now reach the Supreme Court only after the court of appeals has heard the case. Three-judge courts remain in legislative reapportionment cases or when Congress specifically provided for them, as in the Voting Rights Act. A single judge now handles preliminary matters in such cases. When a district judge invalidates a federal statute, the case still goes directly to the Supreme Court; this occurred with the challenge to the federal flag-burning law.

District of Columbia and the Territories. In the District of Columbia there are both the usual national courts—a district court and a court of appeals—and a set of courts more like state courts, which are established under Congress's authority to make laws for the nation's capital (Art. I, Sec. 8, cl. 17). These courts, whose judges serve fixed terms, apply laws passed by Congress specifically for the District and those passed by the D.C. City Council. Prior to 1971, cases from the District of Columbia Court of Appeals did not go directly to the U.S. Supreme Court, as they would from the highest state courts, but instead went to the U.S. Court of Appeals for the District of Columbia. In 1970 a new District of Columbia Superior Court assumed most local jurisdiction, including some cases formerly in the federal district court, and most cases from the District of Columbia Court of Appeals now go directly to the U.S. Supreme Court. Those involving a law "not applicable exclusively to the District of Columbia" still go to the U.S. Court of Appeals.

The district courts in Guam, the Virgin Islands,[16] and the Northern Marianas (the newest federal judicial district) were established under Congress's power to regulate the territories (Art. IV, Sec. 3). The District Court for the Canal Zone, created under the same authority, went out of existence in 1982 when authority over the Zone was transferred to the government of Panama. The territorial courts hear cases under federal and local laws, including appeals from local courts. The early territorial courts were treated much like regular district courts. The judges sometimes had legislative as well as judicial duties but had tenure "during good behavior," that is, for life, under Article III of the Constitution. By the mid-nineteenth century, Congress shifted the basis for creating their positions to Article IV. The territorial judges lost their lifetime positions, and presidents even treated the judges as removable summarily. Judges of the territorial courts now have terms of from four to eight years. When a territory becomes a state, the territorial court is abolished and is replaced by a regular Article III court with lifetime judgeships.

Native Americans. American Indian tribes have been treated as separate, although dependent, nations. For that reason and because of the many treaties signed with them (although often dishonored by the government), relations of Native Americans to the federal judicial system have given rise to special problems.[17] The tribes have traditional courts, consisting of a tribal chief and council of elders. Modern tribal courts, operating under modern tribal legal codes, were established under the Indian Reorganization Act of 1934. They replaced the Courts of Indian Offenses, operated by the Bureau of Indian Affairs and known as CFR courts because they operate under guidelines in the Code of Federal Regulations.

Even though the tribes are not states, decisions of the tribal courts are given deference under the idea of comity and the Full Faith and Credit Clause (Art. IV, Sec. 1). The 1968 Indian Civil Rights Act made available habeas corpus petitions to federal district court to test tribal court orders. The Major Crimes Act (18 U.S.C. §§ 1154, 3242), under which designated offenses by an Indian against an Indian or non-Indian are to be tried in federal court, serves as an additional restriction on tribal courts' ability to try criminal cases. The Supreme Court has had to deal with jurisdictional conflicts when states have sought to assert jurisdiction over certain matters Indians claim to be within tribal court jurisdiction, or have tried to limit Indians' access to state courts unless the Indians allow themselves to be sued there.

Magistrate Judges[18]

The position of U.S. magistrate—renamed magistrate judge in 1990—was created by the Federal Magistrates Act, which was fully effective in 1971. That law reorganized the U.S. commissioner system. The commissioners, about one-third of whom were not lawyers, had limited authority and were paid up to $10,500 under a fee system. There are both full-time magistrates, who must be lawyers and who serve for eight years, and part-time magistrates, who serve for four years. The salaries of full-time magistrate judges are now set by law at 92 percent of district judges' salaries. In the late 1980s, as a result of a trend toward full-time positions, there were 266 full-time and 183 part-time magistrates. Only a few districts have only a part-time magistrate judge; roughly a quarter of the districts have only one full-time magistrate judge. More than two-thirds of full-time magistrate judges serve in the 25 largest district courts. Subject to congressional funding, the Judicial Conference allocates magistrate judge positions to districts on the basis of recommendations from district courts, circuit councils, its own committee, and the Administrative Office.

The magistrate judges themselves are selected by the district judges in the district in which they serve. A provision in the 1979 Magistrates Act requires the district judges to appoint merit panels (with some nonlawyers) to advertise positions, evaluate the applicants, and submit a list of five nominees. The result has been the appointment of more women and minorities, but an earlier pattern of appointing people with close connections to the court (and thus known to the judges) continues.

Magistrates started with all the commissioners' former duties. They were given additional duties by statute or by assignment, to relieve the district judges of their increasing caseload, and such duties have steadily accounted for an increasing proportion of their work. Most magistrates are assigned most tasks the district judges can designate, with handling of Social Security cases and prisoner petitions most likely to be assigned; more are *designated* to perform certain duties than are actually *assigned* them. Depending on the tasks assigned, they may serve as subject-matter specialists (on Social Security and prisoner matters); as "team players," taking cases through the early stages before district judges take them; and as additional judges, handling their own caseload.

Magistrates previously could hear only those criminal cases involving minor offenses (those with a maximum fine of $1,000, a year's prison sentence, or both) and could not hear jury trials. Under the Federal Magistrates Act of 1979 they may now hear, and impose sentence in, all jury and nonjury misdemeanor criminal cases if the defendant waives the right to trial by a district judge, with appeals going directly to the court of appeals. Their juvenile jurisdiction, which depends on the juvenile's consent, is still limited to petty cases and they may not impose a term of imprisonment on juveniles.

Magistrate judges also conduct pretrial criminal proceedings and preliminary review of applications for posttrial relief, and evidentiary hearings on federal habeas corpus petitions. The Supreme Court has said authority may be delegated to a magistrate to hear testimony concerning suppression of evidence as long as the district judge is the ultimate decision maker. The Court then ruled that the magistrate may supervise *voir dire* (jury selection) in felony trials, as long as the litigants consent; consent eliminated any problem in not having all parts of a felony trial conducted by an Article III judge.[19]

Magistrate judges' civil jurisdiction has also been expanded from their pre-1979 duties of conducting civil pretrial and discovery proceedings, acting as special masters in civil cases, and reviewing administrative records in Social Security cases. District judges' referrals of Social Security benefit entitlement cases to magistrates were upheld as "substantially assist[ing] the district judge in the performance of his judicial function, and benefit[ing] both him and the parties."[20] The 1979 statute confirmed existing practice of referring jury or nonjury civil cases, with the parties' consent, to a magistrate for trial.

Prior to the 1979 Act, appeal of a magistrate's order to the district court for trial *de novo* was thought to protect the right to be tried by an Article III judge, even though the district judge usually based a ruling on the magistrate's report. The new statute provided that civil cases tried to a magistrate were to be appealed to the court of appeals, unless, when the case was referred, the parties agreed the appeal would go to the district judge. (When an appeal is taken from a magistrate's decision to the district court, further appeal—to the court of appeals—is not a matter of right but is by petition for leave to appeal.) The 1990 law facilitated referral of cases to magistrate judges by giving the judge the opportunity to remind the party of that option.

Bankruptcy Court

Bankruptcy judges, called referees in bankruptcy until 1973, serve on term appointments. Prior to 1946, they were paid by fees they collected. Now they are salaried, with their salary 92 percent of a district judge's salary and subject to congressional adjustment. Prior to 1978, they were appointed by district judges for six-year terms; they could serve on a full-time or part-time basis. Now they are appointed, by the courts of appeals, to 14-year terms. From 232 bankruptcy judges before 1986, the number grew to 291 by 1990, with another 32 about to be authorized. Those judges must deal with substantial case filings—almost a million (950,000) in 1991, up from 227,000 in 1979.

Most supervision of bankrupts' assets is carried out by bankruptcy trustees appointed by the attorney general, not by individuals appointed by the judges for particular cases. That gave rise to judicial-executive conflict concerning the preferred method of administering such a program. The trustee program was started as a pilot program in 18 districts. When Congress considered making it permanent, the Judicial Conference took the position that there would be potential confusion and overlap as judges handled bankruptcy cases and U.S. trustees separately administered the underlying estates, and that it would be more efficient and cheaper to house such a program in the judiciary. Friction between the judiciary and the bankruptcy trustees has continued.

How the present system came into existence is an interesting story in the politics of the judiciary. The Bankruptcy Reform Act of 1978 changed bankruptcy judges' status in important ways. Starting in 1984, they were to be appointed by the president for 14-year terms; before then, merit screening committees could recommend termination of those whose terms expired, and chief judges could terminate them and appoint replacements. Bankruptcy courts' jurisdiction was also expanded under the new statute, to encompass *all* civil proceedings related to bankruptcy cases, including state law as well as federal law questions. This increased authority led to legal challenges. In 1982, a badly divided Supreme Court ruled that Congress had unconstitutionally granted too much authority to these judges without lifetime tenure. Justice Brennan said judges with most attributes of "judicial power"—including authority over matters normally handled through the common law—had to be Article III judges with the necessary independence provided by lifetime appointments and protection against salary reduction so that they would not slant decisions to increase the chances of reappointment.[21] (He did, however, find constitutional justification for having judges of limited terms—Article I judges—serve on territorial and District of Columbia courts, courts-martial, and courts and administrative agencies established to adjudicate cases involving "public rights," those granted by the government against itself such as pensions.)

But what should the Court do to avoid invalidating prior decisions of bankruptcy judges appointed under the old procedures but exercising authority under the new statute? In a move unusual because the Court usually makes rights effective upon its declaration of those rights,[22] the justices did not make their ruling retroactive but stayed its implementation to give Congress several months either to curtail bankruptcy judges' jurisdiction or to give them Article III status, and extended this stay for several months. At the end of 1982, when Congress was unable to agree on a new statute, the Court refused any further extension. Congressional inaction continued until mid-1984, well past the 1978 statute's March 31, 1984, deadline for authority of the former bankruptcy judges and for presidential appointment of new ones. During this period, matters were made more complicated by challenges to bankruptcy judges' jurisdiction to hear cases, although the Judicial Conference provided guidelines for dividing jurisdiction between the bankruptcy and district courts, and all federal judicial districts adopted emergency interim rules based on the guidelines.

Congressional stalemate stemmed from disagreement about (1) bankruptcy judges' proper status—whether, as the House wished, they should be Article III judges, or, as the Judicial Conference and the Senate preferred, they should have a lesser status, with district judges handling complex matters relating to bankruptcy; (2) whether, if lifetime appointments were involved, one president should be able to appoint a large number of bankruptcy judges; and (3) whether the bankruptcy law's substantive provisions, which had facilitated bankruptcies by individuals, should be changed, with business wanting to make bankruptcy more difficult and labor wishing to eliminate the Supreme Court's ruling in *N.L.R.B. v. Bildisco*, which allowed firms going into bankruptcy to abrogate their collective bargaining agreements with labor.

Congress finally reached a compromise in midyear 1984. The new bankruptcy judges were *not* to be Article III judges but were to be appointed not by the district court or the president, but by the courts of appeals. District courts were given basic bankruptcy jurisdiction but could refer civil cases related to bankruptcy proceedings to bankruptcy judges. Certain orders must be entered by district judges after considering bankruptcy judges' recommendations, but parties may also consent to bankruptcy judges' decision of some matters. Appeals from bankruptcy judges' rulings go first to the district court, unless a circuit establishes a bankruptcy appellate panel (BAP) of bankruptcy judges. Only one circuit (the Ninth) now has one, but the Federal Courts Study Committee recommended other circuits adopt them.

Additional controversy resulted from Congress's failure to agree on the compromise until 12 days *after* expiration of the old bankruptcy courts' authority to keep operating. The Judicial Conference specifically designated U.S. magistrates to handle bankruptcy matters, created the same number of magistrate positions as there had been bankruptcy judges, and gave district courts the option of having the bankruptcy judges serve temporarily as "consultants" until steps could be taken to appoint them as magistrates. Congress tried to handle the problem by retroactively reappointing all bankruptcy judges to serve until there was time for the new appointment process to work. However, the Director of the Administrative Office of the Courts, William Foley, probably acting at the behest of the Chief Justice, refused to pay the judges. He did so on the grounds that Congress, because it cannot appoint judges, had acted unconstitutionally in restoring bankruptcy judges' authority once it had expired. House Judiciary Committee Chairman Peter Rodino threatened hearings into the Administrative Office's action, because it challenged Congress's authority, and some bankruptcy judges refused to work while their pay was being withheld. In many districts, all papers in bankruptcy cases were sent to district judges for their signature—resulting in a massive paperwork problem. After a group of bankruptcy judges sued Foley, he allowed district courts to make whatever arrangements they wished for handling of bankruptcy cases, and agreed to pay their salaries.

By late 1984, matters had worked themselves out, but not before the Department of Justice had intervened in a case brought by debtors to challenge portions of the 1984 compromise, to urge the law be invalidated. However, when a bankruptcy judge did invalidate a part of the new law, the Justice Department did support the statute. In late 1984 federal district judges upheld the constitutionality of Congress's retroactive reappointments and the Fifth Circuit upheld the law in late 1986,[23] apparently bringing matters to a close, although the scope of bankruptcy courts' power is still being litigated.[24]

Other Specialized Courts

There are a number of other specialized trial-level courts. Despite the preference for general jurisdiction courts, specialized courts have been established
throughout our history, when particular problems have been thought to require
focused attention or there have been a large number of cases on a particular issue
at one time. In the mid-nineteenth century, for example, a special court was
established to settle the status of Spanish and Mexican land grants in the territory
ceded by Mexico to the United States in the Treaties of 1848 and 1853.

A number of considerations go into the decision to create a specialized
court. One is the complexity of law judges must apply, and the complexity of
facts to which the law must be applied. Another is the extent to which cases and
issues can be segregated from other issues and cases: tax law is high, patent law
low (because it is mixed with antitrust issues). A third is whether there is a consensus on the objectives in a particular area of law. The lack of consensus about
objectives of the Commerce Court (see pages 60–61) is one reason it lasted only
a short time. The distribution of cases in the courts of general jurisdiction is
another consideration: consolidating cases in a specialty court is more likely to
succeed if each general jurisdiction court has relatively few cases. [25]

One of the oldest specialized courts is the U.S. Claims Court, formerly the
U.S. Court of Claims. It was established in 1855 to provide for suits against the
United States government and to relieve the pressure on Congress from requests
for private bills to deal with claims against the government. Initially, the Court
of Claims could hear only claims referred by the House of Representatives or the
Senate. It lacked authority to award judgments against the government and could
only report its findings to Congress along with a proposed bill authorizing payment. In the 1860s, however, its judgments were made final. Originally an Article I court whose judges had limited terms, the Court of Claims was made an
Article III court in 1953. [26]

Initial determinations in the Court of Claims were made by one of 16 judges
(trial commissioners). In addition to adjudicating cases referred by Congress,
they had functions analogous to those of U.S. magistrates or special masters.
Only the court's Article III judges, who sat together in Washington, D.C., could
enter dispositive orders. They decided major motions and appeals from trial
judges' findings of fact, and handled appeals from decisions of government contract boards. A clearer separation between trial judges' work and that of the Article III judges was created in 1982. The U.S. Claims Court again became an
Article I court of 16 judges and appellate jurisdiction is lodged in the new Court
of Appeals for the Federal Circuit (see page 59). The Claims Court retained the
Court of Claims' jurisdiction, which encompasses claims against the United
States except for tort cases; contract disputes make up the bulk of the Claims'
Court work.

The U.S. Tax Court, created in 1924 as the Board of Tax Appeals, was
renamed the Tax Court of the United States in 1942. Until 1969 an independent

agency in the executive branch, it became a legislative (Art. I) court. Congressional oversight is vested in the House Ways and Means and Senate Finance Committees. The Tax Court has 19 judges, nominated by the president and confirmed by the Senate for 15-year terms with the same salary as district judges. They are assisted by "special trial judges" the Tax Court itself selects. The Supreme Court had to consider the question of whether the Tax Court's chief judge could assign certain complex cases to the special trial judges. In 1991, the Court unanimously agreed that such appointments did not violate separation of powers, but there was a serious division within the Court as to their proper constitutional grounding. The majority said that the Tax Court was a "Court of Law" and thus could make such appointments; another four justices felt that the Tax Court, as an Article I "legislative court," had to be viewed as a government "department" for the head of that department (the chief judge) to be able, constitutionally, to make such appointments.[27]

Although the Tax Court is based in Washington, D.C., single judges hold hearings at 80 cities throughout the United States to decide the more than 30,000 cases filed each year. The chief judge reviews opinions for uniformity; where a case appears inconsistent and the trial judge will not alter his decision, the case becomes a "court-reviewed" one, decided at a conference of the 19 judges. The Tax Court also uses the conference when it must decide how to proceed when a U.S. court of appeals has reversed it and the same issue recurs in another circuit.

The Tax Court shares jurisdiction over tax litigation with the Claims Court and the district courts, which are the exclusive forum (court) for criminal tax proceedings. The Tax Court's basic jurisdiction is over cases in which the taxpayer contests the government's assertions of tax liability in excise tax cases or with respect to income, estate, or gift taxes. In 1974 and 1979, the Tax Court also was given the authority to issue declaratory judgments (statements of litigants' rights before the government takes action against them) on such matters as the tax status of organizations, employee retirement plans, and government bonds.

The Tax Court is the only court to which a taxpayer can bring a case before making full payment of taxes instead of having to pay under protest and then sue to recover. The taxpayer who has overpaid and wishes to recover some of those funds may go either to the Claims Court or to the district courts, which also have jurisdiction over enforcement of tax laws and over liens. In order to centralize trials of tax matters from the district courts, Tax Court, and Claims Court, the Federal Courts Study Committee suggested that the Tax Court be changed to an Article III court with exclusive jurisdiction in trials and appeals over federal income, estate and gift tax cases.

The Customs Court, an administrative body that had evolved into an Article III court, was transformed in 1980 into the U.S. Court of International Trade. The court has nine judges, no more than five of whom may be from one political party. They are appointed by the president with the advice and consent of the Senate. This court's rulings provide the uniformity concerning import transactions required by the Constitution (Art. I, Sec. 8, cl. 1). Most of its work involves hearing challenges to administrative decisions of the Customs Service and the Treasury. In addition to its older appellate jurisdiction over rulings and appraisals on imported goods made by collectors of customs, it now also has exclusive jurisdiction over conflicts arising under certain tariff and trade laws. As often happens when Congress creates a new court or realigns an older one, the Supreme Court has to decide the contours of the new court's jurisdiction, and it ruled that the Court of International Trade did not have jurisdiction over all customs-related matters.[28]

The newest Article I court is the U.S. Court of Veterans Appeals, created in 1988 to review decisions of the Board of Veterans' Appeals. The court will have up to seven judges, who will serve 15-year terms with compensation the same as that of district judges. Either a single judge or a panel of judges can hear cases, and the Federal Circuit will have exclusive jurisdiction over appeals from its rulings on law. A court like it, to review administrative law judges' rulings on Social Security disability benefits, has also been proposed. This Court of Disability Claims would reduce the number of layers of review in disability benefit cases.

Perhaps the most intriguing special court is the Foreign Intelligence Surveillance Court. It is a result of the provision of the 1978 Wiretap Act that court orders must be obtained for telephone and other electronic taps of foreign agents (individuals and embassies) in the United States—including, in exceptional cases, American citizens with information thought essential to the national security. The seven members of the court are to be appointed—to staggered terms—by the Chief Justice after consultation with the chief judges of the circuits; they are regular judges of other courts serving on the FIS Court as well when needed. What makes the court unusual is that it meets in a "secure" courtroom and conducts its work in secret, not writing opinions or publishing rulings, except in one case in which it said that the court's jurisdiction did not extend to searches of private property.

The Courts of Appeals

The U.S. Courts of Appeals, formerly called the Circuit Courts of Appeals, are the general appellate courts for the federal judicial system. They were created in their present form in 1891, as a result of increased federal court caseload and the recognition of the impracticality of having Supreme Court justices sit on circuit. They are required to hear the cases brought to them, that is, they are mandatory jurisdiction courts and as such they engage primarily in "error correction." They also engage in important "law-making" activity, much of which is not reviewed by the Supreme Court. The Supreme Court concentrates on broader policy concerns; courts of appeals, on the other hand, "concentrate on statutory interpretation, administrative review, and error correction in masses of routine adjudication."[29] They handle cases on all types of federal law—"traditional" areas of litigation such as admiralty and antitrust; constitutional issues that are more prominent in the Supreme Court's work; and many cases appealed from federal regulatory agencies, although some agency decisions are reviewed in the district courts. The D.C. Circuit is particularly significant in reviewing agency decisions and is considered the second most important federal court.

The courts of appeals bring some degree of uniformity to national law, providing some oversight of activities once considered primarily local. That is, they perform a harmonizing function, a function once thought to be performed only by the Supreme Court. When the Supreme Court does not review areas of law, the courts of appeals perform that harmonizing function. If the standard by which they review district court decisions is a deferential one, then the district courts develop the law; if the standard of review is strict, the courts of appeals' role is increased, but too strict a standard increases the number of appeals brought to them and hinders their ability to harmonize the law.

The courts of appeals are, however, also a decentralized mechanism, exhibiting considerable diversity; they thus can reflect regional variations in needs and values. As a result of their location in the judicial system,

> they enforce national policies [but] also mediate between national law and various political and professional constituencies in regional communities. . . . As intermediates in many dimensions of responsibility, they look down to district courts and agencies, up to the Supreme Court and the central government, in to themselves, their colleagues and staffs, across to rival appellate courts, and all around to various groups and individuals who compose their attentive publics.[30]

This is but one example of a more general phenomenon seen also in the emphases on commercial litigation in the Second Circuit (New York) and on civil rights in the old Fifth Circuit: each court of appeals becomes "a magnet for certain subjects of federal law by virtue of location, special jurisdiction, and predilections," as well as differing propensities of attorneys and litigants to appeal different types of cases.[31]

There are now 167 authorized judgeships for the courts of appeals, 35 having been added by the 1978 Judgeship Act, 24 more in the 1984 legislation, and 11 in 1991. (There are also 12 judges for the Court of Appeals for the Federal Circuit, a specialized court.) Assisting the circuit judges in deciding cases are the courts' *senior* (semiretired) judges (see pages 91–92), as well as district judges and judges from other circuits who sit "by designation." There are now 12 U.S. Courts of Appeals with general appellate jurisdiction—11 numbered circuits and one for the District of Columbia—in addition to specialized appellate courts (see pages 58–61). Except for the District of Columbia Circuit, each court of appeals covers several contiguous states. The courts range in size from the First Circuit (Massachusetts, New Hampshire, Maine, Rhode Island, and Puerto Rico), the smallest with six judgeships, to the Ninth (Alaska, Hawaii, California, Oregon,

Washington, Idaho, Montana, Nevada, and Arizona, plus Guam and the Northern Marianas), with 28 judgeships. Judges in all but the District of Columbia Circuit reside at various and often widely dispersed locations throughout the circuit. They meet when hearing oral argument and discussing cases immediately thereafter, or when conducting court business. They rely heavily on telephone and electronic mail to discuss cases further and develop opinions.[32]

Until 1980, when the Fifth Circuit (the Deep South) was divided into the Fifth and Eleventh Circuits, no new circuit had been created since the mid-1920s, when the Tenth Circuit (the Rocky Mountain states) was carved out of the Eighth Circuit extending westward from the Mississippi River. California was a one-state circuit in the mid-nineteenth century, when it had its own circuit judgeship before the U.S. courts of appeals were formed. At the same time, one state (Arkansas) was split, with parts in two circuits. With those exceptions, we have not had either one-state circuits or split a state between circuits.

Division of the Fifth Circuit and failure to divide the Ninth Circuit both illustrate political aspects of structuring our judicial system. Prior to 1978, the Fifth Circuit had the largest number of judgeships (15) and was to receive 11 more in 1978. Because a court of 26 judges was thought much too large, proposals were made to divide the circuit. However, enactment was delayed for several years—in fact, delaying passage of the Omnibus Judgeship Act until 1978—by resistance from the NAACP, concerned that a relatively liberal civil rights court would be broken up, and particularly from conservative Senator James Eastland of Mississippi, then chairman of the Senate Committee on the Judiciary. Eastland insisted on having one circuit composed of only Texas and Louisiana, with Mississippi, Georgia, Alabama, and Florida in the other. Then came Eastland's announcement of retirement from the Senate, the appointment of some black judges, withdrawal of NAACP opposition, and support by Senator Edward Kennedy, the incoming committee chair, for a different division (adding Mississippi to Texas and Louisiana). Yet even these changes did not result immediately in a split of the circuit. The Fifth Circuit tried to sit with its full complement of 26 judges, but the logistical difficulties led the court itself to ask that it be divided, and Congress agreed in 1980.

There have been efforts to divide the Ninth Circuit. One proposal would have divided California, which generates roughly three-fifths of the Ninth Circuit's caseload, and that was not politically acceptable. A more recent proposal, to create a smaller northern circuit and a larger southern one from the present Ninth Circuit, is based in part on concern by senators from the northern states about decisions on the environment, particularly rulings that protect the spotted owl by limiting the amount of timber that can be cut. This indicates the connection between policy positions and proposed structural changes, also true in the splitting of the old Fifth Circuit. A major reason that the Ninth Circuit has not been divided is that its judges have worked to keep it intact and to make it an exemplar of an effective large circuit.[33]

When the courts of appeals were created, the judges who sat on them were two circuit judges and a district judge. Most courts of appeals cases now are heard by three-judge panels of changing membership. A panel *is* the court of appeals for the cases it decides, and a panel's ruling is not to be overruled by another panel but only by the court of appeals sitting *en banc*, that is, all of the court's judges sitting. The courts of appeals sit *en banc* to hear particularly important cases, usually after a panel has heard the case, but the mechanism is used infrequently. *En banc* sittings were developed when the Supreme Court gave the appeals courts the responsibility for producing uniformity in legal matters within a circuit. The 1978 Act also allowed large circuits to use limited *en banc* courts of some number less than the entire court. The Ninth Circuit is the only court to have done so, using 11 judges (the chief judge and 10 others drawn by lot). The 1978 Act provided that circuits with more than 15 active circuit judges (then only the Fifth and Ninth) could create internal administrative units, and only the Ninth Circuit did so. Rotation of panel membership, large caseloads, and ideological differences can contribute to inconsistency *within* a court of appeals, limiting the court's ability to produce uniform interpretation of the law.[34]

Roughly 33,000 cases are docketed in the U.S. courts of appeals each year. Caseload has increased 15 times from 1945–89, while the number of judges increased only three times in the same period. More important, the increase in appellate case filings has exceeded the increase in district court filings, and a much higher proportion of district court cases are now appealed than was true earlier.[35] Criminal cases have grown most in recent years and now account for roughly one-third of appeals court caseload. There is no Speedy Appeals Act, but criminal appeals are expected to be handled expeditiously, helping to create a delay in reaching and deciding other types of appeals. Moreover, increases in judges may help reduce backlogs temporarily, but more decisions will be appealed as a result of new district judgeships, and proportionately more cases may be appealed by litigants whose trials are more promptly terminated by those judges, resulting in a continuing heavy appellate court caseload.

All the courts of appeals operate under the Federal Rules of Appellate Procedure but adopt separate Local Rules. They vary in reliance on oral argument. The Second Circuit uses it in almost every case while other circuits dispense with it in a significant portion of cases. Certain appeals that are thought to be "frivolous," having little substance and not raising new issues, and others that are routine are often handled by truncated procedures and receive summary dispositions with unpublished opinions. All circuits now issue high proportions of decisions in Not-for-Publication memorandums, which cannot be cited as precedent by lawyers in other cases.[36] Still other appeals are "ritualistic," brought because of the litigants' demands even when the likelihood of reversing the district court is low. Only a relatively small proportion of cases involve "nonconsensual" appeals "which raise major questions of public policy and upon which there is considerable disagreement."[37]

Among the nonconsensual appeals may be those in which "issue transformation" has taken place as a case moves from the district court to the appeals court. Such issue transformation was found in civil liberties cases and particularly in race relations cases in the Third, Fifth, and Eighth Circuits from 1956 through 1961. Through it the appeals courts, which granted liberties denied in the district courts, enforced a more "national" and less local perspective.[38] However, there was very little issue transformation in cases taken from the district courts to the Second, Fifth, and District of Columbia Circuits in Fiscal Years 1965–67. Only 7 percent of the cases provided an indication that the two levels of judges defined the issues in cases differently. However, the appellate judges filtered issues as they moved up to the Supreme Court. This was part of the intermediate courts' "important functions as gatekeepers, directing traffic in the stream of federal appeals."[39]

The finality of the courts of appeals' decisions is particularly significant. Because very few cases are appealed from there to the Supreme Court, which denies most petitions for review, appeals court rulings are left as the final judicial statement in the great bulk of cases. For example, in the Second, Fifth, and District of Columbia Circuits, only one in five decisions was appealed. The Supreme Court granted review to only one-tenth of the decisions appealed, leaving over 98 percent of appeals court rulings as final—actually closer to 99 percent if we include cases in which the Supreme Court granted review and then affirmed the appeals courts. There are, in short, few "interventions" by the Supreme Court in the appeals courts' work.[40] (There are even fewer by the courts of appeals in the district courts' work.) Because most appeals court actions are not disturbed, they "*make* national law," although "residually and regionally." The Supreme Court remains largely dependent on them to "enforce the supremacy and uniformity of national law," particularly in those areas of law in which undisturbed cases tend to cluster,[41] including such important subjects as workmen's compensation and minimum wage, Social Security, insurance contracts, and even school desegregation. Because the Supreme Court reviews selectively, paying more attention to some circuits such as the District of Columbia Circuit, it seldom supervises areas of litigation in which individual circuits specialize.[42]

Specialized Appeals Courts

Just as there are specialized trial courts, there are some specialized appellate courts. Most notable among them was the Court of Customs and Patent Appeals (CCPA), created in 1910 and absorbed into the Court of Appeals for the Federal Circuit in 1982. The CCPA was initially an Article I court but its judges were given Article III (lifetime) status in 1948. The CCPA had appellate jurisdiction on matters of law over not only the Customs Court but also the Patent Office and Tariff Commission. This made it a semispecialized court. Until the mid-1950s, judges of the Court of Customs and Patent Appeals were nonspecialists not chosen from the patent bar, the lawyers who represent those seeking to obtain patents or defend patent holders against infringement of those patents. These nonspecialist judges tended to defer to Patent Office decisions denying patents because the Patent Office was an administrative agency. In the late 1950s, the patent bar persuaded the president to appoint two patent attorneys to CCPA, which almost immediately changed direction, producing substantially more reversals of the Patent Office and becoming more lenient than the district courts in cases involving issued patents. They continued to be more deferential to the Patent Office than were the "specialist" judges.

This history of the decisions of one specialized court indicates that "specialization may create conditions" such as success in obtaining nominations for certain types of people, "that cause a court to take a distinctive path."[43] However, it does not allow us to say that specialized courts will invariably behave differently from general jurisdiction courts, or that litigant interest groups, particularly if unified, have greater influence over such courts than over courts of general jurisdiction. However, while a generalist court is a buffer between political pressures and citizens, specialized courts, because their judges "are more likely than generalists to identify with the goals of a government program," are more likely to be a "superconductor" of those pressures,[44] and specialized courts may have been proposed "primarily or in part to create more favorable conditions for the federal government in litigation against private parties."[45]

Arguments for creating any specialized court were apparent in the recent move to centralize all patent appeals in one court. A principal argument—by attorneys and federal judges alike—for creating a specialized court for patent cases was that such cases are too technical for generalist judges. One response was that patent cases are no more complex than antitrust or environment cases. Another was that judges who hear only one type of case will lose perspective as they become divorced from developments in other fields of law and will become immune to subtleties in the cases before them.

The idea that patent appeals should be centralized bore fruit in 1981, when Congress created the Court of Appeals for the Federal Circuit, which assumed the existing appellate jurisdiction of both the Court of Claims and the Court of Customs and Patent Appeals, plus all appeals from the district courts in cases involving patents or nontax monetary claims against the United States. In addition to hearing appeals in cases involving contract and eminent domain claims against the government, the court hears appeals from the Court of International Trade (formerly the Customs Court), the Patent and Trademark Office, and the Merit Systems Protection Board (created in the reorganization of the federal government's personnel system). All this jurisdiction makes the Federal Circuit "less specialized than most other specialized courts, but it is much less a generalist than are the courts of appeals."[46]

Perhaps the most significant part of the reorganization is that, while trials in patent cases still take place in the district courts, patent *appeals*, instead of being heard in several courts (the Court of Customs and Patent Appeals, the Court of Appeals for the District of Columbia—for certain types of cases, and other courts of appeals), are now centralized in one court, an example of cases being appealed from a generalist trial court to a specialized appellate court. This is much appreciated by the patent bar, which the Court of Appeals for the Federal Circuit has enlisted in working out its new jurisdiction. The Court has, however, taken a narrow view of its jurisdiction on some topics, so that some issues are "stranded in the regional circuits or the state courts" and limited the Federal Circuit's ability to harmonize the law.[47] By contrast, several paths remain for tax appeals: from the Claims Court to the Court of Appeals for the Federal Circuit, and from the Tax Court to the court of appeals to which a taxpayer would have taken an appeal from the district court; the result is several diverging bodies of tax law.

Review from the Federal Circuit is on certiorari to the Supreme Court. Since the Federal Circuit's creation, there have been far fewer patent cases in the Supreme Court. With the Federal Circuit creating uniformity in patent law, the Supreme Court need not take these cases. It is also possible that the justices "will be handicapped in reviewing the work of a specialized court," which will "evolve a distinctive legal culture that will be hard for any generalist body to fathom," particularly with intercircuit conflict no longer providing differing views on a legal issue.[48]

Some specialized appellate courts have been staffed by Article III judges whose full-time positions are on other courts and who are appointed to the specialized courts by the Chief Justice. This may provide judges of broader perspective but it also can create mixed loyalties. These courts include the Temporary National Emergency Court of Appeals for cases arising under the wage-price control and emergency petroleum allocation programs of the 1970s—created in 1971 and processing cases into the 1990s, so hardly "temporary"; the earlier Emergency Court of Appeals, established during World War II for wage-price cases[49]; and a special court to handle problems under the Regional Rail Reorganization Act of 1973.

There is also the three-judge Foreign Intelligence Surveillance Court of Review, to review applications for electronic surveillance denied by the Foreign Intelligence Surveillance Court (see page 54). Another such court is known as the Special Division of the United States Court of Appeals for the District of Columbia Circuit. Its judges have two-year appointments, with priority given to senior circuit judges and retired Supreme Court justices, and one must be from the D.C. Circuit. That court has the task of designating independent counsel (formerly called special prosecutors) called for under the Ethics in Government Act of 1978 in cases involving the president, vice president, and other high government officials.[50] Although there has been one ruling that the Special Court unconstitutionally carried out nonjudicial functions with respect to the special counsel,[51] the Supreme Court, in *Morrison v. Olson*, upheld the independent counsel statute, including the appointment provisions (see pages 329–30).

An earlier experiment with a specialized court to hear cases from a single administrative agency—the Commerce Court, to hear cases from the Interstate Commerce Commission—was abandoned in 1913 after only a few years because the railroads preferred to deal with the ICC, shippers didn't like interference with the commission, and Congress saw a threat from the court to the commission, which it saw as more its own arm.[52] From time to time, a proposal has been made for a Court of Administrative Appeals, which would handle all appeals from orders of federal administrative agencies, but it has not gained much support.

There is only one Article I specialized appeals court, the Court of Military Appeals. It was created in 1950, under congressional power to provide for the armed forces, to apply the revised Uniform Code of Military Justice (UCMJ). Its five (originally three) civilian judges serve for staggered 15-year terms; no more than three may be of one political party. They must review courts-martial decisions involving general or flag officers, capital punishment decisions affirmed by the Boards of Review in the military services, and cases the service judge advocate generals (JAG) certify for review. Its principal business, however, is discretionary review of courts-martial decisions involving bad-conduct discharges and prison sentences of more than one year, which it considers if a Board of Review approves a petition by the convicted person. The judges grant approximately 10 percent of those petitions and deny the others without explanation. Effective in 1984, the Supreme Court was given the authority to review certain decisions of the USCMA on certiorari. Until then Supreme Court review was restricted to habeas corpus on the limited question of whether the military had jurisdiction over the court-martialed person. However, through use of that jurisdiction, the Court handed down important decisions concerning the military's authority to court-martial civilians or military personnel involved in non-service-connected offenses.[53]

Reexamining the System

Problems generated by increased caseload in both the Supreme Court and courts of appeals, coupled with Chief Justice Burger's greater attention to administrative matters, led to the first serious structural examination of the national court system since the 1920s and to proposals to restructure that system. The most important proposal would have created a new federal appellate court located between the U.S. courts of appeals and the Supreme Court.[54]

The first major proposal was recommended by a study group appointed by Chief Justice Burger and chaired by Harvard Law School Professor Paul Freund. It called for a National Court of Appeals, a "mini–Supreme Court," staffed by present appeals court judges on a rotating basis. The new court would sort cases awaiting the Supreme Court's review and select roughly 400 each year most worthy of the Supreme Court's attention, from which the justices were to select 120 to 150 cases for full-dress treatment. The new court's denials of review and its determinations of legal conflicts between the courts of appeals would have been final. This proposal was shelved, largely because it would have deprived the Supreme Court of the considerable power it has through its finality of denials of review. That the Chief Justice, without legislative involvement, had appointed a committee likely to recommend what he wanted did not help the proposal. Moreover, that failed effort had a continuing effect, making it more difficult for more moderate proposals that followed.

The Commission on Revision of the Federal Court Appellate System, created by Congress, then made recommendations in 1975. Based on its examination of the national court system's capacity for "declaring and defining the national law," it proposed a National Court of Appeals of several judges to be appointed by the president. The Supreme Court could send cases to the new court before deciding them ("reference jurisdiction") and the courts of appeals could send them when a rule of federal law was applicable to recurring factual situations or when federal courts had reached inconsistent decisions on a rule of federal law ("transfer jursidiction"). The new court's refusal to accept cases would not be reviewable, but its decisions of cases on the merits could be reviewed by the Supreme Court on certiorari. This proposal received more substantial support than the Freund Study Group proposal, but was not accepted. Creation of the Court of Appeals for the Federal Circuit, discussed previously, came from the effort to salvage some part of the proposal.

For a while justices continued to speak out on the idea of a National Court of Appeals. Some took issue with colleagues' suggestions while agreeing that something had to be done about workload (see pages 196–99). In 1983 and thereafter, Chief Justice Burger, in a number of forums, including his State of the Judiciary addresses to the American Bar Association, renewed his call for the new tribunal. He even suggested that it be established on an experimental basis for five years. Before being nominated to be Chief Justice, Justice Rehnquist advocated it but without claiming the Supreme Court is overworked or suggesting the Court would shed cases. Bills to establish such an Intercircuit Tribunal of the United States Courts of Appeals were approved by subcommittees in both houses of Congress, and by the full Senate Judiciary Committee in 1986, but no legislation has passed both houses. Proposals have varied, particularly as to the size of the court, and the method of selecting judges has been a bone of contention: Chief Justice Burger wanted them selected by the Chief Justice or the Judicial Conference, while the circuits have opted for selecting their own members of the new court. Chief Justice Rehnquist would have given the appointment power to the president, although that would not be palatable to senators whose party was not in control of the White House. Other proposals have included a single U.S. court of appeals without existing circuit lines but with regionally based general appellate divisions and specialized (subject-matter) divisions that would be nationally based, and intercircuit panels on a regional basis to resolve some intercircuit conflict.

There is concern that the Supreme Court's work will be increased to some extent if, in addition to deciding whether to grant review in a case, the justices have to decide whether a case is of sufficient importance to be heard by the new court but not by the Supreme Court; adding a choice to those available to any decision-making body increases the opportunities for conflict.[55] Knowledgeable lawyers and scholars continue to express the view that any such significant structural change should not be made until after other methods of reducing the Supreme Court's caseload, such as complete removal of diversity of citizenship jurisdiction, have been tried. Critics also suggest that the amount of unresolved intercircuit conflict with which the new court is supposed to deal may be overestimated, and that some of it might be avoided by clearer Supreme Court opinions. Certainly the Rehnquist Court's decision of fewer cases during the term, and its slowness in filling its calendar for each year, indicates that the Court itself has additional "national judicial decision-making capacity" said to be needed.

The most recent examination of the federal courts and of proposals to alleviate caseload problems was undertaken by the 15-member Federal Courts Study Committee, created by Congress in 1988, with its members appointed by the Chief Justice. The Committee made its recommendations in 1990, and some were enacted into law, including a new Court of Veterans Appeals (see page 54). However, most major proposals were not adopted immediately and remained on the legislative agenda. One would have given the Equal Employment Opportunity Commission (EEOC) the power to adjudicate wrongful discharge employment cases and another would have given the Tax Court Article III status (see pages 52–53). Still another, related to the National Court of Appeals idea, would have been an experiment for Supreme Court referral of intercircuit conflict cases to one appeals court for authoritative ruling. The difficulty in obtaining adoption of the proposals, whatever their merit, indicates the politics involved in restructuring the court system.

Judicial Administration

Judicial administration is "the direction of and influence on the activities of those who are expected to contribute to just and efficient case-processing, except legal doctrinal considerations insofar as they dispose of the particular factual and legal claims presented in a case."[56] It is a low-visibility activity, yet neither any single court nor the judicial system as a whole could function without it. It encompasses activities related to processing cases, the judicial branch's personnel needs, budgeting for the judiciary, planning, and research. The federal courts' increasing caseload and Chief Justice Burger's efforts have focused more attention on judicial administration and have helped produce a greater desire to shift from haphazard, inefficient management to more organized and "professional" administration. From the early years, the Chief Justice "received information on the state of judicial business in the far-flung districts,"[57] but only in the twentieth century has serious and protracted attention been given to problems of judicial administration, particularly by Chief Justices Taft and Burger.

Judges' insistence on independence and their resistance to central authority have made it difficult to establish even something seemingly as simple as uniform personnel and salary systems for the federal courts. The judges' independence includes their lobbying of members of Congress to seek support for their own policies. (Judges' communication is supposed to be through "official channels," but the Justice Department has interpreted this statutory requirement to allow individual judges to spend funds to contact members of Congress and legislative committees to express views of legislation.) Pressure has nonetheless been substantial to make the courts' internal operations administratively efficient so that the courts might be more effective in performing their functions. Reformers have sought to improve court administration through "centralization, bureaucratization, and professionalization of judicial administration . . . at the expense of judicial informality and autonomy." Such trends, "accelerated by the law explosion," are "rooted in external demands for efficiency, fiscal accountability, and professional standards of personnel management."[58]

The difficulty in bringing about effective, rational management of the federal court system is demonstrated by the problems in developing methods for assignment of judges to handle cases where their help is needed. Until 1850, a federal judge could not sit outside his district. After 1850, he could be assigned only to a court within his own or a contiguous circuit—and only to help a sick or disabled judge. In the early twentieth century, the Chief Justice could ask that a judge serve elsewhere, but the chief judge of the judge's circuit could refuse the request—and did so. Judges, as a result of their primarily local or state orientation, did not see themselves as part of a national judicial system.

Problems surrounding intercircuit assignment of judges have changed—it is not as easy to block requested transfer—but have not disappeared. If all courts have crowded dockets, it is difficult to find anyone except senior judges, who are willing to be assigned around the country to assist with particularly overloaded districts. Yet, despite Chief Justice Taft's support for the idea, a "pool" or "flying squadron" of federal judges available for assignment anywhere in the system has never been established on a *regular* basis, although the Commerce Court's five judges were available for assignment to trial or appellate work throughout the country after that court was eliminated. Assignments between the circuits must now be cleared by the Intercircuit Assignment Committee, closely responsive to the Chief Justice's wishes. Fear of congressional objection to the expenditure of funds for judges to travel from one part of the country to another—even before Gramm-Rudman—has led the Chief Justice to be chary about approving intercircuit assignments.[59] (The Chief Justice has authority to select judges from another circuit when all the judges of a court of appeals withdraw from a case because a defendant has filed a complaint against them or when they are colleagues of a judge involved in some way in a case. There are no statutory directives about how the Chief Justice can select the replacement judges, giving rise to the claim that selections might be made to produce a desired result.[60])

Particularly important among aspects of judicial administration has been budgeting for the court system. The judiciary's budget is only *one-tenth of one percent* of the total federal budget, despite significant growth since 1950—by over 100 percent in the first three decades, including a 350 percent growth from 1970–1980, before reduced growth (only 61%) in the next decade.[61] That budget, although smaller than Congress's or the Justice Department's, was affected by efforts to reduce the nation's budget deficit. The Gramm-Rudman-Hollings Budget Reduction Act's targeted reductions in budget deficits, and provisions for automatic cuts if Congress did not reach the targeted amounts, applied to the judiciary. In Fiscal Year 1986, an across-the-board 4.3 percent reduction meant that $42 million had to be saved from a $1.1 billion budget. Courts were affected by a reduction in the number of security guards at federal courts, elimination of parking fees for federal jurors, depletion of funds to pay basic juror fees (provided in a supplemental appropriations bill)—a problem that recurred in 1992, and reductions in the courts' staffing levels and in judges' travel allotments. (See pages 306–7.)

For many years, despite the number of people working in the federal judicial branch (over 23,000) little attention was given to the selection, retention, and supervision of personnel necessary to make the courts operate effectively. Hiring of administrative personnel, such as clerks of court, who generally focus on day-to-day aspects of processing of cases and who until recently were fully responsible for administering court activities, was essentially a matter of judges' patronage and was unsystematic. Most court staff positions are now filled through regularized hiring procedures and a 1990 law gave the director of the Administrative Office of the Courts (A.O.) the authority to establish a personnel system for that agency, but employees in the courts are hired under Judicial Conference rules. Court reporters, who record and transcribe what is said in court, were not hired by the courts on a uniform basis until 1944; before then, most courts left it to the litigants to arrange for private reporters.

Other personnel involved in the courts' work are probation officers and U.S. marshals. The former, originally under the supervision of the Bureau of Prisons, are now responsible to the Administrative Office. The U.S. marshals, nominated for each district by the president and confirmed by the Senate, are executive branch employees. They are formally responsible to the attorney general but work closely with the courts. Under an agreement between the A.O. and the General Services Administration (GSA), they are responsible for courtroom security, which is a matter of increasing concern, particularly in larger cities, and the judges' safety, crucial after increased attacks on judges (see page 88); they also enforce judicial orders. Their working relations with the courts are usually smooth, but the question of whether marshals must transport state prisoners to testify in federal court cases ended up in the Supreme Court, which ruled that federal courts had no authority to order the marshals to perform that task.[62]

In addition to administrative personnel serving the court as an institution, there are law clerks, recent top-ranked law school graduates who serve a judge for a year or two years at most. Supreme Court justices have used law clerks since early in this century. Each Supreme Court justice is now entitled to four clerks, but some have preferred to use less than their allotment. To provide expertise and continuity, Justice White keeps one of his clerks for a second year. Law clerks did not appear on a salaried basis in the district courts until the mid-1940s. Now each district judge has two law clerks. In the courts of appeals, where each judge has three law clerks, the courts now also hire staff attorneys, who perform legal tasks for all the judges of the court rather than being assigned to individual judges.

Judges use several methods to select their clerks. Many have open competitions, while some depend on law school professors to make selections for them; others enlist former clerks to screen candidates while making the final selection themselves. Clerks perform a variety of tasks for judges. They examine briefs and court records in cases, research matters of law, and draft opinions; at the Supreme Court, they also summarize petitions for review (see page 210). The extent of their input depends on the judge or justice for and with whom they work; some clerks are able to offer ideas in addition to performing more basic research and writing tasks.

Circuit Councils

The basic units involved in administering the federal judicial system are the Judicial Conference of the United States, the Administrative Office of the United States Courts, and the circuit councils. All were established relatively late in the national judicial system's history, largely as a result of judicial and administrative politics, with the primary reason probably that federal judges wished to retain their independence both of each other and of any central authority. (Only in the early 1990s will the major judicial administration agencies be housed together, in a new judiciary office building near the Supreme Court. It will house the Administrative Office and the Federal Judicial Center, as well as the U.S. Sentencing Commission and the Multi-District Litigation Panel.)

There is a chief judge in each district and circuit. Although the chief judge of a circuit or district used to be the most senior judge of the court under the age of 70, now someone cannot become chief judge after reaching age 65 unless no one else is eligible. The chief judge may serve for no more than seven years and must step down as chief judge at age 70. Because the position is filled on the basis of seniority, there is no guarantee that a chief judge will be good as either an administrator or leader. Getting the judges of a court to work together and to work with or under a chief judge can be difficult, particularly if the "chief" is strong willed. Conflict in the Northern District of Ohio between Chief Judge Frank J. Battisti and his colleagues in 1985 led the Sixth Circuit to rule that Battisti could remain chief judge but policy for the court's operation would be set by a majority of the district's judges.

The basic administrative unit of the federal judicial system is supposed to be the *judicial council* in each circuit. These were created in part to decrease the chance of political attacks on the central judicial establishment in Washington, D.C. (There is also a *circuit judicial conference* in each circuit, which includes all circuit and district judges, other judicial officers, and lawyer representatives and meets once a year to consider a wide range of matters.) Until 1981, the circuit council was composed of all circuit judges on active-duty status, the *en banc* court of appeals wearing administrative rather than judicial hats. Legislation affecting the councils' responsibilities for judicial conduct (see page 93) also changed their structure by adding district judges. No longer are all the circuit judges automatically members of the council. An equal number of circuit judges and district judges now compose the council, chaired by the circuit's chief judge.

In addition to its role in judicial discipline, the council's wide range of powers includes approving judicial accommodations, directing where court records should be kept, and performing other "housekeeping" tasks; consenting to the assignment of judges to courts in other circuits and dividing judicial business in the districts if the district judges cannot agree among themselves; and the far more sensitive business of certifying to the president that because of disability a judge is unable to discharge his or her duties. The council also receives reports from the Administrative Office on the dockets in the circuit's courts and is supposed to take appropriate action on the basis of those reports.

The circuit council is assisted in carrying out its tasks by the *circuit executive*, who assists the chief judge and the circuit council with general administration of the circuit and with special projects. Some circuits have made substantial use of their circuit executives, but it is necessary to do more than appointing someone with such a title to solve administrative problems. Chief judges' inability to delegate responsibility to circuit executives, the executives' involvement in detail, and conflict between the executive and clerk of court, increasingly likely to be well trained, are principal difficulties.[63]

Judicial Conference

Diffusing responsibility among all a circuit's judges serving as the circuit council often led to a lack of willingness to act on important matters or to exercise authority. For this reason and because the councils are more attached "to the ideal of local self-government and an independent judiciary,"[64] they have played a less important role than the Judicial Conference of the United States. Indeed, circuit councils blocked the trend toward a centralized administration for the judiciary.

Establishment in 1922 of the Judicial Conference, originally the Conference of Senior Circuit Judges, was the first official manifestation that authority in the federal judicial system was being centralized. Chaired by the Chief Justice, the Judicial Conference consists of the chief judges of the courts of appeals, a district judge from each circuit except the Federal Circuit, and the chief judge of the Court of International Trade. District judges were not part of the original membership. The Conference meets twice a year. A six-member executive committee acts for the Conference between meetings. The Chief Justice has wielded significant authority in the Conference's work. That authority, initially enhanced because he had to speak for the Conference between meetings, was later strengthened because only he, and not the other justices, participated in the Conference. The other justices have generally not wanted to be involved in such administrative matters, are busy, and, with few exceptions, lacked an administrative background.

The Conference was created to be the chief administrative policymaker for the federal judiciary but "constituted only a first step toward a more integrated administrative system." At first it operated mainly by tying the senior circuit judges into a national communications network. However, it never developed the predominance for which it was intended. Its potential strength was reduced by its infrequent meetings and the later development of committees, which proliferated and became more important under Chief Justice Stone. The Chief Justice's position is strengthened by the fact that the more than 20 standing and ad hoc committees attached to the Conference report to him.[65] Development of the committees left the Conference largely a ratifying body for committee-recommended policies. Such policies covered a wide variety of matters, such as rules of evidence and procedure for the federal courts, the intercircuit transfer of judges, and the need for additional judges to deal with the ever-growing caseload of the federal courts.

The authority of the Conference itself has remained substantial, and it has dealt with such matters as ethical standards for judges and other court personnel, qualifications for those personnel, bankruptcy administration, and most important, the budget for the federal judiciary. The importance of the issues with which the Conference and its committees deal has led to pressure to open up the process by which Conference policy is made, and to require the Conference and its committees and subcommittees, as well as circuit judicial councils, to hold public meetings to transact business. Such efforts have thus far been unsuccessful.

Encompassed in the committees' work is the development of legislation to be submitted to Congress. The judges representing the Conference and its committees and the director of the Administrative Office present legislative proposals to Congress. This allows the Chief Justice to stay away from a direct role in that area, which can cause trouble. When Director of the Administrative Office Rowland Kirks, in the company of an interest group lobbyist, visited Speaker of the House Carl Albert in late 1972 about a bill concerning product safety, Chief Justice Burger was accused of sending a lobbyist to argue against the bill. Denying the charge, the Chief Justice said his only concern was the bill's possible effect on the court system—part of his desire for "court impact statements."

Proposals for limiting use of habeas corpus by state prisoners awaiting the death penalty caused conflict in the Judicial Conference between some of its members and the Chief Justice and illustrates tension within the federal judiciary. Chief Justice Rehnquist had appointed a committee, chaired by retired Justice Powell, which made suggestions on limiting federal habeas corpus. Shortly after the Powell task force issued its report, in October 1989, a majority of the Judicial Conference membership, objecting to Rehnquist's attempt to get immediate approval of the recommendations, voted 17–7 to defer consideration to its March meeting and wrote to the House and Senate judiciary committees to try to assure that the dissenting position of some judges would be heard when the recommendation was forwarded. The Chief Justice nonetheless urged Congress to approve the task force recommendations speedily, and some of the judges who disagreed did testify before Congress. Then in March 1990, the Judicial Conference, by a vote of 14–12, modified the proposal that Rehnquist had sent to Congress so that the limits on habeas corpus would be more moderate. (The Chief Justice's own vote averted further modification.) Not deterred, Rehnquist made a public call for enactment of the limits, and then led a majority on the Court to enact them as decisions of the Court (see page 187). That he could do so indicates further that the Supreme Court and the Judicial Conference are not closely linked.

Another example of the difficulty into which the Chief Justice can get himself in acting for the Conference occurred in 1978 during final stages of consideration of the new bankruptcy statute. Before either House or Senate passed its version of the bill, Chief Justice Burger reportedly made telephone calls to several legislators asking that consideration of the bills be delayed until certain issues could be explored further and the Judicial Conference's opinion on compromise legislation heard. Although his position was based on Conference opposition to giving bankruptcy judges Article III status and having bankruptcy appeals go directly to the courts of appeals, Burger's reported anger—for example, in a call to the Senate subcommittee chairman in charge of the legislation—particularly irritated some members of Congress. They felt that the Chief Justice was going far beyond his proper role and exceeding the powers of the judicial branch. However, this is not the only instance when "Chief Justices . . . have cast aside the judicial robe long enough to press their Court's case before coordinate branches of the national government and even to mobilize public opinion." In so doing, they have at times sought legislation of assistance to the Supreme Court or the judiciary more generally; they have also "entered the political arena to fend off legislation they have perceived as potentially harmful to the Court."[66]

The Administrative Office and
the Department of Justice

From its creation in 1870, the Department of Justice performed day-to-day administrative tasks for the federal courts. Formation of the Judicial Conference did not end the department's involvement. Pervasive conflict over administration has taken place between the department and individual judges. Department field auditors visiting judicial districts to look over books, records, and accounts performed "a communication function as well as an investigative one,"[67] but clerks of court resisted department demands for the reporting of financial transactions. Despite such opposition, the department increased its control over district court clerks and their deputies in 1919, courts of appeals clerks in 1922, and the probation service in 1925. Yet obtaining statutory authority over particular functions did not lessen the need for the department to fight to obtain actual control, and its failure to submit recommendations of the Conference of Senior Circuit Judges to Congress or to support them when submitted did not win the judges' favor.

Considerable change in the administrative center of gravity for the federal judicial system occurred in 1939. In his "Court-packing" plan, President Roosevelt, proposing to reform judicial functioning, had suggested that a proctor (court administrator) be appointed for the Supreme Court. Although the plan to "pack" the Court was defeated, Congress did establish the Administrative Office of the Courts (A.O.). The A.O. is *not* part of the executive branch, and its creation within the judiciary reinforces separation of powers by allowing the judges to handle the administration of their own branch of government. At the same time, integrating administrative functions for the judiciary in the judiciary itself has increased friction between the branches, perhaps a natural result of separation of powers, in part because administration of the judiciary was cut off from the political power base on which it rested while in the Department of Justice.[68]

The A.O.'s director is appointed by the Supreme Court. The provision that the director perform duties assigned by the Supreme Court and the Judicial Conference acting together has, however, served to reduce the administrative role of the Supreme Court as a whole, although the Chief Justice has continued to be important after the director is named. This is true even when a Chief Justice like Earl Warren gives the director a relatively free hand. It is particularly true where there is a close working relationship, as there was between Chief Justice Burger and the directors who served during his tenure. There is no one to deal with the A.O. on the Chief Justice's behalf; the Chief deals directly with the director.

When the A.O. was first established, members of the Judicial Conference acted to limit the authority of the office and its director, intending that the A.O. be "an executive office with strictly limited power" and that it deal with judges and other court personnel only upon authorization of the Conference, circuit councils, or individual courts, and performing housekeeping functions for the courts without employing the court's personnel. However, the A.O. has often initiated policies later considered by the Conference and its recommendations have carried great weight.[69] Despite their complaints, judges at times show considerable deference to the Administrative Office, even on legal matters, instead of using their own staff.

The Administrative Office took over most functions the Justice Department had performed, plus others that the department had not performed. The A.O. has the duty to compile suggested budgets and prepare vital statistics, examine dockets, determine personnel needs and procure supplies, and carry out additional tasks the Supreme Court or the Judicial Conference assigns, for example, establishing federal public defender systems to implement the Criminal Justice Act. The A.O. also serves as the secretariat for the Judicial Conference and its committees and as the liaison between the judiciary and Congress, individual judges, professional organizations, and other government agencies. As a result of the establishment (in 1976) of a Legislative Affairs Office, the A.O. has been able to focus its responsibilities for legislation better and to go beyond information gathering to supplying of information and helping to resolve problems that develop during the process of enacting legislation affecting the judiciary.

The *Federal Judicial Center* is the most recently created (1967) element in federal judicial administration. It was set up to meet research and educational needs of the judiciary. Among the tasks that it has undertaken have been testing calendaring procedures and means of transmitting judicial documents. The Center has studied elements of the court system such as magistrates and circuit executives and such matters as case screening, delays in the filing of transcripts, case management, and adoption of administrative innovations by a court. It has prepared a manual for complex and multidistrict litigation and a "bench book" for judges, and has conducted seminars and other training programs for newly appointed judges, magistrate judges, and probation officers.

The Supreme Court

We are so accustomed to a United States Supreme Court of nine justices that altering that number would be extremely difficult. The Constitution provides for a Supreme Court but does not designate its size, which at first was six. The number of justices fluctuated until well after the Civil War as presidents left seats vacant (Lincoln did so with three seats) and Congress ordered positions not to be filled (during Reconstruction) or increased the number (to 10 during the Civil War, although it is unlikely all 10 sat together). In his Court-packing plan of 1937, President Franklin Roosevelt would have added a justice for each one over the age of 70 who did not retire. Chief Justice Hughes helped defeat the proposal with a statement to Congress that a Court of more than nine justices would be unwieldy and that the Court could not divide into panels or "divisions" to hear cases, as some state high courts do, because the Constitution speaks of "one Supreme Court." Chief Justice Burger suggested in 1984 that the Court have a tenth justice, but the "Associate Justice for Administration," chosen by the Chief Justice from among sitting federal judges, would have no judicial duties.

Original Jurisdiction

Only the Court's original jurisdiction—cases brought to it directly—is detailed in the Constitution. (See Art. III, Sec. 2.) The Court's original jurisdiction accounts for only a very small proportion of its workload; there have been only approximately 150 such cases decided in the Court's history. In *Marbury v. Madison* the Court said that original jurisdiction was limited to the subjects designated in Article III. More important, the Court does not treat its original jurisdiction as mandatory and often changes it into appellate jurisdiction by sending cases brought as original jurisdiction cases to the district court.

> In all Cases affecting Ambassadors, other public Ministers and Consuls, and those in which a State shall be a Party, the supreme Court shall have original Jurisdiction. In all the other Cases before mentioned, the supreme Court shall have appellate Jurisdiction, both as to Law and Fact, with such Exceptions and under such Regulations as the Congress shall make. (Art. III, Sec. 2)

When an original jurisdiction case cannot be resolved on the pleadings, the justices appoint a special master (often a senior federal judge) to hear testimony and to make findings and recommendations; the special master serves as the equivalent of a special trial jury. The justices then decide to accept, modify, or reject them after hearing from the lawyers. Thus the justices act, as usual, in an appellate capacity, with the master really serving as a trial judge, but the Court has not always agreed about how much weight to give to the master's findings.

The Court's avoidance of original jurisdiction cases leaves for that jurisdiction only cases between two states, for example, over boundaries or water allocation, that would be a "cause of war" if the states were sovereigns, or between a state and the national government, like states' suits to test the validity of the 1965 and 1970 Voting Rights Act (*South Carolina v. Katzenbach* and *Oregon v. Mitchell*). Yet even when two states are involved, the Court may try to send cases elsewhere, particularly if the parties' interests would be adequately protected in those courts.

Appellate Jurisdiction

The Supreme Court's appellate jurisdiction accounts for the bulk of the Court's work. The Constitution makes that jurisdiction relatively open-ended and subject to modification by Congress (see pages 316–17). The Supreme Court long had to hear all cases appealed to it that came within its jurisdiction, but large classes of cases were outside the Court's appellate review. In the post–Civil War period, when Congress increased the scope of Supreme Court review of state court rulings, the Court itself, in *Murdock v. Memphis* (1875), interpreted the law narrowly and thus continued the limitations on Supreme Court authority over state law matters. Only state court decisions *denying* federal rights could be heard by the Supreme Court until 1914, when, to provide uniform interpretation of federal law, the high court received authority to review state court rulings *fa-*

voring the federal right. We are accustomed to assuming that criminal cases can be appealed, but for much of our history federal criminal cases were not subject to appeal to the Supreme Court. Only in 1914 were criminal cases from the U.S. courts of appeals subject to the Court's appellate jurisdiction, in addition to the Court's earlier limited civil jurisdiction.

When the Supreme Court had to hear all the cases within its appellate jurisdiction, the cases came to the Court on a *writ of error.* That writ allowed only review of the law, not the facts as a present-day appeal would. Cases could come to the Court when there was a "division of the court" in the lower court: with only two judges (a justice and a judge) sitting, they could split evenly. After the present courts of appeals were established, the Supreme Court was provided its certiorari jurisdiction, the authority to pick and choose the cases it would hear. Litigants with cases they wish the Supreme Court to hear file a petition for a *writ of certiorari,* which is an order to a lower court to send up the records in a case. When the Court issues the writ, it has accepted the case.

Certiorari jurisdiction, initiated in 1914, now accounts for almost all the Court's cases, but at first it was restricted to state court decisions favoring rights claimed under federal law. Two years later, some appeals from state court decisions denying federal rights were shifted to the Court's certiorari jurisdiction. The Judges Bill of 1925 provided substantial certiorari jurisdiction, including state court "federal question" decisions favorable to the federal claim, for example, when a state law is invalidated under the Supremacy Clause, and decisions by the U.S. courts of appeals interpreting or applying the Constitution, treaties, and federal laws or holding that state laws or constitutional provisions are *not* contrary to federal law. At that time, and until 1988, other cases were brought on *appeal.* In theory that jurisdiction was mandatory, but the justices had made it largely discretionary (see pages 203–4). Prior to 1988, cases eligible for appeal encompassed decisions in which either the highest state court or a federal court invalidated a federal law, a U.S. court of appeals struck down a state law, or a high state court denied a federal challenge to a state law, as well as rulings from three-judge district courts (see page 46). The justices themselves called for eliminating all the Court's mandatory jurisdiction, so that the above classes of cases would, like almost all others, come to the Court on petition for certiorari. Responding to objections to the Court's mandatory jurisdiction (see page 204), Congress eliminated such jurisdiction, effective September 1988, for all cases except those coming from three-judge district courts—essentially voting rights cases, including reapportionment—and those which Congress requires the Court to decide, as it did with challenges to the 1989 Flag Protection Act.

Rarely the Court receives a case on *certification.* A lower court faced with a new legal question "certifies" the question for answer by the Supreme Court. The justices have three basic choices: (1) they can refuse the certificate, forcing the lower court to decide the question on its own; (2) they can provide an answer, which the lower court applies; or (3) they may simply take the case and decide it directly without the extra step of returning it to the lower court, as the Supreme Court did with the Japanese Relocation Cases during World War II.[70] (We might call this type of certification "upward" certification, to distinguish it from "downward" certification, a procedure for federal courts to send cases to state courts; see page 184.) Cases can also come to the Supreme Court directly on *habeas corpus*, but this is rarely used, although it is how those who had been court-martialled could test the military's jurisdiction over them.

Supervisory Power and Rule Making

The Supreme Court, as the highest court in the federal court system, affects rulings of the lower courts not only through its interpretations of statutes or the Constitution but also by exercising *supervisory power* over the lower federal courts. This power is implied from the Constitution's providing for a Supreme Court and the reference to other federal courts, to be established by Congress, as "inferior" (that is, lower). An important instance was *Mallory v. United States* (1957), holding that under the Federal Rules a suspect must be taken before a magistrate for arraignment rather than being held by the police so that they can obtain a confession. Another is *United States v. Hale* (1975), ruling that a defendant's silence after being given *Miranda* warnings cannot be used against him. Because these rulings were based on the supervisory power rather than the Constitution, they were not applicable to the states through the Fourteenth Amendment, although the *Hale* ruling was later given constitutional footing.[71] A ruling involving interpretation of the Federal Rules could also be revised by Congress— exactly what happened with *Mallory* (see pages 342–43).

Exercises of the supervisory power are related to another, separate, element of the Supreme Court's work: its role in the development of the rules of procedure for the federal judiciary. Sets of rules (the Federal Rules of Criminal Procedure, Civil Procedure, Evidence, Appellate Procedure, and Bankruptcy) and amendments to them are promulgated by the Court under a grant of authority from Congress, the Rules Enabling Act (28 U.S.C. §2072). An advisory committee, and, more recently, a committee of the Judicial Conference itself aided by several advisory committees, prepares the rules, the Conference adopts them, and the Supreme Court then issues them. Even the Court itself knows that it is "in truth merely a conduit" for the transmission of the rules, although the justices are "nominally the promulgators" of them."[72] The Supreme Court develops its own Rules, announcing changes when it is ready to do so.

Justices Black and Douglas often criticized the Supreme Court's involvement in the promulgation of the rules. They felt that the Court should restrict itself to deciding cases, and that because the Court could not give full consideration to the Conference-proposed rules, the Conference itself should have full power to promulgate them. There have also been occasional disagreements by some of the justices with the substance of the rules transmitted to Congress. For example, when amendments to the Federal Rules of Civil Procedure affecting pretrial discovery were transmitted to Congress in 1980, Justices Powell, Stewart, and Rehnquist stated that the proposals were insufficient to bring about needed changes in civil lawsuits. They feared that acceptance of these rules would deter consideration of more thorough and more effective reforms.

The Rules Enabling Act provided that the rules go into effect unless disapproved by Congress (a legislative veto). Now Congress must pass a bill to defer the rules' effect and the president must sign the bill. For years, Congress accepted new Court-announced rules without debate. However, when new Federal Rules of Evidence were announced with significant changes in 1972, Congress, because of substantive disagreement over a number of the rules, delayed the effective date, subjected the rules to section-by-section reconsideration, and enacted them only in 1975. Congress also doubled the 90-day "waiting period" for congressional consideration of the evidence rules and provided for further extension. In 1988, Congress provided that for rules to go into effect in a given year, they must be submitted to Congress by May 1 of that year, and could take effect no earlier than December 1 (28 U.S.C. §2074). Nor could there be a change in evidentiary privileges without an act of Congress. The new timelines mean that an advisory committee must propose for publication a draft set of rules changes roughly two-and-a-half years before the effective date—and perhaps longer—because of the need for a six-month period of public comment, standing committee approval, and Judicial Conference approval.[73] Congress, which granted the courts the authority to develop and promulgate the rules, can itself change the rules, as it has done from time to time when considering, for example, issues of criminal procedure or, more recently, sentencing.

Judicial Review

The power of *judicial review*—the power to invalidate acts of Congress, the executive branch, and state and local governments—makes the Supreme Court particularly important. This power, not mentioned in the Constitution, was developed by the Court itself. All courts in the United States may exercise judicial review. The Supreme Court, because of its position, has the final judicial word on matters of judicial review concerning the United States Constitution.

Judicial review in the United States had several sources; the idea was not wholly original.[74] Its establishment and development were affected by philosophical views that influenced the Founding Fathers on such matters as the distribution and separation of powers. Also relevant, although not determinative, was the practice concerning the review of decisions made in the American colonies. "Conformity clauses" in state charters required acts of the colonial legislatures to conform to the laws of England and gave the king's Privy Council and its Committee on Appeals the power to disallow the legislation; that power was exercised in fact by the Board of Trade. Such action was, however, review without a written constitution, which England did not have. Thus it did not lead the colonies to associate judicial review with a written constitution. Decisions of the courts in the colonies could also be appealed to the Privy Council when the royal governor granted a request to appeal. Here the Committee on Appeals often based its decisions on the colony's local law.

The Articles of Confederation contained no provision for a separate national judiciary. Congress became the court of last appeal, or the board of arbitration, for controversies between the states and for a limited number of cases involving individual rights. The Constitution's Supremacy Clause was anticipated, however, in the stipulation that the Articles and acts of Congress be accorded the status of law within the states.

No plan submitted to the Constitutional Convention of 1787 conferred directly upon the judiciary any power of passing on the constitutionality of congressional acts. Under one major proposal—the Virginia Plan—judges would have been chosen by Congress. Congress would have had the right to disallow state legislation; a council of revision composed of the executive and a "convenient number" of the judiciary would have had a suspensive veto over national legislation. The major alternate plan made acts of Congress and treaties the "supreme law of the respective States" so that state judges would be bound by congressional acts, notwithstanding state constitutional provisions. Because state courts would initially decide federal cases, the need for lower federal courts would be eliminated. There would, however, be a supreme national tribunal, appointed by the executive, with appellate jurisdiction in certain classes of cases coming from the state courts. The convention eliminated congressional disallowance of state legislation and judicial participation in the veto. A Supreme Court was to be established, with Congress having the power to create lower federal courts, but not a word was said regarding the power of these federal courts to invalidate laws contrary to the Constitution. As with much of the rest of the document, the language was left general—perhaps a necessity if approval of the Constitution was to be obtained.

If the Constitutional Convention's leaders did not foresee that judges would engage in general expounding of the Constitution's meaning, they apparently did believe that the federal judiciary had the right to refuse to recognize unconstitutional federal law. Hamilton, Madison, and Jay, who wrote *The Federalist* papers to secure ratification of the Constitution in New York, argued strongly for judicial review. The Constitution as fundamental law was to be preferred when there was an irreconcilable variance between it and a legislative act, and the courts had a duty "to declare all acts contrary to the manifest tenor of the Constitution" void. There was, however, no direct empowerment to construe laws according to the Constitution's *spirit*. Judicial review was not an exercise of judicial power over the legislative branch. Instead, through judicial review the intention of the people—who ratified the Constitution—would be enforced against the intention of their agents, the legislators; the prior act of a superior authority would be preferred to the subsequent act of an inferior one. They dealt summarily with the Supreme Court's right to overrule state legislation, thus indicating it was less of an issue, at least for them.

The authors of *The Federalist* also noted that state judges were to be incorporated into the operation of the national government and would be bound by oath to support federal laws when those laws concerned legitimate and enumerated objects of federal jurisdiction. The Supremacy Clause was deemed imperative in helping produce needed uniform interpretation of federal law and treaties, as was national court jurisdiction and a supreme tribunal of last resort, to avoid an endless variety of decisions on the same point that would occur without appeal and review of rulings made by state courts of final jurisdiction. All matters of national law would receive this original or final determination in the national courts. However, in an appeal to states' rights interests, it was pointed out that the state courts—which would look beyond their own law in making decisions and would recognize relevant federal court rulings—would retain their former jurisdiction unless specifically limited by Congress, and that this system of initial state court determination with appeals from the state court to the federal courts would actually diminish the number of federal courts.

> This Constitution, and the Laws of the United States which shall be made in Pursuance thereof and all Treaties made, or which shall be made, under the Authority of the United States, shall be the supreme Law of the Land; and the Judges in every State shall be bound thereby, any Thing in the Constitution or Laws of any State to the Contrary notwithstanding. (Art. VI, Cl. 2)

Judicial review of state decisions took place before judicial review of national actions. Despite controversy, it became firmly established earlier. In 1797, in *Ware v. Hylton*, the Court held our treaty of peace with Great Britain superior to Virginia's statute sequestering property. The next year, in *Calder v. Bull*, the Court reviewed a state action challenged under the Ex Post Facto Clause, although it did not invalidate the statute in question. Twelve years later, in *Fletcher v. Peck*, stemming from the Yazoo land fraud, the Court ruled a Georgia statute in violation of the Constitution.[75] The most severe early test of judicial review of state court decisions came when Virginia courts declared unconstitutional a provision of the federal Judiciary Act establishing appeal of state decisions affecting federal rights. Responding in *Martin v. Hunter's Lessee* (1816), Justice Joseph Story ruled that the U.S. Supreme Court had a right to review the decisions of state courts in order to produce uniform interpretation of the nation's "supreme law." Five years later, Virginia's claim that a criminal defendant's appeal from a state ruling violated state sovereignty—part of the early battle over "states' rights"—was rejected in *Cohens v. Virginia*. Chief Justice Marshall stated that the Supreme Court had the right to appellate jurisdiction over decisions of highest state courts in all questions of national power.

The need for uniform national interpretation of constitutional provisions has led to the feeling that the Supreme Court's power to review state decisions may be more important than its power over national government actions. As Justice Holmes put it, "I do not think the United States would come to an end if we lost our power to declare an act of Congress void. I do think the Union would be imperiled if we could not make that declaration as to the laws of the several states."[76] Until we developed an active national government enacting numerous policies, there was less federal legislation for the Supreme Court to review, making judicial review of state legislation more important for that reason as well.

Throughout our history the Court has invalidated state laws more frequently than federal laws. Until the end of the Civil War, only two federal laws—but 60 state laws—were struck down. In the period from 1888 to 1937, over 400 state laws were invalidated, while only 70 national statutes were declared invalid. In the post-1937 period, well over 1,000 state laws were declared unconstitutional, but until the legislative veto case, only a few more than one hundred had received such treatment, with the Warren Court invalidating 19 acts of Congress in 16 years and the Burger Court striking down 29 acts of Congress in the amount of time before the Gramm-Rudman budget ruling and not counting the more than 200 statutes affected by the legislative veto decision (see page 311).

The exercise of judicial review of state laws may be more readily accepted now than in the Court's earliest days, although particular rulings may be disputed. However, opposition to judicial review itself still occurs at times. During the height of resistance to the Court's 1954 desegregation decision, Arkansas Governor Orval Faubus asserted that state governments were not bound by Supreme Court decisions because those decisions were not part of the "supreme law of the land." In the famous Little Rock case, *Cooper v. Aaron* (1958), the Supreme Court rejected this contention and stressed the supremacy of national law, *including* the Supreme Court's interpretation of it. More recently, when a federal judge's efforts to gain compliance with his orders concerning Native Americans' rights to their share of spawning fish (steelhead and salmon) encountered serious resistance from Washington State officials, the Supreme Court had to reiterate that a state's prohibition against compliance with a federal district court's decree could not survive under the Supremacy Clause.[77]

Judicial review of national government actions has been far more controversial. *Marbury v. Madison*, an 1803 case, was the first instance in which the Court invalidated a national statute, but in an implicit recognition of judicial review the Court had earlier upheld a federal statute. In 1796, in *Hylton v. United States*, the Court had ruled a carriage tax imposed by Congress not a direct one that would have had to be apportioned among the population, so the Court did not have to rule on the statute's constitutionality. Four years earlier, in *Hayburn's Case* (1792), Chief Justice John Jay and four other justices, ruling in Circuit Court decisions, said that a statute subjecting Circuit Court decisions on individuals' eligibility for pension benefits to review by the Secretary of War and Congress was invalid because the courts' decisions were not final and thus were mere advisory opinions. When the case came to the Supreme Court, the justices did not reach the constitutional issue but did report in the notes the circuit court rulings on the constitutional question.[78] Sitting as the Supreme Court rather than as circuit justices, the justices ruled to the same effect in *United States v. Todd* (1794).

Nonetheless, it was the *Marbury* decision that established judicial review. In the waning hours of the Federalist administration, William Marbury had been appointed to a minor judicial position but had not received his commission. He sought a writ of mandamus from the Supreme Court to make the new Secretary of State, James Madison, hand over the commission. Chief Justice John Marshall, himself one of the last of the Federalist appointees, found that Marbury had a right to his commission and thus was entitled to a remedy. However, he ruled that the Court could not issue the requested writ because the Judiciary Act of 1789 unconstitutionally added to the Court's original jurisdiction:

> If Congress remains at liberty to give this court appellate jurisdiction, where the Constitution has declared their jurisdiction shall be original; and original jurisdiction where the Constitution has declared it shall be appellate; the distribution of jurisdiction, made in the Constitution, is form without substance. . . .

Marshall insisted that the language of the Constitution be taken seriously. "It is a proposition too plain to be contested," he asserted, "that the constitution controls any legislative act repugnant to it; or that the legislature may alter the constitution by an ordinary act"; there were no other alternatives. The Constitution had to be either a "superior paramount law, unchangeable by ordinary means" or it was like any other law. But Marshall said,

> Certainly, all those who have framed written constitutions contemplate them as forming the fundamental and paramount law of the nation, and consequently, the theory of every such government must be that an act of the legislature repugnant to the constitution is void.

From this he concluded that the courts should invalidate the "repugnant" acts, giving the courts power over the other branches of government when constitutional questions were at issue. In ruling as he did, Marshall gave himself an opportunity to lecture the Jeffersonians and establish judicial review over acts of Congress. This perhaps put the administration on notice that future legislation might be declared unconstitutional.

Marbury was a decision founded largely on political prudence. Jefferson's administration was lectured, but "the actual holding of the case worked to the advantage of the . . . administration" because there was no order for it to disobey; in that sense, it could be seen as "a conciliatory gesture on the part of the Supreme Court" toward the administration.[79] More important, had Marshall *not* acted as he did, it would have been seen as a retreat by the judiciary. Thus "a brief opinion simply denying jurisdiction would not have been a 'neutral' act without important political effects," but "would have been interpreted as the act of a fearful judiciary bending before a triumphant and hostile party that was dominating the legislative and executive branches."[80] As Chief Justice Burger has observed, if Marshall had mandamused the administration and the order had been ignored, the Court would have faced "ridicule, and the ale houses would rock with hilarious laughter."[81] Because Marshall was Chief Justice before we had a stable political system and while there was still a lack of clarity about our fundamental principles, it was crucial that Marshall defend the Constitution to the nation, as he did in his opinion, where he engaged in examination of the Constitution "to support the general argument from the nature of the U.S. government."[82]

Marshall's opinion is open to considerable criticism. Under today's standards, he should have withdrawn from the case because of his earlier involvement; when he was secretary of state, he had failed to deliver Marbury's commission. Had he followed usual procedure and looked first at whether the Court had jurisdiction, he could have invalidated the statute but could not have lectured the administration about not giving up the commission. More important, Marshall could have followed a rule of judicial self-restraint and construed the Act of 1789 to save its constitutionality by saying the items of original jurisdiction enumerated in the Constitution need not be exclusive but could be supplemented by Congress, a view generally accepted in the 1790s.

Nor was Marshall's conclusion the only one he could have reached. There was the alternative position that the courts were limited to looking to see whether the legislature, in passing a law, had used the proper procedures. Judges implementing a law properly passed but in violation of the Constitution were not, by this view, committing an unconstitutional act but only doing what they were required to do. Another argument aimed at limiting the force of judicial review is that each branch of government should decide for itself what is constitutional and then should act on the basis of its own conclusions. Such a position is based on the idea that legislators and executives as well as judges take an oath to support the Constitution and can be thought to be as committed as judges to that oath. President Andrew Jackson, saying he had to make his own judgment, vetoed legislation for a national bank even though Chief Justice John Marshall, in *McCulloch v. Maryland*, had earlier sustained the validity of such a bank. President Jefferson thought Supreme Court determinations about statutes' validity were entitled to respect but were not binding on him as president. Similarly, after *Dred Scott*, President Lincoln said he would again vote to ban slavery in the territories: a ruling not embodying what he conceived to be the Constitution's basic or fundamental values was not a "political rule" he had to follow nor did it command permanent obedience but was to be challenged.[83] And this theory can also be seen in the practice, started by President Bush, of attaching statements to bills, when he signs them, indicating certain provisions he will not enforce as infringements on his authority.

Attorney General Meese, who previously attacked specific Supreme Court rulings (see page 329), said in 1986 that Supreme Court interpretations of the

Constitution were not "the law of the land" and that officials' own views of the Constitution should guide their acts. In so doing, repeating what earlier officials had stated, he restated the view that the Supreme Court and the Constitution are not one and the same. However, he went on to say that a Supreme Court ruling "does not establish a 'supreme law of the land' that is binding on all persons and parts of the government, henceforth and forevermore." The Court's rulings *are* supposed to bind "all . . . parts of government," including the states, not simply "the parties in the case and the executive branch for whatever enforcement is necessary." His statement produced an outcry, not much lessened by a subsequent modification in which he talked of the general applicability of the Court's rulings. Moreover, that he encouraged extension of Supreme Court rulings agreeing with the administration's position suggested a selectivity in those rulings he did not want others to follow.

The position that each branch should look to its own views would make judges' rulings potentially persuasive and would not prevent other policymakers from taking actions they thought appropriate or from trying to enforce laws without the courts' assistance. However, it would still allow judges to refuse to *enforce* policies they thought unconstitutional when those policies came before the courts in "cases and controversies." The Court's ability to rule effectively on challenges to acts of the other branches might not be severely limited because the executive needs to seek judicial assistance in enforcing the law.

Another, related version of judicial review gives each branch the final word about matters directly affecting it or "naturally" falling within its respective special competence. Here there would be "judicial supremacy" only about matters within the judiciary's particular bailiwick. Examples are the jurisdictional question in *Marbury*, the advisory opinion aspect of *Hayburn's Case*, and judicial remedies for constitutional violations, such as desegregation orders. Chief Justice Marshall, of course, went further, to establish judicial review over the acts of the legislative and executive branches affecting the entire government, not simply the judiciary. However, after *Marbury* the Court took no further such action for more than 50 years; this time lapse has, however, been "attributed to lack of provocation rather than to judicial self-restraint" because judicial review "had long since won general public acceptance." [84]

The criticisms of *Marbury* ignored the case's long-term implications for judicial review, and it was Marshall's position that won the day. *Marbury* came to stand for the Supreme Court's power—and by extension the power of other courts—to invalidate acts of Congress and the president. As Marshall asserted, in language the Court was again to use in *United States v. Nixon* in ruling that the president was not the sole judge of when he could invoke executive privilege:

> It is, emphatically, the province and duty of the judicial department to say what the law is. Those who apply the rule to particular cases must of necessity expound and interpret that rule. . . . If a law be in opposition to the constitution: if both the law and the constitution apply to a particular case, so that the court must either decide that

case, conformably to the law, disregarding the constitution, or conformably to the constitution, disregarding the law: the court must determine which of these conflicting rules governs the case; this is of the very essence of judicial duty.

Judicial review was extended the year after *Marbury* to executive orders, in *Little v. Barreme*, but the power was not used again until 1857, when the Court struck down congressional action concerning slavery in the territories in *Dred Scott v. Sandford*. This was only the first instance of national judicial review not dealing with strictly judicial matters. Perhaps in part because of the bad name given to judicial review of other branches of the national government by Chief Justice Taney's ruling in *Dred Scott* that slaves were not citizens and thus could not bring lawsuits, judicial review became common only at the end of the nineteenth century, and was not used frequently until the 1930s. Yet we should remember Justice Cardozo's words: "The utility of an external power restraining the legislative judgment is not to be measured by counting the occasions of its exercise"[85]: judicial review has become fully established even when used sparingly.

Notes

1. *Stuart v. Laird*, 1 Cr. 299 (1803). See Wythe Holt, "The First Federal Question Case," *Law and History Review* 3 (Spring 1985): 169–89.

2. Julius Goebel, Jr., *History of the Supreme Court of the United States: Antecedents and Beginnings to 1801* (New York: Macmillan, 1971), p. 565. For early circuit-riding, see Wythe Holt, " 'The Federal Courts have Enemies in All Who Fear Their Influence on State Objects': The Failure to Abolish Supreme Court Circuit-Riding in the Judiciary Acts of 1792 and 1793," *Buffalo Law Review* 36 (1988): 301–40.

3. Wythe Holt, " 'Federal Courts as the Asylum to Federal Interests': Randolph's Report, the Benson Amendment, and the 'Original Understanding' of the Federal Judiciary," *Buffalo Law Review* 36 (1988): 341–72.

4. The leading Supreme Court case is *United States v. Hudson and Goodwin*, 7 Cr. 32 (1812). See Kathryn Preyer, "Jurisdiction to Punish: Federal Authority and the Criminal Law," *Law and History Review* 4 (Fall 1986): 223–65, and Robert C. Palmer, "The Federal Common Law of Crime," *Law and History Review* 4 (Fall 1986): 267–323.

5. See *Posada de Puerto Rico Associates v. Tourism Company of Puerto Rico*, 478 U.S. 328 at 339 n. 6 (1986).

6. Wolf Heydebrand and Carroll Seron, *Rational Justice: The Political Economy of Federal District Courts* (Albany, N.Y.: State University of New York Press, 1990), p. 48. For an examination of caseload and the factors affecting it, see that volume. See also Heydebrand, "Government Litigation and National Policymaking: From Roosevelt to Reagan," *Law & Society Review* 24 (1990): 477–95.

7. See Joel Grossman and Austin Sarat, "Litigation in the Federal Courts: A Comparative Perspective," *Law & Society Review* 9 (1973): 321–46.

8. Heydebrand and Seron, p. 55.

9. *Thermtron Products v. Hermansdorfer*, 423 U.S. 336 (1976).

10. Published district court rulings, a very small proportion of all those decided, may be found in the *Federal Supplement*, cited as "F. Supp.," as in 535 F.Supp. 234 (E.D.Va. 1986).

11. J. Woodford Howard, Jr., *Courts of Appeals in the Federal Judicial System: A Study of the Second, Fifth, and District of Columbia Circuits* (Princeton, N.J.: Princeton University Press, 1981), p. 39.

12. Burton Atkins, "Interventions and Power in Judicial Hierarchies: Appellate Courts in England and the United States," *Law & Society Review* 24 (1990): 83, 86.

13. Howard, p. 39.

14. Ibid., p. 41.

15. See John R. Bartels, "United States District Courts *en banc*—Resolving the Ambiguities," *Judicature* 73 (June-July 1989): 40–42.

16. See Justice Kennedy's comments in *Barnard v. Thorstenn*, 109 S.Ct. 1294, 1298 (1989).

17. Vine Deloria, Jr., and Clifford M. Lytle, *American Indians, American Justice* (Austin: University of Texas Press, 1983).

18. This section draws on Steven Puro, "United States Magistrates: A New Federal Judicial Officer," *Justice System Journal* 2 (Winter 1976): 141–56; two monographs by Carroll Seron: *The Roles of Magistrates in Federal District Courts* (Washington, D.C.: Federal Judicial Center, 1983), and *The Roles of Magistrates: Nine Case Studies* (Washington, D.C.: Federal Judicial Center, 1985); and Christopher E. Smith, "Who Are the U.S. Magistrates?" paper presented to Midwest Political Science Association, Chicago, 1987. See also Seron, "Magistrates and the Work of Federal Courts: A New Division of Labor," *Judicature* 69 (April-May 1986): 353–59.

19. *United States v. Raddatz*, 447 U.S. 667 (1980); *Gomez v. United States*, 109 S.Ct. 2237 (1989) (no magistrate conducting voir dire in felonies, in situations where consent had not been given); *Peretz v. United States*, 111 S.Ct. 2263 (1991) (such supervision valid with parties' consent).

20. *Mathews v. Weber*, 423 U.S. 261 at 272 (1976).

21. *Northern Pipeline Construction Co. v. Marathon Pipe Line Co.*, 458 U.S. 50 (1982).

22. Another famous instance was the Court's postponement of school desegregation, after its initial ruling in *Brown v. Board of Education* (1954), first by asking for further argument on implementation of the ruling and then, in its 1955 ruling in the case, allowing implementation to proceed "with all deliberate speed," *Brown v. Board of Education* (1955).

23. *In Re Koerner*, 800 F.2d 1358 (5th Cir. 1986).

24. See, for example, *Granfinanciera v. Nordberg*, 109 S.Ct. 2782 (1989).

25. See Federal Courts Study Committee, *Working Papers and Subcommittee Reports, July 1 1990*, Vol. I, pp. 154–232.

26. See *Glidden v. Zdanok*, 370 U.S. 530 (1962).

27. *Freytag v. Commissioner of Internal Revenue*, 111 S.Ct. 2631 (1991).

28. *K Mart Corp. v. Cartier*, 485 U.S. 176 (1988).

29. Howard, *Courts of Appeals*, pp. 58, 76.

30. Ibid., pp. 20–21.

31. Ibid., p. 55.

32. Stephen L. Wasby, "Communication Within the Ninth Circuit Court of Appeals: The View from the Bench," *Golden Gate University Law Review* 8 (1977): 1–25; Wasby, "Communication in the Ninth Circuit: A Concern for Collegiality," *University of Puget Sound Law Review* 28 (Fall 1987): 73–138; and Wasby, "Technology and Communication in a Federal Court: The Ninth Circuit," *Santa Clara Law Review* 11 (Winter 1988): 1–28.

33. See Arthur D. Hellman, ed., *Restructuring Justice: The Innovations of the Ninth Circuit and the Future of the Federal Courts* (Ithaca, N.Y.: Cornell University Press, 1990). For a study of the Fifth Circuit's division, see Deborah J. Barrow and Thomas G. Walker, *A Court Divided: The Fifth Circuit Court of Appeals and the Politics of Judicial Reform* (New Haven, Conn.: Yale University Press, 1988).

34. See Stephen L. Wasby, "Inconsistency in the United States Courts of Appeals: Dimensions and Mechanisms for Resolution," *Vanderbilt Law Review* 32 (November 1979): 1343–73. See also Arthur D. Hellman, "Jumboism and Jurisprudence: The Theory and Practice of Precedent in the Large Appellate Court," *University of Chicago Law Review* 56 (Spring 1989): 541–601, and Hellman, "Breaking the Banc: The Common-Law Process in the Large Appellate Court," *Arizona State Law Journal* 23 (Winter 1991): 915–81.

35. See also Sue Davis and Donald R. Songer, "The Changing Role of the United States Courts of Appeals: The Flow of Litigation Revisited," *Justice System Journal* 13 (1988–89): 323–40.

36. Published opinions of the courts of appeals appear in *Federal Reporter*, now in its second series; it is cited as "F.2d" (when speaking, "Fed Second") so a court of appeals case would be 624 F.2d 325 (5th Cir. 1986). For a study of nonpublication practices in three circuits (4th, 11th, D.C.), see Donald R. Songer, "Criteria for Publication of Opinions in the U.S. Courts of Appeals: Formal Rules Versus Empirical Reality," *Judicature* 73 (April-May 1990): 307–13.

37. Richard J. Richardson and Kenneth N. Vines, *The Politics of Federal Courts* (Boston: Little, Brown, 1970), pp. 118–19.

38. Ibid., pp. 127–29.

39. Howard, *Courts of Appeals*, p. 42.

40. Atkins, p. 87.

41. Howard, pp. 3, 78.

42. See Harold Spaeth, "Supreme Court Disposition of Federal Circuit Court Decisions," *Judicature* 68 (December–January 1985): 245–50.

43. Lawrence Baum, "Judicial Specialization, Litigant Influence, and Substantive Policy: The Court of Customs and Patent Appeals," *Law & Society Review* 11 (Summer 1977): 845–46; see generally 833–46.

44. Richard A. Posner, *The Federal Courts* (Cambridge, Mass.: Harvard University Press, 1985), p. 155.

45. Lawrence Baum, "Specializing the Federal Courts: Neutral Reforms or Efforts to Shape Judicial Policy?" *Judicature* 74 (December-January 1991): 220.

46. Ibid., p. 218 n. 14.

47. Rochelle Cooper Dreyfuss, "The Federal Circuit: A Case Study in Specialized Courts," *New York University Law Review* 64 (April 1989): 34.

48. Posner, pp. 155–56.

49. The Emergency Court of Appeals' exclusive appellate jurisdiction over decisions by the price administrator was upheld by the Supreme Court in *Yakus v. United States*, 321 U.S. 404 (1944).

50. For a thorough discussion of the "independent counsel" provisions, see Mark Bertozzi, "Separating Politics from the Administration of Justice: The Role of the Federal Special Prosecutor," *Judicature* 67 (May 1984): 486–98; and Katy J. Harriger, *Independent Justice: The Federal Special Prosecutor in American Politics* (Lawrence: University Press of Kansas, 1992).

51. See *In re Sealed Case*, 838 F.2d 476, 511–17 (D.C. Cir. 1988).

52. See Ellen R. Jordan, "Should Litigants Have a Choice Between Specialized Courts and Courts of General Jurisdiction?" *Judicature* 66 (June-July 1982): 14–27, for a discussion of this and other specialized courts.

53. See *Reid v. Covert*, 354 U.S. 1 (1957) (no courts-martial of wives of servicemen stationed overseas); *United States ex rel. Toth v. Quarles*, 350 U.S. 11 (1955) (ex-servicemen); *O'Callaghan v. Parker*, 395 U.S. 298 (1969) (non–service-connected offense), reversed, *Solorio v. United States*, 483 U.S. 435 (1987). For an extensive discussion, see Gary N. Keveles, "The Third System of Justice: Military Justice," *Courts and Criminal Justice: Emerging Issues*, ed. Susette M. Talarico (Beverly Hills, Calif.: Sage, 1985), pp. 95–120.

54. See also the proposal for a National Court of State Appeals to review state court decisions in which federal questions were raised. James Duke Cameron, "Federal Review, Finality of State Court Decisions, and a Proposal for a National Court of Appeals—A State Judge's Solution to a Continuing Problem," *Brigham Young University Law Review* 1981: 545–78.

55. See Arthur Hellman, "Caseload, Conflicts, and Decisional Capacity: Does the Supreme Court Need Help?" *Judicature* 67 (June-July 1983): 41, where Hellman thoroughly presents other arguments against establishing the new court.

56. Russell R. Wheeler and Howard R. Whitcomb, "What Is Judicial Administration: A Tedious Effort to Explain Some Basic Concepts," *Judicial Administration: Text and Readings*, eds. Wheeler and Whitcomb (Englewood Cliffs, N.J.: Prentice-Hall, 1977), p. 8.

57. Peter Graham Fish, *The Politics of Federal Judicial Administration* (Princeton, N.J.: Princeton University Press, 1973), p. 8. Fish's book is the source of much material for this section.

58. Howard, *Courts of Appeals*, p. 275.

59. See Peter G. Fish, "Politics Rides the Circuits: State and National Itinerary," *Justice System Journal* 5 (Winter 1979): 115–69.

60. This was raised in the Claiborne case (see p. 95). See *United States v. Claiborne*, 781 F.2d 1327 (9th Cir. 1986) (Reinhardt, J., dissent from denial of rehearing *en banc*).

61. Heydebrand and Seron, p. 87 (Table 4.2).

62. *Pennsylvania Bureau of Correction v. United States Marshals Service*, 474 U.S. 34 (1986).

63. See John T. McDermott and Steven Flanders, *The Impact of the Circuit Executive Act* (Washington, D.C.: Federal Judicial Center, 1979); and Steven Flanders, "Court Executives and Decentralization of the Federal Judiciary," *Judicature* 70 (February-March 1987): 273–79.

64. Fish, *The Politics of Federal Judicial Administration*, p. 408.

65. Ibid., p. 39.

66. Peter Graham Fish, "The Office of Chief Justice of the United States," *The Office of Chief Justice* (Charlottesville, Va.: University of Virginia, 1984), p. 59.

67. Fish, *The Politics of Federal Judicial Administration*, p. 93.

68. See Fish, "The Office of Chief Justice," p. 36.

69. Fish, *The Politics of Federal Judicial Administration*, p. 191.

70. See Peter Irons, *Justice at War: The Story of the Japanese American Internment Cases* (New York: Oxford University Press, 1983), p. 183.

71. *Doyle v. Ohio*, 426 U.S. 610 (1976). Another supervisory powers ruling was *Young v. United States ex rel. Vuitton et Fils S.A.*, 481 U.S. 787 (1987) (district courts could appoint special prosecutor to prosecute for contempt, but could not appoint party's attorneys).

72. *United States v. Abel*, 469 U.S. 45, 49 (1984) (Justice Rehnquist).

73. For an explanation, see Paul D. Carrington, "The New Order in Judicial Rulemaking," *Judicature* 75 (October-November 1991): 161–66.

74. For discussion of roots of judicial review, see Elliot E. Slotnick, "The Place of Judicial Review in the American Tradition: The Emergence of an Eclectic Power," *Judicature* 71 (August-September 1987): 68–79.

75. See C. Peter McGrath, *Yazoo: Law and Politics in the New Republic* (Providence, R.I.: Brown University Press, 1966).

76. Oliver Wendell Holmes, *Collected Legal Papers* (New York: Harcourt, Brace, and Howe, 1920), p. 295.

77. *Washington v. Washington State Commercial Passenger Fishing Vessel Association*, 443 U.S. 658 (1979). Quoting the Ninth Circuit's opinion, the Court observed that, "except for some desegregation cases, . . . the district court has faced the most concerted official and private efforts to frustrate a decree of a federal court witnessed in this century." At 697.

78. An examination of the case is provided in Maeva Marcus and Robert Tier, "*Hayburn's Case*: A Misinterpretation of Precedent," *Wisconsin Law Review* 1988: 527–46.

79. Richard Ellis, "The Impeachment of Samuel Chase," *American Political Trials*, ed. Michal R. Belknap (Westport, Conn.: Greenwood Press, 1981), p. 62.

80. Christopher Wolfe, *The Rise of Modern Judicial Review* (New York: Basic Books, 1986), p. 87.

81. Warren Burger, "The Doctrine of Judicial Review: Mr. Marshall, Mr. Jefferson, and Mr. Marbury," *Views from the Bench*, eds. Mark Cannon and David O'Brien (Chatham, N.J.: Chatham House, 1985), p. 14.

82. Wolfe, *Modern Judicial Review*, p. 84. It also appears that Marshall selectively used precedent in *Marbury*, combining several cases into one to support a position and then ignoring that same precedent when it did not support his position. See Susan Low Bloch and Maeva Marcus, "John Marshall's Selective Use of History in *Marbury v. Madison*," *Wisconsin Law Review* 1986: 301–37.

83. Don E. Fehrenbacher, *The Dred Scott Case: Its Significance in American Law & Politics* (New York: Oxford University Press, 1978), pp. 4–5, 442–43.

84. Ibid., p. 232.

85. Benjamin Cardozo, *The Nature of the Judicial Process* (New Haven, Conn.: Yale University Press, 1921), p. 92.

3 Judicial Selection

Most nominees for federal judgeships are confirmed. However, the process can be far from routine, as rejections of nominations show. A candidate for a judicial position, particularly on the Supreme Court, must travel through a political minefield in which any actions the candidate has taken in the past or statements the candidate has made may be subject to scrutiny.

The Constitutional Convention debated several methods of selecting the justices. These included selection by the Senate alone, by the entire Congress, and by the executive alone. The method ultimately adopted was the one already in use in Massachusetts—nomination by the chief executive with the advice and consent of the Senate. However, the Constitution specifies no formal process by which the president is to choose those to be nominated, and the executive has developed the various processes by which the name of a person reaches the stage at which it is to be sent to the Senate.

Usually a nominee to a federal judgeship does not assume office until after Senate confirmation. However, when a judgeship is vacant, the president may make a *recess appointment* to a vacant judgeship, allowing the person to take office immediately. This has happened over three hundred times and included the appointments of Chief Justice Earl Warren and Justices Brennan, Stewart, and Marshall. A recess appointee may be compensated only under certain circumstances—basically when, toward the end of a Senate session, a vacancy occurs or the Senate rejects a nominee, or a nomination, not that of a previous recess appointee, is still pending when the session ends. These rules are designed to prevent the president from naming as a recess appointee someone whose nomination has been rejected by the Senate or from carrying over a recess appointee from before one Senate term to after its conclusion. When President Carter made the first recess appointment in twenty years—of someone on whose district judgeship nomination the Senate had not acted—a court of appeals panel ruled the judge had not been properly appointed, because a recess appointee, subject to political pressures during subsequent Senate consideration of his nomination, would lack proper judicial independence. However, the full court of appeals upheld the president's authority to make recess appointments.[1]

The Judges, both of the Supreme and inferior Courts, shall hold their Offices during good Behaviour, and shall, at stated Times, receive for their Services, a Compensation, which shall not be diminished during their Continuance in Office. (Art III, Sec. 1)

Attracting, Retaining, and Removing Judges

In the Supreme Court's early years, presidents at times had difficulty obtaining men to serve as justices because of the job's lack of prestige. Some who did serve left the Court after brief service or simultaneously held other government jobs. Now, however, the position of justice of the Supreme Court is thought to be the highest to be attained in the legal profession and is likely to be accepted readily when offered—although Abe Fortas refused President Johnson's initial offer of a position. Justices now only rarely leave the Court for other positions, and then only at the president's urging, for example, when Arthur Goldberg became ambassador to the United Nations.

Attracting lower court judges and particularly retaining them pose somewhat greater problems. Some say the frequency of departure has increased recently and compare 25 resignations between 1958 and 1979 with the more than 40 in the 1980s. (Most judges who resigned had from five to 10 years' service, and several appeals court judges had more than 10 years' service.) The larger numbers do not, however, mean greater frequency, as the number of federal judges is now much larger than in the 1960s and 1970s. Moreover, although most of those resigning entered private practice, some took major government positions—senator, FBI director, secretary of education, solicitor general, attorney general—an indication that for the politically active, a judgeship may mean too much isolation. Also related to politics is evidence that federal judges leaving voluntarily are more likely to do so when the presidency is in the hands of the political party that appointed them.[2]

The large numbers of judgeships may actually be one reason for the departures because it diminishes the status of the position. There are more U.S. court of appeals judges than U.S. senators and more district judges than members of the House of Representatives—and almost 3,000 federal judges if one includes magistrate judges, bankruptcy judges, and administrative law judges. As Gilbert and Sullivan said, "When everybody's somebody, no one's anybody." The Federal Courts Study Committee recently argued that "responsible and efficient performance of judicial duties" requires that the number of judgeships be small enough for the judges to feel that their actions are important and that they have a personal stake in them. Despite the increase in number of judges, there are many highly competent lawyers who would give their eyeteeth to be one, particularly an Article III judge, and the position still retains much prestige and is seen as far better than that of state judges.

Danger is also relevant to attracting judges. The number of serious threats against federal judges has increased in the last few years, and reductions in security guard positions as a result of Gramm-Rudman have increased judges' concern about their safety. Three federal judges have been killed in recent years, and their family members, particularly spouses, have also been at risk. In 1979, a district judge in west Texas, John H. Wood, Jr., was shot and killed, apparently as a result of the severity of his sentences in drug cases. (Also in connection with a drug case in 1982 two men were charged with conspiring to murder a district judge in California.) In 1986, a federal judge in North Dakota who had presided over some controversial trials was the intended target of a pipe bomb that was defused.

Then in May 1988, Judge Richard J. Daronco (S.D.N.Y.), was shot and killed outside his home by the father of a woman whose lawsuit had been dismissed, and in December 1989, Eleventh Circuit Judge Robert S. Vance was killed by a package bomb mailed to his home by someone earlier convicted in federal court for possession of a pipe bomb who held a grudge from that conviction. (Another bomb was mailed to Eleventh Circuit headquarters in Atlanta.) Since the Vance bombing, federal judges have been more cautious about their actions: for example, they do not receive mail at their homes.

Supreme Court justices have also been subject to potential or actual violence. In 1982, a man angry at the Court's rulings struck Justice Byron White several times while White was about to deliver a speech to a bar association meeting in Utah, but the Justice was not injured. There have been death threats against Justice Blackmun, some by a radical, antiabortion group, and a shot was fired into his home in February 1985, although the shot was later thought to be random or a wandering distant shot. Wherever Supreme Court justices attend large meetings, security is tightened.[2]

Salary

The principal difficulty in attracting and retaining judges has been salary. It was cited as at least one reason for departure by many of those who left the federal bench during the 1970s and 1980s, when double-digit inflation resulted in a decrease in federal judges' real income. Fringe benefits such as annuities for judges' survivors were also a problem, but one now remedied for the most part.

In 1975, federal judges' salaries were $42,000 for district judges and $44,600 for court of appeals judges, after their first raises in more than six years. These salaries led over 80 federal judges to pursue litigation. They asserted that the Compensation Clause (Art. III, Sec. 1)—the provision that their pay shall not be reduced during their term in office—had been violated by inflation's erosion of their pay since 1969. (By 1985, inflation reduced a district judge's salary to $26,032 in 1969 dollars.) Despite a $12,000-plus pay increase in early 1977, some judges proceeded with their lawsuit, only to have the Court of Claims rule that the Constitution provided no protection against inflation-caused "indirect" reduction in judges' salaries.[3]

The procedure at that time was that the Commission on Executive, Legislative, and Judicial Salaries proposed salary figures to the president, who made recommendations to Congress which were to go into effect after 30 days unless Congress, by joint resolution (requiring a presidential signature), overturned the resolution or overrode a presidential veto of the joint resolution. Then in four successive years (1976–79) Congress either stopped or reduced statutory automatic cost-of-living increases—twice before the start of the fiscal year, but twice because of congressional delay only after the fiscal year had begun, resulting in a temporary increase followed by a reduction.

When new litigation by the judges reached the Supreme Court, the justices first had to face the problem that with all judges affected by a ruling, no judge could decide it without being involved in a conflict of interest. The Court invoked the Rule of Necessity—that, when every judge has a conflict, some judge nonetheless has to hear a case to assure that plaintiffs' complaints could be heard. (The rule also came into play in the case against Judge Vance's killer, who argued unsuccessfully that *all* federal judges were biased against him so that he could not obtain a fair trial.) Underscoring the Compensation Clause's importance for judicial independence, the Court ruled (*United States v. Will*, 1981) that Congress, which had the authority to set judges' salaries, could change an already-adopted salary formula *only* if the change were made before the beginning of the fiscal year. Thus judges were entitled to increases (4.8% and 12.9%) for two years. (This litigation affected only Article III judges, as others, such as bankruptcy judges and magistrate judges, are not protected from salary reductions, and a lower court upheld Congress's reduction of proposed salary increases enacted ten days into the fiscal year.) By 1985, district judges' salaries reached $78,000 and appeals court judges received $83,200 as a result of the Supreme Court's ruling, further congressional delays in reducing proposed salary increases, and additional increases granted by Congress. Supreme Court justices received $104,100 ($108,400 for the Chief Justice).

Nonetheless, some judges, frustrated about the Judicial Conference's apparent inability to convince Congress of their salary needs, formed a group, the

Federal Judges Association, to lobby Congress concerning pay and fringe benefits, although Chief Justice Burger strongly disapproved of such an organization. Some members of Congress objected to further increases. They said the pool of those both competent and willing to serve is quite adequate, so that making judges' salaries so much higher than those of the "common person" to attract candidates is not necessary. However, inflation, increased costs of college education for judges' children, and availability of far higher compensation in private law practice—high six-figure incomes in major corporate law firms—led to recommendations for even higher salaries.

After Congress in 1987 almost rejected a presidential reduction in the commission's recommendations, 1988 and 1989 brought a crisis. The risk that judicial salaries would be defeated when tied to legislative salaries became reality in early 1989 when the House defeated salary increases for itself—and for judges as well. The judges, who felt they needed (and deserved) this significant increase, were dispirited. In March 1989, Chief Justice Rehnquist held a news conference to try to obtain support for a 30 percent increase, independent of what Congress might (or might not) do for itself.

Efforts like these produced a 25 percent pay increase coupled with cost-of-living increases (7.9% in 1990, 3.6% in 1991, and 3.5% in 1992). Federal judges' salaries effective January 1, 1992, are:

Chief Justice	$166,200
Associate justices	$159,000
Court of appeals judges	$137,300
District court and Court of International Trade	$129,500
Bankruptcy judges and magistrate judges	$119,140

These figures may seem high to the reader. Whether they are high depends, however, on the basis of one's comparison—whether one had been, for example, a state trial judge since one's early thirties with a moderate salary, or had been a partner in a major law firm with a high income. One should also keep in mind that first-year associates in large law firms in major cities receive over $75,000. Receiving $125,000 after 10 years as a federal judge, *after* being a law partner, might well seem very small by comparison. Another part of the problem is that, although in the earliest days of the judiciary, district judges' salaries did differ depending on workload, there is no "locality pay," that is, pay differentials depending on how expensive it is to live in a particular area, so a judge's pay that may seem generous in North Dakota may not seem so in Manhattan or San Francisco. (In 1990 legislation was adopted to provide such differentials for federal white-collar executive branch workers—but not for judges.)

Also relevant to judges' salary is their outside income, limited by the new salary legislation: judges cannot receive income from speaking or from professional, legal, or directors' fees (except book royalties), and income from activities like teaching is limited to 15 percent of their judicial salaries. The 1978 Ethics in Government Act also requires high-level government officials, including judges, to file annual financial disclosure statements, indicating stocks or bonds worth more than $1,000 or savings accounts more than $5,000, but reporting is only within very broad categories. Several judges argued that, as applied to judges, the law violated separation of powers and allowed intrusions on judicial independence, but the Fifth Circuit upheld the law and the Supreme Court refused review.[4] Examination of lower court judges' statements shows that very few have no outside income and more than half reported over $16,600 of such income. The range at the Supreme Court is great, from Justice Thurgood Marshall, who had no outside income and no reportable stocks, bonds, or savings accounts, to Justice O'Connor, apparently the Court's only millionaire.[5]

Discipline and Removal

A problem of potentially greater dimension than retaining judges is getting others to leave the bench when they are old, ill, or not functioning effectively. Within the period of the Burger Court, there were problems with Harlan (failing eyesight) and Douglas (a serious stroke). Douglas was particularly reluctant to leave the Court even after he had formally resigned and Stevens had been named to replace him. (See page 380 on reporting about justices' health.) More recently, several justices (Powell, Blackmun, and Brennan) have had prostate cancer, Brennan had problems with his vocal chords, Justice O'Connor has had breast cancer, and Justice Marshall, before his retirement, had a number of health problems; a small stroke after term's end led to Justice Brennan's retirement. None of these have been stress induced. However, it has been suggested that the defeat in *Baker v. Carr* of Justice Frankfurter's position that federal courts should not hear reapportionment cases may have led to his stroke, and thus to his departure from the Court. The stress of that case on Justice Whittaker, particularly from Frankfurter's lobbying for his position, and from a complex antitrust case in the same term, certainly led to his departure from the Court.[6]

In earlier years, judges and justices died in office. Some were said to have been senile for a time. Unlike some state constitutions, the U.S. Constitution makes no provision for judges' retirement at a certain age.[7] In earlier years, colleagues' entreaties seldom proved successful in getting eligible judges to retire on their then not-very-generous salary, which was the pension until the late 1930s. In 1937 Congress provided that after 10 years of service, on reaching age 70, judges become *senior judges* in partial retirement, continuing to hear cases and able to reduce their workload without having to quit the bench completely. They receive full pay *and* any subsequent salary increases. The law now provides that a judge may take senior status at age 65 after 15 years of service or with any combination of age and years of service equaling 80 (66 + 14, 67 + 13, etc.). Under the 1990 salary legislation, to receive any salary increase beyond cost-of-living adjustments, a senior judge must be certified as working 25 percent of the load of active-duty judges. A judge who resigns from a judgeship—that is, leaves the court completely—after age 70 with at least 10 years' service gets the full salary received at the time of the resignation but no subsequent increases.

Because a judge taking senior status formally vacates a judgeship—but can continue to sit on the court on which the judge was sitting—a new judge is appointed and both the new judge and the senior judge can work on cases. Senior judges' assistance to the federal courts is essential in dealing with the courts' substantial caseloads; they are available to travel to courts that are temporarily in need of additional judges. The federal courts almost lost the services of many senior judges in early 1986 when their salaries became subject to deduction of Social Security taxes and, for those under age 70, to reduction in Social Security benefits and possible loss of Medicare coverage if they earned more than a certain amount. Roughly half the senior judges stopped working, with deleterious effects on court calendars in some districts, until Congress permanently exempted them from Social Security taxation.

Senior status is also available to those with serious disabilities even if they are not yet eligible for regular senior status. With ten years or more of service, these judges receive full pay, but only half-pay if they have less service. They may seek such status voluntarily and receive it if properly certified by the chief judge of the circuit, or they may be certified for it by their colleagues; in some situations the circuit councils have pressed fairly hard for the judges to leave the bench via this route. Senior status cannot be forced on a judge who is not physically or mentally disabled. Thus it is not a solution for the "difficult" judge who continues to serve, and further action is also necessary to terminate the judicial activity of senior judges who wish to continue hearing cases.

A Supreme Court justice who wishes to step down—such as Potter Stewart in 1981 or Tom Clark, who left the Court so that his son, Ramsey Clark, could become attorney general without creating conflicts of interest for both—can sit on the lower courts, and some, including Justice Clark, have; the most recent is Justice Powell. They can also resign outright, as Justices Whittaker (1962), Goldberg (1965), and Fortas (1969) did for different reasons.

Improper Behavior. What happens when we try to deal with venality rather than senility? A number of devices other than impeachment have been used to deal with judges' ethics. One effort aimed at dealing with questions of federal judges' proper behavior, intended to supplement earlier bar association Canons of Judicial Ethics, is the Code of Judicial Conduct for United States Judges, adopted by the Judicial Conference. The Code provides guidelines against which judges' conduct can be evaluated and indicates more clearly to judges what is expected of them. The Code also indicates when judges should disqualify themselves from hearing cases because of potential conflicts of interest, a subject also addressed by statute and on which the Supreme Court finally spoke in 1988. The majority stressed that the purpose of changes in the disqualification statute, to provide for a judge's recusal when his actions "might reasonably be questioned" (not "when the judge believes" they might be) was "to promote confidence in the judiciary by avoiding even the appearance of impropriety whenever possible."[8]

The promulgation of the Code has not, however, served to still all concerns about judicial behavior, and leaves unresolved the problem of dealing with non-criminal, recalcitrant, erratic, or possibly unbalanced judges within the confines of the Constitution without seriously eroding judicial independence. The difficulties of dealing with a problem judge before the present disciplinary system was enacted are perhaps best illustrated by the controversy between District Judge Stephen Chandler (W.D.Okla.) and the Tenth Circuit's Judicial Council.[9] The council, while leaving Chandler his pending cases, distributed new cases to other judges in the district. Chandler, who did not acknowledge the council's authority, argued that under the Constitution, impeachment was the only way to proceed against a judge. The Supreme Court turned away his claims on procedural grounds, but Chief Justice Burger, for the Court, while speaking of "the imperative need for total and absolute independence of judges in deciding cases or in any phase of the decisional function," also said "it is quite another matter to say that each judge in a complex system shall be the absolute ruler of his manner of conducting judicial affairs." Justices Douglas and Black, however, argued that impeachment was the only way to remove a judge. They also spoke out against the circuit council's methods, saying "these efforts of federal judges to ride herd on other federal judges" were "a form of 'hazing' having no place under the Constitution."

The Chandler case and another Tenth Circuit controversy involving Chief Judge Willis Ritter (D.Utah), embroiled in conflict with the Mormon church, led to serious congressional attention to the procedure for judicial discipline, including removal, short of impeachment. Proposals were based on the proposition that appointment during "good behavior" did not necessarily mean "for life" and thus permitted discipline for misbehavior. Some proposals provided for a separate court to deal with disciplinary actions, while other proposals, including those made by the Judicial Conference, provided for filing of complaints with the circuit judicial councils, which argued forcefully for a further chance to deal with the problem.

The 1980 Judicial Conduct and Disability Act reaffirmed the circuit councils' central place in the disciplinary process. Because councils could discipline district judges, district judges were added to council membership (see page 67). Under the statute, any person may file complaints against a judge. Complaints go first to the chief judge of the circuit, who may dismiss a complaint if it simply concerns a ruling in a particular case (likely to be sour grapes), is frivolous, or does not allege "conduct prejudicial to the effective and expeditious administration of the business of the courts" or inability "to discharge all the duties of office by reason of mental or physical disability." The chief judge may also close a complaint upon finding that "appropriate corrective action" had been taken. If a complaint survives this review, the chief judge must appoint an investigating committee—the chief judge and an equal number of circuit and district judges—to report to the judicial council. The council may remove magistrates or bankruptcy judges, and with Article III judges, may issue a public or private reprimand, certify disability, request voluntary resignation, or prohibit further case assignments for a fixed period. If the judge's conduct "might constitute" grounds for impeachment, the council transmits the matter to the Judicial Conference of the United States. The Conference may in turn send the case to the House of Representatives, which it may also do on a judge's conviction of a felony and completion of direct appeals. Any unsatisfied complainants and accused judges may petition the Judicial Conference or its appropriate standing committee to review judicial council actions on their complaints.

Many complaints have been filed under the new disciplinary system. Most concern alleged bias in a judge's handling of a case, although some have claimed racist or sexist comments. Most go no further than the circuit's chief judge, who dismisses them as unfounded or because the underlying issue has been dealt with elsewhere, for example, in the appeal of a case. But actual action against a judge has occurred, and even when a complaint is formally dismissed, the attendant publicity can affect judges' behavior. A judge under attack may even add to the publicity, as Chief Judge Frank Battisti (N.D.Ohio) did in criticizing judicial discipline councils, "ethical zealots," and the media, after a grand jury inquiry produced no indictments and complaints against him were dismissed. The use of the new disciplinary process for ideological reasons can be seen in the complaint, filed by the Washington Legal Foundation, a conservative public interest group, against Judge Abner Mikva of the D.C. Circuit for chairing and recruiting for the "activist" and "politicized" Section of Individual Rights of the ABA. This matter was resolved when Judge Mikva accepted a recommendation from the Judicial Conference Committee on Codes of Conduct that he refrain from participation in membership drives for the section.

Some federal judges have been impeached, convicted, and removed from office. In times past others have resigned under certain threat of impeachment. Impeachment efforts began with friction between Federalists and Jeffersonian Democrats, which led to the sole impeachment of a Supreme Court justice, the Federalist Samuel Chase, for his highly partisan charges to grand juries while on circuit. Chase was, however, not convicted. In the same period, New Hampshire district judge John Pickering, also a Federalist, was impeached and convicted, but he was senile, so his removal expanded the grounds for impeachment to cover that situation.[10]

A question not fully resolved concerning impeachment is whether indictment of a federal judge on criminal charges could precede or only follow impeachment. This is an important separation of powers issue because the executive branch, through the Department of Justice, brings the prosecution of a judge—and could do so against judges it disliked and wished removed from office. The Supreme Court has not ruled on the matter, but when Seventh Circuit

Judge Otto Kerner was tried for behavior predating his judicial tenure, the Seventh Circuit said, "The Constitution does not forbid the trial of a federal judge for criminal offenses committed either before or after the assumption of judicial office."[11] The practice since then has been based on the assumption that indictment need not await impeachment—and lower courts ruled against Judges Claiborne and Hastings on this question. Indeed, impeachment comes after criminal conviction and a judge will not resign.

Until recently, impeachment was thought too difficult to accomplish—there had been no impeachment trial since the Senate convicted Judge Halstead Ritter in 1936—and too severe for most judicial ethics infractions. Then in 1986 Chief Judge Harry Claiborne (D. Nevada), initially indicted for bribery and obstruction of justice, was convicted on two tax counts and sentenced to jail. He refused to resign from the bench and became the first sitting federal judge to go to prison, where he drew his full salary; he promised to return to the bench after his prison term. That behavior moved legislators to impeach him, and the House unanimously voted four articles of impeachment. The entire Senate did not hear the case but instead appointed a 12-member committee to take testimony. The Senate, refusing to hear witnesses, acted on the basis of the committee transcript. After Judge Claiborne's lawyers were turned down both in the lower federal courts and by Chief Justice Rehnquist in their efforts to get a full-blown Senate trial, the Senate convicted by overwhelming margins, thus removing Claiborne from office. While some senators were troubled by the abbreviated procedures, others sought methods that would shorten the process, particularly when other impeachments arose.

The next impeachment—that of Chief Judge Walter L. Nixon (S.D. Miss.), convicted of perjury and sentenced to five years in prison—also involved a judge convicted in a criminal trial. After a unanimous House voted articles of impeachment, the Senate convicted on two articles, but did not reach a two-thirds vote on a count that the judge was a disgrace to the federal judiciary.

The Claiborne and Nixon cases involved convicted judges whose convictions were upheld on appeal. But acquittal does not necessarily end the use of the new judicial discipline procedure to produce impeachment. After Judge Alcee Hastings, the first black federal judge in Florida, was acquitted of bribery, other judges filed complaints against him, including obstruction of justice in his trial and making false claims that he was prosecuted because he was black. The circuit's investigating committee concluded he should be impeached, and sent that recommendation to the Judicial Conference, which told Congress that impeachment of Hastings "may be warranted." Hastings' defense that the impeachment effort was racially motivated did not persuade the Senate, which convicted him by slightly over the necessary two-thirds vote on the conspiracy to bribe charge, but unanimously acquitted him about leaking information to the FBI.

Two more federal judges were convicted of federal offenses in 1991, and await impeachment. Judge Robert Aguilar (N.D. Cal.), originally charged under the racketeering statute, was convicted of unlawfully disclosing a government wiretap and of obstructing justice by lying about it. Judge Robert F. Collins (E.D.La.), another Carter appointee, was convicted of bribery. Because Aguilar is Latino and Collins is black, the government's action led to claims by some that the Reagan and Bush administrations, in addition to their poor record in naming minorities to the federal bench (see page 113), were targeting the ones already there.

The House Judiciary Committee has made clear it would not be an appellate court to which people could turn with disliked decisions when they rejected petitions from over 100,000 Georgia residents to have three Eleventh Circuit judges removed from office for overturning murder convictions because of excessive and inflammatory pretrial publicity. In so doing, the committee reinforced the conduct statute's provision that complaints could not be based on rulings in particular cases. However, concerns about the impeachment process remain.

Responding to such concerns, Congress in 1990 ordered that a commission be set up to recommend streamlining the process. A delay by President Bush in naming his members meant that the commission had not developed any recommendations by 1992 when the Supreme Court accepted Judge Nixon's case to review claims concerning the process. Data from the Claiborne, Nixon, and Hastings impeachments does bear on the question of whether it makes a difference to have only some, rather than all, senators hear the evidence against a judge against whom the House has pressed impeachment charges. Members of the committees that heard the evidence were less likely to vote to convict in those three cases than was the whole Senate. Particularly significant is that in the Hastings case, on *none* of the articles of impeachment did two-thirds of the committee members vote to convict, while roughly three-fourths of the nonmembers voted to convict. In the Claiborne and Nixon cases, however, over two-thirds of both committee members and nonmembers would have convicted on at least some counts.[12]

Selection: The Lower Courts

Vacancies occur in judgeships as judges resign, die, or assume senior status, and as new judgeships are created to keep up with increasing caseload. A highly political issue is the creation of a large number of new judgeships at one time because a president of one party can thus name many judges of similar ideology and party background. Such conflicts go back to the early years of the Republic. The Judiciary Act of 1801, passed during the lame-duck session of the Federalist-dominated Congress before Thomas Jefferson assumed the presidency, provided for 16 circuit judgeships (and also that the next Supreme Court vacancy not be filled). The judgeships would, of course, have been filled by Federalists. However, in March 1802, Congress repealed the 1801 Act, so the circuit judges lost both their offices and salaries.

In recent times, omnibus judgeship bills were enacted in 1961, 1966, 1970, 1984, and 1990. Those in 1961 and 1966, by a Democratic Congress, provided judgeships to be filled by a Democratic president. The 1970 and 1990 acts were somewhat unusual because a Democrat-controlled Congress provided judgeships a Republican president could fill. The Omnibus Judgeship Act of 1978, creating 35 court of appeals and 117 district court judgeships, was not passed until there was a Democratic president, after delay by a Democratic Congress unwilling to have a Republican president name a large number of judges. In 1984, in providing for the addition of more than 80 new federal judges, Congress directed that only 40 could be nominated in 1984. The remainder were not to be selected before the start of the new presidential term in 1985, so that, if the Democratic candidate had won, not all the nominations would already have been filled.

The addition of large numbers of judges at one time means that a president, particularly one who serves more than one term, can name a large proportion of the federal judiciary. Most notable is Franklin Roosevelt's selection of over 80 *percent* of the federal judges. Eisenhower was able to name over half the judges (56.1%) and Nixon almost half (45.7%) but others were able to name smaller proportions—John Kennedy (32.8%) and Lyndon Johnson (37.9%)—and, because of shorter time in office, Gerald Ford (13.1%). Because of the 1978 Omnibus Judgeship Act, President Carter was able to name 40 percent of the federal judges in only one term. President Reagan was able to name a majority of the judiciary, in part by getting "both halves" of the numbers added to the 1984 legislation,[13] and Presidents Reagan and Bush together, 70 percent by 1992.

Congress's delays in adding judgeships that the Judicial Conference claimed it needed led Chief Justice Burger to propose in 1980 that the Judicial Conference be given the authority to establish federal judgeships as they are needed, subject to congressional veto. Such a proposal is politically unacceptable, although the Conference's recommendations, once made every four years but now done every other year, do carry some weight. The Conference's Judicial Statistics subcommittee considers a number of factors, including the district court's weighted caseload per authorized judgeship (the most important factor), the complexity of a district's cases, its backlog, utilization of magistrates, and presence of senior judges.

A judgeship created for a judicial district when caseload demands it but when the permanent need is not clear is considered *temporary*; it may later be made permanent. (The 1990 Act converted eight temporary judgeships to permanent ones.) Filled by an Article III (lifetime) judge, the position is created on a nonpermanent basis. In some instances, the temporary judgeship lapses with the first vacancy in that judicial district, with the judge sitting in the temporary judgeship moving to the vacant judgeship; in others, the position remains until its incumbent departs.

Considerable time can elapse from the creation of a judgeship—and certainly from the Judicial Conference's recommendation that one be created, or the occurrence of a vacancy through death or a judge's assuming senior status—to the filling of that judgeship. Agreement on the nominee a senator will submit may take time. That may be further stretched out by White House staff consideration and investigation by the American Bar Association and then by the Senate Judiciary Committee. The time can be extended even further if Congress is entering an election period when senators wish to get home to campaign. The end of a president's term is also likely to leave some judicial nominations "hung up" as the nonincumbent party wishes to try to save some nominations for its candidate, as happened at the end of President Reagan's term; some of those not approved then were renominated by President Bush. (When a person is nominated for a judgeship, their lives are disrupted—the more so if they are eventually not confirmed.)

Because caseloads justifying a position have already been exceeded when a judgeship is created, not filling a position creates serious caseload problems in some districts, particularly those with few judges where the absence of a single judge is felt more. Some judgeships have remained vacant for well over a year. As of mid-1992, there were only 49 nominations pending for 93 district court vacancies and 14 pending for 22 court of appeals positions. The number of vacancies was so severe that the Judicial Conference was designating courts as having "judicial emergencies" (there were 53 in mid-1992). The president and Congress were arguing over who was responsible for the delays in filling the vacancies, with President Bush blaming the Senate Judiciary Committee and committee chair Senator Joseph Biden (D-Del.) noting that in 1990 nominations were pending in the committee for an average of 68 days, while it took the administration an average of 11 months from the time a vacancy occurred to submit a nomination. Biden also argued that the uneven fashion in which nominations were submitted made the committee's work more difficult.

Selection: President and Senate

The Constitution does not specify either a formal process for the president's selection of judicial nominees or eligibility requirements or selection criteria. Different administrations have given varying weights to factors such as prior judicial experience, age, American Bar Association ratings, "affirmative action" to increase the number of women and minority judges, and ideology. In the first half of the twentieth century, patronage considerations dominated in appellate court nominations when administrations were not concerned about the courts' policy-making possibilities, but a mix of patronage and concerns about professionalism occurred where government's role was limited but judges' role in policy-making was recognized. When, as in FDR's later terms, administrations sought to increase the role of government and also saw judges' possible effects on those efforts, they paid more attention to judges' policy views— their ideology.[14]

More than nine of every 10 times, the selection process for the lower federal courts produces judges of the president's political party. The importance of political party in the selection process was no less true in "merit selection" mechanisms in the Carter administration than in earlier methods of selection, although in states where senators from opposite parties jointly sponsored a selection commission, a portion of the available judgeships went to the party not in the White House. With the Reagan administration, we find the highest level of partisanship in district court appointments since Woodrow Wilson; Reagan appointed *no* Democrats to the courts of appeals, the first time since Warren Harding that had occurred.

The Eisenhower administration explicitly stressed previous judicial experience, particularly for appeals court positions; age; and the ABA's ratings. The Kennedy administration had far less interest in judicial appointments than in social programs, despite judges' potentially great impact on those programs. The Nixon administration paid close attention to ideology in its Supreme Court nominations but not particularly for lower court appointments. The Carter administration gave substantial emphasis to nominees' "demonstrated commitment to equal justice" and to affirmative action, with the president promising to appoint at least one black federal judge in each state in the South. It also emphasized "stringent age and experience requirements," at least for the courts of appeals, meaning 15 years' legal experience and not over 60 years of age. Most important, President Carter altered the structural process by which nominees were chosen for all appeals court seats and for many district judgeships (see pages 101–2).

The Reagan administration paid far more attention than its predecessors since Franklin Roosevelt to judicial nominees' views, perhaps because of its lack of success in getting "social policy" agenda items (abortion and church-state concerns) enacted by Congress or submitted as constitutional amendments. Although factors like age (preference for younger people) and intelligence were also considered, Attorney General Meese said the administration sought those with "the proper judicial philosophy and approach to the bench, which precludes judicial activism, or substituting the courts for the legislature."[15] Meese did not think "any single test should be a disqualifying factor," but a potential nominee's views on the Supreme Court abortion ruling "might be indicative of the way in which that judge would generally approach the whole subject of judicial activism."

Despite Reagan's—and Bush's—choice of many young nominees, done in the hope that their ideological position will be evident on the bench for several decades, it is unclear how long these judges will remain. The opportunity to obtain much higher salaries in private law practice may become increasingly appealing to them as their children approach college age. Moreover, judges appointed in their thirties or early forties might not wish to serve for 25 years or more to be eligible for senior status, when departure after 10 or 15 years on the bench would allow them, in their fifties, to have an extended career as a private attorney.

Process. The basics of the process now used to select nominees were put in place during the Eisenhower administration, but important alterations in selection of names for the president's consideration occurred during the Carter and

Reagan administrations. The president himself is seldom directly involved in the selection process except for Supreme Court vacancies or other matters staff brings to his attention, but White House staff involvement can be great. For both district and appeals court positions, the Justice Department works as the president's surrogate with the appropriate senators, and prior to formal nomination by the president, the department, usually through the deputy attorney general, identifies and screens candidates for the president's consideration. The FBI conducts an intensive investigation of those being seriously considered, and other Department of Justice officials evaluate FBI reports. Prior to the Nixon administration, a background check was run only on the person already selected, but it is now usually performed earlier to ensure sufficient information and to avoid embarrassment. (In part because the announcement of Justice O'Connor's nomination was made earlier than the president first planned to make it, the FBI field check on her was not performed until after the announcement.)

Senatorial Courtesy. The president has the formal constitutional power to make judicial nominations. However, under the practice of *senatorial courtesy,* the executive shares judicial selection with the senator(s) from the president's party in the state in which the appointment is to be made. If there are no senators from the president's party, the state party organization and members of that state's House delegation may be consulted and members of the Cabinet serve as contact points. Senators of the other party may also be consulted, part of a pattern in which minority party senators interact with the president and his representatives about appointments. (New York's senators agreed that the party not in control of the White House would get a proportion of the judgeships.) Judges appointed by the president or by a previous president of his party may volunteer names for judgeships or are invited by the president, senators, or the Department of Justice to make suggestions.

Senatorial courtesy has operated most fully for district court vacancies. Informal allocation of appeals court judgeships within a circuit may have been necessary to obtain congressional approval of court of appeals judgeships, so some seats "belong" to particular states. This makes senatorial courtesy also operative in the courts of appeals except for the D.C. Circuit because the District of Columbia has no senators. For Supreme Court nominations, the sponsorship or at least acquiescence of the senators from the nominee's state is helpful in achieving confirmation, but senatorial courtesy is virtually never operative. Most senators take senatorial courtesy seriously, feeling they should designate the nominee. "Some even take the proprietary view that they own the job." [16] Others, however, play only a minor role in the selection process, perhaps to avoid owing the president a favor. They may do no more than submit a list of acceptable nominees, leaving the final choice to the president's staff. Many senators also do not wish to trade a vote on an issue to obtain approval of a nomination.

Senatorial courtesy does not operate formally until the Judiciary Committee has sent the nomination to the floor of the Senate. Senators once could invoke senatorial courtesy with little challenge simply by stating that, whatever the real reason, an opposed nominee was "personally obnoxious." However, expectations have developed that a senator has to substantiate claims about the nominees rather than merely assert objections.

Until recently, the executive has regularly consulted the appropriate senators and has seldom challenged senatorial choices; either the nominations are noncontroversial or the president later needed senators' votes for his program. But conflict between the White House and senators, even those of the president's party, can occur. Senatorial courtesy has been used defensively to try to block a presidential nominee, not always successfully. However, even its effective exercise does not ensure acceptance of a senator's nominee, and senators have generally lost battles with the president over nominations, often because the successful appointee was sponsored by the state's other senator of the same party.

Delay is one weapon in conflict between president and senators. Both delay and recess appointments have been used to pressure senators. Delay was used effectively by the Kennedy administration in one-fifth of its judicial nominations. It was used again in the Carter administration, when southern senators failed to nominate blacks, but it did not prove an effective tool then. The Reagan administration's delay in moving senators' preferred choices provided a bargaining chip for use when one of the administration's nominations encountered difficulty. Some senators voted for the nominee in return for White House promises to advance the senators' preferences to the nomination stage. Delay in the Bush administration, thought to be the most severe in years, stemmed in part from the executive's examination of potential nominees and their ideology, part of its decreased use of senators' preferences.

Selection Commissions. President Carter's belief that judges should be chosen through "merit selection" and his emphasis on affirmative action brought about a significant change in the selection of names to be forwarded to the president, involving more formal consultative and screening devices. The president had wished to use merit selection for both district courts and courts of appeals, but Attorney General Griffin Bell and Senate Judiciary Committee Chairman Eastland "struck a deal" in which appeals court nominees would be produced by selection commissions established by executive order, put into effect in 1977 and 1978, while senators continued to choose district judge nominees. The 1978 Omnibus Judgeship Act (OJA) gave a push to the use of commission selection mechanisms for district judgeships, which were to be filled on the basis of merit selection guidelines. However, no nomination could be blocked for failure to comply with the standards.

The Carter-initiated change in the selection process for court of appeals vacancies was significant both structurally and in the results produced.[17] Thirteen selection panels were established—one for each circuit, with two each for the not-yet-divided Fifth Circuit and the Ninth Circuit. Each panel had equal numbers of members of the bar and laypersons, and included women and minorities, but panel members were predominantly white and Democratic, with a high proportion of Carter activists. However, panel members opened up the selection process by seeking out potential nominees instead of relying on those who volunteered their candidacies and did not place much importance on a candidate's political activity or on partisan recommendations. Instead they ranked mental health and "character and personality traits" most important.[18] Interestingly, lawyers gave *less* weight to bar association recommendations than did lay members.[19] Panelists' principal complaint was of inadequate time to screen and interview candidates and to debate their qualifications—initially 60 days to submit no fewer than three names or more than five for each position.[20]

The idea of special selection panels for district judgeships also took hold. By 1979, senators in 29 states—20 of them where both senators were Democrats—established either ad hoc or permanent judicial nominating commissions.[21] Commission size and procedures varied, as did the sponsoring senators' role in designating candidates.[22] Most senators defined their affirmative action obligations in terms of search and outreach, for example, expanding the candidate pool with women and minorities, but not doing so to produce a certain proportion of black, Hispanic, or female judges.[23]

Perhaps more important were variations after the panels produced names: some senators sent the full commission-generated lists directly to the executive branch; others, giving themselves greater control over the nomination, reduced the lists first. ("Nontraditional" nominations were more likely when senators sent President Carter a list without designation of a preferred nomination than when senators exercised the nomination choice themselves.) Newer members of the Senate were more likely to accept a greater executive role in the process, undoubtedly a function of their use of the selection commissions; senior senators were more likely to assume a greater role in the selection process.[24] (After President Reagan ended presidential encouragement for district judgeship panels and after the 1980 change in Senate party control, by 1983 there were commissions in only 15 states but senators who did use them really wanted to do so. That may explain why there were greater differences between panel and nonpanel-generated district court nominees in 1981–82 than there had been during the Carter administration.[25])

President Carter's efforts at "affirmative action" in the judiciary, successful in terms of the numbers of women and minorities placed in the federal judiciary (see pages 113–14), also indicate problems a president faces in trying to increase the number of federal judges from groups who do not constitute a large proportion of the legal profession (racial minorities) or are disproportionately "junior" in legal experience (women). Finding appropriate candidates within a small initial pool of nontraditional candidates may not be easy. The pool is even smaller if ABA guidelines are used and nominees are submitted to usual evaluation processes, and there are relatively few alternative nominees available if questions are raised about any particular nontraditional nominee. This situation allowed the white southern establishment, which had refused to handle civil rights cases, opportunities to question the qualifications of black attorneys whose principal legal work was in the civil rights field and to force withdrawal of some nominations.

Use of the selection commission device meant the executive branch and the Judiciary Committee played larger and more independent roles. As a precursor to greater executive involvement in the Reagan administration, the role of the White House staff did increase. Carter's Attorney General Griffin Bell had thought he would take names of possible nominees to the president, but taking them to the "White House" came to mean the White House staff, a committee composed of counsel, congressional liaison, press representative, and chief of staff. The number and variety of participants in the selection process—particularly persons from outside the government—increased. Scrutiny of applicants was greater and also more repetitive. Of particular significance is that commission-selected candidates thought the process was more open than under the more traditional process, where they would have been at a disadvantage because they did not know senators, were politically inactive, or were not "traditional" candidates (older, white males).[26] For example, panels selected a higher proportion of nominees with teaching experience.

Selection under Reagan and Bush. The Reagan administration terminated panels for U.S. court of appeals vacancies in May 1981. The executive branch structure for selecting nominees was also revised and formalized. The basic change was one from the regionalized selection commissions to a centralized process. Justice Department examination of possible nominees was more intensive, including long interviews. The involvement of the president's office increased. Assisted by a special counsel for judicial selection, the assistant attorney general for the Office of Legal Policy, rather than the deputy attorney general, became the principal executive branch official for judicial selection. With the attorney general, these officials met to make recommendations to the nine-person President's Committee on Federal Judicial Selection, which also included the president's counsel, the White House chief of staff, and some assistants to the president. That group, which created a more active White House role in selecting nominees, provided the greatest difference from previous practice. Not merely a "check" on Justice Department suggestions, the President's Committee played an independent role. New names of potential nominees entered the process at that stage and the committee provided a further mechanism for review of a potential nominee's ideology even when such considerations had entered into the Justice Department's earlier examination.

A major result of this new set of arrangements was a decreased role for senators—and friction between senators (even Republican ones) and the administration. Senators who did not accept the Justice Department's view that senators should submit several names were not viewed favorably by the administration, which refused to fill positions until senators submitted names of people whose ideology fit the administration's wishes.[27] There were "pitched and protracted battles over particular nominees" and "hand-to-hand political combat" between the administration and senators who insisted on their prerogatives.[28]

The Bush administration made some changes in institutional arrangements, but the basic elements of the Reagan administration process were retained, including centralization, emphasis on selecting nominees ideologically compatible with the administration, and lessened emphasis on senatorial courtesy. In the Justice Department, the Office of Legal Policy was replaced by the Office of Policy Development, and in the White House, the role of the White House counsel's office increased and the membership of the President's Committee on Federal Judicial Selection was slightly changed. White House insistence on considering more than one name produced conflict between the administration and a Republican senator from Vermont, with the Senate Republican Conference siding with the senator.[29] This illustrates that senators, although not inclined to interfere regularly with district court nominations in other states, may become involved—or may be pressured by interest groups to get involved—in nominations seen as affecting the federal judiciary's quality and image. This illustrates that senators do not accept either the president's or their colleagues' assessments totally at face value and also look at both a nominee's professional competence and policy views or ideology.

The Senate. When a nomination is referred to the Judiciary Committee, there is an equivalent of senatorial courtesy. Senators from the nominee's state are sent a *blue slip.* Failure to return the slip was supposed to kill a nomination automatically, but most senators seldom have used the blue slip except to comment or to sign off, or have delayed returning it to obtain more information or to negotiate over, rather than kill, nominations. Senator Edward Kennedy (D-Mass.), taking over the committee chairmanship in 1976, decided that nominations would not automatically be killed when someone failed to return the blue slip, but the committee would vote on whether to proceed, and that rule has been retained. Individual senators also place "holds" on nominations, saying they wish more time to consider them but often really doing so because of another dispute with the administration. Because of senators' deference to each other, a hold allows a senator to hold disliked nominations hostage—or to delay them sufficiently at session's end to ensure that they are not approved. The committee as a whole can also test the president's will by delaying action on nominations. At the end of 1991, as a result of controversy surrounding the Supreme Court nomination of Clarence Thomas, the administration limited access by Senate Judiciary Committee members and staff to full FBI reports on judicial nominees; in February 1992, the dispute was resolved, at least for the time being, by an agreement between Senator Jopseh Biden (D.Del.), the committee chairman, ranking committee member Senator Strom Thurmond (R-S.C.), and White House counsel C. Boyden Gray.

Apart from the senators from the nominee's state, the members of the Judiciary Committee are the most important senators in the nomination process. The committee's chair can have substantial power. A particularly stubborn chairman like Senator Eastland can force a hard bargain. He can delay consideration of a much-wanted nomination until the president submits others the chairman wanted. The commitee chairman can also set the tone of the committee's questioning and can either encourage or discourage committee members' aggressive approach to nominees. This makes Senate majority party control of the committee quite important, and makes elections to the Senate, such as those of 1986 when party control changed hands and put Senator Biden in the chairmanship, quite important in the judicial nomination process. The committee takes testimony from the nominee, supporters, and opponents, its hearings often held by subcommittees of only a few senators. It can decline to let someone testify, thus relegating objections to the less visible printed record, and can control the sequence of witnesses and the hostile or friendly treatment they receive. In this way, the committee can attune the entire Senate, the media, and the general public to objections against the nominee.

The Judiciary Committee at times is able to affect selection criteria. The committee became involved in issues concerning the ABA's age guidelines (see page 109) and judges' memberships in clubs without minority group members. After a nominee felt that resigning from an all-white group would be admitting that his membership was improper, chairman and ranking minority member Senators Kennedy and Thurmond agreed on a statement that "it is inadvisable for a nominee for a Federal judgeship to belong to a social club that engages in invidious discrimination." The statement led a number of nominees to resign from such clubs, but did not settle the question about sitting judges, many of whom belonged to such clubs.

In the late 1970s, because it was not satisfied with the FBI's investigations, the committee began to conduct its own, using FBI files and financial information about the nominees and then its own questionnaire, to supplement information obtained by the administration. When Republicans controlled the committee, conservative Senators Hatch, Denton, and East sent a questionnaire to a district court nominee asking views on abortion, school prayer, the right to bear arms, the Equal Rights Amendment, and the death penalty. The request for specific answers rather than views on broad topics like federalism or a general discussion of the role of judges led chairman Thurmond to rule out such a questionnaire in the future and to say that senators were to question nominees only during committee hearings.

When Democratic committee members began to focus more attention on marginal nominations that required greater investigation, a bipartisan agreement in late 1985 gave the Democrats more time to investigate, with hearings deferred but, to prevent delay for delay's sake, a vote on noncontroversial nominations was to take place within five weeks of the nomination. (No timetable was specified for controversial nominations.) Agreements like this did not prevent further delay nor disagreements between president and Senate as to who was responsible for the delays. In gaining control of the committee in 1987, the Democrats established their own screening panel to give particular attention to the president's nominees, and its chair, Senator Patrick Leahy (D-Vt.), attacked the competence of the administration's previous nominees as well as its failure to nominate more women and blacks.

After concluding hearings, the committee makes a recommendation to the full Senate. That recommendation has usually been positive, but the Judiciary Committee's more independent examination of nominees has resulted in some nominations being rejected. 1980 marked the first time in 42 years the committee had taken such action. Then in 1986, the committee refused to recommend confirmation of Daniel Manion to the Seventh Circuit, because of his relatively limited legal experience, combined with his conservative ideology and a statement from more than 40 law deans saying he was unqualified. The committee did send the nomination to the Senate where it was approved, 50–49, with the vice president casting the deciding vote.

Shortly thereafter, the committee rejected the nomination to a district judgeship in Alabama of Jefferson B. Sessions III, U.S. attorney in Mobile, who had unsuccessfully prosecuted blacks for vote fraud in what critics thought was an effort to intimidate black voters and had made disparaging remarks about the NAACP and a white civil rights lawyer. Also rejected during the Reagan administration was the nomination of Bernard Seigan to the Ninth Circuit, on the basis of his extremely conservative views. In 1991, in the only Bush nomination to the lower courts to be defeated, the committee blocked the elevation of Judge Kenneth L. Ryskamp (S.D.Fla.) to the Eleventh Circuit. There were complaints he had been insensitive to minorities, and he had long belonged to a country club that appeared to exclude blacks and Jews.

When a nomination goes before the full Senate, often there are only some laudatory comments, little debate, and approval by voice vote, but at times senators debate before voting on the nomination, providing them another opportunity to embarrass the president by questioning an appointment. Anticipating that such questions will be raised, a president may prefer to avoid a particular nomination or even, despite the resulting embarrassment, to withdraw it once made.

The ABA's Role

Lawyers' principal national interest group, the American Bar Association (ABA), has assisted in selecting federal judges since 1946. Its Committee on the Federal Judiciary initially suggested names of candidates but sought to review nominations before they were made public. President Eisenhower's emphasis on "quality" in the federal judiciary led to increased ABA involvement. By 1953, instead of only making recommendations, the committee was evaluating the names of those under "active consideration." From the beginning, there have been objections to the ABA's special access and its alleged ideology masked by its claim to be interested only in judicial competence. Initially the complaint was about the group's conservatism, but more recently conservatives have found the ABA favoring liberals.

The weight given to ABA recommendations by subsequent administrations has varied. ABA participation in judicial selection has been more significant in Republican administrations than in Democratic ones. In Eisenhower's last two years, for example, the ABA committee "had a virtual veto power" so that only those the committee rated Qualified or better were nominated. The Kennedy administration tried to limit the ABA's role. Top Justice Department personnel were unwilling to give in to the ABA when they differed with its committee. Indeed, using "argument and cajolery," the administration was able to get the ABA to change some of its ratings, so that 29 percent of the ABA's informal ratings differed from formal ratings finally announced. In 30 percent of the changes, the rating was upgraded, perhaps as a result of the ABA's desire to appear successful when the administration was intent on a particular nomination.[30] President Lyndon Johnson's initial relations with the ABA were strained, but extremely negative reaction to some of his nominations made him more sensitive to the bar's reaction, and his nominees' rankings improved.

During the Nixon presidency, the ABA's position again strengthened. The president said he would not name someone considered Not Qualified, but late in his administration he broke his word. The ABA's importance in lower court nominations continued into the Ford administration. The bar group seemed quite pleased, at least publicly, with its relations with that administration and with the district judge selection commissions during the Carter administration, with a higher proportion of commission-selected nominees than of nominees not chosen through the commission mechanism rated better than Qualified. Some friction between the administration and the ABA did occur, however, particularly when the ABA twice rated a nominee Not Qualified and made its recommendation public. The Carter administration's use of selection commissions led to decreased reliance on the ABA committee.

Because many women became lawyers at an older age than men and only limited trial work had been made available to them, the Carter administration's emphasis on appointing women conflicted with the ABA's preference that nominees have considerable trial experience, which led the ABA to reject a solicitor in the Labor Department for a judgeship. Attorney General Civiletti, although not directly disagreeing with the ABA, said that certain standards, adopted years earlier, "ought not to be mandatory," so there could be "room for an outstanding or qualified exception under certain conditions."[31] Also noteworthy is that in 1977–79, 72 of 157 white males (but only one woman) were rated Exceptionally Well Qualified, and, although 62.5 percent of all Carter judicial nominees were rated Well Qualified or better, only 30 percent of the women were so rated.[32] Beginning in 1979, the Carter administration allowed the Federation of Women Lawyers Judicial Screening Panel to review nominees for their "commitment to equal justice under law" and sought similar input from other organizations. These practices were terminated by the Reagan administration, although in early 1987 the Justice Department took up an offer from the Federation of Women Lawyers to help the administration find women candidates for judgeships.

Friction between President Reagan's administration and the ABA was obvious. Because of its more thoroughly developed selection process and greater concern for ideology, the administration became the first Republican administration since Eisenhower not to consult the ABA prior to nomination and felt that even Not Qualified ratings should not bind the president.[33] Nonetheless, the administration's nominees received high ABA ratings, making his district court judges "the most professionally qualified group of appointees in the past 25 years"—at least on that measure.[34] However, Reagan appellate appointees also had the highest proportion of the lowest favorable ratings (Qualified) in five administrations. In part this occurred because such ratings were given to appointees who were law professors, despite their distinguished records as legal scholars and in part because the ABA committee was more likely than in the past to announce split decisions (the Qualified/Not Qualified rating).[35]

The administration's conflict with the ABA over the role of ideology—including the ABA's alleged use of ideology in its ratings (see pages 109–10)—continued with the Bush administration, although in mid-1989 the administration started providing single names of nominees to the ABA for evaluation. Bush's appointees received both the largest percentage with the highest evaluation since President Kennedy, and a high proportion (30%) with split (Q/NQ) ratings.

Some nominees not actually confirmed encountered difficulties with the ABA or state or local bar associations, and some were withdrawn. When the New York City Bar Association, one of the nation's most prestigious lawyers' groups, said that James L. Buckley, about to be nominated to the Second Circuit, had failed to prove his qualifications—he failed to meet with the bar group or to answer their questionnaire—the administration instead nominated him to a position on the D.C. Circuit. The Bush administration Justice Department said that *only* the ABA would be given the opportunity to interview candidates for judgeships, and that the New York City Bar Association would not be provided the names in advance of nomination.

Questions have been raised about the ratings the ABA has used. The ratings used by the ABA have been Exceptionally Well Qualified, Well Qualified, Qualified, Qualified/Not Qualified, Not Qualified (originally Not Opposed), and Not Qualified by Reason of Age, which has been dropped. The split Qualified/Not Qualified rating has been used when a majority of the ABA committee rates a possible nominee Qualified and a minority gives the Not Qualified rating. In 1989, when the Senate Judiciary Committee had a hearing on the ABA's committee, the ABA announced it would delete Exceptionally Well Qualified so that Well Qualified, Qualified, and Not Qualified would be the only ratings remaining—although some Qualified/Not Qualified split ratings were still used.

Controversy over an appointment led to reevaluation of another ABA standard. Archibald Cox, Harvard Law School professor and former Watergate prosecutor, was proposed for an appeals court position but the administration rejected him ostensibly for being over 65, although friction between President Carter and Senator Edward Kennedy may also have played a part. Critics soon attacked the ABA's age policy, which provided that no one already a federal judge would be considered for an appeals court judgeship if over 64, and those 60 and over had to be in excellent health and rated Well Qualified or better; a district judge could not be elevated to the court of appeals if over 68. In 1980 the Senate and House adopted resolutions calling for an end to the guidelines, and the ABA committee then discontinued its age guidelines and Not Qualified by Reason of Age rating. The ABA has not had guidelines for *minimum* age. President Reagan chose a high proportion of younger judges—in his second term, 37 percent under age 45—and President Bush's were younger. [36]

The ABA's ratings process was brought into public and negative scrutiny when the Reagan administration nominated J. Harvie Wilkinson III, a former clerk to Justice Lewis Powell and a University of Virginia law professor with no trial experience, to the Fourth Circuit. Straightforward application of ABA criteria would not have won him a Qualified rating. When the rating was thought in difficulty, ABA committee members were lobbied—by Justice Powell, the Justice Department, and by Wilkinson himself (which did not stand him in good stead at the confirmation stage). The committee's 11–5 vote for a Qualified rating brought questions about the pressure's effect. Some thought the committee had improperly waived its standard that judicial nominees be lawyers for at least 12 years and have "substantial" trial work, which the committee had generally been unwilling to waive for women.

Attacks on the ABA from another direction came in 1985 and 1986. The Washington Legal Foundation felt the ABA was obstructing and delaying nominations of conservative candidates and was giving lists of nominees to liberal groups like the American Civil Liberties Union and People for the American Way. Joined by Public Citizen, a public interest group that is not conservative, it sued the ABA Committee on the Judiciary to obtain its lists of prospective nominees and investigation records and sought to attend its closed meetings, and sued the Justice Department for its connections with such a group. The Supreme Court ruled that the ABA committee was not an "advisory committee" to whom the statutory requirements of public meetings applied. Several concurring justices did think the Federal Advisory Committee Act applied, but said that if it did, there would be a serious separation of powers problem of congressional interference with the president's right to select nominees. [37]

That ruling was far from the end of ABA-administration friction, which was exacerbated by the defeat of the nomination of Judge Robert Bork to the Supreme Court after a split ABA rating (see page 122). Receiving attention was language in the ABA's guidelines. In 1980, the group had added language that the committee's evaluation would be "directed primarily" to professional qualifications and that "the prospective nominee's political or ideological philosophy" would not be investigated "except to the extent that extreme views on such matters might bear on judicial temperament or integrity." As a result of criticism that such language was said to open the door to giving low ratings to conservatives because they were conservative, in 1988 the word "primarily" was deleted, the other language was altered to read "Political or ideological philosophy are not considered, except to the extent they may bear upon the other factors," and the ABA Board of Governors also formalized guidelines about leaks to the media and the appearance of impropriety from committee members' participation. That did not, however, satisfy the administration. After a meeting between Attorney General Dick Thornburgh and several ABA leaders, it was agreed that any reference to consideration of "political or ideological philosophy" would be deleted, with evaluation restricted to "professional qualifications—integrity, competence, and judicial temperament," as it had been before 1980.

Judicial Backgrounds

Correlations between federal judges' votes and their background characteristics have not been particularly consistent. Relationships between other factors and judges' voting disappear when political party is taken into account, leaving party affiliation the single most helpful explanatory factor.[38] However, party also does not have a uniform effect, having affected civil liberties decisions of district court judges more "in the wake of the transition from Warren to Burger" when the Supreme Court's cues were changing and more ambiguous than earlier.[39]

Voting records of U.S. courts of appeals judges show that appointees of Democratic Presidents Kennedy, Johnson, and Carter cast votes supporting criminal defendants and prisoners over half the time, while those appointed by Presidents Nixon and Ford did so less than one-third of the time. Differences were in the same direction on sex discrimination and racial discrimination cases. In non-unanimous 1983–84 cases, Carter judges were more than two times as liberal as the Reagan judges in most categories of cases. When Carter and Reagan-appointed judges sat on the same cases and disagreed, Carter's nominees were liberal in 95 percent of the cases, but Reagan's more ideologically homogeneous nominees, who vote much like Nixon and Ford appointees, only 5 percent.[40] There are similar differences in the regulatory sphere. Carter judges vote more frequently for the liberal antitrust position than do Reagan judges, although overall both sets of appointees support the conservative position and one can find Carter judges with predominantly conservative records. In Clean Air Act and Clean Water Act cases, Carter judges more frequently uphold "burden-increasing" agency actions and Reagan judges more frequently support "burden-reducing" actions.[41] Increased partisan differences—between Democratic- and Republican-appointed judges—may result from replacement of Eisenhower appointees (the most liberal among the Republicans) with Reagan and Bush appointees.[42]

Judges also usually support the power of the presidents who appoint them. From 1940 through 1984, Republicans were more supportive of presidential power than were Democratic appointees in nine of 10 policy areas (the tenth was the spending power). The president's law enforcement powers were supported by almost two-thirds of Republican judges, but by only slightly more than one-third of the Democrats. Overall, presidents obtained their strongest support from judges whom they had appointed and who were from their own party.[43]

Whatever their effects on voting, judges' personal and social characteristics—their race, gender, and religion; where they received their legal education; and their prior occupations—are important because of the feeling that in a democratic system judges should be roughly statistically representative of the general population. There is also the important symbolic element that, in a government of all the people, an all-white male judiciary is a slight to women and racial minorities. Some argue for broader representation of women or minorities on the judiciary because their personal experiences may make them more sympathetic to concerns of those who share their characteristics, just as former business lawyers have been, or that, at a minimum, their very presence will serve to remind their white male colleagues of the concerns of such people.

Religion has been given less attention than race or gender. There are differences in religion between Republican and Democratic appointees. Over three-fourths of Eisenhower's appointees were Protestant, more than Kennedy's district court (three-fifths) and appeals court (two-thirds) appointees. Similarly, proportionately more Nixon than Johnson appointees were Protestant. Johnson, like Kennedy, appointed proportionately more Catholics and Jews. President Reagan had a pattern more like a Democratic administration, naming more Catholics and Jews and fewer Protestants than earlier Republican presidents, but religion seemed not to be a factor in Bush's appointments.[44]

Prior Occupation. Federal judges' formal education and their parents' occupations have always been somewhat unrepresentative. During the nation's first century, both the nation's elite and particularly the "common man" were underrepresented in the lower federal courts: two of three judges were from middle-class homes.[45] Despite the small number of federal judges then, many appointees had other family members in the judiciary and even more had kinfolk in public service. Those appointed to the (Article III) district courts were usually of higher social status than territorial judges, who were "ambitious and generally successful middle-class lawyers" often not *from* the territories.[46]

The contemporary period has seen three basic paths to the federal judiciary: private legal practice and national party service or a local sponsor; in-service promotion from a position as U.S. attorney or from a district judgeship to the court of appeals; and lateral entry at an older age, such as from service as U.S. attorney after a career in private practice.[47] The Carter administration's selection methods and affirmative action efforts meant additional paths to judgeships from public interest or civil rights law practice and from law schools.

Presidents' statements emphasizing selection of people with prior judicial experience are not always matched in practice. The Eisenhower administration stressed this factor, but did not do as well in this regard as had the Truman administration. The Hoover administration had a particularly good record in rewarding prior judicial experience: 11 of 16 appeals court appointees came from the district courts. Efforts to promote district judges to the courts of appeals are limited when the presidency changes hands, because the likelihood is small that a president will elevate district judges appointed by a president of the opposite party. District judges are also more likely to be elevated when patronage considerations are central in judicial nominations; not only can senators recognize "one of their own" through the elevation, but they can also create a district court vacancy they can fill. When professionalism is central, nominations go not only to present district judges but also to state judges. The lowest rate of elevation of district judges to the appellate courts comes when policy considerations dominate.[48]

During the Johnson administration and Nixon's first term, only one-fifth of the appeals court nominees and a comparable proportion of district court nominees outside the South had neither prosecutorial nor judicial experience.[49] Both the Carter and Reagan administrations drew heavily on prior state or federal judicial experience in selecting nominees, with the Carter administration having the higher proportion of former judges for district court appointments. "Nontraditional" appointees of the Carter administration were particularly likely to be judges (three-fifths compared to two-fifths of white males), indicating that a judgeship may substitute for other, absent credentials.[50] Prior judicial and prosecutorial experience combined was predominant among Reagan district court appointees, more than 70 percent of whom had one or the other. The Bush administration, like the Reagan administration, took almost half their appointees from the judiciary but had the lowest proportion in six administrations of those with prosecutorial experience.[51]

Eisenhower's nominees were particularly likely to be from relatively large private law firms or from government practice. High-ranking Justice Department officials, who are likely candidates for federal judgeships, accounted for roughly 10 percent of his nominations. More of Kennedy's choices had been either in elective positions or some form of government administration. The private lawyers he nominated were more likely to have been in small law firms or individual (solo) practice. The same differences occurred between the (Democratic) Johnson and (Republican) Nixon administrations; more of Nixon district court appointees were partners in large law firms, more of Johnson's from small firm and solo practice. The pattern has not changed since.

Nomination of a member of Congress can present a special problem—possible violation of Article I, Section 6 of the Constitution, prohibiting appointment of members of Congress to any position "the Emoluments whereof shall have been increased" during their term in office. When Hugo Black's appointment to the Supreme Court was challenged on this basis in 1937, the Supreme Court ruled the plaintiff lacked standing (*Ex parte Levitt*, 1937). A similar challenge arose when President Carter, prompting much conservative opposition, chose Rep. Abner Mikva (D-Ill.) for the Court of Appeals for the District of Columbia. Congress passed a law granting standing to members of Congress specifically to challenge judicial appointments to the D.C. Circuit on eligibility grounds, and Senator McClure (R-Idaho), financed by the National Rifle Association, filed suit, based on an automatic pay raise that went into effect during Rep. Mikva's term but after he had resigned his House seat. Notwithstanding the statute, a three-judge district court denied the senator standing to challenge an approved nomination. The Supreme Court affirmed without comment the lower court's ruling that Congress itself had to decide the eligibility of nominees. [52]

Race. President Eisenhower appointed no blacks to federal judgeships; Kennedy named five, four to the district court and one (Thurgood Marshall) to the court of appeals. In addition to appointing Marshall to the Supreme Court, making him the first black to sit there, Johnson appointed five blacks as district judges and two as court of appeals judges. (One Johnson district court nominee, not confirmed, was later appointed by President Ford and elevated to the appeals court by President Carter.) Nixon named only four black district judges.

Blacks and Hispanics accounted for a higher proportion of nominations in President Carter's administration—roughly one-fifth—than in previous administrations, and Carter also appointed some Asian-American judges in California. More important, President Carter appointed more blacks and Hispanics to the federal bench than the *total number* appointed by all previous presidents. Presidents Reagan and Bush returned to prior patterns. Reagan had only one black appellate appointee among the first 59 judges and four black district judges in over 260 positions—the worst record in appointing blacks since Eisenhower—and Bush's record was worse. Reagan's record in appointing Hispanic judges was better, slightly behind Carter's. [53] Most Hispanic judges were appointed in places with some concentration of Hispanic population.

Some black judges' right to preside over race relations cases has been challenged because of their prior civil rights involvement. Third Circuit Judge Leon Higginbotham, asked by litigants to excuse himself from a civil rights case, refused because to agree would mean that only white judges could hear such cases. Former NAACP lawyers like Judges Constance Baker Motley (S.D.N.Y.) and Nathaniel Jones (Sixth Circuit) have taken the same position. In view of such concerns, does a judge's race make a difference? Appellate judges' voting records show that black male judges were more liberal on criminal defendant and prisoner cases than white males and also more liberal as well on sex discrimination cases, although by a smaller amount. They were *not*, however, more liberal on race relations cases. [54]

Gender. The first woman federal judge was Florence Allen, appointed to the Sixth Circuit in 1934. After her retirement in 1959, there was no new woman appeals court judge until Shirley Hufstedler was named to the Ninth Circuit nine years later; when she became President Carter's Secretary of Education, women were sitting on a majority of the courts of appeals. When President Carter took office, there were only three women district judges, but by mid-1980, there were 31, plus three on the Tax Court and one on the Claims Court. President Carter appointed twice as many women judges—roughly one-fifth of his appeals court nominations and 14 percent of his district court nominations—as had been appointed by all previous presidents. These women were less likely than "traditional" (white male) candidates to have been judges, or to have worked for large, corporate law firms, but were more likely to have been law professors. Nonwhite females were particularly likely to be younger than most nominees.[55] In short, women lawyers could become federal judges if they were "exceptional"—which they became "by escaping their stereotyped legal roles" (such as working in trust departments of banks rather than litigating in court) "and, perhaps, by being at the forefront of professional developments which were altering those very roles during the decade of the 1970s."[56] Like his appointment of members of racial minorities, it was somewhat easier for President Carter to appoint so many women because he could often nominate women and men simultaneously for the multiple vacancies that occurred in a district or circuit under the Omnibus Judgeship Act—easier than appointing a woman or minority group member to a judgeship in a single-judge district.

President Reagan named only six women to district judgeships and none to appellate judgeships by mid-1983, and made only 23 such appointments (20 to the district bench, three to the appeals courts) in his first 287 appointees (roughly 9% overall). However, that meant he had appointed more women than any other Republican president, and it made him second to Carter in number and proportion of women judges; on this criterion, President Bush did even better. Reagan's female appointees differed from Carter's: they were more likely to have been prosecutors—and were more so than male Reagan appointees—and were twice as likely as Carter's to have been politically active. Sex did not appear to affect judges' voting strongly. President Carter's white female appointees were more liberal than white male judges on both sexual and racial equality, although not by substantial amounts. However, they showed no difference in criminal defendant and prisoner cases; a match-up of female with male Carter appointees showed no significant differences.[57]

Whether women who are feminists will act as feminists once appointed to the bench is affected by the same role constraints that affect, and limit, the exercise of ideology by any judge. One interesting finding is that women judges who are not activists are more likely to support the women's rights position than are activist judges, because, with a nonactivist role orientation and feminist ideology, the latter operates.[58] Of particular note is that women Reagan appointed to federal judgeships are *less* likely to feel conflict between their careers and roles as wives and to rank their spouses negatively on support on matters of childcare and housework than are women judges appointed by Carter; whether this was a result of their spouses being different or of the two sets of judges having different expectations is unclear.[59]

The Supreme Court

The Justices' Qualifications

Just as is true with appointments to the lower courts, nothing is said in the Constitution about how the president should select his nominees to the Supreme Court or whom he should select. There is not even a requirement that a Supreme Court justice be a lawyer, although we now take that for granted. The qualifications of Supreme Court justices have been categorized as representational, professional, and doctrinal.[60] To these, as a "bottom-line" measure, one should add confirmability. Given the difficulties encountered by nominees in recent years, whether someone can be confirmed with relative ease is important—unless a president wants to engage in the politics of confrontation with the Senate.

Certainly politics plays a large role in the selection process. We can see that in the selection of Earl Warren as Chief Justice, in part Eisenhower's repaying Warren for his role in helping Eisenhower obtain the presidential nomination, then selecting Brennan because he was a sitting judge to try to calm the criticism over the Warren appointment. And one could see it in the power battle in the Reagan administration over whom to pick after Judge Bork's nomination was defeated—Douglas Ginsburg, advocated by the more conservative members of the administration, or the more easily confirmable Anthony Kennedy, who was in fact chosen after Ginsburg's nomination failed.

One element of representation is geography. Until recently, there have been more justices whose home states were in the East (the older part of the nation) than in the West. Geography once played a larger role; now some effort is made to avoid overrepresentation of any region, but that does not prevent two justices being from the same state or even same city (Rehnquist and O'Connor are from Phoenix), nor is every area always represented. The principal representational qualification has been political party. As with lower court judges, the great majority (90%) of the more than 100 justices have been of the appointing president's party. Low-visibility partisan activity is acceptable, but explicit partisanship could act as a disqualification and is played down. Party affiliation was a much better predictor of voting in the nineteenth century than it is now, because then the parties were more clearly divided on some issues, particularly regional/sectional ones like slavery.[61]

No African American reached the Supreme Court until Lyndon Johnson's appointment of Thurgood Marshall, and no Hispanic or Asian American has served. When President Bush nominated Judge Clarence Thomas to replace Marshall, the president claimed that race had nothing to do with the nomination, but it was immediately clear that the president, despite his complaints about "quotas," was seeking to fill "the black seat" on the Court. (The president seriously considered nominating an Hispanic judge before he chose Thomas.)

The greatest proportion (all but a dozen) of the justices have been Protestant, but for them, religion was not something to which attention was paid. Protestantism was sufficiently dominant that religious influences and those from the general American culture could not be easily separated.[62] Because of their small numbers, the presence of religious minorities has been obvious, although whether those individuals have been chosen because of their religion is disputed. A "Jewish seat" seemed to exist with the appointment of Louis Brandeis. In succession, Felix Frankfurter, Arthur Goldberg, and Abe Fortas served on the Court. Asserting existence of a "Jewish seat" is difficult, however, because Benjamin Cardozo served with Brandeis, Frankfurter was appointed before Brandeis resigned, and Fortas was not replaced by another Jew. Recently, Brandeis and Frankfurter have been portrayed as "outsiders" because of their religion, with Frankfurter seeking to become an insider once he was on the Court.[63]

There has also been decreasing attention to a "Catholic seat." Catholics' religion was a reason they were selected to serve on the Court but not an overriding one. For a potential justice, Catholicism was initially a potential handicap, then a "plus," and finally something explicitly to be sought, before becoming less important.[64] Both Justices Scalia and Kennedy were chosen because of judicial experience and ideology, not religion, although Scalia's religion and ethnic background (he is the first justice of Italian-American heritage) may have made some difference.

Most of the justices have come from upper-middle-class or upper-class surroundings; very few have been of "essentially humble origin." Into the nineteenth century, justices came from "socially prestigeful and politically influential" families of the gentry class; later, professional family backgrounds predominated, and economic rather than political prominence was likely.[65] The nation's more open political system resulting from Jacksonian democracy was not directly reflected in the Court's membership. Members of justices' families were often active in public life, and more than one member of the same family has served on the Court, for example, Stephen Field and his nephew David Brewer (some said this gave Field two votes) and the two John Marshall Harlans, one at the end of the nineteenth century and his grandson in the 1950s and 1960s.

Justices' ages increased as the nineteenth century progressed; this was a result of our political development and the concomitant growth of informal career lines. The likelihood that justices would be older was reinforced by formal law training and greater specialization in the legal profession, so that it took longer to become established in the profession and receive appropriate recognition. Although Justice Douglas was 40 and Justices Rehnquist and Thomas in their forties when appointed, appointments to the Court in an individual's early fifties, as with Stevens, O'Connor and Scalia, or sixties, true of three of the Nixon nominees, has been more typical.

The professional elements by which nominees are judged—by presidents in selecting them and by the Senate in considering whether to confirm them—can be categorized as competence, impartiality, integrity, and temperament, with each of those determined by surrogate measures. For example, for competence, people look at the nominee's pedigree (where attended law school), experience, and testimonials; for integrity, they examine consistency, continuity, and concern about appearances. [66]

Primary professional qualifications are prior judicial and governmental service. The state courts provided most of the Supreme Court justices in the last century, although at the end of the century justices were more likely to have had national rather than local experience; roughly equal numbers have come from state and federal judiciaries. A nominee's judicial experience has always been taken into account, although lack of it has not been a bar to appointment. The American Bar Association focused more attention on this factor and criticized nominees who lacked judicial service, such as Earl Warren. This criticism was compounded by his being chosen Chief Justice, but diminished by his experience as a prosecutor and state attorney general as well as governor.

Most other recent appointees either had judicial experience, had held important government jobs, or were distinguished lawyers. Many, including Johnson appointee Marshall (solicitor general at the time of his appointment), Nixon appointees Burger and Blackmun and unsuccessful nominees Haynsworth and Carswell (earlier a district judge), and Ford appointee Stevens were federal appeals court judges, as were the last six nominees—Scalia, Ginsburg, Kennedy, Bork, Souter, and Thomas—the last two only briefly. Burger, Rehnquist, White, and Scalia all had held major Justice Department positions, and Thomas had headed the Equal Employment Opportunity Commission. Goldberg, Fortas, and former ABA president Lewis Powell were distinguished attorneys. O'Connor had been an Arizona intermediate appellate court judge and state senator but had not been in the national positions common to other recent appointees. [67]

Presidential Expectations

Some presidents appear to have had few expectations of their nominees, but others have placed justices on the Court to do a specific job. Thus Lyndon Johnson put Thurgood Marshall on the Court to do more about social justice, Warren Burger was nominated to implement President Nixon's "law 'n order" concerns, Rehnquist was elevated to Chief Justice because he was then the most conservative justice, and Presidents Reagan and Bush selected conservatives to advance their social agenda. President Franklin Roosevelt's focus in selecting justices was on overturning the Court's rulings on economic regulation, and he chose justices for their opposition to or criticism of the conservative Supreme Court, their support for his Court-packing plan, and their divergence from what the "Establishment Bar" would have chosen. This meant that discord developed among his appointees when the political context and types of cases changed from the late 1930s to the early 1940s. FDR's justices tried to apply the lessons they had learned about the "old Court" but diverged considerably in their applications, further dividing the Court. [68]

The seat being filled may create expectations the president must meet. That helps explain why the vacancy created by Justice Marshall's retirement was filled by another African-American, Clarence Thomas. In terms of doctrine, the perception that Justice Powell had been the "balance wheel" on the Court created expectations that the nominee for that position not be too extreme—an expectation that worked against the Bork nomination. Yet by and large the president operates on the basis of his expectations. He attempts to ascertain "doctrinal qualifications" or ideological affinity from individuals' professional qualifications because presidents now lack personal knowledge of most of those they nominate. Considering this lack of personal knowledge and the fact that some nominees have been without extensive judicial records to be examined, presidents have been quite successful overall in identifying their nominees' doctrinal proclivities, and generally justices have consistently supported the policies of the presidents who selected them. Roughly three-fourths of the justices "for whom an evaluation could be made conformed to the expectations of the presidents who appointed them,"[69] and "judges from the president's party are [more] likely to decide for him than are the judges for the opposition party" in cases involving presidential power.[70] Indeed, the idea that the president will be surprised by the decisions of his appointees has been called a "myth." If a president pays attention to the views of those he selects, surprise is unlikely: "a Chief Executive who knows which issues he cares about and who is attentive can select his nominees with some confidence that he will get what he wants."[71]

Yet presidents' expectations are not always met, as Justice Rehnquist noted in a 1984 speech. For example, for justices appointed by Presidents Eisenhower through Nixon, presidents were "only moderately successful in appointing justices who would later take positions consistent with the appointing president's public statements on civil rights."[72] Some presidents have expended much energy to ensure that those they have nominated will vote the "right" way on key questions. Yet even when care has been taken to appoint the "right" person, the president's expectations may be disappointed. The best-known story involves President Theodore Roosevelt, who selected Oliver Wendell Holmes for the Supreme Court after assuring himself that Holmes would vote "correctly" on antitrust matters. Yet in his first antitrust case, Holmes voted the "wrong" way, provoking Roosevelt to say he could make a judge with a stronger backbone out of a banana. The Nixon nominees failed to reflect the president's position on electronic surveillance (a criminal procedure issue), important aspects of desegregation, aid to parochial schools, and abortion—although abortion may not have been on anyone's minds at the time the justices were appointed. In the end, of course, Nixon's appointees joined in handing down the Watergate Tapes Case that led to his departure from office.

Whether nominees have agendas when they reach the Court is not always clear. Justice Powell, appointed on short notice, and Justice Blackmun appeared not to have agendas. However, both Justice Rehnquist and Justice Scalia—whose agenda could be determined from his law review writings and lower court rulings—appeared to have the same agenda: minimalist government. Justice Thomas, despite disclaiming an agenda, had often staked out conservative positions in speeches made while in the executive branch. Whatever their personal values, those who wish to be selected must deny having an agenda they would implement on the Court, as Justice Scalia did during hearings on his nomination. We could see this more obviously during the Souter and Thomas hearings, particularly when the nominees were pressed on the issue of abortion. (Judge Souter was more forthcoming on questions of general judicial philosophy.)[73] However, in addition to trying to learn a nominee's agenda, others may use the selection and confirmation process to try to shape a potential justice's agenda. In the case of Justice O'Connor, who did not have strong ties to women's organizations, abortion was an issue placed on her agenda.[74] (In choosing her because she was a woman, President Reagan may not have thought through what her perspective on abortion could be, and for all the attention given to abortion at her hearings, Justice O'Connor has not provided the necessary vote to overturn *Roe v. Wade*—indeed, writing in 1992 to affirm it.)

Prior Judicial Experience. Appellate judges are included among potential nominees because their records on some issues likely to come before the Supreme Court can be checked. At least that seemed to be true until Judge Bork's long record of law review articles and court opinions left him vulnerable to attack. That produced a partial shift to nominees with some judicial experience (to satisfy the professional qualification) but not very much: Judge David Souter, not on the First Circuit long enough to have written opinions and before that on the New Hampshire Supreme Court, where major constitutional rulings are not everyday fare, and Judge Clarence Thomas, on the D. C. Circuit for only a year.

Chief Justice Warren Burger is a good example of prior judicial service facilitating a president's choice. Burger's decisions as a court of appeals judge showed a "judicial philosophy . . . generally described in terms of strict construction, conservatism, and judicial restraint." In the policy area in which Nixon was most interested, Burger had decided against the criminal appellant in 25 of 26 nonunanimous arrest and search and seizure cases during the 1956–69 period and in all 14 *en banc* criminal procedure rulings between 1965 and 1969.[75]

When he was nominated to be Chief Justice, Fortas's record on the Court helped not the president but critics of the Court's civil liberties decisions, such as those on obscenity. The same was true with Justice Rehnquist's extremely conservative record for those advocating greater protection for civil liberties and civil rights. The National Organization for Women (NOW) and other women's groups objected to Stevens's and Scalia's nominations because of their judicial opinions. The lower court records of rejected nominees Parker, Haynsworth, and Carswell were attacked by labor and civil rights groups.[76] Carswell's service as a district judge produced complaints that he had handled civil rights cases with hostility and had treated black lawyers and black defendants rudely; his professional competence was also questioned because the Fifth Circuit had reversed him more frequently than all but a few other district judges in the circuit. It was criticism that Carswell had "more slender credentials than any nominee for the Supreme Court put forth in this century" that provoked Senator Hruska (R-Neb.) to proclaim the need to have mediocrity represented on the Supreme Court.

Prior judicial service may assist the president in choosing nominees to the Court, but prior service on the Court itself is not a good basis for selecting a Chief Justice, because such a choice tends to expose animosities and has provoked threats of resignation. This may help explain why, of 20 nominations to be Chief Justice, 16 of which were confirmed, only four nominees to be Chief Justice— Edward White, Harlan Fiske Stone (neither from the president's party), Fortas, and Rehnquist—have come from within the Court. Charles Evans Hughes, earlier a member of the Court, was not on the Court when named Chief Justice. Rehnquist's ability to get along with his colleagues—who stated that they would all be able to work with him—may well have helped him. However, what administration officials may have perceived as Justice O'Connor's "streak of independence" on some issues, at least compared to Rehnquist's more consistent position, served to sidetrack the possibility of her being named Chief Justice.

Ethics. Prior judicial service may also reveal a judge's ethical sense. That has received much attention in recent years, starting with Justice Fortas's resignation upon the disclosure that he had temporarily retained money from Louis Wolfson, a financier in trouble with the government, as part of a contract to be a foundation consultant to Wolfson. This action, which compounded earlier difficulties, created the appearance that Fortas was practicing law for Wolfson while on the Court or perhaps—and worse—trying to influence the government's prosecution of Wolfson. The ABA's ethics committee found that Fortas had violated provisions that a judge should avoid "impropriety and the appearance of impropriety" and that a judge should not undertake work inconsistent with his judicial duties.[77]

Ethics was at the heart of the Senate's rejection of Judge Haynsworth's nomination and had "an important influence on the final vote."[78] He had not recused (withdrawn) from a case in which he appeared to have a financial interest and had purchased stock in a company in a case before him after the case was decided but before the decision was announced. Haynsworth had been cleared of charges of unethical conduct relating to the first matter,[79] but particularly in the aftermath of Fortas's conduct, the second matter hurt his cause.

Focusing on a nominee's ethics has been more acceptable than challenging political philosophy. That is why ethics concerns—on nonjudicial and judicial matters—were central in Rehnquist's nomination to be Chief Justice. One of the most important issues was his refusal to recuse from participation in the case testing Army surveillance of civilian activity, *Laird v. Tatum*, despite his Justice Department involvement as a congressional witness and policymaker on the topic (see pages 225–). In addition, some law professors felt he had not been sufficiently forthcoming about important issues during the hearings, raising questions about his qualifications. Of particular concern to lawyers was whether he had been aware of religious and racial restrictive covenants on his properties and why he had not acted to remove them. His response, that he had not been aware of them because lawyers had handled the transaction, was contradicted by one of the lawyers. That he was assistant attorney general at the time of one of the transactions, said his critics, raised a question of his sensitivity to minorities.

Ethics issues—charges of conflicts of interest while on the White House staff—would have become important in the nomination of Douglas Ginsburg had it not been withdrawn because he had smoked marijuana. The sort of ethics issue that exploded during the Thomas nomination was quite different from previous concerns: sexual harassment claims became the basis for a separate, second round of hearings, after the Judiciary Committee had voted on the nomination—and the committee made no findings on those claims.

Political Activity. Doctrinal qualifications may also be revealed by previous political involvement, which is said to show "judicial temperament" (undefined) or lack of it. Louis Brandeis was said to lack judicial temperament, a claim likely based on anti-Semitism and his advocacy of minimum wage and maximum hours legislation. Hugo Black's membership in the Ku Klux Klan, had it been known before rather than after his confirmation, would have been used against him. His later judicial defense of civil rights led to the comment that "Hugo Black used to go around in white sheets, scaring black people; now he goes around in black robes, scaring white people.") In the 1950s, John Marshall Harlan was questioned about his membership in the Atlantic Union, which supposedly indicated a diminished commitment to United States sovereignty, and about his attachment to the liberal faction of the Republican party. Opposition to Justice O'Connor came from some groups who did not feel her votes as a state senator indicated sufficient antiabortion sentiment.

Judge Parker's campaign statement that Negroes shouldn't vote, apparently an isolated incident that occurred in the political climate of 1920, helped produce the defeat of his nomination. Carswell's racism was evident from a comparable campaign statement after World War II, which was followed by his helping the Tallahassee, Florida, municipal golf course become a private club to avoid desegregation—action he took while U.S. attorney. Both Judge Bork and Judge Thomas also faced opposition based on their extra-governmental statements—Judge Bork's extensive law review articles and Judge Thomas's speeches while chairman of EEOC. Their backing away from those statements hurt them, as it seemed to be a "confirmation conversion" to acceptable views. Judge Thomas's record as chair of EEOC, particularly whether the agency had pursued claims of employment discrimination with sufficient vigor, was another basis for criticism of his nomination.

Complaints about Rehnquist's initial nomination centered on his 1964 opposition to a Phoenix public accommodations ordinance, his Justice Department work on policy concerning electronic surveillance and mass demonstrations (raised again in 1986), and his defense of Carswell's nomination as the administration's spokesman. On his nomination to be Chief Justice, a memo he wrote while in the Justice Department stating objections to the proposed Equal Rights Amendment (ERA) also received attention. So did claims that he had directly challenged black and Hispanic potential voters in Phoenix, a matter that had arisen in the 1971 hearings. Then, although saying he had participated in a voter eligibility (not disqualification) program, he had denied any direct involvement in challenging voters, but in 1986 that claim was flatly contradicted by several direct witnesses.

American Bar Association

Largely as a result of presidential actions, the American Bar Association's role concerning Supreme Court nominations has not been consistent, ranging from evaluating a person already nominated, the usual situation, to evaluating one or more prior to nomination. Probably because its own investigations did not uncover embarrassing information about Haynsworth and Carswell, after those defeats the Nixon administration agreed to allow the ABA committee to evaluate not only the person already selected but all those being considered for a Supreme Court position. This arrangement lasted only a short time, however. After the committee rated one potential nominee Not Qualified and another Not Opposed, President Nixon (unfairly) accused the committee of having "leaked" the nominees' names to the press and dropped the ABA's prior screening of nominees. The vacancy created by Justice Douglas's resignation provided the ABA its desired prior involvement in screening for the first time. Attorney General Edward Levi sent a list of potential nominees to the ABA, which could add to the list, and 15 names were screened over a two-week period. But when Sandra O'Connor was nominated, the ABA was not consulted before the nomination, apparently the case since then as well.

ABA actions have led to problems for itself. Some were related to shifts in the ratings used. Prior to the Haynsworth nomination, after using only the ratings Qualified and Not Qualified for Supreme Court nominees, the ABA adopted the ratings Highly Acceptable, Acceptable, or Not Acceptable, but later readopted the Qualified-Not Qualified standards. A further change in the rating scale was made after the Carswell defeat—to "high standards of integrity, judicial temperament and professional competence," "not opposed," or "not qualified." Other problems were related to conservatives' increased aggressiveness in seeking to obtain confirmation for conservative nominees. When the ABA committee, which had given Robert Bork a high rating when he was nominated to the Court of Appeals for the District of Columbia, was less than unanimous in its rating and then would not explain the negative votes, the administration and other conservatives criticized—and the administration indicated its unwillingness to rely on—ABA ratings. The result was an eventual change in the wording of the ABA guidelines (see pages 109–10). This was part of a transformation in which the ABA is no longer the single dominant group involved in the selection process, because many groups now take part and the president has found he can learn about nominees' views without having to rely on the ABA.

Judges' Involvement

Supreme Court justices themselves at times get involved in selection politics. Chief Justice William Howard Taft frequently exerted pressure on behalf of people he wanted nominated.[80] More recently, Chief Justice Warren attempted to exert some pressure on behalf of Arthur Goldberg and Byron White for the Frankfurter and Whittaker vacancies. In connection with the latter, when President Kennedy sought Warren's advice (through Attorney General Robert Kennedy), Warren strongly opposed two potential nominees because they would be aligned with Justice Frankfurter as "self-restrained" justices.[81] Chief Justice Warren, along with Justices Black and Douglas, encouraged Abe Fortas to join the Supreme Court, and Warren also tried to exert some pressure on behalf of Fortas to succeed him as Chief Justice, but apparently also paid a visit to his old political enemy Richard Nixon to comment against Justice Stewart's effort to succeed him. Chief Justice Burger was apparently not silent concerning Supreme Court nominations.

The most frequent method used in these efforts has been a letter of recommendation or a comparable statement—used by the justices supporting Rehnquist's nomination to be Chief Justice—followed in frequency by personal visits to either the president or the attorney general. Next most frequent has been a presidential request to the justices, in responding to which they are able to supply information and recommendations. Intense lobbying has been used only infrequently. Efforts in favor of a candidate appear to be less successful than those against, although judges' intervention is, of course, only one factor among many affecting the ultimate nomination.[82] Moreover, too much pressure from a Supreme Court justice can drive the president away from a potential nominee, not toward him, as appears to have been the case with Justice Frankfurter's efforts to obtain a Supreme Court appointment for Circuit Judge Learned Hand.[83]

Lower court judges may also try to play a role in the selection of Supreme Court justices. For example, the judges of the District of Columbia Circuit supported Burger's nomination to be Chief Justice, all the judges of the Fourth Circuit supported Judge Haynsworth's nomination, and most district judges in the Fifth Circuit sent the White House a statement endorsing Carswell after the press noted a lack of support for the nomination among his Fifth Circuit colleagues.

President and Senate[84]

Any time a president's nomination is not easily approved, and most certainly when a nomination is rejected, there is tension between the president and the Senate. This certainly was true when the Senate turned down Fortas's nomination to be Chief Justice and then, shortly thereafter, rejected the Haynsworth and

Carswell nominations consecutively. Yet after that, and the confirmation of Justices Powell and Rehnquist, relations seemed to return to normal. And they continued that way through the beginning of the Reagan administration, as the O'Connor nomination was approved without much difficulty. The Senate's rejection of the Bork nomination, with its extensive hearings televised nationally, seemed to usher in a new era of conflict between president and Senate concerning Supreme Court nominations. That conflict was fed after Bork's defeat by his charges in *The Tempting of America* that the process had been politicized and that liberals had ganged up to defeat his nomination.

In one important sense, the Bork nomination was not something new: a president of one party confronted a Senate controlled by the other and chose a controversial nominee, whose nomination stimulated interest groups, often involved in the selection process, to get involved.[85] A heightened level of potential conflict stems from the presence of "divided government" (Senate of one party, president of the other), presidents seeking to achieve a social agenda (abortion, affirmative action, crime control, school prayer) through the courts because they cannot achieve it in Congress, and a Senate more assertive in seeking answers to important questions from nominees.

There are, however, some aspects that did change. One is national television coverage, which had considerable impact as well in both sets of hearings on the Thomas nomination. Another change is that conflict over Supreme Court nominations seems more institutionalized, that is, follows more of a set pattern, since the 1969 failure of Fortas's nomination to be Chief Justice. Since President Reagan took office, and perhaps since President Nixon took office, party and legislative systems have changed: Supreme Court appointments are not seen as only patronage and, within the legislature, senators are more independent-minded, so that to win confirmation, more must be done than pleasing a few dominant figures ("whales"). The growth of judges' authority and the centrality to which the Warren Court period brought the Supreme Court have also made interest group participation more likely.[86]

Yet confrontation is not inevitable. After the Bork nomination was defeated, the Kennedy nomination was confirmed—easily. And, although senators wished to learn more about him, the nomination of David Souter was confirmed without difficulty. If a president lowers the level of rhetoric (for example, does not claim to be transforming the Court with his nominations) and nominates qualified, experienced candidates who are not combative about the Court's prior record, confirmation can be obtained—perhaps not unanimously but with a minimum of negative votes.[87]

The president's position when he deals with the Senate is stronger for Supreme Court nominations than for those to the lower courts. That the president's position is not absolute is shown by the Senate's successive rejections of President Nixon's nominations of Judges Haynsworth and Carswell—the first formal rejections of a nominee since 1930 and the first "double rejection" since 1894, its rejection of Bork, and its near rejection of Thomas. Despite these rejections and the Senate's failure to confirm the nomination of Justice Fortas to be Chief Justice and the nomination of Judge Homer Thornberry that accompanied it (both withdrawn), presidents have done far better in the twentieth century than earlier. Including those of 1894, seven nominations were rejected before 1900, and many more were not confirmed, for example, withdrawn after the Senate's extended delay in acting on them.

Most nominations sail smoothly through the confirmation process. Usually less than two months is necessary from submission of the nomination to the Senate to final Senate vote, and the time was less than three weeks each for Harry Blackmun and John Paul Stevens. Most of the time is consumed in the period between committee hearings and release of the committee's report; once it receives the nomination, the full Senate votes promptly. When a justice retires at term's end in June or July, several months will elapse between nomination and confirmation, but that includes Congress's summer recess.

Judiciary Committee hearings have been perfunctory in most instances, with one-day hearings the pattern, although those for Brandeis occupied 19 days. More than half the post-1950 hearings have occupied at least two days, with more than four days consumed in the hearings on Haynsworth (8 days), Fortas to be Chief Justice and Bork (11 days each), Souter (5 days), and Thomas (12 days). Negative votes have occurred in committee on only one-fourth of the nominations. Bork's nomination received a negative vote in committee (5–9) and the Committee divided 7–7 on Thomas before sending the nomination to the Senate without a recommendation. Rehnquist's nomination to be Chief Justice attracted five negative votes (13–5). There were also close committee votes (margins of four or fewer votes) with three other nominations in this century: Parker (6–10), Brandeis (10–8), and Haynsworth (10–7).

The nominee's actions during the confirmation process, particularly at the committee hearings, may have some effect on the outcome.[88] Harlan Fiske Stone, under fire from Senator Walsh of Montana, offered to appear before the Judiciary Committee—not the custom at the time—and he handled himself quite successfully. Nominees were not called on to appear before the Senate committee until 1939 and their appearance did not become standard until after World War II. Indeed, until 1929, the committee did not have public sessions about the nominations.[89] Stone's success indicates the importance of the nominee's candor with the committee. Prehearing visits by recent nominees with individual senators have apparently aided them. On the negative side, Justice Fortas, in appearing before the Senate Judiciary Committee, not only refused to answer questions about decisions of the Court—either ones he had participated in or others—but also lied about his involvement with President Johnson on a number of policy matters, not least of which was the Omnibus Crime Control Act, reversing several Supreme Court rulings. He gave incorrect answers and far less than complete answers, but at that point the senators did not have the evidence with which to pin him. Although Rehnquist provided affidavits to the committee chairman in 1971 dealing with questions that arose after his hearing, his failure to reappear angered some senators, as did his lack of candor in his 1986 appearance. More damaging, however, were Judge Haynsworth's failure to deal with ethical conduct charges and Carswell's failure to indicate that an important judge had withdrawn his support.

In the 1986 Rehnquist hearings, senators faced a problem of access to both medical records—to evaluate Rehnquist's problems with medication to ease back pain, which at one time led to slurred speech at a Court session—and documents from the nominee's prior government service that they wished to examine. Rehnquist waived any rights to privacy in Justice Department documents concerning his role with respect to Army surveillance of civilians (see page 225), but the administration balked and made them available only after a bipartisan Judiciary Committee majority's protracted efforts and narrowing of an initial broad request. The documents, examined by staff members and senators, were not made public but apparently did not provide much new information.

Without question, Robert Bork's combative style—seen by the entire nation on television—and his willingness to abandon prior positions, along with the position on privacy to which he did adhere, hurt his nomination severely. That he was not telegenic reinforced this, as can be seen from the decrease in support for him during the hearings. The administration learned from that experience, and was very careful to have prepared later nominees for their Senate (and television) appearances. In a combination of style and preparation, both Kennedy and Souter came across as low-key and as reasonable individuals, which helped them, the more so in Souter's case as he had not been known prior to his appointment (the "Stealth nominee"). Clarence Thomas's performance, whether his natural demeanor or the result of preparation, was also effective, particularly in the initial hearings, although his statement that he had not debated the abortion case with anyone and his disavowal of his earlier statements on natural law injured his credibility. His credibility did help him with enough people to allow his confirmation even after the damaging claims of sexual harassment and the separate hearings on those claims (called by some, "Sex, Lies, and Confirmation"), although some appeared to have voted for him despite disbelieving his defense.

The Senate has engaged in no more than two days of debate on all except the most controversial nominations—five days each on Fortas (to be Chief Justice) and Rehnquist (both initially and then to be Chief Justice) and seven days on Haynsworth. Until recently the Senate seldom even bothered with roll calls on the nominations, and Senate votes are often unanimous (Scalia and Kennedy) or nearly so (Souter, 90–9). Few recent votes in favor of confirmation have been close. The 64–33 vote on Rehnquist to be Chief Justice, following the 68–26 vote on his initial confirmation, produced the most negative votes ever for the position of Chief Justice and was the closest until the vote on Clarence Thomas, which at 52–48 was the closest in more than 100 years. However, opposition has generally increased recently. Since 1949, nine confirmed nominees have received 10 or more "No" votes. Opposition has occurred even when senators were nominated, although Black's was the first in 50 years referred to committee. Black and Sherman Minton (a Truman appointee) each received 16 negative votes. (Being from the Senate may actually slightly decrease a nominee's chances.[90]) Prior to the nominations of Rehnquist to be Chief Justice and Thomas, in only three twentieth-century confirmed nominations—Mahlon Pitney, Brandeis, and Charles Evans Hughes to be Chief Justice—did the negative votes approach one-half the positive vote. Until Bork, defeated 42–58, rejections had been relatively close—Parker, 41–39, Haynsworth, 55–45, and Carswell, 51–45.

There are other factors that affect the outcome of Senate consideration of a nominee. One is the conflict over some Reagan lower court nominees. The thoroughness with which Democrats began to examine such nominees was an indication that they would give comparable, if not in fact more thorough, consideration to Supreme Court nominations. This illustrates that nominations to the Supreme Court are not independent events, but are affected by prior events; they also affect what comes after them.

Among the most important factors are the Senate's partisan and ideological composition and the time during a president's term when the nomination occurs. When a set of possible factors affecting nomination outcomes is put together, partisanship (whether the president's party controls the Senate) is the most obvious variable, with presidents far less successful in achieving confirmation of their nominees when the opposition party controlled the Senate than when the president's own party was in control.[91] On nominations from 1955 to 1988, senators' ideology was generally the most important variable, although presidential support was next most important (the most important on the Bork nomination). Senators' region is also important in some nominations. With some nominations (Fortas, Carswell, and both Rehnquist nominations), ideology was the only significant factor, with presidential support and region playing no important part.[92]

Political considerations underlay votes in 14 instances from Brandeis through Rehnquist's initial confirmation in which at least 10 percent of the Senate's votes were negative. Senators favoring confirmation differed from their generally more cohesive Senate opposition on salient policy issues. This made "dissatisfaction with the predicted policy behavior of the nominee . . . the main motive force behind a vote against confirmation."[93] In more than three-fourths of the confirmation votes, more than half of those opposing the nomination were clustered at either the most conservative or most liberal end of the political continuum with respect to the policy area at issue, although the ideology of the nominees' supporters was at the opposite extreme in only five cases.

Timing. Timing is another important element. Nominees have been confirmed roughly 90 percent of the time during the president's first three years in office, but less than two-thirds of later nominations have been successful. However, when there is a partisan difference between Senate and president (the situation for Nixon, Reagan after the 1986 election, and Bush), the president has had a success rate of roughly two-thirds. The rate falls to just above one-fourth in the last year of the president's term. However, the combination of the last year of the president's term with an opposition Senate has not further weakened the president's chances in this century.[94] Independent of this matter of timing, the president's success rate is over 90 percent when his party controls the Senate, but under half when his party is in the minority.[95]

The president cannot control when a vacancy occurs. Warren Harding got four quick vacancies, filling them with Taft, George Sutherland (his campaign manager), Pierce Butler, and Edward Sanford. In the early 1950s, Eisenhower had several vacancies to fill. Nixon was able to fill the Chief Justiceship immediately and another position a year later, followed by two more shortly thereafter. President Reagan also had three selections to make in a short time: Rehnquist as Chief Justice and Scalia, and then Bork (ultimately Kennedy) shortly thereafter. Others have not been so fortunate. Jimmy Carter, who never had a vacancy to fill, was the first president not to be able to make a nomination to the Supreme Court. Carter was not, however, the only one not to be able to do so during his first term. That was FDR's initial problem: although eventually in the course of his three-plus terms, he was able to name more Supreme Court justices than any other president, the first vacancy, that of Willis Van Devanter, did not come until Roosevelt's Court-packing plan was under heavy fire—and Van Devanter's resignation helped undermine the plan.

President Reagan was not able to control the timing of the vacancy caused by Justice Stewart's departure, which was a surprise because Stewart was one of only four justices under 70. However, because the vacancy came very early in his term, President Reagan benefited from an early administration "honeymoon effect" and could make good on his campaign promise to name a woman to the Supreme Court. Yet in the short run a president may be able to affect the timing of a nomination. There is some reason to believe that President Reagan, knowing that it would be difficult to get a new chief justice confirmed late in his own second term, and concerned that the Democrats might gain control of the Senate in 1986, attempted successfully to bring about Chief Justice Burger's retirement. That came a year earlier than most expected—in June 1986 rather than after September 1987, his eightieth birthday and the bicentennial of the Constitution. Burger, with a strong background in Republican politics, may well have responded favorably to a Republican president's appeal that the vacancy be created promptly.

In hindsight, Burger's decision to resign seems to have been a wise one in its timing. Not only did the Democrats capture the Senate, but "Irangate" occurred, further weakening the president and encouraging the Democrats to assert themselves even more. A nomination to the chief justiceship would have had much rougher sledding under these conditions than it did when Burger chose to leave the position. (If President Reagan sought to obtain Chief Justice Burger's retirement, it appears that the unwillingness of Justices Blackmun—and earlier, Powell—to step down may have resulted from the Justice Department's strong ideological stance in key cases; their *not* retiring earlier illustrates that judges are often able to control the president's opportunity to appoint successors.)

Rehnquist's initial nomination was helped by timing, because it came at the end of a Senate session when the necessity of completing normal end-of-session business meant less time for consideration of the nomination, when the Senate was tired from a Cabinet nomination fight, and after substantial effort had been devoted to attacking some anticipated nominations. This suggests that opposition to a nomination may have a carryover effect. Hoover's nomination of John Parker, which occurred late in Hoover's term, was affected by the earlier controversy over Hughes's nomination to be Chief Justice. Liberal opposition to Warren Burger's appointment as Chief Justice was still simmering when Haynsworth was nominated. That displeasure reinforced the deeper liberal and Democratic unhappiness over the Republicans depriving them of the Chief Justiceship by blocking the Fortas nomination and over the Nixon administration's not-well-concealed role in helping drive Fortas from the Court.

Another element of the timing of nominations is the president's use of recess appointments (see pages 86–87) to the Supreme Court. Examples are Eisenhower's appointments of Warren, Brennan, and Stewart. However, this device is likely to produce negative Senate reaction, such as delay in confirming the nominations. Yet there are pressures on the president to fill a vacancy on the Court that arises when the Senate is not in session. To wait to make the appointment until the Senate returns might mean injustice to those with pending cases, which might have to be delayed or reargued. Although the Court's senior justice could serve as de facto Chief Justice, a vacancy in the Chief Justice's position is particularly serious. Coupled with the fact that *Brown v. Board of Education* had been set for reargument when Chief Justice Vinson died, this probably explains the recess appointment of Earl Warren.

Despite the occasional need to make them, recess appointments cause problems for the president, the Senate, and the Court itself. If the Senate were to convene in special session to consider only the recess nomination, more attention would be focused on the nomination than it would otherwise receive, and the Senate's power would increase in relation to the president's. If senators have difficulty getting detailed answers to questions bearing on specific issues when a nominee is not a sitting justice, they have found it almost impossible to get necessary information from an already sitting nominee because ethically the justice cannot respond to questions which touch on cases under consideration by the Court. There are also the possibilities that an appointee concerned about Senate reaction to his or her votes might "pull punches," or that cases in which the nominee is to write the Court's opinion might be "held" until after confirmation. (Two important opinions by Justice Brennan were not announced until nine weeks after his confirmation.)

President's Actions. Often the president does not do more, and need do no more, than announce the nomination. However, not only his timing but also his stance toward the nomination may affect the outcome, particularly if opposition arises. For example, immediately after the grueling fight over Haynsworth, the Senate, as suggested by one senator, was prepared to confirm anyone who had not raped a small child, in public, recently. Thus Nixon's delay in sending the Carswell nomination to the Senate misfired, as it allowed the liberals to regain their strength and to discover much negative evidence about Carswell.

Both Woodrow Wilson's support for Brandeis and Eisenhower's support for Earl Warren (a public statement and a letter to the Judiciary Committee) had positive effects, and President Reagan's radio attack on Rehnquist's critics may have been of some help. President Hoover's calling in several Republican senators for discussions to gain support for the Parker nomination was, however, unsuccessful, and Lyndon Johnson's support of Abe Fortas's nomination to be Chief Justice backfired because Fortas was already under attack as a crony of Johnson. President Nixon failed to help the Haynsworth nomination with his initial heavy pressure: a special news conference repudiating anti-Haynsworth charges in detail, and a statement that senators should not take a nominee's philosophy into account; Republican senators did not like Nixon's "arm-twisting." Nixon's attempt to maintain a "low profile" for the Carswell nomination was not effective, and he overreacted, even claiming, in a letter to Senator (later Attorney General) William Saxbe (R-Ohio), that he had a right to appoint whom he wanted.

> What is centrally at issue in this nomination is the constitutional responsibility of the President to appoint members of the Court—and whether this responsibility can be frustrated by those who wish to substitute their own philosophy or their own subjective judgment for that of the one person entrusted by the Constitution with the power of appointment. The question arises whether I, as President of the United States, shall be accorded the same right of choice in naming Supreme Court Justices which has been freely accorded to my predecessors of both parties.[96]

Challenging the Senate, as the president did in this statement, is particularly unwise politically.

Because the president has effectively shifted attention to the Senate, to which the media also pays more attention, insufficient attention has been paid to *presidential management* (really *presidential mismanagement*) as a major factor in the outcomes of Supreme Court nominations. In addition to instances—of misused timing and inadequate support—already mentioned, one can see mistakes made in the Bork and Thomas nominations, such as representing the nominee as something he wasn't (Bork as a moderate, Thomas as the most highly qualified individual); failing to estimate opposition strength and intensity (although even opponents of Thomas at first thought he was likely to be confirmed easily); and providing too little support until too late, and then too much pressure (in imitation of Nixon in the Carswell nomination).[97]

*   *   *

Each nomination has its own particular aspects, even if none is as extreme or unusual as the separate hearings on claims that Clarence Thomas sexually harassed Anita Hill. Yet there are patterns in the nomination process, even in the conflict between Senate and president, that became more regular starting in the late 1960s. We can say, for example, "When a strong president nominates a highly qualified, ideologically moderate candidate, the nominee passes the Senate in a lopsided, consensual vote. . . . When presidents nominate a less well qualified, ideologically extreme candidate, especially when the president is in a weak position, then a conflictual vote is likely."[98] The question then becomes less why the Senate is divided than why the president nominates those who are not easily confirmable. For example, Souter, a noncontroversial candidate (who puzzled people because he was unknown) was nominated when the president could not afford to alienate Congress, but Thomas was selected when Bush wanted to divide the Democratic coalition.

The president's rhetoric has persuaded many that the president should be able to demand confirmation of his nominee and that senatorial disagreement is improper. Yet the Senate, although lacking a spokesperson equivalent to the president, is part of a coordinate branch of government, and its role in the process of placing people on the Supreme Court was specified in the Constitution in its provision for "advice and consent." Although some think a more assertive Senate is "out of line," the critics are often supporters of defeated (or challenged) nominees, or a defeated nominee himself, like Bork. That should indicate that the argument is not a neutral one. Likewise, suggestions that the confirmation process be improved or streamlined, made after the Thomas confirmation battle, come from a president whose nominee was almost defeated and would generally decrease the Senate's role.

The Senate has been more assertive in recent years, the more so as it is controlled by the party in opposition to the president's party. That assertiveness has shown itself in the Senate's being willing to oppose nominees explicitly for ideological reasons, such as that a nominee would affect the Court's "ideological balance." If some think the Senate too assertive, there are others who think it is still insufficiently assertive—that it has not questioned nominees closely enough and has allowed them to "get away" with vacuous responses to important questions with which the Court will have to deal, or that it has not effectively investigated nominees' backgrounds or charges against them, as the sexual harassment issue in the Thomas nomination illustrates. In this connection, we must recognize that there is no single Senate role: different senators assume different roles in the confirmation process. Among those roles are those of *validator*, who has made a preliminary decision and uses the hearings to validate it; *educator*, who uses hearings to persuade other senators (including fellow committee members) and the public; *advertiser*, who wishes to publicize a policy point; and *partisan*, either positively advocating the nominee (or defending the nominee) or attacking the nominee.[99]

Whatever role individual senators, or the majority of the Senate, adopt, the question will remain whether the burden is on the president, and the president's nominee, to demonstrate that the nominee should be confirmed, or is on the Senate opponents of the nominee to show that the person nominated should not have been chosen. What is clear is that conflict between president and Senate over nominations is likely to persist and that each will attempt to impose a view of the nominee favorable to its own interests, with the president stressing the nominee's qualifications and an opposition Senate trying to cast the nominee as "controversial" in order to increase the chances of denying confirmation.[100]

Notes

1. *United States v. Woodley*, 751 F. 2d 1008 (9th Cir. 1985).

2. Deborah Barrow, Gerard Gryski, and Gary Zuk, "The Institutional Politics of Federal Judicial Regeneration, 1869–1990," paper presented to American Political Science Association, 1991, pp. 8, 11, 15.

3. *Atkins v. United States*, 556 F. 2d 1028 (Ct. Cl. 1977), cert. denied, 434 U.S. 1009 (1978).

4. *Duplantier v. United States*, 606 F. 2d 654 (5th Cir. 1979) and 608 F. 2d 1373 (5th Cir. 1980), cert. denied, 449 U.S. 1076 (1981).

5. See "U.S. Judges Earn Considerably More Than Salary," *New York Times*, June 5, 1989, p. B6.

6. Bernard Schwartz, *Super Chief: Earl Warren and His Supreme Court* (New York: New York University Press, 1983), pp. 427–28.

7. *Gregory v. Ashcroft*, 111 S.Ct. 2395 (1991), dealt with the effect of the Age Discrimination in Employment Act (ADEA) on mandatory retirement for state judges.

8. *Liljeberg v. Health Services Acquisition Corp.*, 486 U.S. 847 (1988). For a discussion of that case and the issue of judges' recusal more generally, see Stephen L. Wasby, "Recusal of Federal Judges: A Discussion of Recent Cases," *Justice System Journal* 14/15 (1991): 525–49.

9. *Chandler v. Judicial Council of the Tenth Circuit*, 398 U.S. 74 (1970). For a thorough treatment of the entire Chandler matter, particularly the underlying conflict between Judge Chandler and his fellow judges, see Joseph C. Goulden, *The Benchwarmers: The Private World of the Powerful Federal Judges* (New York: Ballantine Books, 1974), pp. 234–84.

10. Richard Ellis, "The Impeachment of Samuel Chase," *American Political Trials*, ed. Michal R. Belknap (Westport, Conn.: Greenwood Press, 1981), pp. 57–78.

11. *United States v. Isaacs*, 493 F. 2d 1124 at 1142 (7th Cir. 1974).

12. See David Stewart, "Impeachment by Ignorance," *ABA Journal* (June 1990): 52–55.

13. Sheldon Goldman, "Reaganizing the Judiciary: The First Term Appointments," *Judicature* 68 (April-May 1985): 314 n.1.

14. Rayman L. Solomon, "The Politics of Appointment and the Federal Courts' Role in Regulating America: U.S. Courts of Appeals Judgeships from T.R. to F.D.R.," *American Bar Foundation Research Journal* 1984 (Spring): 285–344.

15. "Q. & A. With the Attorney General," *ABA Journal* 71 (July 1985): 46.

16. Harold W. Chase, *Federal Judges: The Appointing Process* (Minneapolis: University of Minnesota Press, 1972), pp. 36–37.

17. For a description of procedure, see Elliot E. Slotnick, "The U.S. Circuit Judge Nominating Commission," *Law & Policy Quarterly* 1 (October 1979): 465–96, on which I have drawn; Slotnick, "Federal Appellate Judge Selection During the Carter Administration: Recruitment Changes and Unanswered Questions," *Justice System Journal* 6 (Fall 1981): 293–304; Larry Berkson, "The U.S. Circuit Judge Nominating Commission: The Candidates' Perspective," *Judicature* 62 (May 1979): 466–82; and Larry C. Berkson and Susan B. Carbon, *The United States Circuit Judge Nominating Commission: Its Members, Procedures and Candidates* (Chicago: American Judicature Society, 1980).

18. Elliot E. Slotnick, "What Panelists Are Saying About the Circuit Judge Nominating Commission," *Judicature* 62 (February 1979): 322.

19. Ibid., p. 322.

20. Ibid., p. 323.

21. See Alan Neff, "Breaking with Tradition," *Judicature* 64 (December-January 1981): 256–78; Neff, *The United States District Judge Nominating Commissions: Their Members, Procedures and Candidates* (Chicago: American Judicature Society, 1981); and Slotnick, "Reforms in Judicial Selection," *Judicature* 64 (August 1980): 60–73 and (September 1980): 114–31.

22. Neff, "Breaking with Tradition," pp. 265–66.

23. Slotnick, "Reforms in Judicial Selection," p. 116. See also Sheldon Goldman, "Should There be Affirmative Action for the Judiciary?" *Judicature* 62 (May 1979): 488–94.

24. Slotnick, "Reforms in Judicial Selection," p. 67.

25. W. Gary Fowler, "Judicial Selection Under Reagan and Carter: A Comparison of Their Initial Recommendation Procedures," *Judicature* 67 (December-January 1984): 265–83.

26. Neff, "Breaking with Tradition," p. 275.

27. See Steve Alumbaugh and C. K. Rowland, "The Links Between Platform-Based Appointment Criteria and Trial Judges' Abortion Judgments," *Judicature* 74 (October-November 1990): 155.

28. A Friend of the Constitution, "Congress, the President and Judicial Selection: Lessons from the Reagan Years," *Judicial Selection: Merit, Ideology, and Politics* (Washington, D.C.: National Legal Center for the Public Interest, 1990), p. 56.

29. Sheldon Goldman, "The Bush Imprint on the Judiciary: Carrying on a Tradition," *Judicature* 74 (April-May 1991): 294–306, particularly 305.

30. Chase, *Federal Judges*, pp. 130–31, 135.

31. "Q. & A. With the New Attorney General," *American Bar Association Journal* 65 (October 1979): 1502. See also Elliot E. Slotnick, "The ABA Standing Committee on Federal Judiciary: A Contemporary Assessment," *Judicature* 66 (March 1983): 348–62 and (April 1983): 385–93.

32. See Elaine Martin, "Women on the Federal Bench: A Comparative Profile," *Judicature* 65 (December-January 1982): 309.

33. David O. Stewart, "The President's Lawyer," *ABA Journal* 72 (April 1, 1986): 61. See also Goldman, "Reaganizing the Judiciary."

34. Sheldon Goldman, "Reagan's Judicial Legacy: Completing the Puzzle and Summing Up," *Judicature* 72 (April-May 1989): 322.

35. Goldman, "Reaganizing the Judiciary," pp. 322, 326; Sheldon Goldman, "Reagan's Second Term Judicial Appointments: The Battle at Midway," *Judicature* 70 (April-May 1987): 327.

36. Goldman, "Reagan's Judicial Legacy," pp. 323–24.

37. *Public Citizen v. U.S. Department of Justice*, 109 S.Ct. 2558 (1989). See William G. Ross, "Participation by the Public in the Federal Judicial Selection Process," *Vanderbilt Law Review* 43 (January 1990): 1–84, particularly 35–68, for an analysis of the district court and Supreme Court opinions in this case.

38. See Sheldon Goldman, "Voting Behavior on the United States Courts of Appeals, 1961–1964," *American Political Science Review* 60 (June 1966): 374–83; Goldman, "Conflict and Consensus in the United States Courts of Appeals," *Wisconsin Law Review* 1968: 461–82; and Goldman, "Conflict in the U.S. Courts of Appeals, 1965–1971: A Quantitative Analysis," *University of Cincinnati Law Review* 42 (1973): 635–58.

39. C. K. Rowland and Robert A. Carp, "A Longitudinal Study of Party Effects on Federal District Court Policy Propensities," *American Journal of Political Science* 24 (May 1980): 300. See also Robert A. Carp and C. K. Rowland, *Policymaking and Politics in the Federal District Courts* (Knoxville: University of Tennessee Press, 1983).

40. See Jon Gottschall, "Carter's Judicial Appointments: The Influence of Affirmative Action and Merit Selection on Voting on the U.S. Courts of Appeals," *Judicature* 67 (October 1983): 164–73, and Gottschall, "Reagan's Appointments to the U.S. Courts of Appeals: The Continuation of a Judicial Revolution," *Judicature* 70 (June-July 1986): 48–54. For a study of lower court judges' decisions on a set of Title VII (employment discrimination cases), see Vicki Schultz and Stephen Petterson, "Race, Gender, Work and Choice: An Empirical Study of the Lack of Interest Argument in Title VII Cases Challenging Job Segregation," *University of Chicago Law Review* 59 (Summer 1992).

41. See William E. Kovacic, "Reagan's Judicial Appointees and Antitrust in the 1990s," *Fordham Law Review* 60 (October 1991): 49–124, and Kovacic, "The Reagan Judiciary and Environmental Policy: The Impact of Appointments to the Federal Courts of Appeals," *Boston College Environmental Affairs Law Review* 18 (1991): 669–713.

42. Donald R. Songer and Sue Davis, "The Impact of Party and Region on Voting Decisions in the United States Courts of Appeals, 1955–1986," *Western Political Quarterly* 43 (June 1990): 328.

43. Craig R. Ducat and Robert L. Dudley, "Federal Judges and Presidential Power: Truman to Reagan," *Akron Law Review* 22 (Spring 1989): 561–98.

44. Goldman, "Reaganizing the Judiciary," p. 323; Goldman, "Reagan's Second Term," pp. 330, 334; Goldman, "Reagan's Judicial Legacy", pp. 318–30; and Goldman, "The Bush Imprint."

45. Kermit L. Hall, "The Children of the Cabins: The Lower Federal Judiciary, Modernization, and the Political Culture, 1789–1899," *Northwestern University Law Review* 75 (October 1980): 436. See also Hall, *The Politics of Justice: Lower Federal Judicial Selection and the Second Party System, 1829–1861* (Lincoln: University of Nebraska Press, 1979).

46. Kermit L. Hall, "Hacks and Derelicts Revisited: American Territorial Judiciary, 1789–1959," *Western Historical Quarterly* 12 (July 1981): 279, 284.

47. J. Woodford Howard, Jr., *Courts of Appeals in the Federal Judicial System*, p. 113.

48. Solomon, "Politics of Appointment."

49. The data here and some that appear subsequently are drawn from Sheldon Goldman, "Characteristics of Eisenhower and Kennedy Appointees to the Lower Federal Courts," *Western Political Quarterly* 18 (1965): 755–62; and Goldman, "Judicial Backgrounds, Recruitment and the Party Variable: The Case of the Johnson and Nixon Appointees to the United States District and Appeals Courts," *Arizona State Law Journal* 1974: 211–22.

50. Elliot E. Slotnick, "The Paths to the Federal Bench: Gender, Race and Judicial Recruitment Variation," *Judicature* 67 (March 1984): 384.

51. Goldman, "Reagan's Judicial Legacy," and Goldman, "The Bush Imprint."

52. *McClure v. Carter*, 513 F. Supp. 265 (D.Idaho 1981), aff'd sub nom. *McClure v. Reagan*, 454 U.S. 1025 (1981).

53. Goldman, "Reaganizing the Judiciary," pp. 321–22; Goldman, "Reagan's Judicial Legacy."

54. Gottschall, "Carter's Judicial Appointments."

55. Martin, "Women on the Federal Bench," pp. 310, 312; and Slotnick, "The Paths to the Federal Bench," pp. 375–76.

56. Slotnick, "Paths to the Federal Bench," p. 387.

57. Gottschall, "Carter's Judicial Appointments."

58. Elaine Martin, "Women Judges: Daring to be Different," unpublished ms., 1990.

59. Elaine Martin, "Women in the Federal Judiciary," paper presented to Midwest Political Science Association, 1986.

60. Robert Scigliano, *The Supreme Court and the Presidency* (New York: Free Press, 1971), p. 105.

61. John R. Schmidhauser, "Judicial Behavior and the Sectional Crisis of 1837–1860," *Journal of Politics* 4 (November 1971): 615–40.

62. Paul J. Weber, Robin Davis, and Alicia McAdam, "The Protestant Justices: A Boring Majority?" paper presented to American Political Science Association, 1987.

63. Robert A. Burt, *Two Jewish Justices: Outcasts in the Promised Land* (Berkeley: University of California Press, 1988).

64. Barbara Perry, "The Life and Death of the 'Catholic Seat' on the United States Supreme Court," *Journal of Law & Politics* 6 (Fall 1989): 55–92. See also Perry, A *"Representative" Supreme Court?: The Impact of Race, Religion, and Gender on Appointments* (Westport, Conn.: Greenwood Press, 1991).

65. John R. Schmidhauser, *The Supreme Court: Its Politics, Personalities and Procedures* (New York: Holt, Rinehart and Winston, 1961), pp. 31–32.

66. William Haltom, "Rituals of Confirmation for the Federal Courts," paper presented to American Political Science Association, 1990.

67. For examination of each of the justices who served on the Burger Court, see Charles M. Lamb and Stephen C. Halpern, eds., *The Burger Court: Political and Judicial Profiles* (Urbana: University of Illinois Press, 1991).

68. Robert Harrison, "The Breakup of the Roosevelt Supreme Court: The Contribution of History and Biography," *Law and History Review* 2 (Fall 1984): 165–221.

69. Scigliano, *The Supreme Court*, p. 146. His full treatment of the subject is on pp. 125–28.

70. Stuart Nagel, "Comparing Elected and Appointed Judicial Systems," Sage Professional Papers No. 04–001 (Beverly Hills, Calif.: Sage, 1973), p. 25.

71. Laurence H. Tribe, *God Save This Honorable Court: How the Choice of Supreme Court Justices Shapes Our History* (New York: Mentor Books, 1985), pp. 61, 89–90.

72. Edward V. Heck and Steven A. Shull, "Policy Preferences of Justices and Presidents: The Case of Civil Rights," *Law & Policy Quarterly* 4 (July 1982): 333.

73. For a discussion of the Code of Judicial Conduct as it applies to judicial nominees' refusal to answer questions about issues and about pending proceedings, see Albert P. Melone, "The Senate's Confirmation Role in Supreme Court Nominations and the Politics of Ideology versus Impartiality," *Judicature* 75 (August-September 1991): 68–79, particularly 75–78.

74. Beverly Blair Cook, "Justice Sandra Day O'Connor: Transition to a Republican Court Agenda," *The Burger Court*, eds. Lamb and Halpern, pp. 238–45.

75. Charles M. Lamb, "The Making of a Chief Justice: Warren Burger on Criminal Procedure, 1957–1969," *Cornell Law Review* 60 (June 1975): 756, 786. See also Lamb, "Exploring the Conservatism of Federal Appeals Court Judges," *Indiana Law Journal* 51 (Winter 1976): 257–79.

76. The examination here draws on Joel B. Grossman and Stephen L. Wasby, "Haynsworth and Parker: History Does Live Again," *South Carolina Law Review* 23 (1971): 345–59; and Grossman and Wasby, "The Senate and Supreme Court Nominations: Some Reflections," *Duke Law Journal* (August 1972): 557–91. See also Peter Fish, "*Red Jacket* Revisited: Saga of the Case that Unraveled John J. Parker's Appointment to the U.S. Supreme Court," *Law and History Review* 5 (Spring 1987): 51–104.

77. See Robert Shogan, A *Question of Judgment: The Fortas Case and the Struggle for the Supreme Court* (Indianapolis: Bobbs-Merrill, 1975).

78. Donald R. Songer, "The Relevance of Policy Values for the Confirmation of Supreme Court Nominees," *Law & Society Review* 13 (Summer 1979): 939.

79. For a correction and addition to the study by Grossman and Wasby based on correspondence with Judge Haynsworth, see Wasby and Grossman, "Judge Clement F. Haynsworth, Jr.: New Perspectives on His Nomination to the Supreme Court," *Duke Law Journal* 1990: 74–80.

80. See Walter F. Murphy, "In His Own Image: Mr. Chief Justice Taft and Supreme Court Appointments," *Supreme Court Review* 1961, ed. Philip Kurland (Chicago: University of Chicago Press, 1961), pp. 159–93.

81. Schwartz, *Super Chief*, pp. 428–29.

82. Henry J. Abraham and Bruce Allen Murphy, "The Influence of Sitting and Retired Justices on Presidential Supreme Court Nominations," *Hastings Constitutional Law Quarterly* 3 (Winter 1976): 37–63.

83. Bruce Allen Murphy, *The Brandeis/Frankfurter Connection* (New York: Oxford University Press, 1982), p. 320.

84. This is based on Grossman and Wasby, "The Senate and Supreme Court Nominations," updated.

85. Ross, "Participation by the Public," 2–34. See William Haltom and Patti Watson, "Sealing Judge Bork's Doom: The Role of the Usual Suspects," paper presented to Western Political Science Association, 1990. See also Ethan Bronner, *Battle for Justice: How the Bork Nomination Shook America* (New York: Norton, 1989).

86. Mark Silverstein and William Haltom, "Can There Be a Theory of Supreme Court Confirmations?" paper presented to Western Political Science Association, 1991.

87. Paul R. Dimond, "Common Sense About an Uncommon Rejection," *Law & Social Inquiry* 15 (Fall 1990): 794.

88. William G. Ross, "The Questioning of Supreme Court Nominees at Senate Confirmation Hearings," *Tulane Law Review* 62 (November 1987): 109–74.

89. Paul A. Freund, "Appointment of Justices: Some Historical Perspectives," *Harvard Law Review* 101 (1988): 1157–58, and other articles in that issue of *HLR*.

90. Jeffrey Segal, "Senate Confirmation of Supreme Court Justices: Partisan and Institutional Politics," *Journal of Politics* 49 (1987): 1008.

91. Ibid., 1007.

92. John D. Felice and Herbert F. Weisberg, "The Changing Importance of Ideology, Party, and Region in Confirmation of Supreme Court Nominees, 1953–88," *Kentucky Law Journal* 77 (1988–89): 509–31.

93. Songer, pp. 935–36.

94. Segal, "Senate Confirmation," 1011.

95. See Scigliano, *The Supreme Court*, pp. 146–47; updated.

96. Richard M. Nixon to William Saxbe, March 31, 1970, *Congressional Record* 116 (1970): 10158.

97. See John Massaro, *Supremely Political: The Role of Ideology and Presidential Management in Unsuccessful Supreme Court Nominations* (Albany: State University of New York Press, 1990).

98. Charles M. Cameron, Albert D. Cover, and Jeffrey A. Segal, "Senate Voting on Supreme Court Nominees: A Neoinstitutional Model," *American Political Science Review* 84 (June 1990): 532.

99. George Watson and John Stookey, "Supreme Court Confirmation Hearings: A View from the Senate," *Judicature* 71 (December-January 1988): 186–96.

100. See Watson and Stookey, "Supreme Court Confirmation Hearings," and Stookey and Watson, "Doubting Thomas, Borking Bork, and Other Tales of Nomination Controversy: Mapping Supreme Court Nomination Discourse," paper presented to Western Political Science Association, March 1992.

4 Lawyers, Interest Groups, and Appeals

PLAYING A CRUCIAL ROLE in the judicial process are people who initiate cases and particularly their attorneys, who present the cases in court. Lawyers—individual attorneys in private practice, government lawyers, and interest group lawyers— are particularly important for the Supreme Court because of their role in deciding what cases to appeal. Not all types of cases are appealed in the same proportions, and during an appeal lawyers may shift the focus of a case from issues that were central in the trial to other issues. The Supreme Court accepts only cases involving issues of considerable public significance; the role of lawyers is especially important in helping shape those outcomes, which will affect many people in addition to the lawyers' clients, and it is because of their stake in long-run outcomes extending beyond the particular facts of individual cases that interest groups participate in the judicial process and other well-organized actors become involved in cases before the Supreme Court. Some corporations or wealthy individuals can afford the lengthy process of litigation and appeals, but taking a case to the Supreme Court requires most litigants to obtain financial support, at times provided by interest groups.

The government is another party appearing regularly before the courts in general and the Supreme Court in particular. The government acts not only as a prosecutor and defender of its own policies, but also as another major actor trying to affect the Court's shaping of policies in cases in which the government itself is not a party. In this chapter, after some general comments about relations between lawyers and judges, we look first at federal government attorneys—the United States Attorneys, the Attorney General of the United States, and the Solicitor General—and then turn to a more extended examination of the role of private attorneys and interest groups in litigation.

Lawyers, Cases, and the Court

Relations between bench and bar take a variety of forms in and out of court. Lawyers and judges interact not only in formal and regularized ways in the courtroom, but also outside the courtroom in a variety of ways differing in their formality. Lawyers who become judges may withdraw somewhat from frequent contact with former lawyer colleagues, even when they remain in the same city, but not all such ties are severed. Judges continue to participate in national, state and local bar association activities including work on committees that make policy recommendations. Judges also have contacts with the lawyers who serve on advisory committees of both the Judicial Conference of the United States and circuit councils. Lawyer representatives are regularly in attendance at the annual circuit judicial conferences, providing them an opportunity to discuss issues with judges and to criticize their work.

Lawyers' involvement in cases is, of course, crucial to the course of the judicial process and its outcomes. Even though judges may have the final say in a case, the importance of lawyers at all stages of litigation, from initiation to final appeal, cannot be underestimated. Lawyers help determine the cases that will be brought initially and that form the universe from which appeals may be drawn, but decisions to initiate cases are often the result of implicit interaction between lawyers and judges. On the basis of the precedents established by judges' rulings, lawyers may try to discourage clients from pursuing litigation they are sure to lose. Yet where the law is not clear or fully developed, a lawyer wishing to solve a client's problem may bring to the courts questions the judges have not previously considered. Judges may encourage lawyers to bring cases by making hints or suggestions that particular legal issues have not been raised. On the other hand, by showing firmness in disposing of a matter, they make clear that the court wishes to hear no more litigation on that subject.

Moreover, the general policy orientation of a court affects the cases lawyers bring to court and pursue on appeal. With the departure of Earl Warren and his replacement by Warren Burger, for example, conservative lawyers representing public interest law firms and government lawyers who saw the Court as more open to their claims were more likely to appeal cases to the Supreme Court, and one heard civil liberties lawyers talk about taking fewer cases to the Supreme Court. Yet despite their negative perceptions of Supreme Court rulings, liberal lawyers continued to bring cases—because of momentum or habit, because clients pressed them to do so, because the lawyers believed they might achieve victory even if they estimated their chances of doing so to be slim, and because they feared that other lawyers would bring a case raising their issue before they had a chance to do so.

In our supposedly adversary system of justice, courts are expected to make their decisions on the basis of material submitted by the parties. This serves to underscore the importance of lawyers' actions in presenting their cases. Reliance on party-submitted material is greatest at the trial with respect to factual matters, which are doubly important because the trial record serves as the basis for appeals. Thus lawyers' actions at one stage of litigation affect later actions and may even foreclose them. At the appellate level, the court's decision is also supposed to be based on the trial record and the briefs submitted by lawyers and their arguments. To a greater or lesser degree lawyers' positions place constraints on the decisions judges can reach. If both lawyers in a case press the same position or at least focus directly on the same narrow issues, the judges' freedom of action may be decreased. At other times, however, those constraints are not tight, particularly when lawyers plead multiple claims, press procedural and substantive questions simultaneously, or argue broad grounds about which they are personally indifferent. The constraints are further lessened when interested individuals or (more likely) groups file briefs as an *amicus curiae* ("friend of the court") to urge legal positions related to the issues in the case but often somewhat different from those stressed by the direct litigants.

Judges can increase their freedom of action by expanding or contracting issues ("issue fluidity": see page 205), by relying more on arguments made by an *amicus* than by the parties or by developing additional information through research they and their law clerks conduct. Judges' development of information has been criticized for not being consonant with a pure version of the adversary system and because the litigants don't have an opportunity to evaluate material serving as a partial basis for judges' decisions.[1] However, such use of additional material may be necessary if courts, and particularly the Supreme Court, are to issue decisions affecting more than the immediate parties to the case. Only in this way might a judge know, for example, of a case's broader implications and potential effects.

The Government's Attorneys

United States Attorneys

Particularly crucial for the federal judicial process are United States Attorneys and the Attorney General and Solicitor General of the United States. There have been U.S. attorneys, one for each judicial district, and an attorney general, serving as the lawyer to the president, since 1789, although there was no Department of Justice until 1870. U.S. attorneys are formally appointed by the president and confirmed by the Senate, although district judges have the authority to select "court appointees" to fill temporary vacancies and the attorney general designates acting U.S. attorneys. The realities of the appointment process give substantial roles to senators, through senatorial courtesy, which increases U.S. attorneys' local orientations and to the Justice Department, which, in making its choices, takes into account the need to maintain good relations with the bench. (Senatorial courtesy plays a larger role in selection of U.S. attorneys than it now does in selection of district judges. See pages 103–4.) The U.S. attorneys' national orientation is evident in the fact that they generally submit their resignations when a new president takes office, although there have been some instances in which they have refused to do so, thus forcing their removal by the president.[2] The president may also remove a U.S. attorney for misbehavior.

U.S. attorney offices vary greatly in size, roughly paralleling the relative size of a district's federal bench. They range from an office that comprises the U.S. attorney and one assistant to that for the Southern District of New York with well over 100 assistants. In the larger offices, the U.S. attorneys generally act as managers, although some seek to set policy and shape agency priorities; they hire the assistant U.S. attorneys, who carry out the basic work of the office. Although U.S. attorney offices have responsibility for enforcement of federal law, that for the District of Columbia is unusual in having responsibility for enforcement not only of federal statutes but also of laws of local applicability. Because of its location, it also represents many government agencies when their actions are challenged.

U.S. attorneys and their assistants are at the center of a set of relations— with the judges in their districts, other government agencies, and the Department of Justice, which in turn has relations with executive branch agencies (see Figure 4.1). Relations between DOJ (Department of Justice) and the USAs (U.S. attorneys) vary depending on the district and the incumbent. They also vary over time, depending on DOJ efforts at control and the USAs' willingness to resist such control. U.S. attorneys are under the formal supervision of the attorney general, who can control politically sensitive cases—for example, bribery charges against high government officials—or cases in certain categories such as civil rights, for example, police beatings of citizens (the Rodney King case), and can instruct the U.S. attorneys about whether or not to try a case.

In the 1980s, the Justice Department made use of *strike forces* of its attorneys and agents from other government units to go to particular areas of the country to deal with major problems like drugs or organized crime. Policies for the strike forces were set by the Justice Department rather than by the U.S. attorney in the district in which a strike force was working. Although there was some cooperation between U.S. attorneys and the strike forces, the U.S. attorneys disliked the competition and sought to regain control over cases arising in their districts. President Bush's Attorney General Dick Thornburgh, responding to the U.S. attorneys' wishes, ended the organized crime strike forces and shifted their lawyers to organized crime units in the U.S. attorneys' offices.

In areas of law that the Justice Department considers important, great effort is made to establish priorities for U.S. attorneys. Overall policy direction is, or at least can be, established by the attorney general and the assistant attorneys general in charge of the department's various subject-matter divisions: Criminal, Civil, Land and Natural Resources, Civil Rights, and Antitrust. In most instances, however, formal supervision is not matched by actual control of their work so that the federal government has "not yet succeeded in establishing complete domination and control over U.S. attorneys' offices."[3]

Figure 4.1   United States Attorneys' Relations

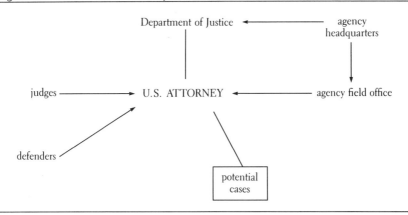

U.S. attorneys have traditionally exercised considerable independence of "headquarters"—and of each other, at times leading to disputes over which U.S. attorney should pursue a case. A few offices, most notably that for the Southern District of New York, have developed significant autonomy—especially symbolic autonomy—because of the high proportion of all federal cases, and particularly of the important federal cases, they handle. Indeed, U.S. attorneys have considerable autonomy within the federal law enforcement establishment because of their resources, including their standing in the community, access to information that others do not possess, and others' dependence on their work. They have considerable discretion in determining what cases they will bring, resulting in considerable variation from one district to another in the way similar cases are handled. Because most federal cases are initiated by U.S. attorneys, without consultation with DOJ or DOJ direction, there is the possibility of divergence between local initiative and action and national policy. Locally initiated cases may also look quite different later, on appeal, than they do when initiated, because of the greater role of the Justice Department after the case moves up the judicial ladder.

U.S. attorneys' activities are affected less by relations with DOJ than by relations with district judges and by interaction with the other federal agencies that initiate cases and on which they may need to rely for information. Because they can refuse to prosecute, U.S. attorneys and their assistants may be in a superior position in dealing with investigative agencies. However, "many of the cases presented leave little room for the exercise of discretion": good cases cannot be turned down and trivial ones cannot be authorized.[4] Moreover, workload affects decisions about what cases to accept: a heavy caseload may lead an office to decline prosecution of cases that an office with greater resources would have accepted. Judges have particularly significant effects on U.S. attorneys' offices: they can affect not only case outcomes but also the way in which cases move through the court, and can supervise the assistant USAs, who spend much time in court. However, relations between judge and prosecutor are not unilateral: cases brought by the U.S. attorney's office are the dominant portion of a district court's caseload and thus affect the conditions of the judge's conduct and the amount of work the judge has.

Attorney General and the Justice Department

The attorney general has several roles to perform. One is to serve as a member of the Cabinet. Another role is that of chief prosecutor of those alleged to have violated the nation's laws. Still another is as administrative head of the Department of Justice (with 60,000 employees in more than 30 divisions, bureaus—including the Federal Bureau of Investigation—and boards) and of the decentralized collection of U.S. attorneys and their assistants, although day-to-day administrative coordination is invariably performed by someone else. The attorney general's tasks as administrator may entail resolving friction not only between DOJ and USAs, but also between lawyers in the department's divisions and the political appointees heading those divisions. An example is the continuing conflict between the department's conservative top leadership and the more liberal career lawyers, particularly in the Civil Rights Division, over the administration's position on civil rights issues and on abortion.

The Attorney General of the United States is often someone personally close to the president or someone closely involved in his political campaigns. There are special assistants to provide supplementary skills and a deputy attorney general to assist in running the Department of Justice, and specialists are chosen as assistant attorneys general. However, an important question is whether a person chosen to be attorney general on the basis of political party or friendship considerations—such as Robert Kennedy, with little previous legal experience; John Mitchell, a Wall Street bond counsel who was Nixon's attorney general; or Reagan's attorneys general William French Smith, a corporate attorney, or Edwin Meese, a long-time friend and close policy advisor to the president—has skills appropriate to being the nation's chief lawyer.

There is also a question whether such people can avoid getting into legal trouble related to their close ties to the president. An independent counsel investigated Meese for actions as a White House adviser and questions were raised about his role as attorney general in the Iran-Contra controversy. The solicitor general and former assistants said he should be prosecuted, and, after he left office, the department's Office of Professional Responsibility found he had violated the ethics rules. President Bush's first attorney general, Dick Thornburgh, also faced criticism from his deputy attorney general, who quit, as did other aides. His remaining in office after it was clear he would run for senator from Pennsylvania also was criticized.

Another issue is the attorney general's ideological commitment and the closeness of his views to the president's policy positions. The president would be expected to choose an attorney general to carry out his policies rather than to be neutral on such matters.[5] However, the attorney general, as the official supervising government prosecutors, may find it difficult to enforce the law in an evenhanded fashion if he pursues a particular ideological platform or if he continues to play a role in policymaking over a wide range of issues. Attorney General Meese and his successors have done so by presiding over the Domestic Policy Council, a cabinet group advising the president on domestic and social issues, with a Justice Department staff member coordinating the Council's activities. The Ethics in Government Act provided for independent counsel to prosecute certain cases because of concern that attorneys general would not be appropriately neutral. Judges have ruled that the attorney general failed to follow that law when accusations had been made against senior federal officials, and others have claimed that the attorney general too easily found "credible evidence" warranting appointment of an independent counsel. Although the attorney general can ask a special court to appoint independent counsel, he can do so himself. (See pages 329–30.)

Relations between the Department of Justice and other executive branch agencies with respect to litigation are not always smooth. The agencies want to control cases they initiate and the Justice Department wishes to maintain a uniform litigation position and assure that only legally sound positions are pursued; it claims this can be accomplished only if it controls the litigation. At times there are disputes between other agencies which can lead to prosecution of the same entity by more than one department; at other times, the dispute is between another agency and DOJ.[6] (There is also conflict *within* the agencies, for example, between general counsel and agency head or simply between factions within the agency.) Conflicts between DOJ and agencies about litigating authority are not new, reaching back to the Justice Department's establishment in 1870. For example, in the New Deal, agency attorneys who had begun to proceed with cases in court found that the Justice Department wished to remove their authority to do so.[7]

Justice Department representation of agencies in court, which puts agencies in the position of being "captive clients," allows the department to control litigation. For example, the Civil Division usually represents administrative agencies in litigation concerning those agencies' regulatory programs. The department has generally pressed hard to increase its litigating authority, so that the agencies have had to deal with its "relentless bureaucratic imperialism." For example, in June 1933, the department, by Executive Order, took away control of litigation authority from all existing agencies. There are, however, situations in which agencies, at times as a result of congressional pressure, have had their own litigating authority increased through a "memorandum of understanding" reached with DOJ.[8] In general, when conflicts arise about whether a case should be brought or how it should be argued (that is, the points that should be emphasized), Justice Department officials end up resolving the disputes. During the Carter administration, a Federal Legal Council was created "to facilitate communication and coordination" among agency general counsel and the attorney general.[9] And the president, through executive orders, can establish guidelines for agency litigation, as President Bush did in 1991 in announcing rules intended to limit government litigation.

A crucial role for the attorney general is that of the "president's lawyer." This role has been retained despite the growth of White House staff, which allows the president to obtain legal advice on his immediate responsibilities from his own staff. The position of White House counsel dates only from the Truman administration. As recently as the Nixon administration, the office consisted of only two lawyers, John Dean (remember Watergate?) and Fred Fielding. As President Reagan's White House counsel, Fielding had eight to 10 attorneys working for him plus several other professionals assisting on security clearance matters.[10] The power possessed by the president's counsel could be seen in the important role played by C. Boyden Gray in President Bush's administration—including some instances where Gray appeared to upstage the president in the making of policy. In the Department of Justice, the work of being the "president's lawyer" is institutionalized in the Office of Assistant Attorney General for Legal Counsel. This office advises the attorney general in the latter's role as the president's adviser, provides legal opinions for the heads of executive branch agencies, and helps to settle legal disputes within the administration, quite likely to arise on major policy matters where policy and political concerns are likely to dominate.

The attorney general, working with the president and the latter's assistants and at the president's direction, is also chief maker of the nation's legal policy. This role includes making decisions to bring cases or to file briefs to establish particular legal points, where the solicitor general's office (see below) acts for the government. Examples were the Reagan administration's participation in cases as part of its efforts to limit school busing; to restrict "affirmative action" plans for hiring of minorities in public employment; and to restrict the breadth of the exclusionary rule in criminal cases. An example from the Bush administration is its argument, in support of the antiabortion group Operation Rescue, that federal courts lacked jurisdiction to issue orders banning that group's activities.

The attorney general's role as maker of national legal policy is particularly visible in changes from one administration to the next in the government's litigation position. For example, after the Reagan administration took office, there were shifts on tax-exempt status for private schools that discriminate against racial minorities (from opposition to the tax exemption to support for it) and on a state's obligation to provide education to children of illegal aliens (where the government terminated its support for nongovernmental litigants seeking such educational aid). (The administration lost both cases.)

In trying to develop national policy, the government continues its efforts even after losing in one or more district or appellate courts. A single court of appeals ruling adverse to the government on a particular point of law is not always accepted as authoritative. Instead the government often is willing to relitigate even within the same circuit if some basis can be found for distinguishing later cases from the initial ones. Usually only when three unanimous courts of appeals decisions have been decided against the government is the government willing to stop litigation on that point of law. This continuous relitigation is part of an effort to create an intercircuit conflict that it is hoped the Supreme Court will accept (see pages 214–15).

Solicitor General

The Solicitor General of the United States is the third-ranking official in the Justice Department. His office is perhaps best known from its appearances before the Supreme Court, where its actions carry great weight. Assisted by five deputies and almost 20 assistant solicitors general, he plays a crucial part in the executive branch's judicial activity, particularly in the appellate courts. Making up the bulk of the work of the solicitor general's office are decisions whether to appeal cases the government has lost in a district court and whether to seek Supreme Court review of adverse appellate rulings; government agency decisions *not* to appeal are seldom reviewed by the solicitor general, much less overturned. Decisions not to appeal government defeats to the Supreme Court may be related to the Court's caseload and the government's general legal policy position, including the desire to restrict the legal effect of the defeat to the district or circuit in which it occurred. The solicitor general must also decide whether to defend the government against appeals from its lower court victories, although this is done routinely, and whether to oppose opponents' certiorari petitions.

These actions are closely related to the Justice Department's overall litigation concerns. They are also crucial for federal agencies, as only a few regulatory commissions, such as the National Labor Relations Board (NLRB) have the authority to go to court on their own to seek enforcement of their orders, and only a few, including the Interstate Commerce Commission and Federal Maritime Commission, have statutory authority to appeal their cases without DOJ approval; even for them, absence of the solicitor general's approval is disadvantageous. If two agencies take opposing positions, the solicitor general may resolve the conflict by allowing one to file its own appeal without his endorsement.

The solicitor general may decide that the government should have lost a case it has won, for example, because of improper actions like illegal wiretapping. In such instances the solicitor general makes a *confession of error,* that is, tells the justices that the government should lose. Among the factors that come into play, foremost is the need to protect the department's reputation and thus to increase the chance of winning later cases. Faced with a statute it believes unconstitutional or otherwise improper, the department also may refuse to defend the provision, leaving Congress to provide a lawyer to defend the statute, as happened with the legislative veto case. When the administration adopts this position after the government has won in the lower court, the Supreme Court may have to appoint someone to present one side of the case. This happened with respect to the issue of tax exemptions for private schools that discriminate on the basis of race (*Bob Jones University v. United States*, 1983).

At least some justices will not automatically accept a confession of error. Several justices have complained about the Court's responses to the solicitor general's suggestions, when it returned to the trial court a case involving promises made to a government witness and remanded cases to the lower court for reconsideration in light of the solicitor general's claims.[11] The critics said "this Court does not, or at least should not, respond in Pavlovian fashion to confessions of error" and have criticized the solicitor general for trying to use the Court to remedy U.S. attorneys' failures to follow Justice Department policy.[12]

Another of the solicitor general's principal functions is to decide, in cases to which the government is not a party, when the government will appear as an *amicus curiae* to urge executive branch policies upon the courts. Here the solicitor general can be highly selective in choosing the cases in which to press new legal arguments. The United States and its agencies (when the solicitor general approves), like state and local governments, do not need to seek approval in order to file *amicus curiae* briefs. Without the consent of both parties, *amicus* participation comes only upon a petition to the Supreme Court itself, so the solicitor general must also decide, in cases in which the government *is* a party, when others will be allowed to appear as *amicus*. The solicitor general's participation as *amicus* before the Supreme Court and the permission granted to others have varied over time, in part reflecting the Supreme Court's preferences. Thus, after the Court seemed in 1949 to want fewer *amicus* participations before the Court, the solicitor general reduced the number of permissions to potential *amici*. Then as the justices seemed to relax their position on *amicus* participation, his consent was given more frequently.[13]

When the government files an *amicus* brief, it may also ask to appear to present oral argument as *amicus*. Private *amici* are rarely granted such permission. The Court frequently gives it to the solicitor general and continues to do so most of the time even after changing its rules in 1980 to eliminate the solicitor general's exemption from the rule that such appearances would be allowed only under "the most extraordinary circumstances." When the solicitor general's office does appear in person, it is more likely to win than when it only files a brief. In addition, the Court may *invite* the solicitor general to present the government's position in a case in which the office has not already done so. Such an invitation might suggest that the justices are unsure of the result they should reach, but the solicitor general does not win more frequently when invited to participate than when he does participate on his own motion.[14]

There is little question that the Court pays close heed to the solicitor general's arguments—and even to his *not* filing a brief, to which it has given weight although not "dispositive" weight.[15] The solicitor general is far more successful than private litigants in getting the Court to accept the government's petitions for certiorari. It does so at a rate of roughly 70 *percent*, and Chief Justice Rehnquist has said that "we depend heavily on the Solicitor General in deciding whether to grant certiorari in cases in which the government is a party."[16] As an *amicus* in support of others' certiorari petitions, the solicitor general is even *more* successful in getting the Court to take cases.[17] In the Court either as a party or as an *amicus*, the solicitor general's won-lost record has also been extremely impressive, with far more victories than losses. For example, in sex discrimination cases in the 1971–84 Terms of the Supreme Court, the direction of the solicitor general's brief was highly related to the direction of the Court's result: a liberal brief meant a liberal result in 90 percent of the cases, whereas a conservative brief meant a liberal result only one-third of the time.[18] When "underdogs"—not likely winners in the Burger Court in any event—were supported by the solicitor general, their chance of prevailing was noticeably increased.[19] In general it can be said, "Although success rates vary across solicitors, presidents, and with the ideological direction of the brief (but not with the issue being adjudicated), the solicitor general typically wins as *amicus* regardless of these factors," at very high rates and "even when siding with respondents" (the side whose victory is being reviewed).[20]

One must be careful not to attribute too much influence to the solicitor general. Influence may instead run in the other direction, with the solicitor general responsive to the Court's wishes and policy positions and "guided by the Court's ideological predilections in carrying litigation to the Court." For example, in the 1960s solicitors general authorized appeals in only a low percentage of cases when the government's position was conservative and a much higher percentage when the government's position—like the Court's at the time—was liberal. With changes in the Court's orientation and with the administration and the new Court majority sharing an ideological orientation, as the Reagan administration and the Burger Court did, one would have expected comparable interaction.[21]

In the Reagan administration, however, the solicitor general's office went further and increasingly presented to the Court positions that directly reflected the administration's conservative ideology without sufficient regard for the Court's position or for more narrowly technical legal considerations. The solicitor general's abandoning the previous administration's position in controversial cases that were not yet resolved, which made some of the justices unhappy, further illustrates the politicization that took place. Some justices, in interviews, even criticized the politicization of the office.[22] And there is evidence of the politicization in the fact that the moderate correlation between presidents' ideology, from Eisenhower through Reagan, and the solicitor generals' position in *amicus* briefs is almost totally explained by the Reagan administration data. "That is, prior to the Reagan administration, there was only a slight relationship between administration ideology and the positions taken by the solicitor's office."[23]

The departure of Solicitor General Rex Lee may have occurred because

Lee, although conservative, did not readily advocate conservative positions before the Court—at least not readily enough for the president's very conservative supporters. When he did argue for a moment of silent prayer in schools, they criticized him for not asking the Court to overturn the school prayer ruling, and thought Lee was not doing enough to press a political agenda and was doing too much to win cases and thus maintain the office's stature in the Court's eyes. Charles Fried, Lee's successor, although denying the politicization of the office, did ask that the Court's 1973 abortion ruling be overturned. He also continued to press the administration's position that there could be no racial preferential hiring and promotion except for specific victims of discrimination, even after all the courts of appeals that considered the position rejected it. His position that voting rights improvements indicated a lack of discrimination against North Carolina blacks prompted a counterbrief from Senate Majority Leader Robert Dole (R-Kan.)—and the administration's position lost. However, despite Attorney General Meese's attack on *Miranda*, Fried did *not* ask the Court to overturn that ruling, perhaps because even the conservative members of the Court seemed to have accepted it and because of Fried's losses when he did directly challenge precedents.

If there was politicization of the solicitor general's office, it came by placing ideological partisans representing the administration's position to supervise the solicitor general's office. The solicitor general did not himself behave in politicized fashion even though, because of the new process, he filed briefs the content of which was more closely related to the administration's ideology. The change in the solicitor general's posture was said "to translate into a lack of willingness on the part of the Court to defer to the Solicitor General's expertise," because if the solicitor general takes obviously "political" (or "partisan") positions in some cases, the justices cannot be sure the office is not doing so in others. [24]

Under President Bush, there was some effort to return the solicitor general's office to a more neutral model. Although the solicitor general continued to ask for the overruling of *Roe v. Wade* and also supported Operation Rescue (see page 145), the ideological oversight of the solicitor general's office seems to have been removed. Not only was there no criticism of the new solicitor general, former circuit judge Kenneth Starr; there was praise for the professionalism of the office.

Private Lawyers, Interest Groups, and Litigation

Private Attorneys

Private attorneys, particularly those associated with interest groups, are also crucial to the federal judicial system's operation. Lawyers who bring cases to the Supreme Court have become associated with those cases in several ways. For example, lawyers in Warren Court reapportionment and loyalty-security cases became involved through friendship with potential litigants, while those in civil rights cases had group affiliations. [25] Lawyers also enter cases at various stages of litigation. Over 85 percent of those who argued reapportionment and loyalty-security cases in the Supreme Court in the late 1950s and early 1960s were involved from the initial trial onward, but less than two-thirds of those who argued civil rights cases were involved in the initial trial and the remainder did not become involved until the Supreme Court stage. In criminal justice cases, where most attorneys became involved through court appointment, slightly over two-fifths were involved at the initial trial, more than one-third appeared in the case at the first appeal, and the remainder were first involved at the Supreme Court level. Lawyers handling federal criminal appeals are now quite likely to enter cases at the appellate level because the Criminal Justice Act of 1964 provides appointed appellate counsel for those who cannot afford to retain their own attorney. However, lawyers who set out to establish particular doctrinal positions by bringing a case in a purposeful challenge to a statute or regulation (a *test case*) are more and more likely to be involved from the beginning of the case.

Certain lawyers appear much more frequently in the Supreme Court than do others. The "Supreme Court bar" of the Court's early days has dispersed, in part because of the ease of getting to Washington, D.C., to argue a case and the temptation to do so. However, lawyers from the solicitor general's office or representing some major civil rights groups, who appear before the Court regularly, possess experience that serves them well when they argue a case. Because that experience was thought to be lacking among lawyers for state and local governments, a State and Local Legal Center was established in 1983 by the National League of Cities and the Council of State Governments to file briefs and to assist those doing so or arguing before the Court, so that they can make a better presentation. The Justice Department has assisted in this effort by loaning a senior attorney to the National Association of Attorneys General to provide comparable assistance.[26]

Not all those who have achieved major Supreme Court victories establishing important precedent set out to do so. Attorneys in the major Warren Court criminal procedure cases were often simply trying to win cases for their clients. In that effort, they argued constitutional questions along with everything else they could find to present, thus giving the Court its opportunity to establish the broad rules it announced. By comparison, attorneys who argued sit-in, reapportionment, and loyalty oath cases were far more likely to be interested in broader goals than winning the case for the client.

Lawyers do not have identical orientations to the law and those orientations affect their choice of cases and appeals as well as the shape of those cases and appeals. Some lawyers act as the client's agent (or "hired gun") and use the law basically to resolve conflicts. Others, whose view of the social good or public interest may play a greater role in determining the course of litigation, see law and clients' cases more as means for bringing about social change. Lawyers in corporate practice are more likely to be in the former group; those in other types of practice—such as criminal, environmental, consumer, labor, and civil rights law, and women attorneys more than men attorneys—are more likely to adhere to the latter view.[27]

The Supreme Court itself helped stimulate an increase in the number of lawyers with a "welfarist" orientation. The Court's ruling in *Gideon v. Wainwright* requiring appointment of counsel for indigents in serious criminal trials, followed and reinforced by establishment of the "War on Poverty" Legal Services Program with its emphasis on "law reform" instead of individual "band-aid" law, helped produce lawyers broadly interested in the problems of the poor. Such lawyers were more likely than others to initiate broad legal challenges, for example, to welfare policy. Their action reinforced the Warren Court's reach toward broad rules, which in turn further encouraged the lawyers.

Lawyers' differing orientations affect not only the types of cases they pursue but also the factors they consider in deciding to appeal and the relative weights they give those factors. One set of federal appellate lawyers studied generally agreed that the chance of success is quite important, and the timing of a case, an organization's concern, and advice by other attorneys are unimportant factors. However, "social welfarists" were more likely than "entrepreneurials" to give the chance of winning greatest weight in deciding whether or not to take a case to the court of appeals, and the "entrepreneurials" gave far less weight to "importance to society" than did the "social welfarists." A greater overall interest in obtaining a forum for publicizing issues led social welfarists to be more willing to file a certiorari petition when there was a low likelihood it would be granted. Women appellate attorneys appeared to want higher "odds" of winning than did the men before they would file a certiorari petition. They were also less likely than men to cite financial reasons, including a client's ability to pay, for appealing and placed more emphasis on strategic concerns than did men.

Interest Groups

Cases are usually brought in the name of individuals. However, *interest groups* are associated in some way with a large proportion of cases, particularly in "public law" cases involving challenges to government actions and in cases brought under new statutes protecting individuals' rights. Many interest groups become involved in the judicial process only infrequently and peripherally, but some have become "repeat players," large-volume litigators able to obtain advantages in the choice of courts in which to bring cases, the choice of cases to pursue, and the pace at which they move cases.[28] Interest group participation in the judicial system occurs in forms specific to the legal system but serves to reinforce the political character of the judicial process.

The norm is that interest groups should not lobby judges the way they lobby members of Congress or administrative officials. Despite occasional violations of the norm, direct contact with judges is generally avoided. The norm also does not prevent many people from writing letters—often critical of particular cases—to the justices. Justice Blackmun, author of the Court's opinion in the 1973 abortion cases, is estimated to have received over 45,000 letters in the 10 years after the decision, most of them unfavorable, with many more since then.

Interest groups involved in litigation include both the "aggressive litigant . . . seeking innovative interpretations of the Constitution" and the "defensive litigant" whose strategy is to convince judges "that prevailing constitutional norms, already favorable to his interests, should be applied."[29] At times, defensive litigants have been at a disadvantage before the Supreme Court. They can be effective in invoking precedent and custom before local judges who share their views, but at times they have not been prepared to deal effectively with the different—and more nationally oriented—values invoked in the Supreme Court by aggressive litigants seeking social change. In the effort to overturn racially restrictive covenants used to prevent the sale of housing to blacks, defensive litigants were successful in enforcing the covenants in state courts. However, they failed in the Supreme Court (in *Shelley v. Kraemer*, 1948), in part because they were not prepared to defend their position in terms of nationally accepted values and lacked as well an appropriate organizational network for defending their position.[30] The same may be said of those southern attorneys general defending school desegregation against the NAACP's attack in *Brown v. Board of Education* and related cases.[31] "Defensive litigants" in those situations were conservatives, but now those defending Warren Court criminal procedure rulings find themselves "defensive litigants" rather than "aggressive" ones.

A noticeable increase in Supreme Court participation by better prepared conservative interest groups started with the Burger Court's first term. During the 1969–80 Terms, either a liberal or a conservative interest group or both participated in half the cases decided by the Court. Liberal interest groups were either direct sponsors of litigation or *amicus curiae* in two-fifths of the cases; conservative groups participated at one-half that rate. Thus, despite the predominance of liberal groups, conservative groups' participation was far from insignificant and it increased during the period. The conservative groups were more likely to be found in cases involving economic regulation, while liberal groups were still more likely to be found in civil liberties cases.[32] However, conservatives' participation was more likely to be as *amicus* than was that of liberal groups. Despite liberal groups' decreasing win rate in the Supreme Court, "underdogs" *increased* rather than decreased their use of *amicus* participation during the Burger Court, an extension of the increases during the Warren Court period so that their filings were almost even with those by "upperdogs."[33]

Beginning with the Warren Court era, many interest groups seeking to produce social change for less advantaged members of society such as racial minorities, women, and the handicapped, or seeking to advance new causes such as environmental protection, played an increasing role in litigation.[34] Labor unions have also long used the courts in pursuit of their goals. However, such groups have no monopoly on interest group participation in the judicial process. A number of groups pursue conservative goals through litigation.[35] For example,

Citizens for Decency through Law seeks to limit obscenity; Americans for Effective Law Enforcement attempts to strengthen the hand of police and prosecutor; and the National Right to Work Legal Defense Fund is engaged in limiting unions' authority. Also increasingly involved in litigation have been conservative public interest law firms, including a set of regional units created by the National Legal Center for the Public Interest and a number of unaffiliated conservative public interest law firms like the Capital Legal Foundation. These are modern-day versions of the dominant social interests favoring the status quo—such as business groups and trade associations—that have long used the legal system to achieve their goals, not only to resolve disputes but also to create rules for their future advantage. In the late nineteenth and early twentieth centuries, they used the courts to attack laws they couldn't defeat in the legislatures; and they were behind the attacks on New Deal legislation during the 1930s, speaking, for example, through the National Lawyers Committee of the American Liberty League.

Until the mid-1960s, groups representing the politically disfavored were unable to achieve national legislation necessary to protect their rights and thus they regularly turned to the courts, where much civil liberties and civil rights policy was made. Passage of the Civil Rights Act of 1964 and the Voting Rights Act of 1965 altered the political environment by requiring group attention not only to maintenance of existing judicial precedent but also to implementation of the statutes through regulations and follow-up litigation. Such groups were, however, not the only ones to use litigation; in short, "political disadvantage" is not an adequate explanation of why interest groups engage in litigation,[36] even if it may explain why civil rights groups made it the primary focus of their activity for an extended period of time. Interest groups turn to the courts not only because they are unable to achieve their goals elsewhere but also because of the *myth of rights*, the idea that litigation can produce statements of rights as well as their implementation.[37] Their belief in this myth is one reason why lawyers return again and again to court even when rights "won" there are not implemented and even when courts like the Supreme Court seem to be less receptive to lawyers' claims.

When interest groups do go to court, the question is whether to proceed in state or federal court. The answer has varied over time and has depended in large measure on where interest groups believe the judges will be more favorable to their position. In the nineteenth century, business turned to the federal courts for protection while state regulators used state courts. At least since the Warren Court's favorable consideration of civil rights and civil liberties claims, interest groups seeking protection for civil rights have gravitated particularly to the federal courts. One reason why a national interest group might prefer federal over state courts—apart from the question of which provided more favorable rulings—is that federal court litigation is "the surest and fastest route to the Supreme Court" for those seeking constitutional precedent.[38] An organizational factor is that litigating in federal court provides a single legal framework (the federal rules of procedure) that allows staff attorneys to bring cases anywhere in the nation and to coordinate local attorneys' work more effectively. The complexities of the multiplicity of state procedural and substantive legal provisions, which would force staff attorneys to devote scarce time to their mastery, are thus avoided.[39] There are, however, some who argue that the perceived lack of "parity" between federal and state courts in their handling of civil liberties cases is not real, and that courts in some states support civil liberties and civil rights claims at least as favorably as the federal courts.[40] Certainly the Burger Court's lessened support for civil liberties claims, as reflected in lower court rulings carrying out the new Supreme Court precedents, might lead an attorney to believe that civil liberties claims stood a greater chance of success in state courts, particularly those using their own constitutions as the basis for decision.

Types of Participation. Interest group participation is of several different types. Lawyers may be interest group "cooperating attorneys" receiving help in preparing briefs and assistance with expenses; a group may provide some or all of the financing for trial or appeal; or a group may provide its own staff lawyers to try a case. Other groups become involved only as *amicus curiae* at the appellate level. This is an effective way for a group to be involved in precedent-making cases while shepherding scarce resources. Conservative public interest law firms, however, have regularly used the *amicus* device even when they had adequate financing to be more directly involved. They seemed primarily concerned to have the conservative perspective brought before the court so that the liberal view would not be the only one presented.

Groups usually become involved in a case as *amicus* because they wish to present a position favorable to one side in a case. However, they may participate at the stage at which the Court is considering whether to grant review, by arguing either for or against granting review. Their briefs at that stage are important because "an *amicus* brief at the agenda-setting stage is a signal by organized interests to the Supreme Court about the practical importance of all cases."[41] (See page 215.)

"Friends of the court" may at first have been thought to serve the court as neutral participants rather than to favor the parties. Over time, there has been a shift in *amicus* participation from neutrality, actually being a friend of the *court*, to advocacy, being a friend of one of the parties.[42] *Amici* do not, however, usually repeat the principal parties' basic arguments and often either adopt a different perspective or argue positions the principal litigants do not wish to emphasize. An *amicus curiae's* approach provides reinforcement for the justices' opinions or even alerts the justices to the importance of certain issues. This may result in a case being considerably transformed in the Supreme Court. For example, in *Mapp v. Ohio* (1961) the argument in the lower courts had centered on the issue of convicting someone for "mere possession" of obscene material (that is, without intent to sell) and on the "shocking" nature of the search that led to discovery of the material, but the defendant's attorney had not urged a change in the rule that improperly seized evidence could be used in the trial. The exclusionary issue was raised in the *amicus* brief filed by the American Civil Liberties Union and the Ohio Civil Liberties Union, but it was not central even to their argument.[43] The Supreme Court, clearly eager to reverse its position on the admissibility of improperly seized evidence, reached out to make the admissibility question the central one of the case, and, without reaching the obscenity issue raised by the parties, handed down a landmark ruling excluding illegally seized evidence from state trial.

Amicus participation, particularly before the Supreme Court—it occurs far less in the lower appellate courts—increased substantially starting in the 1960s and was quite likely to be found in civil liberties and civil rights cases, although less so in criminal appeals.[44] There are multiple briefs in some cases—78 in the 1989 *Webster* abortion case.[45] The Court has been generous in granting requests to file *amicus* briefs when one or the other of the parties has refused to grant participation (see page 146), with the Court's "grant" rate running around 85 percent.[46]

Interest groups increasingly have felt that more direct involvement in cases is necessary and that it is best to provide an attorney from the beginning of a case. Groups such as the American Civil Liberties Union, which tended to focus earlier efforts on appellate *amicus* work, often participate in cases from the beginning and often will not become involved in a case unless they can do so. This gives the group a greater opportunity to control the case by shaping the trial record, instead of having to work on appeal with a record created by lawyers for whom the group's interests may not have been central. Control allows a group to concentrate on issues of particular concern and permits it to file multiple cases raising the same or closely related issues in different courts. This in turn increases the likelihood of having a "good" case available for appeal.

Instead of waiting for potential litigants to come to the group seeking assistance, some interest groups may seek out litigants who have a case raising issues important to the group and who have a "case or controversy," thus satisfying requirements for access to the courts (see Chapter 5). In such cases, despite the use of the names of individual plaintiffs, the group, not the individual, is bringing the case. In such situations, groups like the NAACP and ACLU have been accused of *barratry*, more commonly known as ambulance-chasing. This is the stirring up of litigation in which the instigator has no direct interest, usually for a share of the proceeds. The Supreme Court has made clear that a group, as part of its members' right of association, may help protect their constitutional rights through litigation. That groups such as the NAACP and ACLU have not profited financially from the litigation has undoubtedly been a factor in such rulings.[47] From time to time, groups bring lawsuits in their own name. At times they do so to protect their own members, as the NAACP did in protecting against demands for membership lists. They also do it to assert the group's basic interests, seen frequently in environmental litigation, where cases are brought by the Sierra Club, the Wilderness Society, and the Natural Resources Defense Council.

Resources.[48] Resources are a major problem for many litigating interest groups, both liberal and conservative, although the latter have larger financial backing on which to draw. Interest groups' decisions concerning allocation of whatever resources exist are difficult. These include not only decisions about legal issues on which to concentrate but broader decisions about the relative weight to give to litigation, lobbying the legislature and administrative agencies, and developing public opinion. Such resource-allocation decisions are affected by the relative complexity and length of the contemplated lawsuits as well as by availability of attorneys. Both attorney preferences for certain types of cases and membership concerns affect resource allocation and may lead to placing new topics on a group's litigation agenda.

The cost of major litigation, particularly when groups are involved from the beginning, is very large. The set of cases constituting *Brown v. Board of Education*, the 1954 school desegregation ruling, cost at least $250,000 (in the preinflation dollars of that time), even with much lawyer time donated. The Detroit school cases of the mid-1970s—long in the trial court, in the appeals court several times, and twice decided by the Supreme Court—cost the plaintiffs just under $4 million. The Dayton school cases, also involving two Supreme Court rulings, resulted in an application for fees and costs for the NAACP and retained counsel of $1.8 million.

On the basis of the frequency with which their names appear in the media, groups trying either to defend or advance the interests of minorities and the otherwise disadvantaged may seem to have adequate resources, but the actual situation is one of quite scarce resources, both absolutely and in relation to goals sought. Resources must be stretched if cases are long and complex, true for school desegregation and job discrimination suits and cases challenging conditions in mental institutions and prisons: time is needed to prove a constitutional violation, additional resources are required to develop remedies, and still more time is needed to overcome resistance to implementation of the remedies.[49] Because there are too many lawsuits to be brought in too many different places, organizations may have to pass up cases because their attorneys are "pinned down in the trenches" somewhere else.

Interest groups' in-house legal staffs are not large—perhaps 20 lawyers in most significant liberal groups, and actually much smaller in the conservative public interest law firms. Attorney resources are, however, made considerably greater through use of *cooperating attorneys*. These are lawyers otherwise in private practice who handle cases for the interest group either *pro bono* (for free: *pro bono publico* means "for the public good") or for a fee or honorarium considerably less than their regular hourly rate; the interest group often also assists with expenses. Cooperating attorneys have their own law practices to attend to, and thus often cannot handle long and complex cases, leading to use of staff attorneys. Cooperating attorneys' priorities may not be identical with the groups', so delegating responsibilities to them may cause problems; and reliance on them leads to organizational decentralization. At times, local attorneys are used for cases in state courts, where they are more familiar with the rules, and national staff attorneys handle federal litigation and any Supreme Court cases. At other times, the relationship is sequential: local attorneys take matters through the lower courts and then "hand them off" to national staff attorneys for appeals. Such an arrangement may be necessary when a local lawyer does not seek an interest group's assistance until after the trial. This requires the group's staff attorney to begin the group's work with whatever the local attorney has accomplished—or failed to accomplish.

Interest group resources have been increased through court awards of attorneys' fees. When a group has supplied an attorney for a lawsuit, has prevailed, and has obtained an award of attorneys' fees, those fees can be plowed back into the organization to finance other litigation. The basic *American rule* has been that the winning party in a lawsuit is *not* entitled to attorneys' fees as part of the costs awarded at the end of the trial. However, the idea that individuals or groups serve as *private attorneys general* to enforce existing laws or constitutional rights—and thus are entitled to attorneys' fees—has been embodied in some statutes, such as the Civil Rights Act of 1964.

In 1975, the Supreme Court ruled in the *Alyeska Pipeline* environmental litigation that, because Congress had not specifically provided for them in that type of case, attorneys' fees could not be awarded in cases where the public is said to benefit from pursuit of the lawsuit but where no single individual or small set of individuals may have suffered substantial economic injury. Congress then included attorneys' fees provisions in several substantive statutes. More important, it passed the Civil Rights Attorneys Fees Act allowing the prevailing party in civil rights cases to recover attorneys' fees and the Access to Justice Act allowing recovery of fees from the federal government.[50] Obtaining attorneys' fees is not easy, with litigation necessary to obtain them. The Supreme Court has decided a number of cases covering such questions as what constituted the "prevailing party" entitled to recover such fees and on what claims recovery could occur (those on which the client prevailed plus others sufficiently intertwined), and with what attorneys' fees are appropriate, including the basic method of calculating fees.[51]

Resources can sometimes be stretched by enlisting the assistance of government agencies that share group goals. Groups may shepherd scarce resources by transmitting individual complaints to those government agencies with complaint-processing machinery. And, agencies or factions within an agency may not object to being prodded by interest groups to use their resources in a particular way. Such actions serve to bring government pressure on those the interest group would otherwise have to pursue directly.

Strategy.[52] Talk of choices to be made in allocating resources may imply that litigating groups have a well-developed litigation strategy. If we define strategy broadly as "overall plans, coordination and direction developed for a major area of litigation, general enough to allow for flexibility and adaptability to changing circumstances,"[53] that may be true in some situations. Some groups define in advance the policy positions to which they will give preference in bringing or defending lawsuits for individuals who seek their aid. Some cases are brought at the trial level with the intent to appeal them to the Supreme Court. However, many are initiated simply to obtain a trial court order and not as a part of a "grand plan."

Yet groups are often propelled into a case before a strategy is developed. This occurred with the sit-in cases, where no strategy existed because lawyers for the "Inc. Fund" (the NAACP Legal Defense and Educational Fund) initially had no idea that so many cases would develop.[54] Groups that appear to have a strategy may simply be responding idiosyncratically to cases brought to them or engaging in "an ad hoc search for targets of opportunity,"[55] and some groups conducting much litigation remain largely reactive. Even when a group has a general blueprint, the often unpredictable course of litigation is as influential as the blueprint. The same is true for government agency attorneys trying to bring test cases; like interest groups, those agencies vary in their litigation strategies, and tend to reflect the style of their general counsel.[56]

One reason the existence of interest group strategy in the broad sense is problematic is that groups have a variety of goals they wish to achieve. Some seek to achieve certain outcomes. These might be greater rights for women or minorities, the invalidation of restrictive economic regulations, district judges' detailed rulings on remedies to change public institutions like prisons, or Supreme Court rulings on constitutional principles. Others undertake litigation to achieve leverage for legislation and administrative regulations they want adopted or altered, as Common Cause did in its campaign for election finance laws.

Some interest group litigation goals are short-term because victories are necessary if the groups are to continue to obtain resources. Thus certain actions must be undertaken for organizational maintenance—for publicity purposes, to show supporters that the organization is alive and well, and to reinforce the group's ideological position. (Amicus participation may help in this respect, particularly if the group is short of resources for other types of litigation participation.[57]) Yet attention to short-term concerns may tie up precious resources needed for the longer term and may interfere with development of strategy aimed at achieving long-run goals, which perhaps can be achieved only by a series of cases, each building incrementally on the next but none of them particularly glamorous.

Groups' efforts to achieve their multiple goals are affected by the environment in which groups must act. This includes existing statutes and regulations. In the early 1970s and the 1980s, changes in public opinion, coupled with corollary changes in congressional mood and particularly in the executive branch's posture, produced an atmosphere far less favorable to civil rights interest groups and more favorable to conservative groups than had existed in the 1960s.

Control of cases is central to group strategy. Whether client or group controls a case is an important issue, particularly when an interest group supplies counsel and when it seeks out litigants. Because resources are scarce, a group is not likely to get involved in a case unless its own interests can be advanced. However, the ethics of the legal profession require that an attorney act in the interest of the client. If the client shares the group's interests, there is no problem. But when interests are not identical, the lawyer may elevate group interests over the client's interests. For example, when the client is offered a settlement in a case that might "make new law" if it were to proceed to trial, the lawyer might be tempted to recommend against acceptance of the settlement, as that would require "sacrificing" the group's investment in seeking new legal principle. Most groups say that the case is indeed the client's, not the group's, but instances can be found that indicate that the group has settled for a symbolic victory rather than more concrete rewards for the client, or that the group has emphasized precedent-setting cases at the expense of actions to enforce the rights won in such cases. [58]

Certain elements of interest group litigation are likely to increase separation of client interest from group concerns. Attorneys serving on the staffs of national organizations often have backgrounds and political ideologies different from those of the membership of the groups for which they are working. In addition, professionals such as lawyers often dominate laypeople such as clients. In interest groups such lawyer dominance tends to extend beyond the details of litigation to the general setting of policy and is quite likely if the group has a successful litigation record. There is often considerable geographical distance between an organization's staff attorneys (working at headquarters, usually New York City or Washington, D.C.) and the communities in which the group's members/clients are found. Often there is little if any personal contact between staff attorneys and clients, with local counsel handling the face-to-face interaction with the client. Contact between lawyer and client is further diminished by use of lawsuits on behalf of large classes of people. An organization has to use such *class action suits*—brought in the name of one or more specific plaintiffs on behalf of all those "similarly situated" legally—to stretch scarce resources, but those within the plaintiff class who disagree with the dominant class view are quite likely to be submerged. [59]

Supreme Court decisions on both procedural and substantive issues have definitely affected the course of interest group litigation. An example of the effect of procedural rulings is the obstacle posed for attacks on suburbs' exclusionary zoning by the Court's decision on who may bring lawsuits asserting the rights of disadvantaged individuals (see pages 173–74). However, that ruling did nudge groups toward greater use of state courts, where they received favorable rulings in some states. [60] The Court's decisions on substantive issues also have affected interest groups' litigation strategy, as when NAACP lawyers' efforts received a substantial boost from a ruling that facilitated a new attack on whites-only primary elections. [61] Similarly, the NAACP's shift toward a more direct attack on "separate but equal" facilities came after the Supreme Court ordered desegregation of law schools on the basis of intangible factors, in *Sweatt v. Painter* (1950).

Organizational Factors. Important intra- and interorganizational factors affect litigation strategy and make the existence and course of planned litigation even more problematic. One is a group's *organizational structure*, such as whether it is membership based, with official policy established by representatives at an annual convention, or is limited to a collection of attorneys and an advisory board and is funded by contributions and foundation grants. There has been an increasing number of the latter. They are generally referred to as *public interest law firms*, which exist to serve not only liberal causes, such as the National Resources Defense Council or the Mexican-American Legal Defense Fund (MALDEF), but also the conservative ones mentioned earlier.

A group's *longevity* and continuity allow it more strategic flexibility because a group that has been around for some time and is in no danger of collapse can wait out bad times more easily. Because the group can adjust the pace of its litigation to changing judicial doctrine, longevity affects a group's ability to control litigation. Longevity can, however, lead to inertia, in which a group continues down tried-and-true paths, unable to adapt to changes in judicial doctrine or political environment. Group inertia or momentum can be reinforced by opponents' resistance to earlier judicial victories. It is particularly likely to result from success in the courts: lawyers may feel that "after all, if we've been successful there, we will continue to be." Victorious litigants certainly do not wish to give up, or to be seen as giving up, what they had pressed hard to achieve. Moreover, a group that has developed expertise in presenting cases in court will want to continue to utilize, rather than dissipate, that expertise.

The existence of and *relations with other organizations*, including business groups providing financing (in the case of conservative public interest law firms), are an important part of an interest group's political environment and affect a group's litigation activities. The number of groups litigating in a particular area of the law—thus competing for resources—is part of the interorganizational situation. For example, for a long time the NAACP Legal Defense and Educational Fund (LDF), closely allied with the NAACP, was the dominant if not the sole civil rights litigator, thus having substantial control over litigation when it engaged in planned strategy. Now the NAACP and LDF are separate—and have feuded—and there are many, many civil rights litigating units. These include public interest law firms; private law firms that provide regular fee-for-service lawyering to private clients and also engage in public interest law practice; other private law firms closely affiliated with particular interest groups; individual private attorneys who bring cases, such as employment discrimination cases under Title VII of the 1964 Civil Rights Act, from which they can receive attorneys' fees if they win; and "back-up centers," created through the Legal Services Program, that assist with litigation.

A growing "rights consciousness" has also produced more causes—including women, the poor, the handicapped, and gays and lesbians—for which litigating capacity has developed. The large number of groups in any one of these areas, such as the large number of women's groups, have caused problems of coordinating litigation. Proliferation of litigating units had led to a loss of control by any single litigator and decreased ability to pursue a concerted strategy. Also important is the presence of groups that, as an ideological matter, do not use litigation and may disdain it. In the 1960s, for example, new civil rights groups, whose style was far more activist and confrontational, felt that the NAACP had not accomplished enough through the courts. The activities of groups such as the Congress of Racial Equality (CORE) and the Southern Christian Leadership Conference (SCLC, the Reverend Martin Luther King, Jr.'s group), caused older groups to shift priorities and resources as well as to pay more attention to membership concerns.

In addition to competition and conflict between groups seeking goals in any policy area, there is considerable cooperation. At times lawyers whose organizations are formally "at war" work together toward common goals. This cooperation is true of the small and cohesive "civil rights bar," in which a convergence of perspectives has developed. At times groups work together explicitly, primarily through exchange of information, which is quite important for control of cases as well as for efficient allocation of resources. Representatives of litigating groups also meet to exchange ideas or even to work out strategy. The three primary plaintiffs' interest group litigants in the church-state area (the American Jewish Congress, American Civil Liberties Union, and Americans United [for Separation of Church and State]) have worked together in this way.[62] Similarly, the Heritage Foundation has held monthly luncheons attended by representatives of most conservative litigators. Some groups go even further, perhaps providing auxiliary legal services for other interest groups. Much cooperation is, however, implicit rather than overt. Through awareness of what other groups are doing, groups maintain at least somewhat differentiated central thrusts in which some concentrate on some types of cases while others focus their efforts on other areas. At times, such "comparative advantage" leads to the explicit cross-referral of cases from one organization to another better fitted for the particular task.

Notes

1. Charles M. Lamb, "Judicial Policy-Making and Information Flow to the Supreme Court," *Vanderbilt Law Review* 29 (January 1976): 46–124.

2. On selection of U.S. attorneys, see James Eisenstein, *Counsel for the United States: U.S. Attorneys in the Political and Legal Systems* (Baltimore, Md.: Johns Hopkins University Press, 1978), pp. 35–47. The following paragraphs also draw on Eisenstein's study.

3. Ibid., p. 16.

4. Ibid., p. 156. See also Robert L. Rabin, "Agency Criminal Referrals in the Federal System: An Empirical Study of Prosecutorial Discretion," *Stanford Law Review* 24 (June 1972): 1036–91.

5. See Nancy V. Baker, *Conflicting Loyalties: Law and Politics in the Attorney General's Office* (Lawrence, Kan.: University Press of Kansas, 1992), with its attention to the Advocate and Neutral roles.

6. See Peter H. Irons, *Justice at War* (New York: Oxford University Press, 1983), for a story about conflict between DOJ and the War Department.

7. Peter H. Irons, *The New Deal Lawyers* (Princeton, N.J.: Princeton University Press, 1982), pp. 40–41.

8. See Susan M. Olson, "Comparing Justice and Labor Department Lawyers: Ten Years of Occupational Safety and Health Litigation," *Law & Policy Quarterly* 7 (July 1985): 295; and Olson, "Challenges to the Gatekeeper: The Debate Over Federal Litigating Authority," *Judicature* 68 (August–September 1984): 71–86.

9. Olson, "Comparing Justice and Labor Department Lawyers," p. 290.

10. David O. Stewart, "The President's Lawyer," *ABA Journal* 72 (April 1, 1986): 58–61.

11. *DeMarco v. United States*, 415 U.S. 449 (1974); *Alvarado v. United States*, 110 S.Ct. 2995 at 2997 (1990) (Rehnquist, dissenting); and *Diaz-Albertini v. United States*, 110 S.Ct. 776 at 777 (1991) (Rehnquist, dissenting).

12. *DeMarco v. United States*, 415 U.S., at 451; *Watts v. United States*, 422 U.S. 1032 at 1035–36 (1975) (Burger, dissenting); *Rinaldi v. United States*, 434 U.S. 22 (1977) (Rehnquist).

13. See Robert Scigliano, *The Supreme Court and the Presidency*, pp. 167–68. See also Samuel Krislov, "The Role of the Attorney General as *Amicus Curiae*," in Luther Huston, et al., *Roles of the Attorney General of the United States* (Washington, D.C.: American Enterprise Institute, 1968), pp. 71–104. For a description of the process leading to the Solicitor General's decisions to file or not file *amicus* briefs in the *DeFunis* and *Bakke* affirmative action cases, see Timothy J. O'Neill, *Bakke & The Politics of Equality: Friends & Foes in the Classroom of Litigation* (Middletown, Conn.: Wesleyan University Press, 1985), pp. 179–91.

14. S. Sidney Ulmer and David Willison, "The Solicitor General of the United States as *Amicus Curiae* in the U.S. Supreme Court, 1969–1983 Terms," paper presented to American Political Science Association, 1985.

15. See *Container Corporation of America v. Franchise Tax Board*, 463 U.S. 159 at 196 and n. 33 (1983).

16. *Alvarado v. United States*, 110 S.Ct., at 2997 (1990). See also Gregory A. Caldeira and John R. Wright, "Organized Interests and Agenda Setting in the U.S. Supreme Court," *American Political Science Review* 82 (December 1988): 1109–28.

17. Scigliano, *The Supreme Court and the Presidency*, p. 176.

18. See Jeffrey A. Segal and Cheryl D. Reedy, "The Supreme Court and Equal Protection: The Role of the Solicitor General," paper presented to American Political Science Association, 1975, p. 11.

19. Ulmer and Willison, "The Solicitor General of the United States," p. 19.

20. Jeffrey A. Segal, "Courts, Executives, and Legislatures," *The American Courts: A Critical Assessment*, eds. John B. Gates and Charles A. Johnson (Washington, D.C.: CQ Press, 1991), p. 378. See also Segal, "Supreme Court Support for the Solicitor General: The Effect of Presidential Appointments," *Western Political Quarterly* (March 1990): 137–52.

21. Scigliano, *The Supreme Court and the Presidency*, pp. 191–93, for the earlier period; for a comparison of the actions of three solicitors general, see Karen O'Connor, "The *Amicus Curiae* Role of the United States Solicitor General in Supreme Court Litigation," *Judicature* 66 (December-January 1983): 256–64.

22. Lincoln Caplan, *The Tenth Justice: The Solicitor General and the Rule of Law* (New York: Alfred A. Knopf, 1987). See also Rebecca Mae Salokar, *The Solicitor General: The Politics of Law* (Philadelphia, Pa.: Temple University Press, 1992).

23. Segal, "Courts, Executives, and Legislatures," p. 381.

24. Ulmer and Willison, "The Solicitor General of the United States," pp. 16–17.

25. Jonathan Casper, *Lawyers Before the Warren Court: Civil Liberties and Civil Rights, 1957–1966* (Urbana: University of Illinois Press, 1972), tables 4 and 5, pp. 88–89.

26. See Douglas Ross, "Safeguarding Our Federalism: Lessons for the States from the Supreme Court," *Public Administration Review* 45 (Special 1985): 723–31. For recent examination of states' appearance as *amicus* in the Supreme Court and their relative success, see Thomas R. Morris, "States Before the U.S. Supreme Court: State Attorneys General as *Amicus Curiae*," *Judicature* 70 (February-March 1987): 298–305, and Lee Epstein and Karen O'Connor, "States Before the U.S. Supreme Court: Direct Representation in Cases Involving Criminal Rights, 1969–1984," ibid.: 305–6.

27. Gregory J. Rathjen, "Lawyers and the Appeals Process: An Analysis of the Appellate Lawyer's

Beliefs, Attitudes and Values," paper presented to the Midwest Political Science Association, 1975; Rathjen, "Lawyers and the Appeals Process: A Profile," *Federal Bar Journal* 34 (Winter 1975): 21–41; Susan Ann Kay, "Sex Differences in the Attitudes of a Future Elite," *Women & Politics* 1 (Fall 1980): 35–48.

28. See Marc Galanter, "Why the 'Haves' Come Out Ahead: Speculations on the Limits of Legal Change," *Law & Society Review* 9 (Fall 1974): 95–160.

29. Richard C. Cortner, "Strategies and Tactics of Litigants in Constitutional Cases," *Journal of Public Law* 17 (1968): 288.

30. See Clement Vose, *Caucasians Only: The Supreme Court, the NAACP, and the Restrictive Covenant Cases* (Berkeley: University of California Press, 1959).

31. For the story, see Richard Kluger, *Simple Justice: The History of Brown v. Board of Education and Black America's Struggle for Equality* (New York: Alfred Knopf, 1976).

32. Karen O'Connor and Lee Epstein, "The Rise of Conservative Interest Group Litigation," *Journal of Politics* 45 (May 1983): 479–89.

33. Robert C. Bradley and Paul Gardner, "Underdogs, Upperdogs and the Use of the *Amicus* Brief: Trends and Explanations," *Justice System Journal* 10 (Spring 1985): 78–96.

34. For stories and studies of the work of these groups, see Michael Meltsner, *Cruel and Unusual: The Supreme Court and Capital Punishment* (New York: Oxford University Press, 1973), and Robert Belton, "A Comparative Review of Public and Private Enforcement of Title VII of the Civil Rights Act of 1964," *Vanderbilt Law Review* 31 (May 1978): 905–61, on the work of the NAACP Legal Defense and Educational Fund; Robert Rabin, "Lawyers for Social Change: Perspectives on Public Interest Law," *Stanford Law Review* 28 (January 1976): 207–61, on the NAACP Legal Defense Fund and the American Civil Liberties Union; Frank J. Sorauf, *The Wall of Separation: The Constitutional Politics of Church and State* (Princeton, N.J.: Princeton University Press, 1976); Karen O'Connor, *Women's Organizations' Use of the Courts* (Lexington, Mass.: Lexington Books, 1980) and O'Connor and Lee Epstein, "Beyond Legislative Lobbying: Women's Rights Groups and the Supreme Court," *Judicature* 67 (September 1983): 134–43; R. Shep Melnick, *Regulation and the Courts: The Case of the Clean Air Act* (Washington, D.C.: Brookings Institution, 1983); and Susan M. Olson, *Clients and Lawyers: Securing the Rights of Disabled Persons* (Westport, Conn.: Greenwood Press, 1984).

35. Lee Epstein, *Conservatives in Court* (Knoxville: University of Tennessee Press, 1985).

36. See Susan M. Olson, "Interest-Group Litigation in Federal District Court: Beyond the Political Disadvantage Theory," *Journal of Politics* 52 (August 1990): 854–82, particularly 855–64.

37. Stuart Scheingold, *The Politics of Rights: Lawyers, Public Policy, and Political Change* (New Haven, Conn.: Yale University Press, 1974), p. 5.

38. Sorauf, *The Wall of Separation*, p. 111.

39. For the basic arguments about why civil liberties lawyers favor federal courts, see Burt Neuborne, "The Myth of Parity," *Harvard Law Review* 90 (April 1977): 1105–31, and "Toward Procedural Parity in Constitutional Litigation," *William & Mary Law Review* 22 (Summer 1981): 725–87.

40. For one study, see Robert Solomine and James Walker, "Constitutional Litigation in Federal and State Courts: An Empirical Analysis of Judicial Parity," *Hastings Constitutional Law Quarterly* 10 (1983): 213–53.

41. Caldeira and Wright, p. 1119.

42. Samuel Krislov, "The *Amicus Curiae* Brief: From Friendship to Advocacy," *Yale Law Journal* 72 (March 1963): 694–721.

43. Lynn Mather and Barbara Yngvesson, "Language, Audience, and the Transformation of Disputes," *Law & Society Review* 15 (1980–1981): 802–5, and Fred W. Friendly and Martha J. W. Elliott, *The Constitution: That Delicate Balance* (New York: Random House, 1984), pp. 138–39.

44. See Reginald S. Sheehan and Donald R. Songer, "Parties Before the Courts of Appeals in the 1980s," paper presented to Midwest Political Science Association, 1989; Karen O'Connor and Lee Epstein, "*Amicus Curiae* Participation in U.S. Supreme Court Litigation," *Law & Society Review* 16 (1981–1982): 701–10.

45. Susan Behuniak-Long, "Friendly Fire: *Amici Curiae* and *Webster v. Reproductive Health Services*," *Judicature* 74 (February-March 1991): 261–70.

46. Bradley and Gardner, "Underdogs, Upperdogs," p. 90. For an examination of the types of *amici*, in relation to participation at the review-granting and merits stages, see Gregory A. Caldeira and John R. Wright, "*Amici Curiae* Before the Supreme Court: Who Participates, When, and How Much?" *Journal of Politics* 52 (August 1990): 782–806.

47. See *NAACP v. Button*, 371 U.S. 415 (1963), and *In re Primus*, 436 U.S. 412 (1978).

48. This material and the remainder of this section is based in part on Stephen L. Wasby, "Interest Groups in Court: Race Relations Litigation," *Interest Group Politics*, eds. Allan Cigler and Burdett Loomis (Washington, D.C.: CQ Press, 1983), pp. 251–74.

49. Phillip J. Cooper, *Hard Judicial Choices: Federal District Court Judges and State and Local Officials* (New York: Oxford University Press, 1988).

50. See Karen O'Connor and Lee Epstein, "Bridging the Gap Between Congress and the Supreme Court: Interest Groups and the Erosion of the American Rule Governing Awards of Attorneys' Fees," *Western Political Quarterly* 38 (June 1985): 238–49.

51. *Hensley v. Eckerhart*, 461 U.S. 424 (1983); *City of Riverside v. Rivera*, 477 U.S. 561 (1986). See also *Pennsylvania v. Delaware Valley Citizens' Council for Clean Air*, 478 U.S. 546 (1986).

52. In addition to Wasby, "Interest Groups in Court: Race Relations Litigation," see also Wasby, "How Planned Is 'Planned' Litigation?", *American Bar Foundation Research Journal* 1984 (Winter): 83–138; "The Multi-Faceted Elephant: Litigator Perspectives on Planned Litigation for Social Change," *Capital University Law Review* 15 (Winter 1986): 143–89; and "Civil Rights Litigation by Organizations: Constraints and Choices," *Judicature* 68 (April-May 1985): 337–52.

53. Jeanne Hahn, "The NAACP Legal Defense and Educational Fund: Its Judicial Strategy and Tactics," in Stephen L. Wasby, *American Government and Politics* (New York: Scribner's, 1973), p. 396.

54. For an examination of interest group litigation in the field, see Edward V. Heck and Joseph Stewart, Jr., "Ensuring Access to Justice: The Role of Interest Group Lawyers in the 60's Campaign for Civil Rights," *Judicature* 66 (August 1982): 84–95; and Stewart and Heck, "The Day-to-Day Activities of Interest Group Lawyers," *Social Science Quarterly* 64 (March 1983): 173–82.

55. Scheingold, *The Politics of Rights*, p. 5.

56. See Irons, *The New Deal Lawyers*, pp. 4–5. Irons portrays litigation differences between the Agricultural Adjustment Administration, the National Industrial Recovery Administration, and the National Labor Relations Board.

57. O'Connor, *Women's Organizations*, p. 117.

58. See Stephen C. Halpern, "Assessing the Litigative Role of ACLU Chapters," *Civil Liberties: Policy and Policy Making*, ed. Stephen L. Wasby (Lexington, Mass.: Lexington Books, 1976), pp. 159–68, for a criticism of group strategy.

59. See Deborah L. Rhode, "Class Conflicts in Class Actions," *Stanford Law Review* 34 (July 1982): 1183–1261.

60. *Warth v. Seldin*, 422 U.S. 490 (1975). See Michael N. Danielson, *The Politics of Exclusion* (New York: Columbia University Press, 1976), p. 318; and Geoffrey Shields and Sanford Spector, "Opening Up the Suburbs: Notes on a Movement for Social Change," *Yale Review of Law and Social Action* 2 (Summer 1972): 310.

61. Clement E. Vose, *Constitutional Change: Amendment Politics and Supreme Court Litigation Since 1900* (Lexington, Mass.: Lexington Books, 1972), p. 321.

62. Sorauf, *Wall of Separation*, p. 82. See also Vose, *Caucasians Only*, pp. 58, 151; Meltsner, *Cruel and Unusual*, pp. 114, 238–39.

5   Getting into Court

VERY FEW CASES FILED in federal or state trial courts ever get to the United States Supreme Court, even in the form of a request for review. Most cases that are filed do not proceed to trial. Many are not pursued, a great many civil cases are settled before trial, and most criminal cases end with a dismissal or a guilty plea. Of those cases that reach the trial stage, most never proceed further. Of the relatively small proportion taken to the first appellate level, few are pursued beyond that point. State cases that do move further are first appealed through the state court system. And most taken to the Supreme Court are denied review, like most federal appeals.

In this chapter, we examine the rules the Supreme Court has developed concerning access to the courts and its doctrines concerning relations between federal and state courts. The Court's requirements on access mean that not everyone can get into court to pursue certain issues. Some people with complaints that they wish judges to decide may not be able to satisfy necessary procedural requirements. Because all must take care to assure that the rules are satisfied, particular plaintiffs may have to be chosen for cases or the issues shaped in a certain way.

Access to the Courts

The formal paths along which cases move are clearly delineated (see Figures 2.1 and 5.1). However, before cases may be moved along those paths, requirements concerning which cases can be brought to court must be satisfied. Congress creates some of these rules in statutes establishing procedural rules, such as those on how appeals should be processed, and providing *causes of action*, the substantive legal claims that are the basis of lawsuits. Cases on whether, in the absence of explicit language, Congress intended to allow private citizens to sue to enforce antidiscrimination statutes that provided other remedies, have resulted from Congress's failure to make its intent clear and have seriously divided the Court in recent years.[1] (The Court also established direct constitutional causes of action for certain civil rights claims, against federal agents for improper searches or inadequate medical treatment, and against members of Congress, under the Fourth, Fifth, and Eighth Amendments.[2])

The Supreme Court, through its decisions, also sets many rules on access to the federal courts. If the Court is restrictive in those rulings in granting access, major claims may never reach the lower federal courts, much less the Supreme Court itself. The Supreme Court cannot tell state courts which cases to hear, but it is not bound to accept appeals from state courts unless its own access requirements have been met. Thus an individual who initiated a state case under state rules, but who could not have done so under federal rules, cannot bring the case to the Supreme Court: the Supreme Court will apply the federal rules in deciding whether or not to grant review to such a person. (However, the defendant who loses such a case may be able to obtain review because the state court ruling creates the injury necessary for the losing defendant to satisfy the federal rules.[3])

The Court has also affected access to the federal courts by developing rules intended to keep cases in the state systems. These affect litigants' ability to challenge the actions of state and local legislators and administrators. They ensure that cases are given complete treatment there before being brought to the federal courts, and that once claims are in federal court, review of state court decisions is limited. Included are rules on who should decide issues when federal and state judges have concurrent jurisdiction. Among the rules are those covering use of habeas corpus petitions in federal courts to challenge state convictions, federal courts' authority to issue declaratory judgments and injunctions against state laws, and removal (transfer) of cases from state to federal court.

Many rules on access to the courts revolve around the stipulation in Article III that courts deal with "cases" or "controversies." This is a corollary of the idea that courts are legal institutions operating with a specific set of procedures. Rules on access to the courts are of broad importance and central to the courts' powers in our political system, and should not be dismissed as "narrow technicalities." Before deciding a case "on the merits," that is, before turning to substantive issues such as "Did John Jones discriminate against Sally Smith in considering her employment application?", "Did the Giant Corporation attempt to monopolize the business in its field?" or "Did the government prove that the Porn Corporation transported obscene materials in interstate commerce?", a judge must be satisfied that a number of procedural prerequisites have been met. Indeed, if the prerequisites are not satisfied, the case is ended by procedural considerations without the merits being reached.

Many procedural prerequisites fall into three interrelated categories. They are

- *jurisdiction*, a court's *authority* to hear a case;
- *standing*, whether the right *person* is bringing a case; and
- *justiciability*, whether a *case* is appropriate for judges to hear, which includes the requirements that the parties to a case be adverse to each other and not have manufactured a case to get into court; that the court not be asked for an *advisory opinion*; that the case be both *ripe* (ready for judgment) and not *moot* (the controversy concluded); and that it not entail a *political question* (something to be decided by the other branches).

It is relatively easy to challenge restrictions imposed on an individual. For example, as a defense to a criminal charge, one may question the validity of the law under which the charge has been brought. Thus the arrest or indictment of an individual often allows the person to challenge laws on which that action has been based, but the Supreme Court has recently imposed restrictions on who may challenge an allegedly improper search (see page 172). However, prior to the law's enforcement against that person, if someone wishes to challenge a law and to obtain a *declaratory judgment*, a declaration of legal rights, questions arise on access to the courts. When actions for declaratory judgments and injunctions are filed against government officials for violations of civil rights, such as improperly institutionalizing the mentally retarded, "double-celling" prisoners, or engaging in police brutality, they are brought under 42 U.S.C. §1983 (Section 1983 of Title 42 of the United States Code). Questions concerning access to the courts arise frequently in such "1983 actions" and are at the heart of much Supreme Court activity on the topic.

> Every person who, under color of any statute, ordinance, regulation, custom, or usage, of any State or Territory, subjects, or causes to be subjected, any citizen of the United States or other person within the jurisdiction thereof to the deprivation of any rights, privileges, or immunities secured by the Constitution and laws shall be liable to the party injured in an action at law, suit in equity, or other proper proceeding for redress. (42 U.S.C. §1983)

The Burger Court increased access to federal court for those proceeding against local governments and local officials, but restricted access in other ways. State courts' authority was strengthened by limits on use of the federal courts to decide issues pending in the state courts, and through restrictions on state prisoners' access to federal courts for review of their convictions. These limits were significantly reinforced by the Rehnquist Court. In becoming considerably more restrictive concerning a number of important aspects of access, the justices forced the judicial process toward a more traditional model of our adversary legal system as part of which access rules were initially developed, and toward a more limited role for the courts in our system's separation of powers arrangement, in which they could not easily intervene almost at will in important policy questions.[4] Strong parallels between the Court's access doctrines, for example, those excluding the poor and disadvantaged from the benefits of certain constitutional provisions, and its lessened support for civil liberties/civil rights claims, led dissenters to complain that the Court majority, although talking about access considerations, really based their rulings on the underlying substantive claims.

At times, the justices have treated access rules flexibly to allow them to accept important questions or to reach particular results. The Burger Court majority interpreted the rules on mootness (see pages 176–77) loosely in cases on durational residence requirements for a divorce (where the woman seeking a divorce had already obtained one) and on affirmative action consent decrees (where laid-off workers had been reinstated), and reached a conservative result in those cases (upholding the residence requirement, ruling against layoffs affecting whites negatively). The liberals took a narrower view of mootness, dissenting in those cases, not surprisingly parallel to *their* result preferences.[5] However, before jumping to the conclusion that the Court's rulings on access are mostly a cover for the justices' ideology, we should remember that several other elements might underlie access rulings. They might limit access because of legal or jurisprudential concerns, a belief in courts' limited role, an aspect of judicial self-restraint; or they might do so for reasons more directly "political"—to "evade certain policy choices and [to] indirectly legitimize preferred policy choices made elsewhere"; or they might want to limit access to facilitate the handling of increasing caseload, an administrative concern."[6]

None of these reasons served to explain access rulings for the Court as a whole, in the 1960–75 Terms. However, in varying ways they influenced individual justices, few of whom have been consistent in the direction of their access voting over longer periods. The Court's rulings were partly "a function of an underlying attitude toward access *per se*"—a combination of administrative and legal concerns about proper party and proper forum (court)—and partly a function of attitudes about substantive issues ("political" considerations).[7] Four justices' (including Rehnquist's) access votes were predominantly affected by administrative and legal concerns; two, Brennan and Douglas, were affected predominantly by political concerns; and three, including Chief Justice Burger, showed no dominance of either set of concerns. Three of the four Nixon appointees (Burger, Rehnquist, and Powell), although with differing motivations, were "willing (and ostensibly anxious) to close access," and three justices (Brennan, Douglas, and Marshall, the Warren Court's liberals) were "generally willing . . . to open access," while the remaining three leaned toward closing off access.[8]

Jurisdiction

Jurisdiction is the power of courts to hear a case, that is, their legal authority to do so. Rules of jurisdiction are found either in the Constitution—for example, the Supreme Court's original jurisdiction is stated in Article III—or in statutes. Most detailed matters of jurisdiction are spelled out in the latter. Judges consider matters of jurisdiction so important that they will raise questions of jurisdiction on their own (*sua sponte*) even if the parties have not done so.[9] Yet we must be careful not to assume that the rules on jurisdiction are always clear or that they point in only one direction. "Like other procedural principles, jurisdictional rules may be manipulated to the strategic advantage of private parties and their lawyers"[10]—and to the judges' advantage as well. The rules may be unclear, may be diffuse or "elastic," or may be contradictory (rules, with counterrules, with exceptions). This gives the user, whether lawyer or judge, much flexibility.[11]

Jurisdiction has a number of components—concerning geography, level of court, subject matter, federalism, the parties to a case, timeliness, and the dollar amount at issue. The first, or horizontal aspect, concerns the question, "Which trial court has jurisdiction to hear a particular case?" An example of a question of jurisdiction is whether a person claiming to have been libeled may sue the publisher not where she lives but in another state where the magazine carrying the alleged libel circulated (Yes).[12] A court may have exclusive jurisdiction, that is, a case can be brought only there, true of the Court of Appeals for the District of Columbia for appeals from some administrative agency rulings. In other instances, there are alternate locations in which a case can be brought, for example, where the plaintiff resides or at the site of the headquarters of the agency being sued. The Court recently had to decide whether a federal district court or the Claims Court had jurisdiction to review certain actions of the Secretary of Health and Human Services concerning Medicaid reimbursements (the district court).[13] And after the Federal Circuit was given jurisdiction over all patent appeals, certain questions remained whether the other courts of appeals had jurisdiction over certain patent-related cases, with the Supreme Court having to decide one dispute in which a case had been shunted back and forth between the Federal Circuit and the Seventh Circuit.[14]

Jurisdiction is closely related to *venue*, concerning the proper location for a case when a particular type of court has authority over the particular type of case. The Bill of Rights even specifies venue in criminal trials: "In all criminal prosecutions, the accused shall enjoy the right to a speedy trial, by an impartial jury of the State and district wherein the crime shall have been committed, which district shall have been previously ascertained by law . . ."(Sixth Amendment).

Another element of jurisdiction is a vertical one—which level of court is appropriate. For example, felonies must be tried in district court, but certain lesser offenses can be tried before magistrate judges (see pages 48–49). The libel example illustrates another aspect of jurisdiction—its chronological element. The plaintiff had sued in the only state where the *statute of limitations* still permitted the suit. At times the question is what statute of limitations Congress meant to adopt for the statutory rights it had created, for example, under the antidiscrimination laws. (The answer is state statutes of limitations, but then the question becomes, "*Which* state statute of limitations?"). At other times, the question is "When did the period under the statute of limitations start to run?"— for example, from when a patient realizes a connection between an injury and a doctor's action, or whether the patient knows that action may have been medical malpractice (the former).[15]

Courts must also have jurisdiction of the subject matter of a case, as specified by Article III and, within Article III's limits, congressional statutes. For example, appeals in all patent cases must now go to the Court of Appeals for the Federal Circuit. Courts must also have personal jurisdiction over the individuals who bring the lawsuit and especially those against whom it is brought—a matter of due process. An instance of subject-matter jurisdiction comes from the struggle, in the federal courts' early years, to work out their jurisdiction. Federal courts have only the jurisdiction Congress gives them, and Congress has not given them all the jurisdiction the Constitution would allow. This makes them, despite the wide range of cases they can hear, in a sense courts of limited jurisdiction. A particular problem was whether there was a common law of crimes (see page 42). Supreme Court justices were intimately involved in the process of deciding this issue while deciding cases on circuit before the Supreme Court clearly decided in 1812 against a federal common law of crimes.[16]

The federalism aspect of jurisdiction concerns whether a case is properly brought initially in a state or federal court. Many cases could be brought in either. This indicates that "federal courts have never been primarily tribunals vested with an exclusive special subject matter jurisdiction,"[17] although there are certain federal statutory claims that have no "match" in state law and certain crimes triable only in federal court. (Recently, there has been a trend toward having many drug cases tried in federal court even though they could be prosecuted in state court, and members of Congress have added to federal court jurisdiction drug and gun cases that previously were tried only in state court.) One important category of cases that can be brought in either federal or state court are those involving citizens of different states (*diversity of citizenship* cases) (see pages 182–83); they can be brought in federal court, however, only if at least $50,000 is at issue. A jurisdictional dollar amount, a statutory requirement, was also applied to "federal question" jurisdiction until 1980, when Congress felt that the federal courts should be more open for rulings on federal law.

Sovereign Immunity. Another hurdle to be overcome, related to jurisdiction, is whether one is allowed to sue the entity one blames for one's injury, for example, a governmental unit or official. If someone is immune from suit, the court cannot hear the case, although it will have to rule on whether that person is indeed entitled to immunity. Under the doctrine of sovereign immunity, a government may not be sued without its consent. Sovereign immunity does seem to be antidemocratic in that it appears to put government above the law. One rationale for the immunity is that it allows government to function without having its decisionmakers constantly defending their actions in court, or at least without worrying about having to pay damages for erroneous decisions. Because the government must defend against declaratory judgment and injunction actions, its officials don't stay out of court, and individual officials may find themselves liable for damages even if the government as such is not. Federal court suits (under 42 U.S.C. §1983) seeking declaratory judgments and injunctions against a state for violating personal constitutional rights, such as freedom of speech or the right to associate or property rights, and federal statutes such as the Social Security Act are permissible because they are aimed at *officials* rather than the state itself and are not suits for damages from the state.

The federal courts have had to rule on the extent to which the federal government gave up its sovereign immunity in the Federal Tort Claims Act. The *Feres* doctrine, banning suits by members of the armed services for injuries incurred while in the military, has been particularly controversial because it has been applied to a wide range of situations extending well beyond the battlefield. And it has also been extended to military contractors: "an independent contractor performing its obligation under a procurement contract" involves "the same interest in getting the Government's work done" as does "an official performing his duty as a federal employee."[18]

Passage of the Foreign Sovereign Immunity Act of 1976, which gives U.S. courts jurisdiction over claims stemming from foreign governments' commercial activity, also forces the courts to deal with foreign governments' sovereign immunity as well as with whether the acts in the complaint result from commercial activity and there is a connection (a "jurisdictional nexus") between those business dealings and the acts that are the basis for plaintiff's lawsuit.

The Supreme Court has often been asked to decide whether federal courts may hear lawsuits against states, local governments, and their officials, or whether such suits are barred by the Eleventh Amendment. That amendment, ratified in 1798 to overturn an early Supreme Court ruling, prevents suits against a state by citizens of another state. However, the Court has said it also embodies sovereign immunity, so that a state may not be sued by *its own* citizens without the state's consent,[19] and has continued to apply it to bar a variety of claims. Perhaps most important, the amendment is said to bar suits for payments of refunds, like welfare benefits, that the state has improperly withheld.[20] The Court has also ruled that a state, by accepting funds under a federal statute, did not waive its immunity,[21] but Congress then amended the Rehabilitation Act to eliminate the states' Eleventh Amendment immunity under that law. The Court, however, has ruled that congressional action enforcing the Fourteenth Amendment may remove a state's immunity. In 1978 the Court overturned a 17-year-old decision (*Monroe v. Pape*) and said in *Monell* that local governments may be sued for actions implementing official policy statements,[22] but in the *City of Newport* case (1981), the Court was unwilling to allow an award of punitive damages when municipalities violated people's rights—for example, by canceling a concert by the rock group Blood, Sweat, and Tears. State officials sued in their official capacity are not "persons" subject to liability under §1983, but they are subject to suit under that statute in their "persons."[23]

The Court has also removed at least some of state and local officials' legal immunity for actions violating people's constitutional rights, thus making them personally liable for damages. In *Scheuer v. Rhodes* (1976), stemming from National Guard killings of students at Kent State University in 1970, the Court ruled that state officials' immunity from suit was removed if they violated the U.S. Constitution, but high-level officials received what amounts to executive immunity; the higher an official's position, the more discretion the official is allowed. The Court also said in *Wood v. Strickland* (1975) that superintendents, principals, and school board members would be personally liable if they maliciously or knowingly violated students' rights or did so when they should have known they were doing so.

However, the Court has closed off damage suits against those connected with law enforcement and the courts. Beyond granting judges absolute immunity from suit (see page 4), the Court also granted state prosecutors absolute immunity from civil rights suits for actions at probable cause hearings and at trials, when they were said to use false evidence and to suppress material evidence, and to police officers serving as witnesses who supposedly gave false testimony at trials, so they would not have to spend their time defending lawsuits instead of carrying out assigned duties, but prosecutors were not absolutely immune for legal advice given to police.[24]

Standing

To bring a case, a person must have *standing*, that is, must be a proper party. If no one has standing, the court lacks jurisdiction to hear a case. This leaves the possibility that unconstitutional laws will remain on the books because no one is in a proper legal position to challenge them. Some rules on standing are found in statutes. For example, in passing the law establishing the National Railroad Passenger Corporation (Amtrak), Congress provided that the attorney general should enforce its provisions. The Court said this meant that a railroad passenger group was barred from protesting passenger train discontinuances. The Court similarly limited the ability of trade associations and political action committees (PACs) to invoke Federal Election Campaign Act procedures and restricted the standing of a party national committee to challenge certain election expenditures. An example of expansive interpretation of statutory grants of standing was the Court's ruling that under Congress's open housing legislation, white tenants of an apartment complex have standing to complain about discrimination against blacks.[25]

Most rules on standing are judge-made. As with any judge-made rules on access to the courts, this allows flexibility and makes it more likely that justices' ideologies will affect those procedural rules. The basic rule on standing is that the litigant must show real or potential personal injury or have a personal stake in the outcome. Thus a doctor could not challenge anticontraceptive statutes solely on the basis that they would injure his patients.[26] But at times the rights of others may be asserted to reinforce one's own claim, particularly where there are obstacles to others' asserting their own rights and where the party in court would assert those rights effectively. Thus a white woman, sued for damages for selling her house to blacks in violation of restrictive covenants, was granted standing to assert blacks' rights to purchase housing; whites have been allowed to challenge the exclusion of blacks from juries and men to challenge the exclusion of women; and doctors seeking to recover payment for abortions were allowed to assert the rights of Medicaid patients who wished abortions.[27] The Court was not, however, willing to grant standing to a physician who had entered an abortion case as an intervenor seeking to protect the unborn, nor to a Death Row inmate to challenge the death penalty imposed on another individual who had given up his right to appeal.[28]

The Court has also limited standing to challenge allegedly improper searches. The Warren Court had ruled in the *Alderman* case that suppression of evidence could be urged only by those whose rights were violated by a search, not those against whom evidence is used. The Burger Court built on that by saying that violations of Fourth Amendment search and seizure standards could not be questioned by those who did not own a car that had been searched or its contents or who did not have an expectation of privacy in those parts of the car that were searched (*Rakas v. Illinois*, 1978). The justices promptly extended that ruling to noncar searches, overturning a Warren Court ruling in the process.[29] These rulings are related to the exclusionary rule (see page 12), which the Burger Court majority disliked: if fewer people had standing to challenge searches, the exclusionary rule would be applied less often.

During the late 1960s the Court relaxed the rules on standing. The Court expanded the scope of those "injured," recognizing in *Sierra Club v. Morton* that injury to "aesthetic and environmental well-being" was among interests that could provide a basis for standing. To obtain standing, a group would have to do more than state a general interest in the environment; its members would have to claim injury from the environmentally adverse action—a requirement later tightened by the Rehnquist Court.[30] (The Court has regularly allowed groups to sue on behalf of their own members.)

Prior to 1968, federal taxpayers could not use their taxpayer status to establish standing to sue the government for using money for an unconstitutional project, because there was little to distinguish taxpayer complaints from general citizen grievances, which are not an adequate basis for standing. But in 1968 the Court ruled, in a case brought to test provisions of the 1965 Elementary and Secondary Education Act (ESEA) for assistance to parochial schools, that a federal taxpayer could have standing to sue the government if the challenged program were alleged to violate a specific constitutional prohibition, such as the First Amendment's "establishment of religion" clause (*Flast v. Cohen*, 1968). In

1982, however, in a ruling indicative of the Burger Court's narrower view of who should be able to raise issues in the courts, the Court refused standing to an organization challenging a free transfer of government property to a religious organization, saying there was no personal injury.[31] This echoed an earlier Burger Court ruling refusing standing to a taxpayer trying to force compliance with the Statements and Accounts Clause (Art. I, Sec. 9, cl. 7) of the Constitution because Congress had failed to require the Central Intelligence Agency (CIA) to produce detailed reports of its expenditures; such claims, Justice Powell said, should be brought to Congress, not the courts. Chief Justice Burger added that taxpayers could not use federal courts for general grievances.[32]

The Burger Court's restrained view of standing was perhaps clearest in civil rights cases. Here the Court made it difficult to challenge police and judicial practices, requiring both a showing of likely future injury and a connection between the challenged act and the injury. The Court denied standing to both whites and blacks in Cairo, Illinois, the site of serious racial conflict, when they sued to obtain relief from racially discriminatory judicial bonding and sentencing practices, because the plaintiffs had not shown either that they had already been injured or that they could suffer continuing injury from the practices. This case, O'Shea v. Littleton (1973), showed that multiple aspects of access doctrine may appear in the same case; the Court's ruling was also based on the view that the federal judiciary should not regularly supervise state judges. In a similar ruling (Rizzo v. Goode, 1976), the Court said complainants lacked standing to bring about an overhauling of police disciplinary procedures because their claims of improper police practices against minorities and mishandling of complaints rested on what a small, unnamed minority of officers might do in the future and on incidents that *might* happen to others *if* the police procedures were not changed. The Court went even further in City of Los Angeles v. Lyons (1983): a plaintiff who had been subjected to a police "chokehold" after being stopped for a traffic violation and who feared a recurrence of such police action was denied standing to enjoin police use of chokeholds because the Court said he did not face a real or immediate threat of recurrence nor had he shown the city authorized routine use of chokeholds.

In another civil rights area, access to housing, the Court in Warth v. Seldin (1975) used rules on standing to turn aside all plaintiffs—low- and moderate-income minority residents of a city, a nonprofit corporation trying to alleviate their housing shortage, central city taxpayers, and a homebuilders' association— trying to attack restrictive and exclusionary suburban zoning ordinances. To sue, they would have to indicate specifically both how the challenged ordinances would harm them and how judges could protect their rights. That the majority's position was in part based on the merits can be seen in Justice Powell's comment that "the economics of the housing market," not the ordinances, prevented plaintiffs' move to the suburbs. Despite this ruling, it proved possible to challenge exclusionary zoning ordinances, at least when a specific rezoning request had been turned down—although the Court then found no intentional racial discrimination.[33]

Justiciability

Rules on justiciability—the question of cases appropriate for judges to hear—are, like rules on standing, judge-made; they are even more flexible than the rules on standing. The concept of justiciability includes norms against issuing advisory opinions or deciding feigned controversies, moot or unripe cases, or "political questions." There are also cases that fit in none of these categories, as when the Court ruled challenges by Kent State University student government officers to Ohio National Guard riot control rules nonjusticiable because the requested remedy would engage federal judges in constant review of the executive branch, charged with supervising the Guard (*Gilligan v. Morgan*, 1973).

All the categories but that of "political questions" are based on a fundamental rule, settled early in the Court's history, that the Supreme Court will not issue opinions on abstract legal questions but will decide questions of law only when they are presented in the fact context of a particular lawsuit. This basic principle was stated in the course of deciding that the Court would not issue formal advisory opinions. However, it extends to situations such as cases without adverse parties, cases that are not ripe, and cases that are moot, where the question would be abstract and the result would be the equivalent of an advisory opinion. The judge would not receive adequate information nor would the law be given its operative meaning through facts about the law's application. A law might appear to be constitutional "on its face" but be applied in an improper manner, or a law of dubious validity may have been applied—or interpreted by the lower courts—so as to preserve its constitutionality. This is why judges are reluctant to grant declaratory judgments: prosecution after a violation will bring out fuller sets of facts on the statutes' operation. However, increased decision of cases on summary judgments—cases decided on the pleadings and affidavits—somewhat undercuts this idea.

Advisory Opinions. Narrowly defined, an *advisory opinion* is an opinion given by judges to the legislature or executive about a proposed bill or action. Some state high courts do issue such opinions. However, when President Washington asked the Court for advice on some treaty questions, the justices of the U.S. Supreme Court firmly established a rule against the justices giving advisory opinions. They responded through Chief Justice Jay that they would not do so. Early in the present century, the Court amplified the rule. Congress had passed a law allowing the Cherokee Indians to file suit to test a statute, but in *Muskrat v. United States* the Court said that Congress was seeking a ruling on the law's constitutionality without the presence of a live controversy, therefore in effect asking for an advisory opinion, and the justices would not allow the case to be heard. Because the Court, as the nation's highest tribunal, decides cases intended to be representative of large issues and thus decides more than the particulars of the dispute between the immediate parties, the justices are expected to issue opinions with a reach broader than the facts of the specific case being decided, and thus may make advisory comments.

Some informal exceptions to the ban on advisory opinions have also occurred. In 1822 President Monroe asked several members of the Court about the legality of federal "internal improvements." Justice William Johnson made a general if oblique reply for himself and several other justices, indicating their position that governmental construction of military roads and post roads was constitutional. Certainly Chief Justice Hughes's comment on behalf of the Court about Roosevelt's Court-packing proposal—that the "one Supreme Court" called for by the Constitution could not sit in divisions—could be called an advisory opinion. At other times, individual justices have provided the president with legal advice and have helped draw up legislation, as Justice Frankfurter did for President Franklin Roosevelt and Justice Fortas did for President Lyndon Johnson.

In the course of deciding cases, justices also provide informal advisory opinions when they comment on matters on which the Court is not ruling or give suggestions to the other branches about how to deal with problems. Thus, in striking down a statute regulating a part of the economy, justices have suggested how Congress could deal with the problem by relying on another constitutional clause. More recently, justices have suggested that a statute amending the Voting Rights Act to outlaw at-large municipal elections would be valid and that a statutory revision allowing noncommercial educational broadcasting stations to have affiliates that would editorialize would also pass muster.[34]

Whenever the Court goes beyond the specific facts of a case to anticipate general questions of policy not yet directly presented to it, it can be said to be issuing an advisory opinion, and some other members of the Court are likely to complain. Justices are more likely to make statements of this sort when they write concurring or dissenting opinions than when they write the "opinion of the Court." When the author of the Court's majority opinion does make comments not necessary for the Court's ruling, the statements are called *obiter dictum* (plural: *dicta*), that is, language beyond the *holding* or basic rule of the case—"something mentioned in passing, which is not in any way necessary to the decision of the issue before the Court."[35] Although speculation about hypothetical situations not before the Court is clearly *obiter*, often it is difficult to tell what is *obiter* and what is not, and, in later cases, justices may disagree over what was part of a Court's earlier holding and what was *obiter*.

Feigned Controversies. As part of its effort to have the federal courts avoid handing down advisory opinions, the Court insists that litigation not be made up simply to obtain a ruling on some matter that the parties would like to see settled, particularly to the detriment of a third party not involved in a case. Thus the parties in a case must be adverse to each other. This rule against feigned controversies is aimed at collusive litigation. It does not mean that the litigants have to be "at each other's throats" but only that their interests be opposed; in short, not all "friendly suits" are barred, but the parties cannot be *too* friendly, or cannot bring a suit to exclude the presentation of their real opponents' views.

Nonetheless, there have been efforts to get into court with collusive cases from time to time. An example of the courts *not* throwing out a case as a "feigned controversy" is *Carter v. Carter Coal Co.* (1936), in which the president of a company sued his own company to prevent compliance with the Guffey Bituminous Coal Act. Both sides had lawyers who made strong arguments in the Supreme Court, but the common interest of both parties in getting the law invalidated should have been clear. The possibility of the same problem arose in *Nixon v. Fitzgerald*, on the president's immunity from suit (see page 000), because of a "side payment" from Nixon to Fitzgerald contingent on the outcome, but the Court decided the case nonetheless.

Under the rules existing at the time of *Carter*, the United States—whose statute was at issue—was not a party to the case and was thus at a disadvantage in trying to argue the statute's validity. Because of that situation—in which the Court *did* invalidate the statute—Congress promptly passed legislation that made the United States a party whenever the constitutionality of a federal statute is brought in issue in a case in which the United States is not initially a party. This provision was used in the *Northern Pipeline* bankruptcy case (see page 50) and in an earlier challenge to a union's political expenditures, where the government had not been involved in the lower court but did argue in the Supreme Court after the case was delayed to allow it to do so.[36] States now have the right to become a party to cases in which their laws are being challenged, a parallel to the federal government's right to intervene.

Mootness and Ripeness. Another aspect of the "case or controversy" requirement is that a case not be moot, that is, that a dispute not be completed or that it not be too late for judges to apply a remedy. The rule has, however, not always been interpreted strictly. Prisoners' challenges to their convictions were also made easier when the Court ruled that a prisoner's habeas corpus challenge to a conviction was not mooted by release from prison, because disability resulting from the conviction remained. However, if prisoners were only attacking *sentences* and those sentences expired before a court decided the case, the matter would be moot.[37]

When the government made it difficult to challenge its actions either by voluntarily eliminating a questioned rule in the face of a lawsuit while retaining the option of reinstating the rule or by issuing orders of brief duration, each of which would expire before a court challenge could be made, the Court has been willing to hear cases. The Court has changed its basic direction on mootness to make it easier for courts to decide issues that were likely to recur. Under traditional mootness rules, challenges to election rules, particularly those excluding candidates, were usually moot before they reached the appellate courts because the election had already taken place. However, because the issue involved in the challenge would recur in a subsequent election, when it might again become moot on appeal, the Supreme Court began to rule on some election cases even after the election had passed.[38]

This relaxed interpretation of mootness was applied in the Court's 1973 abortion cases, *Roe v. Wade* and *Doe v. Bolton.* Justice Blackmun, noting that pregnancy was likely to recur, both for the woman challenging antiabortion laws and for other women as well, ruled that, because it was "capable of repetition yet evading review," it was not subject to traditional rules of mootness, under which questions related to pregnancy could never be reviewed on appeal because the pregnancy would be completed. Generally, however, the Court requires that a case be "live" (not moot) when it is filed and that it remain alive through the Supreme Court's proceedings. At times this has forced the Court to search for signs of nonmootness.[39]

A case also cannot be *premature* or *unripe* if judges are to decide it. Ripeness, like mootness, is related to standing. Someone bringing a case that is not ripe lacks standing. Similarly, someone without a definite injury lacks standing because the matter is speculative and thus unripe. For example, because only a subjective "chill" to First Amendment rights, not actual injury, resulted from Army surveillance of civilian political activity, the Court—in *Laird v. Tatum* (1972)—ruled a challenge to that activity not ripe. There are few clear rules concerning ripeness. Its contours are established on a case-by-case basis. For example, the Court held a challenge to anticontraceptive laws not ripe because, although a prosecutor said he would prosecute those violating the law, contraceptives were widely available and there had been no such prosecution for 20 years; thus a declaration of people's rights was not necessary, said the majority. When a doctor opened a birth control clinic, he was arrested, clearly giving him standing to challenge the law and making the matter one of some immediacy, and the Court then invalidated the law.[40]

An important element of the rules on ripeness is that a litigant have previously exhausted available administrative and judicial remedies. The administrative ones should be exhausted before one comes to court, so that the administrative agencies' views on the dispute will be known and so that the dispute might be resolved before ever reaching court. For example, the Court had ruled that challenges to courts-martial cannot be heard by civilian courts until military courts have completed their review, even where the military's jurisdiction to hold the court-martial is the subject of the challenge.[41] The exhaustion doctrine in areas such as welfare may exhaust the individual rather than the remedies. Available judicial remedies should be exhausted before one proceeds to a higher court, to allow the lower courts to play their proper role in the judicial system, leaving appellate courts free to review lower court decisions. One must also make full use of state court remedies before using federal courts to challenge convictions.

"Political Questions." The most ambiguous part of justiciability is the *political question* doctrine. Under it, courts will not decide questions the judges think "belong" to the legislative or executive branches under the Constitution's terms

or would be more appropriately handled there. The doctrine is closely related to judges' perceptions of "activism" and "restraint" (see pages 287–91). When the Court is unwilling to rule on an issue affecting other branches, a restrained posture, the issue may be labeled a "political question," but when the judges are willing to act, the label is missing.

Over the course of its history, the Court has considered a variety of issues to be "political questions." These include whether a state may rescind its ratification of a constitutional amendment, and which of two "regimes" in a particular state was the legitimate one. These were matters that could be dealt with by Congress in determining the ratification of an amendment or the credentials of members of Congress. Others were whether state constitutions may provide for recall of judges and whether or not a president should enforce certain laws—something the justices felt should be left to the executive's discretion.[42]

The Warren Court drastically reduced the "political question" doctrine's earlier content. Although for many years reapportionment had been thought to be a "political question," in 1962 the Court said in *Baker v. Carr* that complaints about malapportioned legislative districts could be heard by the courts. (In 1986, in *Davis v. Bandemer,* the Court went even further by saying that challenges to partisan gerrymanders—purposeful malapportionment to benefit one political party—were justiciable.) The Court also showed itself willing to interfere in previously undisturbed legislative judgments about the qualifications of their own members. In *Bond v. Floyd* the Court overturned the Georgia legislature's refusal to seat Julian Bond because of his antiwar statements and in 1968 ruled that Congress should seat Congressman Adam Clayton Powell (D-N.Y.). The latter ruling, *Powell v. McCormack,* came close to rejecting the "political question" doctrine entirely. When President Nixon claimed that the request for the Watergate tapes was nonjusticiable because it was an "in-house" controversy between president and special prosecutor, the Court in *United States v. Nixon* rejected the claim that there was a "political question" and went on to decide the case (see pages 327–28), just as it did nine years later in overturning the legislative veto.[43]

The political question doctrine is still applied in some situations, almost exclusively involving our relations with foreign nations. The validity of treaties under international law and our recognition of foreign governments are still considered to be "political questions"; thus the courts will not interfere with the executive branch's decisions. The federal courts often used the political question doctrine as the basis for refusing to decide the validity of the Vietnam War under either our own Constitution or international law.[44]

Relations Between Federal and State Courts

Because we have a dual court system, we have a set of problems dealing with the interface between federal and state courts. If we had only one set of courts that applied both state and federal law, these issues would not arise. There are both day-to-day relations between federal and state courts and relations stemming from judicial rulings. With respect to the former, one type of problem stems from prosecutors' actions. An example is drug cases that federal judges believe belong in state court but which have been brought as federal charges, because of crowding in the state courts. They are sometimes prosecuted in federal court by state prosecutors deputized as U.S. attorneys. They add to the increasing number of federal drug cases burdening some districts.

In terms of judicial decisions, friction between federal and state courts has abated substantially since the early years of the Republic, when there was considerable resistance to judicial review of state court rulings (see pages 77–78). Relations are now less difficult, but problems still abound. Examples are conflicts over federal court interpretation of state law and over review of state criminal convictions. At times, as in the 1986 Texaco-Pennzoil case, conflict stems from federal court rulings, prior to completion of state proceedings, that state courts have not adequately protected certain parties' procedural rights. A federal judge's intervention in the proceedings, by significantly reducing the appeal bond required by the Texas courts, was seen as an affront to state judges, and the Supreme Court ruled the judge should have abstained from ruling on Texaco's federal court efforts (*Pennzoil Co. v. Texaco*, 1987).

In a number of states, administrative and policy matters are handled by *federal-state judicial councils*. Most of these were set up after Chief Justice Burger called for them in his 1970 State of the Judiciary message, but many then became inactive. The composition of the councils varies, but usually the chief judge of the federal district court, a resident court of appeals judge, and the state's chief justice are among the members. The councils are primarily mechanisms for exchanges of views, although agreements about how to deal effectively with certain problems may be made. Questions these councils consider include habeas corpus petitions, diversity of citizenship litigation, and transfer of jurisdiction. Administrative matters such as overlapping federal and state jury service and the scheduling of conflicting trial schedules for lawyers have also been dealt with. Some councils have worked out joint judicial hearings—with both a federal judge and a state judge present—for certain special cases.[45]

Friction between state courts and the Supreme Court has resulted when the high court's interpretations of the U.S. Constitution's protection of civil liberties have been at variance with state court interpretations. When the Supreme Court rules that the Constitution *permits* but does not require a certain state practice, such as nonunanimous jury verdicts, the states are at liberty to adopt more rigorous standards (for example, by retaining the requirement of a unanimous jury). However, the justices have said that state courts may not limit state officials' actions to provide greater protection for civil liberties by interpreting the U.S. Constitution differently from the way the Supreme Court has interpreted it. "A State is free *as a matter of its own law* to impose greater restrictions on police activity than those this Court holds to be necessary under federal constitutional standards. . . . But . . . a State may not impose such greater restrictions as a matter of *federal constitutional law* when this Court specifically refrains from imposing them."[46] Such a statement stems from the Supreme Court's views, enunciated in the Little Rock case (see page 78), that not only the Constitution but also the *Supreme Court's interpretation* is the "supreme law of the land."

In 1980, the Supreme Court made good on its promise that state courts could establish greater protection for civil liberties under their state constitutions. The Supreme Court had said only a few years earlier that leafletting in a privately owned shopping center was not protected by the First Amendment. The California Supreme Court then ruled that it had to be allowed under the California Constitution. Writing for a unanimous Court, Justice Rehnquist said that the state court was not prevented from "adopt[ing] in its own Constitution individual liberties more expansive than those conferred by the Federal Constitution."[47] That such a ruling may be made grudgingly is shown by Chief Justice Burger's suggestion in a later case that if state voters don't like state law-based rulings by state judges, they can change that law.[48]

State courts that carefully base their ruling solely on their own constitutions (and statutes) can both avoid Supreme Court review and establish rules different from those the Supreme Court requires under the U.S. Constitution. The Supreme Court seldom used to interfere with state decisions thought to rest on adequate state law grounds, but it has become more difficult for state courts to avoid Supreme Court intervention. The justices have said that unless the state courts make a "clear statement" that their decisions rest on state law, the justices will feel free to treat the state court ruling as based on federal law and thus subject to Supreme Court review.[49] Such a rule resulted in the Court's overturning pro-defendant state court rulings. Although complaining that state judges do not do enough to rest decisions on state law grounds, Justice Stevens has said that the Supreme Court's presuming that it has jurisdiction over state court cases "evidences a lack of respect for state courts and will . . . be a recurrent source of friction between the federal and state judiciaries."[50] The Court has now ruled, however, that when federal courts are considering habeas corpus petitions from state prisoners (see below), they should *not* presume that a state court decision without a "clear statement" is based on federal grounds so as to allow consideration of the habeas petition. Although the Court may seem inconsistent as to when it requires a "clear statement" by state courts as to their use of state law, the result is clearly to defer to state courts and to uphold convictions. (In the case in which it announced the rule, the result was to uphold a death penalty.[51])

Formal relations between federal and state courts, which the Supreme Court interprets, are depicted in Figure 5.1. The Supreme Court has issued a set of decisions delineating relations between federal and state courts. Those concerning habeas corpus and civil rights claims are based on interpretation of federal statutes; others are based on basic conceptions of national court deference to the state judiciary.

Figure 5.1 Relations Between Federal and State Courts

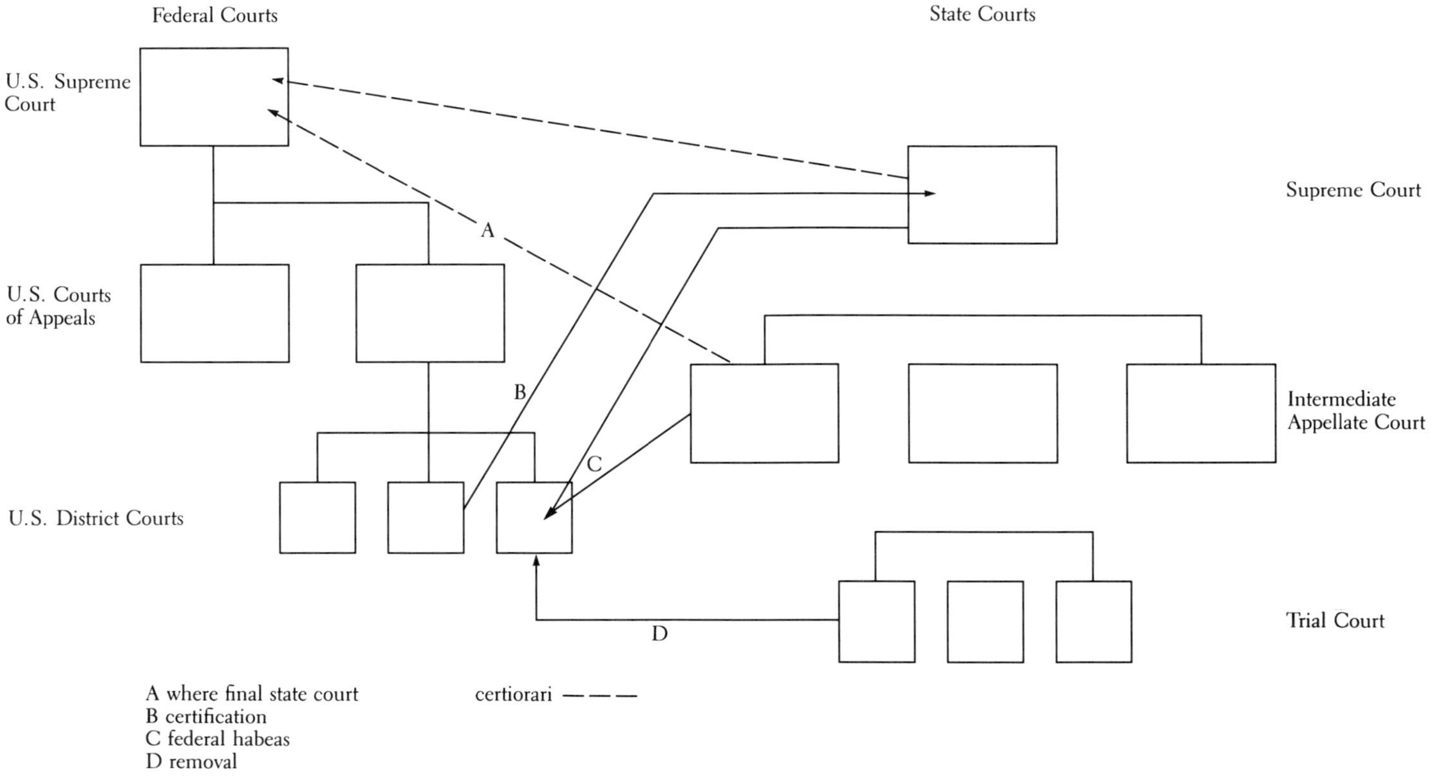

Federal Courts

State Courts

Supreme Court

Intermediate Appellate Court

Trial Court

U.S. Supreme Court

U.S. Courts of Appeals

U.S. District Courts

A
B
C
D

A where final state court
B certification
C federal habeas
D removal

certiorari ------

Diversity and Removal

The basic provisions dealing with diversity of citizenship cases and removal are established by statute. *Diversity of citizenship suits* are those between citizens of one state (including corporations) and those of another. They may be brought in federal court if more than $50,000 is involved. When the amount is not satisfied, a case can still be brought in state court. Federal courts' application of federal rather than state law in such cases has caused substantial friction within the federal system, because it leads to conflicting rules of decision in courts that have concurrent jurisdiction over a matter. In 1842 in *Swift v. Tyson*, the Supreme Court ruled that the federal courts could establish their own common law in diversity cases. The Supreme Court did not reverse itself until 1938. In *Erie Railroad Co. v. Tompkins*, the Court declared that its earlier decision was unconstitutional, that there was no federal common law, and that the federal courts should apply the laws of the states in diversity litigation. This means that federal courts would interpret state law, but the state courts could ignore the federal courts, making their own interpretation of their own laws.

Despite *Erie*, there is still some use of federal common law in other types of cases, such as labor-management disputes. There is also the equivalent of a federal common law of procedure because the federal courts have to have a set of rules as to which state's law to apply when different results would occur ("choice of law" or "conflict of law"), but state law now has much greater authority in diversity suits. Although state substantive law is applied, federal procedural rules—particularly those developed under the Rules Enabling Act (see pages 74–75)—supersede conflicting state procedural rules.[52] This is one reason lawyers prefer federal court; it allows them to work under one set, rather than many sets, of procedural rules.

Federal courts' diversity caseload increased by roughly 50 percent from 1960 to 1976, and increased much further—more than doubling—by 1988. Although the number of diversity cases climbed, they remained relatively constant as a proportion of total federal case filings.[53] Nonetheless they remained a significant proportion of federal judges' caseload, and the workload created by them was said to be equivalent to the total workload of 193 district judges and 22 courts of appeals judges. Chief Justice Burger, along with the Judicial Conference of the United States, suggested eliminating it altogether to reduce federal court caseload. He argued that although diversity was based on the idea that state judges were unfair to out-of-state litigants, that was no longer the case. However, lawyers remain concerned about local favoritism in state courts but not necessarily about a separate bias against corporations. A former attorney general, Griffin Bell, has said he has been "homefried" too often to give up diversity jurisdiction; a state judge has suggested that the increase in the jurisdictional dollar amount will mean that poor people are more likely to be "hometowned" when relegated to the state courts. (Lawyers pick the court, state *or* federal, that will most expeditiously process their cases, and look for judges of high quality, with federal courts given higher ratings.[54])

Another argument is that federal judges have to take considerable time to ascertain (or guess) the state law to apply and have not helped to develop that law. However, others have argued—and many individual federal judges believe—that diversity cases, which present general legal issues like those often heard in state courts, keep federal judges from becoming narrow specialists and have provided them with a broader perspective.[55] Moreover, there is no state mechanism for handling mass tort litigation, which can be consolidated in one federal judicial district through the actions of the Panel on Multi-District Litigation.[56] Another reason for not shifting diversity cases out of the federal courts is that state courts are generally overburdened and state judges would thus not like the additional infusion of cases.[57] However, the Conference of State Chief Justices has argued that federal diversity jurisdiction should be eliminated because it casts intimations of second-class citizenship on the state judiciary. Thus, at both federal and state levels, we see judicial leaders' official positions differing from positions of many individual judges "in the trenches." The Court has tried to impose some limits but Congress, responding to pressure from lawyers and judges and a lack of general public concern, has not yet eliminated diversity jurisdiction, but did raise the threshold from $10,000 to $50,000 in 1989. Preliminary estimates were that about 39 percent of diversity cases filed in federal district court in 1987 would have been left in state court with the new law in effect, but the effect of the new law is said to be more on the amount *claimed* in a case than in the number of cases kept out of federal court.

Diversity jurisdiction and *removal* of cases from state to federal court are related because many diversity cases are started in state courts—where they also can be brought—only to be shifted (removed) to federal court by out-of-state defendants. A recent example of such removal—for the benefit of you sports fans—was the action by the commissioner of baseball to remove Pete Rose's suit against the commissioner from state court (in Cincinnati, where Rose was popular) to federal court (in Columbus). Removal is central to diversity of citizenship jurisdiction but affects other types of cases as well. For example, federal officers may remove cases against them from state court to federal court, and the Resolution Trust Corporation, involved in the savings and loan bailout, may remove state court cases in which it is a litigant to the U.S. District Court for the District of Columbia.

During the 1950s, removal was attempted in another category of cases—those of civil rights workers in the South who argued that they were being arrested and prosecuted in order to harass them. Their efforts to transfer their cases to federal court failed when the Supreme Court, sensitive to the problem of taking cases away from the state courts, took a narrow view of the federal removal statute and allowed removal only when there was a statutorily protected federal right involving racial equality and a state law or rule prevented the protection of rights

in a state trial. An allegation of an unfair trial was an insufficient basis for removal, as errors at trial could be corrected on appeal.[58] (Other limits on removal
are provided by statute, for example, claims under state workmen's compensation
laws and cases under part of the 1933 Securities Act.)

Abstention

Federal judges often apply state law. They do not have to interpret what state
law means when the state law is clear "on its face" or when state courts have
provided a clarifying interpretation (or "gloss"). But for federal judges to decide
the meaning of ambiguous state law not clarified by state courts is considered
inappropriate. Judges have developed the doctrine of *abstention* to avoid federal
court-state court conflict over interpretation of state law. This is part of *comity*—
respect for state courts' ability to decide issues.

Applying abstention, which is one particular way in which federal judges
refrain from deciding cases, federal courts "stay their hand" until state courts
have an opportunity to rule on state law questions, because such state court action might allow federal courts to avoid federal questions or might modify those
questions so that federal court action would be affected. There are several types
of abstention. When there is no state case in progress, the federal court waits
until the plaintiff brings such a case, known as "*Pullman* abstention."[59] When
state proceedings have already started, the federal court waits for the proceeding
to conclude or dismisses the federal case (see below). However, federal courts do
not invariably abstain from deciding cases when state courts may also be involved
in an issue. Justice Brennan has said that abstention was "the exception, not the
rule" because federal courts could not abdicate their duty to decide cases unless
some important countervailing interest was present.[60]

A specific mechanism for prompt state court interpretation of unanswered
state law questions in pending federal cases is for the federal court to *certify* the
questions to the state courts, which then provide an answer the federal court
applies to the case before it. An increasing number of states have provided for
such "downward certification" (different from lower federal courts asking higher
federal courts to answer novel legal questions: see pages 73–74). The Supreme
Court itself has made use of such a mechanism, for example, remanding a death
penalty case to the Georgia Supreme Court for interpretation of that court's opinion.[61] The Supreme Court also returns cases to state courts for rulings on unanswered questions that might provide an "adequate and independent state ground"
to support the state ruling and when it is unclear whether a state court has used
federal law, state law, or both as the basis for a decision, to ascertain whether
there were separate state law grounds for the ruling.

Competing with the preference that state courts decide state law questions is
a preference that all claims in a case be heard by either state or federal courts.
However, the idea is not followed consistently, so the same facts may be heard
simultaneously in federal and state courts, producing duplicative litigation with

potentially inconsistent results. This happens with prisoners' claims embodied in both a habeas corpus petition and a civil rights suit. There is no requirement that state remedies be exhausted in civil rights cases, which can thus move directly to federal court, but the exhaustion rule does apply to habeas claims, taking them back to state courts.[62] At times, the preference for having all claims decided in one court may lead to all claims being decided in federal rather than state courts, the reverse of the result produced by abstention. State matters raised in federal court along with an adequate federal claim may be heard by the federal judge under the doctrine of "pendent jurisdiction." (However, the Court has said that a federal court may not take jurisdiction over a pendent *party* unless Congress has given explicit authority[63]—which Congress then did.) If the federal court then follows normal rules of self-restraint and avoids federal constitutional questions, it may decide the state claim first, thus ironically not resolving the federal questions.

An important issue touching on abstention and comity is whether federal courts should enjoin (prohibit) enforcement of state laws or other action by state officials or should insist that an individual against whom the state has acted use federal claims as a defense in state court, thus assuring that state courts had the first opportunity to rule on such matters and to apply the Constitution. A Warren Court ruling allowing an injunction against state prosecution under a broad statute that infringed freedom of speech, *Dombrowski v. Pfister* (1965), coupled with lower federal court interpretation of the ruling, led to a considerable increase in federal court challenges to state laws; these occurred even where state courts, given a chance, might have enforced federal constitutional rights.

Chief Justice Burger, who felt this practice overused federal courts and denigrated state court authority, was determined to put an end to it. The Court's change of position came when the majority ruled in *Younger v. Harris* (1971) that federal courts were no longer to issue injunctions against already instituted state criminal prosecutions even when the challenged statute was clearly unconstitutional. State court proceedings were to be allowed to continue, except where great and immediate irreparable damage was threatened and that harm could not be prevented by raising the constitutional claims in a later state trial. The Court later extended the *Younger* rule in *Hicks v. Miranda* (1975), ruling that a federal injunction could not be obtained against a prosecution initiated in a state court *after* the federal challenge had been started. This prompted the dissenters to complain that whether you could get an injunction depended on an improper "race to the courthouse" in which the state could start later and get there first. *Younger* was also extended to *civil* proceedings closely related to criminal matters, for example, a state civil nuisance proceeding against a theater showing allegedly obscene movies, and to other matters, both civil and administrative, as well.[64]

If federal court actions against many types of state court actions are barred, state courts also may not prevent the filing of appropriate federal court suits. In 1977 and 1978, the Supreme Court twice had to order a New Mexico judge not to interfere with a litigant's rights to file certain federal cases related to ongoing state litigation concerning obligations under a contract for delivery of uranium in the face of a fivefold price increase.[65]

Federal Habeas Corpus

The most controversial present issue concerning relations between federal courts and state courts is filing of habeas corpus petitions in federal court by those challenging state convictions, often many years after state appeals have concluded. Habeas corpus cases, technically civil cases although they often deal with criminal procedure issues, provide a clear instance of "diachronic or sequential redundancy" in our dual court system; after one level of courts has decided a case, the parties can turn to the other.[66] (After a federal district court denies a habeas corpus petition, the order denying the petition may be reviewed on appeal only if the district judge who examined the petition, a judge of the court of appeals, or the circuit justice issues a certificate of probable cause, which requires a substantial showing that a federal right has been denied.)

Conflict over habeas corpus is not new, and actually was more severe in the past. There was considerable pre-Civil War conflict between federal and state courts over its use when habeas corpus was sought from state courts to free fugitive slaves rather than have them returned to their owners and to release rescuers arrested by federal officials for violating the Fugitive Slave Act. Federal courts used habeas corpus to release federal officers held in contempt of state court for enforcing the law.[67]

Warren Court rulings resulted in a substantial increase in federal habeas corpus petitions challenging state convictions. The Burger Court reduced use of federal habeas challenges to state convictions. Chief Justice Burger said that the lack of finality in criminal cases resulted in considerable extra work for all courts and complained about state prisoners' ability to challenge their convictions repeatedly with multiple, successive habeas filings.[68] These views were put into rulings.

One was that search and seizure claims already reviewed by a state court could not be raised again in federal court (*Stone v. Powell*, 1976). However, the Court was unwilling to extend *Stone v. Powell* to claims that the right to counsel had been improperly denied.[69] The Court has also demanded that deference be given to state court judges when it ruled that, in federal habeas proceedings, state courts' factual determinations must be given a "presumption of correctness" and a federal court overruling such determinations must indicate in writing its basis for doing so.[70]

Another was that a federal habeas petition could not be filed until the specific claim it contained had been brought before the state courts, and that a defendant could not use habeas corpus to challenge aspects of a trial if that issue had not been raised properly in the state proceeding. The petitioner would have to show "cause" for such an omission *and* actual prejudice to rights from the challenged unconstitutional action (the "cause and prejudice" rule[71]) to challenge such state court procedural defaults. The justices also adopted Chief Justice Burger's basic views on successive habeas petitions. They refused to preclude them outright but defined quite narrowly the standard (the "ends of justice") under which they would be allowed.[72]

The Rehnquist Court, in addition to adopting this position on successive habeas petitions, developed a series of rules that made it extremely difficult for a habeas petitioner to benefit from new favorable criminal procedure rules and requiring that matters were to be dealt with at one time rather than in successive petitions. In so doing, the Court overruled *Fay v. Noia*, the 1963 ruling at the heart of the Warren Court's habeas corpus doctrine. Some of the key new decisions came in capital punishment cases and can be seen as part of Chief Justice Rehnquist's desire to shift such cases to the state courts—not as part of an effort to increase protection of rights (as Justice Brennan had sought in urging greater use of state courts) but to limit those rights. The Court ruled that new constitutional criminal procedure rules will not be made retroactive to cover convictions already final and "new law" could not be the basis for a petitioner's habeas claim, so habeas judges may apply only the rules in effect at the time of the conviction. The Court also ruled that to file a second or subsequent habeas petition, the petitioner must satisfy the "cause and prejudice" test for not having raised the issue earlier.[73] The practical effect is that someone convicted in a state proceeding, who has exhausted available state appeals, has only "one shot" in federal habeas court to pursue federal constitutional issues—and then only if they had been raised properly, according to state procedure, in the state case. Later in the 1991 Term, in imposing a tighter standard on those who had failed to develop factual matters in state court proceedings, the Court also overruled another major Warren Court habeas ruling, *Townsend v. Sain* (1963).[74]

These rulings closely paralleled the recommendations of the Powell Study Committee appointed by Chief Justice Rehnquist and an ABA task force; both recommended limits on successive petitions, and limited the time in which habeas petitions could be filed; however, the key was that if states did not provide competent counsel to the defendant to pursue habeas, the possibility of multiple attacks on the conviction would remain. When Congress stopped short of passing a crime bill in late 1991, the bill included a provision limiting the time for filing habeas petitions; President Bush had sought more severe limitations.

Notes

1. See, for example, *Cannon v. University of Chicago*, 441 U.S. 667 (1979).
2. *Bivens v. Six Unknown Federal Narcotics Agents*, 403 U.S. 388 (1971); *Carlson v. Green*, 446 U.S. 14 (1980); *Davis v. Passman*, 442 U.S. 228 (1979).
3. See *Asarco Inc. v. Kadish*, 109 S.Ct. 2037 (1989).
4. See Antonin Scalia, "The Doctrine of Standing as an Element of the Separation of Powers," *Suffolk Law Review* 4 (1984): 881–89.
5. *Sosna v. Iowa*, 419 U.S. 393 (1975); *Firefighters v. Stotts*, 467 U.S. 561 (1984).

6. Gregory J. Rathjen and Harold J. Spaeth, "Access to the Federal Courts: An Analysis of Burger Court Policy Making," *American Journal of Political Science* 23 (May 1979): 366.

7. Ibid., p. 374.

8. Ibid., p. 380. However, another study shows Burger and Blackmun increasing their support for access claims. Burton Atkins and William Taggart, "Substantive Access Doctrines and Conflict Management in the U.S. Supreme Court: Reflections on Activism and Restraint," *Supreme Court Activism and Restraint*, eds. Stephen C. Halpern and Charles Lamb (Lexington, Mass.: Lexington Books, 1982), p. 373.

9. See *Marrese v. American Academy of Orthopaedic Surgeons*, 470 U.S. 373 at 378 (1985).

10. Robert M. Cover, "The Uses of Jurisdictional Redundancy: Interest, Ideology, and Innovation," *William & Mary Law Review* 22 (Summer 1981): 639 n. 1.

11. See Martha Field, "The Uncertain Nature of Federal Jurisdiction," *William & Mary Law Review* 22 (Summer 1981): 686–87.

12. *Keeton v. Hustler Magazine*, 465 U.S. 770 (1984).

13. *Bowen v. Massachusetts*, 487 U.S. 879 (1988).

14. *Christianson v. Colt Industries Operating Corp.*, 486 U.S. 800 (1988).

15. The Court said the former, earlier time. *United States v. Kubrick*, 444 U.S. 111 (1979).

16. *United States v. Hudson and Goodwin*, 7 Cr. 32 (1812).

17. Cover, "Uses of Jurisdictional Redundancy," p. 640.

18. See *Boyle v. United Technologies Corp.*, 487 U.S. 500 at 505 (1988).

19. For a discussion of the application of the Eleventh Amendment to suits against the state, see *Florida Department of State v. Treasure Salvors, Inc.*, 458 U.S. 670 (1982), and *Pennsylvania v. Union Gas Co.*, 109 S.Ct. 2273 (1989), at 2286–89 (Stevens) and 2295–2303 (Scalia).

20. *Edelman v. Jordan*, 415 U.S. 651 (1974); see also *Papasan v. Allain*, 478 U.S. 265 (1986) (trust income for school lands).

21. *Atascadero State Hospital v. Scanlon*, 473 U.S. 234 (1985), and *Pennhurst State School and Hospital v. Halderman*, 465 U.S. 89 (1984), both decided 5–4.

22. The Court has now had to decide what constitutes official policy. See, e.g., *City of Oklahoma City v. Tuttle*, 471 U.S. 808 (1985) (policy of "inadequate training" of police could not be inferred from single incident), and *Pembaur v. City of Cincinnati*, 475 U.S. 469 (1986) (single incident involving instruction from assistant prosecutor can satisfy the test).

23. *Will v. Michigan Department of State Police*, 491 U.S. 58 (1989); *Hafer v. Melo*, 112 S.Ct. 358 (1991).

24. *Imbler v. Pachtman*, 424 U.S. 409 (1976); *Briscoe v. Lahue*, 465 U.S. 325 (1983); *Burns v. Reed*, 111 S.Ct. 1934 (1991).

25. *National Railroad Passenger Corp. v. National Association of Railroad Passengers*, 414 U.S. 453 (1974); *Bread Political Action Committee v. Federal Election Commission*, 455 U.S. 577 (1982); *Federal Election Commission v. National Conservative Political Action Committee*, 470 U.S. 480 (1985); *Trafficante v. Metropolitan Life Insurance Co.*, 409 U.S. 205 (1972).

26. *Tileston v. Ullman*, 318 U.S. 44 (1984).

27. *Barrows v. Jackson*, 346 U.S. 259 (1953); *Peters v. Kiff*, 407 U.S. 493 (1972) and *Taylor v. Louisiana*, 419 U.S. 522 (1975); and *Singleton v. Wulff*, 428 U.S. 106 (1976).

28. *Diamond v. Charles*, 476 U.S. 84 (1986); *Whitmore v. Arkansas*, 110 S.Ct. 1717 (1990).

29. *United States v. Salvucci*, 448 U.S. 83 (1980), overturning *Jones v. United States*, 362 U.S. 257 (1960).

30. See *United States v. S.C.R.A.P.*, 412 U.S. 669 (1973); *Lujan v. National Wildlife Federation*, 110 S.Ct. 3177 (1990); *Lujan v. Defenders of Wildlife*, 112 S.Ct. 2130 (1992).

31. *Valley Forge Christian College v. Americans United for Separation of Church and State*, 454 U.S. 464 (1982).

32. *United States v. Richardson*, 418 U.S. 166 (1974). See also *Schlesinger v. Reservists Committee to End the War*, 418 U.S. 208 (1974).

33. *Village of Arlington Heights v. Metropolitan Housing Development Corp.*, 429 U.S. 252 (1977). However, the plaintiff did win on remand.

34. *Rogers v. Lodge*, 458 U.S. 613 at 632 (1982); *Federal Communication Commission v. League of Women Voters of California*, 468 U.S. 364 at 401 (1984).

35. *Crawford Fitting Co. v. J. T. Gibbons, Inc.*, 482 U.S. 437 (1987).

36. *Machinists v. Street*, 367 U.S. 640 (1971); see Schwartz, *Super Chief*, pp. 371–72.

37. *Carafas v. LaVallee*, 391 U.S. 234 (1968) (challenge to conviction); *Lane v. Williams*, 455 U.S. 624 (1982) (sentences).

38. See *Moore v. Ogilvie*, 394 U.S. 814 (1969).

39. See *Honig v. Doe*, 484 U.S. 305 at 331–32 (1988) (Rehnquist, concurring).

40. *Poe v. Ullman*, 367 U.S. 497 (1961); *Griswold v. Connecticut*, 381 U.S. 479 (1965).

41. See *Noyd v. Bond*, 395 U.S. 683 (1969), and *Schlesinger v. Councilman*, 420 U.S. 738 (1975).

42. *Coleman v. Miller*, 307 U.S. 433 (1939); *Luther v. Borden*, 7 How. 1 (1849); *Pacific States Telephone and Telegraph Co. v. Oregon*, 223 U.S. 118 (1912); and *Mississippi v. Johnson*, 4 Wall. 475 (1867).

43. *I.N.S. v. Chadha*, 462 U.S. 919 at 941–42 (1984).

44. See Anthony D'Amato and Robert O'Neil, *The Judiciary and Vietnam* (New York: St. Martin's Press, 1972).

45. See John W. Winkle, "Toward Intersystem Harmony: State-Federal Judicial Councils," *Justice System Journal* 6 (Summer 1981): 240–53.

46. *Oregon v. Hass*, 420 U.S. 714 at 719 (1975) (emphasis in original) (Justice Blackmun). For a discussion of doctrinal interchange between the U.S. Supreme Court and state courts, with each drawing on the other's views, see Stanley H. Friedelbaum, "Reactive Responses: The Complementary Role of Federal and State Courts," *Publius* 17 (Winter 1987): 33–50.

47. *PruneYard Shopping Center v. Robins*, 447 U.S. 74 at 82 (1980). The earlier case was *Lloyd Corp. v. Tanner*, 407 U.S. 551 (1972).

48. *Florida v. Casal*, 462 U.S. 637 at 639 (1983).

49. *Michigan v. Long*, 463 U.S. 1032 (1983).

50. *Delaware v. Van Arsdall*, 475 U.S. 673 at 690 (1986); *Massachusetts v. Upton*, 466 U.S. 727 at 735 (1984).

51. *Coleman v. Thompson*, 111 S. Ct. 2546 (1991), which Justice O'Connor, for the Court, began with "This is a case about federalism" (at 2552).

52. See *Burlington Northern Railroad Co. v. Woods*, 480 U.S. 1 (1987).

53. Victor E. Flango and Craig Boersema, "Changes in Federal Diversity Jurisdiction: Effects on State Court Caseloads," *University of Dayton Law Review* 15 (1990): 415.

54. See Kristin Bumiller, "Choice of Forum in Diversity Cases: Analysis of a Survey and Implications for Reform," *Law & Society Review* 15 (1980–1981): 749–74; Jolanta Perlstein, "Lawyers' Strategies and Diversity Jurisdiction," *Law & Policy Quarterly* 3 (July 1981): 321–40; and Victor E. Flango, "Attorneys' Perspectives on Choice of Forum in Diversity Cases," *Akron Law Review* 25 (Summer 1991): 1–82.

55. See David L. Shapiro, "Federal Diversity Jurisdiction: A Survey and a Proposal," *Harvard Law Review* 91 (December 1977): 317–55.

56. See Susan M. Olson, "Federal Multidistrict Litigation: Its Impact on Litigants," *Justice System Journal* 13 (1988–89): 341–64.

57. As to how eliminating diversity jurisdiction would affect the state courts, see Victor Eugene Flango, "How Would the Abolition of Federal Diversity Jurisdiction Affect State Courts?", 74 *Judicature* 35–43 (June-July 1990).

58. *Georgia v. Rachel*, 383 U.S. 780 (1966); *City of Greenwood v. Peacock*, 383 U.S. 808 (1966).

59. Because it is based on *Railroad Commission of Texas v. Pullman*, 312 U.S. 496 (1941). There is also *Burford* and *Colorado River* abstention based on *Burford v. Sun Oil Co.*, 319 U.S. 315 (1943), involving federal court intervention in state agency proceedings, and *Colorado River* abstention where there are parallel state courts that can decide the issue and conserve scarce judicial resources. *Colorado River Water Conservation District v. United States*, 424 U.S. 800 (1976).

60. See *Colorado River Water Conservation District*, 424 U.S. at 815–17.

61. *Zant v. Stephens*, 456 U.S. 410 (1982). Another example is *Virginia v. American Booksellers Association*, 484 U.S. 383 (1988), certifying to state court to indicate the scope of coverage of an obscenity statute.

62. *Preiser v. Rodriguez*, 411 U.S. 475 (1973).

63. *Finley v. United States*, 109 S.Ct. 2003 (1989).

64. *Huffman v. Pursue*, 420 U.S. 592 (1975); *Trainor v. Hernandez*, 431 U.S. 434 (1977); *Ohio Civil Rights Commission v. Dayton Christian Schools*, 477 U.S. 619 (1986).

65. *General Atomic Co. v. Felter*, 434 U.S. 12 (1977) and 436 U.S. 493 (1978).

66. Cover, "Uses of Jurisdictional Redundancy," p. 648.

67. See *Ableman v. Booth*, 21 How. 506 (1859), where the Taney Court overturned a Wisconsin Supreme Court ruling holding the Fugitive Slave Act unconstitutional two years after *Dred Scott*, and the earlier *Prigg v. Pennsylvania*, 16 Pet. 539 (1842), a ruling under the pre-1850 Fugitive Slave Act. See Robert Cover, *Justice Accused* (New Haven, Conn.: Yale University Press, 1975), particularly pp. 175–91.

68. See one of his attacks on state prisoners' excessive use of federal habeas corpus, *Spalding v. Aiken*, 460 U.S. 1093 (1983). For a rejoinder, see *Witt v. Wrainwright*, 470 U.S. 1039 at 1043–44 (1985) (Justice Marshall).

69. *Kimmelman v. Morrison*, 477 U.S. 365 (1986).

70. *Sumner v. Mata*, 449 U.S. 539 (1981) and 455 U. S. 491 (1982).

71. *Picard v. Connor*, 404 U.S. 270 (1971); *Francis v. Henderson*, 425 U.S. 536 (1976). The Court did rule that claims of racial discrimination in state grand jury selection *could* be challenged through federal habeas even if the subsequent trial jury had not been improperly constituted. *Rose v. Mitchell*, 443 U.S. 545 (1979).

72. *Kuhlmann v. Wilson*, 477 U.S. 436 (1986).

73. *Teague v. Lane*, 109 S.Ct. 1060 (1989), and *Penry v. Lynaugh*, 109 S.Ct. 2934 (1989); *McCleskey v. Zant*, 111 S.Ct. 1454. The overruling of *Fay v. Noia* came in *Coleman v. Thompson*, 111 S.Ct. 2354 (1991).

74. *Kenney v. Tamayo-Reyes*, 112 S.Ct. 1715 (1992). Further limits on use of habeas corpus, to present claims of actual innocence, came in *Sawyer v. Whitley*, 112 S.Ct. 2514 (1992).

6 The Supreme Court: Its Docket and Screening Decisions

LAWYERS' AND GROUPS' DECISIONS to take cases to the Supreme Court, made within the rules on access to the courts, provide the basic pool from which the Supreme Court, using certain regular procedures, takes its cases. By "skimming off" most cases at early stages and disposing of some others through brief orders (summary dispositions), the Court can concentrate on those it considers worthy of full treatment.

All this is part of *docket management*, which provides the Court with opportunities to engage in strategic actions. Selectivity is crucial to the Court's work—not only administratively but also politically: "It helps to keep the Court abreast of new trends in litigation, and it helps to maintain the Court's flexibility in responding to change."[1] Deciding which cases to accept and which to reject is critical if the justices are to have cases with the best factual settings for rulings they may be predisposed to make and if they are not to have to hand down the wrong decision at the wrong time.

In this chapter, we look first at the cases brought to the Court, that is, the size and content of its docket, and then at the ways in which the justices skim off most of the cases. We turn in the next chapter to the Court's "full-dress treatment" of the cases that remain.

The Court's Business

Docket Size

Some claim that the Supreme Court is overloaded with cases. That claim was made repeatedly in the 1970s and 1980s. It was also made earlier, even when docket size was much smaller, for example, before the courts of appeals were established and again before certiorari jurisdiction was provided. One could even say that Chicken Little runs the court system, because whatever time period we examine, we find judges complaining about the increasing and unbearable workload and the need for relief. Relief is provided in one form or another, there is a temporary downturn in cases and complaints, and then the caseload heads upward again—and the complaints reappear.

To examine the overload claim, we need to examine the Court's caseload—the number of cases filed—before turning to the question of whether that is an *over*load requiring a remedy—that is, more necessary work than the Court can do, or a burden in which the number of filings exceeds a level with which the justices can reasonably cope. We look first at load and then at *over*load. An increased number of filings—even a substantial increase—does not necessarily mean that the Court is overworked, particularly if many of those cases are relatively simple or do not raise important issues of law. Such a judgment depends on what we expect the Court to do with cases brought to it, such as deciding important cases. The fact that the parties, who will have already had at least one appellate review, would like the Court to hear their case does not mean the case is of sufficient importance beyond their own immediate concerns to justify the justices' devoting their time to it.

The idea of "overload" has both subjective and objective components. The subjective ones are the justices' own views of the conditions under which they are working; objective ones might be, for example, increased time from filing to decision, or observers' judgments, based on some agreed-upon standard, of the quality of the Court's output, although many of the standards are themselves subjective. One can agree that Supreme Court justices work hard without necessarily agreeing that they are *over*worked, because the caseload may be manageable, particularly with the management tool given the Court in the Judges Bill of 1925, under which most cases are subject to the Court's own decision as to whether it should hear them. This allows the justices to manage the Court's docket and keep the cases to which it gives full (plenary) treatment at a reasonable level for them, regardless of the number of filings.

A variety of factors in combination affect the number of cases *filed* in the Supreme Court. Some are external to the Court. They include "political, economic, and social forces," which may have a general, perhaps thin, effect on several areas of the Court's docket rather than a focused effect on one area; social problems that are transformed into legal issues, as when concerns about women's position in society led to the women's movement and to sexual discrimination cases; and external events, including some external to the United States, like the Arab oil embargo, which ultimately produced cases concerning federal regulations' preemptive effect on state law.[2] They also include Congress's enactment of new legislation, its creation of new federal judgeships, and people's propensity to initiate cases and to appeal them, which is affected in part by their perceptions of the Court's caseload.

Others are internal to the Court: the Court's own actions affect its caseload. The justices' willingness to rule on a topic increases the number of cases filed, just as consistent refusal to review cases on a particular subject results in review being sought in fewer such cases. Similarly, adoption of certain doctrinal rules serves to make clear to potential litigants that it will not be fruitful to bring certain types of cases. If, while deciding cases, the justices make statements indicating the Court would welcome cases raising questions not presently before the Court, lawyers are likely to try to bring those questions to the Court for resolution. If, as critics suggest, the justices feel compelled to take more cases instead of allowing lower courts to resolve them, if they operate from an apparent presumption that only *they* can decide certain cases, an increase in filings is likely.

References to the Supreme Court's *docket* are really references to its dockets. Until 1970, there were three: the Original Docket, for the few original jurisdiction cases; the Appellate Docket, containing certiorari petitions or jurisdictional statements (for appeals) in *paid* cases, that is, where the petitions or statements have been printed; and the Miscellaneous Docket, containing the unpaid or *in forma pauperis* (i.f.p.) cases from those, often prisoners, who cannot afford the regular fees. The Appellate and Miscellaneous Dockets are now combined in the Appellate Docket, but paid and i.f.p. cases can still be distinguished because different numbering systems are used for each. (There are also separate dockets for special motions, for applications for stays of lower court proceedings, and for disbarment of lawyers who are members of the Supreme Court bar.)

The requirements of a printed submission and the payment of filing fees are waived for someone qualifying for *in forma pauperis* status. Starting in 1983, the Court began to question whether some people asserting that they qualified for i.f.p. status in fact did so, by giving them several weeks to produce additional documentation or, in the alternative, pay the docketing fees. Several justices objected, saying that if the Court was going to reject the petition for review in any event, which they said was true of the petitions in question, it was simply making more work for itself, for it would now have to examine a resubmitted petition again.[3]

Action to limit i.f.p. petitions, at least from individuals who filed large numbers of them, came in 1991. The Court first denied *in forma pauperis* status for filing an extraordinary writ to someone for whom this was the twenty-fourth such filing in the 1990 Term, and then, in a stronger ruling, denied another such individual, who had made 32 i.f.p. filings in three terms, permission to file i.f.p. petitions for extraordinary writs.[4] The Court then reinforced this action with an amendment to the Court's Rules that when a certiorari petition or petition for extraordinary writ was frivolous, the Court may deny the i.f.p. petition. The majority said the new rule was necessary because the filing fee required for "paid" petitions and the damages and costs that could be awarded for frivolous filings in other situations did not deter in the i.f.p. context, justifying the change because it was "vital that the right to file *in forma pauperis* not be incumbered by those who would abuse the integrity of our process by frivolous filings." Justice Marshall objected to the "invidious distinction" of a rule that affected the poor without penalizing "paying" petitioners, who "are a substantial source of these filings."[5]

There are now over 4,000 cases filed each year in the Supreme Court. That makes us forget the Court's early small caseload. From 1790 to 1801, the Court's appellate jurisdiction was invoked in only 87 cases, of which 80 were federal cases (36 diversity of citizenship cases, 35 admiralty cases, and 9 civil cases brought by the government).[6] In the earliest years, the justices' workload was largely a matter of circuit duty, not the Court's own small docket. As late as the Civil War years (1862–66), the Court still was not handing down many decisions: 240 cases were decided in that period. However, paralleling an increase in federal district court caseload, the Court's output grew to 1,125 for the 1886–90 period. This post-Civil War docket growth resulted largely from statutory changes, including provisions for removal of cases to the federal courts and addition to "federal question" jurisdiction. The passage of the act establishing the courts of appeals in 1891 produced an immediate drop in Supreme Court filings—from over 600 in 1890 to 275 in 1892—and the number of petitions for review continued to decline at the rate of 2 percent during the century's last decade.[7]

Despite a rate of increase in filings of roughly 2 to 3 percent for the first half of the twentieth century, as recently as the early 1940s fewer than 1,000 cases were filed annually. The number of filings fluctuated between 1,000 and 1,500 from 1944–54, and then began rather steady increased growth, reflecting an increased annual rate of filings of 5 percent-plus starting at about midcentury. The result was that the Court was dealing in 1971 with three-and-one-half times as many cases as 20 years earlier and roughly seven to eight times the number it had confronted in 1925, when it received full certiorari authority. In the decade ending in 1972, filings grew from 2,200 to over 3,600. The *rate* of increase decreased after 1968, but the larger base meant that absolute increases in filings were substantial. The increase did not continue, with the 1983 Term figure only 16 percent over that for the 1971 Term; had the earlier rate continued, there would have been *almost 6,100 cases* filed in the 1981 Term instead of the actual 4,400 plus.[8] The figure remained relatively stable before climbing to over 5,000 by the 1990 Term, in part a result of the shift from appeal to certiorari (see page 73) but also from general growth.

Caseload increase has had a number of causes. Roughly half the increase in filings in the 1970s was in unpaid cases, primarily prisoner petitions, which increased in part because of the 1964 Criminal Justice Act provision for appointed counsel for indigent federal criminal defendants. New federal statutes containing new causes of action have regularly contributed to the larger "pool" of cases from which lawyers sought review in the Supreme Court. So have the Court's rulings recognizing new substantive rights.

When caseload increases, there are cases not filed because people feel that the probability of obtaining a decision on the merits was not worth the expense or, particularly, the delay. A feeling that the Court has been inundated by filings or is "overloaded" may lead to the existence of a *hidden docket*. However, given the relative ease of filing cases *in forma pauperis* if one is poor, and the existence of many "noncertworthy" petitions now being filed, it is unlikely there are many cases not being brought to the Court that would be plausible candidates for review.

Has the Supreme Court been able to keep pace with the filings? The Court is current with its work in the sense that, except for a few cases set for reargument the next term, all cases argued within a term are disposed of during that same term; in this sense, the Court has no backlog. And in most recent years the Court has disposed of roughly as many cases as have been filed, thus not leaving a growing backlog, leaving unchanged the number of cases not acted upon during the term (carryover + cases docketed − dispositions). The cases remaining at term's end numbered in the high 800s into the early 1980s.[9] By the late 1970s, the Court was carrying over for argument roughly the same number of cases as had been on the argument calendar at term's beginning. For a while, the Court accepted more cases for argument without similarly increasing the number of cases argued so that the argument calendar filled up earlier each year—by Christmas recess in the 1981 Term. However, in the 1982 Term, the Court significantly reduced the number of cases accepted for hearing (179 as against 201 in the 1981 Term), and reduced the figure even more—to around 150—the following term. Under Chief Justice Rehnquist, one could see that the Court had begun to hear fewer cases. This was quite clear in the 1989 and 1990 Terms, when the oral argument calendar for the term was not complete when the term began (and more so in O.T. 90 than in the previous term).

The Court under Chief Justice Burger generally handed down 140 to 150 decisions a year (covering roughly 180 cases, some of which are consolidated in a single decision), up from an average of 115 per term during the 1950s and 1960s. In addition, numerous summary rulings were issued—some 15 to 20 with opinions per term, plus 15 or so summary affirmances with one- or two-line orders, 80 to 90 dismissals of appeals that are rulings on the merits and an additional 40 to 90 rulings in which review is granted and the case is returned to the lower court for further consideration on the basis of intervening Supreme Court rulings. With the Rehnquist Court not filling its calendar by term's beginning, it is not surprising that it decided fewer cases. The 129 signed opinions of the 1989 Term was the lowest in the decade—although it had been lower in the past, as recently as the Warren Court. One explanation may be the elimination of almost all appeal jurisdiction effective in 1988. Another may be that the dominant conservative coalition in place with the appointment of Justice Kennedy had less need to take cases to make its point. (The shift to more affirmances is related to this caseload decrease.)

The recent downturn in the Court's output despite a high and stable rate of filings might suggest the absence of a clear relationship between input and output, filings and opinions, at the Court. However, for the 1948–1985 period (the end of the Burger Court), a 10 percent increase in cases docketed led to an increase of 3.5 percent in the Court's opinions, so output was rising more slowly than input. Put differently, "the Court increased its opinion-writing at one-quarter the rate that its dockets have grown" in this post-World War II period. The productivity increased particularly under Chief Justice Burger, with the Court producing 1.2 percent more opinions for each year he was Chief Justice—perhaps an indication of the effect of his administrative concerns within the Court as well as outside it. [10]

The time the Court has taken to deal with cases has been fairly steady, at least for its initial screening decisions. Screening decisions are generally made within three months of a case's being filed—except when the filing comes late in the term, in which case no decision is reached until October. Except for the October "bulge," screening decisions issue relatively steadily during the term although there is no deadline for ruling on certiorari petitions once they are filed. The lack of a deadline allows the Court to cumulate cases on certain subjects before deciding to which (if any) they will grant review, although it is not done frequently. Cases accepted for review may remain in the system for extended periods of time, but that depends in part on whether they come from the federal or state courts (longer if from federal court), were appeals rather than certiorari cases (longer for appeals), and whether *amicus* briefs are filed (longer if they are). [11]

Overload. Is the Court, as some justices and some observers claim, overloaded? High, even increasing caseload, does not necessarily mean *overload*. Increases in supporting staff, such as law clerks, have enabled the Court to cope with higher caseload and, as just noted, the Court has actually decreased the number of cases to which it gives plenary (full) treatment each term. The Court continues to function effectively even when complaints about caseload might lead one to believe that was not possible. However, the Court's ability to decline easier cases means the justices are left with more difficult ones to decide. Thus even if numbers remained the same, workload would increase.

The "overload" argument was renewed with particular force in the 1970s and 1980s. Concerns were raised about the effect of increased caseload on the *quality* of the Court's work, and serious attention should be given claims that the Court does not have time for adequate deliberation, or, on the other hand, adequate time to devote to screening cases for review. However, it has been argued, "History provides little support for the assertion that a smaller docket leads to wiser adjudications or more illuminating opinions," and decisions handed down only after long consideration—like the School Desegregation Cases of 1954 and 1955 and the abortion rulings of 1973—were much criticized not only for their results but also for lack of craftsmanship. [12] With more time, the justices might write more, adding to the "noise" in the system already created by their multiple opinions. And in evaluating arguments about caseload, we must also remember they may well be a neutral-sounding excuse for the justices' position—particularly as it is the conservative members of the Court who have used the argument when civil liberties claims are turned aside. Their actions undercut the caseload argument when they take criminal cases where the lower court has decided in favor of a defendant in a criminal case.

Some justices have spoken out about workload—even if they do not support a remedy, or any particular remedy, for it. New members of the Court have been more likely to complain about overwork, and to utter such complaints less as they got accustomed to the pattern of work. Justice Douglas said that "no Justice of this court need work more than four days a week to carry his burden," which he claimed was "comfortable" even when he was hospitalized. He argued that the Court was "if anything, underworked, not overworked."[13] Other justices have agreed with him, needling their colleagues for complaining about overwork when they insisted on taking cases of little importance and did not show sufficient respect for decisions of either the U.S. courts of appeals or the state courts.[14]

The Court's creating more work for itself is a situation that has existed over the years. The justices cannot resist taking cases that will allow them to reach particular results. If they really wanted to reduce workload, the justices could find reasons *not* to take cases, but they seem to reach in the other direction. Thus the way the Court has limited the "adequate state ground" doctrine (see page 180) allows the Court to take more, not fewer, cases. In earlier years, the Court interpreted federal question jurisdiction in a way that added to its docket, and it was true years ago as it is now that despite the justices' complaints of overwork, "a few important cases decided differently would have had the effect of discouraging much litigation."[15] As Casper and Posner observe, "A frequently overlooked point is the extent to which the Supreme Court itself controls the demand for its services through its power to recognize a new, or extinguish a recognized, federal statutory or constitutional right by interpreting or reinterpreting a federal statute or constitutional provision."[16] Individual justices also make more work for themselves by writing concurring and dissenting opinions. These are written in addition to, not instead of, their regular "opinions for the Court."

If the Court has in some ways made more work for itself, the justices have also done some things to reduce their workload—just as they did in pressing for the Judges Bill of 1925, which gave them their present discretionary jurisdiction. The justices were at the forefront of the move to eliminate direct appeals from three-judge district courts (see page 46), and to remove remaining mandatory jurisdiction (see page 73). However, removing diversity of citizenship cases from federal jurisdiction (see pages 182–83), which they also favor, would assist the lower federal courts but have very little effect on the Supreme Court's own burden. In areas of the law where the justices perceive a significant increase in filing, they have acted to limit them. A prime example is limiting use of federal habeas corpus by state prisoners, particularly those sentenced to death.

Chief Justice Burger suggested that prospective appellants get approval from the courts before they could appeal their cases, and he led moves within the Court to penalize those bringing "frivolous" appeals. In 1983, acting under a court rule that permits an award of "appropriate damages" to the appellee when appellant's case is "frivolous," the Court made such an award (of $500) in a case.[17] In 1985, Burger renewed his call for more such action "in egregious cases" in order to "discourage many of the patently meritless applications that are filed here each year," but he was met with a rejoinder from four justices that the time necessary to determine which of the meritless petitions warranted sanctions "would be a time-consuming and unrewarding task."[18] The Court has barred those seeking to file frivolous i.f.p. petitions (see pages 193–94).

The revival of concern about overload in the 1970s by Chief Justice Burger and the Commission on the Federal Court Appellate System (the Hruska Commission) has had a specific focus: whether the nation has sufficient judicial capacity to decide cases of national importance and whether the Supreme Court can provide that capacity without assistance from a new court (see pages 61–63). The claim is that issues requiring a uniform national position, such as interpretations of frequently used statutes, have gone undecided, and that intercircuit conflict—conflicts in position between the U.S. courts of appeals—have not been resolved promptly. Pressing this view, the Commission said that the absence of adequate capacity for the declaration of national law led to lack of Supreme Court review for cases that 20 years earlier would certainly have been accepted. Agreeing, Justice Byron White regularly notes what he feels are intercircuit conflicts when he dissents from the Court's denial of review.[19]

The Commission also felt that unresolved intercircuit conflict led to repetitive litigation, further increasing filings in the Supreme Court. Because it was the only court capable of resolving conflicts between the circuits, the Supreme Court would be forced to take cases "otherwise not worthy of its resources."[20] Yet even with a lower caseload, the Supreme Court has not always handed down many decisions in any particular area of the law and, more important, the area in which it has handed down most decisions—Fourth Amendment search and seizure law—has remained one of considerable confusion, not clarity.[21]

There is no consensus as to whether many claimed instances of intercircuit conflict are real conflicts. But not all need immediate resolution by the Supreme Court. Left alone, some disappear: a trend develops and the "minority position" dissolves. Not resolving a conflict immediately also allows "percolation": lower courts' differing positions provide the Supreme Court with a variety of views on a subject on which the justices can draw when they consider the issue. However, some conflicts may be "intolerable" and should be resolved promptly, for example, "when litigants are able to exploit conflicts affirmatively through forum shopping, or when the planning of primary behavior is thwarted by the absence of a nationally binding rule."[22]

A systematic examination of cases to which the Court granted review in the

1982 Term helps us evaluate claims about overload. Cases were divided into three categories, with specified criteria for the categories based on clearly stated assumptions about the Supreme Court's roles (see pages 28–33). Central was the notion that the Court should function as a manager of the judicial system, delegating responsibilities to subordinates and presuming their decisions valid. In particular, much weight was given to "percolation" of issues in the lower courts rather than having the Court accept conflicts as soon as they developed.

Close analysis of the Court's 1982 Term showed that almost half (48%) of the cases to which review was granted belonged on the priority docket, cases that it was imperative for the Court to hear. Included were intolerable conflicts, conflicts with Supreme Court precedents, and resolution of important federalism issues and interbranch disputes. Somewhat more than one-fourth (28%) were located on the discretionary docket, cases the justices need not hear but could reasonably review. Included were cases presenting opportunities to develop federal law. Another *one-fourth* (24%) were found to be improvident grants, where the criteria for the first two categories are absent. Thus "a significant portion of the Court's present capacity is misused, and might be devoted more productively to other types of cases"[23]; had the Court *not* heard these cases, it most certainly would not have been overworked.

Docket Content

The content of the Court's docket is at least as significant as its size. Over time that content has shifted toward cases raising constitutional questions. In the nineteenth century and extending into the twentieth century, the Supreme Court was primarily a private law court. Cases with constitutional questions began to increase in the 1930s, when matters of due process constituted the greatest portion; other constitutional cases then involved the Commerce Clause, impairment of contract, and full faith and credit. Prior to 1960, nonconstitutional holdings made up two-thirds to three-fourths of the Court's rulings. However, as a result of the Warren Court, constitutional cases constituted one-half to two-thirds of the Court's full-opinion decisions. Cases based on the Bill of Rights were only 5 percent of the constitutional cases in the 1930s, but by the late 1950s they made up over one-third of the cases filed, and *half* in the late 1960s. Much of these changes can be explained by the increase in state criminal cases, almost 100 percent of which entailed constitutional questions.[24]

The Burger Court was expected to give less attention to constitutional problems and more attention to matters of statutory interpretation, in part by shifting from civil liberties cases to commercial or regulatory litigation. At first, there was a shift toward economic issues, with a concomitant decrease in criminal and habeas corpus cases and an increase in private civil actions accepted.[25] However, after a few terms, the Burger Court, instead of "deconstitutionalizing" its working docket, showed itself to be largely a constitutional court, and, in particular, to be a *civil rights court*. Cases with constitutional individual rights issues, just over one-fourth of the plenary docket in the 1959 Term, displaced other types of cases on the docket during the 1960s so that by the 1970s they became the plenary docket's largest single component—over two-fifths, and even higher if one adds cases with procedural issues affecting individual rights and those with individual rights as secondary issues.

Criminal procedure cases provided a stable level of business for the Court in the 1970s and 1980s. The predominant issue was search and seizure, even after the Court seemed to cut off federal court habeas review of such issues. But there was also significant attention to right to counsel; self-incrimination; and cruel and unusual punishment—specifically aspects of the death penalty, with 28 cases on that subject in 1986–89. In a rare concentration of attention to a single subject, in the 1974–77 Terms the Court decided more cases on double jeopardy than in the preceding 15 terms. Most federal criminal defendants seeking the Court's review came to the Court as indigents, although there were also numerous "paid" petitions seeking review of federal criminal convictions; somewhat more state criminal defendants seeking review of their cases were paid than was true of federal defendants, but most of the state cases were also "unpaid." As time progressed, the Court took a substantially greater portion of its criminal cases from state courts—nearly half by the late 1970s—but it was interested in cases brought by state *prosecutors* challenging prodefendant rulings.[26] There was thus greater change in who brought to the Supreme Court the cases the justices decided to hear than there was in either the Court's caseload or the composition of that caseload.

In addition to criminal procedure and free expression cases, equal protection cases and cases on access to the courts accounted for most growth in the civil rights component of the Court's plenary docket. The freedom of expression area illustrates that subjects prominent for a while then fade from view as the Court clarifies the law so that it need not take new cases until a new aspect of the problem appears. This was true of a question like access to the ballot by minor political parties and independent candidates. It was also true of obscenity, where there were 20 decisions in the 1959–76 Terms but only three rulings in the seven subsequent terms; the more recent cases dealt with methods for controlling obscenity, not defining it, the earlier focus.

Equal protection cases involving racial discrimination issues increased severalfold from 1959 through the mid-1970s but then declined, remaining as only a small part of the plenary docket. There were, however, few school desegregation cases, with more attention to other aspects of racial discrimination. Although reapportionment received less attention in the 1970s than earlier, there were new areas of equal protection litigation to which the Court gave attention in the 1970s and 1980s: illegitimacy, the rights of aliens, and gender discrimination.[27] (By contrast to its willingness to deal with women's rights issues, the Court has been unwilling to deal with the concerns of homosexuals and lesbians, and when it did do so in 1986, in *Bowers v. Hardwick*, was resoundingly negative.)

Dominance by constitutional individual rights cases did not mean exclusion of other types of cases from the plenary docket. Cases involving separation of powers, in which the Court performs its role as umpire among the three branches, and federalism, where it serves as umpire among the levels of government, although a smaller proportion of the docket, have been present in significant numbers, with separation of powers cases among the most important of the 1980s (see pages 332–35). After the late Warren Court's decrease in interest in federalism issues, interest revived—with a focus on such matters as federal preemption of state powers and whether states had exceeded their authority, especially in matters of interstate commerce.[28]

Cases involving interpretation of federal statutes, earlier accounting for at least 40 percent of the Court's plenary docket, after the 1967 Term took up less than 30 percent of the docket and the subject matter shifted considerably, showing the effect on the Court's docket of laws Congress enacts. New statutes, on environmental protection, occupational health and safety, securities regulation, pension plans, and employment discrimination, along with Freedom of Information Act (FOIA) cases, came to the fore, and older aspects of labor law received less attention in the business regulation area, antitrust provided the largest segment of cases, and there was an obvious decline in Interstate Commerce Commission cases—one "fallout" from deregulation.[29] Among "federal specialties," Federal Employer Liability Act (FELA) cases, once a staple of the Court's business, and admiralty cases were almost totally gone from the docket. Such changes indicate the Court's ability to respond to the need for interpretation of new statutes but also illustrate the "episodic nature of the Court's intervention," which "stands out even more strongly in the realm of statutory law" than elsewhere.[30]

This broad picture of docket content and trends should not obscure the rich variety of particular issues the Court explores in any single term, which contains many business issues, such as tax, antitrust, patent, and regulatory issues, in addition to civil liberties questions. Rarely are there more than one or two cases per term on any single issue, and multiple cases on only a few broad topics such as employment discrimination, search and seizure, or the death penalty. This results from the Court's seldom deciding more than 150 cases with full opinion and its attempt to develop law on the many topics on which people have sought its guidance and direction.

Agenda. The Court's continuing attention to criminal procedure cases, and the Warren Court and Burger Court doing so for different reasons (one to protect defendants' rights, the other to limit those rights), raises the question of whether the Supreme Court has an *agenda* and, if so, how it proceeds to implement it. Certainly the Court does not announce an agenda in the way a president or governor or legislative leader would announce it; instead, the agenda is implicit, to be inferred by observers. We can see that the Court's "agenda building has purposive elements" but also "varies by policy area"[31] when we look at changes in the number of criminal procedure cases decided. Over a 40-year period including the early Burger Court, the changes did not appear to reflect changes in the incidence of crime, media coverage of crime, or public concern about crime or changes in that concern, despite all the attention given to "law and order" starting with the late 1960s. What did make a difference were the controlling justices' differing ideologies and changes in chief justices. The Court was significantly more likely to increase the number of criminal justice decisions when liberals controlled the Court than when conservatives did.[32]

Constraints on implementation of the agenda are at least equally as important as positive efforts to build an agenda. For example, independent of the justices' values, the Court needs to take some cases to correct lower court error or to clarify rules. In some other instances, the action of another branch of government creates the Court's agenda. Such matters have been called the Court's "exigent" agenda—as distinguished from its "volitional" agenda, that is, issues the Court chooses without pressure from its environment.[33] Examples are President Truman's seizure of the steel mills in 1952, President Nixon's refusal to surrender the Watergate tapes for use in a criminal case, and his administration's efforts to stop publication of the Pentagon Papers. Despite the effect of their ideological proclivities on their choice of cases, the justices find that there are some matters they almost *have* to take, at least eventually if not immediately when they are first presented. Included would be certain church-state issues, cases that follow up their 1973 abortion ruling, death penalty procedures, and the challenge to the constitutionality of the "independent counsel" (special prosecutor) provisions (see pages 329–30). Although the Court must take such cases, by placing such matters on its own agenda it can elevate them on the national agenda. Another instance where this clearly happened was school desegregation. With abortion, one might say that the Court put the issue on the national agenda when it wasn't there—or occupied a very low position before the Court decided *Roe v. Wade*.

The Court's agenda is constructed through interaction of the justices' policy views and their views of their roles, on the one hand, and what others active in policy-making bring to the Court. Some of that interaction takes place over time. Because "demands for Court activity are responses to earlier decisions," it takes some time before justices' desires to deal with a particular area of law are reflected in the cases brought to the Court to which review can be granted.[34]

We find that the agenda develops in stages.[35] Past decisions and choices of issues on which to focus affect later agenda. In part this is a result of limiting the space available for new issues. The larger the "exigent agenda," the smaller the "volitional agenda." Over time, issues that began on the volitional agenda may move to the exigent agenda. In addition, "landmark" cases can produce new issues, which must then be dealt with, leading to significant agenda change: the Court's major rulings on libel, obscenity, and search and seizure are examples of this sort of development. When an issue appears on the Court's volitional agenda, it may at first appear only occasionally and not regularly (the Episodic stage); in due course, the Court will regularly hear cases concerning the issue (the Emergent stage). Then, with basic elements of the issue resolved and the justices' having decided how to approach the issue, the Court must face increasingly difficult questions in the Elaborative stage. As aspects of an issue become still more difficult, at the Complex stage, the Court's treatment of the issue with its multiple dimensions may be unstable: in some of these situations, the issue leaves the Court's agenda (Exit). Accompanying these stages may be different voting patterns, with the Court perhaps more nearly unanimous with respect to its exigent agenda than its volitional one, at least at the Elaborative stage.

"Skimming Off": Case Selection

In reaching cases to which it will give full (plenary) treatment, the Supreme Court "skims off" many other cases. It does so by denying review and otherwise deciding cases summarily, generally low visibility dispositions. The sheer numbers of such decisions and the variety of factors potentially playing a part in any particular Court action mask their meaning but do not decrease their extreme importance. This stems from the fact that such decisions account for the bulk of the Court's actions, far exceeding the Court's formal statements of policy. For the Court to make a decision not to hear a case may be as important—not only for the litigants but also for the (unaware) public—as for it to decide particular controversial questions explicitly. This explains why the media often report denials of review, although at times misreporting them as decisions on the merits. The patterns of the Court's actions, reinforced by statements by some of the justices, provide strong evidence that the Court's actions denying review have clear policy implications.

The Court's means for managing its docket have varied. At times the Court has sought additional statutory authority to reduce the proportion of cases it must decide, as when it obtained its discretionary jurisdiction in the 1925 Judges Bill. As early as a hundred years ago, the Court allowed appeals (formerly writs of error) to be affirmed on motion without argument when the appeal appeared to be frivolous or to have been undertaken for purposes of delay. The Court even took its theoretically mandatory appeals jurisdiction and made it discretionary in fact, and also disposed of many appeals summarily, a recognition of the Court's flexibility. The important shift toward de facto discretionary treatment of appeals came in 1928, when the Court requested submission of a *jurisdictional statement* stating why the Court should take the case, later extended to indicating why the federal question was a "substantial" one the Court should take. The Court dismissed a large proportion of appeals cases "for want of a substantial federal question." Slightly fewer were dismissed for want of jurisdiction. Dismissal for want of a substantial federal question was more than a rejection of review, and was formally considered to be a decision on the merits. The Court stated that in such cases "a federal constitutional issue was properly presented, it was within our appellate jurisdiction . . . and we had no discretion to refuse adjudication of the case on its merits. . . . We were not obligated to grant the case plenary consideration; and we did not; but we were required to deal with its merits."[36] Just as the Supreme Court expected lower courts to be bound by full opinion decisions, it expected them to be bound by dismissals for "want of a substantial federal question" even though the Court had not described the facts and issues covered by lower court rulings in such cases or explained the basis for its action. According to Justice Brennan, making such dismissals rulings on the merits also deprived the Supreme Court of lower courts' thinking on complex legal problems: being bound by the dismissals, those courts were expected only to *apply* them, not to explore further the issues in them.

In picking and choosing from among the cases that people wish the Court to consider, the justices select for further action a small proportion of those brought on certiorari—a proportion that has decreased from 17.5 percent in 1941 to 11.1 percent ten years later, to 7.4 percent in 1961, and to below 5 percent since 1971 as the number of certiorari filings has increased while the number of decisions by the Court has remained relatively stable. The justices ruled on about half of those that fall in the appeals category, handling most with summary rulings.

In managing its docket, the Court must reduce the number of cases to a reasonable amount, but in doing so it does not pick cases at random or through some previously adopted formula. The justices must take care not to concentrate their efforts disproportionately in one or only a few areas of case law, for that constrains its ability to take up other issues. There are also some cases that cannot be easily ignored (see page 199), including challenges to major new federal statutes, and instances of extreme resistance to the Court's rulings, such as the Little Rock school desegregation situation. (There the Court not only departed from its pattern of not reviewing cases in that area but also held a special session to hear the case.) As this indicates, accepting cases allows the Court to prevent departure from its policy. Granting review also indicates that aspects of certain issues have not been settled, just as rejecting cases allows the Court to show that certain questions are settled and that it does not wish to comment further on the issues. Thus, in considering whether or not to grant review, the Court keeps an eye on the relation of new action to its own prior rulings, just as the Court must also be concerned with the timing of its decisions in relation to external events such as Congress's consideration of legislation.

Despite these constraints, the Court does have considerable flexibility in case selection. The wide variety of issues that people want the justices to hear does allow the Court to avoid certain fields completely, at least in the short run, and its pattern of accepting cases for review varies from one policy area to another. In some areas the Court accepts virtually all cases, as it did with sit-in cases in the early 1960s, but in others it may take very few, as it did in school desegregation after *Brown*. Docket management also involves selecting cases of desired breadth or narrowness, weeding out cases with peripheral issues, and altering issues presented by the parties. When lawyers seeking review present several questions of varying breadth, the Court can limit its grant of review to one or more of the questions presented. The more issues raised in the request, the more likely the Court is to limit those for which review is granted.

Instead of narrowing its focus, the Court may choose cases that focus directly on a broad issue "to establish a broad precedent applicable to cases percolating in the lower courts or being readied for the 'launching pad' " and thus to "head off large numbers of cases" coming to the Court.[37] The Court can reach the same goal by asking lawyers to address questions not raised in their petitions for review, thus adding issues to cases.[38] If offered only a small number of cases in a particular issue area, the Court can use this ability to increase the number of issues to provide complexity otherwise provided by a larger number (and wider range) of cases. Such issue modification fits well with the discretionary character of certiorari.

This shifting in the issues to which the Court gives attention in a case, which is called *issue fluidity*, can also occur during postargument consideration of a case and development of the Court's opinion. For example, in *California v. Grace Brethren Church* (1982), the issue shifted from the constitutionality of collecting unemployment insurance taxes from religious schools not affiliated with a church—the issue decided in lower court—to whether the Tax Injunction Act permitted declaratory judgments. *Illinois v. Gates* (1983) provides an instance in which the Court appeared to have changed the issue to be decided and then, somewhat embarrassedly, changed its mind again. Certiorari had originally been granted to consider whether a magistrate could properly issue a search warrant on the basis of a partially corroborated anonymous tip. After briefing and oral argument, the Court asked the parties to address whether the exclusionary rule should be modified when evidence was obtained "in the reasonable belief that the search and seizure at issue was consistent with the Fourth Amendment" (the "good-faith exception" issue). Because some justices' hostility to the exclusionary rule was well known, the request did not surprise observers. The case was reargued, but then the Court decided to rule on only the original issue, because a majority found the newer one had not been addressed by the state court.

The justices may decide not to deal with some issues that litigants have briefed and argued (*issue suppression*). Indeed, that the Court has accepted a case to resolve an issue does not mean it will do so; it may yet avoid decision of the issue. That occurred in the 1980s over the question of whether a zoning regulation constituted a "taking" requiring compensation by the government: in a series of cases, the Court said there was insufficient information in the lower court rulings about the use that could actually be made of the land in question, and so declined to answer the question that was the reason for taking the case.[39] The Court may not be well served when it obviously avoids an issue, for example, when it uses a procedural device that precludes reaching the merits, although this insulates it, at least for the time being, from the issue. An example is the

Court's ruling that the *DeFunis* affirmative action case was moot. On the other hand, briefs and oral argument may prompt the justices to consider issues not earlier thought to be present in a case (*issue discovery*), to alter their views of issues' relative importance, or to consider grounds for an opinion not discussed by the parties.[40] This occurs because lawyers' arguments may be based on any matter appearing in the record and appellees may use any appropriate arguments in support of the lower court's judgment.

The Court does not often decide a case on the basis of an issue not presented to it, and particularly if it has not been presented in the lower courts. However, issues *are* added to allow the Court to decide a case the way a majority considers appropriate. Furthermore, if a precedent is thought necessary "to cover a large number of detailed questions being posed in the lower courts" when no case is available posing the question with appropriate breadth, the justices may use issue transformation to develop such a question and then decide it. As this suggests, "The question(s) to which the Court will respond in any given case cannot be known with certainty until the Court's opinion in the case is announced. . . . The Court can expand, contract, suppress or replace issues posed by the litigating parties at various points between initial issue framing and final issue resolution."[41]

Summary Dispositions

The decision to grant review is linked to the decision on how to process a case. Most cases accepted for review proceed to plenary consideration—full briefing, oral argument, and a full opinion signed by the author. However, even after full briefing and argument, the Court may decide not to issue a full opinion, instead dismissing the certiorari petition (see below), perhaps because briefing and argument reveal a situation the justices did not see earlier. Such nonmerits dispositions are a small proportion of cases that are argued because once there is full briefing and argument, the likelihood is a full opinion case. There are also a number of *summary dispositions* given to cases, based solely on the certiorari (or appeals) papers, without full briefing or oral argument. Among these are summary affirmances or reversals, with only a one- or two-line statement issued to explain how the case is decided; remands to the lower court for further treatment (see below); and full, if not extended, unsigned opinions designated *per curiam* ("by the Court").

First used only to indicate cases with "indisputably clear" substantive law, *per curiam* rulings were later also used for orders in original jurisdiction cases, dismissals of appeals for want of a substantial federal question, and obviously moot cases. There are, however, some *per curiam* dispositions that announce substantive law. This was a relatively uncommon event until the mid-1960s, as the Court generally did not write opinions in cases to which plenary treatment (full briefing and oral argument) had not been given. However, it was not uncommon thereafter, particularly with the Burger Court,[42] although there was a steady decline through the 1980s. Usually within the first six weeks of each term of Court, the Court hands down a number of summary dispositions on the merits with brief *per curiam* opinions. In recent terms, many of these rulings have been dispositions of petitions for the Court to review rulings favorable to criminal defendants, and the Court's response has generally, although not always, been a summary reversal supporting the state's position.

A *per curiam* ruling rather than a signed opinion may indicate that a case is considered routine or noncontroversial, or may be used to signal that the outcome is obvious and should receive prompt compliance. That can be true even when the case has been argued, as in the 1969 ruling ending "all deliberate speed" in school desegregation (*Alexander v. Holmes County*). The Court also sometimes uses *per curiam* opinions in argued cases when it is very badly divided or when something during briefing or argument prompts the justices not to reach the merits, for example, when the case appears moot or needs further development in the lower courts.[43]

Another type of disposition short of reaching the merits is the Court's sending a case back to the lower courts so it can be reconsidered on the basis of a Supreme Court ruling rendered after the lower court first decided the case.[44] Here the Court grants certiorari, vacates the lower court ruling, and remands for "reconsideration in light of" a specified recently decided case. These GVR (granted/vacated/remanded) rulings, a phenomenon that began largely in the Burger Court, replaced the Warren Court practice of using summary reversals to dispose of cases that were affected by a new and controlling Supreme Court decision and that had been held by the Court until that decision was handed down. The implication of the GVR order is that something is wrong in the lower court's ruling, but the use of GVR dispositions can also be seen as part of a dialogue between the Supreme Court and the lower courts in which the Supreme Court sends a somewhat ambiguous message, the lower court adds its response, and the parties may take the case back to the Supreme Court again; even if the Supreme Court then denies review, the development of the law has proceeded.[45]

All the types of summary dispositions used by the Court have been criticized for providing insufficient guidance to lower court judges and lawyers. Summary decisions without opinion lead people to try to figure out what the Court meant in its brief order with its citation of one or two cases. With a summary affirmance, one cannot tell whether the Court has merely affirmed the lower court's result or also adopted its reasoning. The lack of an opinion in summary reversals can leave the lower court in the dark about whether it has applied the wrong law or applied the proper law erroneously. Compounding these difficulties is that the Court has indicated that summary rulings are not to be given the same precedential weight as the Court's full opinions.

When the Court, facing a case involving novel legal issues or significantly changing or extending the law, decides it with an opinion announcing new law but without full briefing and oral argument on the basis of only the certiorari (or, earlier, appeals) papers, some justices are quite likely to complain. Such complaints were made when the Court, without full briefing and argument, sustained a 40-year prison term for possession of marijuana against a cruel and unusual punishment claim,[46] and when, in the *Snepp* case, the justices ordered a former Central Intelligence Agency employee to disgorge the profits from his book because he breached his duty to submit material for prepublication review. Recently, dissenters have claimed that the Court's use of such decisions is "one-sided," favoring prosecutors as the Court reverses prodefendant lower court rulings but not proprosecution rulings.[47]

Despite these protests, summary dispositions do provide the justices an additional option in cases for which the Court does not have time for full-dress treatment but on which they wish to act. Summary dispositions also allow the Court to "clean up" a large number of cases in a particular policy area. They may also be used to make clear to lower court judges that their rulings need to be reexamined and cases disposed of more completely in the lower courts. Summary actions may also preserve freedom of action for the justices by providing a result, and thus perhaps an implicit message, without the constraints that full development of doctrinal reasons would impose. However, a summary action's visibility may be too low for the ruling to have its intended effect, particularly when resistance to the Court's policy exists. Thus the Court's mid-1960s attempt to communicate through *per curiam* rulings that desegregation should take place more rapidly was generally ignored, requiring more explicit rulings in 1968 and 1969.

Certiorari: The Process of Choice

The power to grant or deny certiorari (see page 73 for a definition) is fully discretionary. Yet the Court's choice of cases is not random. This leads one to question whether, as is often claimed, the Court is a passive body waiting until someone brings a "case or controversy" for decision. A discretionary jurisdiction court like the Supreme Court *is* active. The ability to pick and choose cases makes it like a fisherman of cases. The Court can't place fish in the stream: that is, it cannot create a lawsuit where none exists, but it may stimulate others to stock the stream when the Court's pattern of granting review or the justices' statements prompt litigation to resolve previously undecided or currently unsettled issues. Particularly when those fishing (the justices) change, there may also be changes in those who stock the streams; for example, the change in membership from the Warren Court to the Burger Court led to a partial shift from defendants seeking to suppress evidence or to reverse convictions to prosecutors seeking to have judges' suppression of evidence reversed. In short, the Court's activity may increase the level of nutrients for certain types of fish more than for others, while for other types of cases the Court may provide "acid rain," killing off—or at least reducing—certain types of fish, although it may take considerable time before the Court's actions have an effect. If we talk the language of economists instead of sports fishers, we could say that the Court can depress the market for a certain type of case by denying review while it can create a market by granting certiorari to other types of cases.

By custom, certiorari (cert. for short) is granted by a vote of at least four justices. This is the *Rule of Four* that had been also applicable to decisions to note probable jurisdiction in an appeal. A decision to "hold" a case to determine whether review should be granted until after the Court has decided another pending case with the same issue requires only three votes. Complication can arise from the intersection of different rules requiring different numbers of votes for different actions. We can see this in Justice Brennan's complaint that a five-justice majority was subverting the rule on "holds" by refusing to continue a stay of execution in a death penalty case until the Court had ruled on the certiorari petition in the case.[48]

An important norm is that once the Rule of Four has been satisfied, the justices who opposed review, if they comprise a five-justice majority, should *not* turn around and vote to dismiss the case; *all* should participate in deciding it on the merits. Yet this norm can be violated. Justice Frankfurter did that in Federal Employer Liability Act (FELA) cases; because he thought the Court should not review those cases, he refused to participate in deciding them. If all the justices followed Justice Frankfurter's practice, the Rule of Four would be a Rule of Five. This was suggested by Justice Stevens as an alternative to adoption of other major changes to deal with the Court's caseload. He said that in between 23 and 30 percent of cases in the 1979–81 Terms, there were only four votes for certiorari. According to Justice Brennan, either the minimum four votes or five votes are cast to hear a case in well over half the Court's screening decisions, with relatively few of the Court's decisions to grant review unanimous (only 9% in the 1972 Term).[49] Adherence to the Rule of Four is generally routine, but controversy can still develop over it, suggesting that the rule's continued vitality is fragile. For example, Justice Rehnquist complained that the Court violated the rule by not considering an issue raised in a certiorari petition when the Court decided a case on other grounds.[50]

There are some instances in which four justices, having satisfied the Rule of Four so that a case can be reviewed, do not insist that the Court hear the case. For example, four justices who regularly voted to grant certiorari in obscenity cases, an area in which the Burger Court's majority was firm, said they would not insist the cases be heard because they knew the other five justices would consti-tute a regular majority on the merits. Justice Stevens has suggested that such an alignment is a sufficient reason for the four to vote to deny certiorari, rather than going through the motions of a separate statement.[51]

The process by which the decision is made to grant or deny certiorari, in a vote at a conference of the justices, for the most part is the result of nine individ-ual decisions. Indeed, we can talk about nine separate certiorari process*es* rather than one process,[52] with relatively little bargaining or vote-trading in the review-granting/denying process. Largely because of the press of time, there is relatively little communication between the justices' chambers about granting review in particular cases before the justices gather at conference, and most of the justices come prepared to vote in most cases. However, there are times when justices seek additional votes for review by circulating a draft dissent from a denial of review; such drafts pick up votes in perhaps 10 to 30 cases per term. There are also times when a justice, not feeling strongly about a case but willing to have it reviewed, will have marked a petition "Join 3"—that is, if three other members of the Court wish the case reviewed, the "Join 3" justice will vote to grant certiorari. (This is, however, not a "courtesy vote" when the potential fourth vote is indifferent, but a somewhat weak proreview position.)

In the earliest years of certiorari review, under the 1891 Act, there were relatively few petitions. Each justice received the printed record and briefs, prepared a memo or note about his views, and discussed each petition at conference. As the number of certiorari petitions increased, detailed conference consideration of each petition was not possible. However, some justices have prepared an outline of issues in the petitions and distributed the outlines prior to the Friday conference, and at times there has also been an assignment of memo writing, occasionally to two justices, prior to consideration of the petitions.

There has been a shift from each justice doing his own screening of all the petitions—with the assistance of law clerks—to use of a "cert. pool." In this arrangement, initiated by Justice Powell and now participated in by almost all the justices, the certiorari petitions are randomly assigned to the combined clerks from the participating justices' offices; the clerk prepares a memo that is then circulated to all the pool justices (and about which nonpool justices' clerks sometimes inquire). Clerks of nonpool justices also prepare memos on cert. petitions, but those memos tend to be less formal than the pool memos. Justice Stevens has his clerks do memos only on cases he considers "certworthy," and Justice Brennan read all the cert. petitions himself once the term began, although he might have asked a clerk to do some research before he made a decision.

A justice with experience in dealing with cert. petitions can reduce a large pile of them to a much more manageable pile in short order, because the justice has a "feel" or educated intuition about a case's certworthiness, or significance. After the justice pays greater attention to the reduced pile, the pile can be reduced still further, for consideration at the conference. No matter how much substance clerks contribute to opinions or to suggestions that a case be accepted for review, it is the *justices*, not the clerks, who are definitely in charge. In stating this, Justice Rehnquist (once Justice Robert Jackson's clerk) once asserted, however, that the clerks' political orientations were more liberal than the justices' and affected the cases the clerks recommended the Court take for review.[53]

Prior to the presence of rapid, reliable photocopying machines, there would be only one copy of the *in forma pauperis* ("unpaid") petitions. The Chief Justice had particular responsibility for the unpaid petitions, as part of his task of making the conference presentation of most cases. Now, however, with effective copying machines, each justice receives a copy of all certiorari petitions. Over time there has been a shift from discussion of every case to discussion of every case not on the *dead list* of cases, not to be discussed at conference—and automatically denied review—unless such consideration was requested by another justice, to discussion of a case only if it is on the *discuss list*. The Chief Justice, whose role is still quite significant, prepares this list, to which all capital punishment cases are automatically added. Cases not on that list are not discussed and are denied review unless another justice specifically requests it, and the requesting justice makes the conference presentation if such a case is an "unpaid" one.

The Chief Justice's job is not merely an administrative one of arranging matters so the conference can proceed efficiently: the Chief Justice's choices can make a difference, because to some extent the other justices defer to him. If someone else were Chief Justice, the discuss list would be at least somewhat different. Although the others can and do add cases to the discuss list, there might be others they would put on it in the first instance were it their responsibility. Although some cases are within the associate justices' "zone of indifference," evidence from the justices' papers suggests that they challenge the Chief Justice as to items on the discuss list "on a significant number of occasions in a term." This is because the discuss list, as part of the process by which the Court's agenda is developed, is not neutral, but its formation "is the initial skirmish in the battle for public policy," so that "the content of the discuss list holds enormous implications for the eventual shape of decisions on the merits." [54]

Although factors accounting for a case's being special-listed are not "easily identifiable," cases on the special list during the tenure of Justice Harold Burton (1947–58) seemed to be those where the certiorari petitions (and law clerks' summaries) contained one or more characteristics that served as "demerits" but "no countervailing considerations in favor of review." [55] Intensive examination of the 1982 Term shows that the justices' ideology plays a part, as does the presence of *amicus curiae* briefs and the government's presence as a participant. Also, the lower courts are in conflict in a far higher percentage of cases on the discuss list than of total filings. Particularly significant is that for almost all cases on the discuss list (95%), the respondent had filed a brief in opposition to the Court's granting certiorari. [56]

Once having granted certiorari in a case, the justices can change their minds. In such situations, they dispose of the writ by dismissing it as "improvidently granted" (DIG). They do so when developments affecting the legal posture of a case occur after certiorari is granted, or when briefs or oral argument present a picture different from the one gained from the certiorari petition, which presents less information. Frequent use of the DIG disposition provokes criticism, and specific instances of its use are also criticized. One occurred when the Court, immediately after *Brown v. Board of Education*, after hearing oral argument in a case involving discrimination by a cemetery association, dividing evenly, and receiving a request for rehearing, dismissed certiorari to avoid deciding the case.[57]

There is also concern within the Court that the DIG disposition will be used to undercut the Rule of Four. Thus Justice Brennan argued that a justice who had voted *not* to grant review should not vote to dismiss the case until and unless all four justices who had favored review agreed in that disposition; but Justice Stevens thought the Rule of Four was satisfied so long as one justice originally favoring certiorari was in the majority voting to dismiss. Later Stevens argued that, while the Court should usually decide a case on the merits once four justices had voted to grant certiorari, there was *"always* an important intervening development that may be decisive in leading a majority to DIG a case—the Court's consideration of the case after full briefing and argument, which might cast new light on it.[58]

Reasons for Granting. The granting of certiorari is discretionary but not random. The Court need not give any reasons in granting, denying, or dismissing review, and seldom does so. A dissent from a *grant* of certiorari is extremely rare; when Chief Justice Burger did this, Justice Blackmun complained that a justice doing so indicates commitment to a result in a case before reviewing most of the materials concerning that case.[59]

Chief Justice Warren claimed that "the standards by which the justices decide to grant or deny review are highly personalized and . . . cannot be captured in any rule or guidelines that would be meaningful."[60] However, references to the idea of certworthiness suggests there are regular criteria on which there is consensus. Because litigants or potential litigants "differ in their capacity to deduce probable review criteria from the pattern of grants and denials and the Court's meager guidelines on review criteria," those with considerable experience and expertise in the process of seeking review ("repeat players") "tend to benefit from the obscurity of standards for review," while those who are inexperienced lack that advantage.[61]

The court only occasionally says much about why specific cases have been accepted for review. At the time certiorari is granted, the Court does not tell why it has done so, although the justices ultimately offer some explanation in the Court's opinion. Seldom is the Court's statement more than "We accepted this case in order [to answer the question presented]." At times the importance of the case is noted or a comment is made about the "substantial" or "novel" question presented. Beyond these usual noncommunicative reasons, the need to resolve a conflict between the circuits is the principal reason frequently mentioned. There are, however, times when the Court does tell us more. For example, the Court granted review because the Federal Reserve System's Open Market Committee said a lower court ruling on prompt access to monetary policy directives under the Freedom of Information Act "could seriously interfere with the implementation of national monetary policy." And it granted review when a lower court ruling "exposes the Federal Government to substantial potential liability" and "implicates important questions about a federal court's remedial powers."[62]

The Court's rules talk of granting cert. before the court of appeals has ruled on a case (known as *certiorari before judgment*) in cases of "imperative public importance" but the justices appear to have done so in other situations as well. Cases falling into the "imperative public importance" category include the Nazi saboteurs case during World War II (*Ex parte Quirin*), the Steel Seizure Case, the Nixon Tapes Case, and the Iran hostage case (*Dames & Moore*). There are instances in which certiorari before judgment is granted so the Court can join a case to others with the same issue already before the Court. The *Bolling* case from the District of Columbia, decided along with *Brown v. Board of Education*, was one such case. In addition, the Court at times takes some cases on this basis when the case is coming back to the Court a second time or did so when the parties erroneously took a direct appeal from the district court.[63]

CONSIDERATIONS GOVERNING REVIEW ON CERTIORARI

1. A review on writ of certiorari is not a matter of right, but of judicial discretion, and will be granted only when there are special and important reasons therefor. The following, while neither controlling nor fully measuring the Court's discretion, indicate the character of reasons that will be considered.

(a) When a United States court of appeals has rendered a decision in conflict with the decision of another United States court of appeals on the same matter; or has decided a federal question in a way in conflict with a state court of last resort; or has so far departed from the accepted and usual course of judicial proceedings, or so far sanctioned such a departure by a lower court, as to call for an exercise of this Court's power of supervision.

(b) When a state court of last resort has decided a federal question in a way in conflict with the decision of another state court of last resort or of a United States court of appeals.

(c) When a state court or a United States court of appeals has decided an important question of federal law which has not been, but should be, settled by this Court, or has decided a federal question in a way that conflicts with applicable decisions of this Court.

(Rule 10, effective January 1, 1990)

In its Rule 10, the Court has set forth an official statement of some factors it will *consider* in deciding whether to grant certiorari. Rule 10 stresses legal considerations, and thus is incomplete. In addition to the matters raised there, the presence of an "adequate and independent" state ground (see page 180) has also always been understood to bar Supreme Court review or, if it were discovered after review had been granted, to serve as a basis for dismissing certiorari. Where it is unclear whether a state court has based its ruling on state or federal law, the Court can defer acting on a certiorari petition until a certificate is obtained from the state court explaining its action (see page 184) or the Court can grant the petition and vacate the lower court ruling and remand it for such clarification.

However, the Court's ruling in *Michigan v. Long* (1983), that state courts must make a clear statement they are relying on state law, means the justices will be likely to rule directly on the petition without use of those options.

Individual justices, in off-the-court statements, have also indicated why they grant review or what the Court looks for in considering petitions for review. Chief Justice Rehnquist has said that the grant of review indicates that at least a number of the justices find the lower court's decision problematic—or perhaps troubling. Chief Justice Vinson once said that the Court does not grant certiorari merely to correct errors of the lower courts, but instead uses the writ to deal with cases with broader effects, "questions whose resolution will have immediate importance far beyond the particular facts and parties involved." And Justice Harlan stated from the bench that "the certiorari jurisdiction was not conferred upon this Court 'merely to give the defeated party in the Court of Appeals another hearing,' . . . or 'for the benefit of the particular litigants,' . . . but to decide issues, 'the settlement of which is of importance to the public as distinguished from . . . the parties.' "[64] More recently, Justice Stevens said he did not "believe that error is a sufficient justification for the exercise of this Court's discretionary jurisdiction," because the Court was "much too busy to correct every error that is called to our attention in the thousands of certiorari petitions that are filed each year."[65] Chief Justice Warren's statement that certiorari jurisdiction was "designed by Congress for a very special purpose . . . not only to achieve control of its docket but also to establish our national priorities in constitutional and legal matters"[66] makes clear that political—and strategic—considerations in the broadest sense are behind the Court's review-granting choices.

The Court's actions may also perhaps be explained by the presence of certain *cues* or characteristics of cases. Some of these cues are relatively fixed (an "index"), while others ("signals") are manipulable (not fixed)—like intercircuit conflicts (not fixed because people disagree about whether there is a conflict).[67] The source of a case and the party seeking review are two index items relevant to whether the Court grants review. As to the former, federal appeals are more likely to be accepted than state appeals, but the proportions of state and federal certiorari petitions accepted are more nearly alike.

The party seeking review has regularly been related to the Court's decision to grant review. In 1947–58, certiorari was granted in 49.1 percent of cases in which the only cue was that the federal government favored review, compared to only 5.8 percent of cases in which all other parties sought review—the same as when no cue appeared.[68] When the U.S. government sought review, at least one justice was likely to vote for review in most cases—impressive in view of the fact that most denials were unanimous.[69] An example of the continuing presence of the government-as-party cue comes in the observation that "in most areas of business regulation, the Court's voice is seldom heard except when the Solicitor General persuades the Justices that an erroneous ruling in the court below threatens an important government program."[70] (See pages 145–46.)

Civil rights or civil liberties issues have been highly correlated with the granting of review, but presence of an economic issue alone did little to improve chances of review being granted.[71] Where the sole cues were disagreement between *judges* in a single court, that is, nonunanimous decisions, or disagreement between *courts*, such as where an appeals court had reversed the trial court, certiorari was granted in 12.8 percent of cases. Disagreement *within* a court of appeals may provide a stronger signal to the justices than disagreement *between* levels, but the findings on this matter are not clear.[72] However, intercircuit conflict—even if some lawyers tend to overestimate its existence—is a "signal" related to the granting of review. A study of the 1947–76 Terms showed that the presence of two types of conflict—of a lower court ruling with Supreme Court precedent, and of lower court rulings with each other—both were related positively to the Court's granting of review. Intercircuit conflict was actually less a relevant cue for the Burger Court than for the Warren Court[73] but once the discuss list had been created, intercircuit conflict was an important determinant— along with the solicitor general's participation and that of *amici curiae*—in the granting of review.[74] (However, counter to other studies, it appears that the type of issue has little effect on whether review will be granted.[75]) Of particular interest is that *amicus curiae* briefs in *opposition* to the grant of review may have a significant effect on that decision. One might even say that those opposing review might be better off if they "held their fire," because the very act of opposition serves to call to the justices' attention that many people consider the case important—one of the factors considered in granting review.[76]

Although the same factors play a role in creation of the discuss list and in granting of review once the list is created, "the considerations at play in [these] two phases differ in a significant fashion," and "the decision on certiorari is not simply a replay of the decision to place a case on the discuss list." Factors (cues) that might have caught the Court's attention and played an important role in the first decision, to create the discuss list, may play a less important role in the second decision, to grant review.[77]

What Does Denial Mean? Formally a certiorari denial means only that the Court has not accepted the case, thus leaving the ruling of the lower court undisturbed. As Justice Frankfurter reminded us some years ago, the justices "do not have to, and frequently do not, reach the merits of a case to decide that it is not of sufficient importance to warrant review here." Thus certiorari denial "imports no expression of opinion upon the merit of the case." Such denial "means only that, for one reason or another, which is seldom disclosed, and not infrequently for conflicting reasons, which may have nothing to do with the merits and certainly may have nothing to do with any view of the merits taken by a majority of the Court, there were not four members of the Court who thought the case should be heard." Or, as Justice Jackson observed in the same case, "denial of certiorari . . . creates no precedent and approves no statement of principle entitled to weight in any other case."[78] As Justice Marshall has argued, "Reliance on denial of certiorari for *any* proposition impairs the vitality of the discretion we exercise in controlling the cases we hear."[79] Certiorari denials do, however, have effects. Chief Justice Warren wrote after his retirement that denials had "a significant impact on the ordering of constitutional and legal priorities. Many potential and important developments in the law have been frustrated, at least temporarily, by a denial of certiorari."[80] He did, however, stop short of saying such action was purposeful.

Many Court observers do not accept statements about the nonmeaning of certiorari denials. Justice Jackson conceded that "the Court is not quite of one mind of the subject," continuing, "Some say denial means nothing, others say it means nothing much." However, he asserted, "Realistically, the first position is untenable and the second is unintelligible."[81] Some infer consideration of the merits of a case from denials of review. Thus, "when the Court consistently leaves undisturbed decisions at variance with principle, or when it denies certiorari in a notorious case . . . the public may well believe that the Court is implementing an unspoken constitutional judgment."[82] Despite Justice Frankfurter's 1953 admonition that "the Bar [was] not to draw strength for lower court opinions from the fact that they were left unreviewed here,"[83] lawyers continue to cite certiorari denials. This further stimulates guesses about the meaning of the denials, although such action by lawyers may be no more than their way of indicating that a legal issue is not settled and should therefore be decided, or it may simply be a matter of form (the citation is not complete without noting the cert. denial).

More fuel is added to the fire when the justices themselves cite the Court's certiorari denials in concurring or dissenting opinions more than as a matter of form. Justice Blackmun speculated in 1973 that dissents from an earlier certiorari denial were "not without some significance as to [the justices'] and the Court's attitude." This provoked an extended response from Justice Marshall, who said justices may simultaneously agree about an issue's importance and feel the case was not the "appropriate vehicle for determination of that issue." As Justice Rehnquist has observed, "Some Members of the Court may feel that a case is wrongly decided, but lacking in general importance; others may feel that it is of general importance, but rightly decided; for either reason, a vote to deny certiorari is logically dictate[d]."[84]

The Court gives reasons for its denial of review even less frequently than when it grants review—indeed, hardly at all. A sample of more than 3,000 denied petitions over 20 years produced fewer than 40 explanations, of which the most common was dismissal on motion of the parties or failure to timely file.[85] In the 1972 and 1973 Terms, 60 percent of the dissenting opinions in certiorari denials stated the need for a national decision to resolve conflicts between lower courts or between the lower courts and the Supreme Court, the presence of statutory questions that needed to be resolved, or "the existence of important questions for decision."[86]

The Court is better off *not* explaining its denials if it wishes to avoid open disagreement from its own members, as occurred twice in 1978. When the Court indicated in denying review that it appears "that the judgment of the Illinois Supreme Court rests on an adequate state ground," Justice Stevens complained that such statements were "inconsistent with the rule that such denials have no precedential value."[87] And when the Court denied a petition "for failure to file the petition within the time provided" by the relevant statute, Stevens, along with Justices Brennan and Stewart, objected because the lack of precedential value of a certiorari denial meant the notation "serves no useful purpose" and because such explanations are offered only "spasmodic[ally]" and without consistency.[88] Justice Jackson felt lawyers could no longer believe denial of review to be meaningless when justices began to file such dissenting statements. Lawyers, said Jackson, "will not readily believe that Justices of this Court are taking the trouble to signal a meaningless division of opinion about a meaningless act." Moreover, he added, "every lower court does attach importance to denials and to presence or absence of dissents from denials."[89]

Justice Stevens has recently questioned the validity of dissents from certiorari denials because the strong, perhaps emotional, case the dissenters make can create the impression that the Court, which does not answer the dissenters, "is not managing its discretionary docket in a responsible manner."[90] Stevens has suggested some possible reasons for denial of review, such as procedural defects, not mentioned in the dissenters' complaints.[91] He also noted that the dissenters' written statements have at times been more persuasive than statements made at the Court's conference and have led other justices to change their votes so that review was granted. However, argued Stevens, such results only justified writing and circulating these memoranda, not publishing them if the dissenters had failed to persuade their colleagues.[92] Going further than Stevens, in separate cases Justices Blackmun and Brennan wrote statements *in support of* certiorari denials—Blackmun disagreeing with dissenters from the denial and Brennan suggesting alternative procedural resolutions of the problem presented by a case.[93]

There has been a substantial increase in the number of dissents from certiorari denials despite the absence of time for writing separate opinions and some earlier norms against their use. Not all dissents deal with the merits of cases, but those that do are an indication that review decisions and rulings on the merits are related.[94] Justices' ideologies help explain dissents from cert. denials, with the liberals Douglas, Brennan, and Marshall frequently dissenting from denials of review, but justices' proclivity to vote for review also helps explain their behavior. Some "review prone" justices, like Justice Douglas, have accounted for much of the increase in dissents, but others, like Burton and Frankfurter, were "review conservative."[95] Justices vary in the degree to which they take the merits of a case into account in decisions to grant or deny review ("merits-consciousness").[96] Where the government has won a criminal case in the lower courts, a justice generally favoring criminal defendants (as shown by his votes in full opinion cases) would vote to grant review, while justices who would support the govern-ment once the case was accepted would vote not to grant certiorari; when the government was appealing from a ruling excluding evidence in a case, the reverse pattern would occur.

A judge's certiorari votes helped predict the judge's votes on the merits in cases accepted in the 1947–56 Terms. Liberal and conservative voting blocs among the justices could be identified not only from votes on the merits but also at the certiorari stage: a justice who voted with one set of justices in full opinion cases was *un*likely to vote with his remaining colleagues at the review-granting stage.[97] Indeed, in selected terms from 1954 through 1975, decisions to grant review in "paid" cases can be explained on the basis of whether petitioners are "Upperdogs" or "Underdogs." Upperdogs did better than Underdogs in getting their cases accepted, but Underdogs' success rate was much higher during the Warren Court (55%) than in the Burger Court (39%), when the justices most clearly differentiated between the two in accepting and rejecting cases.[98] How-ever, judges' attitudes cannot explain the high proportion of unanimous deci-sions on granting or denying review or the fact that cases most often unanimously denied review have tapped dissimilar ideological matters, such as prisoner peti-tions and commercial suits by business interests. Such unanimity is likely the result of shared views about the types of cases to which the Court should devote its attention.

Evidence of judges' strategy in their certiorari votes has also been used to explain certiorari denial in political terms and to suggest that judges may try to disguise their attitudes from their colleagues or that certiorari votes on particular issues can be explained in terms of the strategies of game theory. Schubert sug-gested that during 1942–48 in Federal Employer Liability Act cases, a bloc of four justices (Murphy, Rutledge, Black, and Douglas) voted together on certiorari to achieve victory on the merits. This was parallel to a strategy of never voting for the railroad (the employer) on certiorari but always voting for the worker when the court of appeals had reversed a proworker district court decision, then always voting for the worker on the merits. The four justices had a 92 percent success rate (12 of 13) when they followed that pattern, but only a 73 percent rate (8 of 13) when they voted for workers who had lost in both trial and appeals courts. When the four-justice bloc grew to five, they "won" 13 of 14 cases in the 1956–57 Terms; no justice voted for certiorari in the "lost" case because the appeal was so frivolous.[99]

Justice Burton's docket book showed, however, that members of the "certior-ari bloc" showed a lack of consistency. The Court agreed to hear some cases only through the votes of nonbloc members favoring workers and some justices voted to grant review with little apparent regard for whether the cases would produce policies they wished the Court to announce. That justices favoring workers on the merits did cast a high proportion of their certiorari votes so as to favor workers does indicate the effect of the justices' ideology, but the other evidence shows limited use of strategy. More recently, however, examination of the same Court period showed that justices who voted to grant review and then held to a position of reversing the lower court had a higher rate of success in getting the Court to grant review than were justices who were consistent in supporting affirmance of the lower court. This provides evidence of an "error-correcting strategy" in justices' votes to grant review. The evidence does not seem to support the presence of a strategy in which judges vote to grant review because they can predict who will be on the winning side.[100]

The Court's disposition of cases to which it does grant review provides further evidence of the policy implications of certiorari decisions. A pattern "too definite to have arisen by sheer happenstance"[101] appears in the Court's reversal of the lower courts in roughly two out of three certiorari cases over the 30 years up to the Rehnquist Court. With the exception of only a couple out of the last 10 Burger Court years, the proportion of reversals in full opinion cases hovered around 70 percent, with the proportion higher if *per curiam* rulings are added. In the Rehnquist Court, however, the proportion of affirmances rose to over 40 percent in the 1987 and 1988 Terms, but by the 1990 Term it had returned to a 32.3 percent affirmance rate, meaning that two-thirds of the cases were being reversed.[102] Moreover, when the Court has affirmed a lower court ruling, there was more dissent than when the Court reversed the lower court.[103] The rate of reversal seems to indicate clearly a better-than-even chance that the Court approved of lower court decisions to which it did not grant review. Further confirmation comes from Burton's docket book, which indicates that, despite differences between them, justices were more likely to vote to reverse the lower court in cases in which they had voted to grant review than in those in which they did not cast a vote favoring review, and that the Supreme Court reversed the lower court more frequently when five justices (a majority of the full Court) voted to grant review.[104]

Notes

1. Doris M. Provine, *Case Selection in the United States Supreme Court* (Chicago: University of Chicago Press, 1980), pp. 62–63.

2. Arthur D. Hellman, "Case Selection in the Burger Court: A Preliminary Inquiry," *Notre Dame Law Review* 60 (1985): 996, 998.

3. See *Brown v. Herald Co.*, 462 U.S. 928 (1983).

4. *In re Sindram*, 111 S.Ct. 596 (1991); *Demos v. U.S. District Court for the Eastern District of Washington*, 111 S.Ct. 1569 (1991).

5. *In re Amendment to Rule 39*, 111 S.Ct. 1572 at 1573. For the first application of the new rule, see *Zatko v. California*, 112 S.Ct. 355 (1991).

6. Gerhard Casper and Richard A. Posner, *The Workload of the Supreme Court* (Chicago: American Bar Foundation, 1976), pp. 11–12.

7. Ibid., p. 6. See also Gerhard Casper and Richard A. Posner, "The Caseload of the Supreme Court: 1975 and 1976 Terms," *The Supreme Court Review 1977*, ed. Philip B. Kurland and Gerhard Casper (Chicago: University of Chicago Press, 1978), pp. 87–98, updating their earlier study.

8. Hellman, "Case Selection in the Burger Court," p. 952.

9. For additional data, see the Statistical Tables in the *Harvard Law Review's* annual (November) issue on the Supreme Court's previous term. See particularly Five Year Tables I and II: 82 (November

1968): 310; 87 (November 1973): 310–11; 92 (November 1978): 336–37;   97 (November 1983): 303– 6; 102 (November 1988): 350–58.

10. Joseph Stewart, Jr., and Edward V. Heck, "Caseloads and Controversies: A Different Perspective on the 'Overburdened' U.S. Supreme Court," *Justice System Journal* 12 (Winter 1987): 374, 379.

11. These findings are from William McLauchlan, "Managing the Supreme Court's Business, 1971–1983," paper presented to American Political Science Association, 1986; the data are based on paid petitions.

12. Arthur D. Hellman, "The Proposed Intercircuit Tribunal: Do We Need It? Will It Work?" *Hastings Constitutional Law Quarterly* 11 (Spring 1984): 383–84.

13. *Warth v. Seldin*, 422 U.S. 490 at 519 (1975); *Tidewater Oil Co. v. United States*, 409 U.S. 151 at 174–76 (1972).

14. For complaints about the Court's having taken cases for which certiorari did not appear to be warranted, see *Citibank, N.A. v. Wells Fargo Asia Limited*, 110 S.Ct. 2034 at 2042 (1990) (Rehnquist); and *United States v. Dalm*, 110 S.Ct. 1361 at 1370 (1990) (Stevens).

15. Mary Cornelia Porter, "Politics, Ideology and the Workload of the Supreme Court: Some Historical Perspectives," paper presented to Midwest Political Science Association, 1975, pp. 8, 10.

16. Casper and Posner, *The Workload of the Supreme Court*, p. 31.

17. *Tatum v. Regents of University of Nebraska-Lincoln*, 426 U.S. 1117 (1983).

18. *Talamini v. Allstate Insurance Co.*, 470 U.S. 1067 at 1069–72 (Stevens), 1072–73 (Burger) (1985). See also *Hyde v. Van Wormer*, 474 U.S. 992 (1985).

19. See, in particular, White's statement in *Beaulieu v. United States*, 110 S.Ct. 3302 at 3302–3 (1990).

20. Commission on Revision of Federal Court Appellate System, *Structure and Internal Procedures* (Washington, D.C., 1975), pp. 29–31.

21. Hellman, "The Proposed Intercircuit Tribunal," p. 415.

22. Samuel Estreicher and John E. Sexton, "A Managerial Theory of the Supreme Court's Responsibilities: An Empirical Study," *New York University Law Review* 59 (October 1984): 725.

23. Ibid., p. 709. See also Estreicher and Sexton, *Redefining the Supreme Court's Role: A Theory of Managing the Federal Judicial Process* (New Haven, Conn.: Yale University Press, 1986).

24. Glendon Schubert, *The Constitutional Polity* (Boston, Mass.: Boston University Press, 1970), p. 10.

25. J. Woodford Howard, Jr., "Is the Burger Court a Nixon Court?" *Emory Law Journal* 23 (Summer 1974): 757.

26. Arthur D. Hellman, "The Supreme Court, the National Law, and the Selection of Cases for the Plenary Docket," *University of Pittsburgh Law Review* 44 (Spring 1983): 549.

27. Arthur D. Hellman, "The Supreme Court and Civil Rights: The Plenary Docket in the 1970s," *Oregon Law Review* 58 (1979): 3–60; Hellman, "Case Selection in the Burger Court," pp. 1004–5.

28. See Hellman, "Case Selection in the Burger Court," p. 973; and Hellman, "The Supreme Court, the National Law, " p. 585.

29. For this material, see Arthur D. Hellman, "The Supreme Court and Statutory Law: The Plenary Docket in the 1970's," *University of Pittsburgh Law Review* 40 (Fall 1978): 1–45.

30. Hellman, "The Supreme Court, the National Law," p. 631.

31. Richard L. Pacelle, Jr., "The Supreme Court Agenda Across Time: Towards a Theory of Agenda-Building," paper presented to Midwest Political Science Association, 1986, p. 20. And see Richard L. Pacelle, Jr., *The Transformation of the Supreme Court's Agenda* (Boulder, Colo.: Westview, 1991).

32. Gregory A. Caldeira, "The United States Supreme Court and Criminal Cases, 1935–76: Alternative Models of Agenda Building," *British Journal of Political Science* 2 (1981): 457–61, 463.

33. Richard L. Pacelle, Jr., "The Supreme Court's Agenda and the Dynamics of Policy Evolution," paper presented to American Political Science Association, 1990.

34. Pacelle, "The Supreme Court Agenda Across Time," p. 20.

35. Pacelle, "The Supreme Court's Agenda and the Dynamics of Policy Evolution."

36. *Hicks v. Miranda*, 422 U.S. 332 at 344 (1975), also quoting Justice Brennan, *Ohio ex rel. Eaton v. Price*, 360 U.S. 246 at 247 (1959), to the same effect.

37. S. Sidney Ulmer, "Issue Fluidity in the U.S. Supreme Court: A Conceptual Analysis," *Supreme Court Activism and Restraint* (Lexington, Mass.: Lexington Books, 1982), eds. Stephen C. Halpern and Charles Lamb, p. 339.

38. For Justice Stevens's recent complaint about this practice, see *Gilmer v. Interstate/Johnson Lane Corp.*, 111 S.Ct. 1647 at 1658 (1991).

39. See *MacDonald, Sommer & Frates v. Yolo County*, 477 U.S. 340 (1986); *Williamson Planning Commission v. Hamilton Bank*, 473 U.S. 172 (1985); *San Diego Gas & Electric Co. v. San Diego*, 450 U.S. 621 (1981); *Agins v. Tiburon*, 447 U.S. 255 (1980). The Court did finally reach the issue. See *First English Evangelical Lutheran Church of Glendale v. County of Los Angeles*, 484 U.S. 304 (1987); *Nollan v. California Coastal Commission*, 483 U.S. 825 (1987); and *Lucas v. South Carolina Coastal Council*, 112 S.Ct. 2886 (1992).

40. For an example, see *Batson v. Kentucky*, 476 U.S. 79 (1986) (prosecutors' use of peremptory challenges to eliminate racial minorities), and Chief Justice Burger's complaint, at 1732–33.

41. Ulmer, "Issue Fluidity," p. 322. For discussion of matters related to issue fluidity, see *Yee v. City of Escondido*, 112 S.Ct. 1522 at 1533–34 (1992).

42. See Arthur D. Hellman, "Error Correction, Lawmaking, and the Supreme Court's Exercise of Discretionary Review," *University of Pittsburgh Law Review* 44 (Summer 1983): 825–26.

43. For further development, see Stephen L. Wasby, Steven Peterson, James Schubert, and Glendon Schubert, "The Per Curiam Opinion: Its Nature and Functions," *Judicature* 76 (June–July 1992): 29–38.

44. Arthur D. Hellman, " 'Granted, Vacated, and Remanded'—Shedding Light on a Dark Corner of Supreme Court Practice," *Judicature* 67 (March 1984): 389–401; Hellman, "The Supreme Court's Second Thoughts: Remands for Reconsideration and Denials of Review in Cases Held for Plenary Decisions," *Hastings Constitutional Law Quarterly* 11 (Fall 1983): 17–20.

45. Linda Greenhouse, "Justices' Rulings Have a Ripple Effect on the Law," *New York Times*, March 9, 1989, p. B14.

46. *Hutto v. Davis*, 454 U.S. 370 at 387 (1982) (Brennan).

47. See *Florida v. Burr*, 110 S.Ct. 2608 at 2613 (1990) (Stevens, dissenting).

48. *Straight v. Wainwright*, 476 U.S. 1132 at 1134–35 (1986); *Watson v. Butler* 483 U.S. 1037 at 1038–39 (1987). See also *Herrara v. Collins*, 112 S.Ct. 1074 (1992).

49. John Paul Stevens, "The Life Span of a Judge-made Rule," *New York University Law Review* 58 (1983): 17; William Brennan, "The National Court of Appeals: Another Dissent," *University of Chicago Law Review* 40 (1973): 479.

50. *Thigpen v. Roberts*, 468 U.S. 27 at 33 (1984).

51. *Dyke v. Georgia*, 421 U.S. 952 (1975) (obscenity); *Liles v. Oregon*, 425 U.S. 963 (1976) (Stevens).

52. For much material in this section, I have drawn on two papers by H. W. Perry, Jr. "Indices and Signals in the Certiorari Process," presented to the Midwest Political Science Association, 1986, and "Deciding to Decide in the U.S. Supreme Court: Bargaining, Accommodation, and Roses," presented to American Political Science Association, 1986. See H. W. Perry, Jr., *Deciding to Decide: Agenda Setting in the United States Supreme Court* (Cambridge, Mass.: Harvard University Press, 1991).

53. William H. Rehnquist, "Who Writes Decisions of the Supreme Court?", *U.S. News & World Report* (December 13, 1957): 74–75, reprinted in *The Courts: A Reader in the Judicial Process*, ed. Robert Scigliano (Boston, Mass.: Little, Brown, 1962), pp. 166–69.

54. Gregory A. Caldeira and John R. Wright, "Organized Interests and the Discuss List in the Supreme Court," paper presented to American Political Science Association, 1988, p. 5, n. 4; p. 9.

55. Provine, *Case Selection*, p. 82.

56. Caldeira and Wright, "Organized Interests and the Discuss List," pp. 23–24.

57. *Rice v. Sioux City Memorial Park Cemetery*, 349 U.S. 70 (1955).

58. *Burrell v. McCray*, 426 U.S. 471 (1976); *New York v. Uplinger*, 476 U.S. 246 at 250 (1984). For an account of *Burrell*, see Robert Woodward and Scott Armstrong, *The Brethren* (New York: Simon and Schuster, 1981), pp. 424–25.

59. *Darden v. Wainwright*, 477 U.S. 168 at 205 n. 9 (1986).

60. "Retired Chief Justice Warren Attacks . . . Freund Study Group's Composition and Proposal," *American Bar Association Journal* 59 (July 1973): 728.

61. Provine, *Case Selection*, p. 4.

62. *Federal Open Market Committee v. Merrill*, 443 U.S. 340 at 344 (1979); *Lyng v. Payne*, 476 U.S. 926 at 934–35 (1986).

63. See James Lindgren and William P. Marshall, "The Supreme Court's Extraordinary Power to Grant Certiorari Before Judgment in the Court of Appeals," *The Supreme Court Review 1986*, eds.

Philip B. Kurland, Gerhard Casper, and Dennis J. Hutchinson (Chicago: University of Chicago Press, 1987), pp. 259–316.

64. Fred M. Vinson, "The Work of the Federal Courts," *Courts, Judges, and Politics*, eds. Walter F. Murphy and C. Herman Pritchett (New York: Random House, 1961), pp. 55–56; *Jones v. Mayer*, 392 U.S. 409 at 478–79 (1968) (Harlan).

65. *Idaho Department of Employment v. Smith*, 434 U.S. 100 at 105–6 (1977).

66. "Retired Chief Justice Warren Attacks . . ." p. 728.

67. Perry, "Indices and Signals," pp. 16 ff.

68. Joseph Tanenhaus, Marvin Schick, Matthew Muraskin, and Daniel Rosen, "The Supreme Court's Jurisdiction: Cue Theory," *Judicial Decision-Making*, ed. Glendon Schubert (New York: Free Press, 1963), p. 123.

69. Provine, *Case Selection*, p. 32, Table 1.4, and p. 82.

70. Hellman, "The Supreme Court, the National Law," p. 632.

71. Tanenhaus et al., "Cue Theory," p. 123; Provine, *Case Selection*, p. 82.

72. J. Woodford Howard, Jr., *Courts of Appeals in the Federal Judicial System*, p. 67; Richard J. Richardson and Kenneth N. Vines, *The Politics of Federal Courts* (Boston, Mass.: Little, Brown, 1970), p. 153.

73. S. Sidney Ulmer, "The Supreme Court's Certiorari Decisions: Conflict as a Predictive Variable," *American Political Science Review* 78 (December 1984): 908. For an important earlier study, see Ulmer, William Hintze, and Louise Kirklosky, "The Decision to Grant or Deny Certiorari: Further Consideration of Cue Theory," *Law & Society Review* 6 (May 1972): 637–44.

74. Caldeira and Wright, "Organized Interests and the Discuss List," pp. 27–28.

75. Gregory A. Caldeira and John R. Wright, "Organized Interests and Agenda Setting in the U.S. Supreme Court," *American Political Science Review* 82 (December 1988): 1118.

76. Ibid., 1119.

77. Caldeira and Wright, "Organized Interests and the Discuss List," p. 26.

78. *Brown v. Allen*, 344 U.S. 443 at 491–92 (Frankfurter), 543 (Jackson) (1953).

79. *United States v. Kras*, 409 U.S. 434 at 443 (Blackmun), 461 (Marshall) (1973).

80. "Retired Chief Justice Warren Attacks . . . ," p. 728.

81. *Brown v. Allen*, at 542–43.

82. David Adamany, "Legitimacy, Realigning Elections, and the Supreme Court," *Wisconsin Law Review* 1973: 801, drawing on Jan Deutsch, "Neutrality, Legitimacy, and the Supreme Court," *Stanford Law Review* 20 (1968): 207.

83. *Brown v. Allen*, at 491.

84. *Huch v. United States*, 439 U.S. 1007 at 1008 (1978).

85. Tanenhaus et al., "Cue Theory," p. 114.

86. Commission on Revision, *Structure and Internal Procedures*, pp. 48–49.

87. *Illinois v. Gray*, 435 U.S. 1013 (1978).

88. *County of Sonoma v. Isbell*, 439 U.S. 996 (1978).

89. *Brown v. Allen*, at 542–43.

90. *Chevron USA v. Sheffield*, 471 U.S. 1140 (1985).

91. See *Huffman v. Florida*, 435 U.S. 1014 at 1018–19 (1978); *Vasquez v. United States*, 454 U.S. 975 at 975–76 (1981).

92. *Singleton v. Commissioner of Internal Revenue*, 439 U.S. 940 at 943–47 (1978).

93. *Kerr-McGee Chemical Corp. v. Illinois*, 459 U.S. 1049 (1982) (Blackmun); *James v. United States*, 459 U.S. 1044 (1982) (Brennan).

94. See Peter Linzer, "The Meaning of Certiorari Denials," *Columbia Law Review* 79 (November 1979): 1255.

95. Provine, *Case Selection*, p. 114.

96. Provine, *Case Selection*, pp. 110–13.

97. See S. Sidney Ulmer, "Supreme Court Justices as Strict and Not-So-Strict Constructionists: Some Implications," *Law & Society Review* 8 (Fall 1973): 27–28; and Ulmer, "Voting Blocs and 'Access' to the Supreme Court: 1947–56 Terms," *Jurimetrics Journal* 16 (Fall 1965): 8, 12.

98. S. Sidney Ulmer, "Selecting Cases for Supreme Court Review: Litigant Status in the Warren and Burger Courts," *Courts, Law, and Judicial Processes*, ed. Ulmer (New York: Free Press, 1981), pp. 284–98; see also Ulmer, "Selecting Cases for Supreme Court Review: An Underdog Model," *American Political Science Review* 72 (September 1978): 902–10.

99. Schubert, "The Certiorari Game," *Quantitative Analysis*, pp. 210–54.

100. John F. Krol and Saul Brenner, "Strategies in Certiorari Voting on the United States Supreme Court: A Reevaluation," *Western Political Quarterly* 43 (June 1990): 335–42.

101. Schubert, *Quantitative Analysis*, p. 66; for his data, see pp. 55–57.

102. See Jeffrey A. Segal and Harold J. Spaeth, "Rehnquist Court Disposition of Lower Court Decisions: Affirmation Not Reversal," *Judicature* 74 (August-September 1990): 84–88, which does not include the 1990 Term and thus overstates the Rehnquist Court's affirmance rate.

103. Burton Atkins, "Interventions and Power in Judicial Hierarchies: Appellate Courts in England and the United States," *Law & Society Review* 24 (1990): 96 n. 32.

104. Provine, *Case Selection*, p. 127.

7 The Supreme Court: Full-Dress Treatment

IN THIS CHAPTER WE examine the "full-dress" treatment given cases accepted for review. In describing the Court's basic procedures for reaching decisions, particular attention is given to oral argument, the Chief Justice's practices in opinion assignment, and the release of opinions. Then we analyze disagreement within the Court and the alignments of the justices as they decide cases. The Court's power of judicial review and the considerations the justices take into account in reaching their decisions and writing their opinions—matters of precedent, strategy, and activism and self-restraint—are examined in the next chapter.

Procedure in the Court

In its early years the Court's sessions were brief. For example, in the early nineteenth century, there were only February and August sessions of roughly two to three weeks; by 1840, there was a continuous January-March session, which grew to roughly four months-plus by the post-Civil War period. The Supreme Court's annual term now begins on the first Monday of October, as it has since the late nineteenth century, and now extends formally until the beginning of the next term. However, the Court's public sessions and the announcement of decisions continue only until late June or the first few days of July, with the justices using the summer to prepare for the next term. The justices hear oral argument from the beginning of the term through late March or early April. In special situations such as the Nixon Tapes case of 1974, argument can be heard as late as June, and the Court has also held special sessions—in 1958 for the Little Rock school desegregation case and in 1972 for the Democratic National Convention delegate challenges. Cases to which the Court grants review early in the term are argued in the same term and are decided within the term; those accepted later in the term are not argued until the following term.

Six justices constitute a quorum for doing business. The Court can thus operate during vacancies, illness, and a justice's withdrawal (recusal) from a case. However, if there is no quorum, as happened in a 1988 case,[1] the lower court's ruling is affirmed and no opinion is written, the same as when the Court is evenly divided 4–4 or 3–3. In order to avoid such tie votes, the Court has tried to delay deciding controversial cases that might produce such a division until vacancies are filled and there is a full complement of nine justices. When this cannot be avoided, as when illness causes a justice to miss oral argument, some cases might be "returned to the calendar" for reargument later in the same term or in the next term, and some cases are released as 4–4 affirmances. The Court does not explain why it chooses one option rather than the other. Even when all nine justices are sitting, the Court orders reargument in a number of cases, at times asking for responses to specific questions. That was true in *Brown v. Board of Education* (where there were three rounds of argument), and has occurred more recently as well.[2] (See also pages 205–6.)

A justice's participation in a case solely to create a full Court is not necessarily proper. This is illustrated by a problem involving Justice Rehnquist, used against him during the debate on his nomination to be Chief Justice. Shortly before he initially joined the court, Rehnquist, as assistant attorney general, had testified before Congress on military surveillance of civilian political activity and had commented that a pending case challenging such surveillance was nonjusticiable—the central issue in the case. The lower court had ruled that the case could be heard, and the Supreme Court granted review before Rehnquist began his service on the Court, but did not hear argument until later. Without Rehnquist's participation, the vote would have been 4–4, sustaining the lower court. However, Rehnquist participated and cast the crucial fifth vote to reverse the lower court, thus eliminating the challenge to the government activity (*Laird v. Tatum*, 1972). This prompted the American Civil Liberties Union (ACLU) to petition for a rehearing of the case in which Rehnquist's disqualification was specifically requested. The Court denied the hearing petition without comment—its usual procedure.

Rehnquist, however, wrote a memorandum supporting his participation. He said he had only been the government's attorney, expressing the administration's position, not necessarily his own. He added that someone in government service prior to joining the Court was quite likely to have made statements of opinions on subjects that would arise later in litigation. To have a blank mind on such subjects would, he said, "be evidence of lack of qualification, not lack of bias." The American Bar Association code of judicial ethics showed a clear preference for avoiding even the appearance of impropriety, but Rehnquist stressed a duty to participate, particularly where his vote was necessary to resolve the case.[3] The ACLU again tried to reopen the case in 1986 on the basis of information from government memoranda made available during the process of confirming Rehnquist as Chief Justice. The ACLU claimed that he had not merely served as the administration's spokesperson, as he had said earlier, but had played a role in drafting the surveillance plan. Without comment, the Court refused to rehear the case.[4]

In evaluating this situation, one might keep in mind that there have been earlier situations in which justices had, prior to coming to the Court, participated actively in developing laws, and then as justices, sat to hear cases involving those laws. Rehnquist said that Justice Jackson ruled on an immigration issue he had handled as attorney general, and noted that Justice Black, as a senator, had been an author of the Fair Labor Standards Act (the minimum wage law) and Justice Frankfurter had played an important role in enactment of the Norris-LaGuardia (anti-injunction) Act, yet both sat on cases involving the constitutionality or scope of those laws.

Justices usually recuse without explanation or comment, and it is up to the individual justice to make the decision. They do so because of acquaintance with the parties or their lawyers; financial interest, however small or indirect, usually from ownership of stock; or involvement with a case before the justice began Supreme Court service. For example, Justice White, who had been deputy attorney general before becoming a justice, recused himself from a number of cases involving the U.S. government, as did Justice Thurgood Marshall, who had been solicitor general; Marshall also recused from some NAACP-supported cases because of his long connection with that organization, and did so even many years after he joined the Court. Justices Brennan, Stewart, and Stevens, former appellate judges, removed themselves from cases coming from the courts on which they had sat. Financial holdings apparently accounted for the disqualification of Justice Powell, Justice Stewart, and Stewart's successor, Justice O'Connor, in a number of cases in recent years. In 1980 the Court amended its rules to require that when corporations file papers with the Court, the papers "include a listing naming all parent companies, subsidiaries (except wholly owned subsidiaries) and affiliates of each such corporation" (Rule 29.1). This was apparently done to facilitate identification of cases in which a justice, a justice's spouse, or other close relatives might have a financial interest, after some apparent embarrassments when justices participated without knowledge of such matters.

They no longer ride circuit (see page 41), but each Supreme Court justice still has responsibility for one or more circuits for emergencies and other matters that must be dealt with when the Court is not in session, and they are qualified to sit in the circuit for which they are circuit justice, as Justice Scalia did in the District of Columbia in 1987. Among the matters brought to them have been school board efforts to block busing orders in connection with school desegregation and, more recently, an effort to block a teenager's obtaining an abortion. A circuit justice can order someone released on bail and can stay lower court orders until the full Court has a chance to act on petitions for review. During Oliver

North's trial, the Chief Justice granted a stay that would have temporarily delayed the trial.

Most frequent are requests to stay executions, often at the last moment, as more and more Death Row convicts exhaust their appeals and execution warrants are issued. At the present time, most are denied, so it makes little difference who the circuit justice is. A 1991 change in circuit justices appeared to make a difference unfavorable to those seeking to fend off executions, when Justice Scalia, the new circuit justice in the Fifth Circuit, announced he would not grant extensions of time to file certiorari petitions when a death penalty inmate did not have a lawyer; Justice White, the previous circuit justice for the Fifth Circuit, had regularly granted such extensions.

In recent years, the Court generally has refused stays and has even lifted lower court stays at the state's request, and has complained about "abuse" of the habeas corpus process by the filing of multiple habeas petitions and about the multiple hearings given defendants in state and federal courts.[5] In some instances, the Court has refused to grant stays to condemned prisoners even when their time to file a certiorari petition had not expired or when they raised an issue the Court was going to consider in cases to which it had granted review.[6] Such actions prompted Justices Brennan and Marshall to complain about the Court's "indecent desire to rush to judgment in capital cases" and its "unseemly and unjustified eagerness" to allow the prisoner's execution.[7]

Most requests to a circuit justice are passed along to the full Court. Because the action of "the lower court, which has considered the matter at length and close at hand," is presumed to be correct,[8] a circuit justice acting alone does not decide a case on the merits but grants a stay only when the applicant makes a strong showing that the lower court's decision is erroneous and that irreparable injury would occur without the stay; the circuit justice also decides (really predicts) that the other justices would consider the matter sufficiently serious to grant review. Formal action on a stay request is the circuit justice's alone, but when the circuit justice considers the matter too important for a single justice's decision, colleagues are consulted, at times by telephone.

The difficulties that can arise when a stay is requested in a controversial matter are illustrated by what occurred during the controversy over the bombing of Cambodia. A district judge had enjoined the bombing and the court of appeals had stayed the injunction. Those seeking to stop the bombing sought to have Justice Thurgood Marshall, the circuit justice, set aside the appellate court order, but Marshall said that as a single justice he would exceed his authority if he were to do so because he thought the appellate court had not acted improperly. Then, as sometimes happens when petitioners are unsuccessful with the first justice they contact, the plaintiffs went to another. Justice Douglas did set aside the appeals court stay on the grounds that the case was like any capital punishment case in which one tries to avoid having someone die unnecessarily. Douglas was, however, overruled *the very same day.* Justice Marshall, indicating he had communicated with all other members of the Court, directly stayed the district court injunction.[9] (See page 334.)

Oral Argument

Oral argument, the next major step after briefs are filed, was used long before written briefs. It is now used to supplement the briefs and other records submitted in a case, but the Court attaches considerable importance to oral argument. At one time, argument went on without limits. Then in 1848, the court imposed a limit of *eight* hours per case (two hours per attorney, two attorneys for each side). A significant further reduction to two hours per side came in 1871, with a further reduction to one-and-one-half hours per side in 1911; in some cases deemed less meritorious, the Court limited the parties to 30 minutes per side. During Chief Justice Taft's tenure, the Court reduced the length of argument to one hour per side (in 1925) and also declined to hear the appellee (respondent) if the petitioner's opening argument was not persuasive. Further reduction to the present one-half hour per side came with Chief Justice Burger. Additional time is allowed in exceptional cases or in some cases when the government appears as *amicus* to present argument. Consolidation of several cases on the same issue may mean more attention to basic issues common to the cases, which also occurs when two or more cases on the same subject are heard consecutively. The Court now hears argument on Monday through Wednesday, hearing twelve cases during that period; Thursday is left open so the justices can prepare for Friday conference.

Lawyers wishing to argue before the Court are supposed to be members of the bar of the Supreme Court. If a lawyer who wishes to argue a case is not yet admitted to the Supreme Court bar, that lawyer's admission *pro hac vice* (p.h.v.) for that particular case can be moved by another lawyer or the agency employing the lawyer; such requests are usually granted. Joining the Supreme Court bar—often largely symbolic, as few lawyers really intend to argue cases there—is usually a routine matter. The lawyer must have been a member of the bar in good standing in his or her home state for at least three years, must pay a $100 fee, and must be recommended by two present members of the Supreme Court bar. Only a few applications to become a member of the Supreme Court bar are rejected each year, and those rejections are generally not made public. However, starting in 1979, Chief Justice Burger filed written dissents to the admission of several lawyers who had received disciplinary sanctions or were under investigation for disciplinary violations in their home states. He felt those lawyers failed to meet the Supreme Court's standard that the "applicant appears . . . to be of good moral and professional character" (Rule 5.1) and were using their admission to the Supreme Court bar "to 'launder' their professional records." (When a state disbars a lawyer who is a member of the Supreme Court bar, the Court issues an order leading to the prompt removal of the lawyer from the Supreme Court bar.)

Oral argument, although it may not determine the result in a case, is often quite important in the decision.[10] Justice Harlan stated that there was "no substitute" for this "Socratic method of procedure in getting at the heart of an issue and in finding out where the truth lies," and Justice Brennan said he would be "terribly concerned" were he to be denied the opportunity to participate in oral argument because there had been "many occasions when my judgment of a decision has turned on what happened" there.[11]

The justices' questions at oral argument are particularly important. Lawyers appearing before the Court seldom get to make uninterrupted speeches, and the justices often engage in exchanges with them. Although a lawyer may use notes, the Court has made clear that it does not wish to have a lawyer read from a prepared text (see Rule 28.1). Other aids are generally prohibited, but the Court recently allowed a deaf lawyer—arguing the *Rowley* case concerning the amount of assistance a school district had to supply a deaf child—to use a video display screen from which he could read the justices' questions typed into the system by a stenotypist.

Some justices are more frequent questioners than others, and the Court as a whole usually asks more questions of one side than of the other. For example, in the *Briggs* school desegregation case argued along with *Brown*, John Davis, defending segregation, was interrupted only 11 times, but Thurgood Marshall was interrupted 127 times.[12] The justices not only ask questions; they make statements and suggest positions not raised by the lawyers. In so doing, they often disagree with the lawyers. In the Little Rock school desegregation case, when the state's lawyer tried to gain sympathy for Governor Faubus's position by recalling Chief Justice Warren's service as governor of California, Warren forcefully pointed out that he had as governor abided by rulings of the courts, adding, "I never heard a lawyer say that the statement of a governor as to what was legal or illegal should control the action of any court."[13]

Oral argument performs a variety of functions. Although it is quite likely that the justices have read the briefs, it serves to assure the lawyers—and through them their clients—that the Court has actually heard the case. It also helps both lawyers and judges by forcing the lawyers to focus on the arguments they consider most important. Judges' questions quickly lead to a separation of central from collateral issues. That distinction often is not discernible from the lawyers' briefs, which are organized point after point in correspondence to the facts and statutes involved in the case, and which often intentionally lack emphasis as the lawyer, never knowing which argument(s) might be persuasive, tries to convince the Court in as many ways as possible.

For the judges, for whom it is probably more important, oral argument not only legitimizes their judicial function but can also be used to obtain support for their positions or to assure them about an outcome toward which they are already inclined. Judges also use oral argument to communicate with their colleagues, asking questions of counsel that are of greater concern to their associates than to themselves and debating each other through those questions. A justice hammering on a particularly difficult point may be trying to persuade his colleagues that they will have to resolve that point to decide the case in a certain direction.

Oral argument is basically intended to provide the judges with information. Sometimes they simply want to clarify the lawyers' positions. The differences in rates at which Marshall and Davis were asked questions in the *Briggs* argument can be explained in large part by that need for clarification. However, the particular frequency with which Marshall's 1953 argument attacking the "separate but equal" doctrine was interrupted—53 times in roughly three-quarters of an hour—also resulted from the fact that it was the central part of his case and it derived from his position as the person wishing the Court to adopt a major new position.[14] Oral argument also can provide judges with information to assist them in determining the Court's strategies, that is, how the Court should exercise its broader political role. Questions as to how many people might be affected by a decision and where the Court might be heading if it decided a case a certain way help elicit this type of information.

Conference and After

The justices meet during the last week of September to deal with certiorari petitions that have accumulated over the summer. They meet in conference throughout the term, with the exception of Christmas and Easter recesses and recesses for opinion writing. The Court held Saturday conferences when argument time per case was longer, but now the justices meet Wednesdays and Fridays when the Court is hearing oral argument. The Wednesday conference is devoted to voting and deliberating on the previous Monday's argued cases; the Friday conference disposes of the cases argued the previous Tuesday and Wednesday and certiorari petitions and appeals. At times there may be memoranda exchanged by the justices in advance of the conference at which a case will be considered; a justice may even be assigned to write a memo, with others invited to do so. Consensus may develop from this process, which may also serve to identify the justice who will be asked to write the Court's opinion.

In the conference, the Chief Justice makes the initial presentation concerning a case, including his own comments about it. Each justice, the most senior justice first and the most junior last, then comments. Tradition had been to take a formal vote in order of reverse seniority so that the most junior justice would not be influenced by the senior justices' votes, but in most cases a separate vote is not necessary because the justices' votes are clear from their initial statements. The initial conference vote is considered only tentative, allowing justices to change positions before the final vote is taken later. Thus at times what began as the majority becomes the minority, and vice versa.

After conclusion of discussion, the Chief Justice, if in the majority, assigns the task of writing the Court's opinion. In the past, this was done the day after each conference, but now is done after two weeks of argument and conference. If the Chief Justice is not in the majority, the assignment is made by the most senior justice in the majority. Chief Justice Burger is reported to have tried to control opinion assignment even when not in the majority. Apparently blocked from making this change, Burger is also said to have "passed" his vote at conference until the other justices' alignment was evident, so that he could vote with the majority (even when this did not appear consonant with his conference comments) and thus assign the opinion.[15] Chief Justice Rehnquist, on the other hand, is more open at conference about his position. The justice assigned the opinion circulates drafts to all the other justices for comments, doing so each time changes are made in the opinion. To provide other justices the opportunity to express additional views in a concurring opinion or in a dissent from the majority's views, each justice must see all that every other justice has written. No one assigns the writing of a minority opinion, although dissenters may decide informally among themselves who will write.

Although some justices may engage in joint action in advance of initial conference consideration of a case as they attempt to put together a majority, there is considerable exchange, even caucusing, among the justices between opinion assignment and completion of the opinion. Negotiation may take place, with a justice "holding out" his vote until the author of the opinion adds, deletes, or modifies language. Thus an opinion issued under one justice's name, for example, Chief Justice Burger's opinion in the Nixon Tapes case, may really be an amalgam of several justices' contributions.[16] There may be threats to file dissenting opinions or separate concurring opinions. Well-stated drafts of such opinions may prompt changes in the language of the proposed opinion of the Court, leading the latter's writer to withdraw the opinion.[17] A persuasive draft dissent may even attract votes and lead to reversal of the Court's original position, with the dissent becoming the opinion of the Court. When the justice writing the opinion for the majority loses a majority, the opinion-writing task is reassigned.[18] The justice assigned to write the Court's opinion, upon reexamining the case materials, may also completely change position, perhaps taking the majority along. The ability of the justice writing the Court's opinion—or a justice writing a separate (concurring or dissenting) opinion—to attract other justices to that opinion is an indication of that justice's influence. When a justice decides not to join the opinion of the Court but instead to write a separate opinion, that is an indication that the writer of the opinion of the Court has failed to exercise influence.

In the give-and-take leading to the final result in a case, personal friendships between justices may affect voting, and in particular cases the opinion author may find cross-pressures developing, with pulls in different directions coming from different friends on the Court. Justices also look to the longer run as well, and *may* vote against conscience in a particular case to attract a colleague's support in later cases. More common have been instances when justices, to obtain eventual support on other matters, have ingratiated themselves to colleagues—by writing positive responses in the margins of circulated draft opinions ("returns"). All such exchanges are not surprising in a multimember "collegial" body that is expected to work together cohesively. However, justices (for example, Justice Douglas) may desire isolation from colleagues or may refuse to seek others' votes (said to be true of Justice Stevens); if a justice objects to others' "proseletyzing," obtaining necessary agreement may be quite difficult.

From initial conference and vote to the ultimate outcome in a case, actual shifts can be significant and the Court's decision making at times is highly contingent. A recent important shift occurred in *Bowers v. Hardwick* (1986), in which the Court upheld Georgia's sodomy statute; apparently because Justice Blackmun's proposed opinion was too strong for Justice Powell, who had initially indicated he would vote to overturn the statute, Powell changed his mind and cast the decisive fifth vote for upholding such laws. (Too late to help the defendant, after he left the Court Justice Powell indicated that he had erred in his position in that case.[19]) An example of the contingent nature of the Court's decision process can be found in *Baker v. Carr* (1962), ruling reapportionment controversies to be justiciable (see page 178). Justice Stewart, the necessary fifth vote to set aside *Colegrove v. Green* (1946) (reapportionment a political question), did not want to reach the merits of the case, that is, whether Tennessee's reapportionment was valid, but would only rule that courts could hear such cases. Chief Justice Warren assigned the opinion to Justice Brennan with the understanding that, to avoid losing Stewart's vote, Brennan would not go further than that position. Then Justice Clark, originally in the minority, both shifted to the majority and was willing to reach the merits; had he joined the majority earlier, *Baker v. Carr* would have dealt with the merits *and* the Court would have adopted a different standard for reapportionment than the "one person-one vote" standard adopted in *Reynolds v. Sims* (1964).[20]

For selected terms during Justice Harold Burton's tenure, there was no change from 88 percent of the justices' original conference votes to their final votes; in 3 percent of the votes, changes were made from not casting a vote to voting either to affirm or reverse the lower court, or from such votes to nonparticipation, while in 9 percent of the votes there was *strong fluidity*, a change from a vote to affirm to a vote to reverse or vice versa. In 39 percent of the cases, no justices changed their votes, but at least some shift occurred in the remaining 61 percent. In four-fifths of those cases, only one or two justices changed their votes. The original minority became the ultimate majority in 14 percent of the cases in which there were vote changes. The majority remained intact in the other cases, increasing its size five times as often as it lost size. The picture was much the same during Justice Clark's tenure. Strong fluidity in votes took place 10 percent of the time, weak fluidity 3 percent. In one-sixth of the cases with vote changes, a minority became a majority, but most majorities increased in size—68 percent compared to the 24 percent that lost votes.[21]

On the whole, exchanges among the justices in the postconference period produce increased agreement concerning the way the justices view the cases. As changes are more likely to be in the direction of the initial majority, "the move-

ment suggests that postconference activity led to increased similarity of perceptions, which in turn led to greater agreement." The studying and discussing of
issues after the conference is what produces the increased similarity of perception. During this period the justices do not change their basic values or their
role conceptions—neither of which changes easily—but they can change
perceptions.[22]

Opinion Release

The Court's decisions and the justices' opinions are not final or binding
until announced by the Court. After that, there are to be no further changes
(except in grammar, punctuation, or case citation) in the opinions because that
would deprive other justices of the opportunity to comment on *all* the language
in all opinions. Such instances have, however, occurred. Before present day uniform methods of release of the Court's opinions, Chief Justice Roger Brooke Taney held back his opinion in the *Dred Scott* case and added "a considerable
amount of material that few if any of the other justices heard or read before its
publication,"[23] adding to the friction the case produced. When the Court struck
down limitations on pharmacists' advertising of prescription drug prices, Chief
Justice Burger changed his concurring opinion between the advance sheets (the
initial official released opinion) and the final, bound Court reports. After criticism of his initial description of pharmacists as "no more render[ing] a true professional service than does a clerk who sells lawbooks," the opinion was changed
to delete all reference to "true professional service" and to read: "the pharmacist
performs largely a packaging rather than a compounding function of former
times."[24]

The Court has been particularly careful to assure that its opinions do not
become public until they are officially announced, even maintaining its own
print shop for the printing of opinions, including drafts. The Court's present
wordprocessing system is "integrated with the printing and publishing of final
opinions." This wordprocessing system, access to computerized legal research at
the Court, and a computer system for record keeping by the Clerk's office, are
significantly advanced from the beginning of Chief Justice Burger's tenure, when
the Court lacked even photocopying machines. Such systems are part of the
Court's more general pattern of "maintain[ing] its own administrative and research capabilities rather than rely[ing] on the more generally available administrative support office."[25]

The Court's attention to secrecy in the preparation of its opinions stems
partly from the public embarrassment suffered by the Court when President Buchanan referred to the soon-to-be-announced *Dred Scott* case in his inaugural
address, and partly from fear that people who were able to learn about the Court's
intended decisions, particularly those with financial implications, could benefit
unfairly from such information. After a leak in the 1978 Term, when, two days
before the Court announced the major libel case of *Herbert v. Lando*, ABC

News reported that Justice White had written an opinion for the Court in which the media would suffer a defeat, the Chief Justice fired a typesetter from his job in the Court's printshop. The Court's result in the 1985 Term Gramm-Rudman budget case also appears to have leaked.

Justices once read extended portions of their opinions in open court. This practice has been eliminated; justices now read, at most, short statements of the facts and issues in a case and what the Court has decided, unless they have a dissent about which they feel strongly. Until 1965, the only Decision Day, the day when decisions are announced, was Monday, except when Monday was a legal holiday, with Tuesday used instead. In 1965, under Chief Justice Warren, the Court began to use other days as well, to allow greater media coverage of its opinions; it also moved its public sessions from 12:00 to 4:30 P.M. to a 10:00 A.M. start to help the media meet deadlines. The Court has an information officer, but that person's basic task is only to see that the news media get the opinions, not to explain them or to respond to questions about what the Court or individual justices may have intended. Thus the opinions are released without additional comment—by the justices or other Court personnel. The Burger Court has, however, assisted the press in its task of digesting rulings by having the Reporter of Decisions prepare a case *syllabus* or headnote (a concise summary of facts, issues, and the Court's holding) for every full opinion case and release it when the decision is issued, a change from the earlier practice of not having it prepared until months later for the official reports. (The headnote, not officially part of the opinion of the Court, does not digest any concurring or dissenting opinions.)

The first day of each term, the "first Monday in October," is the day the Court announces the results of the justices' summer labors concerning which cases shall be heard and which denied review, although such decisions are also issued regularly throughout the term. On the first day of the 1990 Term, the Court disposed of over 1,400 certiorari petitions (13 granted; 7 granted, vacated, and remanded; the remainder denied); 1 stay; and more than 90 other matters, including 8 petitions for habeas corpus, 18 for mandamus or prohibition, and 4 for rehearing; nearly 50 case-related matters (petitions to file amicus briefs, to retax costs, etc., and 5 requests by the Court for the solicitor general's view in cases), 7 petitions to proceed *in forma pauperis*, and 7 orders relating to disbarment of attorneys.

Use of Monday as the only Decision Day meant that large numbers of important full opinion cases—not to speak of certiorari denials and other orders—were handed down on the same day. This was a particular problem at the end of the term, when the media were deluged with cases. After the Court shifted in 1965 to using non-Mondays as well as Mondays as Decision Days, the Court initially made only minimal use of non-Monday Decision Days, and Monday remained the only Decision Day toward the end of the term, when spreading out cases might have helped out most because most decisions were handed down then. Thus there were such unusually high outputs as 12 (June 10, 1968), 13

(June 12, 1967), and 14 (May 20, 1968) cases, many announcing significant constitutional doctrine.[26]

Chief Justice Burger used non-Monday Decision Days with increasing frequency, so that more than half the Court's signed full opinion cases are now handed down on non-Monday Decision Days and the Court developed a pattern of handing down cases on several days each week at the end of the term, particularly on the Monday following the Friday conference and on the Thursday following the Wednesday conference. The Court thus succeeded in spreading out cases more when the flow was heaviest. There might be more than 20 signed opinions in a week, but no more than seven were likely to be issued on any one day.

These changes have not been accompanied by changes in the flow of cases through the term. Few opinions can be expected in October, November, and December when oral argument has just begun, but disparities in output between the second three months (January-March) and the last three (April-June) have been considerable. As Table 7.1 indicates, only a small portion of the Court's signed cases appear by the end of December. Less than 40 percent of the Court's full opinions are announced by the end of March.

The Court releases most of its output in the last third of the term, but as much as one-third or more of the Court's entire output for the term is announced in the last six weeks. In the 1984 Term, over 40 percent of that term's output was released in the last month; in the 1986 and 1987 Terms, the proportion was again 40 percent. The proportion was somewhat lower (one-third) in the 1990 Term, but the Court's total output was much lower than in previous years. Spectacular "bursts" of opinions came in the 1986 Term, with one-fifth of the term's output in one week, and the following year, with over one-fourth of the total in two weeks alone. (*Per curiam* rulings tend to be released relatively evenly across the term's trimesters, because, although a brief opinion must be written in such cases, the decision process for them is much less extended than for full opinion cases.)

Consensus and Dissensus in the Court

Unanimity and Dissent

Lack of unanimity among judges of a multijudge court results from a variety of causes. Included are intellectual processes of reasoning about past doctrine, differences in judges' values, attitudes about judicial role, and leadership (or lack of it). Personal animosity also plays a part. Examples are the friction between Justice Frankfurter and several other members of the Court, including Chief Justice Warren, and between Justices Black and Jackson, related to Black's imagined role in Jackson's not receiving the chief justiceship.[27] The desire to have judges put aside personal values and engage in deliberate, logical consideration of cases, so that the result is determined only by the facts of the case and relevant

Table 7.1 Opinion Flow—Signed Cases

		Term								
	1986		1987		1988		1989		1990	
October, November, December	11	7.4%	8	5.5%	9	6.6%	10	7.8%	8	7.1%
January, February, March	45	30.2	37	25.5	46	34.1	41	31.5	30	26.8
April, May, June	93	62.4	90	62.0	80	59.3	79	60.8	74	66.1
Total	149		135		135		130		112	

precedents, makes all these reasons except the first somewhat suspect, and helps explain the sharp criticism of any justice whose decisions seem fully controlled by personal attitudes. Justice Douglas was the target of such criticism, not only for his civil liberties decisions—as predictable in the liberal direction as Justice Rehnquist's have been in the conservative direction—but for his tax rulings as well. For example, in 1959–64, Douglas favored the taxpayer in 73 percent of these cases.[28]

Justices' attitudes regularly are important in Supreme Court decision making. Were this not so, shifts in the Court's direction would not stem, as they do in fact, directly from changes in personnel, although other factors soften or reinforce the effects of these changes. It should also be no surprise that justices, not newcomers to major political issues prior to judicial service, do not decide all cases unanimously and that they disagree about the opinions explaining the Court's results. Such disagreement is not necessarily destructive. Conflict within the Supreme Court "makes for alertness, clarifies issues, raises alternative approaches, and tests the intensity of justices' commitments to given positions." It can, however, be destructive if it "becomes highly emotional and antagonistic."[29] We might recall that Justice Holmes once referred to the members of the Court as "nine scorpions in a bottle."

One would expect division on controversial cases. From that perspective, the alignment in a case like *Bakke*, with Justice Powell casting the deciding vote for two different four-vote groups of his colleagues (in a 4–1–4 alignment) should not cause concern, nor should 5–4 rulings on other major issues. What does cause concern, however, is the perceived lack of stability in the Court's decisions and in the fracturing of majority voting groups so that several concurring opinions appear in addition to the opinion of the Court. (Although there was an opinion for the Court in *Pennzoil v. Texaco* in 1987 and the vote was unanimous, there were *six* separate opinions.)

More serious is having only a *plurality* opinion rather than an opinion of the Court. A plurality or prevailing opinion is one in which some majority justices join the Court's judgment (its decision or result) but not what would otherwise be the "opinion of the Court," thus leaving fewer than five justices supporting the basic opinion. An example would be a case in which the justices divided 5–4, with three of the majority justices favoring one opinion and the other two concurring only in the result—but not the opinion.

Plurality opinions officially have no binding effect, although they have persuasive value. As time passes, people may come to treat them as precedent—long true of Justice Frankfurter's plurality opinion in *Colegrove v. Green* that reapportionment was a "political question." Nonetheless, plurality opinions bring criticism and frustrate the lower courts—trying to apply the Supreme Court's doctrine—as well as the other justices. For example, the Court's longtime inability to produce an opinion of the Court in obscenity cases during the 1960s led Justice Tom Clark to say, with some irritation, that his colleagues were "like ancient Gaul . . . split into three parts." [30] The absence of leadership is likely to increase such outcomes.

The Court at times is so badly split that it must resort to a *per curiam* announcement of the basic policy on which the justices agree. Examples are *Furman v. Georgia*, the 1972 death penalty case, and the Pentagon Papers case (*New York Times v. United States*), in both of which each majority justice appended a separate opinion to the brief *per curiam*; and *Buckley v. Valeo*, the 1976 campaign finance ruling where five justices dissented from at least some parts of the ruling. [31]

Disagreement among the justices does not mean that they *express* that disagreement through dissenting opinions or separate opinions concurring with the majority. Concurring opinions, written less often than dissents because they are less useful to later justices and less frequently cited by them, either provide additional thoughts; agree only with the majority *result* but on the basis of different reasoning; or agree only in part with the prevailing opinion. (A justice may also concur in part and dissent in part.)

Because a justice must write separate opinions in addition to opinions of the Court, they add to a justice's workload and thus limit the frequency with which they are prepared. There are additional constraints as well, [32] some of which are strategic. For example, dissents are said to encourage noncompliance, particularly with controversial rulings like school desegregation. [33] The Court may also be criticized for being divided frequently. A justice contemplating a dissent must also remember that, apart from the fact that open disagreement may be interpreted as an attack on the Court's integrity, a strong dissenting opinion may make the majority opinion more visible and thus more damaging than would silence. And when a justice dissents repeatedly, predicting harsh consequences as Justice Frankfurter did, that "Chicken Little" approach becomes "Wolf! Wolf!": the justice loses credibility. A recent "Doomsday" dissent of some importance was Justice Blackmun's opinion in the *Webster* abortion case in which, after saying, "I fear for the future. I fear for the liberty and equality of the millions of women who have lived and come of age in the 16 years since *Roe* was decided. I fear for the integrity of, and public esteem for, this Court," he ended with the statement that "the law of abortion stands undisturbed. . . . But the signs are evident and very ominous, and a chill wind blows." [34]

Individual justices, or groups of justices, dissent to state principled opposition to the majority's doctrine. Dissents may give the losing side the feeling that someone has listened to their position. By making the majority justices sharpen their reasoning, dissents may allow them to write more forcefully because they do not have to compromise with the dissenting justices. Dissents may also appeal to the dissenter's colleagues and the Court's immediate audience. Dissents may, for example, be written for present lower court judges in the hope that if those judges dislike the Supreme Court majority's position, they will see ways in which to limit it. For example, Justice Brennan suggested that dissents can serve both as "damage control" to limit the sweep of the majority's position and as "practical guidance" to those wishing to circumvent the majority ruling. In a dissent in a criminal procedure case, he wrote that the Court's rule did not "preclude a contrary resolution of this case based upon the State's separate interpretation of its own constitution."[35] In so speaking to state judges, the dissenters may be more persuasive than the Supreme Court's rulings, which are not binding on matters of state constitutional interpretation.[36] A dissenter may also speak to legislators—state or national—who might use the dissent as a basis for correcting legislation.

Dissents may also be speaking to future lawyers and judges. "An effective dissenting opinion is like a spotlight that picks out arguments or facts conveniently overlooked by the majority, that shows how eroded the majority's legal doctrines have become or that lights a path toward alternative theories."[37] As Judge Richard Posner has put it, "Dissenting . . . opinions have played so important a role in the development of the law that it would be a great error to suppress them; it would actually make law less rather than more certain, by concealing from the bar important clues to the law of the future."[38] Although many dissenters are defending an outdated status quo, dissents are indeed potential majority opinions of the future. Certain "Great Dissenters" such as Holmes and Brandeis are certainly well remembered for their contributions in this regard. Although other factors also contribute to the Court's overruling of past decisions, in three-fourths of the Court's overruling actions from 1958 through 1980, justices gave dissents in earlier cases as the basis for overruling those decisions or based overruling opinions on ideas from the prior dissents.[39] Judges vary in the extent to which they continue to state a dissent on a particular issue, being more likely to continue so stating in constitutional than in statutory cases. That they stop making the dissenting statement does not, however, mean they have abandoned their initial position; they are more likely to be acquiescing temporarily in the disliked precedent.

Considerations such as the encouragement of noncompliance and the appearance of attacking the Court's integrity also do not prevent dissenters from directly attacking not only the majority's policy positions but also its intelligence and ability. This is perhaps an extension of friction in the Court's conference meetings, which, according to Justice Blackmun, have been "marked by 'impatience' and 'short temper.' "[40] The present friction is, however, as nothing compared to some past situations. Most notable was the hostility of Justice McReynolds, so anti-Semitic that he left the conference room when Justice Brandeis was speaking; the tension caused by McReynolds's behavior was so great that it caused Justice John Hessein Clarke to resign from the Court.

At times, the language of the justices' opinions becomes rather testy, raising questions about the "respect" in "I respectfully dissent." In a 1978 case, for example, Justice Brennan accused Justice Rehnquist of writing an opinion that "reaches a result supported by neither policy nor precedent, ignores difficult legal issues, [and] misapprehends the significance of the proceeding below." As if that were not enough, he accused Rehnquist of "ignoring wholesale the analytical framework" of a recent important case, of committing "case-reading errors," and of avoiding discussion of certain important issues.[41] In another case, involving the *Miranda* warnings, he wrote that "the Court mischaracterizes our precedents, obfuscates the central issues, and altogether ignores the practical realities of custodial interrogation that have led nearly every lower court to reject its simplistic reasoning" and also criticized the "Court's marble-palace psychoanalysis."[42]

Rehnquist handed out comparable criticism in the 1979 school desegregation cases, where he said of the Court's "lick and a promise" opinions that "perhaps the adjective 'analytical' is out of place, since the Court's opinions furnish only the most superficial methodology."[43] In a particularly sharp attack in a case involving federal preemption of state regulatory action, Justice Blackmun criticized Justice Sandra O'Connor for a "rhetorical assertion" about federalism that was "demonstrably incorrect" if it were to be taken literally. He added that "while Justice O'Connor articulates a view of state sovereignty that is almost mystical, she entirely fails to address our central points."[44] In the 1989 *Webster* abortion case, Blackmun, dissenting, claimed that not "in his memory has a plurality gone about its business in such deceptive fashion" and through its actions "invites charges of cowardice and illegitimacy to our door. I cannot say that these would be undeserved."[45]

The extent of disagreement within the court has varied over the years. In the Court's earliest years, there was no "opinion of the Court," with each justice writing an opinion in each case. Chief Justice John Marshall brought an end to these seriatim opinions. Indeed, he wrote most of the Court's opinions, even when he did not agree with the result: from 1801 to 1804, the Court handed down 26 decisions containing opinions, and Marshall wrote for the Court in 24. The "first dissenter"—in the context of unified opinions—was a Jefferson appointee, Justice William Johnson. His dissents not only served to break Marshall's monopoly but led to present practices of opinion-assignment by the Chief Justice, although pressures remained strong to limit the statement of separate views.

Despite year-to-year variation, the level of disagreement within the Court has generally increased over the years. As expectations of what is appropriate changed, there has been a marked shift from justices acquiescing in all except very major cases to more routine expression of dissent. Because most of the Court's cases in the late nineteenth century did not then give rise to controversy, all but a few were decided unanimously. The period of the Taft Court (1921–29) was also one of few dissents, for example, less than one for each six cases in the 1925 Term—leading to the comment that it "may have been the 'Roaring Twenties' in the speakeasies, but it was the 'Boring Twenties' at the Supreme Court."[46]

The shift from mandatory to discretionary review, by eliminating the less controversial cases, produced more disagreement. After 1925, an increase in dissent first appeared in the appeals jurisdiction, from which less important cases had been shifted to the certiorari category; the more controversial cases which remained naturally produced more dissent. As winnowing progressed in the certiorari cases as well, dissent later increased there, as did the number of concurring opinions.[47] In short, the cases the Court accepted were disproportionately complex or controversial ("hard" cases), likely to produce dissent, contributing to the long-term trend, extending from well before 1925, to an increase in sharply divided cases (those with 5–4 rulings).[48] Here we must remember that the Supreme Court's cases have been said to be the most difficult of the most difficult of the most difficult to the tenth power.

In 1930, only 11 percent of the Court's cases were split decisions. That percentage more than doubled in each of the next two decades. Harlan Fiske Stone's ineffective leadership as Chief Justice (1941–46) produced rates of disagreement between the justices reaching one-third.[49] Dissent rates continued to rise after Stone's tenure, reaching 61 percent in 1950 during Fred Vinson's chief justiceship. After Earl Warren became Chief Justice, the figure rose to over three-fourths of the cases in 1957. Only about two-fifths of the Court's full opinion cases in the early 1960s were unanimous.

The transition to the Burger Court produced an obvious drop in consensus. In Burger's first three terms, the Court achieved unanimity in only roughly one-third of its full opinion cases, a level not exceeded—and in several terms, not met—until 1981. The proportion exceeded two-fifths in both 1983 and 1984 before dropping sharply to over one-fourth in the 1985 and 1986 Terms, then rose to 40 percent (1987 Term), before settling back to roughly one-third for the next several years. That proportion may seem low, but one can see it as high if one takes into account the difficulty of the cases that the Court accepts for review.

The size of majorities may reflect disagreement even more clearly than the proportion of cases that are unanimous. During the 1969 Term, Burger's first, there were wide margins (at least four votes) in 62 percent of the signed cases. The proportion fell to under half the next year, with one-vote margins in over one-fourth of the cases. The proportion of cases decided by wide margins has dropped below half only once in the 1981–90 Terms. (44.5% in the 1986 Term, Rehnquist's first as Chief Justice), was at 50 percent in only two terms, and was at or above 65 percent twice (1984, 1987). (See Table 7.2.) Thus, correspondingly, close votes (6–3 and 5–4) accounted for as much as 55.5 percent (1986 Term) or as little as one-third (1984 Term), with no linear trend. However, the proportion of cases decided by one-vote margins has remained high—over one-fourth of the cases in 1970, and 20 percent or more in 1978 and 1981 through 1982, jumping to over one-fourth in the last Burger term and first Rehnquist term. After the lowest proportion in years (10%, 1987 Term), the proportion was then between 20 and 30 percent.

One factor explaining the high dissent rate is the type of cases the Court decided: cases with constitutional issues were far more likely than those with

Table 7.2 Distribution of Votes—Full Opinion Cases

	1986	1987	1988	1989	1990
Unanimous	26.0%	40.9%	35.8%	33.1%	34.8%
8–1	4.2	9.5	7.5	6.2	7.1
7–2	14.4	14.6	6.7	14.6	16.1
"Wide Margins"	44.5%	65.0%	50.0%	53.8%	58.0%
6–3	25.3	24.8	23.1	16.9	19.6
5–4	30.1	10.2	26.9	29.2	22.3
"Close Votes"	55.5%	35.0%	50.0%	46.2%	42.0%

Note: 8–1 includes 7–1 and 6–1; 7–2 includes 6–2; 6–3 includes 5–3, 5–2, 4–2; 5–4 includes 4–3.

statutory questions to produce multiple dissents. Thus in the 1981–84 Terms, of the constitutional decisions, nearly half had at least three dissenting votes and only a little more than one-fourth were unanimous. By contrast, only one-third of the statutory cases had three or four dissenting votes and nearly half were unanimous. Of 250 civil rights cases decided on the merits during that period, there were not even 40 in which all the justices joined in a single opinion, yet there were 70 statutory decisions with all the justices supporting a single opinion. (Likewise, constitutional questions accounted for all but two of 24 cases in which there was only a plurality opinion instead of an opinion of the Court.[50])

Also part of patterns of disagreement is the number of concurring and dissenting opinions.[51] The number of concurring opinions, 40 in the 1962 Term and 67 ten years later, reached over 85 in the late 1970s; there was an average of almost 70 per term in the 1980s. The period from 1981 through 1990 produced an average of roughly 115 dissenting opinions per term although the figures ranged from 94 (1987) to a high of 144 (1985) and an average of 1.25 dissents per nonunanimous case. The relationship between the number of *votes* and the number of *opinions* shows that the justices were more likely to join in other justices' dissenting opinions than in their concurring opinions. A recent examination of justices' joining in each others' concurring and dissenting opinions, as a measure of influence, showed little overall influence of justices on each other, but in the Burger Court, the liberals mutually influenced each other more, whereas during the Warren Court, the nonliberals had shown higher mutual influence.[52]

Whereas Chief Justice Warren had been an infrequent dissenter, Chief Justice Burger dissented frequently, along with Justice Rehnquist. The liberal justices then became the Court's most frequent dissenters, with Stevens—not Rehnquist—the most frequent *lone* dissenter. However, the level of dissent within the Burger Court cannot be explained solely by the liberals' dissents or by Justice Douglas's prodigious dissent frequency (57 dissenting votes in the 1971 Term, 15 solo, and 60 the following term). In the first Rehnquist Court years, the high rate of dissents by the liberals continued, with Brennan and Marshall having roughly 50 dissenting votes in the 1986, 1988, and 1989 Terms; Stevens, who also had over 50 dissenting votes in 1986, wrote the largest number of dissenting opinions—26 or more in 1986, 1988, and 1989. That this was in part a function of Justice Stevens's style can also be seen in his 16 concurring opinions in the 1989 Term, when he was tied with conservative Justice Scalia, who had 24 concurring opinions the previous term as he stated his different view of the law.

Variation in the frequency of dissent is an indication of the Court's overall alignment. Thus it should be no surprise that those at the ideological extremities of the Court cast the most dissenting votes, with Brennan, Marshall, Rehnquist, and Chief Justice Burger rivaling each other for the "prize" in this regard. The high rate of dissent for the Chief Justice was perhaps more surprising—and certainly more remarked upon—than Justice Rehnquist's behavior, because of our expectation that a Chief Justice will try to "mass" the Court and will cast fewer dissents as part of that effort.

The size of the Court's majorities may be affected by a tendency, noted by students of small-group decision making, for decisions to be made by *minimum-winning coalitions*, that is, the smallest majority necessary. A body threatened from the outside is, however, thought to increase the size of the decision-making coalition. During the period of Justice Burton's Court service, when coalitions at the initial conference vote were smaller than minimum winning, they were likely to become minimum winning by the conclusion of the case, probably because the justices wished an "opinion of the Court." However, when original coalitions were larger than minimum winning, they were unlikely to shrink to minimum-winning size. When justices changed positions, size of majority increased far more often than it decreased. [53]

In the Warren Court, in nonthreat situations, 31 percent of the *decision coalitions*—justices joining in the vote for the result in a case—and 40 percent of the *opinion coalitions*—justices joining in support of the Court's principal opinion—were minimum winning and 17 percent were unanimous. However, under conditions of threat, for example, legislative proposals to limit the Court's jurisdiction, only 13 percent of decision coalitions and 23 percent of opinion coalitions were minimum winning, 44 percent unanimous; the same relations hold if six-justice coalitions are added to combinations of five justices. Furthermore, large coalitions formed under threat conditions were more likely than otherwise to include justices with divergent policy positions, but opinion coalitions smaller than the decision coalitions were more likely than other coalitions to contain ideologically "connected" justices. [54]

Chief Justice: Leadership
and Opinion Assignment

The Chief Justice is expected to play a wide variety of roles. In addition to participating in the deciding of cases, writing a share of the Court's opinions, and serving as the Court's presiding officer, he serves as a circuit justice (for the D.C. and Fourth Circuits), and also is court manager, court defender, third branch chieftain, and statesman. Being court manager entails such duties as allocating circuit justice duties, signing certificates of disability for Supreme Court justices should that be necessary, and working with the Court's officials—the clerk of court, marshal, reporter of decisions, and librarian—and serving as "building manager" for the Court; it also encompasses being a protocol leader and a major host to foreign dignitaries. Serving as court defender means "press[ing] the Court's case before coordinate branches of the national government" and perhaps "mobiliz[ing] public opinion" in order to protect the Court's status. [55] The role of "third branch chieftain," one to which Warren Burger gave great attention, concerns administration of the federal judiciary (see page 18). The "statesman" role is extrajudicial: in it the Chief Justice serves on a variety of commissions (as provided by statute) and may accept additional assignments (see page 296).

With respect to the Chief Justice's colleagues, there are three leadership roles that have to be performed within the Court—roles that the Chief Justice may assume but that may be assumed by other justices. These are task or intellectual leadership; social leadership, through which solidarity is produced among the justices and their "emotional needs . . . as individuals" are attended to; and policy leadership, moving the Court toward a particular position over the long term. The Chief Justice may be the Court's social leader (like Taft) or the task leader, although apart from Hughes it does not appear that chief justices have been the task leader. It is possible that the Chief will perform both social *and* task leadership roles, as Hughes did. When the Chief Justice performs neither role (like Stone), an extremely uncohesive Court results. If the Chief Justice does not perform one of the necessary roles, someone else will; for example, Justice Willis Van Devanter was task leader when Taft was social leader.

Even if the Chief Justice does not perform either role for the Court as a whole, he can perform both roles or neither for a bloc of justices. Chief Justice Burger may have done this for the Nixon appointees during the early years of his tenure, although he did not do so subsequently; criticisms of Burger as a weak Chief Justice were legion. One must, however, take into account his attention to judicial administration; a Chief Justice devoting much attention to matters outside the Court is less likely to be an in-court leader than one who invests most of his energies in the Court itself.

Burger's activities raised the larger issue of how much time we wish a Chief Justice to devote to judicial administration. Sitting on a court where all justices are expected to sit on all cases, the Chief Justice cannot shed some caseload to provide time for administrative duties. The result is thus a trade-off between attention to internal court leadership and to supervision of judicial administration. The Chief's judicial administration efforts may lessen his effectiveness as a within-Court leader, producing more division in the Court's rulings. If we want a Chief Justice to focus on the Court and to be less interested in judicial administration, supervision of judicial administration will have to be accommodated some other way.

If the Chief does not lead, others will fill the vacuum, even in (or particularly in) the Court's most crucial cases, as appears to have occurred in developing the opinion in the Nixon Tapes case. Even where the Chief does lead—clearly the case, from most accounts, of Earl Warren, called the "Super Chief"—others may also play a large role. We must be careful not to assume leadership on the part of the person in the "center chair"; even during Earl Warren's tenure, Justice Brennan was a major influence on the Court's doctrinal landmarks, for example, when a suggestion he made to Justice Douglas became the right to privacy basis of the *Griswold* contraception case, which led directly to the Court's 1973 abortion rulings.[56]

The Chief Justice's leadership is affected by the degree to which he dissents: a dissenter may exercise *policy* leadership, but exercising leadership over colleagues in the short term is difficult if one is often in dissent. Thus Chief Justice

Stone's lack of leadership is reflected in the fact that he dissented in a larger proportion of nonunanimous cases than did any other Chief Justice, and Chief Justice Burger's dissent rate helps explain claims that he did not provide strong leadership. A high dissent rate seemed to be part of Chief Justice Rehnquist's leadership problem in his first term, when as a result Justice Brennan was able to assign many major opinions. After that, Rehnquist's hold on the Court seemed stronger. However, this resulted more from the addition of new conservative justices than from any change in position on the Chief Justice's part: "The comparison of Rehnquist's voting behavior during his tenure as an associate justice with his behavior as Chief Justice shows no change," nor did he "become more influential as Chief Justice than he was as a member of the Burger Court" in terms of getting people to join his opinions.[57]

The dissent rate when earlier Chief Justices presided was affected by "the attitudes of the justices toward dissent or expressing dissent, the varying complexity of cases being decided, and interpersonal feuding in the Court."[58] If the absence of "conflict cases" indicates more effective leadership, Chief Justice John Marshall (1801–35) has the highest place as a leader: 92.7 percent of the cases during his tenure did not reveal conflict. In the second rank (87–90% nonconflict cases) are Chief Justices Salmon P. Chase (1864–73), Morrison R. Waite (1874–88), Edward White (1910–20), and William Howard Taft (1921–29). At the next level (83–85% nonconflict cases) are Roger Taney (1836–63), Melville Fuller (1888–1909), and Charles Evans Hughes (1930–41). Far behind are Chief Justice Harlan F. Stone (1941–46) (almost half the cases during his tenure involved conflict), and Earl Warren and Fred Vinson (1946–53) (with almost three-fourths of the cases involving conflict). A problem with this indicator is that the cases facing the Court have varied over time in complexity and controversiality, as have justices' attitudes toward dissent and the level of interpersonal friction in the Court.

Opinion Assignment. The assignment of opinions by the Chief Justice is one of the ways in which he can attempt to exercise his and his colleagues' influence outside the Court—on the Court's multiple audiences, particularly lawyers. There are, however, numerous constraints on the Chief Justice's choice of an opinion writer for the Court. These include his efforts to influence his colleagues through the assignment of opinions and the necessity of distributing the writing workload evenly among all the justices, something not easy to do if some colleagues are frequently in dissent. Justices are expected to be "generalists," that is, to write opinions in all fields of law, but informal specialization appears from time to time—for example, Justice Stephen Field in land law and, apparently, Justice Powell in business cases.

Cases may also be assigned to justices because of their past positions, for example, Powell as a former American Bar Association president writing on lawyer advertising and lawyer residence requirements for admission to the bar, and Tom Clark, as former attorney general, writing in criminal procedure cases. The

Chief Justice must participate in writing opinions, and he thus retains some cases. It is expected that the Chief Justice will write in some of the Court's "big" cases, but the Court's internal social relations prevent him from keeping all the most important ones.

Danelski has suggested two strategies that the Chief Justice might use in assigning opinions to accommodate some of these pressures:

> Rule 1: Assign the case to the Justice whose views are the closest to the dissenters on the ground that his opinion would take a middle approach upon which both majority and minority could agree.

> Rule 2: Where there are blocs on the Court and a bloc splits, assign the case to a majority member of the dissenters' bloc on the ground that he would take a middle approach upon which both majority and minority could agree and that the minority justices would be more likely to agree with him because of general mutuality of agreement.[59]

Those justices never "closest" to the assigners are usually given unanimous cases or cases in less controversial areas of the law. There are other strategic concerns as well, for example, that of assignment of a case when the Court changes position, where assigning to a prior dissenter may produce too "sharp" an opinion.[60]

In close political cases through 1962, Chief Justice Warren, seeming to follow the strategies suggested by Danelski, "overassigned" cases to justices who joined the majority through votes inconsistent with their usual positions. In the 1962 Term, he also assigned Justice Goldberg, closest to the Court's center of the five reliable liberal votes, six of his twelve opinions in 5–4 rulings. In economic cases, however, Warren assigned opinions to maximize the liberal policy position.[61] When majorities were large, he tended to overassign to those in the mid-majority position. Although assigning justices have generally favored justices "closest to them in various issue areas,"[62] Warren used those large majorities to help create an opinion of the Court considerably different from his own particular position. The rule of assigning cases to moderate justices was evident in Justice Clark's opinions in cases with liberal results, such as *Mapp v. Ohio* on the exclusionary rule for improperly seized evidence, where his background as attorney general was probably thought to produce a better reception in the law enforcement community than if a justice with a predictably liberal record had written for the Court. As had Chief Justice Vinson before him, Warren underassigned to himself, although toward the end of his tenure, he seemed to keep more of the Court's important cases than he had earlier.

Chief Justice Burger allocated the writing of the Court's signed opinions relatively evenly among the justices.[63] Exceptions are explained in part by a justice's illness (Powell's 1984 Term surgery), vacancies, or newness to the Court. As freshman justices, new members of the Court may receive fewer assignments because they are not familiar with the Court's work; if they join the Court in midterm, there would have been cases in which they could not participate because they did not hear oral argument. Indeed, we find that in their freshman terms, Justices Scalia, Kennedy, and Souter were used by Chief Justice Rehnquist a smaller proportion of the time they were available (not in dissent) than were the other justices. Despite the supposed tradition that a new justice's first opinion comes in a noncontroversial, unanimous case, both Justices Powell and Rehnquist wrote for divided courts in their first opinions; the "tradition" was, however, true for Justices Stevens, O'Connor, Scalia, and Thomas.

A justice's speed in writing also affects assignments, and may override the effects of ideology on assignments; at least it appears to have done so in the Vinson Court, where there was "an inverse relationship between the number of majority opinion assignments received by a justice and the average number of days he took to complete the majority opinions."[64] More recently, Justice Blackmun's slow pace in writing is said to have affected the assignments he received—as well as his ability to influence other justices, something that may also be true of Justice Souter.

Ideology has also played an important role in opinion-assignment: Burger definitely used his assignment of opinions to reward Justices White and Stewart, the Court's centrists, and particularly the other Nixon appointees. In the Burger Court, specialists in particular civil liberties and civil rights areas were also the Chief Justice's ideological allies, so that issues specialization can be seen as resulting from assignment based on ideology.[65] Assignment of Rehnquist to write criminal procedure opinions ran counter to the strategy of using mid-Court members, but may have resulted either from the majority coalition's single-mindedness in this policy area or from a feeling that the coalition was sufficiently solid that Rehnquist's positions would not lose votes. The proportion of times Chief Justice Burger assigned a case to each justice when that justice was available did vary, with Burger choosing Rehnquist and White a disproportionately high percentage of the times they were available. The liberal justices were used a higher proportion of the time they were available to the Chief Justice, because their dissents made them less available generally. Brennan and Marshall wrote fewer opinions for the Court than the average in several terms, White and Rehnquist somewhat more than the others.

The liberals received many of their assignments from the ranking justice when the Chief Justice was in the minority, and many of Brennan's opinions for the Court (12 of his 15 opinions in the 1981 Term) came from self-assignment in that situation. Because Brennan controlled many assignments from 1986 through 1989, this self-assignment was an important source of his power within the Court. Justices Blackmun and Marshall also received a significant portion of their opinion-writing assignments from Brennan.

Certain justices at times write for the Court more frequently in particular situations. There appears to be some subject-matter specialization in assignment of opinions from time to time. Table 7.3 shows that some justices write more

Table 7.3   Assignments, 1986–1990 (combined)—Full Opinion Cases*

	Rehnquist	Scalia	Kennedy (1987–1990)	White	O'Connor	Blackmun	Stevens	Marshall	Brennan (1986–1989)
Unanimous	22.4%	29.6%	10.6%	33.8%	44.3%	35.5%	45.3% (33/1)	49.3% (34/1)	23.0%
8–1, 7–1, 6–1	5.3	12.7	12.8 (5/1)	1.2	7.6	14.5	4.0 (2/1)	11.3	6.6 (3/1)
7–2, 6–2	19.7	12.7 (7/2)	23.4 (7/4)	11.8 (7/3)	8.9	11.3 (4/3)	5.3 (2/2)	14.1 (9/1)	21.3 (7/6)
6–3, 5–2	21.1	18.3 (12/1)	29.8 (12/2)	16.5 (12/2)	11.3 (8/1)	19.4 (9/3)	20.0 (10/5)	12.7 (5/4)	16.4 (1/9)
5–4, 4–3, 5–3	31.6	26.8 (17/2)	23.4	31.8 (21/6)	27.8 (17/5)	19.4 (6/6)	25.3 (12/7)	12.7 (1/8)	32.8 (2/18)
Total Assignments	76	71 (66/5)	47 (40/7)	85 (74/11)	79 (73/6)	62 (50/12)	75 (59/16)	71 (57/14)	61 (27/34)

Note: Where two numbers are separated by a slash (9/1), the first number indicates opinions assigned by the Chief Justice; the second indicates those assigned by others when the Chief Justice was in the minority.

*These are inferred assignments, calculated from final vote, not initial vote (data not available). Fluidity might mean assignments have shifted from the original assignment. When the Chief Justice concurred, it is assumed that he assigned and then wrote separately.

frequently when the Court is unanimous or nearly so, others when the Court is more seriously divided. In the Rehnquist Court, Stevens, Marshall, and O'Connor were used more frequently in unanimous cases. It is not surprising that the Chief Justice did not often assign close cases to the liberal justices; many of the close cases in which they did write for the Court were assigned by the senior justice in the majority. The more conservative justices were assigned to write for the court proportionately more in closer cases. However, it appears that Rehnquist, while not keeping opinion assignments as evenhanded as his predecessors with respect to important cases, "has not used his discretion to assign opinions in order to advance his policy goals."[66]

Chief Justice Burger began to self-assign in important cases like the *Swann* and Detroit busing cases and the major obscenity case of *Miller v. California*. Chief Justice Warren had written most often in cases with wide vote margins or unanimous votes. Burger also wrote a high proportion (half) of his opinions for the court in unanimous or 8–1 cases and in fewer "close" cases than some other justices—only 11.4 percent in 5–4 decisions in 1981–86. His successor was far more willing to write for the Court in close cases: only 22.4 percent of his opinions for the Court were in unanimous, and roughly one-third were in the closest, cases. However, Rehnquist did not write in any of the cases through 1990 in which a law was declared unconstitutional and he was in the majority.[67]

Over a longer span of Court history, Chief Justices have assigned majority opinions to themselves relatively more often than they have to their colleagues, but they have done so *less* in the post–World War II period. However, in important cases, all Chief Justices have engaged in higher self-assignment. Here, too, there have been differences between justices, with Stone and Warren using their self-assignment prerogative least and Chief Justices Taft and Hughes "pursu[ing] the relatively most advantageous self-assignment policy in important cases."[68] The Chief Justices have also been likely to assign themselves unanimous opinions and to write less frequently for highly divided courts. This is true even in important cases: they are more likely than their colleagues to write for a unanimous Court in important cases and less frequently for a moderately or highly divided Court. This means that, on the whole, the Chief Justice is not put in the position of writing frequently for badly divided courts in a large proportion of major cases.

Judicial Values and Alignments

The votes of Supreme Court justices are patterned, not random. A number of factors help account for the patterned nature of the justices' votes, which have both a short-term component and a long-term one. The short-term component includes the influence of other justices with whom they serve, the presentation of cases through briefs and oral argument, and the decisional environment, plus political and other events of the time. The long-term component includes the justices' pre-Court socialization, which can be a function of the generation in which they were raised; their experience on the Court; their ideology; and their personality. An important part of the reason for the Court's high level of explicit disagreement is that newer members of the Court know their own minds and do not wait to assert their positions. Perhaps as a result of their past judicial and legal experience, they have spoken out in dissenting and concurring opinions within a short time of reaching the bench. Thus Justice Stevens, despite his nonparticipation in roughly one-third of the cases in his first term, dissented in 19 cases; Justice O'Connor promptly joined the Court's conservative bloc.[69] And Justice Thomas immediately joined Justice Scalia at the most conservative end of the Court.

Attitudes and values are among the central elements in justices' voting. The justices' ideologies or broad preferences as to the proper scope of government and the content of government policy are another. These elements are central but they are not the exclusive causes of justices' voting. The particular fact situations in cases may affect the outcome, and recurrent fact situations may allow us to predict the Court's actions. Thus in the area of search and seizure, thought to be unstable and confused, knowledge of where the search had taken place (e.g., home or business or car), the extent of the search, its prior justification (was there a warrant?), and whether it occurred in connection with an arrest increased substantially one's ability to predict the Court's result, although conservative rulings—by both the Warren and Burger Courts—were easier to predict than liberal ones, and the Burger Court's liberal decisions were harder to predict than the Warren Court's. There was a clear difference in predisposition toward search issues between the Warren and Burger Courts, but, given the differing predispositions, they treated the factors just discussed in roughly the same way.[70]

Background factors are thought to have an effect on a justice's voting. Among those factors are the justice's region, social class, religion, college and law school attended, partisan identification, and previous public service (elected and appointed) including judicial experience. The results of studies of the effect of background characteristics have not been conclusive. They have also been thought to be "time-bound," that is, particular factors have had particular effects over a 40- or 50-year period but not over the life of the Supreme Court.[71] A recent study of justices serving from 1966 through 1988 shows that, for both economic regulation and civil liberties/rights cases, personal attributes of justices can explain 50 percent and 45 percent, respectively, of the variance in the justices' voting.[72]

Personality, although studied less than attitude or ideology, is another major factor that helps explain the pattern of Supreme Court votes, particularly because of its effect on a justice's role conceptions and on interpersonal relations within the Court. Personality is an important explanation, because "a simple, 'rational' explanation cannot account for [a justice's] personal style on the Court."[73] An individual's ability or difficulty in assimilating a wide range of often contradictory information and the individual's ability (or inability) to change an initial mindset about a case clearly will affect the processes of communication and negotiation within the Court, and a justice's willingness to admit error (or a change in position) would facilitate development of the law over time.[74]

Problems in this regard can be illustrated by Justice Felix Frankfurter who, "intense, nervous, arrogant, [and] domineering . . . could not accept serious, sustained opposition in fields he considered his domain of expertise." Thus when he reached the Court, where he could no longer operate as a behind-the-scenes adviser but was "formally committed to sharing power with strong-willed individuals who had ideas of their own," he "reacted to his opponents with vindictive hostility."[75] His suppressed self-doubts made it difficult for him to work out contradictions in his belief system "between his endorsement of judicial self-restraint," for which he is perhaps best known, "and his belief in the existence of a hierarchy of constitutional values."[76] Not only did he "harden his stands," but he became "preoccupied with the motives of his judicial opponents," attributing impropriety to them; colleagues differing on how to decide cases were not simply fellow professionals with whom one had reasonable disagreements but opponents to be battled as if one were under siege.[77] When he was not trying to ingratiate himself to his colleagues (before he gave them up as lost causes), he was deluging them with suggestions both about cases and about court procedures—something that drove them further away instead of attracting them to his position.[78]

Closely related to personality may be biological processes of aging and senescence. These not only cause problems when an older judge becomes ill and is unwilling to leave the Court—true of Justice Douglas after he suffered a serious stroke[79]—but can also affect an individual's thought processes, for example, leading to rigidity of thinking; this may help explain increasing conservatism among judges.[80] Such considerations seem particularly relevant in explaining the increasingly conservative voting behavior of Justice Black, who, like Justice Douglas, was most liberal in mid-career. The shift in Black's judicial behavior in civil liberties cases, like that of some other twentieth-century justices, may also have reflected new types of civil liberties cases facing the Court as well as responses to changes in the Court's action. In Black's case, the new types of cases involved not "pure" free speech (speech not connected with action), but "free speech plus," particularly civil rights demonstrations to which he had a strong negative reaction.[81]

Also affecting such change is personal learning over time. We have seen justices change their positions—both generally and in particular areas of the law. Justice Holmes changed his position on freedom of speech, moving in a more libertarian direction, between the *Debs* case and his *Abrams* dissent with a different application of the "clear and present danger" test he had developed earlier, as he became educated on the importance of free speech as a result of criticism of his earlier opinions.[82] Justice White recently discussed the change in his position in libel cases from the 1964 ruling in *New York Times v. Sullivan* to the *Gertz* case 10 years later.[83] A broad change occurred with Chief Justice Warren, whom we remember as a liberal justice but who did not start out firmly planted in the Court's liberal wing, moving there only after two terms in the Court's center.[84] And, more recently, Justice Harry Blackmun, who started his tenure on the Court closely allied with Chief Justice Burger and with a shared conservative view of the world, with considerable deference to government, moved in the 1980s not only to a more liberal voting pattern but to considerable compassion for individuals (other than criminal defendants) negatively affected by government actions or who lacked the resources to contest those actions.[85]

Most studies of the relationship of justices' values or attitudes and their voting have been based only on the justices' recorded votes, supplemented by their papers and, recently, by their docket books, in which they record initial conference votes. Materials from a justice's experience prior to Court service have been used to shed light on their values such as morality, tradition, or religion—for such experience could affect the justice's perceptions concerning those values. There was a congruence between the values evident in justices' speeches prior to Supreme Court appointment and the justices' judicial positions reflected in solo dissents, but the justices' pre-Court values sometimes caused them internal conflict. For Justice Pierce Butler, these noncongruent values were patriotism and individual freedom. Butler resolved the conflict between them by deciding in favor of patriotism in free speech cases but in favor of individual freedom in criminal procedure cases.[86]

Studies of the justices' voting have been based primarily on their voting interagreement (bloc analysis) and on Guttman scaling. The period used is often that of a *natural court*, that is, a set of nine justices without personnel changes and a period shorter than the broad "Burger Court" or "Warren Court" periods. *Guttman scaling*, based on the idea that the case is a stimulus and the judge's vote a response, is used for testing the consistency of attitudes underlying a set of decisions. Scales are sets of cases in which the justices were aligned so that a consistent underlying attitude accounted for their votes. If attitudes do underlie justices' votes in a set of cases, the Guttman scale will indicate a "breakpoint," the case or cases where a justice's votes shift from support for a value to opposition; and a justice whose value or attitude influences his or her voting will vote consistently on either side of the "breakpoint." (However, when two justices vote the same way, it is not clear whether they are treating the same stimulus or perceiving different ones.)[87]

Most bloc analysis studies have been based on the voting interagreement of pairs of justices. The pairs are arranged in a matrix, with blocs identified from sets of high interagreement scores. However, if a bloc is defined as a cohesive group whose members vote together regularly, so that a "bloc" really exists only if Justices Jones, Green, and Brown vote together frequently and if the three are frequently found alone, bloc behavior may not be very frequent. If they vote together primarily when they are also voting with others, they do not constitute a bloc. Similarly, the members of several pairs of justices do not constitute a bloc unless all the members of the pairs in the set are in high interagreement. For the 1963–65 Terms, for example, it was difficult to determine the identity of blocs that persisted over time, and identifiable blocs "voted together alone less than half the number of times [they] voted together." Moreover, three- and four-justice dissenting blocs seldom joined in the same *opinion* even when they voted together, making tenuous the idea of "stable, persistent and exclusive . . . blocs, whose members interact substantially as a bloc."[88] Even when two (or more) justices vote conjointly, that does not necessarily mean they share an ideology. Perhaps the best example of this phenomenon is Brandeis and Holmes. Both "believed that the executive and legislative should be given wide latitude in the formulation of social and economic policy," but Brandeis's basic premise was that scientific expertise in government could resolve the problems brought to the government for solution. On the other hand, Holmes was a skeptic and a Social Darwinist: the best-fitted would win in the end, so he should not interfere.[89]

Whatever their methods, researchers have regularly discovered blocs in the Supreme Court. For example, in the 1931–35 Terms, the Court that displeased FDR contained a "Left bloc" of Stone, Cardozo, and Brandeis, and a "Right bloc" of Van Devanter, Butler, Sutherland, and McReynolds. Justice Roberts and Chief Justice Hughes were members of the Right bloc in terms of overall interagreement, although in dissent Roberts was independent and Hughes was marginally affiliated with the Left bloc. In the 1935 Term, however, when the Court shifted to the right, Roberts "was closely aligned with the conservative bloc" in cases where bloc voting occurred and Hughes, who had been slightly left of center, moved slightly right of center.[90]

Looking at this period in terms of game theory, Schubert examined whether Hughes and Roberts ("Hughberts," because of their closely joined voting) had done what they should have done in the 1936 Term to increase their power, that is, their ability to determine the outcome of the Court's decisions. A "pure" strategy for them would have been to form a minimum winning coalition of five with the Left bloc when possible, and to join with the Right bloc when the first strategy was not possible, and to join the rest of the Court (Right and Left together) when all agreed, so as not to be isolated. The Hughes/Roberts behavior indeed closely approximated the specified strategy: the two were affiliated with the Left in total interagreement, voting with the Right only when they could not form a majority with the Left.[91]

Part of the "conventional wisdom" concerning the Court's response to FDR's attack was that only Roberts had shifted his position to produce the "switch in time that saved nine." Roberts's own explanation was that he had earlier indicated his change in positions on the validity of minimum wage legislation, but that when a case containing the appropriate challenge did arise, Justice Stone's illness produced a delay in decision of the case, which as a result was not decided until after the Court-packing plan.[92] Schubert's conclusion, reinforced by a radical shift in bloc dissenting rates from the five previous terms to the 1936 Term, is that both Roberts *and* Hughes had shifted; it is based on an entire term of Court, not just a few cases, and thus revealed patterned rather than idiosyncratic behavior.

That "switch in time" episode raises the question of whether any single justice's vote can ever be said to be determinative of the outcome in a case. There are times when evidence from justices' papers indicates that one person switched sides, thus changing the outcome, but in most cases when the vote is 5–4, *any* of the majority votes is determinative. We could say that the vote of the person nearest to the Court's center, as measured by a Guttman scale, is determinative. Beyond that, we have to speculate—but we must be careful not to be too hasty in saying that a particular justice has the "balance of power" or is the "swing vote." Justice Lewis Powell was said to "balance the Court" in the late 1970s, with his vote between two four-justice groups in *Bakke* an example. However, a systematic examination of his voting does not show him attached to either bloc within the Court: he was a regular part of the conservative bloc in civil liberties cases and was also not the deciding vote in 5–4 rulings. More recently, people have tried to decide whether the replacement of Justice Brennan by Justice Souter has made a difference in the outcome of decisions—another frequent type of speculation. An examination of 5–4 cases in the 1989 Term (Brennan's last) does show a dozen cases in which, had Souter been voting rather than Brennan, the case would have "gone the other way."[93]

Justices' interagreement in the Warren Court and afterward indicates the presence of blocs as well as variance in patterns of interaction within and between those groupings. In the Warren Court's first few years, the Chief Justice and Justice Tom Clark voted together in 95 percent of the cases in which both voted and occupied the Court's "center of gravity," while in the 1958–62 period the Court "splintered into warring factions, with no group able consistently to attract the decisive votes of the centrist judges."[94]

The Warren Court's middle period (the 1962–64 Terms) produced a liberal bloc of Justice Douglas, the Court's most liberal member, Black, Warren, Brennan and Goldberg—whose arrival had for the first time provided a reliable fifth liberal vote—and a conservative bloc of Clark, Kennedy appointee Byron White, Eisenhower appointee Potter Stewart, who occupied center position on the Court, and John Marshall Harlan, the Court's most conservative justice.[95] Then in the 1964 Term, the liberals, "having achieved full control over the court . . . broke ranks."[96] When Justice Fortas replaced Justice Goldberg, there was greater fluidity, but fundamental changes in bloc alignments did not occur. Black's movement to a point between the liberal and conservative blocs meant a liberal majority was not assured, but Justice Marshall's arrival led to an extremely cohesive bloc of Warren, Brennan, Fortas, and Marshall—with Douglas a reliable liberal vote even if not a cohesive bloc member.[97]

The departures of Warren and Fortas and Chief Justice Burger's arrival immediately affected voting alignments. Results were, however, unpredictable, as alignments never fully solidified in the "Burger Court." A clear indication of early change was that Justice Black voted with Chief Justice Burger more than with former voting companion Douglas in the 1969 Term. In the 1970 Term Burger and Justice Blackmun, the other "Minnesota Twin," voted together in 90 percent of nonunanimous cases and in all but one criminal procedure case. Once Powell and Rehnquist joined the Court, Burger's highest interagreement was with Rehnquist (95% of the nonunanimous cases). At the same time, Burger voted with Douglas only 4.2 percent of the time, and Brennan only 10.9 percent, a polarization extreme for the modern Supreme Court. Seven pairs of justices had disagreement rates above 50 percent, and the two-thirds Douglas-Rehnquist disagreement rate was "a modern Supreme Court record."[98]

When the Court opposed defendants' criminal procedure claims, the Nixon bloc was in the majority in all but a very few cases over several terms—but when the Court supported defendants' claims, they were in the majority only slightly more than half the time.[99] Apart from the criminal procedure area, "although the Nixon appointees voted together frequently enough to reorient the Court, they disagreed among themselves often enough to ensure that they could not dominate the Court as thoroughly as had Brennan and his allies in the late Warren Court."[100] The most common pattern in nonunanimous cases was the four Nixon appointees plus White and Stewart, who had begun to help the Nixon appointees control the Court starting with the 1971 Term, although they arrived at the centrist position by somewhat different routes: Stewart was more liberal than White on criminal procedure, more conservative on race relations.

The last half of the 1970s showed a Court with fluid blocs, with Justice Stevens, the Court's newest member, adding to the fluidity of the Court's alignments. Only Brennan and Marshall had an interagreement score over 90 percent. Burger and Rehnquist voted together almost 90 percent of the time, but Rehnquist disagreed with Powell and Blackmun in more than one-fifth of the cases. Burger, Powell, Blackmun and White formed a marginally cohesive bloc (interagreement just over 80%).[101] In the 1981 Term, new Justice O'Connor had an interagreement rate with Justice Rehnquist of over 85 percent, slightly exceeding that of Rehnquist and Burger, thus leading to the formation of the "Arizona Twins" (or the "Phoenix Pair"). They did not, however, match the interagreement of Brennan and Marshall (almost 95%). Justice Blackmun's movement away from Burger accelerated when Justice O'Connor joined the Court—in order, Blackmun has said, to maintain the Court's balance.[102]

We can get a different look at the same essentials if we examine alignments in cases in which two justices of widely differing ideology disagreed. Thus in 63 cases in the 1979 Term in which the Chief Justice and Justice Brennan were on opposite sides, Burger and Rehnquist were together in 61 but Brennan and Rehnquist voted together only *twice*. In the 1984 Term, when Burger opposed Brennan 56 times, Rehnquist joined Burger in 51 of those cases (White, 47; O'Connor, 46), while Marshall voted with Burger only twice. In the last five

Burger Court terms, at least three of the four Nixon appointees were together in three-fourths or more of the Court's nonunanimous cases; O'Connor joined them 70 percent or more of the time after her first term. The Minnesota Twins' voting record varied considerably, from a high of almost 70 percent to below two-fifths, but Burger and Rehnquist were regularly together in over three-fourths of the cases, and Rehnquist and O'Connor voted together even more frequently in four of the five terms. Blackmun now voted with the frequently paired Brennan and Marshall more than half the time in all but one of the five terms.

Although the conservatives have dominated the Court in recent terms, the most conservative justices have not always voted together. From the 1986 through the 1990 Terms, Rehnquist, Scalia, White, and O'Connor never voted together as often as 60 percent of nonunanimous cases and did so in as few as 38 percent. (See Table 7.4.) Once Justice Kennedy joined the Court, his votes were little different from what had been expected of Judge Bork had he been confirmed; Kennedy joined these other four in over half the cases in the 1988 and 1989 Terms, and the four of the five justices voted together roughly three-fourths of the time then. However, in the 1990 Term, the five voted together in only 38.6 percent of the nonunanimous cases; Justice Souter and the other five joined in only 30 percent. In the 1991 Term, O'Connor, Kennedy, and Souter became a more moderate conservative grouping, while Rehnquist, Scalia, and Thomas adopted a more strict conservative stance. Yet great cohesiveness was less necessary with six conservative justices and only five needed for a majority. And we find in the 1990 Term that the conservatives' dominance had become so obvious that on some criminal procedure matters, Justice White joined the "liberal" position—and his support for civil liberties claims increased. Among the conservative justices, there were, however, pairs of justices who did vote together quite frequently. Chief Justice Rehnquist and Justice Scalia, for example, regularly voted together in just under 80 percent of nonunanimous cases; Justice Kennedy and the Chief Justice voted together from two-thirds to over 80 percent of the time. Stanford Law classmates Rehnquist and O'Connor were in the 70 percent range in four of these five terms.

We see a similar pattern among the more liberal members of the Court. Justices Brennan, Marshall, Stevens, and Blackmun regularly voted together in more than 40 percent of the nonunanimous cases from 1986 through 1989. Justices Brennan, Marshall, and Blackmun voted together in two-thirds of the nonunanimous cases in two of the terms, slightly lower in the other two; Brennan, Marshall, and Stevens voted together in the 50 percent range, although over 60 percent in the 1989 Term. Once Justice Brennan retired, Justices Blackmun and Marshall increased the frequency of their joint voting.

Data on civil liberties cases, important in the change from the Warren Court to the Burger Court, reinforce the picture provided by voting interagreement. Comparison of justices' votes on all civil liberties cases with their votes on *close* cases—when their votes were more important—indicate that both the more con-

Table 7.4 Vote Patterns, 1986–1990—Nonunanimous Cases
(frequency with which particular groupings of justices vote together)

	Term				
	1986	1987	1988	1989	1990
Rehnquist, Scalia, White, O'Connor	50.9%	47.5%	57.0%	57.0%	41.1%
Above + Kennedy	—	—	55.8	52.9	38.6
Four of above five	—	—	74.0	77.0	65.6
Rehnquist + Scalia	79.6	75.0	79.1	80.5	75.3
Rehnquist + Kennedy	—	—	81.3	66.7	74.0
Rehnquist + O'Connor	73.1	67.5	74.4	78.2	71.2
Rehnquist + Souter	—	—	—	—	65.8
Brennan, Marshall, Blackmun	68.5	67.5	64.0	63.2	—
Above + Stevens	43.9	42.5	43.0	40.2	—
Brennan, Marshall, Stevens	51.2	57.5	58.1	63.2	—
Brennan, Marshall	92.6	90.0	84.9	96.6	—
Blackmun, Marshall	71.0	66.3	54.7	63.2	76.7
Marshall, Stevens	72.0	61.3	59.3	59.8	63.0
	n = 107	80	86	87	73

servative and more liberal justices had more extreme voting patterns in the close cases than for all cases. On close cases Burger and Rehnquist almost never supported civil liberties claims, and Marshall and Brennan almost never opposed the claims. (See Table 7.5 for recent terms.) However, these patterns do not always hold for more specific issue areas.

Studies of the Court's alignments based on Guttman scaling have produced findings comparable to those derived from bloc analysis. The basic scales that regularly appear were the "C" and "E" scales.[103] The C scale covers civil liberties cases, matters of personal rights and freedoms such as the First Amendment, fair trial, and racial equality. In some terms of the Court, the C scale was a general civil liberties scale; at other times it had subcomponents. The E scale includes economic regulation matters: government regulation of business, antitrust, and labor-management cases. In some years, other scales, including one encompassing questions of federalism and another for judicial activism in reviewing decisions of the other branches of government, have also been identified.

By combining justices' positions on the political (C) and economic (E) scales, Schubert identified four categories of justices (see Figure 7.1). Further classification produced three ideological dimensions. One was Equalitarianism/Traditionalism: someone liberal on both C and E scales would hold the Equalitarian ideology, a belief in greater equality of opportunity for all. The Authoritarian/Libertarian dimension dealt with the scope of freedom as opposed to the scope of authority: those holding the Authoritarian ideology were political conservatives and economic liberals. The third policy dimension was Collectivism/Individualism, involving emphasis on the individual human being as against emphasis on society as such, with a political liberal and economic conservative an Individualist. A fourth dimension cut across the others: Dogmatists, those who believed highly in the authority of precedent, and Pragmatists, those less concerned about precedent and more concerned about decisions' effects.

From 1946 to 1962, Traditionalism, Collectivism, Authoritarianism, and Equalitarianism were dominant at different times. The conservatives, but not the liberals, were divided into Pragmatists and Dogmatists. Six of the seven justices who scored positive on the political liberalism dimension also were positive on economic liberalism; four other justices were neutral as to political liberalism but negative as to economic liberalism. Their limited support of civil liberties led them, when the Court was under political attack in 1956 and 1957, to support another cluster of five justices—neutral on economic matters but negative on political liberalism—in limiting the liberals.[104] Because only three justices—including Chief Justice Warren, who became more liberal—changed ideological positions once they joined the Court, shifts in domination of the Court had to come through changes in personnel that altered the three clusters of justices.

For the Warren Court and the early Burger Court, other scholars found that more than 85 percent of the Court's rulings could be explained in terms of a dimension, New Dealism, based on economic activity and two major dimen-

**Table 7.5 Civil Liberties Claims: Selected Recent Terms
(proportion of times favoring the claim)**

	1986		1988		1990	
	All	*Close*	*All*	*Close*	*All*	*Close*
Rehnquist	11.5%	3.6%	29.0%	4.8%	16.7%	— 0 —
Scalia	21.8	16.4	38.0	19.0	22.9	10.0
Powell/Kennedy	34.6	28.6	41.9	17.1	31.3	13.3
O'Connor	25.6	17.9	37.8	9.7	35.4	20.0
White	25.6	13.0	42.9	14.3	45.8	36.7
Souter	—	—	—	—	31.8	17.2
Stevens	67.9	76.9	69.4	69.0	87.5	90.0
Blackmun	72.7	80.4	71.4	73.8	81.3	96.7
Marshall	96.2	100.0	90.4	95.1	93.7	100.0
Brennan	94.9	100.0	88.7	100.0	—	—

Figure 7.1   Judicial Ideologies (based on Schubert)

| | | *Politics* | |
		Liberal	Conservative
Economics	Liberal	Liberal	Collectivist (Statist)
	Conservative	Individualist (Libertarian)	Conservative

sions related to civil liberties—freedom, covering cases involving criminal defendants and those in political "crimes," such as the loyalty oath cases, and equality, covering political, economic, or racial discrimination. Two other relatively minor dimensions—privacy (libel and obscenity) and taxation—also helped explain Warren Court rulings.[105] Six justices were liberal, that is, positive on the three major dimensions, while seven (the four Nixon appointees, Frankfurter, Whittaker, and Harlan) were conservatives, negative on all three. Black was a Populist—negative as to equality but positive as to freedom and New Dealism—and Clark was a New Dealer, positive only on economic matters, negative on the other two dimensions. Stewart and White were considered Moderates.

Guttman scaling studies have also suggested whether the Court's decisions have been based on the justices' attitudes toward a situation (AS) or toward an object (AO), that is, whether they would vote in terms of their attitude toward that type of person regardless of the situation. In the Warren Court's last 11 terms, AS was found to be more determinative in cases involving labor unions and persons exercising freedom of communication; AO was more important in security risk cases and physically injured employees.[106] However, for the 1971–73 Terms, the attitude toward object—support for the individual or for the government—dominated situational variables for eight of the nine justices (all but Powell) in both criminal and noncriminal cases. That three Nixon appointees favored the government over the individual in both criminal and noncriminal situations indicated clearly that their voting resulted not from a narrow and isolated "law and order" stance but from broader ideology.[107]

All these studies are helpful in understanding the Court and its members. However, while showing overwhelmingly that attitude and ideology affect justices' votes, they are also limited and do not show other factors influencing justices' votes. Because scale positions show only justices' positions relative to each other, not in absolute terms, we cannot tell either where the judges on the extremes are going to fall or exactly where the division between majority and minority will occur. The scales, based only on nonunanimous cases, also cannot explain why the Court achieves unanimous decisions not only on noncontroversial legal questions but on important matters of law such as school desegregation and the Nixon tapes.

Based only on votes rather than on the justices' opinions, they also capture only the Court's final product, its decision, not such important matters as the fact that justices who vote together do not necessarily write together, interaction among the justices, and changes in written opinions and results that may occur between the initial conference vote and final announcement of a decision. The result in a case as determined by the vote is perhaps the most important to the litigants, but the doctrine of an opinion is generally thought to be more important for the Court's role as a policymaker. It is to these considerations that enter into writing an opinion that we now turn.

Notes

1. *Haig v. Bissonette*, 485 U.S. 264 (1988) (four justices not participating).

2. See, for example, *Kungys v. United States*, ultimately decided at 485 U.S. 759 (1988), and *Patterson v. McLean Credit Union*, ultimately decided at 109 S.Ct. 2363 (1989). The reargument order in *Patterson* is at 485 U.S. 617 (1988) (whether *Runyon v. McCrary* should be reconsidered).

3. Rehnquist's statement is at 409 U.S. 824 (1972). See John MacKenzie, *The Appearance of Justice* (New York: Scribner's, 1974).

4. *Laird v. Tatum*, 479 U.S. 911 (1986).

5. See *Woodard v. Hutchins*, 464 U.S. 377 (1984).

6. See *Autry v. Estelle*, 464 U.S. 1 (1983), stay granted by Justice White on different grounds, 474 U.S. 1301 (1983); *Maggio v. Williams*, 474 U.S. 46 (1983).

7. *Wainwright v. Adams*, 466 U.S. 964 at 965 (1984) (Marshall); *Maggio v. Williams*, 464 U.S. 46 at 56 (1983) (Brennan). On the Court's procedures for handling stays pending lower court disposition of appeals, see *Barefoot v. Estelle*, 463 U.S. 880 (1983).

8. *Whalen v. Roe*, 423 U.S. 1313 at 1317 (1975).

9. *Holtzman v. Schlesinger*, 414 U.S. 1304 and 414 U.S. 1316; *Schlesinger v. Holtzman*, 414 U.S. 1321 (1973). The court of appeals later ordered the case dismissed.

10. This section draws on Stephen L. Wasby, Anthony A. D'Amato, and Rosemary Metrailer, "The Functions of Oral Argument in the U.S. Supreme Court," *Quarterly Journal of Speech* 62 (December 1976): 410–22. A different approach can be found in James N. Schubert, Steven A. Peterson, Glendon Schubert, and Stephen Wasby, "Observing Supreme Court Oral Argument: A Biosocial Approach," *Politics and the Life Sciences* 11 (February 1992): 35–51.

11. Quoted in Commission on Revision of the Federal Court Appellate System, *Structure and Internal Procedures*, pp. 104–5.

12. Milton Dickens and Ruth E. Schwartz, "Oral Argument Before the Supreme Court: Marshall v. Davis in the School Segregation Cases," *Quarterly Journal of Speech* 57 (February 1971): 39.

13. Anthony Lewis, "Supreme Law of the Land Still Rests in High Court," *Portland Oregonian*, July 14 1974: F3.

14. Dickens and Schwartz, "Oral Argument," pp. 36–37.

15. Woodward and Armstrong, *The Brethren*, pp. 170–72, 179–81, 187–89, 417–22.

16. Ibid., pp. 63, 288–347.

17. For examples see Alexander Bickel, ed., *The Unpublished Opinions of Mr. Justice Brandeis* (Cambridge, Mass.: Harvard University Press, 1957); Bernard Schwartz, *The Unpublished Opinions of the Warren Court* (New York: Oxford University Press, 1985); Schwartz, *The Unpublished Opinions of the Burger Court* (New York: Oxford University Press, 1988).

18. See Saul Brenner, "Reassigning the Majority Opinion on the United States Supreme Court," *Justice System Journal* 11 (Fall 1986): 186–95, for the 1946–52 Terms (the Vinson Court).

19. Linda Greenhouse, "When Second Thoughts in a Case Come Too Late," *New York Times*, November 5, 1990.

20. See Schwartz, *Super Chief*, pp. 410–24.

21. Saul Brenner, "Fluidity on the United States Supreme Court: A Reexamination," *American Journal of Political Science* 24 (August 1980): 526–35, and "Fluidity on the Supreme Court, 1956–1967," *American Journal of Political Science* 26 (May 1982): 388–90.

22. David Danelski, "Explorations of Some Causes and Consequences of Conflict and Its Resolution in the Supreme Court," *Judicial Conflict and Consensus*, eds. Goldman and Lamb, pp. 29, 21–22.

23. Don E. Fehrenbacher, *The Dred Scott Case: Its Significance in American Law & Politics* (New York: Oxford University Press, 1978), p. 321.

24. The original text reads as follows: "In dispensing these items, the pharmacist performs three tasks: he finds the correct bottle; he counts out the correct number of tablets or measures the right amount of liquid; and he accurately transfers the doctor's dosage instructions to the container. Without minimizing the potential consequences of error in performing these tasks or the importance of the other tasks a professional pharmacist performs, it is clear that in this regard he no more renders a true professional service than does a clerk who sells lawbooks." The ultimate opinion covered the same ground in one sentence: "In dispensing these prepackaged items, the pharmacist performs largely a packaging rather than a compounding function of former times." *Virginia State Board of Pharmacy v. Virginia Citizens Consumers Council*, 425 U.S. 748 at 774–75 (1976). For another change, see Justice Brennan's dissent in *Carchman v. Nash*, in which the final version tones down Brennan's criticism of the majority, in which he said "the Court's silence . . . leaves a gaping hole in its analysis." 473 U.S. 716 at 738 (1985). For an examination of the Court's practices with respect to altering opinions, see Mark Tushnet, "Sloppiness in the Supreme Court, O.T. 1935—O.T. 1944," *Constitutional Commentary* 3 (1986): 73–89.

25. Charles W. Nihan and Russell R. Wheeler, "Using Technology to Improve the Administration of Justice in the Federal Courts," *Brigham Young University Law Review* 1981: 667n.

26. Data through the first Burger Court term from Donald D. Gregory and Stephen L. Wasby, "How to Get an Idea from Here to There: The Court and Communication Overload," *Public Affairs Bulletin* 3, no. 5 (November-December 1976); later data developed by the present author.

27. See Bernard Schwartz, "Felix Frankfurter and Earl Warren: A Study of a Deteriorating Relationship," *Supreme Court Review 1980*, eds. Phillip Kurland and Gerhard Casper (Chicago: University of Chicago Press, 1981), pp. 115–42; Dennis J. Hutchinson, "The Black-Jackson Feud," *The Supreme Court Review 1988*: 203–43.

28. Bernard Wolfman, Jonathan L. F. Silver, and Marjorie A. Silver, *Dissent Without Opinions: The Behavior of Justice William O. Douglas in Tax Cases* (Philadelphia: University of Pennsylvania Press, 1975).

29. Danelski, "Explorations of Some Causes and Consequences," p. 34.

30. *Manual Enterprises v. Day*, 370 U.S. 478 at 519 (1962).

31. See also the *Norris* pension plan case, *Arizona Governing Committee v. Norris*, 463 U.S. 1073 (1983), where there were different majorities on the constitutional issue and on the remedy; and *Bazemore v. Friday*, 478 U.S. 385 (1986), on racial discrimination, where majorities varied with each particular discrimination issue.

32. See Steven A. Peterson, "Dissent in American Courts," *Journal of Politics* 43 (1981): 412–34. For an interesting, extended discussion of dissents in various situations, see Maurice Kelman, "The Forked Path of Dissent," *The Supreme Court Review 1985*, eds. Philip B. Kurland, Gerhard Casper, and Dennis J. Hutchinson (Chicago: University of Chicago Press, 1986), pp. 227–98.

33. An important examination of the Court's efforts to remain unanimous is Dennis J. Hutchinson, "Unanimity and Desegregation: Decisionmaking in the Supreme Court, 1948–1958," *Georgetown Law Journal* 68 (October 1979), 1–96.

34. *Webster v. Reproductive Health Services*, 109 S.Ct. 3040 at 3067, 3078 (1989).

35. William J. Brennan, Jr., "In Defense of Dissents," *Hastings Law Journal* 37 (1986): 427–38; *Colorado v. Connelly*, 479 U.S. 157 at 188 (1986).

36. See Robert F. Williams, "In the Supreme Court's Shadow: Legitimacy of State Rejection of Supreme Court Reasoning and Result," *South Carolina Law Review* 35 (Spring 1984): 374–75.

37. Linda Greenhouse, "Supreme Court Dissenters: Loners or Pioneers?" *New York Times*, July 20 1990, p. 87.

38. Richard A. Posner, *The Federal Courts: Crisis and Reform* (Cambridge, Mass.: Harvard University Press, 1985), p. 236.

39. Danelski, "Explorations of Some Causes and Consequences," p. 42.

40. David Lauter, "A New Polarization for the High Court," *National Law Journal*, August 11 1986, p. S–3.

41. *Will v. Calvert Fire Insurance Co.*, 437 U.S 655 at 670 (1978).

42. *Oregon v. Elstad*, 470 U.S. 298 at 320, 324 (1985). See also *United States v. Sharpe*, 470 U.S. 675 at 702–4 (1985).

43. *Columbus Board of Education v. Penick*, 443 U.S. 449 at 493 (1979).

44. *Federal Energy Regulatory Commission v. Mississippi*, 456 U.S. 742 at 761 n. 25 and 767 n. 30 (1982).

45. *Webster v. Reproductive Health Services*, 109 S.Ct., at 3067, 3078 (1989).

46. Russell W. Galloway, Jr., "The Taft Court (1921–29)," *Santa Clara Law Review* 25 (Winter 1985): 2.

47. Stephen C. Halpern and Kenneth N. Vines, "Institutional Disunity, The Judges Bill and the Role of the U.S. Supreme Court," *Western Political Quarterly* 30 (Fall 1977): 471–83.

48. S. Sidney Ulmer, "Exploring the Dissent Patterns of the Chief Justices: John Marshall to Warren Burger," *Judicial Conflict and Consensus*, eds. Goldman and Lamb, p. 55.

49. Russell W. Galloway, Jr., "The Roosevelt Court," *Santa Clara Law Review* 23 (1983): 513.

50. Arthur D. Hellman, "Preserving the Essential Role of the Supreme Court," *Florida State Law Review* 14 (1986): 29–30.

51. Professor (now Judge) Frank Easterbrook has suggested that if we look at "whether the Justices who do not join the majority disagree with the Court's rationale," instead of engaging in counting, one sees far less change in conflict within the Court. Frank H. Easterbrook, "Agreement Among the Justices: An Empirical Note," *The Supreme Court Review 1984*, eds. Kurland, Casper, and Hutchinson (Chicago: University of Chicago Press, 1985), p. 389.

52. Harold J. Spaeth and Michael Altfeld, "Influence Relationships Within the Supreme Court: A Comparison of the Warren and Burger Courts," *Western Political Quarterly* 38 (March 1985): 70–83.

53. Saul Brenner, "Minimum Winning Coalitions on U.S. Supreme Court," *American Politics Quarterly* 7 (July 1979): 384–92.

54. David W. Rohde, "Policy Goals and Opinion Coalitions in the Supreme Court," *Midwest Journal of Political Science* 16 (May 1972): 218–19; Micheal W. Giles, "Equivalent Versus Minimum Winning Opinion Size: A Test of Two Hypotheses," *American Journal of Political Science* (May 1977): 405–8.

55. Peter G. Fish, "The Office of Chief Justice of the United States: Into the Federal Judiciary's Bicentennial Decade," *The Office of Chief Justice* (Charlottesville, Va.: University of Virginia, 1984), p. 59. For a recent exploration, see Robert J. Steamer, *Chief Justice: Leadership and the Supreme Court* (Columbia: University of South Carolina Press, 1986).

56. See Schwartz, *Super Chief*. Schwartz does not emphasize Brennan's role, but provides the evidence for that role. I am indebted to Phillip Cooper for this point.

57. Sue Davis, "The Supreme Court: Rehnquist's or Reagan's," *Western Political Quarterly* 44 (March 1991): 90–91, 97.

58. See Ulmer, "Exploring the Dissenting Patterns," p. 54.

59. David Danelski, "The Influence of the Chief Justice in the Decisional Process of the Supreme Court," *Courts, Judges, and Politics*, eds. Walter F. Murphy and C. Herman Pritchett (New York: Random House, 1974), p. 503.

60. On this and other problems, see Kelman, "Forked Path of Dissent," pp. 290–97.

61. William P. McLauchlan, "Ideology and Conflict in Supreme Court Opinion Assignment, 1947–1962," *Western Political Quarterly* 25 (March 1972): 16–27.

62. David W. Rohde, "Policy Goals, Strategic Choice, and Majority Opinion Assignments in U.S. Supreme Court," *Midwest Journal of Political Science* 16 (November 1972): 667; see also S. Sidney Ulmer, "The Use of Power in the Supreme Court: The Opinion Assignments of Earl Warren, 1953–60," *Journal of Public Law* 19 (1970): 49–67.

63. Harold J. Spaeth, "Distributive Justice: Majority Opinion Assignments in the Burger Court," *Judicature* 67 (December-January 1984): 299–304, for the 1969–80 Terms.

64. Saul Brenner and Jan Palmer, "The Time Taken to Write Opinions as a Determinant of Opinion Assignments," *Judicature* 72 (October-November 1988): 182, 184.

65. See Saul Brenner and Harold J. Spaeth, "Issue Specialization in Majority Opinion Assignment on the Burger Court," *Western Political Quarterly* 39 (September 1986): 520–27.

66. Sue Davis, "Power on the Court: Chief Justice Rehnquist's Opinion Assignments," *Judicature* 74 (August-September 1990): 72.

67. Susan Lawrence, "Justice Rehnquist, Declarations of Unconstitutionality, and Judicial Restraint," paper presented to Law & Society Association, 1990.

68. Elliot E. Slotnick, "The Chief Justices and Self-Assignment of Majority Opinions: A Research Note," *Western Political Quarterly* 31 (June 1978): 224. See also Slotnick, "Who Speaks for the Court?: Majority Opinion Assignment from Taft to Burger," *American Journal of Political Science* 23 (February 1979), particularly pp. 68–72, and Slotnick, "Judicial Career Patterns and Majority Opinion Assignment on the Supreme Court," *Journal of Politics* 41 (May 1979): 640–48.

69. See John M. Scheb II and Lee W. Ailshie, "Justice Sandra Day O'Connor and the 'Freshman Effect,'" *Judicature* 69 (June-July 1985): 9–12. See also Scott P. Johnson and Christopher E. Smith, "David Souter's First Term on the Supreme Court: The Impact of a New Justice," *Judicature* 75 (February-March 1992): 238–43, indicating Souter to be a relatively moderate conservative but definitely part of the Court's conservative bloc.

70. Jeffrey A. Segal, "Predicting Supreme Court Cases Probabilistically: The Search and Seizure Cases, 1962–1981," *American Political Science Review* 78 (December 1984): 891–900, and Segal, "Measuring Change on the Supreme Court: Examining Alternative Models," *American Journal of Political Science* 29 (August 1985): 461–79.

71. S. Sidney Ulmer, "Are Social Background Models Time-Bound?" *American Political Science Review* 80 (1986): 957–67.

72. C. Neal Tate and Roger Handberg, "Time Binding and Theory Building in Personal Attribute Models of Supreme Court Voting Behavior, 1916–88," *American Journal of Political Science* 35 (May 1991): 460–80. See also Tate, "Personal Attribute Models of the Voting Behavior of United States Supreme Court Justices: Liberalism in Civil Liberties and Economics Decisions, 1946–1978," *American Political Science Review* 75 (1981): 355–67.

73. H. N. Hirsch, *The Enigma of Felix Frankfurter* (New York: Basic Books, 1981), p. 211.

74. As a small example, see Justice Stevens's admission of incorrectly characterizing a case, *Spaziano v. Florida*, 468 U.S. 447 at 470 n. 4 (1984).

75. Hirsch, p. 506.

76. Ibid., pp. 136–37.

77. Ibid., pp. 9, 153, 176.

78. Ibid., p. 188. See Dennis J. Hutchinson, "Felix Frankfurter and the Business of the Supreme Court, O.T. 1946—O.T. 1961," *Supreme Court Review 1980*, pp. 143–209.

79. See Woodward and Armstrong, *The Brethren*, pp. 357ff.

80. See Glendon Schubert, "Aging, Conservatism, and Judicial Behavior," *Micropolitics* 3 (1983): 135–79.

81. S. Sidney Ulmer, "The Longitudinal Behavior of Hugo Lafayette Black: Parabolic Support for Civil Liberties, 1937–1971," *Florida State University Law Review* 1 (Winter 1974): 131–53. See also Ulmer, "Parabolic Support of Civil Liberty Claims: The Case of William O. Douglas," *Journal of Politics* 41 (May 1979): 634–39, and H. Frank Way, "The Study of Judicial Attitudes: The Case of Mr. Justice Douglas," *Western Political Quarterly* 24 (March 1971): 12–23.

82. Richard Polenberg, *Fighting Faiths: The Abrams Case, The Supreme Court, and Free Speech* (New York: Penguin, 1987), pp. 218–28.

83. See *Dun & Bradstreet v. Greenmoss Builders*, 472 U.S. 749 at 767 (1985).

84. See Russell W. Galloway, Jr., "The Early Years of the Warren Court: Emergence of Judicial Liberalism (1953–1957)," *Santa Clara Law Review* 18 (1978): 613–22.

85. See Stephen L. Wasby, "Justice Harry A. Blackmun in the Burger Court," *Hamline Law Review* 11 (Summer 1988): 186–89, 194–98.

86. David Danelski, "Values as Variables in Judicial Decision-Making: Notes Toward a Theory," *Vanderbilt Law Review* 19 (1966): 721–40, and Danelski, *A Supreme Court Justice is Appointed* (New York: Random House, 1964).

87. Still more sophisticated methods are used by some scholars. See Glendon Schubert, *The Judicial Mind* (Evanston, Ill.: Northwestern University Press, 1965), for use of "smallest space analysis," and S. Sidney Ulmer, "The Discriminant Function and the Theoretical Context for Its Use in Estimating the Votes of Judges," *Frontiers of Judicial Research*, eds. Joel B. Grossman and Joseph Tanenhaus (New York: John Wiley, 1969), pp. 335–69.

88. Joel B. Grossman, "Dissenting Blocs on the Warren Court: A Study in Judicial Role Behavior," *Journal of Politics* 30 (November 1968): 1083, 1089.

89. Hirsch, *Felix Frankfurter*, pp. 129–30.

90. Russell W. Galloway, Jr., "The Court That Challenged the New Deal," *Santa Clara Law Review* 24 (Winter 1984): 86.

91. Schubert, *Quantitative Analysis of Judicial Behavior*, (Glencoe, Ill.: Free Press, 1959), pp. 192–210. See also Russell W. Galloway, Jr., "The Roosevelt Court: The Liberals Conquer (1937–1941) and Divide (1941–1946)," *Santa Clara Law Review* 23 (1983): 495–96.

92. For Roberts's explanation, see Glendon Schubert, *Constitutional Politics* (New York: Holt, Rinehart and Winston, 1960), pp. 168–71.

93. Janet L. Blasecki, "Justice Lewis F. Powell: Swing Voter or Staunch Conservative," *Journal of Politics* 52 (May 1990): 530–47.

94. Edward V. Heck, "Changing Voting Patterns in the Warren and Burger Courts," *Judicial Conflict and Consensus*, eds. Goldman and Lamb, pp. 71–74.

95. Glendon Schubert, *The Constitutional Polity* (Boston: Boston University Press, 1970), pp. 124–25. See also S. Sidney Ulmer, "Toward a Theory of Sub-Group Formation in the United States Supreme Court," *Journal of Politics* 27 (1965): 133–52.

96. Russell W. Galloway, Jr., "The Third Period of the Warren Court: Liberal Dominance (1962–1969)," *Santa Clara Law Review* 20 (1980): 789.

97. Edward V. Heck, "Justice Brennan and the Heyday of Warren Court Liberalism," *Santa Clara Law Review* 20 (Fall 1980): 845–46, 858–59, and Heck, "Changing Voting Patterns," pp. 77–78.

98. Russell W. Galloway, Jr., "The First Decade of the Burger Court: Conservative Dominance (1969–1979)," *Santa Clara Law Review* 21 (1981): 908.

99. David W. Rohde and Harold J. Spaeth, *Supreme Court Decision-Making* (San Francisco: W. H. Freeman, 1975), p. 109.

100. Heck, "Changing Voting Patterns," p. 82.

101. Edward V. Heck, "Civil Liberties Voting Patterns in the Burger Court, 1975–1978," *Western Political Quarterly* 34 (June 1981): 199.

102. See John A. Jenkins, "A Candid Talk with Justice Blackmun," *New York Times Magazine*, February 10, 1983, pp. 20–24ff.

103. What follows is drawn primarily from Schubert, *The Judicial Mind*.

104. Glendon Schubert, *The Judicial Mind Revisited: Psychometric Analysis of Supreme Court Ideology* (New York: Oxford University Press, 1974), summarized in Schubert, "The Judicial Mind Reappraised," *Jurimetrics Journal* 15 (Summer 1975): 279.

105. Rohde and Spaeth, *Supreme Court Decision-Making*, pp. 137–38.

106. Harold J. Spaeth et al., "Is Justice Blind?: An Empirical Investigation of a Normative Ideal," *Law & Society Review* 7 (Fall 1972): 119–37.

107. S. Sidney Ulmer and John A. Stookey, "Nixon's Legacy to the Supreme Court: A Statistical Analysis of Judicial Behavior," *Florida State University Law Review* 3 (Summer 1975): 331–47.

8   The Court's Opinions

THE PART PLAYED BY justices' *values* in their voting patterns is but one consideration entering into reaching a decision and then writing an "opinion of the Court" through which the Court's policy is most explicitly stated. The justices' views of their roles as justices and of the Supreme Court's place in the American political system also play a significant part in the decisions they reach and in their opinion writing, just as they do in decisions to accept or reject cases. Even if justices' initial reactions to a case are affected by their personal value positions, the decision reached by the Court and the ultimate content of the Court's opinion are also affected by an understanding of what the Court's audiences or attentive publics expect. This is not surprising when we realize that the Court's basic impact on other government units comes through its opinions. The breadth of an opinion, its doctrinal bases, and the other content it contains—including precedent and history to establish continuity with the past as well as social science materials, generally used sparingly—affect not only an opinion's immediate policy effects but also its value as precedent. Whether an opinion is framed narrowly, staying within the grounds urged by the parties or seemingly applicable only to the facts of the particular case, or departs from those facts to embrace other situations, and whether it is confined to a statute rather than reaching a constitutional question, are thus quite important.

Basic Considerations

There are some problems in examining the Court's opinions. One is that there have been important changes over time in the Court's decision-making style—the way the justices have made decisions as well as the overall matrix in which the potential elements of an opinion, or factors influencing it, are taken into account. Giving the Court the power to decide which cases to accept had an important effect on such decision making. When the Court had to decide all cases brought to it but its caseload was still small, the justices could decide each case carefully and deliberately, that is, they could engage in rational decision making. With time to consider each case, the likelihood that they would depart from precedent would be greater than otherwise.[1] When the Court had an increased caseload but still operated under the pre-1925 requirement of hearing all cases, decision making was incremental. Changes from past cases were limited; precedent served as a cue to allow prompt disposition. Instead of making law, the Court was more likely to be engaged in interpretation of existing doctrine.

Once it obtained the power to turn away cases, the Court could return to rational decision making for those cases it accepted, thus allowing more policy innovation. When the caseload grew again, "mixed-scanning" decision making was produced, in which a quick glance is given to most cases before they are rejected, while those accepted get more extended and careful treatment. Here the justices' basic doctrinal attitudes affect not only the Court's full decisions but its decisions to grant review as well. The Court's ability to innovate may, however, be hindered if docket size gets too large and approaches "overload chaos," an unmanageable situation that some justices suggest now exists (see pages 196–99).

What justices write is not necessarily a "true" reflection of their reasons and motives in voting for a particular result. Judges' opinions do not exhibit initial thoughts through rethinking to the ultimate product. The opinions thus seldom indicate the process by which the judge has reached the conclusions presented, the serial iterations in the judge's writing process, or changes resulting from interaction with colleagues. A justice's motivations may be accurately reflected in a solo dissent, but the author of an opinion of the Court is constrained by the need to accommodate colleagues' views. The opinion, a justificatory essay, is likely to state conclusions along with their justifications, the "reconstituted logic" of explanations.

Does this mean, to paraphrase one cynic, that a judge shoots an arrow at a target and then draws the bullseye around the place where the arrow struck, or that opinions are only an elaborate display of erudition serving as window dressing to mask initial gut reactions? Certainly what Justice Oliver Wendell Holmes, Jr., called a judge's "inarticulate major premises" affect the judge's written opinions, and the Legal Realists see judicial decision making as idiosyncratic, affected not only by "the law" but also by case facts and the judge's values. Thus the justice writing for the majority and justices writing concurring or dissenting opinions can write equally persuasive opinions, because each reasons from different premises. Nonetheless, justices *are* affected by having to write opinions and by the expectations they will justify their actions, include certain material in their opinions, and address certain problems. In short, whatever the part played by personal values, the justices are affected and constrained by being *judges* expected to justify their decisions through opinions. Also a constraint is the opinion's function to persuade people outside the Court—first, the parties to the case, and then the legal community and other "court-watchers"—that the decision is a reasonable one, reasonably arrived at, with sufficient guidance in the Court's opinion to allow those affected to control "primary conduct." The greater length of the Court's opinions and greater use of precedent have been attributed to the justices' greater concern to justify the Court's authority in the absence of consensus as to its place.[2]

In the course of reaching a decision and arriving at an opinion's ultimate scope, content, and tone, the Court is expected to consider a number of important matters. In deciding cases and writing opinions, the Court is expected to reach toward *neutral principles*. It is also expected to develop policy incrementally and to rely on *precedent*. The justices must also consider whether the Court should exercise its power of *judicial review* (see pages 75–82), important to the Court's relations with the other branches of government and to the tension between judicial review and democracy. An aspect of judicial review is the extent to which the Court will defer to the states as part of *federalism*. Another aspect of judicial review is whether the Court should exercise *self-restraint* or engage in *judicial activism*; the latter is at the heart of criticism of the federal courts for being unnecessarily interventionist (see pages 3–7). While not fully governing the Court's decisions or justices' opinions, all these matters have some effect, and thus can legitimately be called "considerations" in the justices' work. Indeed, if they are not taken into account, criticism, from inside the Court and from outside, is sure to result. Another concept, not considered separately here, that may serve to pull the other elements together is *judicial role*: how the justices see what they should do in relation to those people and institutions with whom they and the Court must interact affects their votes and decisions.

Still another matter, undergirding the others but not likely to be discussed openly by the justices, is whether and how the Court in attempting to achieve its goals, and the individual justices in attempting to achieve *their* goals, will engage in strategy—already an element in the Court's choice of cases for review and in the decision to give cases summary or full-dress treatment (see pages 203–8). After a discussion of all these matters, we conclude the chapter with an examination of another important reflection of their strategic concerns and role concepts: their off-the-Court activities concerning judicial and nonjudicial matters.

Neutral Principles

People who see the Court as finding law, and even many who recognize that it makes policy, expect of the Court that its decisions should be *principled*. Compromises deriving from pragmatism are for legislators and political executives; courts, on the other hand, must stand for principle, deliberateness, the use of rationality and logic, and detachment from the turmoil and passion of political conflict. As law professor Alexander Bickel said:

The root idea is that the process is justified only if it injects into representative government something that is not already there: and that is principle, standards of action that derive their worth from a long view of society's spiritual as well as material needs and that command adherence whether or not the immediate outcome is expedient or agreeable.[3]

In the most noted statement on the subject, Herbert Wechsler said judicial determinations should rest on "reasons that in their generality and their neutrality transcend any immediate result that is involved." Criteria for decisions had to be exercises of reason, "not merely . . . an act of willfulness or will"[4]; in Justice Marshall's words, "bedrock principles are founded in the law rather than in the proclivities of individuals."[5]

Wechsler had demanded too much even for advocates of the Court's "passive virtues" like Bickel. Bickel argued that if the Court were to have to rest its decisions "only on principles that will be capable of application across the board and without compromise, in all relevant cases in the foreseeable future," with any flexibility built into the principle itself "in equally principled fashion," there would be few such principles. Thus few decisions of other branches of government would be overturned, and the "neutral principles" position would be restraintist. Moreover, because, in the absence of such neutral principles, few cases would be decided, the Court would fail to meet the public's demand that it resolve issues. As Justice Brandeis put it, it is better that some cases be decided than that they be decided right.[6]

The "neutral principles" idea is, however, important because it proposes a goal—principled and reasoned opinions—to which judges should aspire even if they are not able to achieve it. It should be enough, said Bickel, to have "an intellectually coherent statement of the reason for a result which in like cases will produce a like result, whether or not it is immediately agreeable or expedient," with the values having "general significance and even-handed application."[7] This is similar to Judge Posner's call for consistency: "To be a principled adjudicator means more than just being willing to state publicly the true ground of decision; it also means being consistent."[8]

The question of whether the Court was basing its ruling on will or principles came to the surface when a majority overturned recent rulings on the (in)admissibility of victim impact statements in capital cases. As the 1991 decision overruled 1987 and 1989 rulings, dissenting Justice Marshall argued that "Power, not reason, is the new currency of this Court's decision." Justice Scalia, concurring, responded that "what would enshrine power as the governing principle of this Court is the notion that an important constitutional decision with plainly inadequate rational support *must* be left in place for the sole reason that it once attracted five votes."[9]

Precedent

One of the strongest expectations in the legal community is that the justices will adhere to the doctrine of *stare decisis* (literally, to stand on the decision), at the heart of the Anglo-American legal tradition. Precedent performs important functions. It is "the means by which we ensure that the law will not merely change erratically, but will develop in a principled and intelligible fashion" and allows people to see "the judiciary as a source of impersonal and reasoned judgments."[10] Beyond that, it "serves the broader societal interests in even-handed, consistent, and predictable application of legal rules," in short, "in stability, and in the orderly conduct of our affairs."[11] Judges must take care in departing from precedent, because when they do or the Court "makes new law out of whole cloth," "the holy rite of judges consulting a higher law loses some of its mysterious power."[12] Too many sharp deviations and departures, too many unpredictable results disturb the general public and particularly those "opinion leaders" who watch the Court most closely.

The importance of precedent is demonstrated by the time and effort justices devote to explaining why their opinions follow, or why colleagues' opinions depart from, precedent. Such comments may be stimulated by the justices' respective value positions, but if precedent were not considered important, it would not be used as either justification or weapon. Nor would the justices devote so much time to persuading each other—and the publics who read their opinions—of their "readings" of the relevant cases. There is also the element of *personal precedent*, in which a justice is committed, at least within limits, to a position adopted earlier, part of a striving for internal consistency, which may reinforce adherence to a position the Court has adopted and with which, at the time, the justice has agreed, or which may lead a justice to hold to views, once adopted in a dissent, in the face of other justices' contrary rulings.

The expectation that courts base their decisions on precedent, which involves taking the present case, finding past cases that are similar, and then applying the rules from those past cases, creates a number of problems. How does one know which cases are "similar"? On what competing precedents should one rely? How should legal doctrine of the relevant cases be interpreted? And, at the level of the Supreme Court, should precedent be followed as closely as lower courts are expected to follow it?[13] The Court's place as the nation's highest and last court has led it to feel *less* bound by precedent than do the lower courts. In Justice Powell's words, "When governing decisions are badly reasoned, or conflict with other, more recent authority, the Court 'has never felt constrained to follow precedent.' "[14] And Justice White has said that the Court "has not hesitated to overrule decisions, or even whole lines of cases, where experience, scholarship, and reflection demonstrated that their fundamental premises were not to be found in the Constitution."[15]

Precedent has reduced force when the Constitution is being interpreted, because changes in constitutional rulings can be overturned only through the very difficult process of amending the Constitution itself.[16] Because Congress has the power to rewrite statutes and thus correct the Court's interpretation of those statutes (see pages 318–21), the justices are more reluctant to alter precedents based on statutory interpretation even when they recognize that those precedents may be in error.

Illustrating this point is the Court's disposition of Curt Flood's challenge to the reserve clause in professional baseball, the only major professional sport exempted from antitrust coverage (Hi there, sports fans!). The baseball exemption stems from the Court's 1923 ruling, reaffirmed in 1953, that baseball was not commerce and therefore was not subject to the Sherman Antitrust Act. In ruling on *Flood v. Kuhn* (1972), the majority agreed that professional baseball was a business in interstate commerce and that the antitrust exemption for baseball was "in a very distinct sense, an exception and an anomaly," because other courts, on the basis of the Supreme Court's post-1937 broader definition of commerce, had held other sports, particularly professional baseball and professional basketball, subject to the antitrust laws. Nonetheless, said Justice Blackmun, "the aberration is an established one" recognized by Congress, which "by its positive inaction" had allowed the earlier baseball decisions to stand. Thus "if there is any inconsistency or illogic in all of this, it is an inconsistency and illogic of long standing that is to be remedied by the Congress and not by this Court." [17]

Despite these statements, if the legislature has not relied on the Court's past rulings, if past rulings are out of step with still earlier rulings, or if the challenged ruling is out of phase with more recent statements of legislative intent, the Court now reading legislative history differently will be more willing to overrule precedents interpreting statutes. An example is the *Monell* case, in which the Court, only 16 years after initially holding that municipalities could not be sued under the Civil Rights Act of 1871 (42 U.S.C. § 1983) (see pages 170–71) and only five years after reaffirming the initial decision, held that the courts *would* entertain such suits. The majority justified the reversal both on the basis of inconsistency with other civil rights rulings and on the Court's not having adequately considered its earlier position before adopting it.

Justice Rehnquist's comment in the *Monell* case that "this Court is surely not free to abandon settled statutory interpretation at any time a new thought seems appealing" suggests that criticism from other justices and from outside the Court is likely when the Court does overrule a precedent. Such criticism occurs whether the precedent is new or old: if old, the Court is said to be interfering with the "settled ways" of the law; if new, the Court is not allowing the law to develop properly. Recent changes in precedent are also used to block further changes in the law. Justice Rehnquist commented in a post-*Monell* case that "the law in this area has taken enough 90-degree turns in recent years" and therefore should not be changed further. [18]

The majority's failure to explain effectively departure from recently established precedent gives dissenting justices' criticism more force. The Burger Court's rulings on leafletting in shopping centers provide an example. In 1968, the Warren Court had said that picketing a particular store in a large, privately owned shopping center had to be allowed. In 1972, without overruling that earlier case, which it said was different, the Burger Court allowed antiwar leafletting to be banned because the protest was unrelated to the shopping center or its stores. Then in 1976 the Court banned picketing of a shopping center shoe store by workers whose basic dispute was with the store's warehouse. Here the Court explicitly overruled the 1968 case, but in doing so said the overruling had really taken place in 1972 because the 1968 case had not "survived" the 1972 ruling, thus conceding that the first opinion had been overruled *sub silentio*. The inadequacy of this explanation, so obviously at variance with the majority's own 1972 statements, led Justice Marshall to complain that the first case had "been laid to rest without ever having been accorded a proper burial."[19] The same problem arose in the 1989 *Webster* abortion case, where the plurality did not explicitly overrule *Roe v. Wade*, although Justice Scalia, concurring in the judgment, would have done so explicitly. Justice Blackmun, dissenting, thought that the plurality had "repudiate[d] every principle for which *Roe* stands," and thus had done everything *but* overrule it.[20]

Another way to avoid the thrust of precedent without stirring up criticism from an explicit overruling is "strategic differentiation" or the *distinguishing* of cases from one another. In this technique, used by the Burger Court in its erosion of Warren Court rulings, particularly in the criminal procedure area, differences are emphasized and the application of precedent is limited by saying new cases contain facts not identical to those in the older cases. However, even when precedents are expandable and contractable, the earlier cases create limits, so that some opinions stating new policy "won't write." This is one reason the Burger Court was less conservative than expected: Warren Court precedents led to more liberal results than if President Nixon's appointees had been able to write on a clean slate.

Although one's desire to uphold, or abandon, precedent is in part a function of one's like, or dislike, of the precedent itself, precedent definitely affects individual justices. For example, in *Runyon v. McCrary* (1976), Justice Powell went along with the Court's outlawing racial discrimination in admission to private schools, because the Court had considered application of those civil rights statutes to private acts "maturely and recently" in its 1968 *Jones v. Mayer* decision applying post–Civil War antidiscrimination statutes to private housing sales. Justice Stevens indicated he would vote differently "were we writing on a clean slate," but said that "the interest in stability and orderly development of the law" and the fact that the precedent "accords with the prevailing sense of justice today" had "greater force" than the argument that the earlier case was wrongly decided. There was an outcry from many quarters when the Court asked for briefing and argument on whether *Runyon* should be reconsidered. Many members of Congress, state attorneys general, and leaders of the organized bar, plus civil rights groups, called on the Court *not* to overturn the precedent. After considering the matter, the Court reaffirmed it while limiting its application in the employment context.[21]

Justices who agree to abide by particular precedents even when disliking them are sending "mixed messages," one part of which may be an invitation to lawyers to challenge the disliked precedent. At times they go further, openly calling for reversal of disliked precedents. Rehnquist and Chief Justice Burger made long arguments for overturning the exclusionary rule with respect to improperly seized evidence. And, in a major parental consent abortion case, Rehnquist, while joining the majority in upholding precedent because "literally thousands of judges cannot be left with nothing more than the guidance offered by a truly fragmented holding of this Court," announced he would "be more than willing to participate" when "this Court is willing to reconsider" its decision. [22]

Not only did Justice Scalia call for overturning the *Roe v. Wade* abortion ruling, but he also called for overturning the Court's precedent on discharge of public workers for political party affiliation. He said that "all reluctance" to overturn precedent "ought to disappear" "when that precedent is not only wrong, not only recent, not only contradicted by a long prior tradition, but also has proved unworkable in practice." [23] Similarly, Justice White said he "would support a basic reconsideration of our precedents" on the Establishment Clause. In an example of adherence to personal precedent, he noted his argument was "not surprising" because he had "been out of step with many of the Court's decisions dealing with this subject matter." [24]

The Court does indeed overturn decisions. This is likely to result from a combination of new justices joining the Court and changed minds, for example, when the Court quickly reversed itself on the constitutionality of the compulsory flag salute. [25] In the late 1980s and early 1990s, reversals of precedent came from the addition of new justices. As Justice Marshall said, in dissenting from the Court's allowing use of "victim impact statements" in death penalty cases and thus overruling two recent cases, "Neither the law nor the facts supporting [the earlier cases] underwent any change in the last four years. Only the personnel of this Court changed." [26]

There are times when the need for consistency in the law leads the Court to abandon past rulings in favor of a new and clear standard, for example, when there are competing lines of cases that are not easily reconciled. An example comes from the law of search and seizure, when the Court's "dual regimes" of rules for searches of automobiles (not requiring a warrant) and other, more recent rules for searches of containers in cars (requiring a warrant), proved "confusing"; in 1991 the Court adopted one rule covering both situations (allowing searches without warrants if probable cause existed). [27] Overruling may also occur when the Court has ventured into an area of law for the first time and found that later cases cast a different light on the subject, as appears to have happened with the Burger Court's dealing with double jeopardy claims. [28]

The Court's rulings on Congress's extension of the minimum wage to state and local government employees illustrate the overturning of an overturning. The Court first ruled, in 1968 (*Maryland v. Wirtz*) that Congress had the authority to extend the law to certain state and local government employees. Then in 1976, in what looked like a resurrection of the Tenth Amendment in *National League of Cities v. Usery,* the Court overturned Congress's authority, only to have the *National League of Cities* case in turn overruled in 1985 (*Garcia v. San Antonio Metropolitan Transit Authority*). This shows that some rulings may be overturned rather quickly, although others are reversed only after a somewhat longer time.

The Court, throughout its history, has engaged in more than 250 reversals of precedent.[29] Many of the recent overrulings have been by closely divided votes. Although in some cases the overruling took place in less than five years from the date of the original ruling, and at the other extreme, some cases that had stood for more than 70 years were overturned, the average life of the precedents overturned from 1958 through 1980, before they were overruled, was roughly 20 years.[30] Perhaps the period of most frequent reversal was that of the Roosevelt Court, 1937–46, when "the Supreme Court changed its mind about thirty-two precedents" from the previous two decades (1911–30), not counting some cases not overruled but in effect ignored. The cases overturned—roughly one-fourth of which dealt with intergovernmental tax immunity—"could fairly be described as constitutional relics" doomed as soon as FDR was reelected.[31]

The 1990 Term brought new controversy over the reversal of precedent. Some was because of the number of reversals, although earlier terms had seen as many or more, and because they took place in key areas of criminal procedure law. The majority's language was what particularly prompted dispute. Part of the rationale for overturning the victim impact statement cases was that they "were decided by the narrowest of margins, over spirited dissents challenging the basic underpinnings of those decisions. They have been questioned by members of the Court in later decisions, and have defied consistent application by the lower courts." Moreover, said the majority, upholding precedent was more important in property and contract rights cases and less so when rules of procedure and evidence were at issue. Reacting to the "staggering" idea that some precedents were worth more than others, Justice Marshall said the majority had sent "a clear signal that scores of established constitutional liberties are now ripe for reconsideration."[32]

Even when considerable change is taking place, the Court has seen the need to move gradually and to make its rulings appear incremental and to stress continuity. Gradual movement might well characterize the Court's decisions even without precedent. As Shapiro has argued, "The theory of incrementalism may explain, or at least describe, the phenomena of stability and gradual change in law just as well as or better than stare decisis."[33] Most policymakers do not make radical departures from past policy but operate incrementally, developing policy a bit at a time and making changes "at the margin." In the Court, this would result from deciding narrow questions before large ones or making summary disposition of appeals instead of rulings with full opinions. As this suggests, the sequence in which cases come to the Court—and particularly the first case on which the Court decides to issue a full-opinion ruling, is quite important. Dealing with one aspect of a topic first may head the Court down a somewhat different road from the one it would have constructed had another aspect of the subject been decided first.

The school prayer decisions, where the Court first struck down a state-written prayer in *Engel v. Vitale* before eliminating all recitation of school prayer and Bible reading in *Abington School District v. Schempp*, provide an example of incremental action. So does reapportionment, where the Court first demanded equally populated districts for the U.S. House of Representatives (*Wesberry v. Sanders*) and invalidated the Georgia "county unit" system (*Gray v. Sanders*) before ruling, in *Reynolds v. Sims*, that both houses of all state legislatures had to be apportioned on the basis of population. Although policy may be developed incrementally, it may also be developed in "big pieces" and *applied* incrementally, as successive litigation brings the various parts and pieces of a problem to the Court. Thus the Court first provided a broad definition for obscenity in its 1957 *Roth* decision, gradually adding elements to the definition in later cases. After the Court said in *Brown v. Board of Education* that "separate but equal" was not to apply to education, the Court applied this rule to other public facilities (golf courses, swimming pools, and the like) through a series of *per curiam* opinions shortly afterward. These examples also show the incremental development of what *seems* to be a major policy change, as the important elements of the *Roth* obscenity definition were derived from earlier lower court rulings, and *Brown* built on *Sweatt v. Painter*, which invalidated segregation in graduate education because "intangible" factors were not equal.

Strategy

Expectations that the Court seek neutral principles and rely on precedent are traditional, conservative considerations in developing opinions. Quite different is the possibility that the Supreme Court engages in strategy. Changes in the Court's positions—from liberal to conservative, from activism to self-restraint (see below), from the center of the political arena to the periphery and back—are not accidental. Those changes result in part from external forces, such as the arrival of new justices chosen for their ideological proclivities and cases brought to the Court, and in part from internal factors, such as individual justices' attitudinal changes. Through their strategies, individual and collective, the justices contribute another important element to the decision-making process.

Those who believe that justices find law or who seek to have them apply neutral principles find unseemly any talk of judicial strategy. For them, issues are to be confronted directly, regardless of cost to the Court, and not for other concerns is justice for litigants to be sacrificed. Justice Rehnquist has observed that the Court's discretionary jurisdiction should not be used "as a sort of judicial storm cellar to which we may flee to escape from controversial or sensitive cases."[34] And there is no doubt that quite disturbing conflicts between strategy and "justice" exist. Examples are the Court's refusal in the 1950s to decide a challenge to a cemetery's refusal to bury a Native American or to rule on the validity of antimiscegenation (anti-mixed-marriage) laws—even when a black woman went to prison for marrying a white man—or, more recently, its avoidance of persistent challenges to the constitutionality of the Vietnam War, despite the increasing death rate during that conflict.[35] Nonetheless, almost by definition the Court must act strategically, because it is a *political* body acting in an often hostile, or at least nonsupportive, environment.

Courts, no less than other governmental institutions, cannot ignore their environments and must understand them. The justices need to be able to recognize changes in support by relevant publics if they wish their decisions to be accepted. If it is to survive and achieve some of its goals, the Court may have to avoid some controversies, particularly "self-inflicted wounds" like the *Dred Scott* decision legitimating slavery. A justice's 1954 comment, "One bombshell at a time is enough," made when the Court turned away a miscegenation case,[36] was a recognition of the need to concentrate on achieving school desegregation—affecting a large number of people—rather than damage that effort by angering the South with a decision on the mixed marriage laws, affecting relatively few individuals.

The justices themselves provide evidence that the Court takes actions based on strategy. For example, the decision in *Brown v. Board of Education* was delayed to get a vote that was unanimous or more nearly so.[37] When Justice Frankfurter was assigned to write the Court's opinion striking down the "white primary," the Chief Justice was told that, with the South likely to receive the ruling negatively, it would be wiser if the opinion were *not* written by a Jewish immigrant who had taught at Harvard Law School—and the case was reassigned to Justice Stanley Reed, a Kentuckian. Similarly Justice Byrnes, also a southerner, was assigned the opinion in *Taylor v. Georgia* (1940), holding that a Georgia statute violated federal prohibitions against peonage, in order to give the ruling more force.[38]

The justices' demonstrated awareness of their political environment makes it quite likely that, acting on the basis of strategic considerations, they take that environment into account even when they claim not to do so, for example, after FDR's attempt to pack the Court and after congressional efforts in the 1950s to limit its jurisdiction on internal security matters (loyalty oaths and congressional investigations of subversives). The Court thus has acted strategically in responding to threats. It has done this by changing its policy position, refusing to decide more cases on a controversial issue, or deciding cases with larger majorities (see page 244).

Justice Powell, upholding school financing through the property tax in *San Antonio School District v. Rodriguez* (1973), said, "Practical considerations, of course, play no role in the adjudication of the constitutional issues presented," but, showing strategic concerns, commented that to rule otherwise "would occasion . . . an unprecedented upheaval in public education." More recently, Justice Blackmun said he could understand his colleagues' abandonment of past positions concerning state assistance to parochial school education only in terms of "concern about the continuing and emotional controversy and to a persuasion that a good-faith attempt on the part of a state legislature is worth a nod of approval."[39]

Perhaps justices' taking into account the effect of their rulings has been most obvious in the field of criminal procedure. For example, one of several criteria the Court regularly used in deciding whether to apply its criminal procedure rules to past convictions was the effect such application would have upon the administration of justice, and Justice Clark asserted that to apply the exclusionary rule of *Mapp v. Ohio* to past cases "would tax the administration of justice to the utmost."[40] The retroactivity problem has been said to have been guided largely by strategic considerations such as placating those opposed to the Court's new rules.[41] (The Court was also unwilling to apply a ruling retroactively because of its perceived effects on the equalization of men's and women's pension benefits, where the financial burden from retroactivity was involved.[42]) In evaluating these particular instances, one should, however, keep in mind findings that, in the related matter of setting its agenda, that is, deciding what cases to review, the Court "does not respond to increases in the general level of public concern about crime" and does not use public opinion—"either general levels or increments"—as an input into that decision.[43] Nonetheless, if a well-developed societal consensus has formed, it is unwise for the Court to run against it except for very good reason.

To say that the Court acts strategically does not mean that the justices have a complete blueprint to guide their actions. It is more likely that individual justices act strategically than that there is a "strategy of the Court." Justices appear to share the goal of preserving the Court as an institution, which means the Court will try not to get too far afield from public opinion so as to decrease the risk of attack from other institutions, which would make the justices less able to carry out their expected tasks. One may also find that at least some justices share a general sense of direction. Nonetheless, the Court is perhaps best seen as a "mixed-motive" or "mixed-strategy" group.

Strategy encompasses efforts to affect the political world outside the Court or to fend off attacks from outside (*external* strategy), as well as the persuasion and bargaining among justices while a case is under advisement (*internal* strategy) which is necessary to achieve external effects. A justice wishing to accomplish any external goal must attract enough colleagues to get a case accepted for review, then to constitute a majority for affirmance or reversal, and, finally, the most difficult task, to constitute a majority supporting an opinion advancing that goal. The goal seeker must be careful not to take so strong a position that the potential majority is lost, said to have occurred with Justice Blackmun in *Bowers v. Hardwick* on homosexual sodomy. We also know of a justice intentionally taking a strong position in an opinion circulated within the court *in order to* force his colleagues' hands so they would join *another* justice's more limited opinion.[44]

If unanimity is sought, extended discussions and caution to keep potential defectors from deserting may be necessary. This was apparently true after the 1954 school desegregation ruling, when the justices were highly uncertain about the proper way to enforce it or even about its precise meaning. In this situation, unanimity as a conscious strategy "masked the uncertainty" and also "provided a more solid defense to critics." However, because it deprived the Court of the opportunity to be persuasive, unanimity "operated in time to obscure rather than enhance the Court's decisions."[45] This illustrates the difficulties that can result from operating strategically.

A range of tools, usually used in combination, is available to judges wishing to engage in strategy. They are applied not only to a justice's immediate colleagues on the Court but also to the lower court judges so important in implementing the Supreme Court's opinions. At times a justice can assist in the process of selecting new colleagues. Most frequently used, however, are devices necessary to the everyday resolution of cases. Perhaps force of intellect, demonstrated to lower court judges through carefully reasoned and written opinions and to colleagues through draft opinions and arguments in conference, is the one closest to "the law" and furthest from "politics."

Personal intellect is, however, often not a sufficient strategic mechanism. Judges must thus resort to other stratagems including endearing themselves to colleagues, which is important in obtaining votes in cases of lesser importance to those colleagues, and threatening to vote against the majority; however, stating dissenting views strongly in public may damage the Court (see pages 238–39). Negotiation and compromise, at the core of internal strategy, are most upsetting to those who accept the myth of the Court as apolitical. One needs to ask, however, whether one could expect anything other *than* bargaining and compromise as part of the activities of the nation's highest court charged with interpretation of the Constitution, once that court is recognized to be a political actor acting in a political environment.

Whatever may happen in the decision of cases accepted for review, in accepting cases for review the Court tends to be almost like nine separate law firms that go about their own business with relatively little interaction or wheeling and dealing.[46] Yet strategy-related behaviors are brought to bear as the Court chooses issues for decision and the opinions to be written. One way in which the Court has demonstrated strategic concerns, although it now engages in this action less, is its grouping of cases on a single subject, for example, five school segregation cases (*Brown* and four others), six cases on reapportionment, and four cases on confessions obtained without warning defendants of their rights (the *Miranda* decision). Although the individual cases still have to be resolved, this is a way of focusing on broad issues and avoiding being "trapped" by the specific facts of a particular case.

Once it has been decided that the Court will issue a full, signed opinion, important elements in decision making, diminishing the effect of attitude and ideology, come into play. One is pragmatism, which involves "strategic judgments about what professional and lay traffics would bear." This is seen when a justice withholds a dissent even when opposed to the result or writes a concurring opinion rather than a dissent so that the Court's decision can have greater force through a larger majority. Evangelism, the attempt to persuade publics outside the Court of the correctness of the Court's doctrine, certainly influences what justices say. Thus "the demands of persuading colleagues and countrymen in trailblazing cases coalesce with professional habits and personal antagonisms to transform opinion-writing into argument and over-statement."[47]

There are a number of options for the Court and the opinion writer. It is wise for the Court to sound as much as possible like a "law court." Thus opinions should draw heavily on precedent and history where possible and avoid social science evidence, which tends to provoke criticism.[48] Taking aspects of a problem one case at a time, related to the growth of precedent, also allows the Court more flexibility. Instead of outlawing *all* legislative vetos at one blow (see pages 310–11), restricting itself to the particular type of legislative veto in the *Chadha* case, a one-house veto, would have allowed consideration of variants as they appeared, thus permitting "fine-tuning" in the Court's doctrine. Yet if the justices were clear about how they would rule in later cases, they might as well have decided the larger issue, as a matter of docket management.

Opinions vary in their clarity, in their breadth and narrowness, and in the directness with which issues are approached. Ambiguity may be used strategically, to help keep control of policy-making in the Court's hands because unclear decisions force others to come back to the Court to obtain the justices' clarification. Thus ambiguous decisions, while producing "repeater" cases that may cause docket management problems, allow the Court to "monitor" the action of lower courts.

The Court may wish to avoid an opinion so broad it looks "legislative" as well as one so narrow it does not illuminate the law for other lawyers and judges and thus leads to the filing of more cases. However, narrow rulings may be useful as a delaying tactic or as a device to clear away the underbrush before an unmistakable direct attack is mounted on a particular practice. A narrow opinion may also be necessary because a broad opinion may lose judges from the majority; the ultimate opinion is often the lowest common denominator among members of the majority. Thus the Court can achieve its goals without broad opinions, particularly if negative reaction to a straightforward doctrinal ruling is foreseen. Limited grounds—basing a case on its facts or relying on statutory interpretation—can be used instead of dealing with larger, "tougher" constitutional questions. A narrowly focused ruling may be advantageous for the Court by leading the public to focus on the issue decided rather than on larger, more controversial matters. If much of the Court's strategy seems based on avoiding issues or minimizing the degree to which they are confronted, one must remember that this is done so that on the issues the Court considers most important it can act forthrightly. There are times when reaching the principal issues directly is not only what the judges want to do but is also important strategically—to satisfy the demands and expectations of the Court's constituencies.

One can see differences among the justices about the preferred breadth of opinion in the 1989 *Webster* abortion case. Chief Justice Rehnquist's plurality, while upholding a number of challenged provisions, claimed that *Roe v. Wade* had been left undisturbed. Justice Scalia, however, felt the plurality was prolonging bringing an end to *Roe* and he would have explicitly overruled it. Justice Blackmun, on the other hand, felt the disclaimers about leaving *Roe* untouched were "meaningless" and that the plurality not only "obscure[d] the portent of its analysis" but invited charges "of cowardice and illegitimacy" by the way it had considered precedents.[49]

There are also numerous constraints on a judge's ability to accomplish strategic aims. The strongly held myth that the Court finds and does not make law and the special legal framework within which the justices operate serve to limit the degree to which judicial policy-making can be explicit and to which strategy can be openly considered. Beyond those constraints, even if all justices were simultaneously concerned about strategy, each might focus on different aspects of a case or wish to pursue different strategies. Moreover, although a "policy-oriented judge" is "aware of the impact which judicial decisions can have on public policy, realizes the leeway for discretion which his office permits, and is willing to take advantage of this power and leeway to further particular policy aims," not all justices may fit this description: "Probably relatively few justices have had a systematic jurisprudence; more but probably still relatively few have been so intensely committed to particular policy goals as to establish rigid priorities of action that dominated their entire lives; probably few have been able to act only rationally in seeking to achieve their aims." In addition, each judge "has only a finite supply of time, energy, research assistance, and personal influence."[50]

Strategic considerations often compete, and there are standard operating procedures (SOPs) and "bureaucratic routines" that courts, like any other organization, follow. The justices respond to self-imposed deadlines like the one that all cases argued within a term are to be decided by the end of that term, as well as to rules for handling caseload, including technical ones on timely filing and judicial doctrines on the standing of a party to raise an issue. These rules can be ignored when it is felt necessary, but that cannot be done often if the Court is to function effectively. Other constraints on the Court's exercise of strategy include the justices' own positions, interpersonal relations within the Court, the Court's prestige at the time, and external pressures—from interest groups, Congress, and the president.

Requiring particular attention in the Court's exercise of external strategy, and thus constituting serious potential constraints, are lower court judges. A major strategic question is whether, and to what degree, the Court should defer to those judges, particularly state judges. Such deference, like that shown the legislative and executive branches, is necessary because the Supreme Court depends on the lower court judges to carry out its mandates. If the justices interfere frequently with their work, they will be less likely to cooperate. The deference may allow the lower courts to move ahead of the Supreme Court in applying a new doctrine, creating a base on which the Court itself can later build. However, it may also produce delay or noncompliance, with the case being brought back to the Court for further action and thus interfering with docket management. Particularly when the Court has remanded a case with only limited instructions, evasion may also result. The lower court may find an alternative basis for reaching the result it had reached earlier, evading further action by the Supreme Court.[51]

Judicial Review

When to engage in judicial review is another matter with which the Court must concern itself because judges who engage frequently in judicial review will find themselves criticized for being part of an "imperial judiciary" (see pages 3–7) and for being nondemocratic officials encroaching on democratic institutions. The latter concern leads us to look at some fundamental arguments about the propriety of judicial review in a democratic system (see below). These arguments, raised again during the Bork nomination hearings, change somewhat in form over time but are seldom far from the surface. In recent years, they have turned on the extent to which, in interpreting the Constitution, the justices should follow the "original intent" of the framers of the Constitution and its amendments. Among arguments that judicial review is undemocratic,[52] we find judicial review disparaged because life-tenured justices, who often remain on the Court long after they are out of tune with the nation's views, can overrule acts of periodically elected representatives and acts of the executive branch, whose head, the president, is also elected. One response is that when the Court strikes down statutes as "void for vagueness," Congress, because it is being told only that it must act more clearly, not that it cannot act, can rewrite the statutes with clearer prescriptions. Even when the Court invalidates statutes as unconstitutional, such rulings can be overturned. Although some Court actions can be reversed only by constitutional amendment, at times only a statute is necessary to do so. Thus when state action is invalidated for intruding on the federal government's domain in violation of the Commerce Clause, Congress can restore state authority through legislation granting the states authority over the contested subject-matter.[53] Enacting constitutional amendments to overturn the Court is difficult but not impossible, as we see from the Eleventh (no suits against states by citizens of another state), Sixteenth (income tax), and Twenty-sixth (18-year-old vote) amendments and the post–Civil War amendments eliminating slavery, redefining citizenship, and protecting civil rights.[54]

Another response to the claim that judicial review is undemocratic is Alexander Hamilton's *Federalist* #78. For Hamilton, through judicial review the Constitution—the people's will—is enforced over the will of the people's representatives. However, the people whose will is being enforced are long dead, with the ideas of constitution makers of the distant past pitted against views of much more recent legislators. Frequent exercise of judicial review will also, we are told, dampen citizens' demands on legislators and political executives for policy change and legislators' willingness to deal with social problems. In Chief Justice Burger's words, "When this Court rushes in to remedy what it perceives to be the failings of the political process, it deprives those processes of an opportunity to function. When the political institutions are not forced to exercise constitutionally allocated powers and responsibilities, those powers, like muscles not used, tend to atrophy."[55] To the contrary, the Court's action can also help establish an agenda of issues to be given active consideration by the other branches and can stimulate activity to deal with otherwise ignored problems. For example, the Court's reapportionment rulings opened up, rather than restricted, the political process, and state legislatures learned to deal with redistricting.

At the center of the debate about judicial review and democracy is the argument that courts must protect minority rights, as much a part of democracy as majority rule, and can enforce democracy's key demands of free speech and press, assembly, and petition. In a particularly significant statement, in Footnote 4 in the *Carolene Products* case, Justice Harlan Fiske Stone suggested that the usual presumption of validity for challenged statutes might be given less weight when the statutes affected the subject matter of the Bill of Rights. Moreover, heightened judicial scrutiny might be given legislation that "restricts those political processes which can ordinarily be expected to bring about repeal of undesirable legislation" and laws directed at "discrete and insular" racial, ethnic, and religious minorities who were the object of prejudice, because that prejudice would limit use of the political process. Examples are a city charter amendment requiring approval of open housing ordinances (but not other laws) by referendum and passage of a state referendum that limited busing for desegregation (but not for other purposes). Both were held invalid because they restructured the political process to the disadvantage of minorities.[56]

Justice Stone's cautious statement recently became the focus of John Hart Ely's further-reaching "representation-reinforcing theory of judicial review."[57] Ely said that the Constitution saw to it that "everyone's interests will be actually or virtually represented . . . at the point of substantive decision" and "has sought to assure that [an effective] majority not systematically treat others less well than it treats itself." Thus he argued that judges should focus on restrictions on "the opportunity to participate either in the political processes by which values are appropriately identified and accommodated, or in the accommodation those processes have reached"; "unblocking stoppages in the democratic process is what judicial review ought preeminently to be about."[58]

This basic position that the Court must use judicial review, even if incompatible with majority rule, to protect individual rights, is also at the heart of Jesse Choper's argument that the Supreme Court should limit and better focus its exercise of judicial review. Because democratic majorities do not treat personal rights well, "the task of custodianship has been and should be assigned to a governing body that is insulated from political responsibility and unbeholden to self-absorbed and excited majoritarianism."[59] Choper would have the court "pass final constitutional judgment on questions concerning the permissible reach and circumspection of 'the judicial power'" and review state acts violating the Supremacy Clause. However, he would have the Court avoid ruling on states' allegations that Congress has interfered with their authority and on conflicts between president and Congress. Judicial action on the latter lessens the incentives for the two branches to work out matters on their own. If judges abstain from exercising judicial review in these situations, they can be more effective when they exercise it to protect political rights, in rulings likely to provoke and offend other political actors.

Arguments that judicial review is undemocratic may, despite these arguments, be misdirected. For one thing, other governmental institutions may be no more responsive to the public than is the Court, with no one (except perhaps the president) accountable to a majority of the nation's voters. Moreover, our government's institutions operate by means of a system of checks and balances in which each participates in the work of the others and thus limits them. The Court's involvement in these political processes, engaging in strategic actions as a policymaker, thus makes it to some extent a democratic institution; only if it were fully insulated from those processes and if it found the law in total independence of other government bodies would it be undemocratic.

The contemporary argument over how the Constitution should be interpreted is related to the argument over judicial review and democracy in that those urging justices to give close attention to the "original intent" of the Constitution's framers criticize others for injecting their own views into the Constitution and thus acting undemocratically. The argument over reliance on "original intent" has produced much rhetoric without much understanding. Indeed, an examination of Supreme Court decisions indicates that only a very small proportion of explanations are the differing interpretive theories to which the justices subscribe or with which they are associated; important as theories in their own right, they have less effect on actual decision-making than the "hoorah" about them would suggest.[60]

The primary antagonists in the mid-1980s battle were, on the one side, Attorney General Edwin Meese, and, on the other, Justices Brennan and Stevens. Meese's view is that judges should restrict themselves to the Constitution's "original intention," not to its "spirit," because use of the latter would turn the Constitution into a "chameleon." He conceded that the "Constitution is not a legislative code bound to the time in which it was written," but "neither . . . is it a mirror that simply reflects the thoughts and ideas of those who stand before it."[61] Justice Souter, at the hearings on his nomination, said he did not believe in "original intent" because that limited a judge to certain specific applications the Framers intended to be covered. Instead he believed in "original meaning," encompassing the principle embodied in the language adopted. Under the latter, the Equal Protection Clause of the Fourteenth Amendment would allow school desegregation, whereas original intent of the amendment's framers would not.

For Justice Brennan, the Constitution "places certain values beyond the power of any legislature," taking them away from the majority. Ambiguity in the Constitution "calls forth interpretation, the interaction of reader and text." History must be examined, but later interpretation given to provisions must also be considered; so must the "ultimate question": "what do the words of the text mean in our time?" Arguing that from the late twentieth century one could not "gauge accurately the intent of the Framers on application of principle to specific contemporary questions," he stated, "We current Justices read the Constitution in the only way that we can: as Twentieth Century Americans."[62]

The problem with trying to decipher these opposing positions is that the issue is not really about the use or nonuse of "original intent" but about specific value positions. As Grossman observes, "the theory of original understanding . . . turns out to be less a neutral and objective guide to interpretation than a fetish with scarcely concealed ideological premises."[63] Justice Brennan makes the value basis clear: "A position that upholds constitutional claims only if they were within the specific contemplation of the Framers in effect establishes a presumption of resolving textual ambiguities against the claim of constitutional right." Indeed, the position has been called selective original understanding by some, because its adherents accept some parts of the Framers' view but not others and accept some later developments but not others. Meese's value position is evident in his view that the idea the Fourteenth Amendment "incorporated" the provisions of the Bill of Rights as prohibitions against the states was on shaky legal ground. He did later claim, however, that he was not calling for overturning cases incorporating portions of the Bill of Rights, cases through which state criminal defendants have received much protection.

Federalism

The Court has among its roles that of arbiter of the federal system—of conflicts between states and between the national government and the states. Much of the Supreme Court's history can be viewed as a history of its treatment of federalism-related concerns.[64] Of particular significance have been the Warren Court's rulings "incorporating" the provisions of the Bill of Rights in the Due Process Clause of the Fourteenth Amendment as prohibitions against the states, thus nationalizing the Bill of Rights, with the justices interpreting Fourteenth Amendment "due process" (which the states must follow) to be identical with incorporated Bill of Rights provisions.

Questions of federalism have *largely* been settled and thus are less frequently the source of conflict within the Court than they once were. However, they are not *completely* settled. This can be seen most obviously in the line of cases concerning Congress's power to force state and local governments to pay their employees the minimum wage; this started with *National League of Cities v. Usery* (1976), limiting the power, and ended with the 1985 *Garcia* ruling removing the constraints on Congress—and indeed, relegating the states to their representatives in Congress for their protection from such congressional commands. Yet in 1991, in a case involving application of the age discrimination statute to state judges, the Court's majority clearly gave the states more leeway to have some public officials not covered by federal discrimination statutes; this unsettled how much weight the Court would give to state interests.[65] The Supreme Court's other rulings on Congress's power to regulate commerce—and on the states' authority to regulate commerce when Congress has not done so (the "dormant Commerce Clause" cases)—have been particularly important.

Other cases directly posing federalism questions—and particularly significant—are those, occurring throughout the Court's history and quite frequent in recent years, involving the question whether the national government has "preempted" state action on a particular subject. Especially controversial was the Warren Court decision in *Pennsylvania v. Nelson* (1956), setting aside a state conviction for attempting to overthrow the United States government, because the national government had indicated its intention to preempt the field through enactment of the Smith and McCarran Acts. Intense negative reaction led the Court to rule in *Uphaus v. Wyman* (1959) that the states could regulate subversion directed at the states themselves. More recent preemption rulings contributed to the Reagan administration's attack on the Court for undermining state power, an attack also based on the Court's interstate commerce rulings.

The justices vary in the extent to which they defer to the "sovereign" states, but issues of federalism are often present in cases. For example, does Congress have the power to lower the voting age to 18 in both national and state elections? (In *Oregon v. Mitchell*, the Court said Yes for national but No for state and local elections, provoking passage of the Twenty-sixth Amendment.) Or should states, because of their "police power" over matters of health, welfare, and morals, be given more flexibility than the federal government? (The Court, in the *Roth* and *Alberts* cases, treated both levels of government the same, but Justice Harlan pressed for different treatment depending on whether the national or state government was acting.) Even when the focus is on a substantive issue (abortion, obscenity, the death penalty) rather than on federalism itself, federalism questions often come into play beneath the surface. This is particularly likely when an important aspect of the case is whether states may take certain action the national government is not permitted to take.

When state *courts'* actions are under review, questions of federalism and of deference to other judges may reinforce each other. Thus justices have resisted having federal courts engage in close supervision of state courts, whether the issue is alleged racial discrimination in those courts' actions (see *O'Shea v. Little-ton*, 1973) or federal court review of state court criminal cases through federal habeas corpus (see pages 186–87). However, when state courts have ruled in favor of criminal defendants, the Court has not accompanied its rhetoric of re-spect for state court rulings with a "hands-off" approach.

Another issue concerning Supreme Court deference to state courts is whether the state court has explicitly indicated reliance on state law. The Su-preme Court has now required this if the justices are to accept the state ruling as having an "adequate and independent" state ground precluding Supreme Court review (see page 180). However, federal courts considering state prisoners' habeas corpus petitions are *not* to presume that state court rulings are based on federal grounds. In so ruling Justice O'Connor stated, "This is a case about federalism. It concerns the respect that federal courts owe the States and the States' proce-dural rules. . . ."[66]

The Court's rules about reviewing state court rulings have been part of state judges' growing attention to their own state constitutions. Some leading state judges argue that a state court should decide state claims first, because if a right is upheld under the state constitution, discussion of the federal claim is unnec-essary; only if the right is denied does the Supremacy Clause of the U.S. Consti-tution demand consideration of the federal right. By contrast, if the federal claim is discussed first and the claimed right is upheld, any discussion of state law would be *obiter dictum*. Despite this position, state courts vary in the extent to which they rely on the U.S. Constitution and on federal judicial precedent.

The presence of these issues does not mean that conceptions of federalism have been the primary influence in the Court's rulings generally. Examination of the 1969–77 Terms shows that despite occasional statements about leaving mat-ters to the states, the Burger Court was *not* "an overwhelming example of judicial restraint." The justices deferred less to the states on questions of economic regu-lation than they did to federal government regulatory actions, with some deci-sions definitely affected by whether the state policy being reviewed was probusi-ness or antibusiness. Three of the four justices who supported probusiness decisions most strongly (three were President Nixon's appointees) became re-markably unsupportive of antibusiness state policy. Only Justice Rehnquist "defer[red] to the states enough to qualify . . . as an advocate of judicial re-straint," but his "conservative economic bias" showed nonetheless. The pattern of greater support for the federal government than for state governments also appeared in civil rights and civil liberties cases extending through early 1979. Support for state policy was roughly equal to support for the federal government only in search and seizure cases.[67]

Activism and Restraint

Closely related to judicial review and the deference the Supreme Court should give to lower courts is the extent to which the Court, in dealing with other actors in the political system, should be "self-restrained" or "activist." (See pages

4–7.) Because of the absence of clear definitions, controversy over whether the Court has been sufficiently "self-restrained" or too "activist" has been almost continuous. Each concept has several dimensions, but there is some general agreement on the terms' basic dimensions. There are "two major premises that serve as underpinning [for] . . . a limited role for the courts": that judicial policymaking "conflicts with the very essence of a democratic society" and "that courts simply are not equipped to make wise policy."[68]

A federal appellate judge has observed, "Appropriate judicial humility weighs against judicial activism" because on policy questions "the judge can never be justifiably certain that he or she is right even when the judge happens to be right."[69] And Judge Richard Posner has stated:

> (1) A self-restrained judge does not allow his own views of policy to influence his decision. (2) He is cautious and circumspect, and thus hesitant about intruding those views. (3) He is mindful of the practical political constraints on the exercise of judicial power. (4) His decisions are influenced by a concern lest promiscuous judicial creation of rights result in so swamping the courts in litigation that they cannot function effectively. (5) He believes that the power of his court system relative to other branches of government should be reduced.[70]

This fits with Justice Stone's admonition that "the only check upon our own exercise of power is our own sense of self-restraint."[71] As Chief Justice Burger commented, "It is not the function of the judiciary to provide 'effective leadership' simply because the political branches of the government fail to do so."[72] And Justice O'Connor has said that when congressional legislation is not as polished, or complete, as some justices might wish it to be, "it is not the function of this Court . . . to apply the finishing touches. . . . Our job does not extend beyond attempting to fathom what it is that Congress produced, blemished as the Court may perceive that creation to be."[73] Such statements are not made only by conservative judges. Justice Marshall has argued, "The fact that Congress might have acted with greater clarity or foresight does not give the courts a *carte blanche* to redraft statutes. . . . Nor is the judiciary licensed to attempt to soften the clear import of Congress's chosen words whenever a court believes those words lead to a harsh result,"[74] certainly a restraintist comment.

The Court's basic operational rules of self-restraint were spelled out most explicitly by Justice Louis Brandeis in his opinion in the *Ashwander* case. They are not rules in the sense of being formally promulgated, but, although only stated in a concurring opinion, have been given considerable weight. The Court will not rule on challenged legislation in a nonadversary proceeding nor will it decide a complaint made by someone not injured by the statutes or by someone who has benefited from the action being challenged. A constitutional issue will not be decided if other bases for decision, such as statutory construction, are available; in short, the Court will not anticipate a constitutional question unnecessarily nor will it formulate a rule broader than required by the facts of the case.[75] Thus the Court exercises self-restraint by approaching cases cautiously and by exhibiting hesitancy in reaching the merits, for example, by denying review to some cases and, perhaps more important, by developing rules as to who may bring cases and under what conditions they may be brought (see Chapter 5). Considerable disagreement has, however, occurred over whether the Court has followed such "rules" of self-restraint. Some justices argue there are situations when some departure from the *Ashwander* rules is sensible. One is not deciding the statutory question before the constitutional one where one would have to "torture" the statute to save it.

Justices' votes raise questions about whether they *practice* self-restraint to the extent they *advocate* it, whether it actually motivates those who make claims in its behalf, or whether ideology is the actual determinant of their actions. On one side, we see the breadth of the Court's criminal procedure doctrine has been related to the particular justices' goals. On the other, in the 1969–77 Terms of the Court, out of a possible 40 situations—10 justices deciding cases in four categories (regulatory commissions, federalism, access, and civil rights and civil liberties)—in only 10 did activism or restraint influence justices' voting, and only Justice Douglas "manifested activism or restraint in more than a single category."[76]

Of particular interest is Justice Felix Frankfurter, in recent times the Court's foremost advocate of judicial self-restraint. He argued that the Court should stay out of the reapportionment issue because it involved "political entanglements" and the "clash of political forces in political settlements" (*Baker v. Carr*, 1962). Civil liberties and labor cases in which Frankfurter participated often included questions closely related to self-restraint like jurisdiction and deference to other units of government. With such Denial of Judicial Responsibility (DJR) matters present, his vote was always against the civil liberties claim in civil liberties cases and against the liberal position in 16 of 18 labor cases. However, without the DJR element, Frankfurter's position in civil liberties cases relative to other justices remained to the right of center, indicating he was obviously a conservative rather than an apostle of self-restraint. This poses the question whether self-restraint controlled ideology even when the DJR issue was present.[77]

There has been a change over time in the meaning and effect of self-restraint and activism. The pre–New Deal (Taft) Court had "used judicial power actively to police the legislative and executive branches of federal and local government, in order to enforce the Justices' commitment to laissez-faire economic policies," while assuming "an almost entirely passive posture in civil liberties cases, in striking contrast to its constitutional activism in economic cases."[78] In that situation, "activism" produced a "conservative" result: assistance to the business community. "Self-restraint" meant not disturbing legislation regulating the economy, producing "liberal" results. It also meant that after Franklin Roosevelt won his battle with the Court, it began to uphold New Deal legislation. On the other hand, in the area of civil liberties, a "hands off" approach preserved statutes and other actions infringing individual freedoms, while "activism" generally protected civil liberties, at least through the end of the Warren Court.

Richard Nixon criticized judges for having "gone too far in assuming unto themselves a mandate which is not there, and that is, to put their social and economic ideas into their decisions," and pledged to appoint "strict constructionist" judges who would not encroach on areas belonging to Congress and the president.[79] However, his remarks about Supreme Court decisions setting free "patently guilty individuals on the basis of legal technicalities" meant he did not want self-restrained judges when activism could aid the "peace forces" rather than the "criminal forces." Nixon's Republican successors Presidents Reagan and Bush certainly have also claimed they sought "restrained" judges who would not "legislate" but would only uphold the law.

When pro–law enforcement policy goals would be aided by so doing, Nixon's appointees adopted a "self-restrained" posture by deferring to legislative and executive actions. For example, the Court stated that "a prosecutor should remain free before trial to exercise the broad discretion entrusted to him to determine the extent of the social interest in prosecution," even when he had reindicted the defendant on higher charges after the defendant had refused to plead guilty (*Goodwin*, 1982). The Burger Court was also deferential and "self-restrained" toward those in charge of institutions, with the Court moving back toward the "hands-off" doctrine on prison policy. As Rehnquist asserted, "prison administrators . . . should be accorded wide-ranging deference in the adoption and execution of policies and practices that in their judgment are needed to preserve internal order and discipline and to maintain institutional security."[80]

Because the Burger Court enforced the underlying premises of many Warren Court precedents, the Warren Court's activism was "solidified" rather than undercut. Those unhappy with that legacy recognized that judicial restraint, in the sense of adherence to precedent, would not assist in achieving their political agenda. Instead some "negative activism" was necessary. And the Court's majority was not hesitant to be unabashedly (although not explicitly) activist in reaching out to overturn state court rulings that favored defendants' rights (see page 19). It was not only in the area of criminal procedure that the Burger Court was not self-restrained. Measured in terms of statutes invalidated, it was no more deferential than its predecessor to Congress or to state regulatory efforts affecting commerce, and its rulings "significantly constrained" what the states could do.[81] And the justices were not hesitant to rule in separation of powers cases against the actions of other branches of government.

Politicians have managed to join "activism" and "liberalism" at the hip, but conservative activism has certainly been demonstrated by both the Burger and Rehnquist Courts. When the conservative justices achieved a clear majority, that majority then severely limited or overturned criminal procedure precedent; supported prosecutors but showed little deference to state judges whose rulings favored defendants; and limited the prior interpretations of civil rights laws that assisted those claiming discrimination on the basis of race or sex. Some of the members of the conservative majority called for reversal of still other precedents, most notably on abortion (see page 273). While they were doing this, Justice Scalia introduced a new basis for sustaining government action claimed to violate individual rights. Absence of the tradition of a particular right was also a reason for not enforcing it; if government practice had a long tradition, that tradition should be given weight against claims that the practice violated rights. For example, the long use of political patronage was, for Scalia, a reason not to prohibit elected office holders from discharging public employees because of their political party affiliation.[82]

The argument for self-restraint has been made forcefully in recent years. Yet the argument for "affirmative activism" is also a strong one, particularly when such activism takes the form of "an effort by the Court to redress minimally the political imbalance between bureaucrats and those who are subject to bureaucratic power but are typically impotent to reform or influence it."[83] Such a position is closely related to Justice Stone's *Carolene Products* footnote and to use of the courts by those who need governmental assistance to prevent being deprived of their rights. Just as government has grown, so has the possibility of challenges to government action and thus judicial activism to restrain that action.

Adoption of a strongly activist position with respect to individual freedoms is not necessarily realistic for the Court as a political actor. Despite approval by some segments of the public, the Warren Court's decisions were frequently attacked and often disobeyed. Indeed the Court almost lost some of its jurisdiction and perhaps would have suffered severe damage had it not avoided some issues and retreated on other occasions. The absence of attacks on the Burger and Rehnquist Courts, a result of the greater congruence of their decisions with the nation's civil liberties orientation, suggests approval of the Court's recent actions, whether self-restrained or activist, and the advantages flowing from its being able to persuade most people that it is indeed acting from a self-restrained position.

Off-the-Court Activity

The Court's opinions—and the justices' separate concurring and dissenting statements—provide the principal mechanism by which the justices participate in policy-making, and the principal way in which they carry out their strategies. They are, however, not the only ones. There is also judicial participation in matters outside the Court. Here we can see off-the-bench "activism" related to justices' on-the-bench activism.

A justice who has been politically active is not likely to slacken interest in political issues once on the Supreme Court nor to sever all contacts with the political world. For example, completely ceasing contacts with the president is unlikely. Thus justices have informally continued as presidential advisers. Chief Justice Vinson did this with President Truman and Justice Abe Fortas did it with President Lyndon Johnson on such topics as Vietnam, steel price increases, and strikes. It is not clear whether, as alleged, Vinson advised Truman that the latter had the authority to order an emergency seizure of the steel mills, an action the Court later determined to be invalid (see pages 333–34).

Even when prior personal contact has been limited, as in Richard Nixon's acquaintance with Warren Burger during Burger's Justice Department service, contact may later expand, particularly in the case of the Chief Justice. Thus Burger apparently met on occasion with the president or with Attorney General Mitchell, but whether these discussions went beyond matters of judicial selection and judicial administration to comments about the school busing cases is unresolved. Whatever its scope, the role of presidential adviser is likely to be submerged and kept screened from the public to avoid the considerable criticism generated by public knowledge of such relations. Although at the time of his nomination to be Chief Justice, Justice Fortas misstated his involvement with President Johnson, he did not conceal all his contacts. For example, he appeared at the president's signing of a bill and was present at meetings with many of the president's other advisers.[84]

By comparison with activities in the Court's early years, justices' present political activities, such as contacts with the president, are very limited. Over the course of the Court's history, roughly two-thirds of the justices have engaged in some such activity, "either informally or in response to official government requests," and the justices were viewed "as valuable resources to be employed in a wide variety of public services bearing little or no relationship to their judicial function."[85] There has, however, been considerable variation in the general level of that activity, with some, like Chief Justice Melville Fuller (1888–1909), taking the equivalent of the veil, even avoiding Washington social contact. There has also been variation in the norms about the extent of such activity and in justices' sensitivity to those changing norms. Changes in the norms are in part a function of public reaction to the extent of previous extrajudicial activity. The norm generally moves toward lessened out-of-Court involvement after criticism, relaxing somewhat after criticism abates, and then, in something of a ratchet effect, tightens further in the next similar cycle. However, in times of war and crisis the norm of noninvolvement tends to recede to allow the justices to "undertake any necessary informal extrajudicial tasks that might be useful to the nation."[86]

The Court's present traditions were not immediately established. Many of the first justices had sat in the Continental Congress, the Confederation Congress, or even in the new U.S. Congress; the others had been in state ratifying conventions. The early justices, having developed a distinction between what they could do as an institution (the Court) and what they could do as individuals, were willing to serve as commissioners to handle pensions, as individual citizens but not as justices. Moreover, "Individually, judges continued to give advice to both president and Congress, despite the possibility that the subjects involved could later come before the courts."[87] Justices were often also active participants in partisan activity, and spoke openly on partisan subjects, particularly when they were "on circuit." As the only federal officers with regular, continuing contact with all parts of the country, they had to instruct citizens on the structure and operation of the government and on the meaning of new laws. They played this role of being "republican schoolmasters" in giving charges to grand juries, when they tended "to issue political broadsides and thus enter into the heated debates raging between Federalists and Jeffersonian Republicans."[88] Indeed, it was activities of this type that led to the impeachment and trial (but not conviction) of Justice Samuel Chase. Also participating was Chief Justice John Marshall, who, using a *nom de plume*, wrote essays defending his decision in *McCulloch v. Maryland*.

From 1810 to the Civil War, judges' extra-Court speeches and public letters were less partisan. Perhaps to help repair the damage from the *Dred Scott* case, they became even more quiet after the Civil War. However, at the end of the nineteenth century, when the Court's prestige again improved, there was an "explosion" of speeches and writing. After the Depression, the level of oratory again fell and has generally remained low. Exceptions remain, with perhaps the most extensive being Justice Douglas's book writing and statements on conservation and the environment.

Not until after the Civil War did the justices themselves begin to look askance at justices' close ties to political parties or interest groups. Indeed, up to that time, justices had failed even to adhere to a norm of not talking about the Court's cases outside the Court. Until late in the nineteenth century, justices had regularly courted high political office from their positions on the Court. There have been few such instances in the twentieth century, the best known being Charles Evans Hughes's departure from the Court to run unsuccessfully for president. That his nomination came while he still sat on the Court was thought to injure its nonpartisan image, although it did not prevent his later being nominated and confirmed as Chief Justice. There was off-and-on again discussion of the candidacy of Justice William O. Douglas, who also offered to resign from the Court to campaign for President Truman if Truman had decided to run in 1952. An indication of changed norms is that the very discussion provoked criticism.

After the justices cut most political party ties, it took longer before they could be weaned from contacts with interest groups. Most twentieth-century out-of-Court activity not concerning judicial administration has focused on issues rather than partisan elections. Examples are provided by the extrajudicial activities of Justices Louis Brandeis, Felix Frankfurter, and Abe Fortas. Once Brandeis became a justice, he maintained his interest in the issues, both political (such as the concentration of big business) and more specifically religious (Zionism), that he had advanced earlier, and he continued to talk about them with those involved in politics and government. We cannot be sure whether he wished to feed an insatiable appetite for knowledge of "current events" or he continued to influence legislative policy indirectly.

We do know that between 1916 and 1938, Brandeis, an extremely wealthy man, provided to then Harvard law professor Felix Frankfurter regular payments totaling roughly $50,000 (worth many times that amount in current dollars) to assist Frankfurter's engaging in political activity, which would otherwise have been difficult because of medical expenses for his chronically ill wife. Many communications passed back and forth between Brandeis and Frankfurter; Brandeis's political positions apparently appeared in print as editorials in *The New Republic*, for which Frankfurter regularly wrote; Frankfurter served as Brandeis's representative at Zionist conferences; and Frankfurter apparently worked on legislation of interest to Brandeis, including legislation on subjects that had been before the Court or would come before it. Moreover, a number of Frankfurter's proteges (the "Happy Hot Dogs") went to work for the Roosevelt administration and could espouse there Brandeis's positions as transmitted to them from Frankfurter.

We may have here no more than a commonality of interests between the two men or Brandeis's intellectual and personal influence on the professor to work on matters of joint concern, not Frankfurter's taking direction from Brandeis. Whether the payments made him a "paid political lobbyist and lieutenant"[89] is conjectural. Frankfurter also worked on matters of primary interest to himself, including some—most notably FDR's Court-packing plan—on which he and Brandeis disagreed. Even if Brandeis's actions would not be ethically acceptable for a Supreme Court justice in the 1990s, did he exceed the bounds of propriety then? His strong (if behind-the-scenes) efforts to correct the injustice of the Sacco-Vanzetti conviction put him in the position of having to disqualify himself when that case came to him and then to the Court. Whether Brandeis took specific positions on New Deal policies that would have hindered his performance as a justice is unclear. He did deal with major political figures through intermediaries, perhaps as a matter of personal style, but perhaps a smokescreen to conceal his activity. When cases involving statutes on which he had given advice came before the Court, he did not recuse but instead took "only a very minimal role in the ultimate judicial decision"[90]—perhaps resulting from his view of the cases rather than an effort to conceal political activity. Whatever our evaluation, we should be careful not to read 1980's standards—on matters of political activity and recusal, justices' financial interests, or their participation in judicial selection—back into those earlier years.

Frankfurter's political activity also did not cease when he became a member of the Court. Indeed it was more open than Brandeis's. He continued his interests in affecting the staffing of particular government departments, and also put considerable energy into the American war effort and into helping develop the international order for the postwar years. Frankfurter's ability, and his efforts, to affect the executive branch declined after World War II, particularly as a result of President Roosevelt's death. Frankfurter used "strong arguments, indignantly put" to stifle criticism of his activities,[91] about which he seems to have been far more concerned than Brandeis had been.

Whatever Frankfurter's own views, it is difficult not to be concerned about recent revelations by his former clerk Philip Elman about conversations with the justice during the Court's consideration of the *Brown* school desegregation case, when Elman was a senior attorney in the solicitor general's office and was principal author of the government's briefs in the case.[92] Justice Frankfurter told Elman about his colleagues' concerns about the case. This led Elman to write into one of the government briefs an argument he says he would not otherwise have made. Elman says the conversations took place before the government entered the case as *amicus curiae*, but both he and the justice could have anticipated such action in a case of such importance. Despite the closeness that does develop between justices and some of their clerks, the problem of a justice revealing in-Court confidences remains serious.

The most recent extended and extensive political activity while on the bench was that by Justice Fortas, which involved extended contact with President Lyndon Johnson. Evidence available since his departure from the Court under a cloud of ethical impropriety (for having received and not promptly returned a significant sum of money from a friend who was in trouble with the government) indicates that Fortas never gave up his role as a close adviser to the president. There he was not merely a dispassionate expert but a strong advocate for certain positions. After his first year on the Court, "Fortas worked his way into much the same advisory role he had enjoyed during the years before his judicial appointment." That included serving as "political adviser, speechwriter, crisis manager, administration headhunter, legal expert, war counselor, or just plain cheerleader."[93] (At one point, he actually skipped oral argument at the Court to go to the White House for a conference at the president's request.) He certainly dealt with matters likely to come before the Court, such as whether the president could send federal troops to help with the Detroit riots without the governor's request; when the president asked "for nothing less than an advisory constitutional opinion, . . . Fortas had no hesitation in answering."[94] It is now also clear that Justice Fortas, while on the bench, attempted to discredit former Attorney General Robert Kennedy and in the process violated court ethics by providing information to the president about a case.[95]

The involvement of justices in nonjudicial governmental positions has been a source of continuous controversy because of their absence from the Court and their involvement in matters that could later come before the Court.[96] When the Court's workload was not heavy, outside activity did not interfere with the Court's work. Both Chief Justice John Jay and Justice Oliver Ellsworth were involved in treaty negotiations; Jay, also a candidate for governor of New York, served as secretary of state. In the nineteenth century, Melville Fuller and David Brewer arbitrated a boundary dispute between Venezuela and British Guiana, five justices served on the commission to help resolve the disputed 1876 Hayes-Tilden presidential election, and Stephen Field served on a commission to revise state laws in his native California.

More recent "calls" from the president to take on extra-Court jobs have encountered more objections because such jobs interfere with disposition of the Court's increased workload, and because it has been feared that the Court's independence would be injured if it appeared that justices would readily serve at the president's bidding. During Franklin Roosevelt's presidency, Justice Reed chaired a committee to improve the civil service, Owen Roberts conducted an investigation of Pearl Harbor, and Robert Jackson was chief U.S. prosecutor at the War Crimes Trials in Nuremburg.[97] Jackson's failure to consult his colleagues before accepting the assignment and his extended absence brought conflict within the Court and produced a number of 4–4 results and rearguments. It also produced criticism for thrusting a judge into a simultaneous prosecutorial position. Another result was Chief Justice Stone's decision to turn down Roosevelt's requests to assume other tasks, such as investigating the nation's rubber supply. (During Taft's Chief Justiceship, Stone, a former attorney general, had been willing to serve on the Wickersham Commission investigating crime, but Taft had resisted.) Chief Justice Warren, who generally stayed away from most extra-Court activity as a matter of propriety, headed the commission to investigate the assassination of President Kennedy, but he did so only after resisting President Johnson's request. Subsequent questions about the commission's report, including Senate Intelligence Committee revelations that the FBI and CIA withheld information, and the questions raised by the movie *JFK*, reinforce the case against this type of extrajudicial activity.

Most recently, Chief Justice Burger became chairman of the Commission on the Bicentennial of the American Constitution, a topic that was close to his heart, and remained in that position after stepping down as Chief Justice; indeed, he said he left the Court so that he could devote his energies to the Commission. However, even a subject as neutral-sounding as the Constitution's bicentennial provoked controversy when the commission, whose staff director was Burger's former Supreme Court administrative assistant, held meetings in private and was sued for violating the law requiring advisory committees to hold public meetings.

No one challenged Burger's chairing the commission, but challenges have been made to having federal judges sit on other government bodies, including the President's Commission on Organized Crime (Second Circuit Judge Irving R. Kaufman and retired Justice Potter Stewart) and the United States Sentencing Commission, created under the 1984 Crime Control Act to develop uniform guidelines for sentencing federal offenders. Judges were to be named to this commission. After Chief Justice Burger indicated that his naming them raised constitutional questions, the law provided that the Chief Justice would suggest the names of six judges, with the president appointing three to the Commission. Only lower court judges were named. However, when the Supreme Court ruled on the propriety of their service in *Mistretta v. United States* (1989), it spoke about all federal judges, and in doing so drew on the history of Supreme Court justices' extrajudicial service.

Speaking for the Court, Justice Blackmun found no constitutional prohibition on such service by judges, either explicitly or by inference; certainly there was no restriction on their doing so in their individual capacities. In serving on the Sentencing Commission, "the judges, uniquely qualified on the subject of sentencing, assume a wholly administrative role," and the judges would not be wearing judicial and administrative hats simultaneously. Nor did such service "threaten the integrity of the Judicial Branch" or compromise judicial independence. Although there had been concern that such service by active-duty judges would deprive their courts of badly needed personnel, Justice Blackmun thought "widespread judicial recusals" unlikely. He did, however, find more troubling the claim that such judicial service "undermines public confidence in the disinterestedness of the Judicial Branch"; he satisfied himself on that point by noting that work on sentencing was "a neutral endeavor" "performed exclusively by the Judicial Branch." Nor did he think the president's power of appointment to the Commission could serve to influence judges in their decisions on cases.[98]

Justices' off-the-Court activity has included teaching at seminars for judges and in law school. Justice Story taught at Harvard and both the first Justice Harlan and Justice Brewer taught at the predecessor to George Washington Law School. The "flap" over Justice Fortas's receiving $15,000, raised by friends, to teach a law school seminar, about which he did not make a full disclosure when questioned during his confirmation hearings to be chief justice,[99] along with judges' increased public speaking, led the Judicial Conference in 1969 to adopt rules limiting lower court judges' acceptance of fees. Later, in connection with pay increases (see page 90), acceptance of honoraria was barred and the amount of earned income from teaching was severely restricted.

Drafting legislation affecting the courts and commenting on matters directly affecting the Supreme Court are activities more directly related to the justices' regular tasks. This is like judges' activities on the Judicial Conference and its committees (see page 68); that activity is not "extrajudicial" but it is not directly tied to deciding cases. Justice Willis Van Devanter drafted the Judiciary Act of 1915 modifying the Court's appellate jurisdiction, and Justice McReynolds, helped by Justices Van Devanter and Day, drafted the 1916 Judiciary Act. Chief Justice Burger was instrumental in initiating examination of the need for a new level of national appellate court (see page 61). All his colleagues responded to the Hruska Commission's preliminary proposal for a National Court of Appeals, and several made statements supporting or opposing the creation of the new court. Justice Rehnquist, on his nomination to be Chief Justice, strongly supported its creation and suggested how its judges were to be chosen (see page 62). Yet even in taking positions on matters on which they are thought to be expert, such as this major restructuring of the court system, there is a view that judges should restrict their comments to Congress to institutionalized channels like the Judicial Conference.[100] There has, however, been departure from this norm to the extent that individual judges disagree with the Judicial Conference's position. Their unhappiness about their pay (see pages 89–90) led to the formation of the Federal Judges Association, which lobbies on behalf of its members' interests. And the more a topic diverges from judicial administration, the more informal and more covert the communication.

Perhaps coming to be more and more expected as a form of extra-Court activity—and certainly permissible under the Code of Judicial Conduct—are the Chief Justice's comments about the "state of the judiciary"; proposals have been made that such an address be made to Congress. Chief Justices William Howard Taft and Charles Evans Hughes appeared at bar association meetings and at the American Law Institute (ALI) to discuss the "state of the judiciary." Such presentations were revived by Chief Justice Warren, who preferred the ALI as his forum because of ABA criticism of the Court's decisions. However, as noted earlier, Chief Justice Burger, in addition to making numerous appearances to stress the importance of court administration, regularly delivered a State of the Judiciary address at ABA meetings, a practice later discontinued by Chief Justice Rehnquist.

Burger's willingness to speak out was not matched by a willingness to engage in debate. His many formal appearances were held under strict conditions of his choosing, and he would not otherwise meet with the press, justifying this in terms of a First Amendment "right to be left alone." The American Bar Association, after at first acceding to Burger's wishes that his State of the Judiciary addresses to them not be televised, later decided he would not be allowed to control media coverage of *their* activities, and the Chief Justice adjusted his position. These matters raise, and leave unresolved, the question of how "public" a figure the Chief Justice is expected to be. Perhaps a Chief Justice who is going to venture into the "outer world" beyond the Court has to accept more graciously the "costs" of having to deal with the media and others in part on their terms.

Within the last few years, we have seen what amounts to an outpouring of public commentary by other justices as well. This has included television interviews and extended newspaper interviews. Some did not speak to the media until after they left the Court; among these were Justice Powell and Justice Brennan, the latter being interviewed in *Playboy*.[101] Others, however, did speak to the press while they were still on the Court. In the latter situation, some comments, like Justice Stewart's, were general in nature, uncontroversial, and harmless. The bicentennial of the Constitution produced even more public appearances by some of the justices. This included Justice Blackmun appearing at the end of "Superior Court," urging people to read the Constitution. He was also interviewed for a full hour by Bill Moyers as part of the PBS "In Search of the Constitution" series, as were Justices Brennan and O'Connor; and eight sitting justices spoke to *Life* magazine at that time.

More substantive was Stewart's later speech on freedom of the press[102] and Justice Black's talk of his "constitutional faith" (his doctrinal beliefs). In a television interview, Chief Justice Rehnquist even wrote a book about the Supreme

Court,[103] but it is mostly about its history, with no examples from after the post–World War II Vinson Court, so as not to involve people still engaged in the Court's work. The book does, however, also discuss selection of cases, the conference, and oral argument. Justice Blackmun spoke openly of relations among the justices, alignments within the Court, and particularly about his relationship with the Chief Justice; nor was Justice Rehnquist, although less open about matters of internal strategy, hesitant to talk about the Court's decision-making process. Justice Brennan, in an interview with one of his law clerks, discussed his appointment to the Court, his reputation as a "playmaker" (consensus builder), his close relationship with Chief Justice Earl Warren, Justice Douglas's independence, how a new justice is courted by other justices, and the role of a justice's religion in his decisions.[104]

Justice Blackmun also appeared as a panelist on a Public Broadcasting System series on difficult choices in health care in America. While careful not to make any statements reflecting a position on matters that might come before the Court in cases, he did discuss doctor-lawyer relationships and problems of trying medical questions in court, and expressed his confidence in American physicians. Justice Scalia, shortly after joining the Court, *did* discuss a hypothetical case about unauthorized disclosure of government secrets, at a university panel discussion.

There has even been commentary on specific Court cases. In particular, in speeches at the Second Circuit Judicial Conference reported in the press, Justice Marshall regularly openly criticized his colleagues and applauded important Second Circuit civil liberties rulings that Marshall's Supreme Court colleagues had reversed. Marshall also criticized celebration of the bicentennial of the Constitution for overstating the Constitution's perfection, and ranked President Reagan's civil rights performance as the lowest.[105]

Justice Stevens, at a law school dedication, criticized the Court's majority for overreaching to achieve results in civil rights and defendants' rights cases. Other justices also used speeches at universities to make important points about the judiciary. Attracting particular attention was Justice Rehnquist's University of Minnesota Law School speech during the 1984 presidential campaign, in which he said there was nothing wrong with presidents trying to name justices who shared their views. Although he mentioned neither President Reagan nor Democratic candidate Walter Mondale, and although he noted that nominees do not always act as predicted, the speech produced criticism—from the liberals, predictably—for intruding the Court into partisan politics. Causing criticism of a justice, and some embarrassment, was a letter Justice O'Connor wrote to an Arizona conservative Republican, citing several cases for the proposition that the United States was a "Christian nation." She said she regretted having sent the letter. Scholars said she was wrong in her interpretation, and the incident raised the question of her distance from Republican politics.[106]

An earlier study found that, despite the end-of-nineteenth-century outpouring of commentary by judges, there seemed to be no relation between the level of off-Court commentary and either the Court's prestige, the policy direction of its decisions, or the judges' own liberal or conservative tendencies.[107] We cannot be sure what explains the recent increase in justices' speaking out, not merely to other judges but to broader publics. One suggestive explanation is that *The Brethren*—with its revelations of the justices as "real live" people, engaging not only in bargaining but also in bickering—instead of causing them to put on the "false face" of congeniality, may have actually lowered the barriers to communicating what "actually" goes on in the Court. Thus, after the unwanted exposure by the book, the justices may have felt less restraint in addressing the realities of the situation.[108] Moreover, much of the content of the recent spate of remarks seems tied to the justice's ideology.

Notes

1. The argument is that of S. Sidney Ulmer and John Alan Stookey, "How Is the Ox Being Gored: Toward a Theory of Docket Style and Innovation in the U.S. Supreme Court," *University of Toledo Law Review* 7 (Fall 1975): 1–28.

2. Robert A. Burt, *Two Jewish Justices* (Berᵍ ᵉley: University of California Press, 1988), p. 90.

3. Alexander Bickel, *The Least Dangerous Branch* (Indianapolis, Ind.: Bobbs-Merrill, 1962), p. 58.

4. Herbert Wechsler, "Toward Neutral Principles of Constitutional Law," *Harvard Law Review* 73 (November 1959): 19, 11.

5. *Vasquez v. Hillery*, 474 U.S. 254 at 265 (1986).

6. *Burnet v. Coronado Oil & Gas Co.*, 285 U.S. 393 at 406 (1932).

7. Bickel, *The Least Dangerous Branch*, p. 59. See also Bickel, "The Supreme Court's 1960 Term, Foreword: The Passive Virtues," *Harvard Law Review* 75 (November 1961): 40–79.

8. Richard A. Posner, *The Federal Courts* (Cambridge, Mass.: Harvard University Press, 1985), p. 205.

9. *Payne v. Tennessee*, 111 S.Ct. 2597 at 2619 (Marshall), 2614 (Scalia).

10. *Vasquez v. Hillery*, 474 U.S., at 265 (1986) (Marshall); *Moragne v. States Marine Lines*, 398 U.S. 375, 403 (1970) (Harlan).

11. *Thomas v. Washington Gas Light Co.*, 448 U.S. 261 at 273 (1980) (Stevens); *Thornburgh v. American College of Obstetricians*, 476 U.S. 747 at 780–81 (1986) (Stevens).

12. Walter F. Murphy, *Elements of Judicial Strategy* (Chicago: University of Chicago Press, 1964), p. 204.

13. See *Rodriguez de Quijas v. Shearson/American Express*, 109 S.Ct. 1917 at 1921–22 (1989) (lower court should leave overruling to Supreme Court).

14. *Vasquez v. Hillery*, 474 U.S., at 269.

15. *Thornburgh*, 476 U.S., at 787.

16. See *Webster v. Reproductive Health Services*, 109 S.Ct. 3040 at 3056–57 (1989).

17. The first part of Justice Blackmun's opinion contains a history of baseball, "Casey at the Bat," and a list of Blackmun's favorite players, from which he may have omitted at least one. See Woodward and Armstrong, *The Brethren*, pp. 189–92. The second part of the opinion begins with Flood's batting and fielding averages. At the end of the opinion, there is the following notation: "The Chief Justice and Mr. Justice White join in the judgment of the Court, and in all but Part I of the Court's opinion." Did they have no sense of humor? Don't they like baseball (White played professional football)? Or did they have a different "All-Star Team"?

18. *City of Oklahoma City v. Tuttle*, 471 U.S. 808 at 819 n. 5.

19. The three cases are *Food Employees v. Logan Valley Plaza*, 395 U.S. 575 (1968); *Lloyd Corp. v. Tanner*, 407 U.S. 551 (1972); and *Hudgens v. National Labor Relations Board*, 424 U.S. 507 (1976). See also *Press Enterprise Co. v. Superior Court of California*, 478 U.S. 1 at 29 (1986) (Stevens) (open pretrial hearings), overturning part of *Gannett v. DePasquale*, 443 U.S. 368 (1979).

20. *Webster v. Reproductive Health Services*, 109 S.Ct., at 3077.

21. Stuart Taylor, Jr., "High Court Gets An Unusual Plea Not to Reverse Key Rights Ruling," *New York Times*, June 24, 1988, pp. A1, A14; *Patterson v. McLean Credit Union*, 109 S.Ct. 2363 (1989).

22. *Bellotti v. Baird*, 443 U.S. 622 at 652–53 (1979). The earlier case was *Planned Parenthood of Central Missouri v. Danforth*, 428 U.S. 52 (1976).

23. *Rutan v. Republican Party of Illinois*, 110 S.Ct. 2729 at 2756 (1990).

24. *Wallace v. Jaffree*, 472 U.S. 38 at 91 (1985).

25. *West Virginia Board of Education v. Barnette*, 319 U.S. 624 (1943), overruling *Minersville v. Gobitis*, 310 U.S. 586 (1940).

26. *Payne v. Tennessee*, 111 S.Ct. 2597 at 2619 (1991). In one of the cases overturned by *Payne*, Justice Scalia, calling for such action, had observed, "Overrulings of precedent rarely occur without a change in the Court's personnel." *South Carolina v. Gathers*, 109 S.Ct. 2207 at 2218 (1989). On the Court's more frequent overturning of precedent when there is a significant change in the Court's personnel, see Christopher P. Banks, "The Supreme Court and Precedent: An Analysis of Natural Courts and Reversal Trends," *Judicature* 75 (February-March 1992): 262–68.

27. See *California v. Acevedo*, 111 S.Ct. 1982 at 1991 (1991).

28. In 1978 the Court overturned a 1975 opinion with the same justice (Rehnquist) writing both opinions, and in another 1978 ruling, the Court decided no longer to follow some earlier decisions. *United States v. Scott*, 437 U.S. 82, overruling *United States v. Jenkins*, 420 U.S. 358 (1975); *Burks v. United States*, 437 U.S. 1 at 12 (1978). See also the cases on disproportionality of noncapital sentences to the crime charged, with *Harmelin v. Michigan*, 111 S.Ct. 2680 (1991), overturning *Rummell v. Estelle*, 455 U.S. 263 (1980), and *Solem v. Helm*, 463 U.S. 277 (1983).

29. Terry Eastland, "260 Precedents That Bit the Dust," *Wall Street Journal*, July 10, 1991, p. A12.

30. David J. Danelski, "Causes and Consequences of Conflict and Its Resolution in the Supreme Court," *Judicial Conflict and Consensus*, eds. Sheldon Goldman and Charles Lamb (Lexington: University Press of Kentucky, 1986), p. 38.

31. Robert Harrison, "The Breakup of the Roosevelt Supreme Court," *Law and History Review* 2 (Fall 1984): 215.

32. *Payne v. Tennessee*, 111 S.Ct. 2597 at 2610–11 (Rehnquist, for the Court), 2619 (Marshall). The overturned cases were *Booth v. Maryland*, 482 U.S. 496 (1987), and *South Carolina v. Gathers*, 490 U.S. 805 (1989).

33. Martin Shapiro, "Stability and Change in Judicial Decision-Making: Incrementalism or Stare Decisis?" *Law in Transition Quarterly* 2 (Summer 1965): 155.

34. *Ratchford v. Gay Lib*, 434 U.S. 1080 at 1081 (1978).

35. *Rice v. Sioux City Memorial Cemetery*, 349 U.S. 71 (1955); *Jackson v. Alabama*, 348 U.S. 888 (1954); Anthony D'Amato and Robert O'Neil, *The Judiciary and Vietnam* (New York: St. Martin's Press, 1972). Full discussion of this point and most of the argument in this section can be found in Stephen L. Wasby, Anthony A. D'Amato, and Rosemary Metrailer, *Desegregation from Brown to Alexander: An Exploration of Supreme Court Strategies* (Carbondale: Southern Illinois University Press, 1977).

36. Murphy, *Elements of Judicial Strategy*, p. 193. Murphy's discussion of strategy remains the best available.

37. S. Sidney Ulmer, "Earl Warren and the Brown Decision," *Journal of Politics* 33 (August 1971): 697.

38. Alpheus Thomas Mason, *Harlan Fiske Stone: Pillar of the Law* (New York: Viking Press, 1956), pp. 614–15; Chief Justice Burger, 409 U.S. xxxv at xvi (1972).

39. *Committee for Public Education v. Regan*, 444 U.S. 646 at 665 (1980).

40. *Elkins v. United States*, 364 U.S. 206 (1960) (search); *Gregg v. Georgia*, 428 U.S. 153 at 180 (1976), and *Woodson v. North Carolina*, 428 U.S. 280 at 299 (1976) (death penalty); *Linkletter v. Walker*, 381 U.S. 618 (1965) (*Mapp* retroactivity).

41. G. Gregory Fahlund, "Retroactivity and the Warren Court: The Strategy of a Revolution," *Journal of Politics* 35 (August 1973): 570–93.

42. See *Arizona Governing Committee v. Norris*, 463 U.S. 1073 at 1106–7 (1983).

43. Gregory A. Caldeira, "The United States Supreme Court and Criminal Cases, 1935–1976: Alternative Models of Agenda Building," *British Journal of Political Science* 2 (1981): 461; in italics in original.

44. The case was *Bell v. Maryland*, 378 U.S. 226 (1964), on the constitutionality of the sit-ins.

Justice Clark's opinion reversing participants' convictions was intended to obtain a majority for Justice Brennan's opinion, avoiding the merits because Congress was considering "public accommodations" legislation. The strategic action was successful. See Schwartz, *Super Chief*, pp. 522–24. Discussing the sit-in cases later, Justice Brennan said, "We decided to wait and see what Congress would do." Bill Moyers, Interview with Justice Brennan, "In Search of the Constitution," PBS series, May 19, 1987.

45. See Dennis J. Hutchinson, "Unanimity and Desegregation: Decision-Making in the Supreme Court, 1948–1958," *Georgetown Law Journal* 68 (October 1979): 87.

46. H. W. Perry, Jr., "Agenda-Setting in the U.S. Supreme Court," paper presented to Midwest Political Science Association, 1985, p. 23 n.10.

47. J. Woodford Howard, "The Fluidity of Judicial Choice," *American Political Science Review* 62 (March 1968): 49–50.

48. See Richard Lempert, "Between Cup and Lip: Social Science Influences on Law and Policy," *Law & Policy* 10 (April-July 1988): 189.

49. *Webster v. Reproductive Health Services*, 109 S.Ct., at 3064 (Scalia), 3067, 3077 (Blackmun).

50. Murphy, *Elements of Judicial Strategy*, pp. 4–5.

51. See Note, "State Court Evasion of United States Supreme Court Mandates," *Yale Law Journal* 36 (1947): 574–83, and Jerry K. Beatty, "State Court Evasion of United States Supreme Court Mandates During the Last Decade of the Warren Court," *Valparaiso University Law Review* 6 (Spring 1972): 260–85.

52. For an extended treatment, see Howard Dean, *Judicial Review and Democracy* (New York: Random House, 1966).

53. For example, see the regulation of insurance: *United States v. South-Eastern Underwriters Association*, 322 U.S. 533 (1944) (interstate insurance a form of commerce); the passage of the McCarran-Ferguson Act confirming state authority to regulate insurance; and *Prudential Insurance Co. v. Benjamin*, 328 U.S. 408 (1946), sustaining the act.

54. Reversing, respectively, *Chisholm v. Georgia*, 2 Dall. 419 (1793); *Pollock v. Farmers Loan & Trust Co.*, 157 U.S. 429 (1895); *Oregon v. Mitchell*, 400 U.S. 112 (1970); and *Dred Scott v. Sandford*, 19 How. 393 (1857).

55. *Plyler v. Doe*, 457 U.S. 202 at 253 (1982).

56. *Hunter v. Erickson*, 393 U.S. 385 (1969) (housing ordinances); *Washington v. Seattle School District No. 1*, 458 U.S. 457 (1982) (busing).

57. John Hart Ely, *Democracy and Distrust: A Theory of Judicial Review* (Cambridge, Mass.: Harvard University Press, 1980), p. 181.

58. Ibid., pp. 77, 100–101, 117.

59. Jesse Choper, *Judicial Review and the National Political Process* (Chicago: University of Chicago Press, 1980), p. 68.

60. Glenn A. Phelps and John B. Gates, "The Myth of Jurisprudence: Interpretive Theory in the Constitutional Opinions of Justices Rehnquist and Brennan," *Santa Clara Law Review* 31 (1991): 567–96.

61. Quoted in *Washington Post*, November 16, 1985, p. A2 (speech of November 15).

62. William J. Brennan, Jr., "The Constitution of the United States: Contemporary Ratification," speech at Georgetown University, October 12, 1985, pp. 4–5.

63. Joel B. Grossman, "Bork's Law and the Closing of the Judicial Mind," *Law & Social Inquiry* 15 (1991): 811.

64. John C. Schmidhauser, *The Supreme Court as Final Arbiter in Federal-State Relations, 1789–1957* (Chapel Hill: University of North Carolina Press, 1958).

65. *Gregory v. Ashcroft*, 111 S.Ct. 2395 (1991).

66. *Coleman v. Thompson*, 111 S.Ct. 2546 at 2552 (1991).

67. Harold J. Spaeth and Stuart H. Teger, "Activism and Restraint: A Cloak for Judicial Policy Preferences," *Supreme Court Activism and Restraint*, eds. Stephen C. Halpern and Charles Lamb (Lexington, Mass.: Lexington Books, 1982), pp. 283, 296; data at pp. 288–94.

68. Charles M. Lamb, "Judicial Restraint on the Supreme Court," *Supreme Court Activism and Restraint*, eds. Halpern and Lamb, pp. 9, 12.

69. J. Clifford Wallace, "The Jurisprudence of Judicial Restraint: A Return to the Moorings," *George Washington Law Review* 50 (1981): 6.

70. Posner, *The Federal Courts*, p. 207.

71. *United States v. Butler*, 297 U.S. 1 at 79 (1936).

72. *Plyler v. Doe*, 457 U.S., at 243.

73. *Federal Bureau of Investigation v. Abramson*, 456 U.S. 615 at 644 (1982) (O'Connor, dissenting).

74. *United States v. Locke*, 471 U.S. 84 at 95 (1985).

75. For a recent discussion and application of these rules, see *United States v. Locke*, 471 U.S. 84 (1985).

76. Harold J. Spaeth and Stuart H. Teger, "Activism and Restraint: A Cloak for the Justices' Policy Preferences," *Supreme Court Activism and Restraint*, eds. Halpern and Lamb, p. 296.

77. Joel B. Grossman, "Role-Playing and the Analysis of Judicial Behavior: The Case of Mr. Justice Frankfurter," *Journal of Public Law* 11 (1962): 285–309. See also Harold J. Spaeth, "The Judicial Restraint of Mr. Justice Frankfurter—Myth or Reality," *Midwest Journal of Political Science* 8 (February 1964): 22–38; Harold J. Spaeth and Michael F. Altfeld, "Felix Frankfurter, Judicial Activism, and Voting Conflict on the Warren Court," *Judicial Conflict and Consensus*, eds. Goldman and Lamb, pp. 86–114, particularly pp. 93, 95.

78. Russell W. Galloway, Jr., "The Taft Court (1921–29)," *Santa Clara Law Review* 25 (Winter 1985): 1.

79. James Simon, *In His Own Image: The Supreme Court in Richard Nixon's America* (New York: David McKay, 1973), p. 227.

80. *Bell v. Wolfish*, 441 U.S. 520 at 548 (1979).

81. Simon, pp. 198–99.

82. See *Rutan v. Republican Party of Illinois*, 110 S.Ct. 2729 at 2748, 2757 (1990). The cases limiting patronage were *Elrod v. Burns*, 427 U.S. 347 (1976), and *Branti v. Finkel*, 445 U.S. 507 (1980).

83. Stephen C. Halpern, "On the Imperial Judiciary and Comparative Institutional Development and Power in America," *Supreme Court Activism and Restraint*, eds. Halpern and Lamb, p. 225.

84. Bruce Allen Murphy, *Fortas: The Rise and Ruin of a Supreme Court Justice* (New York: William Morrow, 1988), pp. 206, 243.

85. Bruce Allen Murphy, *The Brandeis/Frankfurter Connection: The Secret Political Activities of Two Supreme Court Justices* (New York: Oxford University Press, 1982), p. 7; Fish, "The Office of the Chief Justice," p. 112.

86. Murphy, *The Brandeis/Frankfurter Connection*, p. 352.

87. Maeva Marcus and Emily Van Tassel, "Judges and Legislators in the New Federal System, 1789–1800," *Judges and Legislators: Toward Institutional Comity*, ed. Robert A. Katzmann (Washington, D.C.: Brookings Institution, 1988), p. 43.

88. Marcus and Van Tassel, p. 32; Ralph Lerner, "The Supreme Court as Republican Schoolmaster," *Supreme Court Review 1967*: 127–80; "Preface," *Views from the Bench: The Judiciary and Constitutional Politics*, eds. Mark W. Cannon and David M. O'Brien (Chatham, N.J.: Chatham House, 1985), p. xv.

89. Murphy, *The Brandeis/Frankfurter Connection*, p. 10. For criticism of Murphy's use of source material and interpretations and inferences drawn from those materials, see, for example, Robert Cover, "The Framing of Justice Brandeis," *The New Republic*, May 5, 1982: 17–21, and David J. Danelski, Review, *Harvard Law Review* 96 (November 1982): 312–30.

90. Murphy, *The Brandeis/Frankfurter Connection*, p. 55.

91. Ibid., p. 253.

92. Philip Elman, "The Solicitor General's Office, Justice Frankfurter, and Civil Rights Litigation, 1946–70: An Oral History," *Harvard Law Review* 100 (February 1987): 817–52.

93. Murphy, *Fortas*, p. 235. For another thorough treatment of the justice, see Laura Kalman, *Abe Fortas: A Biography* (New Haven, Conn.: Yale University Press, 1990).

94. Ibid., p. 394.

95. "Justice Fortas Told President about Case, Researcher Says," *New York Times*, January 23 1990; Glen Elsasser, "Ex-Justice Caught in Supreme Court Breach," *Albany Times-Union*, February 11, 1990.

96. Russell Wheeler, "Extra-Judicial Activities of the Early Supreme Court," *Supreme Court Review 1973*, ed. Phillip Kurland (Chicago: University of Chicago Press, 1973), pp. 122–58.

97. For further examination, see Jeffrey D. Hockett, "Justice Robert H. Jackson, The Supreme Court, and the Nuremburg Trial," *The Supreme Court Review 1990*: 257–99.

98. *Mistretta v. United States*, 109 S.Ct. 647 at 671–74 (1989). Note, however, that one of the

commission members was elevated from the district court to the court of appeals; the desire for such elevation might serve to sway a judge's views, although there is no evidence that occurred in this instance. Federal judges have not been hesitant to speak out in criticism of the Sentencing Guidelines. See David Margolick, "Chorus of Judicial Critics Assail Sentencing Guidelines," *New York Times,* April 12, 1992.

99. Murphy, *Fortas,* p. 503.

100. See John W. Winkle III, "Judges Before Congress: Reform Politics and Individual Freedom," *Polity* 22 (Spring 1990): 443–60, on changes in habeas corpus in the 1950s.

101. Alain L. Sanders, "The Marble Palace's Southern Gentleman," *Time,* July 9, 1990, pp. 12, 14; Nat Hentoff, "The Justice Breaks His Silence," *Playboy,* July 1991, pp. 120 ff.

102. Potter Stewart, "Or of the Press," *Hastings Law Journal* 26 (1975): 631–37.

103. William H. Rehnquist, *The Supreme Court: How It Was, How It Is* (New York: William Morrow, 1987). Rehnquist has also written another book: *Grand Inquests: The Historic Impeachments of Justices Samuel Chase and Andrew Johnson* (New York: William Morrow, 1992).

104. John A. Jenkins, "A Candid Talk with Justice Blackmun," *New York Times Magazine,* February 20, 1983, pp. 20–24ff.; John Jenkins, "The Partisan: A Talk with Justice Rehnquist," *New York Times Magazine,* March 3, 1985, pp. 28–33ff.; Jeffrey T. Leeds, "A Life on the Court," *New York Times Magazine,* October 5, 1986, pp. 24–27, 74–79.

105. Stuart Taylor, Jr., "Marshall Sounds Critical Note on Bicentennial," *New York Times,* May 7, 1981, pp. A1, B18; Taylor, "Marshall Puts Reagan at 'Bottom' Among Presidents on Civil Rights," *New York Times,* September 2, 1987, pp. A1, A22.

106. See "O'Connor Embarrassed by Letter on U.S. as 'Christian Nation,'" *Los Angeles Times,* March 16, 1989, p. 23; Alan M. Dershowitz, "Justice O'Connor's Second Indiscretion," *New York Times,* April 2, 1989, p. E15.

107. Alan F. Westin, "Out-of-Court Commentary by United States Supreme Court Justices, 1789–1962: Of Free Speech and Judicial Lockjaw," *An Autobiography of the Supreme Court: Off-the-Bench Commentary by the Justices* (New York: Macmillan, 1963), pp. 28–29.

108. See Ronald J. Fiscus, "Studying *The Brethren:* The Legal-Realist Bias of Investigative Journalism," *American Bar Foundation Research Journal* 1984 (Spring): 487–503.

9 The Supreme Court and the Other Branches

OUR EXAMINATION OF JUDICIAL review should make clear that one of the Supreme Court's major tasks is to rule on issues concerning the separation of powers between legislative, executive, and judicial branches. The Court has done so in some important cases and it has also been content to let other lower court rulings on the subject stand. Increasingly, the courts are called upon to resolve conflicts between the president and his subordinates and Congress—or at least certain members of Congress, who have brought suits challenging executive action or inaction. Judicial rulings interpreting statutes or administrative regulations, far more frequent than instances of judicial review, have produced friction, even conflict.

The interaction between the judiciary and other branches of government, including the other branches' response to the courts' actions, is examined in this chapter. That examination should help us understand to what extent the Supreme Court is an independent force within our governmental system—or a dependent institution. After examining the branches' interaction over operation of the judiciary we turn to the Supreme Court's overall treatment of congressional actions. This is followed by an analysis of Congress's responses to those decisions and to other Court rulings with which it disagreed. We then turn to the Supreme Court's rulings on the presidency, and the chapter ends with a discussion of judicial rulings on regulatory agency decisions.

The Court and Congress

In the early years of the Republic, federal judges were unsure about their relationships with Congress, as the Constitution gave little guidance. They sought to walk a line between independence, stemming from the separation of powers idea, and assisting in promoting the new government. They developed "a distinction . . . that preserved an independent stance for the judiciary at the same time that it allowed justices to maintain political relationships with both the executive and legislative branches of government."[1] Only over the years did an "arm's-length relationship" develop between federal judges and Congress, and it was largely the judges who brought it about.[2] Yet even in the early days, while making informal contacts with members of Congress, when the judges "wished to make a formal presentation to Congress as a body, they did it through the president."[3]

In the present, apart from judicial rulings on legislation, judges and legislators are in frequent contact over matters of judicial administration, but for the most part, those contacts are institutionalized, with the judiciary approaching Congress through the Judicial Conference of the United States (see pages 67–69). Matters at issue include the number of judgeships and administrative support positions, judges' salaries, the courts' jurisdiction, and rules of procedure and evidence—the last generally promulgated by the judiciary under the Rules Enabling Act (see pages 74–75). Judges lobby over major legislation affecting the court system, as in the Judges Bill that gave the Supreme Court its discretionary jurisdiction, changes in the bankruptcy courts (see pages 49–51), proposals for a National Court of Appeals (see pages 61–62), and additions to federal criminal law. Judges and legislators also have contacts about substantive legislation, but such contacts are likely to be informal because of the general judicial position that judges should not get directly involved with the legislature in making the law. Despite existing contacts, communication between members of the two branches is "sporadic and imperfect," and members of each branch feel misunderstood by the other. Underlying this, and helping to explain legislative unwillingness to deal with judges' salary and other concerns, is that members of Congress, who must run for reelection, are jealous of life-tenured federal judges. Recognition of the communication problem, even as to matters of judicial administration, and recognition that Congress passes bills with workload implications for the courts and that courts face problems in dealing with legislative materials, has led to some conferences, outside the context of particular proposals, in which judges and legislators have tried to bridge the gap.[4]

Court Budget

A crucial part of judicial-legislative interaction concerns the judicial budget. Because that budget is a very small part of the total federal budget, it is not likely to command legislators' attention. Prior to the 1939 creation of the Administrative Office of the Courts, the judiciary's budget requests were handled by the Department of Justice. While the judicial budget is now included in the budget the president sends to Congress, the courts really deal only with the Congress over budget matters because the Office of Management and Budget in the executive branch is prohibited by law from changing the Judicial Conference's recommendations, creating judicial independence in budget matters. Despite the Judicial Conference's role, "the process once dominated by civil servants in the Executive Branch has come to be dominated by civil servants in the Third Branch," specifically the personnel of the Administrative Office.[5] Although "separation from the Executive Branch has certainly been achieved" concerning the budget,[6] there is an aspect of judicial administration where it has not: the courts are dependent on the General Services Administration, the federal government's "housekeeping" agency, for the space judges and staff occupy in courthouses and other federal buildings. In part because GSA gives courts a low priority, judges are quite unhappy about the situation, which raises serious separation of powers concerns, and legislation has been introduced to turn control over judicial "space" to the judiciary itself.

Interaction between judiciary and Congress on budgetary matters, like most other judicial-legislative interaction, is carried out through regular, institutionalized means.[7] On the judges' side, the Judicial Conference's Budget Committee is the focal body. To assist the judiciary in attaining its financial goals, the committee's members are chosen because they come from states represented on relevant congressional committees, thus facilitating contact, or because they have legislative (and particularly congressional) experience. The key congressional body is the relevant subcommittee of the Appropriations Committee, as its recommendations are generally enacted without much change. If the Judicial Conference believes the House has cut the judges' requests too deeply, it may ask the Senate to restore some of the funds.

The judiciary's budget for Fiscal Year 1992 (FY 92) was $2,330,672,000, up from $1.2 billion five years earlier and from $2.0 billion in FY 91. For the FY 1969–85 period (before Gramm-Rudman), the judiciary received—after House cuts and Senate restorations—"an average annual increase of almost 16 percent." That was "a rate higher than the average annual growth in the entire federal budget," perhaps because the judiciary's requests—"an average increase of slightly more than 20 percent over the previous year's appropriations"—were "quite modest."[8]

Judicial budget totals can be explained largely in terms of the number of permanent personnel positions, because the judiciary is a "labor-intensive" organization. The number of cases filed in the courts is a better indicator of the judiciary's *needs*. A better predictor of budget amounts is a three-year lag between caseload and budget dollars. That lag exists for several reasons: the lapse of time between the beginning of the judiciary's budget process (well before the start of the budget year) and actual caseloads, and Congress's failure to appropriate funds immediately for requested increases, as it adopts a "wait and see" attitude (Does the increase in caseload continue?) and a related outlook of "See if it keeps up" (Does the increase trend continue?). Moreover, judgeship and staff positions created at one time may not be filled immediately and increases in salaries are not always effective immediately.[9]

Judicial Review

An examination of separation of powers between judiciary and legislature shows that federal courts impinge directly on Congress's actions, not only by invalidating statutes but also by examining matters internal to Congress. The Court, interpreting and applying provisions of the Constitution, has:

• ruled on the qualifications of members of Congress—or at least on Congress's right to expel its members;

• defined "legislative" functions subject to protection under the Speech and Debate Clause (Art. I, Sec. 6), which provides immunity for legislators' official activities, and in so doing has constrained legislators by expanding the area of their liability;

• ruled that members of Congress may be held liable for racial discrimination in choosing staff (*Davis v. Passman*, 1979); and

• taken action to control congressional proceedings, particularly committee investigations and the exercise of the contempt power against witnesses at legislative hearings.

Another major effect, of course, is that produced by the decision that districts for the House of Representatives could be based only on population (*Wesberry v. Sanders*, 1964). This changed the composition of the House, from "a disproportionately rural House . . . into one with a large metropolitan majority," and had policy effects as well with respect to the allocation of government benefits: in particular, a shift in regulatory policy to predominantly nonrural interests like consumer and environmental regulation.[10]

Faced with Congress's refusal to seat Representative Adam Clayton Powell, the Court held the issue not to fall under the "political question" doctrine and then ruled that the Speech and Debate Clause, although preventing a suit against members of Congress for their votes not to seat Powell, did not bar a suit against Congress's employees. In the *Gravel* case (1972), the Court said that a grand jury could not question a senator's legislative assistant about activities related to the senator's legislative work. But it also said that the act of arranging to have a private company publish the Pentagon Papers was *not* legislative activity and thus the senator's assistant, and probably the senator himself, could be questioned about that subject.

The meaning of "legislative activity" was limited by the *Gravel* decision and the Court's holding in *United States v. Brewster* that acceptance of a bribe—by Senator Daniel Brewster (D-Md.)—was not part of a legislator's official duties and thus could properly be the basis for an indictment. However, the Court strengthened Speech and Debate Clause protections in the 1979 *Helstoski* case in ruling that evidence of a representative's legislative acts could not be used in a prosecution of that representative for accepting a bribe, and that the legislator had not waived the clause's protection by testifying before the grand jury and voluntarily producing legislative documents. The Court also limited what constitutes a "legislative" act when it held in *Doe v. McMillan* that circulation outside Congress of a House committee report on the District of Columbia schools was not part of the legislative process, and when it ruled in *Hutchinson v. Proxmire* (1974) that senators and their assistants were not protected from libel suits for transmitting allegedly defamatory material in press releases.

The Court has also defined the scope of congressional investigations—at times supporting an expansive reading of Congress's authority, at times restricting Congress's power to punish those who have objected to or hindered investigations.[11] In one of its most important internal security rulings, *Watkins v. United States*, the Warren Court invalidated a contempt citation resulting from a witness's refusal to answer the House Un-American Activities Committee's questions because the relationship between the questions and the committee's investigation had not been made clear. The Chief Justice severely criticized both the committee and Congress for failing to control the committee's activities. However, after Congress had threatened to remove the Court's jurisdiction over internal security matters, (see page 317), the Court seemingly backed down. In the *Barenblatt* case (1958) it rejected the claim by a witness at a congressional hearing that because of the First Amendment, he could refuse to answer questions.[12]

The Court has also dealt with questions of the procedure by which legislation is enacted. One recent issue was whether a particular law was a revenue-raising measure and thus, under the Origination Clause (Art. 1, Sec. 7, cl. 1), had to originate in the House of Representatives. In the 1990 *Munoz-Flores* case, a unanimous Court found that a $25 special assessment for the Crime Victims Fund, for each count on which an individual was convicted, was not a revenue measure. Perhaps more important than the specific ruling was the Court's decision that, although the House could enforce the Origination Clause by refusing to pass a bill violating it, the Court would nonetheless hear constitutional challenges on the question—just as it does with other separation of powers claims where one branch could have resisted the claimed intrusion.

Despite all these rulings, courts are still hesitant to deal with internal congressional matters. In recent years, rulings by the Court limiting standing to sue have also served to block some cases challenging Congress's actions or failure to act; even when they grant standing to members of Congress to challenge legislative actions, they often decline to decide the cases.

Judicial Review of Statutes. Despite the conflict between President Franklin Roosevelt and the Hughes Court over judicial review of New Deal legislation, neither before that time nor later—except for the legislative veto (see below)—has the Court regularly struck down many congressional acts in a short period. The total number has been considerable, however. Prior to the Civil War, decisions invalidating acts of Congress "occurred on an episodic, nonsystematic basis." Over the long run, "periods of aggressiveness toward Congress have not occurred on a very regular basis." Swings from intervention to passivity have, however, grown larger over time, in proportion to increases in the frequency of the exercise of judicial review. There has also been a "very high correlation" between invalidation of congressional acts and those of state legislatures, with the greatest judicial activity concerning state legislation coming early in the twentieth century as part of judicial resistance to state economic regulation.[13]

Judicial review has been "significantly shaped by such political considerations as the degree of party difference between Congress and the Court, the nature of the party in power in the national government, and the party affiliations of the individual judges deciding specific cases."[14] Excepting the New Deal period because of the extremely high rate at which the Supreme Court invalidated recent legislation, the Court has been more likely to invalidate a law in periods of partisan stability than during partisan shift. For the 1930s and 1960s, state policy invalidated high proportions of issues "which cut across existing lines of ideological cleavage in the major parties" and were related to political realignment; this was not true for the post–Civil War and end-of-nineteenth-century realignments. A high proportion of the invalidated policies were enacted by majorities of the political party opposite that controlling the Supreme Court.[15]

1937 did not mark the end of the Court's invalidating of federal statutes. The Warren Court prohibited removing someone's citizenship for such acts as desertion from the military or remaining abroad to avoid military service, and the Court prohibited courts-martial of civilians in a number of circumstances and of service personnel for non-service-connected offenses.[16] Registration provisions that forced people to incriminate themselves under other federal laws or state law were struck down under the Fifth Amendment.[17] Social Security Act durational residence requirements for welfare benefits were set aside in *Shapiro v. Thompson* for interfering with the right to travel. And the Lindberg (kidnapping) Act death penalty provisions were invalidated (*United States v. Jackson*, 1968).

Burger Court acts of national judicial review, which at times occurred through summary affirmance of lower court decisions, were scattered across a wide range of policy areas. The Court's invalidation of the 1978 bankruptcy statute led to a difficult time for both Congress and the courts before new legislation was passed (see pages 50–51). Other rulings covered limits on who could receive food stamps and discrimination in benefits on the basis of gender and illegitimacy; Post Office methods for screening obscenity and bans on demonstrations on U.S. Capitol grounds and on displaying the flag on the grounds of the Supreme Court itself; and Federal Election Campaign Act limits on individual's expenditures on behalf of candidates of their choice.[18] In the first instance since FDR's 1937 battle with the Court that regulatory legislation based on the Commerce Clause had been struck down, in *National League of Cities v. Usery* (1976) the justices invalidated the extension of the minimum wage law to state and local government employees, but the Court reversed its position in 1985.

In recent years there has been an increase—a rebirth—of major separation of powers cases. They result from several factors, with a major explanation "divided government," in which one party holds the White House while the other party controls Congress, particularly as the president wishes to accomplish his program and Congress resists for both institutional and partisan reasons. One of the most sweeping instances of judicial review of legislative action in the Court's history came in 1983, when the Court invalidated the *legislative veto*, under which executive branch actions can be rejected by a resolution of one house of Congress (the "one-house veto") or by a concurrent resolution of both Senate and House of Representatives. The Court's ruling affected both the trend toward increased presidential power and the countertrend of increased assertion of congressional authority. Availability of the legislative veto, a part of over 200 statutes, allowed Congress to give the president broad authority while retaining controls over exercise of that authority, indicating the conflict between a formal view of separation of powers and the realities of the everyday working relations of Congress and the president. Some provisions limited the president's authority to use American troops overseas (War Powers Act of 1973), reorganize the executive branch, or defer expenditure of funds appropriated by Congress (Budget and Impoundment Act of 1974); many concerned foreign policy matters. Others allowed Congress to reject agency regulations.

In 1983 the Supreme Court, in *Immigration and Naturalization Service v. Chadha*, ruled that both two-house and one-house legislative vetoes violate the separation of powers doctrine and the Constitution's specific provisions concerning enactment of legislation, including *presentment* (presentation to the president) and *bicameralism* (both houses must consider legislation). As it tried to move toward alternatives such as joint resolutions of approval or disapproval, which require the president's signature, Congress continued to pass bills containing legislative veto provisions, doing so 53 times in the 16 months after the ruling, but it did so not out of spite or resistance but because it didn't know what else to do. Even when not including a formal legislative veto requirement, Congress continued arrangements for "reprogramming" of funds or inserted provisions equivalent to the legislative veto, like requiring agencies to notify congressional committees before taking action or including riders in appropriations bills, which the president can't delete from the bill before signing.[19]

The Court next invalidated a key program of the Balanced Budget and Emergency Deficit Control (Gramm-Rudman-Hollings) Act of 1985; Congress's effort to deal with rising budget deficits. The law set targets and provided that, if Congress did not meet those targets, automatic budget cuts would go into effect based on a determination by the Comptroller General of the United States on advice of the Congressional Budget Office (CBO) and Office of Management and Budget (OMB). In an example of members of Congress challenging their colleagues' handiwork, several of them—and a union of government employees—challenged the Act. In *Bowsher v. Synar* (1986) the Supreme Court ruled, 7–2, that execution of the laws could not be placed in the hands of someone responsible to Congress, like the comptroller general, who was removable on passage of a joint resolution of Congress and was "consistently viewed" by Congress "as an officer of the Legislative Branch."

Congress did not replace the invalidated provision. The Gramm-Rudman target figures still serve to push members of Congress toward expenditure reductions. Yet, with the comptroller general out of the picture, the director of the Office of Management and Budget, the "president's man," although told to look at Congressional Budget Office figures, makes the necessary financial determinations. Congress, although recognizing the figures are constructed with smoke and mirrors, must accept them. The clear result of the Court's ruling thus is that the presidency has received more power.

Gramm-Rudman applies to the judiciary, and its mandatory reductions have had their effects. For example, in 1986, some courts said they were without funds to pay jurors' fees. When the supervision of jury trials was challenged as interference with the right to a jury trial, at least some courts ruled there was a violation. However, further constitutional conflict over such effects was avoided by the passage of a supplementary appropriations bill, mooting the cases. The problem recurred in 1992.

After *Bowsher*, the next separation of powers case involved a challenge to the constitutionality of the Sentencing Commission created by Congress to develop sentencing guidelines for federal judges to apply. The commission's unusual characteristics—the statute placed it in the judicial branch but it was an independent agency rather than a court, and judges served on it (see pages 296–97)—did not lead the Court to invalidate it, with Justice Blackmun saying, "Our constitutional principles of separated powers are not violated . . . by mere anomaly or innovation" (*Mistretta v. United States*, 1989). This indicated a far less formalistic position than the Court had taken in *Chadha* or *Bowsher v. Synar*.

One other separation of powers issue has been the circumstances under which the president may exercise the pocket veto. In 1929, when the president had been given a bill less than 10 days before adjournment at the end of the first session of a Congress, the Court ruled in the *Pocket Veto Case* that the bill had been properly pocket-vetoed because adjournment prevented return of the bill.[20] President Nixon pocket-vetoed the Family Practice of Medicine Bill during a congressional adjournment for the Christmas holidays—a during-session adjournment. The courts ruled he had acted improperly but the decision was not taken to the Supreme Court.[21] In 1985, after President Reagan pocket-vetoed a bill requiring him to certify human rights progress in El Salvador, members of the House, joined by the Senate, argued that the pocket veto had been improperly used. After the district court upheld the president, the D.C. Circuit ruled against him, but the Supreme Court said the case had become moot while it was pending and thus did not decide it.[22]

Statutory Interpretation

Most of the Court's decisions affecting Congress involve statutory interpretation—"supplementary lawmaking" as the courts interpret, apply, and flesh out statutes. It is judicial policy-making although not as explicit as when the Court rules in constitutional cases. Statutory interpretation is not easy work because the less clear statutes are more likely to be litigated, and justices do not agree as to how to interpret statutes, particularly on how to use legislative materials (or *legislative history*) in a search for Congress's intent—with Justice Scalia rejecting use of such materials. As Justice Stevens observed in a recent case, "In recent years the Court has vacillated between a purely literal approach to the task of statutory interpretation and an approach that seeks guidance from historical context, legislative history, and prior cases identifying the purpose that motivated the legislation." He argued that the former produced no legislative response, while, "when the Court has put on its thick grammarian's spectacles and ignored the available evidence of congressional purpose," the congressional response had been to overturn the Court.[23] The Court seemed to emphasize different modes of statutory interpretation in different policy areas, depending on the number, specificity, and complexity of statutes in the policy area.[24]

During statutory interpretation, the Court may explicitly suggest what Congress must do to make a statute valid. Overturning a law regulating grain futures transactions, Justice Taft said that Congress could not regulate the transactions unless it saw them as directly interfering with interstate commerce. Congress then placed such an explicit declaration in the Grain Futures Act, which the Court upheld. Even more indicative of the Court's influence are statutes into which Congress has written language the Court has already approved. In enacting the surveillance provisions of the Omnibus Crime Control and Safe Streets Act of 1968, Congress used procedures for wiretapping under a warrant the Court had spelled out in *Berger v. New York*. Similarly, when the Court ruled in *McCarty v. McCarty* (1982) that property settlements in divorces could not include military pensions, but said that Congress could provide otherwise if former spouses were to receive more protection, both houses of Congress took the Court up on the invitation by passing the Former Spouses' Protection Act. But it turned out that Congress had only partially rejected the *McCarty* rule: the Court, while recognizing the statute and Congress's intent, nonetheless ruled that state courts could not treat military retirement pay as community property unless Congress explicitly gave the states that authority.[25]

At other times, the Court interprets a statute so rigidly that the statute looks ridiculous (the "trap pass"), in the hope that Congress will be provoked to change the law.[26] An example is the famous "snail darter" case, in which the Court ruled that under environmental protection law, a major dam, largely constructed but still incomplete, would have to be stopped to protect the snail darter fish (*Tennessee Valley Authority v. Hill*, 1978). Congress then both specifically provided for completion of the dam *and* altered the statute to provide procedural flexibility—probably exactly what the Court had in mind.

Congressional Response

What has Congress's response been to judicial review and statutory interpretation? "Supreme Court abrogations of majority-sponsored activities have been the primary source of retaliation, real and seriously threatened, by the national political branches . . . against the federal judiciary."[27] However, as time has passed, there have been fewer broad-gauge congressional attacks on the Court. Action has usually been directed to particular rulings or sets of rulings. Even the efforts of the early 1980s to restrict federal courts' or the Supreme Court's jurisdiction stemmed primarily from the Court's "social issue" rulings—on school prayer, school desegregation, and abortion. In general, conflict between Congress and Court has been more likely to arise on matters where "constitutional language is unclear and . . . on which public sentiment has been largely unsettled"; where interest groups see vital interests at stake; and where the Court has threatened Congress's authority.[28]

Until the 1980s, undoubtedly as a reflection of the focus of the Court's caseload, action reversing the Court occurred more frequently in the economic sphere than in the civil liberties domain. Excluding the present period, economic regulation issues were involved in four of seven periods in which proposals to curb the Court were frequent, but civil liberties issues were involved in only two such periods. Moreover, the presence of intensely held economic or civil libertarian interests meant less success for Court-curbing than occurred in the areas of separation of powers or federalism, where Congress could take into account policy factors outside the Court's concern.[29] Starting with 1981, with conservative presidents committed to a social agenda they cannot achieve in a Congress controlled by the other party, Congress has been successful in overturning rulings in the field of civil liberties and civil rights (see page 321).

Important reversals on issues of federal-state relations have been quite case-specific. Congress acted to reverse the Court's ruling that the offshore oil lands belonged to the national government, passing "quit claim" legislation giving the lands to the states.[30] Congress also kept state regulation of insurance in force when the Court held in the *South-Eastern Underwriters* case that insurance was part of interstate commerce and thus subject to national regulation. In both instances, the Court, explicitly acknowledging Congress's intent to overturn the Court's initial decisions, sustained Congress's reversal action. At times Congress has also allowed the states to act after the Court has said the federal government had "preempted" an area and prevented state regulation. For example, when the Court said a state could not regulate interstate labor disputes even in the absence of National Labor Relations Board action,[31] Congress rewrote the law to allow such state activity. And when, in the *Garcia* federalism ruling, the Court said that states' protection must come through their representation in Congress, the states did "call their legislators" and within nine months, Congress, which had created the states' problem initially in the minimum-wage law, amended the statute and exempted state and local governments from it.

Negative congressional reaction to the Court's rulings has taken a wide variety of forms: criticism, sometimes in the form of nonbinding resolutions like one calling for a moratorium on busing; attempts to overrule the Court by amending the Constitution or by limiting the Court's appellate jurisdiction; and

refusal to provide compensation required by the Court's rulings. The latter occurred in the Yazoo land fraud case (*Fletcher v. Peck*) and much more recently
after the Court had struck down, as a bill of attainder, an appropriations bill rider
stipulating that three alleged subversives not be paid (*United States v. Lovett*,
1946). In addition, there have been proposals for such basic structural change as
requiring that federal or state laws could be declared invalid only by a vote of at
least seven justices, allowing Congress to override declarations that a federal or
state law was constitutionally invalid, or limiting justices' tenure.

Negative reaction is also evident in resistance to increasing the justices' salaries, in attempts to impeach justices—as in the unsuccessful effort to remove
Justice Douglas—and in resistance to confirming presidential nominees to the
Court, most obvious in the instance of Justice Fortas's nomination to be Chief
Justice. It is *not* likely to take the form of refusal to provide additional judges for
the federal courts because the senators want to have the patronage from additional judges, and because new judges might decide cases counter to the way
those presently on the courts do so. Not providing new judges is, however, a
partisan matter, with Democrats not wanting a Republican president to be able
to appoint a large number of new ones, and vice versa (see page 97).

The Eleventh, Sixteenth, and Twenty-sixth Amendments, as well as the
post–Civil War amendments on slavery and the status of blacks—all initiated by
Congress—were passed to override Court decisions. After the Court limited
Congress's power to regulate the use of child labor either through the power over
interstate commerce (*Hammer v. Dagenhart*, 1918) or taxation (*Bailey v. Drexel
Furniture*, 1922), Congress submitted for ratification a constitutional amendment prohibiting child labor. The Court's post-1937 shift, which included upholding the Fair Labor Standards (minimum wage) Act with its child labor provisions in *United States v. Darby* (1941), eliminated the need for the
amendment, still open to ratification because it contains no termination date—
unlike later amendments, including the Equal Rights Amendment (ERA),
which was not ratified.

Many more such efforts have also failed. These include attempts in the
1960s to overturn reapportionment and school prayer rulings. The latter effort
was renewed after 1980 in the drive to allow "voluntary" prayer in the schools.
Continuous activity to limit school desegregation through constitutional amendment was part of a larger set of legislative efforts aimed at achieving that goal,
including limits on federal judges' power to order busing and prohibitions on
executive branch initiation of desegregation. Similarly, extensive effort to repeal
the Court's 1973 abortion ruling through constitutional amendment—such as
defining when life begins and turning over abortion policy to the states—has
been only one aspect of legislative action aimed at limiting abortions. Perhaps
the best known is the Hyde Amendment—a ban on Medicaid payments for abortions except to save the life of the mother, upheld by the Court itself in *Harris v.
McRae*. That ruling is an indication of an extended dialogue that can be said to

go on between the Court and Congress, in which each speaks in turn, considering what the other has just said.

That dialogue can also be seen in the Court's treatment of the flag-burning issue. After the Court first struck down laws banning desecration of the flag, on First Amendment grounds, in *Texas v. Johnson* (1989), the Senate passed a resolution expressing "profound disappointment" in the ruling and the president asked the attorney general to recommend what to do about it. The Senate Judiciary Committee, in part to head off a proposed constitutional amendment overturning the ruling, recommended a new statute, which passed both houses of Congress 12 weeks after the Court had ruled. That law provided for direct review in the Supreme Court, on an accelerated schedule, of any district court ruling invalidating the new law. After the Supreme Court invalidated this statute in *Eichman v. United States* (1990), 10 days later the House voted on a constitutional amendment to prohibit desecration of the flag, but the vote fell short of the necessary two-thirds majority.

Attempts to limit the Court's jurisdiction have been less successful than efforts to overturn rulings by amending the Constitution. Only once has Congress successfully removed some of the Court's appellate jurisdiction. In the aftermath of the Civil War, the Reconstruction Congress, at odds with President Andrew Johnson and fearful of the Court's potential action concerning questionable detentions of citizens, passed a law removing the Court's jurisdiction over cases arising under the Habeas Corpus Act. The Court complied, in *Ex parte McCardle*, dismissing a case already argued. However, the Court examined congressional action before complying, and its compliance did not foreclose other Court actions to protect the individual. Moreover, when Congress removed the Court's jurisdiction in claims cases involving proof of former Confederate soldiers' present loyalty—ordering the Court to treat acceptance of a presidential pardon as proof of aid to the Confederacy but to ignore the pardon in determining loyalty—the Court struck down the limitation in *United States v. Klein* (1872). That case is said to stand for the proposition that Congress may not withdraw jurisdiction when the intent is to dictate a specific result, as some current congressional efforts are thought to do. The Court again dealt with this question in 1992, in *Robertson vs. Seattle Audubon Society*, but held that the challenged congressional action, concerning the environment, was not improper.

Congress does have the power to withdraw jurisdiction over the lower federal courts, which Congress established. The Supreme Court has sustained limited withdrawals of such jurisdiction. For example, it has upheld withdrawal of the power to issue injunctions in labor disputes (the Norris-LaGuardia Act) and approved Emergency Price Control Act procedures under which review of the Price Administrator's actions was routed through the Emergency Court of Appeals, which was deprived of the power to grant injunctions.[32] Removal of *all* federal court jurisdiction, however, like removal of the Supreme Court's appellate jurisdiction, leaves no final authority to resolve disputes over the affected subjects. It thus leaves standing divergent interpretations of constitutional provi-sions by the lower courts, either state (if all federal jurisdiction is removed) or both federal and state (if only Supreme Court appellate jurisdiction is with-drawn), without a judicial body to reconcile them. No definitive answer is now available to the question of whether such removal of authority, regardless of the subject matter or the effect of such action, is constitutional. *McCardle*, the most relevant case, does not provide such an answer.[33]

In the late 1950s, Congress made a serious attempt to restrict the Court's jurisdiction over internal security matters such as legislative investigations, the executive's loyalty-security programs, state control of teachers and admission of lawyers to the practice of law, and federal preemption of state internal subversion legislation. None of these bills passed, although the Senate vote was very close (a one-vote margin) and the Court appeared to retreat in the face of the attack.[34] When Ronald Reagan was elected president and the Republicans gained control of the Senate in 1980, there was another substantial attack on the Court's appel-late jurisdiction and on all federal court jurisdiction over subjects like school busing, school prayer, and abortion. That effort was somewhat undercut when President Reagan's own attorney general, although approving limits on particular federal judicial remedies, argued that Congress could not limit the Court's juris-diction when the effect is to "intrude upon the core functions of the Supreme Court as an independent and equal branch in our system of separation of powers."

None of the strong efforts by congressional (and particularly Senate) con-servatives in 1982 or 1983 prevailed, because of preoccupation with budget mat-ters, the absence of strong presidential support, and the effectiveness of the lib-erals' filibusters. More generally, broad attacks on the Court have not succeeded because disliked rulings, and most of the Court's actions, involve the states rather than Congress. Legislative delegations from states whose laws have been struck down may be unhappy, but delegations from other states whose policies were supported tend to oppose attacks on the Court; this produces a cross-cutting effect rather than monolithic opposition within Congress or between Congress and the president. When the president did have supporters in Congress for his attacks on the Court, the Court had its own supporters in Congress, interest groups, and the legal establishment.[35]

Legislative proposals to limit jurisdiction have been attacked by many, in-cluding legal scholars, the American Bar Association, and even some who strongly oppose the rulings at which the legislation is aimed—because they feel limiting jurisdiction violates the Constitution's spirit and is unwise. Eliminating Supreme Court review would be short-sighted because it would leave disliked rulings in place and would remove the possibility that the Court itself, perhaps with new appointees, would modify or overrule its "errors."[36] The Conference of State Chief Justices has also complained that the efforts insult state judges be-cause of the assumption that, free of Supreme Court review, they would not honor the Constitution as the Supremacy Clause requires them to do. (In 1958, by contrast, the then far more conservative state chief justices criticized the Supreme Court's internal security decisions, some of which restricted state authority to deal with subversion, as activist interference with states' rights.)

Congressional efforts to rewrite or reenact statutes have affected only a small proportion of the Court's rulings. However, they have been far more frequent and far more successful than efforts either to amend the Constitution or to limit the Court's jurisdiction.[37] For example, between 1944 and 1960, the Court's actions were revised 50 times. Among the decisions altered were 34 instances in which the Court overturned 60 statutes.[38] However, only a small portion of bills intended either to reverse or to modify are enacted; only 13 percent of 176 bills introduced between 1950 and 1978 to react to Supreme Court decisions handed down between 1950 and 1972 were the subject of any congressional action, and less than one-third of those were enacted.[39]

Most efforts to overturn the Court start immediately after the ruling, but the efforts may take a while before success is achieved. However, at times there can be a considerable lag between the Court's ruling and efforts to rewrite the statute. An example is provided by the Eisenhower administration's attempt to rewrite 18 U.S.C. §§ 241 and 242 (on depriving someone of his or her civil rights) to undo the Supreme Court's narrow reading of those provisions in *Screws v. United States*. Although *Screws* had been decided in 1945, the efforts to alter the statutes did not begin until 1956—and were not fully achieved until 1967.[40]

Sponsors of bills reacting to Supreme Court rulings vary in their aims. Some, but not many, want to write the judicial decision into law. And Congress has also prevented the executive branch from arguing for the overturning of Supreme Court doctrine—in the antitrust field.[41] A Court ruling may be written into the law as a result of ideological agreement with the Court's action; an example would be efforts in 1991 to write into a new crime bill limits on state death row inmates' use of federal habeas corpus and statements that evidence obtained without a proper warrant under the Court's "good faith" exception were to be admissible in federal courts. Incorporation of a ruling may also take place at the time law is codified, perhaps shortly after the ruling but not in direct response to it.[42]

The effort to limit habeas corpus illustrates the relationship between interbranch and intrabranch politics. Chief Justice Rehnquist was interested in seeking to limit death penalty convicts' use of federal habeas. Congress, moving in the same direction, sought recommendations from the judiciary. The Chief Justice appointed a task force, chaired by retired Justice Powell, which recommended considerable limits on such use. However, members of the Judicial Conference opposed some of the recommendations, and a majority voted to overturn some of them. Snubbing his judicial colleagues, the Chief Justice sent the full set of recommendations to Congress. After the legislation that would have embodied such limitations was delayed, in a series of cases in 1991 an undaunted Chief Justice led a Supreme Court majority to severe restrictions on state prisoners' use of federal habeas corpus during the time when Congress was considering the bill (see pages 000). He thus accomplished doctrinally what he had not been able to achieve through legislation or judicial rulemaking.

Some bills supplement or clarify the Court's rulings, but more generally the legislators feel the Court has improperly interpreted the statutes. Thus, after the judiciary has altered the law, Congress has frequently returned the law to its original state.[43] After the Court held the 1934 version of the Railroad Retirement Act unconstitutional as a taking of property in violation of the Fifth Amendment and as exceeding Congress's Commerce Clause power,[44] Congress enacted a new version in 1935 under the power to tax and spend for the general welfare. After a district court enjoined that statute, Congress enacted still another version, the Railroad Retirement Act of 1937. Congress's reaction to Warren Court rulings excluding certain types of evidence was to enact statutory provisions making such evidence—confessions and eyewitness testimony—admissible. Part of the response to the famous *Miranda* ruling was legislation allowing use of voluntarily given confessions in federal trials, with the trial judge determining voluntariness based on five factors specified by Congress; however, federal prosecutors were hesitant to use this provision.[45]

Another instance, in the aftermath of a ruling on a technical element of procedure, exemplifies the already noted dialogue between Court and Congress. In *Finley v. United States* (1989), the Court had limited lower federal courts' ability to hear pendent and ancillary claims (those attached to claims over which the court had jurisdiction). The Federal Courts Study Committee recommended restoration of the pre-*Finley* situation. Codifying "supplemental jurisdiction" (a new term including pendent and ancillary jurisdiction), Congress generally followed the recommendation; in so doing, it drew on a pre-*Finley* ruling of the Court (a voice from the past in the dialogue?), and the exception to full return to before *Finley* was itself based on another Supreme Court decision.[46]

Some new provisions are enacted because a changed balance of legislative power favors an interpretation of the law different from that initially intended. After the Court defined "employee" in the National Labor Relations Act to exclude foremen, a conservative Congress reversed that interpretation when it passed the Taft-Hartley Act. In another instance of Court ruling-response-ruling-response from the labor field, the Court upheld "hot cargo" agreements (that workers would not have to handle nonunion goods) voluntarily entered into by labor and management. In the Taft-Hartley Act, Congress then prohibited them. Later, however, reacting to the Court's ruling that picketing a general contractor's entire project to protest the presence of a nonunion contractor was an illegal secondary boycott, Congress created a construction industry exception to the ban.[47]

Recent instances of Congress's reversal of the Supreme Court's rulings included issues of federal employees' legal liability, criminal law, and veterans policy. When the Court ruled in 1988, in *Westfall v. Erwin*, that government employees do not have absolute immunity for torts they commit in the scope of their employment, Congress gave that absolute immunity to government employees in the Liability Reform Act of 1988.[48] When the Court ruled in the *McNally* case that a mail fraud conviction required a tangible loss and rejected the theory that people were being defrauded of an intangible like "good government" when an official accepted a bribe, Congress amended the law to cover the situation— but not before a number of convictions, including that of former Maryland Governor Marvin Mandel, were reversed by the lower courts.

Two reversals involved veterans. In one, the question was whether veterans could pay attorneys *more than* $10 to assist them in obtaining benefits; the $10 amount, from the Civil War period, was intended to prevent bilking of impoverished soldiers. The Court upheld the constitutionality of the statute in 1985, leading Congress to provide partial relief: the Veterans Judicial Review Act of 1988, which created the Court of Veterans Appeals (see page 54), allowed attorneys to be paid for services after the Board of Veterans Appeals had rendered its final decision.[49] (A district judge then struck down the original $10 cap as applied to service personnel exposed to radiation from nuclear explosions.) Then the Congress authorized the Veterans Administration (now Department of Veterans Affairs) to extend the period in which veterans' benefits would have to be used when alcoholism prevented use of those benefits. This reversed the Court's ruling in *Traynor v. Turnage* (1988), which had allowed the government to deny such extensions to alcoholics because their behavior was "willful misconduct."

Some important reversals have occurred in the area of civil liberties and civil rights. Indeed, in recent years Congress has become the battleground on which liberals have sought to overturn conservative Court rulings. One thus had a change in the relation of the Supreme Court to Congress, from a situation in which conservatives attacked Warren Court decisions, even after Congress began to pass major civil rights statutes, to one in the 1980s when the two institutions reversed roles and Congress was the greater protector of rights. After the Court ruled in the *Miller* case that a depositor had no Fourth Amendment interest in bank records subpoenaed by the government, the Right to Financial Privacy Act provided for notification of subpoenas of bank records and the right to challenge them.

Rewriting of the Court's rulings can be found on First Amendment subjects as well. The Court's ruling in *Zurcher v. Stanford Daily* (1978), allowing searches of newsrooms without prior notice, was reversed in part through enactment of the Privacy Protection Act of 1980, which limited government searches and seizures of documentary material in the possession of journalists not themselves suspected of being involved in a crime. And after the Court had found one version of legislation concerning "dial-a-porn" unconstitutional because it reached too far and regulated "indecent" communications, Congress reacted quickly, amending the law by regulating instead of banning "indecent" speech.[50]

In the religion portion of the First Amendment, when the Court upheld military regulations prohibiting the wearing of a yarmulke by an observant Jew while he was on duty (as a psychologist), Congress overrode the Court (and the regulations) to permit wearing of such apparel. [51]

A reversal of considerably greater effect came after the Court ruled, in *General Electric v. Gilbert* (1976), that failing to provide disability benefits to pregnant women was not discrimination based on sex. Congress, after a strong campaign by women's groups, passed the Pregnancy Discrimination Act to make clear that Title VII of the 1964 Civil Rights Act (concerning employment discrimination based on race or sex) covered that situation, and the Court recognized that Congress had sided with the *Gilbert* dissenters. [52] The voting rights area provided another instance of Congress's reversing the Supreme Court, with the Court then upholding Congress's action: after the Court had adopted a restrictive test for "discrimination," when it renewed the Voting Rights Act Congress returned to an earlier test that was easier for plaintiffs to satisfy. [53] And after the Court's *Grove City College* ruling that the antidiscrimination provisions of Title IX (sex discrimination in education) applied only to specific programs that received federal funds, Congress said that if an institution received any federal funds the antidiscrimination laws applied to all of it.

The most striking instance of Congress's reversing the Supreme Court came in late 1991. After considerable resistance from President Bush, who claimed it would require "quotas" in employment, the Civil Rights Act of 1991 was passed. That one law reversed *five* rulings from the 1988 Term (June 1989) that had made far more difficult the filing of employment discrimination claims and two rulings from the 1990 Term. At the heart of that law was a provision that restored the standard for proving employment discrimination that the Court had announced in *Griggs v. Duke Power Co.* in 1971 but which it had significantly limited in *Wards Cove Packing Co. v. Atonio* (1989). [54]

These instances suggest that Congress has the last word. However, at times after Congress rewrites a statute it feels the Court has misinterpreted, the Court has resisted the new statute instead of going along with it. A famous instance from this nation's labor history involved the Court's application of the antitrust laws to unions' secondary boycotts in the *Danbury Hatters* case. Congress then protected such activity in the Clayton Act—or thought it had. But then in *Duplex Printing Press v. Deering*, the Court insisted the activity was still an improper restraint of trade. Only with New Deal labor protective statutes was the matter resolved as Congress wished.

At other times, when the Court's rulings permit further legislative action, Congress at times does nothing. A principal reason is that much of what the Court does falls within Congress's "zone of indifference." This means that the members are satisfied to accept the Court's action without taking any further action of their own. In this situation, doing nothing may be a mark of a lukewarm reaction, whether positive or negative. Another reason for legislative inaction may be that although feelings are strong, legislative forces are so evenly balanced that no agreement can be reached on a new statute. Congress's temporary failure to respond to the Court's invalidation of the new bankruptcy statute resulted from disagreement both over the proper status of bankruptcy judges and over whether further changes in the substantive provisions of bankruptcy law were needed (see pages 50–51). Here we must remember that getting Congress to move to the point of action is not easy. The Court thus makes a mistake when it treats legislative nonaction after one of its rulings as "ratification" of that ruling, as the justices often do. Yet the Court's reluctance to overturn statutory precedents (see pages 271–72) is based in part on the "ratification" idea.

Congressional nonaction after a Court ruling can itself have consequences. For example, the *Toth* decision preventing courts-martial of ex-servicemen for in-service offenses did not preclude a statute allowing them to be tried in federal district court. Such a law was never enacted, allowing some of those involved in the My Lai massacre to remain beyond the government's reach because their involvement was not discovered until after they were discharged from the service. *Branzburg v. Hayes*, in which the Court said that although the First Amendment itself did not provide protection for news media personnel refusing to reveal confidential sources to a grand jury, federal and state "shield laws" were permissible, provides another example, because Congress has not provided such protection although many states have. Nor did Congress take action after the decision in the *Flood* case that Congress would have to act if professional baseball were to be subject to the antitrust laws. A few representatives, perhaps hoping to force the return of baseball to Washington, D.C., did introduce bills on the subject. (Yes, sports fans, Washington once did have a team, the Senators, whose performance led to the saying, "Washington: First in War, First in Peace, and Last in the American League.") Congressional action became unnecessary when the baseball players themselves forced an arbitration that resolved the issue—largely in their favor.

Congress's *reaction* to the Court should not make us forget its *use* of judicially developed doctrine. Both point to the question of whether and to what degree Congress should defer to the Court's judgment. Here it is important to remember that although attacks on the Court are not prevented, "reversal bills" have been less likely to pass when arguments about the Court's sacrosanct nature have been used frequently. Broad attacks on the Court also produce more arguments that the Court should remain inviolate than do "decision-reversal" proposals.[55]

In addition to using the Court's legitimacy to support their positions, members of Congress rely on the Court to resolve difficult problems. For example, in debating a ban on "dial-a-porn," the chief sponsor of the ban said, "Nobody really knows what the outlook is constitutionally. People want it banned. Let the Supreme Court rule on constitutionality. Congress's role is to adopt public policy that measures the will of the people."[56] When an issue is particularly complex,

Congress may stop when it has made a general policy statement, usually a result of legislative compromise, and thus leave it up to the justices to make policy as they apply the laws. Views that can be found in Congress include the "tripartite" position, whose holders feel that Congress itself should decide matters of constitutionality and think that such questions are raised seriously, and the "judicial monopoly" position, according to which questions of constitutionality should be referred to the courts for decisions by judicial experts. Those adopting the latter position, who have been more likely to think that constitutional issues are raised primarily as political maneuvers, are particularly likely to wish to refer matters to the courts when the Court has not ruled on them.[57] However, a strong argument can be made that Congress has in fact debated vigorously on constitutional issues, such as the Bank of the United States, Congress's investigative power, the war-making power, removal from office, and the legislative veto, *before* the courts ruled on them.[58]

Moreover, in recent years, Congress as a whole has done more to monitor court decisions affecting itself and has provided the capacity to defend its position in court. The Senate created the Office of Senate Legal Counsel and there are several attorneys on the staff of the Clerk of the House. This allows the legislators to learn of cases affecting institutional interests as those cases progress through the lower courts and thus to submit *amicus* briefs indicating congressional concerns. It also allows the Congress to present its position when the Department of Justice (which usually defends federal statutes and Congress's prerogatives) fails to do so or withdraws as cases approach the Supreme Court, and Congress's lawyers have participated in major recent cases.

We might also note that Congress's different committees react differently to court rulings. For example, members of the House Interior Committee react only to rulings with constituency impact, but those on the Judiciary and Energy Committees pay heed to cases with national policy consequences. The Judiciary Committee also "treats the courts with more deference" than do members of the other committees, but pay closer attention to the rulings, which committee staff, not outsiders (including constituents), are likely to bring to their attention. Judiciary also has formal rules against interfering with ongoing litigation.[59]

The Court and the Presidency[60]

In ruling on actions by the president, the Supreme Court has established important legal doctrine on matters like his ability to remove officials and, more recently, executive privilege. At the same time, the Court has exercised self-restraint and stayed out of most issues of foreign policy and national security or has upheld the president's power in those fields. Even when a challenge to executive authority is taken to the Supreme Court, the justices have often decided not to accept it. For example, when President Carter's enforcement by executive order of wage-price guidelines through government procurement policy—canceling contracts or prohibiting businesses from bidding if they did not comply with the guidelines—was challenged, and after the Court of Appeals for the District of Columbia ruled there was an adequate statutory basis for the president's action, the Supreme Court refused to grant review.[61] The Court similarly denied review when members of the House of Representatives argued that the president should have submitted to both houses of Congress the Panama Canal treaty under which our control of the Canal Zone was terminated; the appellate court had ruled that treaties were a constitutionally proper way of disposing of property.[62] The Court came closer to involvement in the challenge to President Carter's unilateral termination of the 1954 Mutual Defense Treaty with Taiwan. A district judge ruled that a defense treaty could be terminated only by two-thirds of the Senate or a majority of both houses of Congress, but the court of appeals promptly ruled in the president's favor. The Supreme Court then ordered the suit dismissed (*Goldwater v. Carter*, 1979). Four justices said the case posed a "political question," while another said the question was not ripe for review. Only one justice voted to affirm the appeals court and two more would have heard argument. Somewhat the same result occurred in 1985 in the El Salvador pocket veto situation (see page 312). Such self-restraint means that the constitutional dispute between the president and Congress continues, but with the judiciary often not central to the process.

Decisions on topics like the removal power and executive privilege are only one part of the relations between president and the judiciary. A key element of executive-judicial relations is, of course, judicial selection (see Chapter 3). Recently the Court avoided a constitutional question when it ruled that the Federal Advisory Committee Act did not apply to the American Bar Association's Standing Committee on the Judiciary when it was considering evaluation of federal judges; had the Act applied, the Court would have had to decide whether Congress could thus interfere with the president's obtaining of advice concerning his function of nominating judges. (Justice Kennedy, concurring, said there would be such interference.)[63]

One type of activity considered highly unusual was the surveillance by the Federal Bureau of Investigation (FBI) of the Supreme Court from 1932 to 1985, primarily during the tenure of Director J. Edgar Hoover. Court employees were used as sources, and the conversations of several justices were overheard—although perhaps during surveillance of others rather than directly of the justices themselves. The result was over 2,000 pages of files kept by the FBI. In addition, a biographer of Hoover stated that Chief Justice Burger sought FBI assistance in selecting court administrators who would somehow restrain appellate court opinions—a claim denied by someone speaking for the former Chief Justice.[64]

Naming individuals to the courts gains "access" to the judiciary by having someone predisposed to one's position. Presidents wishing to have the Supreme Court adopt a particular policy agenda will find themselves at a disadvantage if vacancies do not occur. This was FDR's problem in the 1930s, when no vacancy occurred during his first term. Having access through one's appointees is important, as informal contacts are limited, and direct formal contact is limited to such occasions as the members of the Court being invited to a White House dinner. This makes most interaction between the president and the Court indirect and the result of official, public actions when the justices rule on executive department actions and on challenges to presidential policies after Congress has enacted them into law and implementing regulations are promulgated. However, an increasing number of lawsuits against the executive branch are being brought not by private citizens or business but by members of Congress, particularly over exercise of the war and appointment powers and certain agency activities.

Famous confrontations between president and Court have been few but they have received considerable attention because we tend to focus on negative actions, when the Court strikes down the president's acts or the president appears to defy the Court. More important is that the president makes independent judgments on the constitutionality of policies—as President Andrew Jackson did in vetoing the bill for a national bank after the Court had upheld the constitutionality of such an entity. Also important, but of lower visibility, is when the president fails to exhibit leadership in enforcing Supreme Court rulings. Perhaps the clearest example is President Eisenhower's never having made a positive statement about *Brown v. Board of Education*[65]; a contrast is provided by President John Kennedy's explicit support for the Court's widely criticized school prayer rulings.

The conflicts between president and Court include President Lincoln's rejection of Chief Justice Taney's order to release a prisoner imprisoned by Lincoln after his suspension of habeas corpus. Even President Andrew Jackson's famous statement, "Mr. Justice Marshall has made his decision; now let him enforce it," seemingly the epitome of resistance, involved not direct defiance but reluctance to assist in enforcing a Supreme Court mandate directed at the State of Georgia. Only five presidents (Jefferson, Jackson, Lincoln, Franklin Roosevelt, and Nixon) have been engaged in direct conflict with the judiciary. Only one administration (Nixon) was frequently involved in litigation, when the courts regularly were asked to invalidate the president's acts or to force him to do what he had not done. Many of these controversies never reached the Supreme Court because the administration did not appeal adverse lower court decisions, hoping thus to limit their legal effect.

Major conflicts seem to have occurred more frequently after a change in the political party controlling the presidency. Conflicts between Jeffersonian Democrats and Federalists came after the former displaced the latter, although Marshall finessed the conflict in *Marbury* (see pages 78–80); Franklin Roosevelt's problems certainly stemmed from justices appointed by a Republican president. On the other hand, Nixon's troubles came with a Court including his own appointees.

Another type of conflict does not involve the presidency per se but the president's policies. The association of the president or his administration with specific policies may be so great that they are seen as an extension of the presidency. This is particularly so when the solicitor general files briefs directly and clearly embodying the administration's earlier positions, such as those on affirmative action and abortion in the Reagan administration (see pages 147–48). When the administration so obviously "puts itself on the line" and the Court rebuffs the administration's position, the Court's ruling is properly seen as a defeat not merely for the policy but for the president.

The best-known conflict between Court and president prior to President Nixon's troubles involved Franklin Roosevelt and the Hughes Court. Roosevelt, angry about the Court's invalidation of New Deal legislation, raised the Court as an issue in the 1936 campaign, but did not indicate what he would do if the Court did not change direction. In 1937, he proposed that for every justice over the age of 70 who did not retire, an additional justice could be named. The president clearly wished to use the new appointments to neutralize justices opposed to his program, although he said that the change was needed in the interest of judicial efficiency. That premise was undercut by Chief Justice Hughes's letter to the Senate Judiciary Committee that the Court was current in its work. While developing the Court-packing plan with Attorney General Homer Cummings, Roosevelt had paid little attention to signs of potential opposition to the proposal. Thus he was caught unprepared by the strong disapproval that arose even among his own supporters.[66] That disapproval, coupled with the Court's shift in position on major economic regulation issues and Justice Van Devanter's announcement of his retirement, led to the plan's defeat. (When the Court upheld the Wagner Act, in the *Jones & Laughlin* case, Roosevelt lost more than 4 percent of the public opinion, and he lost more than another 5 percent when Justice Van Devanter resigned.[67]) However, it can be said that FDR won his "campaign" because the Court—with new members replacing the conservative justices—sustained a wide variety of economic regulatory measures.

Nixon Cases. Impoundment of funds and executive privilege were at the heart of President Richard Nixon's extended court troubles. Generating a large number of cases was the issue of funds allotted or appropriated by Congress and then impounded by the president because he felt priorities must be given to other programs or that the expenditures would be inflationary. The government lost *over 30* lower court decisions involving funds for education programs, mental health centers, highways, and environmental programs. Then the justices unanimously ruled against the president's actions on the basis that Congress, intending to spend the money to solve what it thought were important problems, would not have undercut itself by giving the president unlimited impoundment power (*Train v. City of New York, Train v. Campaign Clear Water,* 1975). The president's loss was in a way anticlimactic because of the Impoundment Control Act of 1974, which allowed impoundment or deferral of appropriated funds only after congressional consideration. When President Reagan tried to defer spending for domestic programs, saying that to block the deferral Congress would have to pass a law subject to his veto, the lower courts eliminated the deferral provision of the 1974 Act, thus defeating the president's efforts.

Far more serious than impoundment were the continuous confrontations over the release of the Watergate tapes. Prior to the Watergate cases the administration had asserted that the Department of Justice, not the courts, should determine the relevance to a prosecution of conversations overheard during electronic surveillance. The Supreme Court refused to accept the department's own determination of nonrelevance and held, in the *Alderman* case (1969), that a defendant alleging improper interception of conversations was entitled to inspect the "logs" of those conversations. The administration's response was to threaten not to tell the courts of the existence of foreign intelligence surveillance the department thought irrelevant. Not intimidated, the Court refused to change its position. The Court also handed the administration another defeat when it unanimously ruled in *United States v. U.S. District Court* (1972) that electronic surveillance in *domestic* security cases could not be conducted without a proper warrant, because Congress had meant to restrict the 1968 Omnibus Crime Control Act's exceptions to the warrant requirement. Perhaps more important, the Court said that surveillance had to be controlled by judges: the executive branch could not be the sole judge of whether surveillance should take place.[68]

In initial action concerning the Watergate tapes, lower courts ruled that, because the need for information for criminal proceedings was superior to the president's claims of authority to withhold material, a *judge*, not the executive acting alone, must decide the president's claim that certain materials should be withheld. The president at first said he would comply only with a "definitive ruling" from the Supreme Court (meaning a vote of at least 7–2). This meant the president reserved to himself the power to accept or reject matters of constitutional interpretation. Having ascertained that apparently only Justice Rehnquist and possibly Chief Justice Burger would have voted for his position, the president chose not to appeal to the Supreme Court. Compliance with a lower court ruling came only after the "Saturday night massacre" in which Special Prosecutor Archibald Cox and the attorney general were fired (by Solicitor General Bork, as acting attorney general).[69]

The Supreme Court's definitive ruling in the Watergate tapes matter, the unanimous decision in *United States v. Nixon*, came when the president refused to comply with Judge Sirica's subsequent order for production of a much larger number of tapes for the Watergate cover-up trial. The justices emphasized their power to determine the constitutionality of claims made by other branches of government, whether pursuant to express or implied constitutional provisions. Chief Justice Burger twice used Chief Justice Marshall's *Marbury v. Madison* language that it is "emphatically the province and the duty" of the Court "to say what the law is." The Court did legitimize "executive privilege" by recognizing that the president needed the "complete candor and objectivity from advisers" which confidentiality of communications would assist. However, balancing that interest against the requirements of the criminal process, the Court struck the balance against the president, who could not be above the law. The decision, with which the president complied, helped send him from office. The recognition of executive privilege may, however, have been a more far-reaching result of the case.

Closely related was the Court's legitimation of absolute immunity for the president from civil damage suits, which did not come until long after Nixon had left office. By a 5–4 vote the Court ruled in *Nixon v. Fitzgerald* (1982) that the president had absolute immunity from civil suits for damages for acts within the "outer perimeter" of his official responsibility, unless Congress authorized such lawsuits. Our system of checks and balances, including impeachment, was available to constrain the president, who, because of his "unique status," could be treated differently from other executive officials. Presidential assistants, however, were entitled to only qualified (limited) immunity from suit, although those involved in national security and foreign policy work might be entitled to absolute immunity (*Harlow v. Fitzgerald*, 1982). The *Fitzgerald* litigation led to failure of some suits against Nixon administration officials for improper electronic surveillance, but the Supreme Court ruled that the attorney general was entitled to only qualified immunity when sued for acting unconstitutionally in connection with his national security duties.[70] The issue of President Nixon's pardon by President Ford did not reach the Supreme Court,[71] but the Court had said in *Schick v. Reed* (1974) that the president had broad discretion to treat individually each commutation and pardon he chose to issue and to attach conditions, even those not mentioned in the statutes.

After Congress, in the Presidential Recordings and Materials Preservation Act, set aside President Nixon's agreement with the General Services Administration (GSA) on disposition of his presidential papers and provided for screening of materials by archivists and return of purely private material, with safeguards against disclosure of materials affecting confidential communications with the president, the Court sustained the Act in *Nixon v. Administrator of General Services* (1977). The law was not a bill of attainder because the president was a legitimate "class of one" on which Congress, acting to protect materials, not to punish, could legislate.

The Court then ruled in *Nixon v. Warner Communications* (1978) that neither a common law right of access nor the First Amendment required release of the tapes; the lower courts could use their informed discretion in providing procedures for release of materials that had been used in judicial proceedings and in limiting release of those materials. Even this ruling did not end Nixon's resistance to release of materials. In 1982 the Court of Appeals for the District of Columbia upheld allowing the public to listen to the president's tapes, including those from the cover-up trial, after archivists had reviewed them in accordance with statutory procedures. After each new set of regulations concerning screening and release of materials other than the tapes, court orders have been sought blocking release of material. Some of the Nixon papers were made available only in late 1986. Many of the most sensitive documents are still unavailable.

Reagan Administration. As a candidate, President Reagan inveighed against the Court's "abuse of power." There was no direct conflict between the Supreme Court and the presidency during his administration, but criticism of the Court's position, particularly from Justice Department officials, continued almost unabated, even increasing in volume in his second term, as the president, like Roosevelt 50 years earlier, tried to rein in a meddlesome Court. In September 1986, Assistant Attorney General for Civil Rights Bradford Reynolds attacked Justice Brennan for trying to attain "a radically egalitarian society" that was a "threat to individual liberty" and also criticized Brennan's noninterpretivist reading of the Constitution. Most criticism focused on specific rulings. Particularly attacked were *Miranda*, which Attorney General Meese said in 1986 should be overturned, and rulings on church-state relations. The attorney general said those on school and religion were "bizarre," and Secretary of Education William Bennett complained that released-time and shared-time decisions failed to recognize the importance of Judeo-Christian values—and gave school districts a year in which to comply.

The Iran-Contra affair raised a number of issues concerning relations between the president and the judiciary. One was executive privilege, which was asserted to block Admiral Poindexter's efforts to obtain ex-President Reagan's diaries after a judge had ordered them turned over to Poindexter. Another was whether the president could be made to testify in a criminal case. Although his appearance at the trial of Col. Oliver North had been blocked, he did present a deposition in the Poindexter case, in a courtroom near his California home. (The reversal of the North and Poindexter convictions was on other legal grounds, relating to the protection given by legislative grants of immunity.) Still another issue was whether the government would release classified information sought by defendant Joseph Fernandez under the Classified Information and Procedures Act (CIPA); when the administration refused to do so, the case against Fernandez was dismissed.

The last issue indicates the unwillingness of the Justice Department to cooperate with the independent counsel ("special prosecutor") pursuing the Iran-Contra cases. The constitutionality of appointment of such prosecutors was challenged, and, after several negative lower court rulings, was upheld in a case not connected with Iran-Contra. The basic legal issues were whether a prosecutor (usually considered an executive branch official) could be appointed by federal judges, and whether limits on removal of independent counsel, imposed by Congress in the Ethics in Government Act, improperly constrained the president. (Lawrence Walsh, the Iran-Contra special prosecutor, had also accepted a separate appointment from the Department of Justice to avoid such a challenge to his authority.)

In *Morrison v. Olson* (1988), the Court rejected the challenges to the independent counsel provisions, saying there was no violation of the Appointments Clause (as "inferior" officers, they could be appointed by "courts of Law"), of Article III (judges could appoint prosecutors), or of the separation of powers. Although more doubtful about judges' ability to remove independent counsel than to appoint them (there was no problem with interbranch appointments), the Court did not find the removal provision "a significant judicial encroachment upon executive power or upon the prosecutorial discretion of the independent counsel." Likewise, limits on the attorney general's power to remove independent counsel (limited to "good cause") were acceptable because Congress had not imposed them to increase its own power; the president's power over prosecutors was *reduced* but the attorney general retained adequate control.

The administration's policy concerning enforcement of certain laws brought it into regular conflict with the lower federal judiciary; the Reagan administration thumbed its nose at those courts. For example, the Office of Management and Budget instructed government agencies not to follow the "invalid provisions" of the Competition in Contracting Act, authorizing the General Accounting Office (GAO) to review disputed contracts. When a federal judge ordered the Secretary of Defense and the Director of OMB to comply, Attorney General Meese argued that the administration had the constitutional authority not to obey a statute approved by Congress and signed by the president, prompting bipartisan legislative criticism. The Supreme Court did not rule on the contracting statute, granting review to a ruling against the president but then dismissing it at the parties' request.[72] President Reagan had taken to adding statements to bills when he signed them into law, as to his understanding of what those laws meant—to counter statements of "legislative history" by members of Congress. President Bush, taking the practice further, added statements that he would not enforce certain provisions he regarded as infringements on the president's authority.

More frequent conflict occurred over the Reagan administration's policy of "nonacquiescence" in disliked judicial decisions, where the primary battleground was Social Security disability benefits. When the administration, saying the disabled had the burden of proving they were still disabled, removed large numbers of people from the disability benefit rolls, a number of courts ruled against the Department of Health and Human Services (HHS). Although other agencies generally follow adverse court of appeals rulings within the same circuit, HHS, under its "nonacquiescence" policy, neither appealed defeats to the Supreme Court for a definitive ruling nor considered the lower court rulings binding beyond the individual involved in the case. Judges blasted the department, saying its position undermined the rule of law and violated the Constitution; one appellate judge called it like the discredited policy of "nullification" of disliked laws. The U.S. attorney for the Southern District of New York, a former Reagan administration deputy attorney general, refused to defend the government in some of its Social Security disability cases because of this position. Finally Congress passed a bill changing the burden of proof with respect to removing people from disability benefits and applying the standard to those involved in class actions. The Social Security Administration also changed its policy, giving somewhat more weight to court of appeals rulings if the agency's own rules would lead to a denial of benefits. But it still was unwilling to follow judicial determinations throughout all its own processes.[73]

The "nonacquiescence" controversy should not lead us to overestimate the extent to which the executive branch disobeys the courts or to which the president and the courts are in conflict. There are many instances in which the president, despite conflict with the courts over other matters, follows what the Court requires. For example, after the Court provided that the Takings Clause of the Constitution was applicable when a government regulation affecting the use of property was overturned, President Reagan issued Executive Order 12630, "Governmental Actions and Interference with Constitutionally Protected Property Rights," to change federal policy to make it congruent with the Court's rulings.[74]

Overall, presidents have fared well in the federal courts, although presidential power has been supported more in some areas than in others.[75] Of over 400 federal court cases from 1949 through 1984, 70 percent were decided in the president's favor. The most successful president was Lyndon Johnson (92%), while Nixon was the least successful (58%). The third and fourth decades after World War II showed lower support for presidential power than the two decades immediately after the war. The decreased support was accompanied by a long-term upward trend in litigation involving presidential power. That trend holds even if we remove litigation against the Nixon administration. Foreign affairs issues constituted the largest number of cases, with the war power next, but the foreign affairs area was the one in which the president was most successful (losing only 19 of 100 decisions). Presidential power is likely to be rejected or limited in issues of spending, where Nixon impoundment actions accounted for many of the cases, and executive privilege and confidentiality. If one looks at all federal cases, trial and appellate, the judges appear to react to "two presidencies"—one domestic, one foreign. That distinction does not apply for district court rulings alone.

A more recent test of federal judges' support for the president can be found in abortion policy, which Presidents Reagan and Bush made a part of their election platforms and then looked more closely at prospective judges' positions on that subject and other aspects of the "social agenda." Indeed, we find that President Reagan's judicial appointees were less likely than President Carter's appointees to support social regulation or criminal defendants' claims—but there was little difference concerning economic regulation and voting disputes, which were not part of the campaign platform. Reagan's appointees show *much* greater resistance to abortion rights, not only compared with Carter's appointees (77% resistance to 13%) but even compared with Republican President Nixon's appointees (21%, much closer to Carter's judicial selections). Other factors do, however, play a role, with Catholic appointees of each president more resistant to abortion than non-Catholics and Southern judges by far more likely than Northern judges to be resistant.[76]

Areas of Presidential Power. The Court's rulings on presidential power have come in several major areas. One is the appointment power. Particularly significant have been the Court's adverse rulings on the president's right to dismiss employees. Although the Court, in *Myers v. United States* (1926), speaking through Chief Justice (and former President) William Howard Taft, upheld the president's authority to discharge a postmaster, the justices ruled, in *Humphrey's Executor v. United States* (1935), that Congress could limit the president's power to discharge members of regulatory commissions on grounds of political disagreement as the commissioners were expected to play a quasi-judicial role requiring their independence. This was the decision that most infuriated President Roosevelt.[77] The Court has also ruled that although the president cannot insist on the right to remove members of a commission, he is entitled to be involved in the appointment process when commission members have enforcement and administrative powers making them "officers of the United States" (*Buckley v. Valeo*, 1976).

Another subject was delegation of authority, whether Congress could turn over considerable policy-making authority to those administering the law. The only two rulings against the president went against FDR. In the *Panama Refining* case, with liberal and conservative justices agreeing, the Court overturned Congress's grant of authority to embargo shipments of oil produced in excess of state quotas ("hot oil") because Congress had not provided standards by which the president could determine when to act. "This is delegation run riot," said Justice Cardozo. The Court also ruled in the *Schechter Poultry Corporation* case that the National Industrial Recovery Act, under which "codes of fair competition" were developed by industry groups and promulgated by the president, was infected by improper delegation. (The chickens in the case were also infected.) Because the NIRA was at the heart of Roosevelt's economic program, the ruling was even more important than *Panama Refining*, but as his attention had shifted to other programs by the time of the ruling, he may not have been particularly distressed by the Court's action. At almost the same time, the Court upheld delegation without standards in the foreign affairs area in the *Curtiss-Wright Export Corporation* case, a challenge to another presidential embargo (on the sale of arms to warring Latin American countries) imposed pursuant to a congressional grant. In so doing, the Court underscored the executive's relative independence in foreign policy under the Constitution.

Curtiss-Wright is still the law—Col. North tried to use it to justify his actions—but in domestic policy the Court has repeatedly accepted delegations of authority couched in terms at least as broad/vague as those involved in *Panama*. For example, the Court sustained actions by Presidents Nixon and Ford increasing fees on imported oil because the statute had authorized the presidential action, standards had also been provided, and the president's actions were limited so that he could do only what was necessary to prevent damage to the national security.[78] More recently, in dealing with the constitutionality of the Sentencing Commission, charged with providing sentencing guidelines for federal judges, the Court strongly endorsed the delegation of authority "under broad general directives" so that Congress could obtain necessary assistance in dealing "with ever changing and more technical problems."[79]

War Powers and Foreign Policy. Judges have generally been quite unwilling to challenge the president's war-making authority, at least until after a war is over. As Rossiter observed, "Whatever limits the Court has set upon the employment of the war powers have been largely theoretical, rarely practical," and the impression left by the Court's rulings has generally been that "as in the past, so in the future, President and Congress will fight our wars with little or no thought about a reckoning with the Supreme Court."[80] *Ex parte Milligan*, invalidating the practice of trying civilians at courts-martial when the civilian courts were operating, contained stern words applying the Constitution to the president (Lincoln), but it came after the Civil War had ended. During the war, the Court had ruled in *Ex parte Vallandigham* (1864) that it lacked appellate jurisdiction over military court proceedings. Moreover, in a case involving the blockade of the South, the Court sustained Lincoln's ability to wage war without a congressional declaration of war in *The Prize Cases* (1863), and, in *Texas v. White* (1869), upheld his theory of the relation between the seceded states and the Union.

In World War II, the Court sustained use of a military commission to try German saboteurs who had landed in the United States (*Ex parte Quirin*, 1942), and in the *Korematsu* case President Franklin Roosevelt's relocation of the Japanese-Americans was sustained, not on limited grounds of "military necessity" but specifically as valid under the Constitution. (The Court did say in *Ex parte Endo* that, once found to be loyal, a relocated citizen must be released.) The Court did refuse to uphold the imposition of martial law in Hawaii, but did not issue that ruling until after the war's end.[81] In the mid-1980s, lower court judges set aside the 40-year-old convictions of the Japanese-Americans tried for curfew and relocation violations because the government had withheld from the courts information bearing on the validity of the underlying orders.[82] The Supreme Court deferred a suit for compensation on behalf of those relocated, ruling it had been appealed to the wrong lower court (*United States v. Hohri*, 1987). Congress did enact a reparations statute for those interned in World War II, and in 1988 made those payments an "entitlement" under the budget law. This indicates the extended time that can elapse before a major issue plays out fully.

In 1952, President Truman seized the steel mills to avoid their shutdown as a result of a labor dispute tied to wage-price control problems, basing his action in part on the war power: if the mills closed, our national security would be endangered. But in court his lawyers insisted on the president's "inherent power," not grounded in specific statutes or constitutional provisions, to make the seizure. This argument led the Court to invalidate the seizure in *Youngstown Sheet & Tube Co. v. Sawyer* (1952), because Congress had provided means for handling such situations, particularly where there was no real emergency, and moreover had refused to enact the broader provisions Truman had requested. Justice Black, in his opinion for the Court, directly rejected the president's "inherent powers" argument. The concurring and dissenting opinions together, however, show that a majority of justices did not denounce such powers outright, leaving the possibility of their use where Congress had not spoken. Truman's compliance was immediate, but the Court's ruling may have taught the president to use with business and labor "several lesser sanctions none of which is as potent as seizure but the cumulative impact of which enables the President to prevail."[83]

Many efforts were made to challenge the war in Vietnam because Congress had not declared war and because the war was said to violate international law.[84] Using the "political question" doctrine or ruling that by making appropriations Congress had acquiesced in the war, lower courts refused to interfere. The Supreme Court consistently refused to grant review, despite consistent dissents by Justice Douglas, joined occasionally by Justice Stewart and once by Justice Harlan. The Supreme Court also avoided a ruling after Representative Elizabeth Holtzman (D-N.Y.) obtained an injunction against further bombing of Cambodia because the bombing lacked congressional authorization. After an appeals court stay of the injunction, Justice Marshall, as circuit justice, would not act but did say both that the issue might be justiciable and that the president could not wage war "without some form of congressional approval" except in extreme emergencies. When the plaintiffs persuaded Justice Douglas to vacate the stay, the Defense Department threatened noncompliance, and the entire Court overruled Douglas the same day, directly staying the district court injunction. The result of this maneuvering was the usual one of judicial noninterference in war matters.[85]

The agreement that ended the Iran hostage crisis obligated the United States to terminate all legal proceedings in U.S. courts involving claims against Iran and its state enterprises and to nullify attachments against Iranian property. Under implementing regulations, the president allowed judicial proceedings against Iran but no entry of judgment. When a district judge issued orders of attachment, the Supreme Court decided a challenge eight days after oral argument, only slightly more than two weeks before the deadline for transfer of Iranian assets. The virtually unanimous Court, confining its ruling "only to the very questions necessary to decision of the case," upheld the broad authority given the president by Congress, even though his action in dealing with a foreign policy emergency had restricted judicial power (*Dames & Moore v. Regan*, 1981). The president had authority to settle claims when settlement "has been determined to be a necessary incident to the resolution of a major foreign policy dispute between our country and another, and where Congress acquiesced in the President's action." Thus the Court again did not interfere with the president. The justices were, however, careful to note that courts were not being stripped of their jurisdiction.

We have hardly seen the last conflict before the judiciary over the president's war powers and foreign policy authority. Controversy over the sending of military advisers to El Salvador, the invasion of Grenada, and, in particular, the controversy over our Marines' presence in Lebanon, led some Senate leaders, joined by White House officials, to think about bringing a test case to obtain a Supreme Court ruling on the constitutionality of the War Powers Act, but it was not brought. Nor did challenges to Operation Desert Storm, including a suit by 45 House Democrats to bar President Bush from offensive action in the Gulf without a declaration of war or other explicit authority, get anywhere, in part because of the fast pace of military events in Iraq.

In any event, the rulings by the courts and their refusal otherwise to decide cases would seem to provide further evidence that "the rare decision" in which the justices "shout 'Check!' at the President" has not "had the presumably salutary effect of keeping the Presidency in rein, to say nothing of rendering it [check]mated. The most effective restraints upon both the Presidency and the Congress have been those imposed by other components of the national political system."[86]

The Courts and the Regulatory Agencies

The regulatory commissions and executive branch departments performing regulatory tasks handle many more cases than do federal district courts. In the commissions' early years, courts were often hostile to them. Now the lower courts and the Supreme Court allow them and executive agencies considerable discretion. Because agency and court jurisdictions overlap at times, the courts also have to help distribute responsibilities among agencies, or, as in the field of labor law, among agencies, arbitrators deciding cases closely related to agency jurisdiction, and courts.

The Supreme Court initially restricted agencies' jurisdiction and the weight to be given their determinations. Decisions like the one stating that the Interstate Commerce Commission could determine only whether railroad-proposed rates were reasonable led the ICC to concede that "by virtue of judicial decisions, it has ceased to be a body for the regulation of interstate carriers."[87] Similarly, the ruling in the *Gratz* case that methods of unfair competition unknown before passage of the Federal Trade Commission Act were not within the FTC's jurisdiction, and that the courts would identify those methods, led the commission to stop trying to prohibit new unfair trade practices. However, when the Court held in the *Winstead Hosiery* case that the FTC could deal with false advertising and misbranding, the commission's level of activity on those subjects increased. The Court's later decision that the FTC could deal with only false advertising that was both unfair *and* a method of competition had to be overruled by Congress. Only in 1934 in the *Keppel Brothers* case would the Court give weight to the FTC's determination of what practices would be considered unfair.

The courts' later more deferential approach to agency action resulted both from judges' greater familiarity with the agencies, new judges' more favorable attitudes toward regulation, and a greater recognition of the necessity of letting the agencies operate with less supervision lest the courts be swamped with cases appealed from the agencies. Instead of having the courts subject even the agencies' factual determinations to *de novo* review, Congress developed doctrines, enforced by the courts, that decreased judicial oversight of the agencies' work. Judicial review has been ruled unavailable in some situations; in others, courts have insisted that various steps must be followed prior to judicial review (*exhaustion of administrative remedies*); and courts examining agency rulings have generally limited themselves to determining whether "substantial evidence" supports agency actions. Courts interpreting the law applied by the agencies and commissions do continue to determine whether agencies are acting within the scope of authority granted them by Congress. For example, the Supreme Court ruled, in *Hampton v. Mow Sun Wong* (1976), that the Civil Service Commission's exclusion of aliens from federal government employment, far from the commission's core duties, had not been explicitly authorized. (The president then issued an executive order embodying the appropriate authorization.)

The courts now sustain agency actions in a high proportion of these cases, and courts have available a battery of rules to assist them in sustaining agency actions challenged in court. One rule is to give great weight to agency interpretations of the statutes under which they operate. Thus, in reviewing Department of Justice "preclearance" decisions under the Voting Rights Act of 1965, the Court has shown substantial deference to the attorney general's rulings on whether changes in voting procedures have the purpose or effect of discriminating against minorities. The Court's position and the agency's stance *converged* through interaction, making it easier for the Court's majority to draw upon the executive's position. This is similar to the pattern found in appeals court rulings on the Federal Power Commission.[88] Likewise, judicial decisions on the Clean Air Act shaped agency programs. Not only did specific court rulings have an effect but "anticipation of judicial review . . . influenced the EPA's regulations. . . ."[89] As Justice Stevens has observed, "The relationship between the Courts or agencies, on the one hand, and Congress, on the other, is a dynamic one," with Congress "leav[ing] open spaces in the law that the courts are implicitly authorized to fill" and having the responsibility for making further changes.[90] With division in government about the proper course of policy, judicial rulings assist some "players" to achieve their goals. Within the EPA, the courts' rulings "helped political executives gain control over lower levels of the bureaucracy."[91]

The Court also initially restricted the agencies procedurally. While the Court finally came around to giving administrators greater freedom of action, the Court's restrictive rulings caused reexamination of the agencies' procedures and helped lead to their codification in the Administrative Procedure Act of 1946. Holding action or inaction not subject to judicial review under the Act or other statutes helps the agency. The Act's "substantial evidence" standard and closely related tests, such as whether agency actions are "arbitrary and capricious," generally produce deference to the agencies.[92] The Court says that it does not weigh the evidence presented to an agency, except to see whether there is enough to support the agency's result, and that it does not judge the "wisdom" of the agency's action. Sometimes, however, the justices manage to send an agency "multiple messages" by saying they support the agency position while indicating strong misgivings. For example, in voting to sustain a Federal Communications Commission order, Chief Justice Burger said he was unsure that the FCC had made the right decision, but that as a justice of the Supreme Court, he could not "resolve this issue as perhaps I would were I a member of the . . . Commission."[93]

Generally, the Court has said that agencies need to explain how they have reached their conclusions, even if they do not produce the ultimate in clarity. To reinforce this, the justices have invalidated agency orders not linking findings and conclusions. These rules apply to decisions to deregulate by eliminating regulations (which the courts say is not the same as not issuing a regulation in the first place) as well as decisions to regulate, as can be seen in the Court's ruling that the National Highway Traffic Safety Agency had not properly rescinded the "air bag" rule.[94] Also quite important for executive efforts to deregulate was a 1990 ruling of the Court striking down efforts by the Office of Management and Budget (OMB), closely tied to the president, to use the Paperwork Reduction Act to review proposed agency regulations (for notifying those exposed to potentially hazardous substances). In *Dole v. Steelworkers* (1990), holding that the Act did not provide OMB with the authority it had exercised, the Court could be seen as sending a further message that efforts to deregulate or limit regulation must follow proper legal procedures.

Application of the Freedom of Information Act (FOIA), which has a general policy of disclosure but contains many exemptions, has also provided tests of the Court's deference to agencies' use of exemptions to withhold information. In its first FOIA ruling, *Environmental Protection Agency v. Mink* (1973), the Supreme Court upheld the EPA's refusal to provide members of Congress information about an underground nuclear test because relevant documents, classified Secret or Top Secret, were exempted from disclosure. The Court also said that courts could not examine the questioned materials but should accept agency determinations concerning classification. Congress thereupon limited the materials that could be withheld as classified and provided for judicial examination of the documents, thus giving the courts authority the Supreme Court had declined to exercise. By and large, the court strengthened the agencies' hand by ruling that they need not release documents that were not final opinions. However, the justices have also ruled in favor of disclosure of final opinions and of materials that would not produce a "clearly unwarranted" invasion of privacy, and have decided that private companies, such as government contractors, could not prevent release of information otherwise obtained by the government.[95]

As this suggests, the court's deference to agencies has limits. For one thing, the Court does not always follow agency interpretations of statutes. In the *Gilbert* case (see page 321) the Court refused to follow Equal Employment Opportunity Commission guidelines treating pregnancy as a disability. Particularly significant was the Court's invalidation of Occupational Safety and Health Administration's (OSHA) rules on occupational exposure to benzene because the secretary of labor had not made the required threshold determination that the particular toxic substance posed a significant workplace health risk.[96] That ruling, coupled with the Reagan administration's emphasis on deregulation and the availability of fewer research dollars for OSHA, was said to have made it extremely difficult to develop the data needed to meet the Court's burden of proof.[97]

The Court can also limit agency discretion by requiring due process protections for those affected by agency actions, but has not done this frequently. Typical are procedural rulings in which the Court refused to require full hearings for all aspects of new drug applications, allowing summary proceedings instead, and did not require the secretary of transportation to make formal findings in making his determination that there was no "feasible and prudent" alternative route for an interstate highway scheduled to go through a park. The court will also not allow lower courts to demand more procedurally than the Administrative Procedure Act requires.[98]

Perhaps the most notable application of due process came in the Court's 1970 *Goldberg v. Kelly* and *Wheeler v. Montgomery* rulings that welfare benefits could not be terminated without a prior evidentiary hearing even though a full HEW "fair hearing" need not be held until after termination. However, in *Mathews v. Eldridge* (1976) the Court refused to extend its earlier rule to termination of disability benefits. The test developed by the Burger Court in that case "balances the harm to legally protected rights of the individual against the costs and burdens on the agency, using the criterion of whether increased procedures would improve the accuracy of the fact-finding process."[99] This test and other recent cases contravene the conventional wisdom that the federal courts, including the Supreme Court, interfere with administrative agencies and do not allow the managers of those agencies sufficient discretion: "Recent cases indicate an increasing judicial sensitivity to management problems and priorities."[100]

Related to deference to administrative agencies is the Supreme Court's deference to the lower courts, particularly the courts of appeals, that rule initially on agency actions. Yet the Court had not hesitated to overturn lower court rulings on the basis of its own examination of the relevant statute and administrative action—even when the lower court is the U.S. Court of Appeals for the District of Columbia, the most important court of appeals for administrative law because of the high proportion of administrative agency cases it reviews.

Particularly in the 1970s, the D.C. Circuit's essentially liberal and activist posture toward the agencies led it on a path different from the Supreme Court's, making deference by the Supreme Court less likely. For example, after the Federal Communications Commission decided that market forces should prevail and that it would not consider changes in program format (from rock to jazz or from jazz to classical music) in a license renewal application, the D.C. Circuit held that the FCC's policy violated the Federal Communications Act. "Unconvinced" that the lower court's doctrine was "compelled by the Act," the Supreme Court sustained the commission, which had "provided a rational explanation for its conclusion that reliance on the market is the best method of promoting diversity in entertainment formats."[101]

As this case indicates, where agency and lower court differ, the Supreme Court can "have its pick" of policies, dressing up its conclusion in the language of deference—to the agency or to the lower court as appropriate. When lower court judges fail to recognize a Supreme Court change in posture and do not shift their positions accordingly, the justices, to try to make their point, may have to reverse those courts frequently. This was true when the Court of Customs and Patent Appeals resisted Supreme Court changes on the validity of patents.[102]

Overall Support. The Supreme Court's rate of affirmance of agency rulings has usually been in the vicinity of 70 to 80 percent. During the 1947–56 Terms, average support for the agencies was 69 percent; for the 1960–65 Terms, it was 78 percent; for the 1967 Term, the rate went to 84 percent, a further indication of term-by-term variation. Even with the Burger Court's conservative tendencies in economic regulation, 76 percent of agency actions challenged in the Supreme Court were sustained there in the 1971–73 Terms,[103] and the rate remained over 70 percent. The high level of support is particularly striking because only a very small percentage of the regulatory agencies' rulings are appealed to the courts and even fewer—the "difficult" and controversial decisions—to the Supreme Court, which denies certiorari in most cases. This means that the support level for the agencies is extremely high, with very, very few of their decisions overturned. We must, however, remember that there are situations in which the Court's rulings have no effect. These are situations in which,

> while administrative lawyers harangue each other concerning the fine points of the Supreme Court's or the D.C. Circuit's most recent procedural ruling, billions of dollars per year are being transferred, for good or ill, by an invisible army of bureaucratic adjudicators to whom court decisions may have absolutely no relevance.[104]

Not all agencies have been supported at the same level. During the Roosevelt Court, the basic range of support ran from a high of 86 percent (NLRB) to a low of 60 percent (FTC), but the FCC won fewer than half its cases before the Court. The Federal Power Commission and the Federal Trade Commission were supported at rates of over 90 percent during 1957–68, and the NLRB and Internal Revenue Service won about three-quarters of their cases, but the ICC was supported less than two-thirds of the time and the Immigration and Naturalization Service won only 56.3 percent of its cases. These differences are explained largely in terms of the agencies' substantive policies. At least through the

Warren Court, Schubert has argued, the Court supported the agencies because the agencies decided cases in the same liberal direction to which the justices were favorably inclined. Thus, where agency results were conservative, the Court was more likely to overturn the decisions.

A different look at the Warren Court's agency support scores shows that when the agency decisions were probusiness, the Court supported the agency just slightly more than half the time (52%), but when the agencies were antibusiness, support increased to almost two-thirds (65%). The Court supported two-thirds of prolabor agency decisions, but only 53 percent of antilabor rulings. The Burger Court was more likely to overturn liberal agency actions. When the NLRB was prolabor, the Burger Court supported it only 53 percent of the time, but did so in *80 percent* of the board's antilabor cases. Support for probusiness or antilabor agency decisions was higher than for prolabor and antibusiness decisions (63% to 51%).[105] For the combined Warren Court–Burger Court period (1953–88), there was a high rate of overall support for the agencies (supported almost three-fourths of the time), with little difference between the type of agency appearing before the Court (economic or social). This supports "the legal model which suggests that the Court is more concerned with procedural and evidentiary matters . . . and thus is more willing to defer to the agencies as long as they adhere to proper procedure." However, there are differences in Supreme Court outcome, dependent on whether the agency decisions are liberal or conservative, with statistically significant differences for social agency decisions (Warren Court support higher when rulings liberal, Burger Court when rulings conservative). This is a clear indication "that ideology does have an impact on Supreme Court decisions" in this area of law.[106]

The Court's overall supportive position toward the agencies can mask differences among justices. For the 1947–56 Terms, all except Black were consistent in overall support for the agencies. However, justices' value preferences appeared to affect their voting in some situations. Examples were Black and Douglas (prounion) and Chief Justice Vinson (antiunion) in labor cases and Black and Douglas in business competition cases. Black, Douglas, and Frankfurter were more likely to oppose an agency ruling when a person's freedom was involved than when it was not. All the justices were more likely to support the agencies when evidentiary questions were involved than when they were not, but some (Jackson, Reed, Burton) were particularly likely to do so. During 1957–68, differences between justices followed the Court's overall pattern. The justices' basic substantive policy attitudes had a greater effect on their voting than "due process" and "statutory authority and interpretation" dimensions of cases.[107] One could also find differences among Burger Court justices. Even among the four Nixon appointees, two (Burger and Powell) showed a relative lack of deference to the agencies, while Blackmun and Rehnquist were more deferential. Some justices are deferential in particular categories of cases—Powell when agency decisions were probusiness, Marshall when they were prolabor—while only two (Blackmun and White) seemed restrained or deferential across all categories of cases.[108]

Overall, the picture we find in examining Supreme Court judicial review at the national level is that the Court only infrequently reverses the actions of Congress, the president, or the regulatory commissions and executive branch agencies. However, it is not hesitant to do so and can have considerable effect when it does. Yet, despite an apparent lack of reaction to many of its decisions and more willing compliance in other instances, Congress rewrites statutes and at times takes more severe reversal action, and the regulatory agencies have shown themselves quite capable of resisting the High Court through delay and persistence. Judicial review certainly did not cease after 1937, although the focus of such actions shifted from economic regulation to other matters, most notably in areas of civil liberties policy. These actions and their aftermath show the Court important but not all-powerful.

Notes

1. Maeva Marcus and Emily Field Van Tassel; "Judges and Legislators in the New Federal System, 1789–1800," *Judges and Legislators: Toward Institutional Comity*, ed. Robert Katzmann (Washington, D.C.: Brookings Institution, 1988), p. 31.

2. Ibid., p. 33.

3. Ibid., p. 45.

4. See Robert A. Katzmann, "The Underlying Concerns," *Judges and Legislators*, pp. 7–30.

5. Jonathan P. Nase, "Of Dollars and Justice: The Appropriations Process of the Federal Judiciary," *Justice System Journal* 10 (Spring 1985): 72–73.

6. Ibid.

7. Thomas G. Walker and Deborah J. Barrow, "Funding the Federal Judiciary: The Congressional Connection," *Judicature* 69 (June-July 1985): 50.

8. Ibid.

9. Nase, "Of Dollars and Justice," pp. 63–64, 66.

10. Matthew D. McCubbins and Thomas Schwartz, "Congress, the Courts, and Public Policy: Consequences of the One Man, One Vote Rule," *American Journal of Political Science* 32 (May 1988): 389, 410ff.

11. See Louis Fisher, *Constitutional Conflicts Between Congress and the President* (Princeton, N.J.: Princeton University Press, 1985), pp. 184–95.

12. See Irving R. Kaufman, "Court as Court: The Role of the Judiciary in Protecting Witnesses' Rights," *Judicature* 71 (December-January 1988): 184–85, 224–26.

13. Gregory A. Caldeira and Donald J. McCrone, "Of Time and Judicial Activism: A Story of the U.S. Supreme Court, 1800–1973," *Supreme Court Activism and Restraint*, eds. Halpern and Lamb, pp. 111–13, 120–21.

14. Stuart Nagel, *The Legal Process from a Behavioral Perspective* (Homewood, Ill.: Dorsey, 1969), pp. 248, 259.

15. Bradley C. Canon and S. Sidney Ulmer, "The Supreme Court and Critical Elections: A Dissent," *American Political Science Review* 70 (December 1976): 1215–18; Richard Funston, "The Supreme Court and Critical Elections," *American Political Science Review* 69 (September 1975): 795–811; and John B. Gates, "Partisan Realignment, Unconstitutional State Policies, and the U.S. Supreme Court, 1837–1964," *American Journal of Political Science* 31 (May 1987): 259–80.

16. *Trop v. Dulles*, 356 U.S. 86 (1956), and *Kennedy v. Mendoza-Martinez*, 372 U.S. 144 (1963) (citizenship); *Reid v. Covert*, 354 U.S. 1 (1957), *United States ex rel. Toth v. Quarles*, 350 U.S. 11 (1955), and *O'Callaghan v. Parker*, 395 U.S. 258 (1969) (courts-martial); the last was overruled in *Solorio v. United States*, 483 U.S. 435 (1987).

17. For example, *Marchetti v. United States*, 390 U.S. 39 (1968) (gambling), and *Leary v. United States*, 395 U.S. 6 (1969) (marijuana tax).

18. *U.S. Department of Agriculture v. Murry*, 413 U.S. 508 (1973), and *U.S.D.A. v. Moreno*, 413 U.S. 529 (1973) (food stamps); *Weinberger v. Wiesenfeld*, 420 U.S. 630 (1975), and *Jimenez v. Weinberger*, 417 U.S. 628 (1974) (benefits); *Blount v. Rizzi*, 400 U.S. 419 (1971), *Chief of Capitol*

Police v. Jeannette Rankin Brigade, 409 U.S. 972 (1973), and *United States v. Grace*, 461 U.S. 171 (1983) (free speech); *Buckley v. Valeo*, 424 U.S. 1 (1976).

19. Louis Fisher, "Judicial Misjudgments about the Lawmaking Process: The Legislative Veto Case," *Public Administration Review* 45 (Special 1985): 706. The question recurs whether, when a legislative veto provision is invalidated by the courts, the substantive statute of which it is a part should be retained. See *Alaska Airlines v. Brock*, 480 U.S. 678 (1987). For the full story of *Chadha*, see Barbara Hinkson Craig, *Chadha: The Story of an Epic Constitutional Struggle* (New York: Oxford University Press, 1987).

20. See also *Wright v. United States*, 302 U.S. 583 (1938) (president's return of bill to Senate during three-day recess but with Senate official designated to receive messages).

21. *Kennedy v. Sampson*, 364 F.Supp. 1075 (D.D.C. 1973), 511 F.2d 430 (D.C.Cir. 1974).

22. *Burke v. Barnes*, 479 U.S. 361 (1987), vacating *Barnes v. Kline*, 759 F.2d 21 (D.C.Cir. 1985).

23. *West Virginia University Hospitals v. Casey*, 111 S.Ct. 1138 at 1153–54 (1991) (Stevens, dissenting).

24. See Beth Henschen, "Judicial Use of Legislative History and Intent in Statutory Interpretation," *Legislative Studies Quarterly* 10 (August 1985): 353–71.

25. *Mansell v. Mansell*, 109 S.Ct. 2023 (1989).

26. Walter Murphy, *Elements of Judicial Strategy*, pp. 129–31.

27. Jesse H. Choper, *Judicial Review and the National Political Process*, p. 143.

28. Nagel, *The Legal Process*, p. 275; Walter F. Murphy, *Congress and the Court* (Chicago: University of Chicago Press, 1962), pp. 257–58.

29. Nagel, *The Legal Process*, p. 266.

30. Lucius J. Barker, "The Offshore Oil Cases," *The Third Branch of Government*, eds. C. Herman Pritchett and Alan F. Westin (New York: Harcourt, Brace, and World, 1963), pp. 234–74.

31. *Guss v. Utah Labor Relations Board*, 343 U.S. 1 (1957).

32. *Lauf v. E. G. Shinner & Co.*, 303 U.S. 323 (1968); *Yakus v. United States*, 321 U.S. 414 (1944).

33. See Edward Keynes, with Randall K. Miller, *The Court Vs. Congress: Prayer, Busing, and Abortion* (Durham, N.C.: Duke University Press, 1989), pp. 122–23.

34. Murphy, *Congress and the Court*, is an account of Congress's action.

35. Stephen M. Griffin, "Politics and the Supreme Court: The Case of the Bork Nomination," *Journal of Law & Politics* 5 (Spring 1989): 590, 592–93.

36. For a discussion of some of these points, see Kenneth R. Kay, "The Unforeseen Impact on Courts *and* Congress," *Judicature* 65 (October 1981): 185–89; Charles E. Rice, "The Constitutional Basis for the Proposals in Congress Today," ibid., 190–97; Telford Taylor, "The Unconstitutionality of Current Legislative Proposals," ibid., 198–207; and Carl A. Anderson, "The Government of Courts: The Power of Congress," *American Bar Association Journal* 68 (June 1982): 686–90.

37. An earlier version of part of this material appeared in Stephen L. Wasby, *The Impact of the United States Supreme Court: Some Perspectives* (Homewood, Ill.: Dorsey, 1970), pp. 203–13. A recent thorough examination of congressional efforts to override Supreme Court decisions is Richard A. Paschal, "The Continuing Colloquy: Congress and the Finality of the Supreme Court," *Journal of Law & Politics* 8 (Fall 1991): 143–226.

38. Samuel Krislov, *The Supreme Court in the Political Process* (New York: Macmillan, 1965), p. 143.

39. Beth Henschen, "Statutory Interpretations of the Supreme Court: Congressional Response," *American Politics Quarterly* 11 (October 1983): 441–58.

40. Michal Belknap, *Federal Law and Southern Order: Racial Violence and Constitutional Conflict in the Post-Brown South* (Athens: University of Georgia Press, 1987), pp. 41ff., 205ff.

41. Michael W. Dolan, "Congress, the Executive, and the Court: The Great Resale Price Maintenance Affair of 1983," *Public Administration Review* 45 (Special 1985): 718–22.

42. See, for example, incorporation of criteria from *Sanders v. United States*, 373 U.S. 1 (1963), on consideration of successive habeas corpus petitions, into 28 U.S.C. § 2244(b). *McCleskey v. Zant*, 111 S.Ct. 1454 at 1480 (Marshall, dissenting).

43. See Note, "Congressional Reversal of Supreme Court Decisions: 1945–57," *Harvard Law Review* 71 (May 1958): 1336.

44. *Railroad Retirement Board v. Alton Railway Co.*, 295 U.S. 330 (1935).

45. Earlier, after *Mallory v. United States*, 354 U.S. 449 (1957), interpreting the Federal Rules,

Congress made confessions admissible if the defendant was arraigned within six hours. And after *United States v. Wade*, 388 U.S. 218 (1967), Congress made eyewitness testimony admissible regardless of whether the accused had an attorney at the lineup at which identification had been made.

46. The earlier cases are *United Mine Workers v. Gibbs*, 388 U.S. 715 (1966), and *Owen Equipment & Erection Co. v. Kroger*, 437 U.S. 365 (1978).

47. The cases are, respectively, *N.L.R.B. v. Denver Building Construction Trades Council*, 341 U.S. 675 (1951), and *Local 1976, United Brotherhood of Carpenters v. N.L.R.B.* (Sand Door), 357 U.S. 93 (1958). See *Woelke & Romero Framing v. N.L.R.B.*, 456 U.S. 645 (1982).

48. Congress did this by making the Federal Tort Claims Act the exclusive remedy for torts by government employees in the scope of their employment. See *United States v. Smith*, 111 S.Ct. 1180 at 1183–84 (1991).

49. The case was *Walters v. National Association of Radiation Survivors*, 473 U.S. 305 (1985).

50. *Sable Communications of California v. F.C.C.*, 492 U.S. 115 (1989).

51. *Goldman v. Weinberger*, 475 U.S. 503 (1986).

52. *Newport News Shipbuilding & Dry Dock Co. v. E.E.O.C.*, 462 U.S. 669 (1983). On the campaign to overturn *Gilbert*, see Joyce Gelb and Marian Lief Palley, "Women and Interest Group Politics: A Comparative Analysis of Federal Decision-Making," *Journal of Politics* 41 (May 1979): 385–87.

53. *City of Mobile v. Bolden*, 446 U.S. 55 (1980); *Thornburg v. Gingles*, 478 U.S. 30 (1986).

54. In addition to *Wards Cove Packing Co. v. Atonio*, 109 S.Ct. 2115 (1989), the cases include *Lorance v. AT&T Technologies*, 109 S.Ct. 2261 (1989); *Patterson v. McLean Credit Union*, 109 S.Ct. 2383 (1989); *Price Waterhouse v. Hopkins*, 109 S.Ct. 1775 (1989); *Martin v. Wilks*, 109 S.Ct. 2180 (1989); *West Virginia University Hospitals v. Casey*, 111 S.Ct. 1138 (1991); and *E.E.O.C. v. Arabian American Oil*, 111 S.Ct. 1277 (1991). For a listing of instances in the field of civil rights where Congress has reversed the Court, see *Patterson v. McLean Credit Union*, 109 S.Ct., at 2385 n. 9 (Brennan).

55. Harry Stumpf, "The Political Efficacy of Judicial Symbolism," *Western Political Quarterly* 19 (June 1966): 293–303, and "Congressional Response to Supreme Court Rulings: The Interaction of Law and Politics," *Journal of Public Law* 14 (1965): 376–95.

56. Irvin Molotsky, "5-Year Extension of Education Law Adopted by House," *New York Times*, April 20, 1988, p. B11.

57. See Donald G. Morgan, *Congress and the Constitution: A Study of Responsibility* (Cambridge, Mass.: Harvard University Press, 1966), pp. 10–11.

58. See Louis Fisher, "Constitutional Interpretation by Members of Congress," *North Carolina Law Review* 63 (1985): 707–9.

59. Mark Miller, "How Congressional Committees Differ in Their Reactions to Federal Court Decisions," paper presented to Northeastern Political Science Association, 1989.

60. For greater detail, see Stephen L. Wasby, "The Presidency Before the Courts," *Capital University Law Review* 6 (December 1976): 35–73, in which some of this material was first presented.

61. *A.F.L.-C.I.O. v. Kahn*, 618 F.2d 784 (D.C.Cir. 1979), cert. denied, 443 U.S. 915 (1979).

62. *Edwards v. Carter*, 445 F.Supp. 1279 (D.D.C. 1978), 580 F.2d 1055 (D.C.Cir.), cert. denied, 436 U.S. 907 (1978).

63. *Public Citizen v. Department of Justice*, 109 S.Ct. 2558 (1989).

64. See Alexander Charns, "How the FBI Spied on the High Court," *Washington Post*, December 3, 1989, pp. C1, C4; Philip Shenon, "Book Says Hoover Was Asked to Tilt Courts," *New York Times*, October 16, 1988, p. 25. The book is Athan G. Theoharis and John Stuart Cox, *The Boss: J. Edgar Hoover and the Great American Inquisition* (Philadelphia, Penn.: Temple University Press, 1988).

65. For accounts, see Belknap, *Federal Law and Southern Order*, pp. 27–52; Taylor Branch, *Parting the Waters: America in the King Years, 1954–1963* (Simon and Schuster, 1988).

66. See Michael Nelson, "Presidents, Politics, and Policy: A Theoretical Perspective on the Court–Packing Episode of 1937," paper presented to American Political Science Association, 1986.

67. Gregory A. Caldeira, "Public Opinion and the U.S. Supreme Court: FDR's Court-Packing Plan," *American Political Science Review* 81 (December 1987): 1148.

68. When the administration again failed to follow statutory procedures for authorization of surveillance orders, the Court also ruled against the government in some cases. *United States v. Chavez*, 416 U.S. 562 at 580 (1974); see also *United States v. Giordano*, 416 U.S. 505 (1974).

69. Even the firing of the special prosecutor was found illegal by a lower court because the presi-

dent had violated Justice Department regulations "having the force of law." *Nader v. Bork*, 366 F.Supp. 104 (D.D.C. 1973).

70. *Mitchell v. Forsyth*, 472 U.S. 511 (1985).

71. A federal judge in Michigan, however, did rule the pardon constitutional, saying it was within the letter and spirit of the presidential pardon power as well as a "prudent public policy judgment." *Murphy v. Ford*, 390 F.Supp. 1372 (W.D.Mich. 1975).

72. The Court had earlier returned the case to the lower courts to be reconsidered in light of the Supreme Court's Gramm-Rudman ruling. On that reconsideration, the Third Circuit upheld the statute against claims that the law amounted to a usurpation of executive power, saying the statute was a proper exercise of congressional power. *Ameron v. U.S. Army Corps of Engineers*, 809 F.2d 979 (3rd Cir. 1986).

73. See the Supreme Court's actions concerning stays of lower court rulings, *Heckler v. Lopez*, 463 U.S. 1328 and 464 U.S. 879 (1983), and Susan Gluck Mezey, "Policy-making by the Federal Judiciary: The Effects of Judicial Review on the Social Security Disability Program," *Policy Studies Journal* 14 (March 1986): 343–61.

74. The rulings are *First English Evangelical Lutheran Church v. Los Angeles County*, 482 U.S. 304 (1987); and *Nollan v. California Coastal Commission*, 483 U.S. 825 (1987).

75. The material in this paragraph is drawn from three papers by Craig R. Ducat and Robert L. Dudley: Ducat and Dudley, "Presidential Power in the Federal Courts During the Post-War Era," American Political Science Association, 1985; Ducat and Dudley, "Federal Judges and Presidential Power: Truman to Reagan," *Akron Law Review* 22 (Spring 1989): 561–98; and Ducat and Dudley, "Federal District Judges and Presidential Power During the Postwar Era," *Journal of Politics* 51 (February 1989): 98–118.

76. Steve Alumbaugh and C. K. Rowland, "The Links Between Platform-Based Appointment Criteria and Trial Judges' Abortion Judgments," *Judicature* 74 (October–November 1990): 153–62.

77. See Nelson, "Presidents, Politics, and Policy," p. 12.

78. *Federal Energy Administration v. Algonquin SNG*, 426 U.S. 548 (1976).

79. *Mistretta v. United States*, 109 S.Ct. 647 at 654–55 (1989).

80. Clinton Rossiter, *The Supreme Court and the Commander in Chief* (Ithaca, N.Y.: Cornell University Press, 1951), pp. 127–28, 131.

81. *Duncan v. Kahanamoku*, 327 U.S. 304 (1946).

82. *Hirabayashi v. United States*, 828 F.2d 591 (9th Cir. 1987), and *Korematsu v. United States*, 584 F.Supp. 1406 (N.D.Cal. 1984). See Peter Irons, *Justice at War: The Story of the Japanese American Internment Cases* (New York: Oxford University Press, 1983), and Irons, *Justice Delayed: The Record of the Japanese American Internment Cases* (Middleton, Conn.: Wesleyan University Press, 1989).

83. Arthur S. Miller, *The Supreme Court and American Capitalism* (New York: Free Press, 1970), p. 100. For a complete account of the case, see Maeva Marcus, *Truman and the Steel Seizure Case: The Limits of Presidential Power* (New York: Columbia University Press, 1977). See also Alan F. Westin, *The Anatomy of a Constitutional Law Case* (New York: Columbia University Press, 1991 [reissue]).

84. See Anthony A. D'Amato and Robert M. O'Neil, *The Judiciary and Vietnam* (New York: St. Martin's, 1972).

85. *Holtzman v. Schlesinger*, 414 U.S. 1304 and 414 U.S. 1316; *Schlesinger v. Holtzman*, 414 U.S. 1321 (1973). The appellate court then held that Congress's extending the fund cutoff date for funding of the bombing was approved by Congress, 484 F.2d 1307 (2nd Cir. 1973), and other courts held there was no need for judicial decision because the August 15 date indicated an absence of interbranch conflict. See *Drinan v. Nixon*, 364 F.Supp. 854 (D. Mass. 1973).

86. Glendon Schubert, *Judicial Policy-Making* (Glenview, Ill.: Scott, Foresman, 1965), pp. 59–60.

87. Quoted in Merle Fainsod, Lincoln Gordon, and Joseph Palamountain, Jr., *Government and the American Economy*, 3d ed. (New York: Norton, 1959), p. 260.

88. Daniel J. Fiorino, "Judicial-Administrative Interaction in Regulatory Policy-Making: The Case of the Federal Power Commission," paper presented to American Political Science Association, 1975.

89. R. Shep Melnick, *Regulation and the Courts: The Case of the Clean Air Act* (Washington, D.C.: Brookings Institution, 1983), p. 87.

90. *Commissioner of Internal Revenue v. Fink*, 483 U.S. 89 at 105 (1987) (Stevens, dissenting).

91. Melnick, p. 152.

92. The Court has defined "substantial evidence" as not meaning "a large or considerable amount of evidence, but rather 'such relevant evidence as a reasonable mind might accept as adequate to support a conclusion.'" *Pierce v. Underwood*, 487 U.S. 552 at 565 (1988).

93. *United States v. Midwest Video Corp.*, 406 U.S. 649 at 676 (1972).

94. *Motor Vehicle Manufacturers Association of the United States v. State Farm Mutual Automobile Insurance Co.*, 463 U.S. 29 (1983).

95. *Renegotiation Board v. Grumman Aircraft*, 421 U.S. 168 (1975); *N.L.R.B. v. Sears, Roebuck*, 421 U.S. 132 (1975); *Department of the Air Force v. Rose*, 425 U.S. 352 (1976); *Chrysler Corp. v. Brown*, 441 U.S. 281 (1979).

96. *Industrial Union Department v. American Petroleum Institute*, 448 U.S. 607 (1980).

97. Albert R. Matheny and Bruce A. Williams, "Regulation, Risk Assessment, and the Supreme Court: The Case of OSHA's Cancer Policy," *Law & Policy* 6 (October 1984): 441–42.

98. *Weinberger v. Hynson, Westcott & Dunning*, 412 U.S. 609 (1973) (drug application); *Citizens to Preserve Overton Park v. Volpe*, 401 U.S. 420 (1971) (interstate highway); *Vermont Yankee Nuclear Power Corp. v. Natural Resources Defense Council*, 435 U.S. 519 (1978) (procedural requirements).

99. Phillip J. Cooper, "Due Process, the Burger Court, and Public Administration," *Southern Review of Public Administration* 6 (1982): 85.

100. Phillip J. Cooper, "Conflict or Constructive Tension: The Changing Relationship of Judges and Administrators," *Public Administration Review* 45 (Special 1985): 643.

101. *Federal Communications Commission v. WNCN Listeners Guild*, 450 U.S. 582 at 593, 595 (1981).

102. On patent law, see Martin Shapiro, *The Courts and Administrative Agencies* (New York: Free Press, 1968), pp. 143–226; Lawrence Baum, "The Federal Courts and Patent Validity: An Analysis of the Record," *Journal of the Patent Office Society* 56 (December 1974): 758–87.

103. Joseph Tanenhaus, "Supreme Court Attitudes Toward Federal Administrative Agencies," *Vanderbilt Law Review* 14 (1960–1961); 473–502; Bradley C. Canon and Micheal Giles, "Recurring Litigants: Federal Agencies Before the Supreme Court," *Western Political Quarterly* 25 (June 1972): 183–91; Glendon Schubert, *The Constitutional Polity* (Boston, Mass.: Boston University Press, 1970), pp. 37–38.

104. Jerry L. Mashaw, *Bureaucratic Justice: Managing Social Security Disability Claims* (New Haven, Conn.: Yale University Press, 1983), p. 19.

105. Harold J. Spaeth and Stuart H. Teger, "Activism and Restraint: A Cloak for the Justices' Policy Preferences," *Supreme Court Activism and Restraint*, eds. Halpern and Lamb, pp. 299, 278–80. See also Harold J. Spaeth and Michael F. Altfeld, "Felix Frankfurter, Judicial Activism, and Voting Conflict on the Warren Court," *Judicial Conflict and Consensus*, eds. Goldman and Lamb, pp. 86–114.

106. Reginald Sheehan, "Administrative Agencies and the Court: A Reexamination of the Impact of Agency Type on Decisional Outcomes," *Western Political Quarterly* 43 (December 1990): 879, 880.

107. Tanenhaus, "Supreme Court Attitudes"; Canon and Giles, "Recurring Litigants," pp. 189–90. See also Spaeth and Altfeld, "Felix Frankfurter," pp. 98, 104, on justices' union attitudes.

108. Spaeth and Teger, "Activism and Restraint," p. 282.

10 The Supreme Court's Impact

THE EXPECTATION OF IMMEDIATE, unbegrudging, and total obedience to the Supreme Court's rulings is widely held, particularly by those who fail to recognize that the Court is an actor in a political system. Compliance receives little attention and noncompliance is newsworthy—a further indication of the expectation that compliance should be the norm and the belief that it is. Recognition of the Court's political role should carry with it an understanding of the inevitability of negative reaction to its rulings, including noncompliance with them, particularly when important constitutional questions are at stake or controversial issues are being decided. Abundant hostile rhetoric aimed at the Court's rulings interpreting, sustaining, or overturning federal and state statutes is thus not surprising. But that rhetoric is not always representative of broader response. For example, one gets two very different estimates of reaction to the abortion rulings by looking at (a) the hate mail received by Justice Blackmun after he wrote the opinion, demonstrations at the Court against the rulings, efforts to amend the Constitution to prohibit abortions, and the wide variety of "Right to Life" activities following *Roe v. Wade*, (b) public opinion polls showing significant support for a woman's right to obtain an abortion, not to mention (c) the increase in the number of abortions performed—even if only part of that increase is attributed to the Court's rulings.[1]

The Court's Effects

Supreme Court decisions, individually or cumulatively, have had definite impact (effects). Some rulings have produced support and compliance; others have resulted in opposition. Search warrants are now obtained where police would not have bothered to do so earlier; police now give the "*Miranda* warnings." Despite such clear effects, it is often difficult to tell whether the Court has produced social change, increased its pace, merely served as a catalyst, or had no effect because the Court's rulings are often only one of multiple causes of events. Southern schools became desegregated, but how much as a result of *Brown v. Board of Education* and how much as a result of the statute providing for the cutting off of federal funds to government units that discriminate is hard to tell. Except in the Deep South, changing public opinion, itself a result of World War II, might have led to some change without court rulings, and that changed national opinion certainly made it easier for the Court to rule as it did. Before Congress acted, *Brown* itself did not produce much activity except resistance in the Deep South. This made it largely a symbolic ruling but it served to stimulate the civil rights movement, in part because the lack of tangible results led to direct action. Parts of the 1964 Civil Rights Act and the subsequent desegregation guidelines issued by the Department of Health, Education and Welfare (HEW) might not have occurred without *Brown*.

The Court's decisions on desegregation and the perhaps even more widely disobeyed school prayer rulings were highly visible and affected many people, average citizens as well as officials. Other rulings, such as those on reapportionment or criminal procedure, have had their basic direct effect on government officials, through structural or organizational changes, although changes in policy may ultimately affect the citizens. Some effects can be relatively diffuse, for example, when the Court focuses attention on a subject like abortion and thus affects the nation's political agenda. At other times, effects are specific, or limited to a particular industry or individual company. For example, the Court's 1987 ruling upholding the requirement that Texaco post a bond before it could appeal an adverse multi-million-dollar state court ruling pushed Texaco closer to seeking bankruptcy protection.

Most decisions have an economic effect. At times, the effect may be costs removed, as in the 1976 invalidation of the federal minimum wage for state and local employees, important because the Fair Labor Standards Act covers the 7,000,000 full-time employees of all the states, 3,000 counties, 19,000 townships, 15,000 school districts, and 29,000 other special districts. In other situations, economic activity may be limited, speculated to be the effect of the Court's 1987 ruling (*CTS Corp. v. Dynamics Corp. of America*) sustaining state laws limiting takeovers of corporations. Or economic activity may be stimulated—or at least allowed to operate unconstrained. The Court's 1895 invalidation of the federal income tax meant that stupendous fortunes went untaxed until the Sixteenth Amendment was passed, and the Court's ruling the same year that manufacturing was not in commerce and thus not subject to the Sherman Antitrust Act (*United States v. E. C. Knight Co.*), coupled with its later ruling on what constituted reasonable restraint of trade (*Standard Oil v. United States*, 1911), made antitrust laws a "nuisance, if that."[2]

Attracting more attention is the imposition of costs, for example, an increase in the number of people eligible for welfare or large damage awards after

Supreme Court rulings allowed antitrust actions against cities.[3] The latter led to countervailing action: Congress passed legislation exempting municipalities, their officials, and private units acting under their authorization from Sherman Act damage awards. And rulings that local government activities authorized by the state would be exempt from antitrust laws might have led to increased work-loads for state legislative and executive agencies engaged in supervision of local governments, but that burden was lowered when the Court ruled that active su-pervision by the states is not required for local governments to be exempt from antitrust attack.[4] When the Court struck down so-called shared-time provisions under which school districts, with federal funding, had provided parochial schools with some services, concern about parochial schools' ability to fund the remedial programs led to efforts—by and large successful—to delay implemen-tation of the Court's ruling.

Other economic effects on the public fisc resulted from the Court's ruling that states must refund taxes the states knew or should have known were uncon-stitutional, with estimates that the amount to be refunded might be $6.5 billion as to taxes declared unconstitutional, added to another $2 billion resulting from unconstitutional state taxation of pensions of retired federal workers.[5] Some saw strains on Medicaid from a ruling that hospitals could sue over rates for Medicaid to obtain "reasonable and adequate" reimbursement.[6] These instances indicate that the Supreme Court's rulings can affect the operation of our governmental structure.

The Court is not all-powerful, although we overestimate its effect, as when we tend to make it a scapegoat for phenomena like increased crime rates that we cannot easily explain and attribute to it more power than it would have when put to the test. Measuring impact can be quite difficult. We do not even know whether certain laws or other government actions struck down by the Supreme Court "would have soon fallen at the hands of the political process even without judicial intervention." Separating the effects of Supreme Court rulings from other events is difficult in any event. It becomes more difficult over time, as "the repercussions of all government actions ramify indefinitely and interrelate with other phenomena, both public and private, many of which simply cannot be quantified and indeed often cannot even be identified."[7] Actions attributed to the Supreme Court may result from other, less visible or less immediate, matters. Civil liberties are less likely to decrease from Supreme Court rulings than from war and depression or from panics over drugs and AIDS. The difficulty of deter-mining impact is evident when rulings are said to have produced opposite or competing effects. For example, the Court's decisions have been said to have produced segregation—or retarded it; to have increased crime—or protected people's rights; to have expanded free speech—or allowed our morals to sink by facilitating the sale of indecent literature.

We must recognize that the Court by itself cannot produce impacts. What will happen is problematic. The Court cannot always effectively control the con-sequences of the policy enunciated in its opinions and must rely on others to implement them, that is, to put them into effect. In the early years of the Republic, after the Court made a strong statement on behalf of federal authority when a state law had defied a federal court decree affirming title in a prize ship captured and sold during the Revolution, it took a federal posse (2,000 marshals) plus a strong word from President Madison to enforce Chief Justice Marshall's ruling (*United States v. Judge Peters*, 1809). This indicates the need for strong backing by president and Congress for enforcement of some Supreme Court rulings. A century later, the Court's ruling that activities of meat packing houses were clearly in interstate commerce (*Swift & Co. v. United States*, 1905) had almost no effect on the Beef Trust; only the Packers and Stockyards Act of 1921 plus a consent decree and much subsequent litigation produced some effect from the Court's 1905 ruling.[8] Put another way, the Supreme Court may make law, or the law may be what the Supreme Court says it is, but *only after all others have had their say*. The Court's decision of cases does not end political controversies that arrive at the Supreme Court, which often are far too deep-seated to be ended by a single or even several pronouncements from nine justices, as the abortion dispute illustrates.

A focus on controversial rulings, particularly on civil liberties and civil rights matters like school prayer, abortion, criminal procedure, and school desegregation—on the impact of which most studies have focused—may provide a picture emphasizing the lack of the Court's effect. For example, the history of abortion policy since *Roe v. Wade* has been one of state legislation to undercut that ruling through a variety of devices, but the relative lack of impact in those areas—where the Court's effect is nonetheless substantial—serves to understate the Court's effect. Tax and patent issues, for example, may be uninteresting to most, except members of the business community, but they are important, and compliance with rulings on those topics occurs, almost without question. Primary actors will follow rules, in part because what is important is having rules to follow. Like many private citizens, members of the business community, and many public officials, we are willing to follow orders from those we acknowledge as superiors, granting them legitimacy—and on most matters we grant the Court that position.

We begin this chapter with a brief look at some historical instances of impact. This is followed by an examination of the Supreme Court's place in public opinion, both historically and in recent years. Then we turn to a discussion of terms like "impact" and "compliance." This is followed by a detailed look at channels through which decisions might be communicated to those expected to know about and follow them, and at some of the factors that help to explain both communication and impact across different policy areas.[9]

Impact in History

Supreme Court decisions have produced controversy (one type of impact) and other substantial effects throughout the nation's history. Perhaps the first was the Eleventh Amendment, a direct and immediate result of *Chisholm v. Georgia*

(1793), allowing a suit against a state. The growth of a national economy was aided by Chief Justice Marshall's broad interpretations of national government power in sustaining the National Bank against state efforts to tax it (*McCulloch v. Maryland*, 1819), and of commerce when striking down a state steamboat monopoly in *Gibbons v. Ogden* (1824). The economy was also affected by the *Dartmouth College* case (1819) on the sanctity of contracts, which states could not abridge, and the *Charles River Bridge* case (1837), allowing establishment of competing transportation companies. Charles Warren stated years ago, "To untrammeled intercourse between its parts, the American union owes its preservation and strength. Two factors have made such intercourse possible—the railroad, physically; the Supreme Court, legally." [10]

The court has also had long-term effects on American federalism, not infrequently creating adverse reaction "particularly when it has validated exertions of national power against the plaint of states' rights." It has thus helped create enemies willing to join those "who oppose judicial activism in defense of personal liberties," [11] where most noncompliance has occurred in recent times. Among rulings prompting negative state response were those that Congress's jurisdiction over fugitive slaves was exclusive; that a federal statute on the subject preempted conflicting state law; and that a state court lacked the authority to order federal officials to commit an act in conflict with a federal court decision. [12] Indeed, conflict has been quite likely whenever the Court has ruled that federal activity prevents the states from taking action.

The 1920 decision in *Missouri v. Holland* that a federal treaty (with Canada) concerning migratory waterfowl supplanted Missouri's hunting regulations was another important ruling on federalism that stirred the anger of those supporting "states' rights." The Court's statement that in implementing a treaty the national government could go beyond the constitutional powers it would have in the treaty's absence led to later attempts to amend the Constitution to limit the president's treaty-making power. More recently, a ruling that the national government, in setting aside a particular national forest, had not reserved certain uses of river waters, "had the effect of maintaining in state hands title to a potentially valuable and arguably federal resource"; this "created a potential instrument for state influence upon national forest management," [13] thus affecting the bargaining between federal and state levels of government.

One of the most important instances of impact was *Dred Scott*. By saying that Congress could not limit slavery in the states, the Court destroyed congressional compromise. The decision had a number of other impacts, one of which is said to have been that the Court badly damaged itself. However, the extent to which the ruling "undermined the Court as an institution has in fact been greatly exaggerated." Those opposed to the decision wanted to change the Court's membership (and decisions) but "not its structure and functions"; moreover, "hostility to the Supreme Court as a whole . . . was confined to a small though at times highly vocal minority." [14] As is often the case, "the response to the decision proved to be much more important than its direct legal effect." Because of the Civil War itself, the expansion of slavery permitted by the decision did not occur; the owner of the slave whose freedom the Court had denied manumitted him (set him free). However, by legitimating the South's proslavery argument, thus increasing its confidence and making it more inflexible, and by increasing Northern hostility to the *South* (instead of to slavery as such), "as a public event, the decision aggravated an already bitter sectional conflict and to some degree determined the shape of the final crisis." [15]

Not only did the Court, in *Dred Scott*, contribute to the Civil War, but after the war and Reconstruction, it helped upset the civil rights protections that Congress had provided in connection with the Thirteenth, Fourteenth, and Fifteenth Amendments. Most notable was the Court's ruling in the *Civil Rights Cases* (1883) undercutting the 1875 Civil Rights Act, which had provided the first national "public accommodations" legislation.

The Supreme Court and Public Opinion

Opinions about Supreme Court decisions, whether held by newspaper publishers, political elites, members of the "attentive public," and "average citizens," are an important element of impact, as is public opinion about the Court itself, for example, the confidence that people express in it. The media often report criticism of the Court; general support for the Court is heard only infrequently although some decisions may be defended. Political campaigns for over 25 years, starting with George Wallace's and then Richard Nixon's "law and order" campaigns, have included criticism of the Supreme Court. Ronald Reagan openly criticized particular decisions and potential Republican candidate Pat Robertson even challenged the Court's very position in our system, saying that its rulings were "not the law of the land." Such attacks potentially affect public opinion about the Court.

What do we know about public opinion with respect to the justices and their Court? What do people believe about the Court?

In a course on the Supreme Court, students, when asked, "What do people believe about the Supreme Court?" gave the following responses:

• The Supreme Court is "lofty."

• The Court is "political": "After all, it is in Washington, D.C., the center of national politics."

• The Court is "arbitrary" in its decisions; that is shown in the changes in the Court's rulings over time.

• The Court is out of touch. It isn't familiar with current technology. More important, the justices are out of touch because they are older—and haven't experienced what younger people have.

• "The Supreme Court is supposed to provide justice for all, but takes only big cases."

These responses touch on some of the larger themes to be examined in this section, where we look at a number of aspects of public opinion about the Court. After treatment of editorial reaction to some of the Court's major rulings, we turn to extended treatment of public opinion polls—both those of the general public and more specialized and focused surveys. Through such polls, we examine the Court's overall rating in the eyes of the public, the public's confidence in the Court, and public reaction to specific decisions. We also can learn the extent to which people have information about the Court on which their opinions might be based; their belief (or disbelief) in the "myth" that the Court finds rather than makes the law; and elements—apart from information—that underlie the extent of their general and specific support of the Court.

Early History and Editorial Reaction

The Supreme Court's decisions produced effects on public opinion long before the days of public opinion polls. Public reaction to the decisions was often mixed. When the Court invalidated state fugitive slave statutes, "the decision was equally unsatisfactory to both pro-slavery and anti-slavery men"; the former were upset at the blow to states' rights and the latter, who disliked the federal fugitive slave law, thought the Court was backing the South.[16] The Court's reversal in the Legal Tender Cases hurt it in the public eye; the reversal came shortly after the Court was enlarged and only a year after it had held that the Union government could not require that debts made before the passage of the Legal Tender Act be paid in paper money. The legal community felt that the Legal Tender Act was constitutional, but reopening of the case was "a mistake which for many years impaired the people's confidence, not in the honesty, but in the impartiality and good sense of the Court."[17]

Divided reaction was again evident in the New Deal period. When the Court invalidated the National Industrial Recovery Act, "the more conservative sections of the press welcomed it as putting an end to unsound experiments in government regulation of industry," labor opposed the decision, and the business community was divided.[18] However, more and more elements of the public were alienated by the Court's continued striking down of New Deal legislation; "each new adverse decision in the winter and spring of 1936 brought new bursts of hostility."[19] Invalidation of the Agricultural Adjustment Act upset farmers; the voiding of the Bituminous Coal Act irritated workers; and the minimum wage rulings "alienated nearly everybody"—including supporters of earlier decisions. Only 10 of 344 editorials approved the decision on the minimum wage, with some 60 papers, including a number of conservative ones, calling for a constitutional amendment on the subject.

Editorial reaction to decisions is an indirect but useful measure of public opinion. After three of four major Supreme Court church-state decisions, 24 large-circulation newspapers generally favored separation of church and state; the exception was the *Zorach* ruling upholding released time programs, which the papers favored. The *McCollum* ruling striking down religious classes on school property was the most favorably received (eight papers favoring and two opposing), with editorials on the school prayer case closely divided (13 favoring, nine opposing). Support for the *Zorach* ruling may have resulted from that program's milder link between church and state, more conservative public attitudes toward civil liberties in 1952, liberal Justice Douglas's authorship of the Court's opinion, and the general tendency of newspapers to support the Court. Newspapers' editorial positions on church-state matters were affected by a city's political climate (the more Democrats, the more likely a paper to favor church-state separation), the publisher's politics (same relationship, but stronger), and the publisher's religion (higher support for the Court if he was Catholic or Episcopalian).[20] The Court still obtained general support from editorial writers for leading daily newspapers in later cases. Either a plurality or majority of editorial writers approved of most of 11 leading church-state cases,[21] but majorities did oppose the school prayer ruling and one major aid to parochial school case (*Wolman v. Walter*, 1977).

Contrary to public outcry, in 17 race relations cases a majority of the editorial writers for the major daily newspapers approved of the decisions, and a plurality approved of all the others but one—when the Supreme Court avoided a decision by declaring moot the first affirmative action case it accepted for review (*DeFunis v. Odegaard*, 1974). A plurality approved of each subsequent affirmative action case. Editorial confusion was evident in the responses to the *Bakke* ruling, in which the Court was severely divided.[22] Editorials on race relations cases could not be explained in terms of partisan affiliation of the papers, but such partisanship did serve to explain reactions on defendants' rights, where "responses . . . are much more 'bipolar' than responses to race cases."[23]

More in line with general public opinion was the editorial and cartoon reaction of 63 papers of a wider range of circulation. Opposition to the school prayer ruling was stronger in the Upper Midwest papers, with more Southern papers neutral or favorable. Editorial reaction among these same papers to the Court's first reapportionment decision was generally favorable, with the papers' editorial position affecting news coverage: those supporting the Court presented a more restrained account of the Court's rulings in both headlines and reportage of critical reaction to the decisions than did papers opposing the decision.[24]

Public Opinion Surveys

No unified statement about public opinion about the Supreme Court has yet been developed, in part because of the difficulty of determining that public opinion. A basic, but complex, picture can be assembled from scattered items in Gallup and Harris surveys and from more intensive social science studies, which we must piece together because of different samples used.

Ratings. Overall ratings of the Supreme Court remained fairly constant in the mid-1960s. In November 1966 the public gave the Court an overall negative rating (46%–54%) (Harris Poll). Younger people, the better educated, and blacks backed the Court; southerners, older people, and the less well educated were the Court's severest critics. Similar results appear in a 1967 Gallup Poll. There was an almost even balance between favorable and unfavorable reactions: the Court's work was rated excellent by 15 percent, good by 30 percent, fair by 29 percent, and poor by 17 percent. How quickly opinion shifted was evident in June 1968 (Gallup Poll). Evaluations had shifted to 36 percent favorable, 53 percent unfavorable; only 8 percent rated the Court's work as excellent. Republicans were most critical, and those with less than a college education were also negative; Democrats and those with a college education were evenly divided.

The Burger Court's criminal procedure rulings, while more in tune with public opinion, did not improve the Court's overall rating, which was only slightly higher in 1973 than in 1969 (Gallup Poll)—and much lower than the mid-1960s ratings. Who liked the Court had changed. Decreased approval of the Court was now shown by the college educated, those 21 to 29 years old (showing the greatest drop), westerners and easterners, and Democrats, but ratings were up among those age 50 and over, southerners, and Republicans (up 12%).[25] In 1986 a poll found 46 percent rated the Court's work as either excellent (7%) or good (39%) (*New York Times*/CBS News), considerably higher than the 37 percent Gallup Poll figure of 13 years earlier and even marginally higher than the 43 percent Gallup figure of 25 years before. Nonetheless, more rated the Court fair or poor than rated it good or excellent. More of those who found the Court conservative approved the Court's work than did those who saw it as too liberal.

Polls also show shifts in the public's confidence in the Court as an institution. A 1966 Harris Poll majority (51%) expressed a great deal of confidence in the Court—almost 10 percent more than did so for either Congress or the executive branch, but less than for medicine, colleges, or the military. A 1967 Gallup Poll indicated that almost half the public thought the Court had been impartial, but 30 percent—particularly older citizens, Republicans, and southerners—believed the judges showed favoritism toward some groups.

The extent of variation in public confidence in the Court can be seen from 1972 poll results showing only 21 percent of respondents expressing a great deal of confidence in the Court (Harris Poll). Confidence rose from 1972 through 1974 (to 40% expressing a great deal of confidence) before dropping substantially—back to 22 percent in 1976—and then rebounding to 31 percent in early 1978, where it stayed through the mid-1980s. In general, the proportion expressing confidence in the Court was higher than the proportion expressing confidence in other government institutions, and when confidence began to increase from its low point, the Supreme Court registered larger gains than did Congress or the president. This indicated that the Court's place in public opinion, although partly a function of confidence in all government institutions, is to some extent independent of the public's view of those institutions. Confidence in the Court was also responsive "to the happenstances of political events" such as Watergate and President Nixon's resignation and to inflation, although bad economic times had little effect. Of particular interest, because of public attention to the Court's criminal procedure rulings, is that increases in the FBI's crime index had no effect on the public's view of the Court. However, the Court's decisions favoring criminal defendants did cause the public to lose confidence in the Court.[26]

In 1975 38 percent of the respondents felt that those in charge of the Supreme Court "really know what most people they represent or serve think and want," somewhat better than Congress, the White House, or the executive branch. However, more (43%) said the Court was out of touch with those it served, and 19 percent did not know, higher than for any other institution (Harris Poll). By 1977, 47 percent said the Supreme Court was "mostly out of touch." Three years later, almost half said that the Court's decisions were in line with American values and beliefs but 38 percent found the rulings out of step (*National Law Journal*).

In 1981, only 17 percent said the Supreme Court had too much power, with more than twice that proportion (39%) saying the Court was carrying out proper responsibilities. Almost a decade later, although 9 percent thought all three branches were equal in power, the Court was thought most powerful by the second highest proportion—31 percent, compared to 38 percent for Congress, and only 21 percent for the president. Here it is interesting to note that more think the basis for the Court's rulings to be factors like political pressures and personal and political beliefs of the justices (47%) than think the rulings are based on facts and law (44%) (*National Law Journal*).

The public also reacts to specific decisions. Thus in 1966 the public, despite its overall negative rating of the Court, favored rulings on reapportionment (76%–24%) and desegregation of schools and public accommodations (both 64%–36%) (Harris). The school prayer and *Miranda* rulings were disliked (30%–70%, and 35%–65%). In 1973, 58 percent favored the Burger Court's conservative ruling on obscenity, but roughly the same percentage disapproved of the Court's 1972 invalidation of the death penalty (Gallup Poll). (President Nixon's appointees, who had dissented, were closer to public opinion.) Majorities also opposed rulings denying news reporters a First Amendment right to protect confidential sources and invalidating aid to parochial schools.

In early 1981, 74 percent of the public opposed busing their children to another part of town for desegregation, but a year later, a majority opposed a federal law prohibiting the Department of Justice and federal courts from ordering school busing to achieve racial balance, evidence of conflicting or unstable views. With respect to what is perhaps the most controversial recent issue apart from abortion, a 1991 poll indicated that a somewhat larger proportion disagreed with the Court's rulings on flag-burning than supported those rulings (46% against the ruling, 40% supporting), but that 63 percent supported a constitutional amendment to prohibit flag burning (*National Law Journal*).

The public's opinion on a particular issue can be shifted by a Supreme

Court ruling, but this hardly happens all the time. For one thing, there would be no shift if the Supreme Court's decision is consonant with public opinion. And for 146 rulings from 1935–1986 where a comparison is possible between poll items and the rulings, "some 62 or 63 percent of the Court's decisions were consistent with the polls when a clear poll majority (or plurality) existed." Even for other cases, the Court's rulings "seldom greatly influence American public opinion either over the short term or the long term." The rulings that do have an influence are, however, of a particular type: they are liberal and activist, and some time will have elapsed between the ruling and the poll measuring public opinion to allow opinion to shift. A ruling is more likely to have "staying power" in public opinion if it is "unanimous, liberal, consistent with the polls, and occurred during non-crisis times"; a smaller proportion of "countermajoritarian" decisions than majoritarian rulings had staying power.[27]

Opinions of those in the legal community might be particularly important because lawyers might be able to affect average citizens' opinions. At the present time, the American Bar Association, the lawyers' principal national organization (although containing far fewer than half the nation's attorneys), generally supports the Court, but that has not always been so. Indeed, the ABA's unwillingness to back the Court against its critics during the early Warren Court—the period of liberal internal security rulings and of desegregation—and reports by ABA committees criticizing the Court's controversial decisions led Chief Justice Warren to resign his ABA membership.[28] Lawyers in a specific community (Providence, Rhode Island), were more dissatisfied with the Court in 1970 than was the Gallup Poll's national sample of the same time. They were also more undecided than the national sample's college-educated and business and professional groups, but their indecision came from indifference rather than ambivalence. The criminal procedure decisions seemed most important for lawyers criticizing the Court. They tended to hold a "traditional" attitude toward the Court, including the idea that the Court only finds law, and wanted "strict constructionist" judges. Those favoring the Warren Court were more likely to approve of judges engaging in lawmaking.[29]

In early 1977, two-fifths of federal judges, state supreme court judges, and lawyers responding to a *U.S. News & World Report* survey thought the Court was still deciding issues they preferred to be left to the legislative or executive branches of government, but 84.2 percent thought the Burger Court less likely to do so than the Warren Court, and only 2.4 percent thought the Burger Court *more likely* to do so. Over half approved the Court's making it more difficult for citizens to use the federal courts to obtain redress of grievances and just under half (48.4%) said that the Court *was* making it more difficult. A majority of those surveyed approved of the Burger Court's decisions and direction in all areas except obscenity and pornography.

In 1967, four-fifths of the police officers in four medium-sized Wisconsin cities disapproved of *Miranda*. There was no relationship between attitude and amount of formal education, but those with least police experience approved of the decision the least.[30] Five years later, Illinois and Massachusetts small-town police chiefs did not show this same resistance to *Miranda*, as most officers had learned to live with the ruling. However, although Massachusetts officers generally favored the (*Mapp*) rule excluding illegally seized evidence from trials, it was hard to find an Illinois officer who could say anything good about that doctrine. The chiefs' views were not related to their formal education, but those who had had law enforcement training before becoming officers were somewhat more likely to view the rule positively. A study of officers in 29 St. Louis area police departments carried out at the same time, however, showed weak relationships between training and attitudes.[31]

Information. Detailed local, state, and national surveys indicate low levels of knowledge about the Court, broad general support, and low specific support. The public generally lacks knowledge about the legal system, including specific knowledge about the Supreme Court. In a typical finding, in a 1990 survey, "Less than one-fourth of the respondents knew how many justices there are, and nearly two-thirds of them could not name a single member of the Court." If they could, it was likely to be Justice O'Connor, the Court's only female justice.[32] In July 1986, when the nominations of Justice Rehnquist to be Chief Justice and of Judge Scalia to be an associate justice were pending, only 26 percent of those questioned could identify Rehnquist as a Supreme Court justice and only 16 percent could identify Scalia as a nominee.[33]

"Only a few cases were sufficiently dramatic to rise above the public's threshold of attention."[34] In a 1966 Wisconsin test of knowledge about decisions, only 2 percent of respondents had all items correct and only 15 percent had more than half correct; 12 percent had every answer wrong. This lack of awareness extended even to criminal procedure decisions about which there had been open controversy and to reapportionment despite redistricting in the state. This indicates that people have difficulty relating decisions to their personal lives.[35] Less than half (45.2%) of those in the 1964/1966 national University of Michigan Survey Research Center (SRC) postelection survey could name any Supreme Court decision they liked or disliked; however, by 1975 over 60 percent of those in the same sample who had been located indicated specific knowledge of Supreme Court decisions. Yet in both years less than half could answer open-ended questions about specific likes and dislikes.[36] Another aspect of this lack of awareness is that people say the Court has decided noteworthy cases that in fact have never been brought to or near it. This misattribution is, however, an indication of the power we consider the Court to have: after all, if a case is important, the Court must have decided it.

A recent survey in metropolitan St. Louis, Missouri, provides further information about the public's awareness of Court rulings. "The public is neither universally ignorant nor universally informed about Court decisions," but the visibility of a decision is strongly related to public awareness of it: "There is a nearly four-fold increase in awareness from the least to the most visible decisions." Awareness is affected by people's general knowledge of politics, by the frequency with which they engage in political conversations, and their use of news media—particularly for less well-known cases. Moreover, awareness does not seem to "decay" over time. Also positively affecting awareness are a ruling's "underlying salience," "the perceived importance of the decision, and the response of political elites" to it.[37]

By comparison, more than three-fourths of the attentive public (those generally better informed about public events) could indicate specific likes and dislikes among the Court's rulings. Elite groups—congressional administrative assistants and Princeton students—had still higher recall levels: 86 percent could name a recent Supreme Court policy they liked or disliked; not surprisingly, 99 percent of lawyers could do so.[38] Similar differences between the general population and the politically active were evident in a 1976 Wisconsin survey. Overall, only one-fourth of the inactives could identify a Supreme Court decision, but over half of those politically active had such knowledge. Yet only slightly more than one-fifth of the activists identified more than one subject on which the Court had ruled. This supports the proposition that likes and dislikes about the Court are based on limited aspects of the Court's work.[39]

School prayer rulings have been among the most salient of the Court's decisions and, along with civil rights rulings, account for more than two-thirds of the 1964 likes and dislikes about the Court. Indicating volatility in the public's views, by 1966 most likes and dislikes were accounted for by criminal procedure decisions. In 1975 reinterviews, references to school prayer had decreased but other issue areas salient in 1966 (civil rights, school prayer, criminal defendants' rights) were still salient; specific references to capital punishment (on which the Court had begun to rule in 1972) had increased. The school prayer decisions were "unknown only to the same seemingly irreducible number of persons who have managed to remain unaware of the segregation decisions."[40] However, some in a Missouri survey who did not read newspapers knew of at least one Court decision; it appears that "issues which gain the court renown (or notoriety) are so salient that they come through even to people virtually isolated from the printed word."[41]

Support. "There is . . . little evidence of widespread public support for the justices' specific decisions; and the Court does not appear to command sweeping generalized approval."[42] In earlier national surveys, those giving the Court diffuse (general) support outnumbered four to one those giving it specific support (that based on particular decisions), with only about 20 percent negative as to diffuse support. However, one-third were negative on specific support and almost three times as many people named only decisions they *dis*liked as named only those they liked. Some of those opposing particular decisions provided general support, as did some of those least knowledgeable about the Court—who also seemed most trusting of government; and among 1966 SRC respondents reinterviewed in 1975, "In the aggregate, diffuse support for the Supreme Court, despite tremors that shook the entire political system, proved comfortingly resilient."[43] Moreover, "public orientations toward courts apparently change slowly over time if at all, as decisions and popular policy preferences (and other factors) interact."[44]

The relationship between diffuse support (for the Court as an institution) and support for the Court's specific rulings (specific support) has been unclear, but a recent analysis, based on a 1987 panel survey, shows *no* connection between the two. Diffuse support, predicted by the broad political values people hold, such as support for democratic norms, and by the attention people pay to the Court, appears to be "fairly substantial among the mass public," which will oppose efforts to damage the Court despite feeling that the Court "continually makes decisions that the people disagree with." Considering oneself a liberal or conservative, a Democrat or Republican, is not related to diffuse support; positions on some policy issues (support for abortion, opposition to segregation) and diffuse support are related, but not strongly. Interestingly, there is a stronger relationship between satisfaction on policy preferences and support for the Court among elites than among the general public; thus for elites diffuse and specific support are not separated.[45]

Higher knowledge about the Court has regularly seemed to correlate with greater *dis*approval of the Court. This relationship might be complex. For example, a person's support for procedural rights might affect what that person heard and read about the Court, which in turn would affect support for the Court. Level of knowledge of the Court and race are related, affecting blacks' support for the Court. The 1966 SRC survey showed a majority of blacks to be among those unaware of even the desegregation decisions, and for more blacks than whites, the Supreme Court "as a regime institution is not salient,"[46] but a 1975 survey of students at Kentucky universities showed that blacks attributed more legitimacy to the Supreme Court than did whites.[47]

Differences based on race declined in the 1970s but significant differences appeared in a 1987 survey. African-Americans remained "predominantly favorably oriented toward the Supreme Court as an institution," but were less supportive than whites, were more likely to be uncertain about the Court, and had decreased their support of the Court, relative to whites. Yet even when dissatisfied with the Court's policies, African-Americans did not weaken their diffuse support of the Court. This is in part generational, as those influenced by the Warren Court and its liberal rulings showed a higher level of support than did younger blacks and appeared to be less affected by the Court's later specific rulings.[48]

Degree of political activity seems to correlate with support. Wisconsin activists indicated opposition to most major Supreme Court decisions, but nonetheless provided higher levels of specific support than those politically inactive.[49] In Wisconsin in 1976, among the politically inactive the level of hostility exceeded 80 percent for both Republicans and Democrats, with Republicans somewhat more hostile. Differences between Democrat and Republican activists were much greater, with the Democrats far more favorable to the Court's decisions (59.3%–39.5%).[50] Political party identification affected attitudes toward the Court in some but not all surveys. In some situations, the relationship was indirect, for example, being a Democrat influenced what one heard, affecting current attitudes, or Republicans' unhappiness with the Court stemmed from Democratic control of the White House.[51] However, 1975 SRC reinterviews produced no evidence that the public evaluated the Court in terms of who was president; more important, party identification was "useless in explaining change in diffuse support."[52] Respondents' attitudes (liberal/conservative) best explained support for the Court in the SRC national surveys. Congruence between liberals' political positions and the Warren Court's decisions meant that liberals gave the Court more support at that time; in the 1976 Wisconsin survey, the combination of liberalism *and* activism, not activism alone, operated to provide strong commitment to the Court.[53]

Related to diffuse and specific support is public belief in the myth that the Court is a legal rather than a political body. One-sixth of a Missouri sample associated the Court directly with the Constitution or constitutionality; just under one-third each referred to law and to courtlike functions. Because less than one-fourth of all responses showed that the Court was seen primarily as a political institution, one can conclude that "the Court's myth enjoys widespread diffusion." Education *increased* rather than reduced belief in the myth: those who did not believe in the myth were not more politically sophisticated but actually were less well socialized into prevailing norms.[54] Likewise, in the 1976 Wisconsin survey, there was a higher proportion of myth holders among the more politically active. And in the 1975 Kentucky universities survey, whites, who "exhibited a greater mythical belief" than did blacks, and those from higher status families "seem to accept conventional political values and attribute fine qualities to the Court" more than blacks and lower-status whites.[55] A book like *The Brethren*, revealing to a large audience the inner workings of the Court and the bargaining and compromise that takes place there, might well lead to a decreased belief in the myth of lawmaking, particularly among those of higher education, who would have been more likely to have read at least parts of the book.[56]

It can be thought proper for the Court to produce changes in governmental structure or process, such as those required by the reapportionment decisions, that is, to "legitimate regime change," only for those who satisfy three conditions: they must perceive, that is, be aware of, the Court; recognize that it may properly interpret and apply the Constitution; and feel that the Court was acting competently and impartially. According to the 1964/1966 surveys, 40 percent satisfied neither of the first two conditions, while roughly one-fourth satisfied both; only about one-eighth satisfied all three. Ten years later, asked to indicate their preference as to whether Congress or the Supreme Court should resolve disagreements over national policy, more Wisconsinites chose Congress (40.4%–35.3%

overall), although the politically active chose the Court by a 6–5 ratio. Perhaps a reflection of Watergate, far more respondents picked the Court over the president (54.2%–19.4%); activists were even more likely to choose the Court.[57]

Those who think the Court's performance is poor are "most likely to act to change a decision" but "they are neither numerous nor particularly rebelliously inclined."[58] In Wisconsin only a few of those who said they would do something to change a disliked Supreme Court decision would try to develop further opposition among the public. Half would work through members of Congress, and another one-fourth would "act within the established legal processes." Virtually no Illinois or Massachusetts small-town police chiefs said they would refuse to go along with a court ruling. While over half the Illinois officers said they would do something about a decision they disliked, for most this was only to talk about the disliked decisions, complain, and "gripe." In Massachusetts, most spoke of writing to the authorities, including their commanding officers or other chiefs, in order to express their opinions, while a couple would have acted through the legal system.

These responses lead to the remark made about the Wisconsin sample: "This is quiescence indeed" and to the conclusion that "the decisions of the Supreme Court have had more effect on the reputation of the Court than the activities of its antagonists."[59] Yet we have seen repeated attacks on the Court. The Court's abortion ruling produced clear, even violent, opposition; the ruling aroused Right to Life groups and propelled them into politics. (In somewhat the same way, the Court's school prayer rulings helped to stimulate religious fundamentalists' entrance into political activity.) There were annual demonstrations against the Court on the anniversary of *Roe v. Wade*; interference with those seeking to enter abortion clinics; and even bombings of clinics where abortions took place. Continued legislative efforts to overturn the abortion rulings also demonstrated that those opposing a ruling could indeed become active. In response, those supporting a "pro-choice" position demonstrated in support of the ruling, although it was not until the *Webster* ruling directly threatened *Roe v. Wade* that pro-choice groups significantly increased their state-level legislative activity—and then achieved some victories.

In the face of active opposition, "the complex interaction between ideological activists, ideological elites, the nation's institutional and structural arrangements, and the character of dominant political majorities in the United States" protects the Court.[60] Liberal activists provide support for the Court. That support reinforces liberal officeholders' will to resist attacks and to use the complexity of the policymaking process (such as the number of points that a proposed statute or constitutional amendment must "clear") to delay and defuse opposition attacks. The requirement of extraordinary legislative majorities and strong executive support to enact anti-Court policy works to liberals' advantages as they seek to protect the Court, evident in liberal senators' filibusters against school prayer and abortion measures.

If disagreement with a Supreme Court ruling can bring about action against it, the ruling can also bring about compliance—or at least lead people to take no further action after such a ruling. Indeed, the Court "has a slight edge in generating acceptance of its decisions," at least when compared to actions by a local legislature or a local judge. The Court may even be able to produce tolerance of unpopular actions; among those who initially were inclined to block a demonstration, almost one-half "report being less so inclined after a decision by the Supreme Court." And diffuse support, discussed above, assists in this process of producing compliance: "Those who are supportive of the Court are significantly more likely to comply with its decisions even when they are disagreeable."[61]

Impact and Compliance

Impact and *compliance* both refer to effects of Supreme Court rulings but do not have the same meaning.[62] One can distinguish them by saying that impact stands for the consequences of a policy—including but not limited to compliance—while compliance refers to the process, which occurs prior to impact, by which individuals accept decisions; the process by which decisions are enforced can also be called *implementation*. Saying that a person cannot comply with a law unless that person knows of its existence, one can define compliance as obedience to a ruling *because* of that ruling, particularly when a person through either opposition or neutrality did not previously intend to take the action required by the decision. One could say that a person is compliant when the person's behavior is parallel to, in *conformity* with, or congruent with, the requirements of the Court's ruling—when the person would, in any event, have done what the Court requires. However, that weakens the meaning of compliance; at best one can say the person is *not noncompliant*. Put differently, saying someone is "in compliance with the law" is not the same as "complying with the law." One can further distinguish between "acceptance decisions," involving changes (or nonchanges) in attitude, and "behavioral responses," involving changes (or maintenance of) policies.[63]

Compliance is relevant when decisions *demand* or *require* certain actions; other *permissive* decisions *allow* governments or private actors to take certain actions, called *adopting* behavior: because no one is required to do anything, there can be no noncompliance, only impact. Thus, after the Court, in *Ginsberg v. New York* (1968), upheld New York's statute prohibiting the sale to children of materials "harmful" (a standard less strict than "obscene") to them, several states adopted that type of statute. Cases on jury size and unanimity are other examples of permissive decisions: when the Court ruled that state noncapital criminal juries could be smaller than 12 people (*Williams v. Florida*, 1970) and nonunanimous (*Johnson v. Louisiana*, 1972), the Court was saying only that nonunanimous juries and juries of less than 12 were acceptable, not that they were required, so a state retaining unanimous, 12-person juries was *not* disobedient.

Even when part of a ruling is mandato.y, some implications may be permissive, leaving certain actions optional. For example, *Roe v. Wade* told states to stop criminalizing abortions, at least during the first trimester of pregnancy if the woman and her doctor thought an abortion appropriate, and placed strict limits on regulation of abortions during the second trimester. Because the Court did not order doctors or hospitals to participate in abortions, on this score the ruling was permissive for hospitals. Nonetheless, the decision "appears to have had a substantial impact on hospital abortion policies"; almost half changed policy. Most of those expanded abortion services to include elective as well as therapeutic abortions, with a smaller number changing from no abortion services to providing elective abortions.[64] The result, however, was that less than half of hospitals provided abortions, making nonhospital (e.g., clinic) providers increasingly important. Moreover, providers of abortion services were far from evenly distributed throughout the nation: "as late as 1985, a full 82% of all U.S. counties, with 30% of women of reproductive age, had no identified abortion service provider."[65] Just as one cannot speak of compliance with a permissive ruling, one also cannot do so if the Supreme Court has not spoken to a particular point. As *Roe v. Wade* said nothing about consent of spouses or parents to a woman's abortion, immediately post-*Roe* statutes requiring such consent did not fail to comply with *Roe*, even if one could argue that they did not follow from the spirit of that ruling.

Determining what is compliant is difficult. However, there is little question that noncompliance exists. One type of noncompliance is resistance. One can say that compliance is the opposite of defiance. An example of defiance is Virginia's plan of Massive Resistance to school desegregation in the 1950s and its closing of schools in Prince Edward County. That noncompliance is not necessarily resistance can be seen in Congress's continuing to include legislative vetoes in legislation after *Chadha* (see page 311), because this results principally from Congress not being able to develop effective alternatives. This situation also illustrates inertia after a Supreme Court ruling, with all actors continuing to act as before because no one can see an acceptable way out of the situation.

Other types of resistance, such as attempts to override the court by constitutional amendment, may be accompanied by compliant behavior. This mix of compliant and defiant behavior, which when combined appears to fall between outright defiance and full acceptance, is *evasion*. Evasion also occurs when the Court's ruling is accepted, but only literally and narrowly, while other ways are sought to achieve goals with which the ruling has interfered. For example, after the Court said in 1917 that whites could not enact laws to prevent blacks from residing in particular neighborhoods (*Buchanan v. Warley*), whites developed private racially restrictive covenants and enforced those covenants in state courts. Another type of evasion is the misapplication of Supreme Court standards or the substitution of other standards for the Court's by those who do "not admit their noncompliance but rather attempt to portray their decisions as consistent with previous Court decisions and the standards enumerated in them."[66]

When those affected move only a small distance from invalidated statutes, evasion is close to disobedience. Many statutes enacted after the 1973 abortion ruling, particularly those that outlawed the use of saline solution for abortions and thus interfered with medical decisions, fell in this category, and the large number of states with restrictive abortion statutes also suggested that "evasion" here was close to defiance: by 1976, three years after *Roe*, 34 states had adopted laws concerning abortion, with most of those containing restrictive provisions, and by 1985, 49 legislatures had passed 65 state laws affecting abortion rights.

Impact includes all effects resulting from a decision regardless of whether people knew about the decision. Impact involves not only one-way effects of Court on relevant populations but also feedback, the transmission of reactions back to the Court, in short, reciprocal interaction over time among the Supreme Court, lower courts, legislatures, and executive branch agencies. An important part of the feedback is *anticipatory compliance*, in which lower courts, in an example of interlevel interaction, see the direction in which the Supreme Court is heading and hand down rulings that take the law beyond the last Supreme Court decision, with the Court then adopting this forward movement as its own. Evidence of this behavior is quite clear in libel law where the Supreme Court itself invited lower courts to extend the test it had developed in *New York Times v. Sullivan* (1964), limiting public officials' ability to obtain libel judgments.[67]

There may, of course, be situations of "non-impact" in which nothing happens. For example, after the Court ruled that states may block construction of nuclear power plants, there was no apparent effect on construction. And, five years after the *Bakke* affirmative action ruling, there appeared to be little effect one way or the other in the proportion of minority students in college or professional school—although effects of the ruling could have been offset by other phenomena. Ten years after the ruling, there was some increase in the minority proportion of medical school and law school enrollment, but it was hard to determine how much of that to attribute to affirmative action programs; the rulings seemed to have "left aggressiveness in admitting members of minority groups a matter of a school's predilections rather than a matter of law."[68]

Another instance of "non-impact" is seen when the Court upheld New York's provision allowing appeal of search questions in a case despite a defendant's having entered a guilty plea.[69] There was little or no adoption of this mechanism by other states, although it was touted as reducing appeals of convictions by allowing the focus on the allegedly improper search. When the Court in *Cox Broadcasting Co. v. Cohn* (1975) allowed the use of the name of a rape victim by the media if that name was in public court records, newspapers for the greatest part continued to adhere to the older ethic of not reporting the name: nothing much changed as a result of the decision.

In another instance, after the Court upheld Illinois' "group libel" statute prohibiting unfavorable references to minority racial or religious groups (*Beauharnais v. Illinois*, 1952) no other states adopted a similar statute. Many years later, however, *Beauharnais* regained visibility when colleges and universities and some governments adopted "anti–hate speech" rules and laws in the late 1980s and early 1990s in an effort to reduce racial/ethnic/gender friction. The Court's now nearly 40-year-old ruling was used in support of such efforts at control, although others argued that the Court's major constitutional ruling on libel, *New York Times v. Sullivan* (1964), not *Beauharnais*, now governed, and the Court then struck down most "bias crime" laws in 1992 (*R.A.V. v. City of St. Paul*).

Impact may well begin *before* the Court hands down a decision, perhaps even before litigation commences, as a controversy produces a series of effects on those involved. In one instance, the tax status of the Roman Catholic Church as a charity, contributions to which were deductible under the Tax Code, was challenged because of the Church's stand on political issues. The U.S. Catholic Conference became more careful about its stands and issued directives to bishops and priests about the stands they had taken about particular candidates for elective office, even before the courts had dealt with the question of whether the challengers had standing to bring such a suit. Impacts may also be unintended, such as extra work for federal district judges as a result of changed standards for deciding habeas corpus petitions, or "white flight" after desegregation rulings. Another was the complete stop in the building of public housing in Chicago after the Court in *Hills v. Gautreaux* (1976) ordered a desegregation of public housing in the Chicago area. (Ultimately some 3,500 black families had moved to rent-subsidized private apartments in 118 suburbs in six counties.[70])

Impact includes a wide variety of behaviors. When a statute from one state is struck down, officials elsewhere may reexamine their own laws to determine whether they remain valid. This is part of the Court's ability to affect others' *agendas*: a Supreme Court ruling may well force legislative, or executive, attention to issues that had been ignored or neglected. *Brown v. Board of Education* certainly placed school desegregation on the agenda of school boards and state legislatures, and *Reynolds v. Sims* forced legislatures to deal with reapportionment, just as the 1986 *Davis v. Bandemer* ruling on partisan gerrymandering will prompt greater attention to districting. In a recent instance, the losing party to a Court case founded a group that lobbied to change the law that had been the basis of the case, certainly an instance of agenda-setting.[71]

If, after a Court ruling, it is not clear whether statutes or regulations differ in significant particulars from those on which the justices have ruled, uncertainty will result, as it does when the Court's ruling is not comprehensive and thus does not encompass laws elsewhere. For example, when the Court ruled in the 1982 *Rowley* case that a school district did not have to provide a sign language interpreter for a deaf fourth-grade child, school administrators were unsure what services school districts would have to provide to handicapped children.

An important element of uncertainty is fear of litigation. Fears of a Court ruling's effects, which are often highest immediately after the decision, may later be seen to have been exaggerated and to have resulted from claims made in defending the challenged action. For example, fears that the Court's ruling requiring Texas school districts to provide tuition-free education for children of illegal aliens (*Plyler v. Doe*, 1982) would result in substantial enrollment increases were not borne out at the beginning of the 1982–83 school year. Similarly, when the Court ruled in *Baxstrom v. Herold* (1966) that prisoners could not be retained in an institution for the criminally insane beyond the end of their maximum prison sentence unless they were provided a hearing to determine their dangerousness, the state feared that dangerous individuals would create violence in mental hospitals outside the prison system or would be assaultive if released into the community. Again, none of these fears was borne out: levels of violence in civilian mental hospitals were less than expected, and there was less assaultive behavior, both there and "outside," than expected.[72]

There are both first-order and second-order impacts, which parallel the distinction between impact and outcomes. For example, the *impact* of a judicial ruling ordering desegregation would include not only immediate resistance to or acceptance of the decision but also the actual desegregation of schools. Second-order impact or *outcomes* would include desegregation's effect on children's education, including increased disciplinary action against black children; removal of black teachers and administrators; and population movement, such as "white flight" to the suburbs. If the impact of reapportionment is redrawn legislative districts and increased numbers of minority legislators, outcomes would include public policy changes enacted by the newly constituted legislature, such as increased welfare benefits or general state expenditures that were not as substantial as some anticipated.[73] If the impact of the Court's 1973 abortion ruling was invalidation of most criminal abortion statutes and changes in hospital policy, outcomes included a substantial increase in abortions, although the increase was at a slower rate than in the pre-*Roe* years; nonetheless, in 1985, there were 2.7 times the number of abortions that had taken place in 1972.[74] The Court's ruling did not command but did facilitate abortions for women desiring them.

To get a full picture of impact one must look at both short-term and long-term effects of cases and at the effects of *sets* (or a "line" of) decisions in a policy area. Thus to determine impact in the criminal justice area, we would look not only at *Mapp* or *Miranda* but at the whole set of rulings "nationalizing" defendants' rights, which as one effect led state court judges to master federal law. Some impacts definitely occur very soon after a Supreme Court decision. The ruling that there was no Eighth Amendment (cruel and unusual punishment) violation in executing a mentally retarded person if mental retardation had been considered as a mitigating factor at sentencing led Texas and Georgia to seek to execute some people of low IQs. Jehovah's Witnesses ceased asking 25 cents for their magazines, to avoid taxation, after application of state sales and use taxes to religious items and books was upheld. And after the Court overturned state discipline of a lawyer for showing his specialty on his letterhead, states immediately started reconsidering their regulation of lawyers' advertising of their certification as specialists in particular fields of law.[75] When the Court allowed libel suits based on expressions of opinion, thus removing what some had thought was a limit on libel claims, a number of such claims were filed.[76]

In the other direction, after the Court required that intent be shown to prove certain cases of racial discrimination, victims of racial discrimination were deterred from filing cases, with the effect larger than was visible from the proportion of cases claimants won or lost.[77] When a ruling like the one requiring intent is made during the course of other litigation, those other cases will be affected, with plaintiffs' claims at times completely thrown off track. The longer a case is in court—and many civil rights discrimination cases are in court for many years—the more likely a Supreme Court case will have such an impact.

There are also numerous long-term effects. We saw one in the 1988 presidential election campaign as a result of Democratic candidate Michael Dukakis having vetoed a compulsory flag-salute law; although the veto was the direct result of the Supreme Court's 1943 ruling on the subject and an advisory opinion of the Massachusetts Supreme Judicial Court based on that earlier decision, President Bush criticized Dukakis nonetheless.[78] And 10 years after the Court had said that faculty associations at some private colleges could not use the provisions of the National Labor Relations Act, discord continued over faculty participation in college and university governance; the ruling, in N.L.R.B. v. Yeshiva University (1980), had quickly led to a decrease in faculty unions at private colleges and universities.[79]

The school prayer issue also illustrates continuing effects, rather than great short-term controversy followed by compliance and quiet. More than 20 years after the ruling, the Bible was read, prayers were recited, and hymns sung in some schools. In many more, there was a moment of silence—continued after it, too, was struck down by the Court when the legislature enacting it intended it as prayer (Wallace v. Jaffree). Efforts to amend the Constitution to allow "voluntary" prayer or silent meditation have been made regularly, as have statutory efforts. A bill sponsored by Senator Jesse Helms (R-N.C.) to prevent federal court challenges to organized prayer in public school was defeated in September 1985.

Law Enforcement Effects

The Court's rulings also had a long-term impact on the environment in which law enforcement personnel operated. *Gideon v. Wainwright*, requiring representation of indigents at trial, played a major role in shaping this environment. It led to creation or expansion of public defender programs and, coupled with other Warren Court broad rulings on confessions and searches, to attorneys' greater persistence in pursuing criminal cases, particularly at the appeals stage. Courts interpreting *Gideon* had usually adopted a narrow view of its requirements. However, a year after *Argersinger v. Hamlin* (1972), which extended the right to counsel at trial for any situations in which a jail term was imposed, most jurisdictions except for rural southern counties were complying with the Court's directive. They appointed counsel even in traffic cases where imprisonment was a reasonable possibility, although they did not do so for nonserious traffic cases.

Compliance with *Argersinger* may have been only "token," with judges encouraging waiver of counsel and with "no coherent development of defense systems to meet the need for quality representation" that the spirit of the ruling demanded. Appointed counsel—often assigned immediately before a trial— were frequently inexperienced and not well prepared to represent their clients.[80] In the early 1980s, state funding cutbacks seriously affected both public defender agencies and reimbursement of appointed counsel. Appointed counsel resisted working without pay, and in at least one state (Missouri) judges had to impose compulsory service without compensation on attorneys so that defendants would be represented. Almost three decades after *Gideon*, experts reported that too few defendants were receiving competent counsel, with criminal defense attorneys assigned to indigents being overworked and some judges resenting lawyers' effective arguments.[81]

Even increases in appointment of counsel under *Argersinger* did not make the trial process more adversary in nature. Public defender staffs increased in only a small proportion of all counties, primarily the larger ones. This increased staffing did *not*, however, produce the expected great increase in nonguilty pleas in misdemeanor cases. Rates of guilty pleas were somewhat—but not much— lower than in the absence of counsel, nor did presence of defense counsel result in more frequent trials. However, provision of counsel may have delayed or "stretched out" the guilty pleas that most misdemeanor defendants intended to enter when they came to court, and more frequent case dismissals and charge-and-sentence concessions may have benefited defendants. Misdemeanor judges did not believe greater use of defense counsel hindered their ability to handle their caseload.[82]

Exclusionary Rule. Giving us an opportunity to examine a range of impacts in one area of policy is one of the two most crucial Supreme Court criminal procedure decisions, *Mapp v. Ohio* (1961), imposing the exclusionary rule on the states. (*Miranda v. Arizona*, 1966, on the admissibility of confessions, was the other.) Police chiefs, prosecutors, defense attorneys, judges, and American Civil Liberties Union (ACLU) officials indicated that as a result of *Mapp*, search and seizure questions were raised more frequently at trial but there had been no overall change in police effectiveness. Attitudes were reported to have altered. Agreement that the same rules should exist for federal and state police increased, but there was also the belief that more flexible search warrants were needed and that safety should be emphasized more and liberty less.[83] Increased police adherence to legality in searches between 1960 and 1963 was reported; there was a high positive correlation between increased police education on search and seizure and adherence to legality. Over time many officers saw the exclusionary rule as creating problems; frustration and irritation resulted from the granting of motions to suppress evidence.

Mapp also produced a substantial increase in police education, including development of courses at police academies, adult education programs, colleges, and universities, and was among the "key factors in increasing the attempts at centralization and formalization of police training procedures.[84] Training improved in states that previously had no exclusionary rule, and the FBI increased its training of state and local officers. However, the exclusionary rule did not guarantee that good police training on arrest and search would take place: pre-*Mapp* exclusionary rule states were among those doing the least, and four years after *Mapp*, training remained "very spotty in both quantity and quality."[85]

Courts in states with a pre-*Mapp* exclusionary rule seem to have been *less* likely to adopt federal search and seizure precedents after *Mapp*, particularly if they had already begun to develop their own lines of precedents. Thus "where a state judiciary *anticipates* a federal rule, but with variations of its own, those variations are going to prove very hard to kill."[86] Yet states with a previous exclusionary rule had seldom invoked it or had interpreted it narrowly. This leaves "virtually no relationship between adoption and implementation of *Mapp*."[87] Nor was there a great deal of judicial action to implement *Mapp*. State supreme courts did not provide the law enforcement community with statements on much of what constituted an unreasonable seizure; 18 states did not deal with more than two of 16 basic search and seizure questions. For only three questions did two-thirds or more of the state courts rule evidence inadmissible; five of the questions were settled in a manner limiting *Mapp's* application, which was in line with judges' explicit resistance to *Mapp*, as they indicated they had little use for the ruling.[88]

Mapp's most important possible effect was on police actions, but disagreement abounds about those effects. In a study most often cited by *Mapp's* opponents, Dallin Oaks, relying primarily on data from Chicago and Cincinnati, concluded that "the data contains little support for the proposition that the exclusionary rule discourages illegal searches and seizures, but it falls short of establishing that it does not." However, in a stronger statement, he argued, "As a device for directing or deterring illegal searches and seizures by the police, the exclusionary rule is a failure." Police conduct not leading to prosecutions was unlikely to be affected by the rule, he said, with little deterrent effect on prosecution-oriented activity.[89]

Arrest, warrant, and disposition data for the immediate post-*Mapp* period and for later years (to allow the decision's long-term effects to be ascertained) raise doubts about Oaks's conclusions.[90] In 74 cities without a pre-existing exclusionary rule, few search warrants had been used, but the proportion of constitutional searches, although varying from city to city, increased after the Court's decisions. Officials in large-city police departments attributed the increase in search warrants primarily to the increase in narcotics traffic, evidence that changes in arrest and search warrant practices could have resulted from interplay between increases in particular types of crimes (guns, gambling, drugs) and the Court's decision. Police decisions to use search warrants in particular instances reflected the existence of the exclusionary rule, but increased narcotics use largely explained substantial increases in search warrant use from the late 1960s through the early 1970s. Less of the change is accounted for by increased numbers of police, better training, and other judicial rulings. Court decisions were not thought to have had much effect on recent increases in search warrants in roughly one-third of the cities, but judicial action was thought to be a major if not the total cause in approximately one-fourth of the cities. There was little evidence of widespread police violation of the exclusionary rule, but also little evidence that the rule was having a very substantial effect.

Debate about effectiveness and costs of the exclusionary rule continued in the 1980s, with some saying the costs of the rule were too high to retain it, while other noted costs and benefits are not involved "in the vast majority of criminal cases" because there is no seizure of evidence.[91] (The exclusionary rule issue came to the surface again as a key element in the 1991 dispute over a proposed crime bill. A provision in the bill allowed use of evidence seized by officers in "good faith" reliance on warrants later found to be defective—the Court's *Leon* position—but the president wanted a general "good faith" exception for warrantless searches as well.)

Despite attention given the subject, one cannot yet determine which of several possible effects of the exclusionary rule has been predominant. The rule "might have induced police officers to observe Fourth Amendment requirements" or it might have led them to lie about improper searches, with defense attorneys unable to penetrate the perjury. On the other hand, the defense attorneys may not have worked hard to overturn improper searches. Still another possibility "is that evidence has been rarely suppressed because judges and prosecutors have winked at Fourth Amendment violations."[92] A 1980 National Center for State Courts study in several locations suggests that all these effects may have occurred. Because police found the warrant process "burdensome, time-consuming, intimidating, and confusing," search warrants were sought only infrequently, and police often found alternative ways to conduct searches; few challenges to warrants (to suppress evidence) were made.[93] Such a picture suggests that the Supreme Court's shift to a "good faith" exception to the exclusionary rule made relatively little difference.

An important General Accounting Office (GAO) study showed that prosecutors dropped less than 1 percent of cases because of search and seizure problems and that motions to suppress evidence, which were filed in less than one-fifth of the cases, led to exclusion of evidence in only 1.3 percent of federal prosecutions. The motions were denied most of the time when they led to formal hearings. A subsequent Senate Judiciary Committee study that focused on 13 state jurisdictions where the greatest effect of the rule had been alleged also re-vealed a low proportion of cases dropped at the prosecution screening stage be-cause of due process problems and little overall impact on prosecutions. Such findings may mean either that the rule's opponents exaggerated the extent to which the rule has resulted in "criminals running loose on the street because of technicalities," or that cases came to prosecutors in better shape because police have "cleaned up their act" because the rule was effective. However, there are other possibilities—and other arguments. A 1983 National Institute of Justice study, based on late 1970s California data, concluded that the rule did affect felony case processing in important ways, accounting for up to 5 percent of pros-ecutors' rejections of felony charges across the state, more in large cities like Los Angeles and San Diego, with effects greatest in drug cases (where seizure issues are most likely to occur and to be raised).[94] That study, however, has been se-verely criticized for relying on statistics showing what proportion of the *reasons for rejection* were search related rather than focusing on the proportion of *arrests rejected* because of improper searches, and thus for being misleading. Attention to the rejected arrests measure, a critic suggests, indicated rejection of less than 1 percent of all felony arrests and only 2.4 percent of drug arrests because of im-proper searches.[95]

Communication of Decisions

The range of impacts just discussed involves several relevant "populations" and their subpopulations: an "interpreting population," usually a lower court, that refines—makes clearer—the higher court's policy; an "implementing popu-lation" that applies the Court's basic policy directive; a "consumer population" for whom the directive was intended and to whom it is applied; and a "secondary population." This last group includes the general population not included in the consumer population—for example, for school desegregation, perhaps those without children in school, as well as both governmental and nongovernmental "attentive publics"—those interested in but not directly involved in the particular policy and its implementation.[96]

Communication and response or impact are intimately related. In some instances, people may not know much about the actual outcomes resulting from the Court's rulings, but may respond to the Court because of effects the media attribute to a decision. Yet those expected to respond to a decision cannot do so if they do not learn of the ruling. If they receive an incomplete or otherwise distorted version, their response may diverge from what the Court wished to ac-complish. However, although communication and compliance are related, communication does not control compliance, so compliance or impact will vary even if justices' opinions come through "loud and clear." Few among those who might be affected by rulings—whether police affected by criminal procedure de-cisions or booksellers by decisions on the meaning of "obscenity"—seek out in-formation about the rulings. Thus it must be brought to them if they are to obtain it, making quite important the means by which decisions or information about them are communicated.

Only a "small minority" of booksellers in one multistate survey knew about the Supreme Court's obscenity decisions, and only 3 percent of those responding sought legal advice on more than "isolated occasions" about sexually explicit books they sold. Newsdealers in 18 communities that had experienced censorship campaigns did know the Supreme Court had handed down rulings on obscenity and that those rulings "restricted 'obscenity' to a very narrow class of publications," but they were nonetheless "generally unclear about specifics."[97] The relationship between information about the Court's rulings and other factors is complex. For example, in the multistate study, those who did know about the rulings and who allowed their activities to be regulated engaged in "self-censorship," that is, they were the most restrictive in their attitudes toward what they would sell. In the 18-community study, however, "attitudes of the wholesalers and retailers toward sexual speech yield[ed] very limited insight into merchandising practices." On the one hand, some retailers did not have to self-censor because their wholesalers did so; on the other, customer demand for sexually explicit material made it difficult for retailers to limit the items they made available for sale, and publishers exerted pressure on sellers to stock disputed items. Even if wholesalers' and retailers' rights could not be defended "without great cost or anguish," they recognized that demands of censorship groups often became excessive if they cooperated with them, so they had to resist even if they were in an economically marginal situation.[98]

The basic channels through which information about the decisions might flow are depicted in Figure 10.1.[99] One obvious means would be the Court's own opinions. These are available in several forms, including the "slip opinions" handed out on Decision Day, the advance sheets published by private companies soon thereafter, and, in due course, bound volumes. These circulate among at least some attorneys and others interested in the Court's work. The actual availability of the decisions at the local level where people might want to use them is generally unsatisfactory, particularly in the more rural states: a set of the *United States Reports* may be found only in the few larger cities. In many counties in the United States, a set is simply not available, and the reported decisions of the courts of appeals and district courts are even less likely to be accessible. However, even in larger cities, only a few of the larger law offices—and the county law library—may have copies. In 1990, the Court began Project Hermes, a pilot project operated by a nonprofit consortium, through which opinions were to be provided on-line electronically to those who subscribe to the service.

Lower Courts

The court system itself is a means of communication. The Supreme Court's decision is generally sent to a lower court for "proceedings not inconsistent with this opinion." As a result, "the formal judicial structure . . . provides an impor-

Figure 10.1

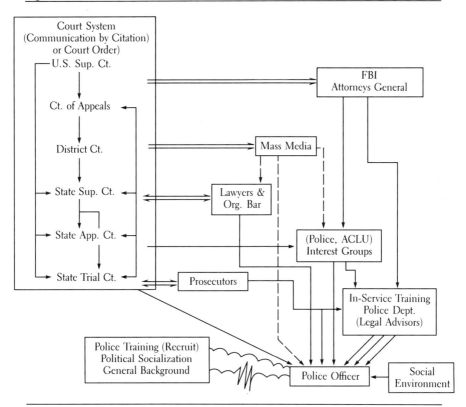

Source: Stephen L. Wasby. *Small Town Police and the Supreme Court* (Lexington, Mass.: Lexington Books, 1976). p. 43.

tant channel through which a ruling is transmitted to those directly under obligation to act."[100] But Supreme Court decisions often are not communicated directly to others, instead slowly working their way down to implementing populations through intervening layers of federal and state courts. At least as measured by lower court rulings, at times not even the trend in the higher court's decisions gets adequately communicated. Despite the court system's official structure, the relationship of the highest court and the courts below it is not hierarchical and bureaucratic. Indeed, "communication channels may be so poor that subordinates do not become aware that a superior has issued a directive," particularly the further away they are from the Supreme Court.[101]

Notwithstanding these difficulties, major changes in law, particularly if they are clear, can be heard and understood by the lower courts. Thus when the Supreme Court gave a liberal reading to private causes of action under the securities law, "it is hardly surprising that the lower courts did encourage private litigation and the statutes were read very flexibly indeed."[102] And when the Court ruled that pretrial proceedings could be closed to the public, judges closed their courtrooms much more frequently. This indicated, although it did not prove, that they were aware of the ruling, one to which they were likely to pay more attention because it directly affected their control of the courtrooms. There will be less effect when rulings are not clear. For example, Burger Court rulings weakening *Miranda* "did not result in as much erosion of the *Miranda* principles by state supreme courts as observers seemed to expect."[103]

Appellate judges also obviously hear the Court's rulings. For example, despite the major change in libel law the Supreme Court directed in *New York Times v. Sullivan*, the U.S. courts of appeals and state supreme courts complied in 86 percent of their relevant cases, with federal courts complying somewhat more than the state courts. This appellate court compliance was particularly important, because the press was likely to lose in libel cases that went to trial, with the juries often awarding punitive damages.[104] No court of appeals decision defied the *New York Times* ruling, which was accepted as binding. In a few cases, examples of "decisions which are technically or narrowly compliant with the Supreme Court precedent but which attempt to provide an unsympathetic interpretation which will limit the scope of the Court's impact," important sections of the ruling were interpreted "in such a narrow manner that defendants actually received little added protection for their rights of expression." In the other direction, some courts of appeals used the Court's ruling "to justify making pro-defendant decisions in cases in which it may be inferred the defendants would have lost" earlier. And support for libel defendants increased substantially, not only in the five years after *New York Times* but even more in the five years after that.[105]

Lower courts' acceptance of Supreme Court rulings can also be seen after the Court reverses the lower courts and then remands a case. Somewhat more than a majority of those who won in the Supreme Court in civil as well as criminal cases were able to preserve that victory on remand. Civil liberties and criminal procedure cases received less support than economic regulation decisions, partly because the Supreme Court gave the lower courts considerable discretion in criminal procedure cases. We do, however, see instances where someone who loses in the Supreme Court in a noncriminal case does win when the case returns to the lower courts.[106] Among recent instances are one in which the lower court, which had originally decided that a woman was improperly denied partnership in an accounting firm on impermissible gender-discrimination grounds, again decided for her even under a Supreme Court standard that was harder to satisfy, ordered her admitted to partnership and also ordered $371,000 back pay. After the Supreme Court had decided that the domicile of a Native American woman's children is the tribe, which therefore could decide on their adoption, the Tribal Court judge gave custody of the child in the case to the (white) adoptive mother.[107]

After the Court had said in *Cruzan v. Missouri Dept. of Health* (1990) that Missouri could require "clear and convincing evidence" that someone did not wish to remain alive in a persistent vegetative state and denied Nancy Cruzan's parents' request that their daughter be disconnected from the tubes keeping her alive, further testimony was introduced in the trial court; the state attorney general, having won his case on the principle involved, withdrew; and the court sided with the parents, so that the feeding tube was removed. However, the parents and the hospital did have to contend with protests from Operation Rescue, an organization active in blocking access to abortion clinics—an indication of the linkage between policy areas. Another victory, but not in the lower courts, came in the important religious freedom case of *Oregon v. Smith* (1990), in which the Court had ruled that laws regulating use of peyote could be applied to members of the Native Americans' church. In June 1991, Oregon enacted a new law permitting sacramental use of peyote by Native Americans in that state.

There were no differences in outcomes on remand between federal and state courts, but courts two levels away from the Supreme Court were less supportive than were those only one level away, such as the U.S. courts of appeals. There were results different from the original trial in a majority of the over 1,100 criminal cases in fiscal years 1975–79 that resulted in reprosecution, but the changes resulted largely from actions of prosecutors, not the judges; motions filed by U.S. attorneys produced most of the changed results. In those instances where there was a retrial to final verdict, however, only one-fourth resulted in acquittals. In addition, the longer the time after the Supreme Court's ruling, the less likely was the Supreme Court victor to prevail on remand.[108]

High state courts often follow the Supreme Court's rulings, but state judges have nonetheless engaged in sarcasm or injected "organizational contumacy" into communication channels by criticizing the rulings, by stating concern for the effect of those decisions on the public's safety, and by challenging the factual premises underlying the rulings. At times they have gone beyond criticism to urge lower state courts not to extend disliked Supreme Court rulings beyond absolute necessity so as not to unsettle the state judiciary. Even when not criticizing, courts which act less on "genuine enthusiasm" and more on "a sense of hierarchical duty," indicating they are acting because they have to do so, are not likely to kindle much enforcement activity by implementing populations.[109]

State court criticism of the Supreme Court was particularly likely to occur when the latter was too liberal for state judges. What happened when the Supreme Court became more conservative? Some state courts, taking their lead from Justice Brennan's suggestion that protection of rights was more likely to come from state courts interpreting their own state constitutions (see pages 18–19), avoided the thrust of the Supreme Court's conservative rulings by restricting themselves to state law in providing greater protection for civil liberties. Some state courts, like those in Oregon, New York, and New Jersey, became known for the primacy they gave to their own constitutions. A look at all state high courts shows, however, that in cases from the late 1960s to 1989, they were more likely to adopt rulings of the Burger and Rehnquist Courts as state law than to reject them: "for every state high court decision repudiating U.S. Supreme Court doctrine there are at least two cases enforcing it," true in criminal procedure as in other areas. In short, "the dominant approach is active incorporation of conservative Supreme Court doctrines."[110]

Trial court judges are crucial in the transmission of the Supreme Court's rulings to particular recipients, such as the police. "To the average officer 'the law' concerning arrest, search, and other police practices is in large measure represented by his direct and indirect knowledge of the attitudes of the local judiciary."[111] Yet the trial judge seldom explains his decision, most trial court decisions are either unwritten (announced from the bench) or unpublished, and few local government units have established methods for systematically gathering and transmitting information from the courts.

Most trial court judges are not likely to obtain information about Supreme Court rulings through vertical channels. They are more likely to learn about them "horizontally" or laterally from other judges at the same jurisdictional level, who thus can be crucial in the transmission of the rulings. However, even when trial judges correctly apply the Supreme Court's rulings, they may do so narrowly, perhaps taking their lead from higher state courts, to which they are likely to pay more attention. Lower court judges who did not like the *Escobedo* ruling—that a suspect being interrogated had to be allowed access to his lawyer—refused to apply *Escobedo* to anyone who did not already have a lawyer. Similarly, judges who did not like the *Miranda* ruling did not require warnings to be given to those not in custody, and then defined "in custody" as narrowly as possible. They were thus much like state supreme court justices in their interpretation of *Escobedo*. Only four state supreme courts followed the letter and spirit of *Escobedo*, while 37 followed the letter but violated the spirit by refusing to extend the ruling beyond its specific facts; five openly criticized the decision. On the other hand, all but two of the courts interpreting *Miranda* complied, with 14 classified as "liberal" in their interpretation.[112]

State judges at the same jurisdictional level may vary in general orientation to legal matters, to their local community, and to important "relevant others" with whom they interact. For example, in the area of juvenile justice, courts differ in the extent to which proceedings are adversary in character and emphasize treatment. Some local criminal courts are characterized more by "community mediation" than by imposition of formal penalties. One would expect Supreme Court rulings requiring increased due process requirements (see *In re Gault*, 1967) to be more readily accepted and implemented in those courts with a more formal orientation—although the judge's ideology about defendants' rights would also have an effect.

At times pressures on judges from their local "constituency"—whether or not the judges are elected—can be strong. That constituency pressure can support acceptance of Supreme Court rulings, for example, when liberal lower court judges, if elected, might be hesitant to diverge from Burger Court criminal procedure rulings for fear of being labeled "soft on crime." The pressure also works against acceptance of the Court's mandate. That was true for Southern judges, both state and federal, asked to enforce desegregation in the decade and more after *Brown v. Board of Education.* Some were aggressive, active enforcers of individual rights. Others were more gradualist; although probably having personal attitudes not congruent with the rights required by the Constitution and statutes, they would enforce the law if they were given enough evidence. Similarly, although some state supreme court judges (States' Righters) emphasized local needs and problems and stressed the primacy of state law and state judicial processes, others (Federals) were willing to take their cues from higher federal courts and from the Supreme Court's interpretation of the national Constitution.[113] Some local judges needed a "hierarchy of scapegoats" as well as more specific guidance about how to achieve desegregation if they were to do what the Supreme Court wanted and to resist pressures from the communities to which they had ties.[114] State judges could more easily sustain civil rights if they could avoid mentioning the U.S. Constitution and could emphasize state legal symbols (the state constitution and state cases).

Lower court resistance to controversial Supreme Court civil liberties decisions undoubtedly overstates their negative reaction. Lower court judges' preferences and interests do run in opposite directions from Supreme Court rulings from time to time, particularly in new areas of the law. Also, some trial judges do not pay much heed to the Supreme Court, particularly if they have adopted a position on an issue before the Court has spoken or if their attitudes are "unfavorable to the intrusion of 'law' into court proceedings which are highly routinized."[115] In the broad range of cases, however, resistance occurs relatively seldom. Most policies enunciated by the Supreme Court fall within lower court judges' "zone of indifference," the area in which their feelings are not strong. Because the judges have been socialized to accept the authority of higher courts—coupled with the potential sanction of reversal—they usually do what is expected of them. They are led to do so because "the judge's sense of professionalism and obligation will overcome any personal reaction he or she might have to the higher court's policy."[116]

Lawyers

Lawyers make use of rulings in dealings with their clients and in pursuing cases. For example, after the Court's libel rulings, libel lawyers and lawyers for the media paid closer heed to stories to check them for accuracy before they were printed or aired, and lawyers in libel suits made greater use of the discovery process ever since the *Herbert v. Lando* decision that journalists' "state of mind" was relevant to the "actual malice" test.[117] Lawyers play an important role in communicating Supreme Court rulings, both to clients seeking advice about the legality of past or proposed behavior, and to judges as well. Few judges monitor higher court decisions, so a Supreme Court ruling may come to a judge's attention only when cited by a lawyer. Partly because of work pressures that limit their reading, many judges wait for attorneys to bring new legal doctrine to their attention, so if the cases are not cited, judges may never be apprised of new rules. Some trial lawyers' negative feelings about their clients serve to limit their learning about the rulings, but lawyers regularly arguing appellate cases are quite likely to know about relevant higher court decisions. Attorneys practicing a particular specialty may have an informal organization for circulating information about relevant cases. Nonlawyers generally must rely on interest groups to which they belong for such information, but most interest groups provide it only sporadically.[118]

Attorneys general and prosecuting attorneys play a most important role in communication of Supreme Court rulings. The advisory opinions of state attorneys general, which may incorporate Supreme Court rulings, are often given great weight by officials contemplating the legal ramifications of proposed actions, although the opinions do not have the force of law. However, the advisory opinions usually are issued only upon a public official's request and are not widely circulated, which limits their use as a means of communication. More important are informational meetings the attorney general's office may hold on new developments in the law and bulletins developed for law enforcement officials, in which Supreme Court decisions are related to state statutes and judicial rulings and thus made more relevant to local officials' immediate concerns. Lawyers in a government agency's legal division can play an important role, not only in communicating the requirements of a court ruling to agency employees but also in developing alternatives to the court's ruling or rationales for retaining previous agency policy.[119]

Local prosecutors could play a large role in the communications process. However, they may not be knowledgeable even as to the subjects of cases they have tried. For example, Wisconsin district attorneys involved in obscenity cases felt some books and magazines "cleared" by the Supreme Court were legally obscene. Other prosecutors gave many wrong answers to factual questions about Supreme Court obscenity cases, with only 20 percent of the prosecutors rated as having high perception of Court policy (medium perception: 42%; low: 20%).[120]

On criminal procedure, however, where their knowledge may be better, their support of rulings favoring law enforcement might be important. In 1979 prosecutors in counties with 100,000 or more population strongly supported *Miranda*; younger prosecutors were more strongly supportive than older ones. The prosecutors also supported the Burger Court's changes in requirements for compliance with *Miranda*, of which they were well aware. However, they did not think the changes significant, nor did they believe the Burger Court rulings had had "a significant, or even a moderate, effect on their decisions to prosecute." Over half reported that Burger Court *Miranda*-related rulings had had limited or nonexistent effects, and less than 10 percent said their prosecutorial decisions had been significantly affected. The greatest change came where the Supreme Court's change had been clearest—in allowing use of improperly obtained statements to impeach a defendant's credibility. Yet even on this point, less than half the prosecutors were more likely to use confessions this way.

Even where the police would like them to do so, prosecutors rarely undertake the task of telling police about Supreme Court decisions or about how police practices might be altered to comply with them. Regular links with local police departments through which the information could be transmitted are lacking, leaving informal contacts the principal way for officials to obtain legal information from the prosecutor. A number of large police departments have remedied this problem by hiring police legal advisers—lawyers whose task includes interpretation of Supreme Court decisions, the development of teaching materials, and training within the department.[121] Small departments, which cannot afford to hire these advisers, remain without systematic means of acquiring appropriate legal information.

Media

Sources outside the judicial system and legal community are also important in communication of Supreme Court decisions. Although the electronic media have made repeated efforts to obtain access to the Court to cover its oral arguments and announcement of decisions, especially for such important cases as the *Webster* abortion case or the challenge to the Gramm-Rudman-Hollings budget law, there is no radio or television coverage of the Supreme Court. Chief Justice Burger said television coverage would not occur "until after my funeral," and his colleagues apparently agreed, as did the membership of the Judicial Conference. Yet several members of the Court, including Chief Justice Rehnquist, attended a "demonstration" at the Supreme Court itself of new technology that would be used to broadcast proceedings, and several members of the Court have advocated a change in the policy. We may thus be moving closer to television coverage of the Court. An experiment was initiated in 1991 in a small number of lower federal courts to allow electronic media coverage of civil cases. Allowing electronic media into the lower courts is a major change and may prefigure television at the High Court. However, even if the experiment is viewed as a success, there is no promise the Supreme Court will be "opened up."

The mass media serve as an important initial source of information about cases. For most members of the general public, television is the principal source as well as the source given most credibility. Newspapers, most of which rely on the wire services for coverage of the Court, rather than using their own reporters or even their own Washington, D.C., bureaus, provide more detail. Media in other languages may be quite important, particularly where there are concentrations of people speaking or reading only those other languages. Thus many refugees from Central America did not learn about the Supreme Court's ruling on the standards for obtaining political asylum (*I.N.S. v. Cardozo-Fonseca*, 1987) for some time after it was handed down, when Spanish-language newspapers, many of them weeklies, began to publish information about it.

In the 1960s, reporters covering the Supreme Court were frequently criticized for not being well trained, and for being passive and uncritical in their reporting of the Court.[122] The accuracy of reporting has increased since then; most reporters covering the Supreme Court for major newspapers, the wire services, and the television networks either have law degrees or have spent some time studying law. This results in greater legal sophistication in coverage of the Court. Yet one still finds, both on the network national news and in newspaper stories, such errors as reporting a denial of review as a full decision of the Court.[123]

The public seems not to expect accurate reporting about the Supreme Court. Or perhaps the public's low level of knowledge about the legal system makes it difficult for the newspaper reader or television viewer to know whether information presented is accurate. There does not even appear to be an expectation of *complete* reporting about the justices' activities, unlike expectations that the media will report the work of Congress and the president and of the president's activities fully and *accurately*. Reporters covering the Court did not mention a speech problem (stammering, slurred words) exhibited by Justice Rehnquist in 1982 until after he was hospitalized. Only from George Washington University Hospital's spokesman were other doctors able to identify the drug (for a back problem) that had probably caused the difficulty. Nor did reporters complain publicly when the Court's Information Officer was typically uncommunicative about the matter, and the Court did not issue a clear or full statement of the sort the reporters would *demand* of the president's press secretary. Some commentators actually defended the silence, saying the Court was sufficiently close-knit to take care of the problem. However, given the Court's difficulty in getting a disabled Justice Douglas (like other disabled justices before him) to leave even when the Court's work was being affected, such statements ring false.

The wire services have been and continue to be the principal source of information about the Court for newspapers and to some extent for television as well. A study of *Baker v. Carr* and the School Prayer Cases in the early 1960s showed that 23 of 25 papers carried reports of the reapportionment ruling on Decision Day, with 14 stories coming from AP, five from UPI, one from the *Herald Tribune* News Service, and only two from the papers' staff writers. The picture was roughly the same for the school prayer rulings. However, starting with the second day after the opinion, although wire service domination continued, more stories were written by staff writers.[124]

The media do not transmit Supreme Court decisions intact; few newspapers even print portions of the most important cases.[125] Nor could they, not only for reasons of space but because the Court's opinions are too complex in their original form to be understood by most people. But a result is that much of the "richness"—including the rationale or reasoning—of the Court's opinions is lost during transmission. The media's reporting filters the Supreme Court's rulings in other ways. Some rulings are lost in the deluge of rulings toward the end of each term and are not treated at all. Some decisions are handled more carefully or more sympathetically than others. In general, the media are part of a translation process in which changes are introduced and different elements of a decision and its context are emphasized. Justice O'Connor has observed, "The summaries of the opinions of this Court carried in the media . . . frequently provide a perspective, not only on the work of the Court but also on the perceptions and judgment of the reporters and their editors,"[126] and Justice Brennan has suggested that the media's attacks on the Court's decisions affecting the media themselves are unreasonable, unintelligent, and inaccurate.[127]

Each medium differs in what it emphasizes about what happens at the Court. The wire services cover the Court on more days than the newspapers (relatively close behind) or the television networks and appear to have the greatest capacity to handle "raw word flow." Individual newspapers vary considerably, but wire-service and newspaper coverage is closely related to the Court's output (television coverage is not). Changes in the pattern of coverage occur when output increases, more so for television than for the other media: more attention paid to impact and somewhat less to legal principles. When output reaches a certain level, the ability of the media to expand coverage to match that output ceases and coverage loses most of its "depth," tending to summaries of individual cases.[128]

Each medium also seems to have a different "profile" in relation to "Court time": wire services and television give relatively greater emphasis to predecision coverage; newspapers, to postdecision coverage. Television seems to add more "contextual information" than do the other media, and to report least on "informational content" about the decisions. Newspapers, on the other hand, seem to be most balanced in coverage of various elements, including not only predecision material and the decision itself, but also material on the Court as an institution and trends in the Court's decisions. Inclusion of this other material makes it difficult for people to learn what the Court has said: they may be able to read about the decision's impact without knowing what is having the impact. Yet if a decision is to be applied to a variety of circumstances, its rationale—not merely the facts and the holding—must be communicated.

Television coverage of a major case, like the *Bakke* affirmative action ruling, can be substantial. Such coverage "was quite extensive, with 60 stories spread relatively evenly across all three commercial network news broadcasts," and those stories "were relatively lengthy." However, more than half were broadcast *prior* to the Court's ruling, and there was a "central focus" on the individual in the case, which helps explain why "nearly half (45%) of the *Bakke* stories lacked any specific content about his legal claim or the factual scenario surrounding the case." Coverage of the prevailing (Powell) opinion in *Bakke* on Decision Day was judged to be "accurate, albeit quite oversimplistic," but the other justices' opinions were given "quite spotty and sketchy" coverage. Only one of the three networks made clear that the ruling favored some affirmative action programs, not merely Allan Bakke as a person; those looking to "understand[] the case's background and substance" would have found little context for that purpose. Further taking away from attention to the ruling itself was the focus "in great detail . . . on reaction to that decision among numerous actors and in several different settings," including reaction in the civil rights community. [129]

Specialized audiences find television and even newspapers inadequate as a source of needed operational information. (However, a television advertisement can call attention to a particular matter, as when Shearson Lehman Hutton encouraged viewers to call about a ruling on taxation of municipal bonds. [130]) Specialized magazines thus must perform an information-communication function about judicial decisions. Most occupational groups' trade journals can carry such information and some do, but it usually is available only sporadically and is not well developed. Specialized material prepared for use in training can be a partial remedy. In such material, the law can be related to problem situations faced by those who must implement the rulings. And training, which takes a variety of forms, including degree programs at two-year and four-year colleges and much shorter two-day or three-day or one-week in-service programs, does serve as a major means of communicating the law (statutory materials as well as court cases) to specific occupational groups. Police officers tend to rank training as the most effective means of learning about the law. Yet education and training programs must cover many subjects, so that coverage of legal matters is likely to constitute only a very small percentage of a total program; only rarely is it devoted solely to the law.

Communication to the Police

Most of our knowledge about communication of Supreme Court decisions comes from the field of criminal justice, and particularly from a study of four police departments in medium-sized Wisconsin cities. The greatest proportion (more than one-third) of the officers in the least professionalized department (Green Bay) found out initially about the *Miranda* decision from a newspaper. About three-fourths cited the newspaper and a superior officer as either an initial or later source. Only slightly fewer were exposed to the case by television, and somewhat over 60 percent heard of it in training sessions. This evidence confirms that "people who have no formal connection with the judiciary may be a more important source of information than any judicial authority," [131] although a full 40 percent of the department's officers did ultimately read the opinion itself. In the most professional of the four departments (Madison), the newspaper was also the most common initial source, and roughly three-fourths of the officers heard about the ruling from each of three sources—newspapers, a superior officer, and the attorney general—but more than 90 percent of the officers there were exposed to the decision in conference-and-training. A high proportion of the officers in Racine, where there was a captain of detectives on whom others relied for legal information, received their first information about *Miranda* from superior officers—who were also the predominant overall source of information.

In all four departments, conference-and-training was rated the best source of information by the most people, whether they approved or disapproved of the decision, but those approving of the decision were more likely to have received information at training sessions. In small (two- and three-officer) Wisconsin departments, the primary initial source of information about criminal justice rulings again was the newspaper; it was also the predominant general source of information and the one thought best. Conferences and training sessions, attendance at which gave the officers prestige, were mentioned in connection with *Miranda* and received high ratings.[132] In large city departments throughout the country, three types of sources of information about Court decisions predominated: the decisions themselves, specialized police publications, and the district attorney. The media were cited as a source by only about 10 percent of the departments.[133]

The greater the larger department's professionalism, the larger the number of sources of information and the greater the percentage of officers who received information from training sessions. Formal law enforcement sources were stressed more in the more professionalized departments; and none of the departments had much contact with "outside" information that might have proved helpful in understanding the decision. Professionalization tended to bring about well-developed lines of intradepartmental communication but not increased contact with nonpolice groups. The more professionalized departments did listen to outside groups more frequently because the groups furnished information that reinforced professional ideology. Thus professionalization affected the way *Miranda* was communicated and received. Yet after the decision as before, "there was no real hierarchy through which binding directives regarding the implementation of the *Miranda* decision could flow." Thus *Miranda* "did not basically change the decentralized and often unsystematic communications processes used to inform police departments about innovation."[134]

Small-town police chiefs in southern Illinois and western Massachusetts interviewed in 1972 were most likely to have found out about Supreme Court decisions from bulletins and other specialized or professional literature. They saw the Court's decisions—which they believed nonlawyers could understand—as the most effective means of communication, with state and local prosecutors a close second.[135] Mass media and personal friends were thought highly *in*effective means of communications. Written communications were seen by most as more effective than oral communications, although some thought a combination (training materials discussed at a conference) better still. The officers seemed to want something like a regular (monthly) bulletin or newsletter that digested cases and provided updated information for the individual officer, not just the department. They saw the local prosecutor—in Massachusetts, along with the attorney general—as having responsibility for providing legal advice to the police, but many officers said they were not provided sufficient material or access to it.

Even where, as in the medium-sized Wisconsin cities, police knowledge of *Miranda's* requirements was relatively high, the decision appeared to produce little change in the conduct of interrogations. Compliance was "formal, perfunctory or rhetorical" without behavioral changes. Police department statements of rules and procedures for interrogators to give warnings to suspects before interrogation were undermined by the interrogators' discretion and by their habit of giving the warnings but not following through on department policies of allowing counsel to be present at interrogations. Detectives said that *Miranda* had changed the way they had to obtain evidence, particularly by forcing them to obtain it prior to beginning interrogation. Observations suggested instead that "all the departments continued to rely first on interrogations. If that failed, either because of lack of relevant information or because of a lawyer's refusal to allow questioning, only then were alternative methods relied upon."[136]

Factors Affecting Communication and Impact

Communication of the Supreme Court's rulings and the impact of those rulings are affected by a variety of factors that alter messages before they reach their intended audience and by the ways in which those audiences respond to the rulings. At times such factors are strong enough to "wash out" most of a decision's intended effect, but we do not know the exact effects or relative importance of these factors.

Attitudes

Attitudes of those affected by decisions appear to play a particularly important role in the decisions' impact. Views of the Court's legitimacy are relevant, with distaste for the Court leading people to pay less attention to its decisions. A feeling that the Court is not ruling fairly on a subject or is not ruling on the basis of adequate knowledge can also interfere with the reception given its decisions. For example, the Court's competence and hence its legitimacy was questioned by law enforcement officers who thought *Miranda* showed the Court was acting without reference to the actualities of police work. Such perceptions made it increasingly likely that the personal and organizational goals of the police would differ from the goals embodied in the Court's ruling. On the other hand, when the *Terry* "stop and frisk" case showed recognition of the dangerous situations in which police find themselves, there was less hostility to the decision in the law enforcement community.

An individual's general commitment to "obeying the law," including the dictates of the Supreme Court, plays a limited role in the Court's impact when other factors enter the picture. Some people alter their attitudes to bring them more in line with the Supreme Court's position. In responding to the school prayer ruling, the "converts" came to believe in the Supreme Court ruling and were committed to enforcing it, while the "liberateds" softened their views about religion in the school and moved toward convergence between their own views and what the Court required. (The "reverse liberateds," however, became more rather than less favorable to schoolhouse religion; they moved away from the Court's position, not toward it.)[137] Many others develop a variety of techniques that allows them to retain their policy preferences without adhering to the Supreme Court's doctrine. The "backlashers," committed to defiance of the Court's ruling, tried to bring religious activities into the schools whenever they could and took a negative stance toward the Court itself. On the other hand, the "vindicateds" were critical of "schoolhouse religion" both before the decision and afterward.

Among techniques used by those who did not change views are attacks on those who are seeking to enforce the decisions (condemning the condemners); appeals to a "higher morality" (an authority higher than the Supreme Court); denial of responsibility for the present situation, perhaps coupled with a claim that others are preventing compliance from coming about; and beliefs that those the decision is intended to protect (whether blacks or criminal defendants) have not really been injured or are instead the *real* menace to society. Others who did not change their personal views complied with the decisions because they generally believed or led themselves to believe that they had no choice but to comply; these were the "nulists."

Prior attitudes about policy affect people's reaction to a Court ruling. This can be seen in responses to the abortion rulings, which also illustrate multiple responses rather than a single unitary response to some rulings. Support for abortion when health considerations were involved increased among those who had heard of *Roe v. Wade*. However, among nonwhites and Catholics, opposition to "discretionary" abortions increased, and women moved from greater support of to slightly greater opposition to abortion than men.[138] Such changes did not occur among those who had not heard of the ruling, indicating that the changes were likely the result of the Court's ruling rather than of some other factor. Attitudes of community leaders also influenced the effect of *Roe v. Wade*. Community leaders' attitudes were related to post–*Roe v. Wade* changes in hospitals' abortion policies and played a larger role in such changes than did demands for abortions or the activities of interest groups. Similarly, the attitudes of hospital governing boards and of doctors and nurses working in the hospitals heavily determined hospital abortion policies.[139]

Sometimes attitudes are superseded by judgments of whether "the utility of noncompliance is greater than the utility of compliance, that is, of engaging in the available alternative activity expected to yield the greatest net gratification." Although basic attitudes help explain parental resistance to desegregation, and decisionmakers' attitudes can somewhat moderate local opposition to desegregation, desegregation of Georgia school districts provided strong evidence to support a cost-benefit explanation: "In communities in which the costs of compliance were perceived to be high and rewards low, the most severe coercion was required."[140]

Clarity

Characteristics of the Court's ruling itself and the place of the ruling in a pattern of decisions are also important. Decisions must be highly visible if those expected to implement decisions are to hear about them. Because at times people become aware of rulings only after they have traveled through lengthy communication channels, the initial signal must be strong to overcome interference and delays. Otherwise the message becomes garbled, as in the game of "Gossip." A unanimous opinion is thought easier to transmit than are several opinions from a single case, and thus increases impact. However, if unanimity is achieved at the cost of a murky, unclear compromise, communication will be more difficult and impact may be lessened. Concurring and dissenting opinions not only increase the information to be transmitted but also make it easier for potential opponents of the majority's view to resist compliance. A plurality opinion makes it particularly difficult for others to determine the Court's intent. The addition of more and more cases on a topic will by itself increase the amount of "noise" in the communication system, as do gaps in doctrine. Such gaps are inevitable because the number of cases decided by the Supreme Court, very small in relation to the total number of issues on which it is asked to rule, may also create ambiguity.

The relative clarity or ambiguity of even a single opinion also affects its communicability. Greater clarity is generally thought to produce greater compliance; ambiguity, more noncompliance. However, state supreme court reaction to establishment of religion cases did *not* show a relationship between Supreme Court clarity and lower court compliance.[141] There are few decisions that, like *Miranda*, can be reduced to four or five warnings to be put on a "Miranda card." Even when a decision is clear initially, it may become less clear as the Court later explicates or limits it. Thus, the initial clarity of *Miranda* was blurred by rulings on use of confessions obtained without warnings or resumption of questioning after it had been stopped. Differences in the types of confession-related cases that prosecutors were likely to pursue closely paralleled the relative clarity of the Court's rulings: the less the clarity in Burger Court rulings, the less likely the prosecutors to use a confession obtained under the circumstances covered in the Court's opinion. But local judicial standards were more important than the Supreme Court's clarity in its effect on prosecutors' actions. Because local judges either had not relaxed *their* application of *Miranda* or had become more strict since the first Burger Court ruling (1971), "the Burger Court's weakening of *Miranda* has not been duplicated at the local level."[142]

Because the Court's initial action may be unexpected, its first case in a policy area may set off far more of a furor, even if that case has limited scope, than do later, more far-reaching cases. *Engel v. Vitale*, although invalidating only state-written prayers in schools, drew far more heated reaction than *Abington School District v. Schempp*, which outlawed school prayer and Bible reading, which were far more prevalent. Affecting reaction to these cases was the Court's greater care in delineating its second holding—in saying that not all teaching about religion had to be excluded from the school—than it had been in its first opinion, where important qualifications appeared only in a footnote. Similarly, less negative state court reaction to *Miranda* than to *Escobedo* may have come both from a realization that *Miranda* was likely to follow and from the *Miranda* opinion's greater clarity.

Situation

The ongoing situation into which a Supreme Court decision is injected affects the receipt of communications and the decision's impact. A decision handed down in the midst of a crisis, unless itself perceived as contributing to the crisis or producing one, is likely to receive less attention than one announced in "normal" times. Compliance with a ruling is facilitated if the ruling "comes well after the deep feelings in the community [provoked by the litigation] have subsided."[143] However, if substantial change in the law has taken place immediately prior to the Court's ruling, obtaining further change from the ruling is difficult. Likewise, judges are less likely to go along with the Supreme Court when invalidating local practices is thought likely to be disruptive. On the other hand, getting people to pay attention to the courts in bringing about substantial short run change is also difficult when the law is well settled.

Both a community's long-term history and events of the immediate past may attune potential recipients to what the Court has said. A community with fewer major crimes is less likely to be "up" on criminal law than one in which a murder has recently occurred or in which the police want to make a major drug "bust." A community's general belief system also affects communication of decisions and receptivity to them. Officials in communities that pride themselves on being "up-to-date" or "professional" might be more likely than other communities to seek out information about court decisions and to work to bring local government action into accord with those rulings.

There were major regional differences in compliance with the school prayer ruling. The practice was least likely to be given up where it had been most widespread, in the East and particularly in the South, and was far more likely to be discontinued in the Midwest and West. Areas that had adopted the practices without explicitly requiring them found it easy to give them up. Those areas that retained school prayer were likely to have had constitutional or statutory requirements underlying the practices. In the East, formal requirements were eliminated, leading to compliance. But in the South, requirements were not removed and were at times supplemented, making it unlikely that the practices would be changed.[144]

Among the factors related to organizations that play a part in the communication of and compliance with court decisions are "the cost of the policy or program changes to the agency, . . . whether the policy conflicts with an agency's goals or mission, whether the policy conflicts with preferences of key personnel, and whether the agency can effectively resist judicial pressure to implement a policy."[145] Availability of agency resources for that purpose is particularly important. Organizational structure and location are other relevant factors. An organization may be so large that specialists or others at the "top" of the organization who learn about judicial rulings cannot effectively transmit information to the "bottom." Where units are small, division of labor and specialization may be insufficient to have a person assigned to monitor judicial rulings. A small unit located near other units may acquire information from those units "horizontally," but if the small unit—like a rural police department—is geographically isolated, it may have few contacts through which to acquire information. Political isolation may be as important as geographical isolation in determining communications received, and community influence in the form of daily pressure also affects how an agency responds to a judicial ruling. Community pressures vary with the size and homogeneity of the community and are particularly severe in small, homogeneous communities where role expectations reinforce each other. And an agency operating in a supportive environment may be more resistant to outside rules that demand change than an agency that is politically vulnerable and may comply to protect its position.[146]

"Follow-Up"

The "follow-up" to a ruling—*who* responds and how they respond—is another important part of the postdecision situation. Average citizens and government employees may pay greater attention to subsequent communications about a ruling supported by elites. The absence of criticism—when relevant officials maintain a neutral posture—may also be important, but even official support of a disliked Supreme Court ruling such as school prayer may have no effect on communities with homogeneous populations. And if prominent officials immediately oppose a ruling, further communication about it may well fall on plugged if not deaf ears. Agency officials' reactions to the Court's rulings are likely to be a function of the distance between the organization's policy and what the Court suggests, and of the agency's commitment to its own program. The greater the change the agency thinks the Court requires, the greater the likelihood the agency will search for alternative policies. Here organizational norms come into play: the norm that the organization should make decisions independently, not subject to an external "superior," would encourage noncompliance.[147]

Follow-up is also affected by community pressures that are an important part of an official's "work situation."[148] That work situation also includes the people from whom the official takes cues about how to behave—the official's "reference group"—that is particularly important when community expectations are contradictory, thus allowing the individual more discretion as to how to act. Some government employees ("locals") take their cues primarily from their own communities, while others ("cosmopolitans," particularly professionals), such as lawyers and doctors, look to those in the same occupation. If, like police officers, individuals spend much time in the company of colleagues and feel the Supreme Court is hurting their work, they may wish to avoid becoming "sore thumbs" or deviants and thus will attempt to follow rules adhered to by their fellow workers. Such social pressure is increased when the work subculture becomes organized into units or comparable interest groups.

Because the Court's rulings are usually not self-enforcing, the degree to which government officials enforce or attempt to enforce those rulings, part of "follow-up," is critical. People are not encouraged to learn about or to follow the rules if there are no sanctions or only limited ones for not knowing the law, and little if any reward for following Court-established rules. Local prosecutors' inaction concerning police violations of search and seizure rules does little to encourage compliance with those rules, as does prosecutorial talk to police about how to "get around" a ruling (called "negative advocacy"). (Even where the decisions are self-enforcing, such as decisions allowing sale of material of greater sexual explicitness, officials' actions in responding to or rejecting demands from community groups opposed to the rulings or abstaining from taking action themselves are important in that situation as well.[149])

Executive branch officials may severely damage possibilities for compliance by refusing to take firm action to implement Supreme Court decisions—true of school desegregation in the Eisenhower, Nixon, and Ford administrations. Eisenhower's attorneys general supported desegregation in the courts, but "the President's ambiguity and the administration's general inactivity . . . encouraged white Southern leadership to believe that the federal executive branch would take no forceful action to enforce the courts' orders." The increase in the number of militant segregationist governors after *Brown* also seriously hindered compliance.[150]

Local and state officials played a key role in deflecting the requirements of the school prayer rulings. Superintendents who opposed the practices were able to use the Supreme Court's ruling to change local practices but needed the decision to do so. Far more numerous were officials, often with other, more important goals to achieve, who wanted to avoid conflict with small-town local power structures. The large number of local districts provided necessary opportunities for noncompliance that must accompany depth of feeling for noncompliance to occur. Many officials either presumed compliance was taking place and did not check for violations or turned their heads after making a perfunctory statement that prayer and Bible reading were to be stopped, thus allowing teachers to continue the practices. Yet school policies did have an effect; only 4 percent of teachers in schools that opposed the prayers said them, compared to 43 percent of teachers in schools favoring the prayers (and 40 percent in schools with no policy).

Teachers' own religious practices offset policy and thus affected compliance: those who attended church more frequently were more likely to lead prayers in the classroom—both before and after the Court ruled. Conservative Protestants were most likely to have said prayers before the ruling and were least likely to comply with the Court's rulings. Jews and Catholics, who, along with liberal Protestants, were less likely to have led classroom prayer before 1963, were most likely to comply. A teacher's seniority also had an effect on compliance: the greater the seniority, the less the change in practice.

Lawsuits were the only practical way of challenging the practices, but few were filed because they were extremely expensive, had few supporters, and those in the minority on this emotional issue were unwilling to subject themselves to the pressure they would have felt had they attacked local practices.[151] Where policy was made primarily at the state level, compliance was more likely both because there were fewer actors to be constrained and because the education "establishment" actively enforced compliance.[152]

Concluding Comments

Compliance with the Court's decisions does occur despite all the obstacles, both to communication of the Supreme Court's rulings and to compliance with those rulings, that have been enumerated and discussed here; those decisions have substantial impact. If that were not the case, we would hear far less objection to them. More important, without them, racial and sexual equality, freedom of speech and religion, and defendants' rights, as well as economic regulation, would not take their present form. The resistance to implementation of those decisions serves all the more to remind us that the Supreme Court is not merely a "finder" of the law but an active policymaker.

Many people have views of the Court which do not cast it in a policy-making role, and generally lack awareness of what the Court has done and even how it operates. Yet the justices maintain a commanding presence. Even when publicly adopting a general posture of "self-restraint," the Court has not been hesitant to strike down the actions of both of its coordinate branches at the national level of government and of the state government as well. Other officials must at least take them into account before they act. In perhaps the most important test, attacks on the Court's major rulings have only very infrequently been successful, although the Court has at times backed off from some of its strongest positions. It is doubtful that we have "judicial supremacy" as the Supreme Court's harshest critics have argued from time to time, but we do have in the Supreme Court of the United States a body of individuals who, operating within the constraints of the nation's legal system, through both the full-dress treatment given some cases and the variety of other, less visible actions they take, regularly make policy for that system and the larger political and social system.

Notes

1. For an examination of the impact of the abortion ruling, see Charles A. Johnson and Bradley C. Canon, *Judicial Policies: Implementation and Impact* (Washington, D.C.: Congressional Quarterly Press, 1984), pp. 4–14.

2. This is based on correspondence to the author from Leonard Levy.

3. *City of Lafayette v. Louisiana Power & Light Co.*, 435 U.S. 389 (1978); *Community Communications v. City of Boulder*, 455 U.S. 40 (1982).

4. *Town of Hallie v. City of Eau Claire*, 471 U.S. 34 (1985). See Stephen Chapple, "*Community Communications v. City of Boulder:* An Intergovernmental Paradox," *Public Administration Review* 45 (Special 1985): 732–37.

5. *McKesson v. Division of Alcoholic Beverages and Tobacco (Florida)*, 110 S.Ct. 2238 (1990); *Davis v. Michigan Department of Treasury*, 109 S.Ct. 1500 (1989). See Stephen Wermeil, "High Court Had Billion-Dollar Impact," *Wall Street Journal*, June 28, 1990, p. B1.

6. *Wilder v. Virginia Hospital Association*, 110 S.Ct. 2510 (1990). See Linda Greenhouse, "High Court Rules Hospitals Can Sue on Medicaid Rates," *New York Times*, June 15, 1990, pp. A1, A15; and Robert Pear, "Ruling Likely to Increase Strains on Medicaid," Ibid., p. A15.

7. Jesse Choper, "Consequences of Supreme Court Decisions Upholding Individual Constitutional Rights," *Michigan Law Review* 83 (October 1984): 7.

8. Based on correspondence to the author from Leonard Levy.

9. Some of the material presented here, revised and updated, was first presented in Stephen L. Wasby, *The Impact of the United States Supreme Court* (Homewood, Ill.: Dorsey, 1970).

10. Charles Warren, *The Supreme Court in United States History* (Boston: Little, Brown, 1922), vol. 1, p. viii.

11. Jesse Choper, *Judicial Review and the National Political Process*, pp. 321–33.

12. *Ableman v. Booth*, 21 How. 506 (1859); *Prigg v. Pennsylvania*, 16 Peters 539 (1842).

13. Jeff Romm and Sally K. Fairfax, "The Backwaters of Federalism: Receding Reserved Water Rights and the Management of National Forests," *Policy Studies Review* 5 (November 1985): 423–24. The case was *United States v. New Mexico*, 438 U.S. 696 (1978), involving the Rio Mimbres and the Gila National Forest.

14. Don Fehrenbacher, *The Dred Scott Case*, pp. 454, 576.

15. Ibid., pp. 3, 449, 493.

16. Warren, *The Supreme Court*, vol. 2, p. 358.

17. Ibid., vol. 3, p. 244. That Justices Strong and Bradley, who helped produce the second decision, were named to the Court on the day of the first decision did not help matters.

18. Merle Fainsod, Lincoln Gordon, and Joseph Palamountain, *Government and the American Economy*, pp. 540, 541.

19. Arthur M. Schlesinger, Jr., *The Politics of Upheaval* (Boston: Houghton Mifflin, 1960), p. 489.

20. Stuart Nagel and Robert Erickson, "Editorial Reaction to Supreme Court Decisions on Church and State," *Public Opinion Quarterly* 30 (Winter 1966–67); 647–55; also in Nagel, *The Legal Process from a Behavioral Perspective*, pp. 285–93.

21. William Haltom, "Editorialists and the High Court: Race, Crime, and Religion," paper presented to New York State Political Science Association, 1986, p. 5.

22. See William Haltom, "Virtues Passive and Active: Supreme Court Opinions and the Attentive Public," paper presented to American Political Science Association, 1985, p. 12.

23. Haltom, "Editorialists," pp. 4, 9.

24. Chester Newland, "Press Coverage of the United States Supreme Court," *Western Political Quarterly* 17 (March 1964): 15–36.

25. See Richard Claude, "The Supreme Court Nine: Judicial Responsibility and Responsiveness," *People vs. Government: The Responsiveness of American Institutions*, ed. Leroy N. Rieselbach (Bloomington, Ind.: Indiana University Press, 1975), particularly Table 1, p. 123.

26. Gregory A. Caldeira, "Neither the Purse Nor the Sword: Dynamics of Public Confidence in the Supreme Court," *American Political Science Review* 80 (December 1986): 1219–23.

27. Thomas R. Marshall, *Public Opinion and the Supreme Court* (Winchester, Mass.: Unwin Hyman, 1989), pp. 78, 151, 156, 178.

28. See account in Bernard Schwartz, *Super Chief*, pp. 282–86.

29. Edward N. Beiser, "Lawyers Judge the Warren Court," *Law & Society Review* 7 (Fall 1972): 139–49.

30. Neal Milner, *The Supreme Court and Local Law Enforcement: The Impact of Miranda* (Beverly Hills, Calif.: Sage Publications, 1971).

31. Stephen L. Wasby, *Small Town Police and the Supreme Court: Hearing the Word* (Lexington, Mass.: Lexington Books, 1976), p. 82; Dennis C. Smith and Elinor Ostrom, "The Effects of Training

and Education on Police Attitudes and Performance: A Preliminary Analysis," unpublished ms., 1973, p. 11.

32. Marcia Coyle, "How Americans View High Court," *National Law Journal*, February 26, 1990, p. 1.

33. "What America Really Thinks About Lawyers," *National Law Journal*, August 18, 1986, p. S-6.

34. John H. Kessel, "Public Perceptions of the Supreme Court," *Midwest Journal of Political Science* 10 (May 1966): 175.

35. Kenneth Dolbeare, "The Public Views the Supreme Court," *Law, Politics and the Federal Courts*, ed. Herbert Jacob (Boston: Little, Brown, 1967), pp. 194–202.

36. See Joseph Tanenhaus and Walter F. Murphy, "Patterns of Public Support for the Supreme Court: A Panel Study," *Journal of Politics* 43 (February 1981): 24–39.

37. Liane C. Kosaki, "Public Awareness of Supreme Court Decisions," paper presented to American Political Science Association, 1991, pp. 11, 12, 14, 16.

38. Walter F. Murphy and Joseph Tanenhaus, "The U.S. Supreme Court and Its Elite Publics," paper presented to International Political Science Association, 1970, p. 22.

39. The 1976 Wisconsin survey is reported in David Adamany, "Public and Activists' Attitudes Toward the United States Supreme Court," paper presented to American Political Science Association, 1977, and David Adamany and Joel B. Grossman, "Support for the Supreme Court as a National Policy Maker," *Law & Policy Quarterly* 5 (October 1983): 405–37.

40. Dolbeare, "The Public Views the Supreme Court," p. 199.

41. Gregory Casey, "The Supreme Court and Myth: An Empirical Investigation," *Law & Society Review* 8 (Spring 1974): 397.

42. Adamany and Grossman, "Support for the Supreme Court," p. 409.

43. Tanenhaus and Murphy, "Patterns of Public Support," p. 29.

44. Kenneth Dolbeare, "The Supreme Court and the States: From Abstract Doctrine to Local Behavioral Conformity," *The Impact of Supreme Court Decisions: Empirical Studies*, eds. Theodore H. Becker and Malcolm Feeley, 2d ed. (New York: Oxford University Press, 1973), p. 203.

45. Gregory Caldeira and James Gibson, "The Etiology of Public Support for the Supreme Court," *American Journal of Political Science* 36 (August 1992): 635–64.

46. Edward N. Muller, "A Test of a Partial Theory of Potential for Political Violence," *American Political Science Review* 66 (September 1972): 940.

47. Dean Jaros and Robert Roper, "The U.S. Supreme Court: Myth, Diffuse Support, Specific Support, and Legitimacy," *American Politics Quarterly* 8 (January 1980): 100.

48. James Gibson and Gregory Caldeira, "Blacks and the American Supreme Court: Models of Diffuse Support," *Journal of Politics* (forthcoming).

49. Adamany and Grossman, "Support for the Supreme Court," p. 412.

50. Ibid., p. 428.

51. Kenneth M. Dolbeare and Phillip E. Hammond, "The Political Party Basis of Attitudes Toward the Supreme Court," *Public Opinion Quarterly* 31 (Spring 1967): 23–24.

52. Tanenhaus and Murphy, "Patterns of Public Support," p. 36.

53. Ibid., pp. 415, 418.

54. Casey, "An Empirical Investigation," pp. 398, 402.

55. Jaros and Roper, "Specific Support and Legitimacy," p. 95.

56. See Ronald J. Fiscus, "Studying *The Brethren*: The Legal-Realist Bias of Investigative Journalism," *American Bar Foundation Research Journal* 1984 (Spring): 487–503.

57. Walter Murphy and Joseph Tanenhaus, "Public Opinion and the United States Supreme Court: Mapping of Some Prerequisites for Court Legitimation of Regime Change," *Frontiers of Judicial Research*, eds. Joel B. Grossman and Joseph Tanenhaus (New York: John Wiley, 1969), p. 282; and see also Walter F. Murphy, Joseph Tanenhaus, and Daniel L. Kastner, "Public Evaluation of Constitutional Courts: Alternative Explanations," Sage Professional Papers No. 01–045 (Beverly Hills, Calif.: Sage Publications, 1973); Adamany, "Public and Activists' Attitudes," p. 26. For a recent statement of their findings, see Walter F. Murphy and Joseph Tanenhaus, "Publicity, Public Opinion, and the Court," *Northwestern University Law Review* 84 (Spring/Summer 1990): 985–1023.

58. Dolbeare, "The Public Views the Supreme Court," p. 208.

59. Kessel, "Public Perceptions," p. 191.

60. Adamany and Grossman, "Support for the Supreme Court," p. 426.

61. James L. Gibson, "Understandings of Justice: Institutional Legitimacy, Procedural Justice, and Political Tolerance," *Law & Society Review* 23 (1989): 477, 481, 489.

62. Discussion of terminology can be found in Wasby, *The Impact of the Supreme Court*, pp. 27– 42; in several of the articles in *Compliance and the Law*, eds. Samuel Krislov et al. (Beverly Hills, Calif.: Sage Publications, 1972); and in Robert V. Stover and Don W. Brown, "Understanding Compliance and Noncompliance with Law: The Contributions of Utility Theory," *Social Science Quarterly* 56 (December 1975): 363–75.

63. See Johnson and Canon, *Judicial Policies*, pp. 14–15.

64. Jon R. Bond and Charles A. Johnson, "Implementing a Permissive Policy: Hospital Abortion Services after *Roe v. Wade*," *American Journal of Political Science* 26 (February 1982): 4.

65. Robin Wolpert and Gerald N. Rosenberg, "The Least Dangerous Branch: Market Forces and the Implementation of *Roe*," paper presented to American Political Science Association, 1990, p. 8.

66. G. Alan Tarr, *Judicial Impact and State Supreme Courts* (Lexington, Mass.: Lexington Books, 1977), pp. 54–55.

67. John Gruhl, "Anticipatory Compliance with Supreme Court Rulings," *Polity* 14 (Winter 1981): 308–9.

68. Joseph Berger, "The *Bakke* Case 10 Years Later: Mixed Results," *New York Times*, October 13, 1988. For a thorough discussion, see Gerald N. Rosenberg, *The Hollow Hope: Can Courts Bring About Social Change?* (Chicago: University of Chicago Press, 1991).

69. *Preiser v. Newkirk*, 422 U.S. 395 (1975).

70. William E. Schmidt, "Moving Out of Projects and Toward a Future," *New York Times*, February 3, 1989, p. A32.

71. The case was *Michael H. v. Gerald D.*, 109 S.Ct. 2333 (1989) (state may presume child of married woman to be her husband's child, although another man is the child's natural father). The man who had sought to establish his rights to see his child got the law changed to allow unwed fathers to request visitation when the mother was married to another man. See Marcia Coyle, "After the Gavel Comes Down," *National Law Journal*, February 25, 1991, pp. 1, 24–26.

72. See Henry Steadman and Joseph J. Cocozza, *Careers of the Criminally Insane* (Lexington, Mass.: Lexington Books, 1974), and H. Steadman and G. Keveles, "The Community Adjustment and Criminal Activity of the Baxstrom Patients: 1966–1970," *American Journal of Psychiatry* 129 (1972): 304–10.

73. See Roger A. Hanson and Robert E. Crew, Jr., "The Policy Impact of Reapportionment," *Law & Society Review* 8 (Fall 1973): 70–93.

74. Wolpert and Rosenberg, "The Least Dangerous Branch."

75. The cases are, respectively, *Jimmy Swaggart Ministries v. Board of Equalization of California*, 110 S.Ct. 688 (1990); *Penry v. Lynaugh*, 109 S.Ct. 2934 (1989); and *Peel v. Attorney Disciplinary Commission of Illinois*, 110 S.Ct. 2281 (1990).

76. *Milkovich v. The Lorain Journal*, 110 S.Ct. 2695 (1990).

77. Theodore Eisenberg and Sheri Lynn Johnson, "The Effects of Intent: Do We Know How Legal Standards Work?" *Cornell Law Review* 76 (September 1991): 1151–97.

78. David Margolick, "Pledge Dispute Evokes Bitter Memories," *New York Times*, September 11, 1988, pp. 1, 30; some in the 1940s cases were still alive.

79. Debra E. Blum, "10 Years After High Court Limits Faculty Bargaining, Merits of Academic Unionism Still Hotly Debated," *Chronicle of Higher Education*, January 31, 1990, p. A15.

80. Sheldon Krantz et al., "The Right to Counsel in Criminal Cases: The Mandate of *Argersinger v. Hamlin*," Summary Report (Washington, D.C.: National Institute of Law Enforcement and Criminal Justice, Law Enforcement Assistance Administration, Department of Justice, 1976), pp. 2–3.

81. "*Gideon's* Unmet Ideal," *ABA Journal* 77 (October 1991): 40.

82. Barton L. Ingraham, "The Impact of Argersinger—One Year Later," *Law & Society Review* 8 (Summer 1975): 616; James J. Alfini and Patricia M. Passuth, "Case Processing in State Misdemeanor Courts: The Effect of Defense Attorney Presence," *Justice System Journal* 6 (Spring 1981): 114.

83. Stuart Nagel, "Testing the Effects of Excluding Illegally Seized Evidence," *Wisconsin Law Review* 1965 (Spring): 283–310; also in Nagel, *The Legal Process from a Behavioral Perspective*, pp. 294–320.

84. Milner, *The Court and Local Law Enforcement*, p. 52.

85. Wayne R. LaFave, "Improving Police Performance through the Exclusionary Rule: Part II: Defining the Norms and Training the Police," *Missouri Law Review* 30 (Fall 1965): 594–95.

86. David Manwaring, "The Impact of *Mapp v. Ohio*," *The Supreme Court as Policy-Maker: Three Studies on the Impact of Judicial Decisions,*, ed. David Everson, (Carbondale, Ill.: Public Affairs Research Bureau, Southern Illinois University, 1968), p. 26.

87. Bradley C. Canon, "Reactions of State Supreme Courts to a U.S. Supreme Court Civil Liberties Decision," *Law & Society Review* 8 (Fall 1973): 126–27.

88. Ibid.; and Canon, "Organizational Contumacy."

89. Dallin H. Oaks, "Studying the Exclusionary Rule in Search and Seizure," *University of Chicago Law Review* 37 (Summer 1970): 655, 667.

90. Bradley C. Canon, "Is the Exclusionary Rule in Failing Health? Some New Data and a Plea Against a Precipitous Conclusion," *Kentucky Law Journal* 62 (1973–74): 708–9. See also Canon, "Testing the Effectiveness of Civil Liberties Policies at the State and Federal Levels: The Case of the Exclusionary Rule," *American Politics Quarterly* 5 (1977): 56–82.

91. Albert W. Alschuler, " 'Close Enough for Government Work': The Exclusionary Rule After Leon," *The Supreme Court Review 1984*, eds. Kurland, Casper, and Hutchinson, p. 368.

92. Ibid., p. 349.

93. Richard Van Duizend, L. Paul Sutton, and Charlotte A. Carter, *The Search Warrant Process: Preconceptions, Perceptions, Practices* (Williamsburg, Va.: National Center for State Courts, 1984).

94. National Institute of Justice, *Criminal Justice Research Report—The Effects of the Exclusionary Rule: A Study in California* (Washington, D.C.: Department of Justice, 1982).

95. See Thomas Y. Davies, "A Hard Look at What We Know (and Still Need to Learn) About the 'Costs' of the Exclusionary Rule: The NIJ Study and Other Studies of 'Lost Arrests,' " *American Bar Foundation Research Journal* 1983 (Summer): 611–90.

96. Charles A. Johnson, "The Implementation and Impact of Judicial Policies: A Heuristic Model," *Public Law and Public Policy*, ed. John A. Gardiner (New York: Praeger, 1977), pp. 107–26. See also Johnson and Canon, *Judicial Policies*, pp. 15–20.

97. James P. Levine, "Constitutional Law and Obscene Literature: An Investigation of Bookseller Censorship Practices," *The Impact of Supreme Court Decisions: Empirical Studies*, ed. Theodore L. Becker (New York: Oxford University Press, 1969), pp. 129–48; Harrell R. Rodgers, Jr., "Censorship Campaigns in Eighteen Cities: An Impact Analysis," *American Politics Quarterly* 2 (October 1974): 376.

98. Rodgers, "Censorship Campaigns," pp. 376, 378.

99. An earlier version of this section, which has been updated, appeared in Stephen L. Wasby, *Small Town Police and the Supreme Court*, chapter 2, pp. 25–55.

100. Richard Johnson, *The Dynamics of Compliance* (Evanston, Ill.: Northwestern University Press, 1967), p. 61.

101. Walter F. Murphy, "Lower Court Checks on Supreme Court Power," *American Political Science Review* 53 (December 1959): 1017–31; Lawrence Baum, "Implementation of Judicial Decisions: An Organizational Analysis," *American Politics Quarterly* 4 (January 1976): 94.

102. Barbara Ann Banoff and Benjamin S. Duval, Jr., "The Class Action as a Mechanism for Enforcing the Federal Securities Laws: An Empirical Study of the Burden Imposed," *Wayne Law Review* 31 (1984): 21.

103. John Gruhl, "State Supreme Courts and the U.S. Supreme Court's Post-Miranda Rulings," *Journal of Criminal Law & Criminology* 72 (Fall 1981): 911.

104. John Gruhl, "Patterns of Compliance with U.S. Supreme Court Rulings: The Case of Libel in Federal Courts of Appeals and State Supreme Courts," *Publius* 12 (Summer 1982): 109–26; Gruhl, "The Supreme Court's Impact on the Law of Libel: Compliance by Lower Federal Courts," *Western Political Quarterly* 33 (December 1980): 502–19.

105. Donald R. Songer and Reginald S. Sheehan, "Supreme Court Impact on Compliance and Outcomes: Miranda and New York Times in the United States Courts of Appeals," *Western Political Quarterly* 43 (June 1990): 306–7, 309.

106. Richard L. Pacelle, Jr. and Lawrence Baum, "Supreme Court Authority in the Judiciary: A Study of Remands," *American Politics Quarterly* 20 (April 1992): 169–91.

107. See, respectively, *Price Waterhouse v. Hopkins*, 109 S.Ct. 1775 (1989), and *Mississippi Band of Choctaw Indians v. Holyfield*, 109 S.Ct. 1597 (1989). See Coyle, "After the Gavel Comes Down," pp. 24–26.

108. Pacelle and Baum, "Supreme Court Authority"; Robert T. Roper and Albert P. Melone, "Does Procedural Due Process Make a Difference? A Study of Second Trials," *Judicature* 65 (September 1981): 136–41.

109. Bradley C. Canon, "Organizational Contumacy in the Transmission of Judicial Policies: The *Mapp, Escobedo, Miranda,* and *Gault* Cases," *Villanova Law Review* 20 (November 1974): 69.

110. Barry Latzer, "The Hidden Conservatism of the State Court 'Revolution,'" *Judicature* 74 (December/January 1991): 190–91, 194.

111. Wayne LaFave and Frank Remington, "Controlling the Police: The Judge's Role in Making and Reviewing Law Enforcement Decisions," *Michigan Law Review* 63 (April 1965): 1005.

112. Neil T. Romans, "The Role of State Supreme Courts in Judicial Policy-Making: *Escobedo, Miranda* and the Use of Judicial Impact Analysis," *Western Political Quarterly* 27 (March 1974): 38–59.

113. Charles Hamilton, *The Bench and the Ballot: Southern Federal Judges and Black Voters* (New York: Oxford University Press, 1973); Kenneth N. Vines, "Southern State Supreme Courts and Race Relations," *Western Political Quarterly* 18 (March 1965): 5–18.

114. J. W. Peltason, *Fifty-Eight Lonely Men: Southern Federal Judges and School Desegregation* (Urbana: University of Illinois Press, 1971 [1961]), pp. 245–46. See also Kenneth Vines, "Federal District Judges and Race Relations Cases in the South," *Journal of Politics* 16 (May 1964): 337–57; Micheal W. Giles and Thomas G. Walker, "Judicial Policy-Making and Southern School Segregation," *Journal of Politics* 37 (November 1975): 917–36.

115. Baum, "Implementation of Judicial Decisions," p. 95.

116. Lawrence Baum, "Lower-Court Response to Supreme Court Policies: Reconsidering a Negative Picture," *Justice System Journal* 3 (Spring 1978): 208–19. See Johnson and Canon, *Judicial Policies,* p. 38.

117. Michael Massing, "The Libel Chill: How Cold *Is* It Out There?" *Columbia Journalism Review* (May/June 1985): 31–43. See also Susan P. Shapiro, "Libel Lawyers as Risk Counselors: Pre-publication and Pre-broadcast Review and the Social Construction of News," *Law & Policy* 11 (July 1989): 281–309.

118. Alan Schechter, "Impact of Open Housing Laws on Suburban Realtors," *Urban Affairs Quarterly* 8 (June 1973): 439–65.

119. See Johnson and Canon, *Judicial Policies,* p. 100.

120. Thomas E. Barth, "Perception and Acceptance of Supreme Court Decisions at the State and Local Level," *Journal of Public Law* 17 (1968): 308–50.

121. See Gerald Caplan, "The Police Legal Adviser," *Journal of Criminal Law, Criminology, and Police Science* 58 (September 1967): 303–9, and Frank Carrington, "Speaking for the Police," ibid., 61 (June 1970): 244–79.

122. See David L. Grey, *The Supreme Court and the Mass Media* (Evanston, Ill.: Northwestern University Press, 1968).

123. An instance occurred in November 1989, when the Court denied review to a challenge to settlement of the major civil case against A. H. Robins Company for injury to women from the Dalkon Shield contraceptive device. The *New York Times* headline read, "Justices Reject Challenges to Dalkon Shield Settlement," which implies "considered and ruled on the merits to reject," not merely denied review, although the article did state, "Without comment, the Court refused to hear challenges. . . ." (November 7, 1989, p. D1). Worse was the headline in another newspaper, "Court affirms Dalkon Shield settlement," *Albany Times-Union,* November 7, 1989, p. 1. (Making a second error in the same set of headlines, the paper stated, "Anti-takeover law supported" when, again, the Court had only denied review—as the story from the *Los Angeles Times* service indicated.)

124. Chester Newland, "Press Coverage of the United States Supreme Court," *Western Political Quarterly* 17 (March 1964): 15–36.

125. For excellent discussion of the media's coverage of the Court, see Elliot E. Slotnick, "Media Coverage of Supreme Court Decision Making: Problems and Prospects," *Judicature* (October-November 1991): 128–43.

126. *F.B.I. v. Abramson,* 456 U.S. 615 at 641 n. 12 (1982).

127. William Brennan, Address at Rutgers-Newark School of Law, October 17, 1979, *Rutgers Law Review* 32 (July 1979): 173–83.

128. See David W. Leslie, "The Supreme Court in the Media: A Content Analysis," paper presented to the International Communication Association, 1976; and Leslie and Hornby, *The Supreme Court in the Media: A Theoretical and Empirical Analysis* (Final Technical Report to National Science Foundation, 1976, Grant GS 38113).

129. Elliot Slotnick, "Television News and the Supreme Court: 'Game Day' Coverage of the *Bakke* Case," paper presented to Midwest Political Science Association, 1991.

130. "The Supreme Court has said Congress has the power to tax municipal bonds. Should you be concerned about this? Call Shearson Lehman Hutton for the message, 'The Impact of interest on municipal bonds.'" Advertisement on network, May 4, 1988.

131. Milner, *The Court and Local Law Enforcement*, p. 47.

132. Larry Berkson, "The United States Supreme Court and Small-Town Police Officers: A Study in Communication," unpublished manuscript, 1970.

133. Data from a study by Bradley C. Canon, reported in Stephen L. Wasby, *Small Town Police and the Supreme Court*, p. 96.

134. Milner, pp. 52, 226.

135. Data from Illinois and Massachusetts from Wasby, *Small Town Police*, chs. 5 and 6, pp. 119–98, passim.

136. Milner, *The Court and Local Law Enforcement*, pp. 229, 217.

137. See William K. Muir, *Prayer in the Public Schools: Law and Attitude Change* (Chicago: University of Chicago Press, 1967).

138. Charles H. Franklin and Liane C. Kosaki, "The Supreme Court and Public Opinion: The Abortion Issue," paper presented to Law & Society Association, 1986.

139. Bond and Johnson, "Implementing a Permissive Policy," pp. 13–19.

140. Stover and Brown, "Understanding Compliance," pp. 369–70; Harrell R. Rodgers, Jr., and Charles S. Bullock III, *Coercion to Compliance* (Lexington, Mass.: Lexington Books, 1976), p. 65.

141. Tarr, *Judicial Impact*, p. 199.

142. John Gruhl and Cassia Spohn, "The Supreme Court's Post-Miranda Rulings: Impact on Local Prosecutors," *Law & Policy Quarterly* 3 (January 1981): 29–54.

143. Frank Sorauf, *The Wall of Separation*, p. 287.

144. Kenneth Dolbeare and Phillip Hammond, *The School Prayer Decisions: From Court Policy to Local Practice* (Chicago: University of Chicago Press, 1971).

145. Johnson and Canon, *Judicial Policies*, p. 94.

146. Michael Ban, "The Impact of *Mapp v. Ohio* on Police Behavior," paper presented to Midwest Political Science Association, 1973, p. 33 (study based on Boston and Cincinnati).

147. Charles A. Johnson, "Judicial Decisions and Organizational Change: Some Theoretical and Empirical Notes on State Court Decisions and State Administrative Agencies," *Law & Society Review* 14 (Fall 1979): 27–56.

148. For a discussion of the police work situation, see Neal A. Milner, "Supreme Court Effectiveness and Police Organization," *Law and Contemporary Problems* 36 (Autumn 1971): 467–87.

149. Bond and Johnson, "Implementing a Permissive Policy," pp. 13, 15.

150. Harold C. Fleming, "Brown and the Three R's, Race, Residence, and Resegregation," *Journal of Law & Education* 4 (January 1975): 10; Earl Black, *Southern Governors and Civil Rights: Racial Segregation as a Campaign Issue in the Second Reconstruction* (Cambridge, Mass.: Harvard University Press, 1976).

151. See Johnson, *The Dynamics of Compliance*. Among the other important studies are those by Donald Reich, "The Impact of Judicial Decision-Making: The School Prayer Cases," *The Supreme Court as Policy-Maker*, ed. Everson, pp. 44–81; and Robert Birkby, "The Supreme Court and the Bible Belt: Tennessee Reaction to the Schempp Decision," *Midwest Journal of Political Science* 10 (August 1966): 304–19.

152. Sorauf, *The Wall of Separation*, p. 304. See also Gordon Patric, "The Impact of a Court Decision: Aftermath of the McCollum Case," *Journal of Public Law* 6 (Fall 1967): 455–65; Frank J. Sorauf, "Zorach v. Clauson: The Impact of a Supreme Court Decision," *American Political Science Review* 53 (September 1959): 777–91.

Table of Cases*

*All cases the names of which appear in the text are included here, as are other important cases appearing in the notes. When the case name is not mentioned in the text, the reference is to the notes at the end of each chapter, from which the reader can refer to the appropriate place in the text.

Index